# 100
## GREAT LI\

This is a well-documented set of a hundred short biographies of people who have left their footprints on the sands of Indian history, in different ways. The figures included lived in the last two hundred years, but are no longer alive. Included are persons from almost every field of activity—writers, artists, scientists, social reformers, educationalists, politicians and freedom fighters. Several Britishers who spent a major part of their adult lives in India and contributed in a major way to the country are also included.

This is a unique volume for all those interested in the larger-than-life figures in India's turbulent history over the past two centuries.

**H.D. Sharma** was educated in the Universities of Punjab, Delhi and Michigan. He was the recipient of the prestigious Fulbright scholarship twice. He has worked as a librarian and taught library science in universities in India and abroad. He has also authored and edited a number of books.

# 100
# GREAT LIVES

H.D. Sharma

RUPA

Published by
Rupa Publications India Pvt. Ltd 2006
7/16, Ansari Road, Daryaganj
New Delhi 110002

*Sales centres:*
Allahabad Bengaluru Chennai
Hyderabad Jaipur Kathmandu
Kolkata Mumbai

ISBN: 978-81-291-0736-7

Ninth impression 2018

15 14 13 12 11 10 9

Typeset by Midways Design, New Delhi

Printed at Yash Printographics, Noida

# Contents

# Preface

*Lives of great men all remind us*
*We can make our lives sublime*
*And departing leave behind us*
*Footprints in the sands of time.*

— LONGFELLOW

This anthology presents short biographies of one hundred persons who lived during the last two hundred years and who are no more. It is difficult to assess the greatness of a living person; his fame could be ephemeral. Hence, the omission. A great variety of persons are portrayed: politicians, statesmen, freedom fighters, writers, philosophers, scientists, painters, dancers, social workers and reformers, religious leaders and Indologists (Indian and also Britishers who lived part of their lives in India). Thus, in a way, this anthology is different from most others which lay more emphasis or cover exclusively leaders like Gandhi, Nehru, Patel, Rajagopalachari, Subhas Bose, Jinnah and Maulana Azad. Of course, they have been included, but there are several others who are lesser known and seldom written about but are 'great' in their own way because they gave their entire lives for a cause. There is Khuda Bakhsh, who spent his life collecting rare manuscripts, spending a fortune and built one of the finest libraries in the country almost single-handedly. Today, the Khuda Bakhsh Library (Patna) is a public library. There is Zorawar Singh, one of the greatest military generals, whom any country would be proud of.

He annexed Ladakh from the Chinese in the nineteenth century and even invaded Tibet, where he died fighting in extremely inhospitable climate near Kailash Mansarover. Bhagat Puran Singh devoted every single day of his adult life helping the crippled and 'discards' of the society and built an institution called *Pingalwada* (home of the crippled) in Punjab. There are several others who deserve homage from the society they served, but have been unjustly forgotten and pushed into oblivion. The book is an attempt to remind people about those great souls.

Individuals do matter in history but the sum total of their lives cannot replace systematically written history, for history is not a game of personalities but constitutes the interplay of several divergent forces. However, this book may throw light on some of the fringes of history, which a history book ignores.

Indians are notorious for writing hagiographies rather than biographies. They do not want to reveal failures and unpleasant facts about a person. They relish in presenting a person as an icon and a demigod. Such biographies, according to critics, are invariably colourless and dull, besides presenting untruth. This book has followed Voltaire's advice: "One owes respect to the living; to the dead one owes nothing but truth". We have tried to avoid hearsay and have mainly depended on documented source material. This applies, especially to political personages. In the process, if long held myths about some persons come tumbling down, facts and truth have to be blamed.

I believe that three things are necessary in a biography: it should tell enough about a person; it should throw some light on the times when a person lived and finally, it should be readable. Towards this end, I have tried.

I am indebted to so many persons who helped me in various ways during the three years which it took me to write the book, that it will not be possible to thank them all. A few of them, however, stand out. Most of the research work was done in the Banaras Hindu University Library. B.N. Singh, the acting librarian, and my erstwhile colleague, was most helpful and without his help, it would have been extremely difficult to complete the book. The other library staff, including people who carried the heavy volumes, were also very helpful. Dr. Mohd. Ziauldin Ansari, director, Khuda Bakhsh Oriental Public Library, Patna, was prompt in sending me the literature about its founder and providing me details about the latest developments in the library. R.K. Singh, chairman, Swami Sahajanand Saraswati Research Centre, Varanasi, threw much light on the life and work of the Swami. To all these persons, my grateful thanks. My unassuming research assistant, S.P. Mukherjee a retired professional librarian himself, was of great help in my search for biographical material. I have to thank my two typists, Bimlendu Bhattacharya and Onkar Nath Sharma, who had to type each of the seven hundred odd pages at least three times without losing patience. I must thank my publisher for suggesting the title and for waiting three long years for me to complete the book. Lastly I am indebted to the editors Sugeetha Roy Choudhury, Disha Mullick for painstakingly going through the manuscript and for giving extremely useful suggestions which saved me for committing many smaller and some major errors.

# Bhimrao Ramji Ambedkar

## (1891-1956)

The life of Ambedkar is a saga of struggle against myriad odds. He showed undaunted courage in facing them. He was a reformer who tried to cleanse Hindu society of its ills, especially that of untouchability and the caste system, on the lines of reformers like Raja Ram Mohan Roy, Swami Dayanand, Jotirao Phule and others. Failing in his efforts and in disgust, Ambedkar opted for a solution which shook Hindu society to its foundations. As a result, he has been maligned and hated by millions of Hindus and revered by millions of others.

Bhimrao was born on 14 April 1891 at Mhow in the erstwhile princely state of Indore. He was the fourteenth child of his parents Ramji Sakpal and Bhimabai. The family belonged to the 'untouchable' Mahar caste. However, among the 'untouchables' Mahars were considered as a martial race and had played an important role in the Maratha army from the time of Shivaji. Many of them had also joined the British army. His grandfather, father and six uncles were in the British army, holding the rank of subedar-major. His father, Ramji, was serving as a teacher in the Army School when Bhim was born. He retired from service after a couple of years and took his family to Dapoli, a village in Ratnagiri district, and then to Satara where he could get a job.

A child's first school is always the family. Bhimrao grew up in a religious atmosphere. His father was a religious man who recited couplets from the *Ramayana* and the *Mahabharata* daily like any devout Hindu. Bhimrao's formal education started at Dapoli but he finished his primary education at Satara. In school, he had the traumatic experiences which an 'untouchable' suffers in orthodox Hindu society. Students and teachers alike shunned him, heaping untold humiliations on the young Bhim. His attitude towards Hinduism and the curse of untouchability could be traced to these ugly degrading experiences in his childhood. While studying at Satara, Bhim used Ambavadekar as surname, which was derived from their ancestral village Ambavade. A teacher, whose name was Ambedkar, changed Bhim's surname to Ambedkar in the school records because he liked the meek but disciplined boy. From Satara the family moved to Bombay, where Ramji got a job. Bhimrao was enrolled in Elphinstone High School from where he passed the matriculation examination in 1908. He was an average student but at a young age he had developed the habit of reading widely, beyond textbooks. Even before he had passed the matriculation examination, he was married to Ramabai, an eight-year-old girl.

After school Ambedkar joined the Elphistone College and passed the Intermediate examination from there. In school, as well as in college, the orthodox Hindu teachers did not allow Bhim to opt for Sanskrit as an elective subject and he was compelled to take Persian. However, with his own efforts and with the help of some broadminded Pundits he acquired a good knowledge of Sanskrit, which enabled him to study and interpret Hindu scriptures. Surprisingly, leaders like Gandhi and Nehru had hardly any knowledge of Sanskrit. Ambedkar was contemplating discontinuing his studies due to financial difficulties when he received a scholarship of twenty-five rupees per month from the Maharaja of Baroda, Sayaji Rao Gaikwad, which enabled him to graduate in 1912. For further studies he went to America on a Baroda State Scholarship and joined Columbia University, New York from where he obtained a Master's degree in 1915, and a doctorate in philosophy in 1916. While at Columbia University, he wrote three dissertations: *Ancient Indian Commerce; Caste in India* and *National Dividend in India*, which were later published in the form of a book. From the US Ambedkar went to England and joined the London School of Economics and Political Science in October 1916 as well as

Gray's Inn for legal studies. While he was still studying, the tenure of his scholarship expired and he had to return to India. He was, however, determined to go back to complete his studies. Back in Bombay, he taught at the Syndenham College for two years (1918-1920); saved some money, borrowed some more and returned to London to resume his studies. He was awarded an M.Sc. degree in Economics in 1921 and D.Sc. in 1923. In the same year, he was called to the Bar and qualified as a barrister. On his return to Bombay he started legal practice but his heart was in doing social work for the emancipation of the downtrodden 'untouchables'. When he had returned to India the first time from England he had started a fortnightly *Mooknayak* (Leader of the Dumb) in Marathi with the help of Sahu Maharaj. He had addressed several conferences expressing his views, which had been well-received. His education completed, he was drawn more and more towards social and political activities. His first concern was the eradication of untouchability and instilling confidence and dignity in the untouchables. For that purpose, he set up the Bahishkrit Hitkarni Sabha in July 1924. The Sabha gave priority to education of the depressed classes and opened free schools, libraries and hostels. Within five years, the Sabha was running four boarding houses in the Bombay Presidency, where students belonging to the lower strata of society could live, as the students belonging to higher castes had refused to stay and dine with them.

Ambedkar started a few journals and newspapers to spread his message. A Marathi fortnightly, *Bahishkrit Bharat*, was started in April 1927. The same year, in September, he founded the Samaj Samata Sangh to preach social equality and started publishing its organ *Samata* in March 1929. Still another journalistic venture of his was *Janata*, a weekly started in November 1930. None of these, however, survived for long as Ambedkar became involved in social, educational and other activities.

In a country like India where a vast majority of people are illiterate, a person cannot become a leader of the masses through his writings and speeches alone. The leader has to take recourse to some dramatic action in which people can participate in large numbers, as was demonstrated by Tilak and Gandhi. With that purpose in mind, Ambedkar resorted to a form of *satyagraha* to fight for the right of 'untouchables' to drink water from 'Chavdan Talen' (sweet water tank) a public tank in Mahad, inaccessible to the lower castes. Ambedkar and his followers walked upto the tank on 20 March 1927 and drank water from it. The high caste Hindus were furious and attacked them. But Ambedkar advised his followers to stay calm and not retaliate. The case was referred to the court, which the 'untouchables' won after a long wait in 1937 from the Bombay High Court. Ambedkar led another satyagraha in March 1930 demanding the right of all Hindus of all castes to enter the famous Ram Mandir (Kalaram temple) in Nasik. From these events, Ambedkar emerged as the leader of the weaker sections of Hindu society. In recognition of this, he was nominated to the Bombay Legislative Assembly where he served from 1926 to 1934, fighting for the cause of the scheduled castes in the Assembly. In 1928, he was appointed a lecturer in the Government Law College, Bombay, and subsequently its principal. In 1935, he was made Perry Professor of Jurisprudence, a highly coveted chair in academics.

Ambedkar was a delegate to the three Round Table Conferences held in London during 1930-32, as representative of the scheduled castes. In these conferences he pleaded for separate electorates for the 'scheduled castes', as there were for Muslims, Sikhs and Christians. During the Second Round Table Conference, Ambedkar came into direct confrontation with Gandhi who claimed to represent all castes and communities in India as the sole representative of the Congress. As the delegates could not arrive at an agreed solution to problems confronting India, the British government announced their own decision on 17 August 1932, known as Communal Award. In it the scheduled castes were given separate electorates. This was unacceptable to Gandhi and most Hindu leaders like Madan Mohan Malaviya. Gandhi went on an indefinite fast in Yervada jail, where he had been interned. A pact was signed between Ambedkar and Madan Mohan Malaviya (on behalf of the caste Hindus) known as the Poona Pact. Under this pact separate electorates for scheduled castes was rescinded and additional reserved seats in legislatures were provided for them. Thus division among Hindu society was avoided. This is rightly considered as a great contribution of Gandhi. However, unwittingly, Gandhi and the Congress party had accepted Ambedkar as the leader of the scheduled castes.

The years 1934 and 1935 proved to be quite significant in the life of Ambedkar. In 1934 he moved to his new house in Bombay which he had designed himself and named it as 'Rajgruha'. It was large enough to accommodate his vast collection of books. On 27 May 1935 his wife Ramabai died and he performed all the rites prescribed by Hindu *shastras* including the shaving of the head to the chagrin of orthodox Hindus. By now Ambedkar was convinced that it was not possible to reform the Hindu society and its hideous customs like untouchability. The only alternative he could think was to leave the Hindu fold and get converted to any other religion, which could offer the untouchables better social status and equality. He announced this on 13 October 1935 at a public meeting at Yeola, district Nasik. He vowed that, "I am born a Hindu because I could not help it but I assure you that I will not die a Hindu." He exhorted his followers to do likewise. He spent several years studying the social set-up of various religions; Sikhism, Islam and Christianity. To his horror he found that some kind of discrimination, some sort of caste system, existed in all these religions. Conversion was therefore postponed.

Ambedkar now wanted to enter politics to represent the depressed classes as well as the poor peasant and labour. He founded the Independent Labour Party in October 1936. The party was confined to the Bombay province. It fought elections in February 1937 for the provincial assembly and won thirteen out of fifteen seats reserved for the scheduled castes (the term used for the depressed classes in the 1935 Act). In 1942, he founded the Scheduled Castes Federation as an all India party bringing all the scheduled castes under its banner. However, it did not do well in the elections for two reasons: One, there are several castes and sub-castes even among the scheduled castes and all the castes were not with Ambedkar who was a Mahar; two, some powerful leaders of the scheduled castes like M.C. Rajah (a pariah) and G.A. Gavai (a Mahar) had joined the Congress and opposed whatever Ambedkar did.

Then came the Second World War in September 1939. Ambedkar was nominated as Labour Member of the governor general's Executive Council. As he was cooperating with the government in the war effort he was made a member of the Defence Advisory Committee. The need for manpower in the defence forces compelled the government to change their policy towards recruitment in the army. Under the pressure of the high castes the British government had stopped recruiting low caste people in the forces by the turn of the nineteenth century. Now they had to change their policy by allowing all castes to join the armed forces. Ambedkar exhorted the scheduled castes to join the army in large number. The British raised a Mahar regiment after half a century. This contribution of Ambedkar has not been accorded its due by his biographers.

In July 1945, the People's Education Society was founded by Ambedkar. The society opened several schools and colleges, the most important college being Siddhartha College, Bombay, founded in 1946. Another college was Milind College, Aurangabad, the foundation stone of which was laid by Rajendra Prasad, president of India in 1950. This college became the nucleus of the Marathwada University.

As the Scheduled Castes Federation did badly in the 1946 elections, the British government did not allow Ambedkar to take part in the final negotiations for the transfer of power, i.e., the Simla Conference (1945) and Cabinet Mission (1946). However, he was elected to the Constituent Assembly from Bengal and in July 1947 from Bombay. The Constituent Assembly started functioning from 9 December 1946, even before the transfer of power. Ambedkar was appointed chairman of the Drafting Committee and played a pivotal role in drafting the constitution. He was also made law minister in the Nehru Cabinet. "He brought to bear upon his task of drafting a vast array of qualities, erudition, scholarship, imagination, logic and expertise as a legal luminary. He may not be a modern Manu but he was the last word on interpretation". Immediately after the work of drafting the constitution was over, Ambedkar started drafting the Hindu Code Bill, and worked on it for one year with his usual diligence. As law minister, he introduced the Bill in Parliament in February 1951. Nehru had promised his support for the Bill but when the time came he dragged his feet and the Bill could not be taken up for discussion and lapsed. This hurt Ambedkar. In disgust, he resigned from the Cabinet. *The Times of India*, Bombay reported on his resignation: "Bereft of the crown of Manu, Dr. Ambedkar nonetheless leaves the Government with a considerable record of achievement behind him. The Cabinet is not overburdened with talent, and the departure of this discerning scholar and industrious student of public affairs cannot but dim its limited lustre".[1]

For quite sometime Ambedkar was not keeping good health. In 1948, he went to Bombay for treatment and was admitted to hospital. Soon after on 15 April 1948 he married a doctor, who was working in the same hospital. His wife Sharda Kabir was a Sarswat Brahmin. They led a happy married life for the remaining eight years of Ambedkar's life. She died on 29 May 2003 at Mumbai at the age of ninety-four.

His achievements notwithstanding, Ambedkar was a frustrated man as he could not do much for the eradication of untouchability. He remembered his declaration which he had made in front of thousands of his followers at Yeola way back in 1935, "that he will not die a Hindu". He felt that the time to redeem his pledge had now come. He had studied Sikhism, Islam and Christianity and had rejected all the religions. In his later years, he had been taking an interest in Buddhism and its philosophy. He had attended a few international conferences on Buddhism at Rangoon, Colombo and Kathmandu. The rational religion had appealed to him. On 14 October 1956 he converted to Buddhism along with his wife and thousands of his followers at Nagpur. On 16 December the same year Ambedkar died in his sleep in Delhi. His body was brought to Bombay and cremated. He was a Buddhist only for two months. The rest of his life he remained a Hindu, the religion which he detested.

Ambedkar was a prolific writer. He wrote highly critical and controversial books on caste and Hinduism: *Caste in India* (1917), *Annihilation of Caste; What the Congress and Gandhi Have Done to the Untouchables;* (1945); *Who Were the Sudras?* (1946); *Untouchables: Who Were They* (1948); *Riddles of Hinduism* (published posthumously in 1987). He also wrote on economic topics like *Problem of the Rupee* (1923); *Evolution of Provincial Finance in British India* (1924). On politics his most outstanding book remains *Thoughts on Pakistan* (1941) and its second edition, *Pakistan or the Partition of India* (1946). He was perhaps the only leader who saw the inevitability of the partition of the country way back in 1940; analysed the problem in detail and suggested that partition seemed to be the only solution alongwith the complete transfer of population of the two communities. The country was partitioned in 1947 but the complete transfer of population did not take place as advocated by Ambedkar.

Ambedkar remained a controversial personality during his lifetime and remains so even after his death, not for what he said but largely for the way he said it. By using a little tact and somewhat refined language he could have avoided strong reactions from the people. Still nobody doubts his greatness. "Ambedkar was a man of principles, a man with a spine, a true patriot, a realist, a loyal shepherd to his community, a scholar in his own right, a man for whom words had a definite meaning".[2] The nation's highest award, the Bharat Ratna, was conferred on him in 1990. An impressive statue of Ambedkar greets the visitors to the Parliament House reminding people about his contribution to the Indian Constitution and to the nation.

## References

1. Keer, Dhananjaya. *Dr. Ambedkar: Life and Mission*. Bombay, Popular Prakashan. 1962, p.437.
2. Elst, Koenraad. *Dr. Ambedkar: A True Aryan*. New Delhi, Voice of India. 1993, p.1.

# Charles Freer Andrews

## (1871-1940)

C.F. Andrews was one of those Britishers who identified themselves with India and the Indians and worked for their social and political emancipation. While Sister Nivedita had beome a Hindu and Annie Besant a Theosophist (the two other Britishers who worked for the same cause), Andrews remained a devout Christian to the end.

Charles Freer Andrews was born on 12 February 1871 at Newcastle-on-Tyne. He was the son of a Christian minister (priest) belonging to very orthodox apostolic church. In 1876 the family moved to Birmingham where Andrews attended King Edward VI School. He was fond of poetry and painting while in school. In 1890, he won an open scholarship and joined Pembroke College at Cambridge from where he obtained the Classical Tripos in first class, and in 1895 the Theology Tripos. Due to the influence of his Christian friends at Cambridge, he broke with the orthodox church of his father and was ordained in the Church of England in 1896. Like a true Christian, he started working for the poor. After a year of working among them in the north of England, he came to London and started doing social work in the East End where the poor lived, under the aegis of the Christian Social Union.

Andrews decided to come to India when he learnt about the death of a missionary Basil Westcott, who had gone to India to serve the Indian Mission. Westcott, in his writings, had spoken highly of India, placing it alongside Greece. Andrews reached India on 20 March 1904 to join the Cambridge Brotherhood and to teach at St. Stephen's College, Delhi. Years later he claimed this date as, 'a second birthday in my life'. Here he met Sushil Kumar Rudra, an Indian Christian, who was vice-principal of the college at that time. A very fruitful friendship between the two ensued, which continued even when Andrews left the college after eight years. In 1907, Hibbert-Ware, the principal of the college, was offered bishopric in one of the British colonies. Andrews was offered the post of the principal. He declined and pleaded that Sushil Rudra, who was the vice-principal at the time and his senior at the college by many years, should get it. Till then no Indian Christian had been appointed as principal of the college. Andrew's forceful plea was considered, and with lot of misgivings Rudra was appointed principal by the management. Rudra became very popular with the students and the staff and was an admirable host. Many national leaders used to visit him and some even stayed with him. Through Rudra, Andrews came to know leaders like Gokhale, Lajpat Rai and Shraddhanand. Gandhi used to stay with Rudra whenever in Delhi after his return from South Africa till Rudra's death in 1925. It was also through Rudra that Andrews came to understand India and love the country and her people. Years later Andrews wrote, "I owe to Sushil Rudra what I owe to no one else in the world; a friendship which has made India from the first not a strange land but a familiar country". At St. Stephen's, Andrews became the most admired teacher. He could teach any subject in the humanities but he enjoyed teaching English poetry and history most. Even during his stay at St. Stephen's, Andrews used to visit the *'chamar basti'* (cobbler's slum) nearby to help the poor cobblers and their families.

In 1912, during his visit to England, Andrews attended a small private gathering where W.B. Yeats, the famous Irish poet, read some of Tagore's poems from the English version of *Gitanjali*. Like others present, Andrews was much moved by the poetic vision of Tagore. The same evening Andrews had an intimate conversation with the poet and a bond was forged between the two which became stronger with the passage of time. Tagore's poems, thought Andrews, contained a message for the West. Tagore, ten years senior to Andrews, became *gurudev* (the sublime teacher) for Andrews.

On returning to India, Andrews met Gokhale, who asked him to visit South Africa and help Gandhi in finalising the agreement with the South African authorities. Andrews, along with another British missionary Rev. W. Pearson, reached Durban on 2 January 1914. Gandhi, along with some of his followers, was at the docks to receive them. This was Andrews' first, meeting with Gandhi and Andrews 'quickly and unobtrusively bent down and touched Gandhi's feet, the Indian way of showing respect. They became friends and started informally addressing each other as Mohan and Charlie. Andrews helped Gandhi to arrive at an honourable end to his satyagraha, working through Lord Gladstone, governor general of South Africa (son of William E. Gladstone, prime minister of England). Andrews had known the Gladstone family in England and with their help "he was able to infiltrate the entire government of South Africa". Mission completed, he returned to India via London. During this period he had studied Tagore and before embarking, he gave two lectures on Tagore in Cape Town, one in the City Hall and the other in the University of Cape Town (February 1914). Andrews was indeed greatly attracted to Rabindranath Tagore and found his peace and permanent abode in Shantiniketan, which he first visited in April, 1914. The poet welcomed him with a song that he had composed for Andrews. Andrews joined Shantiniketan in 1915 and it was his home till his last days. In addition to teaching, Andrews helped Shantiniketan in various other ways. When the institution was in financial trouble, he went literally from door to door to raise funds for it. He helped Sriniketan, the agricultural wing of Shantiniketan, to develop and worked in nearby villages to help the poor farmers. He accompanied Tagore when he visited China and Japan in 1916. The letters that passed between Andrews and Tagore, project the deep bond of friendship and love they had for each other. In a letter to Tagore on 23 May 1914 Andrews wrote: "Your letters have been coming to me morning by morning. They have brought me a vision of a larger, fuller life than I had ever known". From Paris, Tagore wrote to Andrews on 7 September 1920. "Your letters always bring the atmosphere of Santiniketan round my mind, with all its colour and sound and movements. Your letters are great gifts to me. I have not the power to repay them in kind".[1]

Nehru met Andrews for the first time in 1920 when he visited Shantiniketan along with Gandhi. Nehru wrote about their meeting: "I remember C.F. Andrews giving me some books which interested and influenced me greatly. They dealt with the economic aspects of imperialism in Africa. About this time or a little later, Andrews wrote a pamphlet advocating independence for India. I think it was called *Independence, the Immediate Need*. This was a brilliant essay and it seemed to me not only to make out an unanswerable case for independence but also to mirror the innermost recesses of our hearts".[2]

Andrews admired Gandhi and was fascinated and surprised at the respect and reverence in which he was held by the masses. As already described earlier, he first met Gandhi in South Africa early in 1915. He worked with Gandhi in the Champaran district of Bihar in 1917, to help the indigo workers. Later, he was with Gandhi during his serious illness in 1918 and 1934, nursing him round the clock. During the Round Table Conference in London (1931) he was with Gandhi explaining his views to the English people, bureaucrats and the media. He was with Gandhi whenever the latter required 'Charlie's' help. But his admiration and friendship notwithstanding, he was highly critical of Gandhi about his certain policies and idiosyncrasies. He opposed Gandhi for going from village after village to get recruits for the British army during the First World War and criticised him for his double talk and going against his own principles of non-violence. Andrews, along with Tagore, came down heavily on Gandhi when he made a dramatic bonfire of foreign clothes during the Non-Cooperation Movement. "What advantage there was in burning the noble handiwork of one's fellow men and women", he asked. "I almost fear now to wear the *khaddar* you have given me", he wrote, "lest I should appear to be judging other people as a Pharisee would, saying I am holier than thou". Once again he was critical of Gandhi, along with Tagore and others, for asking students to leave their educational institutions. In the words of Tagore: "it was like utilizing the fire from the alter of sacrifice in incendiarism". Andrews felt that the movement should not be run by a rabble and criticised Gandhi for his greed to enlarge his following with men of doubtful integrity. Andrews also felt dismayed when Gandhi attacked Christian missionaries (he being one of the tribe) and wrote strongly to Gandhi about it.

Few had realized at the time that Andrews' spirit of nationalism was more militant than that of Gandhi. Even during the Non-Cooperation Movement the Congress leaders, including Gandhi, were not sure what actually they meant by swaraj. The maximum they could concieve of was some kind of dominion status. But on 9 January 1921, addressing a large meeting of the Calcutta students, Andrews advocated "independence, complete and perfect, as against the soulsapping white-supremacy". It was left for an Englishman, and a Christian missionary at that, to come out with a clear statement about the objective of the freedom movement. Andrews was to repeat this later from hundreds of platforms and in his numerous articles published in India and abroad.[3] It took the Congress another nine years to spell out this theme during the Lahore session (1929-30).

Wherever poor Indians were ill-treated and discriminated Andrews rushed to their help, not only in India but also in foreign lands. This mission of his took him to South and East Africa several times. It was the evil of indenture labour under which the Indian labourers were transported to various British colonies, where they were treated like bonded labourers. To get them justice, Andrews visited Fiji in 1915 and again in 1917. In 1929, he made a personal investigation about their problems in the West Indies and British Guyana. In India, he fought for the rights of the labour class. In 1918, he intervened in the strike of Madras cotton-workers and in 1919 he helped organise relief work among unemployed tea-estate workers stranded at Chandpur (now in Bangladesh). In 1920, he brought to the attention of the government, the plight of forced labour in Rajputana and Simla hills and in 1921-22 identified himself with the cause of striking railway workers at Tundla (Uttar Pradesh). In 1925, he was elected president of the worker's union at Tata factory at Jamshedpur, got the union recognized and the dispute settled with the company. In 1925 and 1927 he was elected president of the Indian Trade Union Congress.

He was equally concerned with the plight of the 'untouchables' and criticised Gandhi for not doing enough for them by frittering away his energy in political work. "Independence", he wrote, "can never be won if the millions of untouchables remain still in subjection". The sympathy with the untouchables made him join the Vykom satyagraha in 1925, getting the road leading to the temple opened for them. He also worked with Ambedkar in formulating the Harijan demands in 1933.

Andrews was a delightful eccentric. He had no sense of possession and was often seen in clothes which did not fit him well, giving him a sloppy appearance. He often walked barefoot even to the offices of high officials. "Andrews was one of those quiet men who wear authority like an invisible garment. He had entry into places rarely entered by missionaries. He would sit down over a tea cup with a prime minister, and the next day, without any warning, there would be an official proclamation, or an order in Council, signed by the prime minister and written with the stub of Andrew's pencil".[4]

From 1935 Andrews divided his time between India and England. He also once again began to exercise his Christian ministry. He had never ceased to regard himself as a fully-committed member of his church, notwithstanding his discarding missionary robes in 1914. Christ remained the centre of his life. Devotion to Him was Andrews' outstanding characteristic, and the source of his inspiration and strength. During the last months at Shantiniketan he often expressed the hope that in this place, where the civilisations of the world can share with each other the bases of their strength, there might be established a 'Hall of Christian Culture' similar to the 'Cheena Bhavan'.

Like in the case of most Britishers in India the climate did not suit him. Insomnia was another of his problems. Over the years he had become very lean and thin and lost much of his vitality. He was operated upon on 31 March 1940 at Dr. Riordan's Nursing Home in Calcutta and died of complications on 5 April 1940. In his will he had written: "I wish to be buried in the Christian faith, a Christian, near St. Paul's Cathedral, Calcutta — if possible with the blessing of the Metropolitan (archbishop) — as a priest of the Christian Church and minister of the Christian faith which I hold with all my heart". The Metropolitan did come to bless him before he died. He is buried in the Lower Circular Road cemetery. Gandhi in a statement to the press said: "He (Andrews) will live through those thousands who have enriched themselves by personal contact or contact with his writings. In my opinion Charlie Andrews was one of the greatest and best Englishmen".

# References

1.  Jaggi, O.P. *Friends of India*, p.7.
2.  Nehru, Jawaharlal, *An Autobiography*. OUP. 1980, p.66. (First pub. Bodley Head, London, 1936).
3.  Ray Chaudhury, P.C. *Gandhi and His Contemporaries*. New Delhi, Sterling. 1986, p.46.
4.  Payne, Robert. *The Life and Death of Mahatma Gandhi*. New Delhi, Rupa. 1997, p.267. (First pub. 1969 by Dutton, New York).

# Abul Kalam Azad

## (1888-1958)

Abul Kalam Azad was born in Mecca (Arabia) in 1888, where his father Maulana Khairuddin had migrated from India earlier. There he had married an Arab lady, Aliya. Their second son was given the name Firoz Bakht, but he was called Muhiyuddin during his childhood, and later came to be known as Maulana Abul Kalam Azad. He coined the name Abul Kalam Azad himself, when he started his journalistic career, just before the First World War. His parents came to Calcutta when he was about two years old. His mother-tongue during his childhood was Arabic as his mother Aliya did not know any other language but Arabic.

Abul Kalam Azad did not have any formal education, not even in a *madrasa*. Initially, he was taught by his father, who was a scholar of Arabic and Persian. Later, tutors were arranged for the young boy who taught him various subjects like philosophy, mathematics and logic in Arabic, besides the Islamic scriptures. He completed this informal education by the age of sixteen, which resulted in his mastery over Arabic and Persian. It was easy for him to learn Urdu, its script being the same as that of Persian and became a competent and forceful writer in these languages. His speeches in chaste Urdu drew attention and respect among the Urdu speaking people. However, with his somewhat Persianised Urdu he could never have a mass following. His claim that he learnt English on his own and could read books in English on philosophy and history, is not supported by the events of his later life. He was not able to converse in English with the English officials and statesmen; an interpreter always accompanied him. The only book in the English language which stands in his name (*India Wins Freedom*) was dictated by him in Urdu to Humayun Kabir, who translated it into English. Azad never learnt Hindi in the Devnagari script, even after it had become the national language in 1950. Azad even used to sign the official files in Urdu while serving as education minister in Nehru's Cabinet.

Azad had a sharp intellect and was eager to learn. He decided to get out of the rigid orthodoxy of the Muslim theology, as preached by his father and other *ullamas* (Muslim scholars). This was the time he changed his name to 'Abul Kalam Azad', marking his 'freedom' from orthodoxy. After completing his studies, he began to move in wider circles, which broadened his views. The partition of Bengal by Lord Curzon in 1905 had agitated the Bengalis and a terrorist movement had started in Bengal under the leadership of Aurobindo Ghose and others. Azad claims that "he had been attracted to revolutionary politics and joined one of the groups", but there is no record of his joining any revolutionary group in the annals of the freedom movement. In 1908, Azad visited Iraq, Egypt, Syria and Turkey and as a result, he was attracted to the concept of Pan-Islamism. On his return to India, Maulana Azad started a weekly *Al-Hilal* (the crescent) from Calcutta in Urdu in 1912. This was the time when the Balkan Wars started, in which Turkey was involved. His paper carried a strong campaign along with *Comrade* of Muhammad Ali, in favour of Turkey and became the mouthpiece of the anti-British propaganda. In the pages of *Al-Hilal*, Azad highlighted the belief that Abdul Hamid of Turkey was the universal Caliph of the Muslim world and that the territorial integrity of his empire should be preserved at all costs. He argued that the institution of Caliphate was necessary to secure the organic unity of the Muslim world. The writings of Sir Syed Ahmed asserting that Abdul Hamid was not a Caliph for Indian Muslims were attacked by him.[1] The anti-British tirade became even harsher when Turkey lost most of the European territory to the Christian nations in 1913. The government banned the publication of *Al-Hilal* in 1914, and confiscated the security amount. Thereupon, Maulana Azad started another weekly journal, *Al-Balagh*, in 1914. By that time, the First World War had started and Turkey was fighting against the British on the side of the Central Powers. *Al-Balagh* took off from where *Al-Hilal* had left. The denunciation of British imperialism and the importance of the Khalifa who was also the Sultan of Turkey continued. *Al-Balagh* met the same fate as that of *Al-Hilal;* the press was confiscated by the government in 1916 and the paper banned. Maulana Azad was interned and kept at Ranchi till December 1919. The First World War ended in 1918 with the defeat of the Central Powers, which included Turkey. Under the Treaty of Sevres, the Ottoman Empire was liquidated. The Pan-Islamic leaders led by the Ali brothers and Maulana Azad started the Khilafat movement in November 1919 against the treatment of the Khalifa by the British. Its central demand was that the Khalifa retains the control of places sacred to Islam and be left with sufficient territory to enable him to defend the Islamic faith and holy places. The Khilafat Conference considered the feasibility of non-cooperation with the government to achieve its end. The movement was strengthened when Gandhi joined hands with the Khilafat leaders and started a Non-Cooperation Movement, adding Punjab atrocities and swaraj to the agenda, for wider support. Gandhi had, thus, reduced the Congress party to the status of an extension of the Khilafat Committee, pushing it in the direction of a conflict with the government, as directed by the Khilafists. The Khilafat movement came to an end in 1922, when the Khalifa was ousted from Turkey by the Turkish people themselves, putting Gandhi, Azad and other Khilafat leaders in an embarrassing situation. The Non-Cooperation Movement was also suspended by Gandhi in February 1922. When this Pan-Islamic movement fizzled out, the Ali brothers (Muhammad and Shaukat) deserted the Congress gradually but Maulana Azad stayed on in the Congress party. As a reward, he was elected to preside over the special session of the Congress in September 1923 at Delhi. As a Congressman, he was imprisoned several times during the agitations sponsored by the Congress party from time to time.

During his internship at Ranchi, Azad had started translating the Quran in the Urdu language, which was published in 1930 as *Turjuman al-Quran*. It contains a clear "exposition of his religious thought in its maturity". It was later translated into English by Dr. Syed Abdul Latif and is considered a monumental work of its kind.

In 1928, Azad presided over the Nationalist Muslim Conference. In 1937, he was appointed a member of the Congress Parliamentary Sub-Committee to guide the Provincial Congress Ministries working under the 1935 Act. Maulana Azad came into the limelight when he was elected president of the Congress party in 1940. He devoted the best part of his presidential address on 19 March 1940, to the communal question, and assured the Muslims of fullest guarantees to the rights and interests of the minorities in any future constitution, and leaving it to the minorities to decide the form of safeguards needed by them. He observed that eighty or ninety million Muslims could not be treated as a political minority though they formed only twenty-five per cent of the population. Moreover, they were more homogeneous and strong as compared to other communities. He further added that any constitution for an all-India federation would provide full autonony to the provinces and arm the federal centre with only all-India matters such as foreign relations, defence, customs etc. Three days later, the Muslim League passed the famous resolution at Lahore demanding separate areas for the Muslims, which was attended by over a hundred thousand Muslims.

Even after his election as Congress president, Maulana Azad did not adhere to all the tenets of Gandhism. He did not spin regularly as was required by the Congress constitution. Azad also did not believe in non-violence. In his opinion, opposing violence with violence was fully in harmony with the natural laws of God, in circumstances under which Islam permits the use of violence. In a letter to Jawaharlal Nehru on 13 July 1942, Gandhi wrote: "This is my plea about Maulana Saheb. I find that the two of us have drifted apart. I do not understand him, nor does he understand me. We are drifting apart on the Hindu-Muslim question as well as on other questions. I have also a suspicion that Maulana Saheb does not entirely approve of the proposed action (Quit India Movement). Therefore I suggest that the Maulana should relinquish Presidentship but remain in the Committee. The Committee should elect an interim President and all should proceed unitedly".[2] Such views deprived Azad of a large Hindu following. During the parliamentary elections, he had to stand from constituencies in North-West Frontier, Rampur and Gurgaon, where there was a large presence of Muslim voters. Fortunately for Azad, the Congress leaders, including Gandhi and Azad, were arrested the following month and the question of Azad resigning as president was postponed indefinitely. In fact, he acted as president of the Congress till June 1946. During this period, being the Congress president, he was spokesman too. He participated in the negotiations during the Cripps Mission (March-April 1942), Simla Conference (June 1945) and Cabinet Mission (March-June 1946). His role as the principal negotiator of the Congress, however, has come under a cloud. "It will always remain a matter of speculation whether it was a blessing or the reverse that at this crucial phase of India's history Maulana Abul Kalam Azad happened to be the President of the Congress", wrote V. Shankar, editor of Sardar Patel's correspondence.[3] While the Cripp's Mission was rejected by the Congress and the Simla Conference failed on flimsy grounds, the greatest boon offered to the Muslims was by the Cabinet Mission proposals. It was stipulated that the Muslim majority areas will be grouped in a way that the whole of Punjab, Bengal and Assam will be included in it; that there will be a very weak centre having jurisdiction to foreign affairs, defence and communications only; and the rest of the subjects will be directly under the provinces, which will have an option to cede after ten years; that Muslims will have fifty per cent seats in the legislature (Parliament) and in the executive (ministry). The Maulana could see that Muslims could never have a better bargain and was so excited at the proposal that he wrote to the Mission members that he would get the proposals accepted by the Congress, even if Gandhi and others opposed them. Stafford Cripps (a member of the Mission) sent this letter to Gandhi, through his emissary Sudhir Ghosh. Gandhi had just finished reading the letter when the Maulana walked in. Gandhi asked the Maulana if he had written such a letter. The Maulana, with a straight face, denied it. Gandhi was stunned. The Maulana had lost Gandhi's trust. Later, Gandhi in a letter to Nehru on 24 July 1947 wrote that he should drop the Maulana from his Cabinet. Nehru did not heed the advice as he needed persons like Azad and Rafi Ahmed Kidwai as a bulwark against the rising tide of, what he termed as, "Hindu communalism and revivalist outlook of certain leaders like Purushottam Das Tandon, Rajendra Prasad and others". Nehru was very unhappy at the victory of this group in getting Hindi, in Devanagari script, recognised as the official language of India in the Constituent Assembly, in spite of his opposition. The victory of Rajendra Prasad as president of India (1950) and of Purushottam Das Tandon as Congress president (1950) over Nehru's candidates should also be seen in this light. To spite the *Hindi-wallahs*, he had appointed Azad who did not know Devanagari nor much about Indian culture as education and cultural minister. Maulana Azad remained so till his death in 1958, although he could not attend office during the last two years of his life, due to ill-health. It must be said to his credit that during his tenure as education minister two education commissions, the University Education Commission (1948) and the Secondary Education Commission (1952) were appointed. During this period several other educational and cultural institutions were created: University Grants Commission; Indian Council of Cultural Relations, "to foster goodwill between India and Pakistan and to create communal harmony"; three academies, Sahitya, Sangeet Natak and Lalit Kala. The Delhi Public Library was established in 1950 with the help of UNESCO. He took great interest in ICCR. The building in which it is situated is called Azad Bhavan. But he did not take much interest in the development and working of the other institutions, including the academies.

His claim of being a secular Muslim leader must be taken with a pinch of salt because even after independence he continued to help the Muslim cause. He brought many Muslim officers, holding high positions, back to India, who had migrated to Pakistan. In his ministry, all the key posts were held by Muslims: Humayun Kabir, K.G. Saidayin, Ashrafaque Hussain, Nurul Hassan. In speech after speech, he advised the Muslims not to migrate to Pakistan because "it will weaken the Muslims of India". During the post-Partition days, he exaggerated the death and plight of the Muslims in Delhi, oblivious of the pitiable condition of millions of Hindu and Sikh refugees. Along with Mountbatten, he incited Gandhi to undergo a fast unto death for the release of fifty-five crore rupees to Pakistan, a country at war with India, against the declared policy of the government. Gandhi's fast was camouflaged as being meant for Hindu-

Muslim unity though there were no riots in Delhi at that time. Lord Mountbatten has spilled the beans, asserting in his memoirs that the fast was essentially to force the government to release fifty crore rupees to Pakistan.[5]

However, the character of Maulana Azad is revealed to a greater extent in the pages of his memoirs *India wins Freedom*. The first edition of the book was published in 1959 and the fuller version which included the most controversial thirty pages, in 1988. In this, he has reviled persons like Gandhi, Rajendra Prasad and even Nehru, his benefactor and faithful friend. But his worst venom was reserved for Sardar Patel, whom he called communal, anti-Muslim and worse, on page after page. The Maulana received brickbats for writing such a book from unexpected quarters. Rammanohar Lohia, while reviewing his book, wrote, "Maulana's book contains at least one lie on each page and it is wholly unreliable in respect of historical interpretation. The whole story is an uninteresting lie". While comparing Azad with Jinnah, Lohia wrote, "In calling Maulana Azad a better Muslim than Mr. Jinnah, I am not concerned with their religiocity. I am only concerned with the extent to which they served the interests of the Muslims in India. Both of them strove outwardly very outspokenly but also perhaps with inward passion, to realize Muslim interests as distinct from the interests of the Indian people as a whole. The Maulana was a better servant of Muslims than was Mr. Jinnah".[6] About so called 'Nationalist' Muslims like Maulana Azad, Ambedkar wrote, "It is extremely doubtful whether the Nationalist Musalmans have any real community of sentiment, aim and policy with the Congress which marks them off from the Muslim League. Indeed, many Congressmen are alleged to hold the view that there is no difference between the two and that the Nationalist Muslims inside the Congress are only an outpost of the communal Muslims.[7] According to Rajmohan Gandhi, "Pride was Azad's failing. We glimpse it in *India Wins Freedom* in the form of 'I-was-wiser-than-the-rest.' He refers several times to the errors of Gandhi, Nehru and Patel and not less frequently to his own sounder judgement. 'Later events proved how justified my apprehensions were'. We encounter such sentences a shade too often".[8] But whatever his own assessment of himself, Maulana did not wield much influence in the decision-making process of the Congress. That remained primarily with Gandhi, Nehru and Patel. "His presence was at best a vindication of the Congress claim that it also represented Muslims".

As a person, he was a personification of dignity; tall, slim and fair with well-trimmed moustache and goatee, and with a Faiz cap covering his head, he looked more like a Muslim divine than a politician. He was a loner and had few friends. He was a chain-smoker and according to M.O. Mathai, a heavy drinker and would not like attending a meeting or dinner party after six in the evening, a time for his rendezvous with the bottle. He did not have much of a family life. His wife Zuleikha Begum gave birth to a baby boy, who died soon after birth. Zuleikha died in 1943, while the Maulana was interned in Ahmednagar Fort during the Quit India Movement. He did not go to Calcutta for her last rites but wrote a very sentimental letter to one of his friends about her, to unburden his feelings, showing his humane side. During the last years of his life he was keeping indifferent health. Around 1946, he fell down, broke his backbone and could not walk without help. He died at the age of seventy, on 22 February 1958. He is buried in the lawns outside Jama Masjid, Delhi.

## References

1. Nagarkar, V.V. *Genesis of Pakistan*. Allied. 1975, pp.98-99 and A.C. Banerjee: *Two Nations; Philosophy of Muslim Nationalism*. New Delhi, Concept. 1981, p.209.
2. *Collected Works of Mahatma Gandhi*. Vol. 76, p.293.
3. Shankar, V. ed. *Sardar Patel; Select Correspondence, 1945-1950*. Vol. I. Ahmedabad, Navajivan. 1976, p.58.
4. *Collected Works of Mahatma Gandhi*. Vol. 88, p.408.
5. Collins, Larry and Dominique Lapierre. *Mountbatten and the Partition of India*. New Delhi, Vikas. 1983, p.52.
6. Lohia, Rammanohar. *Guilty Men of India's Partition*. Hyderabad. 1970, pp.12, 16.
7. Ambedkar, B.R. *Pakistan or the Partition of India*, Bombay, Thackers. 3rd. ed. 1945, p.408.
8. Gandhi, Rajmohan. *Eight Lives; A Study of Hindu-Muslim Encounter*. New Delhi, Roli Books. 1986, p.251.

# Chandra Shekhar Azad

## (1906-1931)

Chandra Shekhar was one of the most daring revolutionaries to sacrifice his life for the freedom of the country.

Chandra Shekhar was born on 23 July 1906 in Bhavra village, which is now in the Jhabua district of Madhya Pradesh. His father, Sita Ram Tiwari, was a watchman in a state garden, on a salary of ten rupees a month. His mother Jagrani had given birth to three children prior to him, who did not survive; Chandra Shekhar thus got special love and care from his poor parents. As a child he attended the village school but did not take much interest in studies and used to roam about and play with tribal boys, using bows and arrows as toys. The village life somehow did not interest him and one day he left without informing his parents. He was fourteen at the time. His worried parents were relieved when they received a letter from their son telling them that he was in Kashi, studying Sanskrit in a *pathshala* (school). As board and lodging was free, he had no worry about his daily needs. It is believed that he lived in a room adjacent to the Batuknath temple in Kamachha locality of Varanasi for some years.

In 1920, the Congress party under the leadership of Gandhi started the Non-Cooperation Movement. The young Chandra Shekhar participated in the movement and took part in picketing. He was arrested and tried before a magistrate. When asked his name by the magistrate he said: 'Azad'; his father's name?, 'freedom'; his address? 'prison'. The magistrate was furious and he ordered fifteen lashes to be inflicted on Chandra Shekhar's bare body. After every lash, he uttered *Bande Matram*. He was only fifteen when this happened. This incident made Chandra Shekhar somewhat of a celebrity in Kashi and from that time on he came to be known as *Azad*. Important citizens of Kashi, like Shiv Prasad Gupta, admired the bravery of the boy and he was felicitated at a meeting of the Congress party soon after.

After the failure and suspension of the Non-Cooperation Movement, there was overall frustration among the people. There was a revival of revolutionary activities, spread over the whole of north India from Bengal to Punjab. A meeting of the revolutionaries was held at Kanpur in October 1924, which was attended by revolutionary leaders from different parts of India. An all-India organisation was set up under the name of Hindustan Republican association, later called Hindustan Socialist Republican Association or Army. Chandra Shekhar joined this association. In Uttar Pradesh, it was led by Ramprasad Bismal. In the Punjab, it was guided by Bhagat Singh and his associates. As the association needed money to survive, they planned dacoities. But instead of looting innocent individals, they decided to loot the government treasury. The most notable exploit was the dacoity on 9 August 1925 in a railway train, proceeding from Kakori towards Alamnagar near Lucknow. Ten young men stopped the train, fired to scare the guard and passengers, broke open the iron safe and disappeared with a large amount of money. Chandra Shekhar was one of these ten young men and had taken a leading part in the dacoity. The government launched a vigorous search for those responsible for this daring act. Indiscriminate arrests were made and the police was able to uncover the whole plot. The leaders were put on trial. Ramprasad, Roshan Singh and Ashfaqulla were hanged. Twelve others were sentenced to various terms of imprisonment. Chandra Shekhar had escaped, adopting several guises. The aftermath of the Kakori incident had a very adverse effect on the movement of the revolutionaries in UP. "Chandra Shekhar Azad, the sole remaining absconder of the Kakori Conspiracy Case took the leading part in re-organizing the revolutionary movement. The name of the Association was changed to Hindustan Socialist Republican Association with a Socialist State in India as its objective".[1] All this was planned with the help of Bhagat Singh whom Chandra Shekhar had met in the office of *Pratap*, (edited by Ganesh Shankar Vidyarthi) in Kanpur. Some of the exploits thereafter were performed in collaboration with Bhagat Singh and his colleagues. In 1926, Bhagat Singh along with Chandra Shekhar planned to rescue the prisoners of Kakori case but the plan fell through. The first overt act of importance of the newly organised association was the murder of Saunders, assistant commissioner of police, Lahore on 17 December 1928, who was mistaken for Scott, believed to be responsible for *lathi* blows on Lala Lajpat Rai during the anti-Simon Commission demonstration in Lahore. This was planned by Bhagat Singh, Rajguru and Chandra Shekhar but the shots were fired by Bhagat Singh. All the three left Lahore immediately after the murder, Chandra Shekhar in the guise of a *sadhu*.

Like the Kakori case earlier, the Lahore Conspiracy Case also adversely affected the activities of the Hindustan Socialist Republican Association. Almost all the prominent leaders were either dead or in jail, with the exception of about half a dozen who had managed to evade arrest. In this dark hour, Chandra Shekhar emerged as the leader of the group and organised the association. Their first activity was an attempt to murder the viceroy. A few bombs exploded under the viceroy's special train near Delhi in December, 1929. The train was damaged but the viceroy escaped unhurt. Next, Chandra Shekhar planned an armed revolution and for that purpose looted Rs. 14,000 in an armed robbery on a firm in Delhi on 6 July 1930. In the course of investigation the police got information about the secret plans of Chandra Shekhar. One of his trusted lieutenants was arrested a few days later with a large stock of arms, and the police discovered a bomb factory in Delhi with a stock of chemicals enough to make six thousand bombs. Chandra Shekhar fled towards Punjab and his presence there resulted in the explosion of a series of bombs which killed and injured a few officials. The police made a vigorous but fruitless search for him in the course of which they arrested a number of revolutionaries and discovered several depots of arms and small bomb factories. The government instituted two cases: the Second Lahore Conspiracy Case and the New Delhi Conspiracy Case. Chandra Shekhar was the principal accused but he succeeded to stay in hiding. The government offered a reward of ten thousand rupees to anyone who could help in the capture of Chandra Shekhar, dead or alive.[2] He was constantly on the move, still trying to put new life in the association with the help of those who were not yet arrested. But there were not many left and new recruits were hard to come by. He was a worried man. In an effort to elicit the sympathy and guidance from the Congress leaders, Chandra Shekhar met Jawaharlal Nehru in February 1931. Nehru describes the meeting thus: "I remember a curious incident about this time which gave me an insight into the mind of the terrorist group in India. A stranger came to see me at our house, and I was told that he was Chandra Shekhar Azad. I had never seen him before, but I had heard of him ten years earlier, when he had non-cooperated from school and gone to prison during the N.C.O. movement in 1921. A boy of fifteen or so then, he had been flogged in prison for some breech of gaol discipline. Later, he had drifted towards the terrorists, and he became one of their prominent men in north India. All this I had heard vaguely, and I had taken no interest in these rumours. I was surprised, therefore, to see him. He had been induced to visit me because of the general expectation (owing to our release) that some negotiations between the Government and the Congress were likely. He wanted to know if, in case of a settlement, his group of people would have any peace. Would they still be considered and treated as outlaws; hunted out from place to place with a price on their heads, and the prospect of the gallows ever before them? Or was there a possibility of their being allowed to pursue peaceful vocations? He told me that as far as he was concerned, as well as many of his associates, they were convinced now that purely terrorist methods were futile and did no good. He was not, however, prepared to believe that India would gain her freedom wholly by peaceful methods. I tried to explain to Chandra Shekhar what my philosophy of political action was, and tried to convert him to my viewpoint. But I had no answer to his basic question: what was he to do now"?[3]

Dejected with Nehru's reply, Chandra Shekhar had no alternative but to continue the struggle with the help of a few remaining revolutionaries. His movements and activities during the last year of his life are not chronicled properly. He must have remained in U.P., visiting places like Kanpur and Varanasi. However, we know that in February 1931 he was in Allahabad. Most of his revolutionary comrades of the time believe that Azad was betrayed by an associate who turned traitor. On 27 February 1931, his presence in Alfred Park was communicated to the police who then surrounded it. For quite sometime he held them at bay, firing from his pistol. Two police officials were seriously wounded in the gun battle which lasted for half an hour. Ultimately, his body was riddled with police bullets and he died on the spot.[4] Thus ended the life of a great revolutionary. While the country was mourning the death of this martyr, twenty-four days later news came from Lahore that Bhagat Singh, Sukhdev and Rajguru had been hanged. The four were revolutionary comrades in life; and martyrs in death.

## References

1.  Majumdar, R.C. *History of the Freedom Movement in India*. Vol. III. Calcutta, Firma KLM. 1988, pp.423-24.
2.  Ibid p.430.
3.  Nehru, Jawaharlal. *Autobiography*, OUP. 1936, pp.261-62.
4.  Azad, Prithvi Singh, Chandra Shekhar Azad, in *Dictionary of National Biography*, ed. by S.P. Sen. Calcutta, 1972.

# Bahadur Shah II (Zafar)

## (1775-1862)

Bahadur Shah is considered as the last Mughal king, though he was only *de jure* king by the courtesy of the East India Company. Bahadur Shah's grandfather Shah Alam II and father Akbar II were pensioners of the East India Company. So was Bahadur Shah, getting one lakh rupees as monthly pension. However, like his father the Company had allowed him to be the titular head of a non-existing 'empire'.

Bahadur Shah's earlier name was Abu'l Zafar and he was born in 1775. Little is known of Abu'l Zafar's childhood. There is no certainty even about the place of his birth and where he spent his childhood. He received instruction in Urdu, Persian and Arabic from private teachers and also learnt military arts of horse-riding, swordcraft and shooting with firearms and bows and arrows. We get only faint glimpses of him during his youth. His father Akbar II did not want him to succeed, and preferred his younger son Jehangir, who even tried to poison his elder brother twice, perhaps with the connivance of their father. However, the East India Company intervened and declared that they would recognise only the elder brother as heir apparent. Besides, being younger, Jehangir was of doubtful character. "There is no doubt that he (Bahadur Shah) was the best fitted of Akbar's sons to succeed".

During the period of his youth, Bahadur Shah "appears throughout the records as a man of culture and upright character". In 1806, when he was thirty-two, and his father was trying to pass him over in favour of Jehangir, he was described as a 'very respectable character' by Charles Seton, the British Resident in Delhi. As a prince, he lived and dressed simply; was of spare figure and stature and always dressed plainly without ostentation. These habits he retained during his reign as well. In the palace-diary of later years, there are glimpses of him spending whole days reading and writing, studying the Koran, and composing verses. Bahadur Shah was educated to the life of a mediatised prince, and the role fitted him perfectly. Whether he could have developed the qualities of action, we shall never know, for he was denied all opportunities in his early years and the Mutiny experience came far too late. But as a philosophic prince he would have adorned any country.[1] Bahadur Shah's interests and tastes were essentially literary and aesthetic.

On ascending the throne in 1837, when he was sixty-two years old, he assumed the name Abu Zafar Mohammad Sarajuddin Bahadur Shah Ghazi. However, he has come to be known as Bahadur Shah Zafar — Zafar being his nom de plume. As he was only a *de jure* king he had not much administrative work to do. But as king of India, he looked upon the British as his subjects, owing allegiance to him under the terms of the Diwani of Bengal, signed by his grandfather, Shah Alam in 1765. The East India Company and the British authorities, however, treated him as their pensioner whom they had granted a nominal status of a king, whose jurisdiction did not extend beyond the walls of the Red Fort. A regiment of Company guards always camped in the Red Fort. Bahadur Shah accepted this humiliating status stoically. Though a religious man, he was no bigot. He did not suffer from the vice of addiction to strong drink but he was a gourmet and loved a variety of food. He married several times and had in addition a number of concubines, slave girls and mistresses, whom he had accumulated during his long life. His favourite wife, however, was Zeenat Mahal whom he married late in life and who shared, though unwillingly, the misfortunes of his last years in exile.

But above all, Bahadur Shah was a poet and a literary patron. He seriously tried to write Urdu poetry under the guidance of first Zauq and later Ghalib — two outstanding poets of the era. "He composed several volumes of lyrics, some of which attained considerable popularity. Though not quite in the same rank as Ghalib and Zauq, he has his niche in the Urdu literary pantheon and his merit cannot be denied. It is this gift, much more than his crown, which gave him his place in the life of Delhi, and it is this even more than his political misfortunes, which has caused him to be affectionately remembered by the people."[2] He used to have *mushairas* (poetic gatherings) in his palace which were attended by leading poets and intellectuals of the city. Life in the city was placid and the majority of the citizens, rich and poor, seemed to be contented. Bahadur Shah did not interfere in the administration of the city and let the British do the job in his name. It gave the British an aura of legality and Bahadur Shah got unfettered time to indulge in poetic, and aesthetic pursuits, secure in receiving his pension regularly, though it was inadequate to maintain his large establishment. He appealed to the British authorities several times to increase his pension but each time the appeal was rejected.

Then came the Mutiny in 1857 when Bahadur Shah was an old, infirm man of eighty-two. A body of mutinous sepoys and officers from Meerut (about forty miles from Delhi) marched to Delhi and forced their way into the Red Fort on 11 May 1857. The soldiers forced leadership on the reluctant Bahadur Shah and compelled him to sign documents under his seal. The rebels killed forty-nine Europeans, mostly women and children who were hiding in the Red Fort. They also killed many Christians living in nearby Darya Ganj. The rebels also searched every corner of the city for Christians and killed all those they could lay their hands on. Bahadur Shah watched all this helplessly. "Although the assumption of leadership by Bahadur Shah gave the mutiny of sepoys in Delhi a general character of popular revolt, it was nothing of the kind. Bahadur Shah had no real heart in the business and only yielded to the importunities of the sepoys. He had not the capacity to lead the sepoys and was really led by them".[3] The reluctance of the king was more than compensated by the eagerness of his sons (princes), especially Mirza Mughal, to join the rebels and to provide them with fractured leadership. But the turbulance of the rebels knew no bounds. They paid scant respect to the king and often insulted him. In the city itself, the sepoys indulged in loot and extortion and the people at large had no sympathy for the mutineers. The leaderless mob became a curse for the city and the citizens prayed for the return of the Company rule. The mutineers insisted that the king hold a durbar every day and he was paraded by them through the streets of Delhi.

Jiwan Lal, (whose 'Diary' is one of the most authentic sources of the events of 1857) wrote:

> From house to house the unwilling king was distracted by the cries and petitions — now from the servants of Europeans who had been murdered, now from the shopkeepers whose shops had been plundered, now from the higher classes whose houses had been broken into — all looked to the king for immediate redress. However, seated on a howdah through the streets of Delhi, 'he was like a cork on the swelling waves of mutiny'.[4]

Within four months it was all over. British enforcements poured into Delhi from Meerut and other nearby areas and the British re-took Delhi by the end of September. Bahadur Shah escaped to the Humayun Tomb but surrendered when the British forces surrounded the tomb, and brought him back to the Red Fort. He was tried under the military commission constituted under Act XIV of 1857, contrary to all established norms of national and international laws. The trial started on 27 January 1858, and lasted till 18 September. During his captivity in Red Fort, he was treated disgracefully huddled in two small, filthy rooms. Bahadur Shah was found guilty and was sentenced to transportation for life. He was not executed like his two sons, including Mirza Mughal, because Lt. General Sir Archdale Wilson had promised Bahadur Shah his life before arresting him and taking him into custody.[5]

In October 1858, Bahadur Shah was exiled to Rangoon. The royal assemblage left Delhi on 7 October 1858 in the dead of the night. The entourage of the emperor consisted of his beloved wife Zeenat Mahal, her minor son Mirza Jumma Bakht, another wife, four harem women, and sixteen attendants, both male and female. The royal caravan travelling in bullock-carts and palanquins took several months to reach Rangoon, where he lived for a little more than three years, pining for his beloved

Delhi and writing some memorable plaintive Urdu verses, which are sung to this day by millions of Indians:

*Lagta nahin hai ji mera ujde dyar mein*
*Kis ki bani kai alme nepaiedar mein*
*Hai kitna badnasib Zafar dafn ke liye*
*Do gaz zameen bhi na mili koi-i-yar mein*

[I am not at ease in this devastated shelter,
But whoever has been happy in this fleeting world?
How unlucky is Zafar that for his burial he could not get two yards
of land in his beloved's place (meaning Delhi).]

His poetry has kept alive his memory. Indian opinion never regarded him as a rebel, and always showed compassion towards him. With the passage of time even a halo of martyrdom and an aura of romantic sympathy has collected round the aged figure. But Bahadur Shah was neither a hero nor a villain. "His role in the uprising of 1857 has been grossly exaggerated by some Indian historians. Bahadur Shah was too weak, too ignorant, too inexperienced in the art of warfare and too resourceless to have taken an effective part as king and leader of a campaign against the British forces. His trial and conviction were clearly a travesty of justice and in the nature of a reprisal."[6] There was an ample proof of his unwillingness to do anything against the British. Still, the Company treated him badly, which led to a fate that certainly he did not deserve.

# References

1.  Spear, Percival. *A History of Delhi Under the Later Mughals*. Delhi, Low price publications. 1990, p.73. (First pub. 1951).
2.  Ibid. p.74.
3.  Majumdar, R.C. *History of the Freedom Movement in India*, Calcutta, Firma KLM. Vol.1. 1988, p.134.

4. Llewellyn, Alexander. *The Siege of Delhi*. London, Macdonald & Janis, 1977, p.42.
5. Agarwal, B.R. *Trials of Independence*. New Delhi, National Book Trust, 1991, p.7.
6. Khosla, G.D. in *Dictionary of National Biography*. ed. by S.P. Sen. Calcutta, Institute of Historical Studies. Vol.1. 1972, p.101.

# Surendranath Banerjee

## (1848-1925)

Surendranath Banerjee was a distinguished teacher, a great orator and one of the foremost leaders of the Indian National Congress for three decades after its inception.

Surendranath was born in Calcutta on 10 November 1848. He was second of the five sons of Durga Charan Banerjee, a reputed medical practitioner. Surendranath's early schooling was in a *pathshala* but at the age of seven he was sent to Parental Academic Institution, Calcutta, attended mainly by Anglo-Indian boys. He graduated from the Calcutta University in 1868. The same year, he left for England along with R.C. Dutt and Bihari Lal Gupta, to compete for the Indian Civil Service. He passed the competitive examination in 1869. There was some problem about his age, which was resolved in his favour. He qualified in the final examination in 1871 and returned to India. He was posted as assistant magistrate at Sylhet. His British superior, Mr. Sutherland, contrived to show defects in his official work, and complained to the higher authorities. A commission of enquiry was appointed; the charges were investigated and Surendranath was found guilty of serious dereliction of duty. He was dismissed from service and was sanctioned a pension of rupees fifty per month. He went to England to appeal to the India House but did not succeed. Not only was the grievous injustice not undone, but he was also debarred from enrolling at the Bar. Surendranath stayed on in England for another year (April 1874 to May 1875), devoting himself to the study of the works of Western social and political thinkers. In June 1875, he returned to India as a frustrated man, but did not lose heart and started thinking about another career. As it was proved later, the loss of the Indian Civil Service was a huge gain for the country. Surprisingly, in 1882, seven years after his dismissal, he was made an honorary presidency magistrate of Calcutta and a Justice of Peace.

Soon after his return from England, he accepted the post of a professor of English at the Metropolitan Institution at the request of Vidyasagar. In addition, he also started serving on the staff of the City College, when it was established in 1879. In 1880, he left the Metropolitan Institution and joined the Free Church College, where he stayed till 1885. In the meantime, in 1882, he had taken charge of a school known as Presidency Institution, which was later upgraded to a college and renamed Ripon College (now known as Surendranath College) after the viceroy, Lord Ripon and continued teaching there. As a teacher, he became very popular among students and inspired them with a new spirit of political consciousness. He served as a teacher for thirty-seven years from 1875 to 1912, when he was elected to the Imperial Legislative Council. "It was with great reluctance," he said, "that I ceased to be a teacher, for I loved the students and rejoiced in their company." While working as a teacher he had also been taking part in political activities and had combined a teaching career with a political career, with amazing success in both.

In 1876, he along with Anand Mohan Bose and others, formed the Indian Association, to create a strong body of public opinion about the problems facing the country. This was achieved to a great extent by the all-India political tour undertaken by Surendranath, under the auspices of the Indian Association, soon after its formation. The apparent purpose of the tour was to organise a public protest against the reduction of the age-limit of the competitors for the Indian Civil Service examination from twenty-one to nineteen years, but the real purpose "was the awakening of a spirit of unity and solidarity among the people of the different parts of India, through a sense of common grievance". He visited many important towns of north India, as far as Lahore. The following year (1877-78) he covered Bombay and Madras Presidencies. "The propaganda tour of

Surendranath from one end of the country to another constitutes a definite landmark in the history of India's political progress. It clearly demonstrated that in spite of differences in language, creed and social institutions, the English educated people of this great sub-continent were bound by a common tie of ideals and interests, creating a sense of underlying unity which enabled them to combine for a common political objective. For the first time in living memory, even historical tradition, there emerged the idea of India, over and above the congeries of states and provinces into which it was divided".[1]

Surendranath began to address and educate a much larger audience when he took up the editorship of the *Bengalee*, in January 1879, which was started by W.C. Bonnerji. Soon, it became a powerful organ of public opinion and a vehicle of mass education. It was subsequently converted into a daily and specially came into prominence during the Ilbert Bill controversy (1880s) when it ably met the diatribes of the Anglo-Indian press. He remained the editor of *Bengalee* till 1920. While Surendranath was in the midst of Ilbert Bill controversy, he happened to criticise J.F. Norris, chief justice of the Calcutta High Court, who had insisted in the production of *Saligramshila* (image of Lord Shiva) as witness in a case. Surendranath wrote that it hurt the religious sentiments of the orthodox Hindus. He was charged with contempt of court and was imprisoned for two months (May-July 1883). It raised a storm of protest throughout the country, which amply demonstrated his popularity as a national leader. After his release, Surendranath again toured the country. Taking advantage of the newly awakened sense of political unity of India, he organised under the auspices of the Indian Association the first ever all-India Political Conference in Calcutta, on 28 December 1883 which was attended by one hundred delegates from different parts of the country. This was followed by the second National Conference in December 1885, a few days before the Indian National Congress was formed in Bombay. The National Conference, headed by Surendranath forestalled the Indian National Congress in all essential aspects. He could not attend the first inaugural session, but after that, he was one of the most conspicuous and respected leaders of the Congress, till his resignation from its membership in 1918. The National Conference merged with the Indian National

Congress after 1885. Henceforth, Surendranath played a leading part in the Congress and twice presided over its sessions of 1895 (Poona) and 1902 (Ahmedabad).

The partition of Bengal in 1905 threw up several leaders who tried to mould the public opinion against this act of Lord Curzon. Surendranath was perhaps the most prominent among them. "The strong leadership and personality which he displayed throughout that memorable campaign, particularly at the Barisal Conference, made him the uncrowned king of Bengal".

Surendranath was a member of the Calcutta Corporation from 1876 to 1899. He was a member of the Congress deputation, which toured England in 1890 to plead for the representative government by reconstitution of legislative councils. He was twice elected by the Calcutta Corporation and twice by the Presidency Division to the Bengal Legislative Council, where he was a member for eight years. In 1909, he was the only member from India to attend the Imperial Press Conference. In 1912, he was chosen a member to the Imperial Legislative Council for the period 1913-16, where he moved several important resolutions.

Surendranath was a moderate like Dadabhai Naoroji, Pherozeshah Mehta, Gokhale and others. They believed in British dispensation and generosity and advocated constitutional methods as a means for achieving a representative form of government. The schism between the Extremists who believed in agitation and the Moderates, which came out in the open at the Surat session in 1907, weakened the Congress which was controlled by the Moderates like Surendranath, Pherozeshah Mehta and Gokhale. The decline in the popularity of the Congress also resulted in the unpopularity of its leaders like Surendranath and others. Thus, he reached the climax of his political career in 1906, and then set in his decline. After 1916, the Congress party came under the control of the Extremists. When the Montague-Chelmsford reforms were announced in 1918, the Congress leadership decided to oppose the reforms. On the other hand, the Moderates led by Surendranath wanted to try the reforms as they believed that the proposed reforms were a step towards representative government. When a special session of the Congress was held in Bombay in 1918 to discuss the issue, Surendranath and other Moderates boycotted it. They held a separate conference on 1 November 1918, under the presidentship of Surendranath. It was styled as the 'All-India Conference of the Moderate Party' which became the nucleus for the 'National Liberal Federation of India', formed soon after. Thus, Surendranath walked out of the Congress party which he had nurtured for more than three decades. Consequently, he practically walked out of the history of India's struggle for freedom. His becoming a minister of local self-government and health in the Bengal cabinet in 1921 and being knighted the same year, further tarnished his image as a great national leader. He came down from once famous 'Surrender Not Banerjee' to 'Sir Surrender', in the eyes of the masses.

Being a man of principles he supported the Montague-Chelmsford reforms in the *Bengalee* and wrote a series of articles against Gandhi's Non-Cooperation Movement. In one of the articles, he wrote, "Non-cooperation is nowhere as compared to the influence that swadeshism exercised over our homes and our domestic life. There are innumerable villages in Bengal where the *churkha* and *khaddar* are unknown. An industrial movement linked with political controversy may receive a momentary impulse, but in the long run it suffers by such association. An industry must be conducted on business lines. Capital, organization and expert knowledge, these constitute the basic foundations of an industrial enterprise". He further criticised Gandhi for his manic craze for Hindu-Muslim unity. In the same article he wrote, "Of course, we admire the supreme solicitude and the earnest efforts of Mr. Gandhi to secure Hindu-Muslim unity. But in judging of the communal strifes, which we all deplore, let us not, for the sake of historical justice, forget the part non-cooperation movement had in fostering and promoting it".[2]

However, Surendranath was no more the idol of the masses. His unpopularity was demonstrated by his crushing defeat in the elections for the Bengal Legislative Council by the young Bidhan Chandra Roy of the Swarajist party. The fire that burnt in Surendranath during the swadeshi movement had deserted him. He retired from active politics and spent lonely years of his remaining life like his contemporary B.C. Pal, who also had dared to challenge Gandhi. It was an extremely gracious gesture, however, on the part of Gandhi to visit Surendranath in Calcutta a few months before his death. About this visit Gandhi wrote in *Young*

*India* (14 May 1925) under the title *'The Sage of Barrackpore'*: "I was privileged to visit Sir Surendranath Banerjee at his residence at Barrackpore. I had heard that he was ailing and that age had told upon his steel frame. I was anxious, therefore, to pay my respects to him. Though he might not approve of some of my activities, my regard for him as a maker of modern Bengal and a Nester of Indian politics has not suffered any diminution. I remember the time when educated India hung on his lips. Sir Surendranath has a magnificent mansion situated on a river bank among beautiful surroundings. All around there is a great quiet. I expected to see him lying in bed, weak and care-worn. Instead, I found myself in the presence of a man standing erect from his seat to greet me affectionately and talking to me with the buoyancy of youth".[3]

Gandhi also wrote the obituary of Surendranath on the same lines when he died soon after on 6 August 1925.

The last two years of Surendranath's life were spent writing his autobiography *A Nation in the Making*. He concludes his autobiography with a plea for "cooperation and not non-cooperation, assimilation and not isolation. Any other policy was fraught with peril to our best interests and was suicidal. That is my message to my countrymen, delivered not in haste or impatience, but as the mature result of my deliberations and of my lifelong labours in the service of the motherland".

That proved to be his swansong.

## References

1. Majumdar, R.C. *History of the Freedom Movement in India*. Calcutta, Firma KLM. Vol. 1. 1988, p.328.
2. Roy Chaudhury. *Gandhi and His Contemporaries*. New Delhi, Sterling. 1972, p.229.
3. *Collected Works of Mahatma Gandhi*. New Delhi, Publications Division. Vol. 27, pp.58-59.

# Annie Besant

## (1847-1933)

Annie Besant was born as Annie Wood in London on 1 October 1847. While her mother Emily was full Irish, her father William Page Wood was half English half Irish. Annie was proud of her Irish parentage and always called herself an Irishwoman and had certain pronounced Irish traits in her character. Her father was a doctor, but he died when Annie was five years old, leaving his wife Emily to bring up her two children, Henry and Annie. Emily moved to Harrow and ran a boarding house for some Harrow boys. So in her childhood Annie had lot of boys for company and was "as good a cricketer and climber as any of them". But soon, one Miss Marryat took responsibility for Annie's education with the permission of her mother. She was taught Latin grammar, French and German, which she perfected during her seven months stay in Paris and on the Rhine respectively. She read widely and cultivated a love for knowledge, which lasted her life time. In 1863 Annie completed her education with Marryat and returned to Harrow. "Here she devoted to archery and croquet, and danced to her heart's content with junior masters, who could talk as well as flirt. Never had a girl a happier home life".[1]

At the age of twenty, Annie Wood married Rev. Frank Besant, a Cambridge man, who was a clergyman in a small church in a suburb of London. They had two children, son Digby and daughter Mabel. Mrs.

Besant found that "the position of a clergyman's wife was only second to that of a nun". The couple separated and her struggle in life began. She could not get custody of her two children because of her views and a small annuity was sufficient for 'respectable starvation'. But she was a free person now, not tied down to the dogmas, rituals and myths of orthodox Christianity, which her rational mind discarded. She became an atheist and wrote a tract, *My Path to Atheism*. She was now twenty-six and in search of a job, when she met Charles Bradley, a Labour MP who liked her views and offered her a small weekly salary and a place on the staff of the *National Reformer*, which was the official mouthpiece of the National Secular Society of England. She became a co-editor of the journal and thus began a journalist career which lasted till the end of her life. This was in 1874. Along with writing for the *National Reformer*, she indulged in prolific literary activity, writing books and pamphlets in abundance during the period 1878 to 1886. Some of them are *Freethinker's Text Book; History of the French Revolution; Sins of the Church of England;* a popular treatise on *Light, Heat and Sound*. Besides, there were innumerable tracts on all sorts of subjects. She also started to work for social reform in many directions including the labour unions. During this period she was busy holding public debates on religion and politics and travelling all round the country lecturing. She became one of the best orators in England, a fact conceded even by her enemies. From 1885, she became closely associated with the Fabian Society and came in contact with such famous people like Sydney Webb, G.B. Shaw and later, Ramsay MacDonald. The same year, she organised the strike of 'match girls' and won the fight for them.

Then turning point in her life came while she was reviewing Madame Blavatsky's *Secret Doctrine,* for *Review of Reviews*. "The moment she read the book, it was as if a long lost synthesis of truth suddenly flashed out in her mind. She asked for an interview with the author, and from that first sight of Madame Blavatsky, Annie Besant's whole life was changed".[2] She joined the Theosophical Society, which was founded by Blavatsky and Colonel Olcott in 1875 in New York and became the most devoted and brilliant disciple of Blavasky. Blavatsky died in 1891, passing over leadership of the society to Annie Besant, who became the president of the society in 1907, an office she held till her death. Annie Besant represented theosophy at the Parliament of Religions in 1893 in Chicago, where she met Swami Vivekananda "in one of the rooms set apart for the use of the delegates, and was highly impressed by the personality and speech delivered by the Swami". From America, she came straight to India, landing here on 16 November 1893, and making it her permanent home. In India, she did not confine her work to the Theosophical Society, the headquarters of which were established at Adyar near Madras. Soon, she started to work for the social, religious and cultural reforms in her adopted country. She started living like an Indian: wearing a sari instead of a skirt, sitting cross-legged for hours and eating with her hands.

The main thrust of her activities, during this period, was in the educational field. She came to Banaras (Varanasi) in 1895 and lived there till 1907. She learnt Sanskrit to understand the Hindu scriptures and soon translated the *Bhagvad Gita* with the help of Dr. Bhagwan Das. A branch of the Theosophical Society was opened in Varanasi. But her greatest contribution towards the city was the establishment of Central Hindu College in 1898. The principal object of the college was "to combine moral and religious training in accordance with the Hindu shastras with secular education". The college started in a rented small building but soon moved to its new campus in Kamacha, gifted by the Maharaja of Banaras. The institution became a model for other schools and colleges in the country. The Central Hindu College later formed the nucleus for the Banaras Hindu University (1916).

There were several other activities that she was involved in for the cause of education, even after she had settled in Adyar near Madras. In 1915, she established the National College at Madanpalle in the Madras Presidency on the lines of the one started by the nationalists in Calcutta in 1906. In 1917, she started the 'Society for the Promotion of National Education'. In 1918, the National University was established by her at Adyar. The chancellor of the University was Rabindranath Tagore and vice-chancellor S. Subramania Iyer. Dr. G.S. Arundale was the principal. She also established several schools for boys and girls. In 1917, she started the Women's Indian Association, which later was transformed into the All India Women's Conference. In 1918, she organized the Indian Boy Scouts Movement where the boys wore Indian turbans and sang Indian songs, while in other ways obeyed the Scout's laws. There was no constructive work done during the forty years of her active service in India of which, if not the originator, she was not one of the most powerful supporters.

Besant perhaps will be remembered most for her political work in India. She entered the political arena in 1913. She founded a weekly newspaper, *The Commonweal* in January 1914 and a few months later she purchased the *Madras Standard*, a daily paper, and changed the name to *New India*. Through these two papers, which soon gained popularity, she conveyed her political views and the aspirations of the Indian people. She declared, "I am an Indian tom-tom, waking up all sleepers so that they may wake and work for their motherland". With that aim, she launched Home Rule League at Madras in September 1916. Tilak, who had already formed his own Home Rule League in April of the same year, did not agree to Annie Besant's proposal for a merger of the two Leagues. However, both worked in tandem. Through her Home Rule League she preached swaraj for India by which she meant 'self-government within the Empire'. The Home Rule movement made a swift and strong impression on the country. Though her demand was modest enough, her advocacy was militant. Through her speeches and writings she created an awakening in the country. Swaraj was now in the air. Gandhi in a speech at the Gujarat Political Conference in November 1917 said, "The air is thick with cries of swaraj. It is due to Mrs. Besant that swaraj is on the lips of hundreds of thousands of men and women. What was unknown to most men and women only two years ago, has by her consummate tact and her indefatigable efforts, become common property for them. There cannot be the slightest doubt that her name will take the first rank in history among those who inspired us with the hope that swaraj was attainable at no distant date."[3] The government wanted to crush her movement; asked her to abandon the compaign or leave the country. She did not agree to either of the options. In order to stifle her propaganda the government first forfeited the securities of her two papers and demanded additional deposit. She complied. As a last resort they interned her on 16 June 1917 alongwith her two colleagues. B.P. Wadia and G.S. Arundale at Ooty. Protest meetings for her release were held throughout the country and in England. She was released after three months. The imprisonment added to her fame, as it often does. She was made president of the 1917 Calcutta session of the Indian National Congress. While concluding her stirring presidential address she said:

"To see India free, to see her hold her head high among other nations, to see her sons and daughters respected everywhere, to see her worthy of her mighty past, engaged in building a yet mightier future — is not this worth working for, worth suffering for, worth living and worth dying for? Is there any other land which evokes such love for spirituality, such admiration for her literature, such homage for her valour, as this glorious mother of nations, from whose womb went forth the races that now, in Europe and America, are leading the world. Has any land suffered as our India has suffered — and having suffered, and having survived all changes, unbroken India, who has been verily the crucified among nations, now stands on this her resurrecting morning, the immortal, the glorious, the ever-young, and India shall soon be seen, proud and self-reliant, strong and free, the radiant splendour of Asia, as the light and blessing of the world."

Then came Gandhi on the political horizon of the country. He promised swaraj in one year, and started the Non-Cooperation Movement asking lawyers to boycott the courts, students to walk out of schools and colleges, government servants to resign from their jobs and everyone to burn foreign made clothes. The reason for starting the Non-Cooperation Movement was ill-treatment to the Khalifa of the Muslims of Turkey by the British and atrocities committed by the government in Punjab. The saner elements in the country including Tagore, Bipin Chandra Pal, Madan Mohan Malaviya, M.A. Jinnah, and Annie Besant were horrified. Besant warned the nation that what Gandhi was preaching would lead the nation to lawlessness and anarchy. She went around the country preaching against the Non-Cooperation Movement and was hooted down at almost every place where she spoke, including Bombay and Allahabad. With saintly cunning, Gandhi had seen to it that the old lady was insulted. Gandhi could not bring swaraj in one year and the Non-Cooperation Movement fizzled out by 1922.

Though Besant became unpopular and lost her position as a leader, she still went on with her work for India. She organized the 'National Convention' with an aim to draft a bill. She succeeded when in 1925 the 'Commonwealth of India Bill' was drafted. She took it to England and got it accepted by the British Labour party and one of its members presented it to Parliament but it could not be enacted. Her political career had come to an end. She was already in her eightieth year.

The remaining years of her life were spent in Adyar involved in the work of the Theosophical Society. But her health was deteriorating slowly. She passed away peacefully on 21 September 1933.

Annie Besant was a prolific writer. It will be impossible to enumerate all the books, pamphlets and tracts which she wrote. Some of the more important ones are: *My Path to Atheism* (1877); *Autobiography* (1893); *Radicalism and Socialism* (London, 1887); *Education as a National Duty* (Banaras 1903); *The Religious Problems in India* (Madras, 1909); *Hints on the Study of the Bhagavad Gita* (Adyar, 1906); *Universal Textbook of Religion and Morals*, 3 Vols (Adyar 1911-15); *Social Problems* (Adyar, 1912); *How India Wrought Her Freedom; The Story of the National Congress Told from Official Records* (1915); *The Ideals of Theosophy* (Adyar, 1912); *Principles of Education* (Madras 1918); *Man's Life in Three Worlds* (Adyar, 1919); *Lectures on Political Science* (Adyar, 1919); *The Future of Indian Politics* (Madras, 1922): *World Problems of Today* (London 1925).

## References

1.  Stead, W.T. *Annie Besant; a Character-Sketch*, Madras, Theosophical Publishing House, 1946, p.19.
2.  Ibid, p.89-90.
3.  *Collected Works of Mahatma Gandhi*. Vol. 14, p.50.

# Homi Jehangir Bhabha

## (1909-1966)

Bhabha was a great scientist and an equally great institution builder. He played a decisive role in putting India on the atomic energy map of the world.

Homi Jehangir Bhabha was born in Bombay on 10 October 1909, in a well-to-do Parsi family. His father, Jehangir Hormusji Bhabha, had been educated at Oxford and later qualified as a lawyer. On his returning to India, he joined the judicial service in Mysore. But after his marriage to Meherbai Framji Panday (granddaughter of Sir Dinshaw Maneckji Petit), he moved to Bombay, where he was associated with the Tata industrial house. The Bhabha family came close to the Tata family when Jehangir Hormusji's sister Meherbai married Sir Dorab Tata, son of Jamshedji Tata. The Tata connection proved very useful to Homi Bhabha in his later life.

Homi started his education at the Cathedral and John Cannon High School in Bombay, from where he passed the Senior Cambridge examination with honours. Later, he joined Elphinstone College and subsequently, the Royal Institute of Science, Bombay. Homi was not really interested in sports, though he did take part in rowing and played tennis while studying at Cambridge. From the very beginning, he was inclined academically and won several prizes in school as well as in college. He supplemented his formal education by reading a wide variety of books on art, music, literature and science, which were available in the personal collections of his grandfather and father. At an early age, he developed a great interest in science and his parents bought hundreds of books on science to satisfy their son's urge for scientific study. It is said that by the age of sixteen, Homi Bhabha had studied and understood the special theory of relativity. Homi had not even completed his eighteenth year when his parents decided to send him to England for higher studies. Bhabha joined the Gonville and Caius College, Cambridge in 1927, courtesy Dorab Tata, who had studied in the same college and had created a trust by donating twenty-five thousand pounds to the college. Homi studied engineering, conceding to the wishes of his father, and obtained a first class in the Mechanical Science Tripos in June 1930. After that he worked as a research student in theoretical physics, the subject which was more to his liking. After completing the Mathematics Tripos, Bhabha won the Rouse Ball Travelling Fellowship in 1932, which enabled him to travel to other places and work there. Thus, he was able to work with some of the leading physicists in Europe: Wolfgang Pauli in Zurich and Fermi in Rome. His own research work had come to the notice of the scientists and as a result he was awarded the Isaac Newton Studentship, which he held for three years. He worked mainly at Cambridge with a short spell in Bohr's Institute, Copenhagen. By 1935, Bhabha had completed the requirements for the Ph.D. degree. In 1937, he was awarded the Exhibition Scholarship, which enabled him to continue his research work at Cambridge.

In 1939, Bhabha was in India on a holiday. In the meanwhile, the Second World War broke out and England became a dangerous place to live. He had to abandon his plans to return to England to continue his research work. By now, he had lived and studied in England for thirteen years. Now, Bhabha had to opt for a career in India. He accepted the post of a Reader, Department of Physics, in the Institute of Science, Bangalore, which had been established by Jamshedji Tata way back in 1911 and was a premium science institute in the country. An added attraction for Bhabha was the presence of C.V. Raman in the Institute, as the head of the Department of Physics. Bhabha became a professor in 1944. Homi Bhabha specialized early in quantum theory and cosmic radiation. The

Dorab Tata Trust gave him a small grant with which he established the Cosmic Ray Research Unit in the department. He had published his first scientific paper in October 1933, in which he had described the part played by electrons in the absorption of cosmic rays. He wanted to continue research in the newly established Cosmi Ray Research Unit. His contribution in the field of cosmic ray research was recognized by the world and he was elected Fellow of the Royal Society of Britain in 1941. In 1943, he was awarded the Adams Prize by the University of Cambridge for his work on cosmic rays. He was also noted for being the first person to calculate the cross-section for electron/positron scattering, which is known as the Bhabha Scattering. He discovered cosmic particles, with a hundred times greater energy than any other previously known. He announced his discovery at the International Technical Conference at Stockholm in September 1952.

By now, Bhabha had made ambitious plans in his mind and for that, the Institute at Bangalore seemed inadequate to him. Bhabha approached the Dorab Tata Trust once again, with plans for an institute fully devoted to nuclear sciences, and which could play a leading role in offering world class research facilities for Indian scientists. As a result the Tata Institute of Fundamental Research (TIFR), Bombay, came into being in 1944. Bhabha now moved to Bombay, after spending 'six very happy and fruitful years' in Bangalore. After the Second World War, it became clear to Bhabha that Indian industry and economy on the whole would require a tremendous amount of energy, which was not possible to procure from the conventional sources of energy. The answer lay in using nuclear power, derived from fuels developed from India's vast resources of uranium and thorium. He devoted his time and energy toward that end. From a research scientist he became an institution builder and almost retired from research in physics. His institution building career had essentially one aim in his mind — to develop atomic energy for peaceful purposes. The Tata Institute of Fundamental Research was the first step in that direction. The research done there had to be translated into concrete form. To make that possible, assistance from the Government of India in various forms, was necessary. It must go to the credit of Jawaharlal Nehru that he assured full support of his government to Homi Bhabha.

Through Bhabha's efforts, the Indian Atomic Act was passed in 1948 by the Parliament and the same year the Atomic Energy Commission was constituted, which was essentially a policy-making body. A full-fledged atomic energy programme obviously could not be carried out and overseen on day-to-day basis by it. For that, a regular department of the government was necessary. The prime minister agreed to Bhabha's proposal and the Department of Atomic Energy was created in 1954, with Bhabha as secretary. The department 'would fund, create and operate all the facilities needed for the atomic energy programme'. Bhabha was also the director of TIFR. So far, the atomic energy programme was being executed with the help of TIFR and its scientists. As TIFR was conducting multiphasic research in its laboratories besides atomic research, at the suggestion of Bhabha, a new laboratory was created at Trombay, near Bombay, for the exclusive purpose of atomic research. It was called the Atomic Energy Establishment. The name was later changed to Bhabha Atomic Research Centre (BARC), which started functioning in 1954. At the suggestion of Bhabha, the Department of Atomic Energy was shifted to Bombay, so that work at the Department, TIFR and BARC could be coordinated expeditiously. In 1954, Bhabha decided that Atomic Energy Establishment, Trombay (AEET) should have a Swimming Pool Reactor to conduct atomic research. The assembly of the systems commenced sometime in 1955 and the reactor itself went into operation in August 1956. Nehru dedicated the reactor to the nation and gave it the name APSARA, which is still functioning. APSARA was a major milestone for the generation of atomic power because the reactor had been designed and built in India. The fuel element alone came from England.[1] It was made clear by the Government of India that atomic power will be used for peaceful purposes only.

Bhabha attended the first 'Atoms for Peace' conference in Geneva, under the auspices of the United Nations and was elected its president. After the Geneva Conference, an International Atomic Energy Agency was created, with its headquarters at Vienna. Bhabha became a member of its Scientific Advisory Committee and remained so till his death.

Under the expert guidance of Bhabha, two more reactors, Cirus and Zerlina, were built. Construction of the country's first atomic power station began at Tarapore in 1963. Unfortunately Bhabha did not live to see its commissioning, which was done a year after his death. Bhabha also played a pivotal role in conceiving and planning the Indian space programme and helped in setting up the Indian National Committee for Space Research, under Dr. Vikram Sarabhai. Bhabha was also chairman of the Government Electronic Committee. He also promoted research in radioastronomy and microbiology. The radio telescope at Ootacamund is one of his creations in this direction.

Bhabha died in a plane crash on 24 January 1966 at the age of fifty-seven. He died a bachelor.

Bhabha was a great lover of music, especially western classical. He was also drawn to painting, literature, architecture and landscaping. His paintings and drawings are of considerable merit and some of them are preserved in British art galleries. He was a born artist and had acquired refined tastes. The flower beds, the landscaping, the architecture of the building of the Tata Institute of Fundamental Research, all bear witness to the keenness of Homi Bhabha's perception of colour, form and design.[2] However, he will be remembered most as the chief architect of Indian atomic energy establishment, on which the future of our country largely depends.

In conclusion: "Bhabha was a brilliant scientist, imaginative visionary, shrewd planner and organizer, able administrator, sensitive artist, devotee of music and literature, and a passionate lover of trees and gardens. Many are the examples of people who have achieved excellence in one or two areas but seldom one comes across a person so versatile as this".[3] He was indeed one of the few universal men of our age. C.V. Raman called him the Indian Leonardo da Vinci. He was awarded the Padam Bhushan by the president of India in 1954. Bhabha was awarded honorary doctorates by several universities including Cambridge, London and Perth, besides several Indian universities. Bhabha wrote scores of scientific papers. His publications include: *Quantum Theory, Elementary Physical Particles* and *Cosmic Radiation*.

## References

1. Venkataraman, G. *Bhabha and His Magnificent Obsession.* Hyderabad, Universities Press. 1994, pp.150-51.
2. Kumar, Rajee N. *Homi Jehangir Bhabha* in *Remembering our Leaders*, New Delhi, CBT. 1998, p.176.
3. Venkataraman, G. op. cit. p.200.

# Bhagwan Das

## (1869-1958)

Bhagwan Das was born on 12 January 1869 (he shared the year of his birth with Mohandas Karamchand Gandhi) at Banaras in a well-to-do Vaish family. He was the second of the six children of Madho Das and Chameli Devi. An ancestor of Bhagwan Das, Sah Manohar Das, was the commissariat agent of the East India Company when the battle of Srirangapatnam was fought between the British and Tipu Sultan. After the death of Tipu, general loot took place and Manohar Das, taking advantage of it, acquired considerable wealth, left Mysore and settled permanently in Banaras. The family owned valuable property in Bara Bazar, Calcutta and extensive cultivable land, mostly in the Jaunpur district near Banaras. The family took to banking and usury. The affluence of the family could be judged from the fact that during Bhagwan Das' time, the family had twenty domestic servants.

Bhagwan Das' education started at the age of three. His first teacher was a Muslim *maulvi* (a religious instructor) who taught him Urdu and Persian and love for Islam, which he carried throughout his life. At the age of about five, he was admitted to a private school, founded by the famous Hindi poet Bhartendu Harish Chandra near their home, where he learnt Hindi and some English. At the age of seven, he was admitted to the Government Queen's College. He was an extremely precocious child. At the age of twelve he passed the Entrance (matriculation) examination and four years later, the Bachelor of Arts examination with a distinction. He had opted for English, Sanskrit and Philosophy as subjects. In 1886, at the age of seventeen, he passed the M.A. examination of the Calcutta University in mental and moral sciences. He developed great interest in Hindu religion and philosophy, an interest which he maintained throughout his life. He devoted the next four years fully to study these subjects and learnt Sanskrit from Kashi pandits to read the scriptures in the original. However, at the insistence of his father, he joined government service in 1890 as a *tehsildar* (subordinate revenue officer) and in 1894, he was promoted as deputy collector and magistrate. He was posted at various places in Uttar Pradesh. The period of his government service was eventless because his heart was not in it, though he proved to be a man of integrity and was devoid of prejudices. His father died in 1897 and he resigned from government service in 1898.

The same year (1898) Annie Besant, the president of the Theosophical Society, founded the Central Hindu College "to rehabilitate all that was great and glorious in the Oriental culture". She felt that religion was the foundation of all true education as it was the foundation of the family and the state. The existing schools, she felt, were not imparting proper education. Bhagwan Das completely agreed with her views and started working with her in the college as well as in the Theosophical Society, a branch of which was opened in Banaras by Annie Besant. The school proved to be a success; the number of students increased every year and it became a model school for the country. One important contribution of the college was the publication of the *Sanatan Dharma Series* of Hindu religious textbooks. These books give, in a form suitable for students, a graduated outline of the fundamental principles of the Hindu religion. It is quite likely that Annie Besant took the help of Bhagwan Das in planning and writing these textbooks. Bhagwan Das had written the book *Sanatana Dharma; An Advanced Textbook of Hindu Religion and Ethics* in 1904, supplementing the *Sanatan Dharma Series* of textbooks. He, jointly with Annie Besant, published the translation of *Bhagvat Gita* in 1906, giving original Sanskrit verses and the English translation alongside and a concordance of Sanskrit words at the end. To this day it remains one of the best translations of the *Bhagvat Gita*. Bhagwan Das served the Hindu

College as honorary secretary for fifteen years (1899-1914). He was also active in the Theosophical Society and played a significant part in the development of the Banaras branch of the society. However, the main interest of his life by now had became the study of Hindu scriptures like the *Vedas* and the *Manusmriti* and their interpretation through his books and articles for the scholar as well as for the layman. A continuous stream of books flowed from his pen year after year and Bhagwan Das became famous as a highly learned man and a Vedic scholar.

Through the study of the Hindu scriptures, he came to the conclusion that there was no valid reason to believe and practice untouchability and that all castes should be allowed to enter Hindu temples without any restriction. He also advocated that the *varnas* (four divisions of Hindu society) should be decided by karma (actions) and not by birth. Thus armed, he took active part, along with Madan Mohan Malaviya, in the movement against untouchability and restrictive temple entry.

From the mid-1920s onwards, Mahatma Gandhi had started preaching against untouchability and supporting the temple entry movement. Whenever Gandhi was in doubt about the verdict of the scriptures (as he hardly knew Sanskrit) he used to refer to Bhagwan Das for his opinion. Gandhi used to address him as 'Dear Baboo Bhagwandas' or simply as 'Dear Babooji'. From their correspondence, it is evident that Gandhi had great respect for Bhagwan Das. When the latter started writing to Gandhi through his secretary Mahadev, instead of writing to Gandhi direct, Mahatma Gandhi wrote to Bhagwan Das, "I know you want to save my time by writing to Mahadev, but it is as well not to do so. It may cause delay and your letters are no strain on me".[1] When Gandhi was undergoing a fast unto death against the verdict of the Communal Award which recommended separate electorates for the scheduled castes, Bhagwan Das went to Poona to meet Gandhi in Yervada Jail. He remained in Poona for three weeks and met Gandhi in Yervada Jail almost daily. About these meetings Gandhi later wrote to Bhagwan Das on 7 January 1933, "I cannot tell you what a joy it was to have you with me for so many days. It was all so unexpected and therefore a double pleasure".[2]

Annie Besant collaborated with Madan Mohan Malaviya in the establishment of Banaras Hindu University and merged the Central

Hindu College in the proposed university, which started functioning in 1916 in the College Campus itself. Bhagwan Das was nominated as one of the five honorary joint secretaries of the Management Committee of the university. He was also nominated as a member of the University Court, Senate and other bodies. But soon after, he started criticising the working of the university and its vice-chancellor, Madan Mohan Malaviya. He wrote articles and 'open letters' expressing his views, which were published in the *Leader* in 1917. The confrontation came to a head in the Court meeting of December, 1920 and he crossed swords with Annie Besant and Malaviya on various issues. The amendments moved by him were lost by heavy margin and consequently he withdrew his membership from the Court, the Council and other bodies of the university.[3]

It was during 1919-20, at the age of fifty, that Bhagwan Das was drawn to politics for the first time. In 1919, he was president of the U.P. Social Conference. In 1920, he presided over the U.P. Political Conference, and soon became an important member of the Indian National Congress. He took part in the Non-Cooperation Movement launched by Gandhi in August 1920 and was sentenced to a nine month imprisonment. However, he was released after two months. When Kashi Vidyapeeth was founded in 1921, Bhagwan Das became its *kulpati* (vice-chancellor). He also used to teach philosophy there. He was nominated as chairman of the Banaras Municipal Board in 1923 and served in that capacity for about three years. During his tenure, the municipality functioned efficiently and its debt was considerably reduced.

In March 1931, serious communal riots took place in Kanpur, after the execution of Bhagat Singh and his two comrades in the Lahore Jail. According to the official estimate 165 persons were killed and 480 injured. Among the killed was Ganesh Shankar Vidyarthi, president of the U.P. Congress. An enquiry committee was constituted by the Congress to go into details of the riots, with Bhagwan Das as chairman. After several months of enquiry and interviews, the Committee submitted a report. About this report well-known historian R.C. Majumdar wrote, "Bhagwan Das submitted a report in a bulky volume. It began with a long historical introduction with sole object to prove that the Muslim rulers were the most tolerant in respect of other religions. A more ridiculous parody of history it is difficult to imagine, and yet bore the signatures of several Hindus who should have known better. It was a piece of pure political propaganda".[4] To placate the Muslims the Committee had to resort to untruth and negationism. Fortunately, for the good name of the Congress, and of the authors of the Report, it was proscribed by the government.

In 1935, Bhagwan Das was elected unopposed to the Central Legislative Assembly. His term lasted for two years but he did not leave any impact on the Assembly proceedings and hardly made any speeches. His son and biographer, Sri Prakasa writes, "My father had no practice of extempore speaking. He was a great writer, but not a speaker. Whenever he had to say anything, he wrote it out with great care and labour, and read it out in the Assembly. He spent most of his time in the lobbies reading and writing. He never asked any questions. My father delivered very few speeches either".[5] His limitations as a speaker could be the reason for his not taking active part in politics. He was essentially a scholar, a philosopher and a writer. He has written more than forty books, mostly on religion and philosophy, and almost all in English. Some of these are: *The Science of Emotions* (1900) (translated in several European languages); *Science of Peace* (1904); *Sanatana Dharma;* translation of the *Bhagavadgita,* jointly with Annie Besant (1905); *The Science of Social Organization* or *The Laws of Manu in the Light of Theosophy; Religion of Theosophy* (1910); *The Psychology of Conversion* (1917); *The Meaning of Swaraj,* jointly with C.R. Das (1921); *Philosophy of Non-cooperation* (1922); *Krishna or the Theory of Avataras* (1924); *Mystic Experiences* (1928); *The Dawn of Another Renaissance* (1931); *The Essential Unity of All Religions* (1932); *The Science of Self* (1938); *Concordance Dictionary of the Yoga Sutra of Patanjali and Bhasya of Vyas* (1938). Most of these books were published by Theosophical Publishing House, Adyar.

Unfortunately, he was a difficult writer to understand. It seems too many ideas gushed out of his mind at the same time, confounding the writer and the reader alike. If he had not acquired a style of writing which was involved and difficult to comprehend, he would have been a much more popular as a philosopher and thinker. He himself confesses at one place, "I feel keenly and regret exceedingly that Nature has withheld from me the very valuable gift of lucid, bright, attractive and pleasing expression and exposition. Even those kind friends who happen to like my reinterpretations and new versions of the ancient words and thoughts, often take me to task for obscure and involved sentences".[6] However, there is no gainsaying the fact that he was one of the most important thinkers and philosophers produced by this country in the twentieth century. According to S. Radhakrishnan, "I have been an admiring student of Dr. Bhagwan Das' works. His attitude to our ancient works is one to be followed by others: trust tempered with criticism. He had great faith in the central ideas of Indian thought and he was an effective critic of the deviations which took place spoiling the purity and strength of our religion".

Bhagwan Das was cast in the mould of great *rishis* (sages) and his luxurious beard imparted grace and dignity to his personality, rivalling that of Rabindranath Tagore. Though he was not a good speaker, he must have been a good conversationalist and a charming host, as many persons used to visit him and enjoy his hospitality. These included Gandhi, Nehru, C.R. Das, C.F. Andrews, Anand Coomaraswamy and many others, both Indian and foreigners. However, he was not a spendthrift and was not lavish of his purse. Nor did his wealth tempt him to be a philanthropist. In spite of his intellectual pursuits he was very fond of physical exercise and used to do scores of push-ups and sit-ups daily, which would have shamed many a wrestler. After seeing Bhagwan Das for the first time, Jawaharlal Nehru remarked, "He has the straightest back I have ever seen." And that back remained straight even when he touched his eightieth year.

Bhagwan Das was awarded doctorate degrees *honoris causa* by the Banaras Hindu University (1929) and Allahabad University (1937). In 1955, he received the Bharat Ratna. In 1959, he died at Banaras. His marble statue greets the visitors to the offices of the Municipal Corporation of Varanasi. His son Sri Prakasa was the first Indian high commissioner in Pakistan (1947-49) and later served as governor of Assam, Madras and Bombay (later Maharashtra).

# References

1. *Collected Works of Mahatma Gandhi*, Vol. 53, p.255.
2. Ibid Vol. 52, p.381.
3. Dar, S.L. and S. Somaskandan. *History of the Banaras Hindu University*. Varanasi, BHU Press. 1966, p.519.
4. Majumdar, R.C. *History of the Freedom Movement in India*. Calcutta, Firma KLM. Vol.3, pp.316-17.
5. Sri Prakasa. *Bharat Ratna Dr. Bhagwan Das*. Meerut, Meenakshi. 1970, p.118.
6. Bhagwan Das. *Autobiography*, in *Shradhanjili Souvenir*, Delhi, Dr. Bhagwan Das Memorial Trust, 1961, p.32.

# Subramania Bharati

## (1882-1921)

Subramania Bharati is considered the greatest Tamil poet of the twentieth century. He wrote one of the best patriotic poems in the Tamil language, besides other poetry. His poems created an immense wave of nationalism in Tamil Nadu and inspired people to join the freedom movement.

Subramania (Subbiah to his family and friends) was born on 11 December 1882 to Chinnaswami Iyer and Lakshmi Ammal at Ettayapuram in the Tirunelveli district of Tamil Nadu. Theirs was a middle-class family. His father, a learned Brahmin, was attached to the Ettayapuram Zamin. He was also interested in industry and had installed the first textile mill at Ettayapuram in 1880. Subramania's mother, Lakshmi Ammal, died when he was hardly five years old. His father married a second time, but his step-mother treated him well, just like her own son.

Subramania started his primary education at Tirunelveli. He was a precocious child in a limited sense. While he loved and mastered the Tamil language at an early age, he did not like other subjects, especially mathematics. He started composing poetry while still in primary school. He would skip classes and wander about, admiring nature and writing simple, short poems in Tamil. Thus, he had become a Tamil scholar very early in life, though without much of a formal education. When he was eleven years old, he was invited to the court of the Raja of Ettayapuram to recite his poems. The noted poets present at the court were amazed at the quality of the lyrics which he recited. They started calling him 'Bharati'.

In 1897, Subramania was married to a seven-year-old girl, Chellammal, who later shared the agonies and ecstacies of his life. The following year, his father died and he went to Banaras to live with his aunt Kuppammal. He passed the entrance examination of the Allahabad University. During his stay at Banaras, he learnt Hindi, Sanskrit and English. His stay there brought a change in his appearance too. He began to sport a thick moustache on the lines of a warrior and an ample turban on his head, tied in a distinct and unorthodox style. Banaras also brought about a change in his outlook, and he began to write patriotic poetry and about the pathetic condition of India under unsympathetic foreign rule. After four years, he went back to his home town Ettayapuram but he was disheartened by the caste ridden and orthodox society. To get away from the suffocating atmosphere he took up a temporary teaching post as a teacher of Tamil at Madurai Setupati High School. He soon left for Madras and took up the job of an assistant editor of a popular Tamil daily, *Swadesamitram*, which was founded by G. Subramaniya Iyer in 1882. There he was responsible for translating into Tamil, news appearing in English dailies. Besides brushing up his English, this job gave him a better idea of the political and social developments in the country. He began to write political poems urging people to wake up from their slumber and to take their destiny in their own hands. He was moving more and more towards writing about the political regeneration of the country. His passion-filled patriotic poems enthralled the people of Tamil Nadu and they started taking active part in the freedom movement. During those days he met Sister Nivedita, a disciple of Vivekananda, and a great nationalist. She blessed him and exhorted him to devote his poetic talents for the emancipation of the country. As a gesture of gratitude, Subramania dedicated two of his poetry books to her.

In 1907, Bharati attended the Congress session at Surat. He was openly with the Extremists led by Tilak, Bipin Chandra Pal and Lajpat Rai. He believed that the situation called for a revolutionary approach and the policy of appeals and representations would not lead the country to freedom. His poems and writings started becoming more and more volatile and no publisher was prepared to publish his books. Even the editor of *Swadesamitram* stopped publishing his extremist views. Bharati resigned from the paper and started publishing his own weekly, *India*, in 1907. In that he began publishing his poems and stories, some of them satirical. The Swadeshi movement in Bengal, and to a lesser extent in other parts of the country, started as a reaction to the partition of Bengal, was gathering momentum. The government had unleashed repressive measures and hundreds of revolutionaries and freedom fighters had been arrested and imprisoned. Even national leaders like Lajpat Rai, Tilak and Aurobindo had not been spared. Fearing arrest, Bharati fled to Pondicherry, a French enclave, in 1908. Here he spent ten years in extreme poverty and isolation and was harassed by British spies. Once his house was ransacked and some valuable manuscripts were stolen. He was forced to discontinue the publication of *India*. But still, he was able to write some brilliant prose and poetry in the beautiful surroundings of Pondicherry. Most of his devotional songs and nature poetry belong to this period. However, tired of long stretch of an exile's life, he returned to British India. The British administration was prompt in arresting him but released him after a few days unconditionally. Bharati first went to his hometown but was out of place in an orthodox society, as was his experience on an earlier occasion. He came to Madras and once again joined the editorial staff of the *Swadesamitram*. After a long time, Bharati began to live on regular, though meagre income. But not for long. He used to visit a temple in Triplicane and offer a coconut to the temple elephant. One day the elephant was in rut and hit him with its trunk, while Bharati was offering a coconut. Bharati was badly injured and died after a few days on 12 September 1921.

Bharati was a true nationalist and left behind a considerable body of brilliant poetry. His poems could be divided into three categories: patriotic poems, devotional songs and miscellaneous poems. Under the first category, come his collection of poems *Swadesa Gitangal* (1909) and *Janma Bhoomi* (1909). Both these books were dedicated to Sister Nivedita, a source of inspiration for many Indians. In these poems, he describes the grandeur of India and her spiritual greatness. He exhorts Indians to work for freedom in true spirit, abjuring political propaganda, and to cast away fear and timidness. Some of the poems in this category describe the lives of great men of India and their great deeds as a source of inspiration for the present generation and the generations to come. His devotional songs are addressed to Lord Krishna, including poetry devoted to Goddess Shakti and poems expressing vividly the ideals of human oneness and universal love as preached by the *Vedas*. That Bharati was a deeply religious man is evident from these poems, in spite of his abhorrence of senseless rituals and customs. Thus the "most significant group is formed by his poems on Shakti, Bharati's *isht devata* (personal god) the primordial power that makes and unmakes the whole universe". The Kali worship witnessed in Banaras, his meeting with Sister Nivedita, the powerful poem *Vande Matram* of Bankim Chandra — all influenced his Shakti poems. His approach is personal and approximate the, mother-child relationship. Her many aspects are caught within the arc of his poetic creation. "*Oozhi-k-Koothu* is the most audaciously frenzied and most poetically articulate piece in the Bharati canon. It is a description of the Mother's terrible dance of destruction which is at last arrested by the advent of Shiva in his auspicious form, and they unite to recreate the world once again".[1]

His miscellaneous poems include ones whose subject matter is social reform, scientific and rational thinking and the emancipation of women and so on. He also wrote poems for children. This was prompted by his younger daughter Sakuntala and her friends. He sang for them *The Child's Song*. He set it to music and children love to sing '*Odi vilaiyadu pappa*' even today. Written in very simple Tamil, Bharati's poems budded with rhyme and rhythm, which even a non-Tamil speaking person could enjoy. His drum-beat song, also popular as a dance piece, proclaims *Vetri yettu thikkum yetta* (all human beings are equal). His other important epic poems are *Kannan Pattu* (1917); *Panchali Sapatham* (1912 and 1924 in two parts) and *Kuyil Pattu*. The last song composed by Bharati and sung by him at a public meeting at the beach in Madras, a few weeks before his death, is one of his most popular poems: *Bharatha samudayam vazhgave* (Long live Bharat Commonwealth).

Bharati also wrote short stories and an unfinished novel, *Chandrikayin Kathai*. His wisdom tales on the lines of *Panchtantra* and *Hitopadesh* are still popular in Tamil Nadu. Bharati also wrote English poetry and prose, which have been collected in *Agni and Other Poems and Translations* (1937) and *Essays and Other Prose Fragments* (1937).

But today Bharati is remembered most for giving a simple and appealing style to Tamil poetry. He showed that the spoken rhythms in Tamil can be easily transferred to the written page. He was one of the first poets of any merit to speak of India as one entity and of her people sharing a common heritage. In poem after poem he describes the best in each region, the sum of which make India. He exhorts the Indians to eschew regionalism to make India great.

Subramania Bharati has inspired many poets and writers like Bharati Dasan (1891-1964) who absorbed the revolutionary zeal of Bharati and chose the pseudonym to underline his affinity with the great poet. In the memory of Subramania Bharati stands the Bharati Mandap at Ettayapuram, his native place. There is a statue of Bharati at the Madras seashore. "The rhythmic roar of the undying waves seems to recite and repeat his poems". About Bharati, C. Rajagopalachari has said, "The body of national thought that he wove into song was that which preceded Gandhi; it was Vivekananda's and Dadabhai Naoroji's and Tilak's India that forms the material of Bharati's poetry". Bharati is known as a national poet and his fame is not confined to Tamil Nadu. He has lived upto what his name depicts — 'Bharati'.

## References

1.  Nandakumar, Prema. Subramania Bharati in *Dictionary of National Biography* ed. by S.P. Sen. Calcutta, Institute of Historical Studies, 1972.

# Vinoba Bhave

## (1895-1982)

Among all the apostles of Gandhi, Vinoba was the only one who blazed his own trail. After Gandhi's death, most of his followers faded into oblivion, with the exception of Vinoba. He did most of the constructive work, for which he is remembered, after the death of Gandhi. He was a thinker and a saint, who believed in doing and not preaching.

Vinoba Bhave was born Vinayak Narhari Bhave, 11 September 1895 at Gagode in the former Baroda state, now in Kolaba district of Maharashtra. His father was Narhari Shambhurao Bhave and mother Rukmani Devi. His father Narhari was a textile technologist and worked in the dyeing department of Buckingham Mills for some time and was credited with producing the first *khaki* cloth. But later, he shifted to Baroda permanently and served as a senior typist-clerk in a government office. Later in life, he developed great interest in music and even wrote books on Indian music. He lived alone in Baroda till 1903, when he brought his family there. Thus, for the first eight years of his life, Vinayak was influenced by his grandfather Shambhurao and his mother, to whom he was very much attached. Vinoba was the eldest of the five children of his parents. One brother and a sister died early, leaving three brothers, Vinayak, Balkrishna (Balkova) and Shiva, to share the love and affection of their parents and grandfather. All the three brothers did not marry and with them ended the Bhave family.

Vinayak started his formal education in a Baroda school and was admitted to Baroda High School later, from where he passed the matriculation examination in 1913. He was not a brilliant student but was good at mathematics and had a knack for learning languages. His English was good and so was his French, which was an optional subject at school. He also knew Marathi, Gujarati and Sanskrit. He then joined Baroda College for his intermediate, for which he had to go to Bombay (1916). During his train journey he changed his mind and instead of reaching Bombay, he took a train to Kashi (Varanasi). He wanted to learn Sanskrit. It is believed that he burnt his school certificates so that he would not be able to continue his college education. There were not many certificates to burn, anyway. He started studying the *Vedas* and the *Upanishads* from some pundits in Kashi, but he did not stay there for long. He had heard about Gandhi and about his controversial speech, which he had delivered at the inaugural ceremony of the Banaras Hindu University, lambasting the princes present on the dais. He wanted to meet Gandhi and reached his Kochrab Ashram at Ahmedabad (Sabarmati Ashram was established later in 1918).Vinayak liked the austere life being led by the ashramites and soon became one of the favourite disciples of Gandhi. The very first day Vinayak met Gandhi, the latter wrote to Vinayak's father Shambhurao on 7 June 1916, "Your son Vinoba is with me. Your son has acquired at so tender age such high-spiritedness and asceticism as took me years of patient labour to do". It is rather surprising how Gandhi could gauge the inner qualities of Vinoba during his very first meeting with Vinoba. The name Vinoba was obviously given to him after he had joined the ashram. At the ashram, Vinoba did all the menial work which was required of all the inmates. It is often claimed that even scavenging was being done by the inmates, including Gandhi. This claim must have a qualified acceptance, as a sweeper had been employed to do the scavenging. In fact, one day, when the sweeper was ill, he had sent his twelve-year-old son to do the scavenging. When the boy could not finish the work, he began to cry. It was at that time that Gandhi decided that the inmates should do the scavenging work. This was in 1920.[1] Vinoba taught mathematics and Gujarati to the students in the Rashtriya Shala (national school) and also acted as a hotel superintendent. Gandhi used to discuss with him the intricacies of the *Gita* and the *Upanishads* and was much impressed by the depth of his knowledge and understanding of Hindu scriptures. Gandhi was so impressed by Vinoba that we find him writing to Vinoba on 18 February 1918, "Your love and your character fascinate me and so also your self-examination. I am not fit to measure your worth. You seem almost to have met a long felt wish of mine". It seems that the hard work in the ashram was telling on Vinoba's health. There could be some other reasons also, which we would never know. Vinoba left the ashram in February 1917 and went to his ancestral place, Wai. There for six months he brushed up his Sanskrit and studied the *Upanishads, Brahmasutra* etc. from a learned pundit. For the next six months he visited several surrounding villages on foot and also visited some historical places. Exactly after one year he returned to Sabarmati Ashram and started doing the daily chores, including teaching, once again.

In April 1921 Vinoba was deputed by Gandhi, at the request of Jamnalal Bajaj, to take charge of the Satyagraha Ashram at Wardha, which was earlier looked after by Ramniklal Modi. Soon, he extended the activities of the ashram. He founded other ashrams in nearby villages; one at Nalwadi, a Harijan village and another in Pavnar, five miles from Wardha. He also started a Mahila Ashram at Wardha. In 1923, he took part in the Flag satyagraha at Nagpur and was imprisoned for three months. He also took part in the Waikom satyagraha, (Kerala) in 1924. He stayed in and around Wardha for thirty years. He ran the ashrams founded by him according to his own beliefs, which were akin to Gandhi but differed in certain important details. There was better discipline, for one thing and greater emphasis on Harijan work. Vinoba had several temples and wells opened for Harijans and also founded a tannery for them near Nalwadi in 1935. He had now a team of dedicated workers which enabled him to put into practice what he believed. To better organise the activities in his ashrams, Vinoba founded the Gram Seva Mandal in 1934. He also opened the Maharogi Seva Mandal at Datapur near Wardha, for service to the lepers.

In October 1940, when Gandhi launched the individual civil disobedience movement, Vinoba Bhave was chosen as the first satyagrahi. He was arrested thrice during this satyagraha and sentenced to various terms of imprisonment each time. When the 'Quit India' movement was started in August 1942, Vinoba was among the leaders who were arrested. He was kept in Vellore and Seoni jails for three years. Back in his ashrams, he started constructive work. After the death of Gandhi in January 1948 the Congress leaders were looking to Vinoba for help in transforming the society in independent India. A conference of top political dignitaries and constructive workers was held at Sewagram Ashram. Nehru, Rajendra Prasad, Azad and others attended. It was then that the concept of 'Sarvodaya Samaj' was formulated. The importance of Vinoba Bhave and his work was being realized by the government as well as social workers. After the conference, Nehru invited Vinoba to Delhi to help in the relief and rehabilitation work for the refugees, who had been ousted from Pakistan leaving everything behind. One purpose of Nehru was to help Meo Muslims of Gurgaon near Delhi to get back their land which had been occupied by Hindu and Sikh refugees when they (Meos) had migrated to Pakistan. Nehru himself had brought them back to India and was now in a dilemma how to get the land vacated without inviting the ire of the Hindus and Sikhs. The sermons of Vinoba, coupled with the unsympathetic attitude of the Nehru government, succeeded in ousting the Hindu and Sikh refugees, thus fortifying the secular image of Nehru.

To spread the message of *sarvodaya*, he started the monthly *Sarvodaya* on 15 August 1949. Vinoba's preachings as well as community work must have come to the notice of people outside India. They had not yet forgotten the devastation caused by war, and were looking for methods which would lead the world to permanent peace. They saw some hope in the teachings of Vinoba. The World Pacifist Conference was held at Sevagram in January 1950 in which delegates from several countries participated. Vinoba inaugurated the conference, and Rajendra Prasad presided. In 1950, he began his experiment of *Kanchan Mukti* — freedom from gold or money economy, which ended in failure for obvious reasons.

Vinoba Bhave is best known for 'Bhoodan' — a gift of land by the big landlords to the landless. The movement was born accidentally in 1951, when he visited the Telangana area where communists were active. In the village Pochampalli, the landless Harijan entreated him to give them land so that they could eke out their livelihood. Vinoba, half in earnest, asked in his prayer meeting if any one could give them land, all the eighty acres which they need. To everyone's surprise a young man, Ramchandra Reddy, stood up and said, "I make a gift of one hundred acres of land." Vinoba realised that it was possible to get land from the big farmers by begging and it could be then distributed to the landless. That was the birth of the 'Bhoodan Movement'. He and a band of his followers marched from one village to another on foot, persuading landlords to donate their surplus property. They travelled from one corner of the country to the other in a 'sweet-tempered fury', demanding land from landlords. It was a sight to see the "frail old man with a goat beard striding ahead, lean and sinewy, wearing tennis shoes and carrying a staff". Vinoba and his movement were propelled to the front pages of newspapers the world over. Prime Minister Nehru lauded his efforts in the Parliament. *New York Times* wrote a three column story on him and his unique movement. The *Time* magazine featured this 'man on foot' in its cover story. The 'Bhoodan March' of Vinoba continued for more than thirteen years covering a total distance of 36,500 miles. During the *padyatra* (travels on foot) he collected 4.4 million acres of land as free gifts, out of which about 1.3 million acres were distributed among landless farm workers.[2] The number of his followers swelled, which included Jayaprakash Narayan, their difference in the later stages notwithstanding. The Bhoodan movement led to some other related movements like Gramdan, Sarvodaya. For his exemplary work, Vinoba received the Magsaysay Award in 1958.

During his *padyatras*, Vinoba Bhave influenced the thinking of many people who met him or heard about him. This included even dacoits of the Chambal Valley. In May 1960, Vinoba, accompanied by Major General Yadunath Singh, toured the dreaded Chambal ravines, which is the safe abode of several dacoits. Word went around among the dacoits and some of them came for his *darshan* and were converted. The first one was the notorious Lachhi, who surrendered at his feet. He had read in the newspapers that the 'Baba' (Vinoba Bhave) wanted them to repent and surrender. Within a few days twenty more dacoits, led by the formidable Lukka and Man Singh-Rupa gang surrendered. In a prayer meeting after their surrender Vinoba said, "Two thousand and five hundred years ago we witnessed such an incident when Angulimal was turned into a saint by the touch of Lord Buddha. People say that such happenings are not possible in this Kaliyug, the age of evil. This is nothing but (a) miracle of the Almighty."[3]

All these years Vinoba had also been working for the eradication of untouchability and caste restrictions and the propagation of *khadi*. But for the last twenty years he had been feeling that he had done all that an individual could do. Still, he could not resist the temptation of doing something to stop cow slaughter, before death overtook him. In February 1982, at the age of eighty-eight, he went on a fast and led a satyagraha to secure a total ban on cow slaughter. He did not succeed. On 15 November 1982 he breathed his last in his Ashram. Mahadevitai, his adopted daughter, lit the funeral pyre.

Vinoba Bhave wrote several books or pamphlets, mostly on spiritual and religious topics. His *Gita Pravachanen,* translated in English as *Talks on the Gita*, is a collection of his talks which he delivered in Dhula jail in 1932. Others include *Swaraj Shastra* or *A Grammar of Politics* (1940) and *Gitai* (a simple rendering of Gita in Marathi verse). His speeches and articles have been collected by his disciples: *Bhoodan* (8 Vols), selected and edited by Nirmala Deshpande; *Shikshan Vichar* or *Thoughts on Education* and many others.

Vinoba learnt much from Gandhi and even imitated him in some ways but his thinking and constructive work went beyond Gandhian teachings. He clarified this during the Sevagram Constructive Workers Conference in March, 1948. He said, "Gandhiji gave me freely, but I also received from others. Whenever and whatever I got, I made my own. It now forms part of my capital. I do not have separate accounts as to what part of it was derived from Gandhiji and what from others. Of the ideas I read and heard, whatever appealed to me and were imbibed by me, became my own. Hence I am a man of my own ideas."

Today, nobody talks about Bhoodan or Vinoba Bhave. The Naxalites have taken over once again and have expanded their area of action. The number of landless labourers has increased since Vinoba's death. Land is being grabbed by the powerful and the unscrupulous. More and more persons are pushed down the enigmatic 'poverty line'. The problem of poverty and landless people is a colossal one. Vinoba tried to do the impossible. But he showed a way.

# References

1. Tandon, V. *Acharya Vinoba Bhave*. New Delhi, Publications Division, 1992, p.21.
2. Pandya, Jayant. *Gandhiji and his Disciples*. New Delhi, NBT, 1994, p.52.
3. Narayan, Shriman, Vinoba. *His Life and Work*. Bombay, Popular Prakashan, 1970, p.279.

# Jagadis Chandra Bose

## (1858-1937)

During the twentieth century, India has produced some eminent scientists but Jagadis Chandra was unique in many ways. His biophysical and plant physiological researches are a metaphysical attempt at fitting empirical results into the Vedic doctrine of unity in diversity. Thus, he became the only Indian scientist to be admired and eulogised by non-scientists like Vivekananda, Gandhi, Tagore, Sister Nivedita and others. Even literary men in Europe, like G.B. Shaw, Galsworthy and W.B. Yeats, showed great interest in Bose's scientific experiments.

Jagadis Chandra Bose was born on 30 November 1858 at Mymensingh, now in Bangladesh. His father Bhagawan Chandra Bose was in government service, working as deputy magistrate. In spite of his high government position, Bhagwan Chandra was an admirer of Indian culture and traditions. Thus, it was not surprising that Bhagawan Chandra sent his son to a local school instead of sending him to an English school. "He should learn his mother tongue before he learnt a foreign language", argued his father. This early learning of Bengali proved an asset for Jagadis in later life, while popularising science among the masses. At the age of nine, Jagadis joined Hare School in Calcutta and soon after was admitted to St. Xavier's School and College, passing the Entrance Examination of Calcutta University in 1875 and B.Sc. in 1879. The following year he left for England to study medicine but had to switch to Natural Science because of ill health. He studied at the Christ College, Cambridge. There he was fortunate to have famous scientists like Lord Rayleigh, a physicist and Sydney Vinis, a botanist, as his teachers. Rayleigh's inspiring lectures and careful experimentation contributed greatly to the making of the physicist Jagadis Bose. In 1884, he passed the Natural Science Tripos of Cambridge as well as the B.Sc. examination of the University of London.

Jagadis returned to India in 1885 and was appointed as assistant professor of Physics at the Presidency College, Calcutta. He protested against the discriminatory pay scales — white teachers being paid almost twice as much as Indian teachers. Jagadis did not draw his salary for three years and ultimately won his case: the College paid all the arrears as that being paid to the British teachers. Along with teaching, J.C. Bose wanted to do research work. But he was saddled with a heavy schedule of class lectures. He was also "subjected to continuous annoyances and petty difficulties — with the evident earnest desire of those who were about him to end his distinction which was personally galling to them", wrote Sister Nivedita, his friend and admirer. However, a determined Bose overcame all these difficulties and found time to do research work staying up late into the night. He built a small laboratory for the purpose, designing and fabricating his own tools and instruments in an ingenious ways. In this modest laboratory, his research career started around 1894, when his interest in electric waves was roused by the work of German physicist, H.R. Hertz, as explained in a small book by Oliver Lodge. Hertz had shown the existence of electromagnetic waves in free space, and found their speed to be the same as that of light. Hertz further showed that such waves had all the usual optical properties i.e. the properties of visible light waves. Hertz died in 1894 and Bose started his research work on the same lines as that of Hertz. Lodge had also started working on similar lines. Bose devised a series of experiments to demonstrate the optical behaviour of electric waves such as reflection, refraction, total reflection, polarisation, diffraction and so on. He even managed to polarise the electromagnetic waves in order to further lay bare their identity with light rays. "By his contrivance of a wide variety of delightfully simple and yet wonderfully ingenious instruments he proved the underlying unity of electrical and optical beams. As early as 1895, he demonstrated at a public lecture in Calcutta, how electric waves could travel from his radiator in the lecture room to another seventy-five feet away, where his receiver managed to pick up enough energy to ring a bell and fire a pistol. To accomplish this amazingly remarkable feat with his feeble radiator, Bose anticipated the lofty antennae of modern wireless telegraphy".[1] Today's radio and broadcasting stations are based on the experimentation and theories as propounded by Hertz and Bose. The results of his investigations appeared in leading scientific journals, *Proceedings of the Royal Society, Electrician, Journal of the Asiatic Society of Bengal.* Thus, by the end of 1895, Bose ranked high among the successors of Hertz. Further, Bose concentrated on short radio waves reducing the waves to the millimetre level, unlike Hertz, who dealt with decimetre waves and Lodge who studied the centimetre waves. Bose was successful in making devices for receiving the polarisation of electric waves using simple material such as jute fibre. These receivers were called 'coherers'. He was able to make a perfect coherer, which he could have commercially exploited. His contemporary, Marconi, who worked with other European scientists, exploited his research venture in the same field by designing a long distance radio signalling device, patented it and made a fortune. But Bose had an antipathy towards commercialising science for pecuniary gain. This attitude of Bose was called 'unpractical quixotism' by some Westerners, but did not move Bose to change his attitude.

Bose wrote a paper based on his research, 'The Determination of the Wavelength of Electric Radiation by Diffraction Grating' and sent it to the University of London as a thesis for the degree of Doctor of Science. Bose was awarded the D.Sc. degree. The university even waived the requirement of his presence at the examination, which was a great honour.

Lord Rayleigh had suggested to Bose vide a letter that he should visit England and meet the scientists there and talk about the work he had done. Bose reached England in October 1896. With the presentation of a paper on 'Electric Waves' at the Liverpool meeting of the British Association, Bose made his debut in England as a scientist. He was an immediate success, and brought, in its wake, an invitation to deliver a series of Friday Evening Discourses at the Royal Institution. 'It was during these discourses, with his free exhibition of all his appliances, that

Bose revealed his characteristically ascetic trait that astonished many and even disappointed a few'. For he never thought of patenting his apparatus, like his improved 'coherer' — an instrument for the reception of radio waves — which had made him justly famous.

Surprisingly, when he was earning laurels as a pioneering physicist he left this field, 'which was still replete with undiscovered nuggets, and ventured into another altogether new one — biophysics or the physics of life.' Bose spent less than five years doing research in physics in a ramshackle laboratory fitted with ingenuously made instruments and earned praise from leading physicists of the world. Bose was really the pioneer in utilising the Hertzian waves for signalling purposes, and laid the foundation of wireless telegraphy. Bose did not care to follow up his great achievement, as his attention was now diverted to an entirely different type of research, which evidently he regarded as of even greater importance. The switchover was accidental. While doing research with the coherer, he found that continuous exposure of metals to electric waves was causing fatigue or less of sensitivity of the metal. He hypothesised that it was similar to the muscular fatigue of animals. These and many other instances of similitude between the responses of the living and the inert that he discovered, encouraged Bose to take up the study of life. During the remaining years of his life, Bose, to prove his point of unity in diversity (between metals, plants and animals), brought into biophysics the quantitative precision of a physicist. He did so by introducing new experimental methods and inventing many delicate and sensitive instruments for demonstrating the effects of sleep, air, light, food, drugs, irritation etc. in plants, in order to prove a complete parallelism between the responses of plants and animals and even between plants and inanimate materials like metals. This he tried to prove with the help of the cresograph, a supersensitive instrument for recording plant growth by magnifying a small movement as much as ten million fold. His first demonstration was at the International Congress of Physics in Paris in July, 1900. Swami Vivekananda was also present at the Congress. He congratulated Bose after the demonstration and called him the 'heroic son of India'. An even greater compliment came from the French writer and philosopher Romain Rolland, "You have made us enter into the Kingdom of the universe of silent life, which till yesterday was thought as dead and buried in the night." Bose visited England and Europe several times on scientific deputation. He lectured at Oxford, Cambridge, London, Aberdeen, and Leipzig. During 1923-24, Bose visited Europe for the sixth time. This time the audience of his lecture at the India Office, London, included Ramsay Macdonald, the prime minister, Lord Hardinge, former viceroy and George Bernard Shaw. The topic was the 'Phenomenon of the Growth of Plants'. After the lecture, Bernard Shaw presented Bose a special edition of his collected works bearing the inscription "From the least to the greatest biologist." The synthetic philosophical outlook that underlay Bose's scientific work had a natural appeal for the sensitive men of literature.

But Bose had his detractors too. They considered his biophysical and plant physiological researches as a metaphysical attempt at fitting empirical results into the Vedic doctrine of unity in diversity. Among such critics were Dr. Waller and Burdon Sanderson, who had even succeeded in persuading the Royal Society not to publish Bose's paper. "He was blamed for having been carried away by a sort of enchantment exercised by verbal ghosts, like fatigue, sleep, exaltation, irritability, of his own conjuring". But the urge to satisfy his longing to bring about the unity of animals and inanimate nature, sustained Bose in the midst of all the criticism that his biophysical work provoked. And during his life time, undaunted by criticism, Bose continued to try to obliterate the boundry lines and establish new points of contact between the domains of the living and the inert. However, his assumption that the phloem tissues in plants are equivalent to nerves in animals was disproved by later investigations.

Jagadish Chandra Bose had married Abala Das, daughter of Durga Mohan Das and a cousin of C.R. Das, in 1887. They had only one child, who died in infancy. The childless couple led a very happy married life. Abala was always by the side of her husband whenever he was in difficulty and often accompanied him during his frequent lecture tours to Europe and America. She was a gracious hostess and acted as a mother to Bose's students, some of whom stayed with them. After Bose's retirement from Presidency College in 1915, Abala founded Nari Siksha Samiti devoted to the education and welfare of women.

Bose had many admirers outside the scientific circle, the greatest of them being Rabindranath Tagore and Sister Nivedita. Bose was in constant correspondence with Tagore, who was always anxious to know about the progress of Bose's research and their response among scientists as well as non-scientists. In all, eighty-two letters were exchanged between the two, all written in Bengali. Tagore also immortalised Bose through many essays and poems including the one on Mimosa (*chhui-mui* plant) used by Bose in many of his experiments and demonstrations. What really brought them together was the fact that both were in quest of an ultimate cosmic unity in the midst of diverse manifestations of Nature. "Another sphere," wrote Tagore, "where Jagadis felt affinity towards me was his profound patriotism".[2] Tagore was three years younger than Bose and outlived him by four years.

Another great friend was Sister Nivedita, who played an inspiring role in the life of Bose. Bose's wife Abala was equally attached to Nivedita and the latter found solace in their company and was a frequent visitor to the Bose's home. Actually Nivedita died in Bose's summer resort at Darjeeling in 1911. Before her death, Nivedita had urged Bose to build a research 'institute epitomising the renascent wisdom of India'. The Bose Research Institute did come into existence in 1917 through the generous donations of the people as well as substantial grant from the government, "where scholars would ceaselessly pursue the quest for truth". An inaugural song was composed by Tagore. The famous painter Nandlal's mural decorated the walls of the lecture hall.

During his life time, Bose was showered with national and international honours. He was knighted in 1916 and was elected Fellow of the Royal Society in 1920. In 1926, he was nominated a member of the League of Nations Committee on Intellectual Cooperation. In 1928, he became corresponding member of the Vienna Academy of Science. He was honorary member of several scientific societies of Europe and America. He was the general president of the 1927 session of the Indian Science Congress.

Bose authored a number of books and papers, both in English and Bengali. Some of them are: *Response in the Living and Non-Living* (1902); *Comparative Electro-Physiology* (1907); *Researches in Irritability of Plants* (1913);

*The Physiology of Photosynthesis* (1924); *The Nervous Mechanism of Plants* (1926); *Collected Physical Papers* (1927); *Motor Mechanism of Plants* (1928); *Growth and Tropic Movement of Plants* (1929). He also edited several volumes of the *Transactions of the Bose Research Institute*. Bose also tried to popularise science by writing scientific essays in Bengali. In 1921, he brought out a collection of these essays titled *Avyukta* (the unmanifest), written since 1894 and published in various magazines.

Bose had been suffering from diabetes and high blood pressure for many years, which had affected his health. Only his love and enthusiasm for research work sustained him through those years. He died on 23 November 1937.

## References

1.  Singh, Jagjit. *Some Eminent Indian Scientists*. New Delhi, Publications Division. 4th ed, 1991, p.24.
2.  Mukherji, Visvapriya. *Jagadis Chandra Bose*. New Delhi, Publications Division. 2nd ed. 1994, pp.52-53.

# Rahmat Ali

## (1897-1950)

"A person who for the first time demanded partition explicitly, loudly and persistently, and who produced a clear-cut plan, was Chaudhry Rahmat Ali". Saad R. Khairi, *Jinnah Reinterpreted*.

Rahmat Ali was born on 16 November 1897 in the village Balachaur about thirty miles from Jalandhar in East Punjab, in a Gujjar middle-class family. It is believed that their ancestors were converted to Islam during the times of Aurangzeb. Rahmat Ali's father Shah Muhammad married twice. Rahmat was the eldest among the three children of Shah Muhammad's second wife. The other two were, his younger brother Mohammad Ali and a sister who died in infancy.

Rahmat Ali's education started in a primary school in Balachaur and continued in Rahon, a small town few miles from his village, which boasted of a middle school. To continue his education further, Rahmat Ali had to go to Jalandhar, the district headquarters and an important city in the area. There in 1910, he enrolled himself at the Saindas Anglo-Sanskrit High School, which was managed by the Arya Samaj. From there he passed the Matriculation examination in 1912. From Jalandhar he went to Lahore to pursue higher studies and joined the Islamia College, one of the string of colleges founded under the Aligarh movement. Rahmat Ali graduated from this college in 1918, getting a second division with Economics, English and Persian as his subjects. It took him six years to graduate which in the normal course takes four years. During these six years he also tried his hand at journalism and served on the staff of *Paisa Akhbar* and *Kashmir*, besides pursuing his studies.

After his graduation, Rahmat Ali continued to live in Lahore, the capital of Punjab, a seat of learning and political ferment. Most of the Muslim elite of Punjab lived there. Ali lived in Lahore till 1930. He wanted to join the Law College but could not, perhaps due to a paucity of funds. Instead, he accepted a tutorship in Aitchison College, a public school for the education of the sons of rulers and chiefs of the province. While serving as a tutor, he came in contact with the Nawab of Bahavalpur whose son he taught. Later he also taught the sons of the Mazari family, who were prominent landlords. He got close to the family and became their legal adviser after attending classes in the Law College (from where he could not earn any degree). The Mazari family paid him well and he lived a life of ease and some affluence. His social contacts widened and the village lad absorbed the culture and etiquette of urban life with ease. Niaz Muhamad Khan, who knew Rahmat Ali during his Lahore days, describes him as, "well dressed, a joy to listen to, with a discriminating taste in cuisine, with impeccable manners and habits, experienced in the way of the world".[1] Another friend describes him in one Urdu word 'banka', the nearest English translation of which would be a 'dandy'.

Rahmat Ali had always nurtured a desire of going to England, which he called his 'mission' in life. The dream materialised in 1930. With the connections that he cultivated in Lahore, he did not find any difficulty in getting prominent Punjabi friends to write to men of influence in England about his plans. Armed with these recommendatory letters, Rahmat Ali left for England on 31 October 1930. He was already thirty-three years old. He decided to become a barrister and joined the Inn of Court, the Middle Temple. But for some unexplained reason he could not be called to the Bar until January 1943, taking thirteen years, which normally aspirants complete in two or three years. It seems he abandoned the idea of qualifying as a barrister soon after and joined Emmanuel College, Cambridge in January 1931. He passed the Law Tripos examination in June 1932. It took him another seven years to get an M.A. degree in October 1940. His other academic accomplishments remain obscure at Cambridge. However, he came into the limelight after the three sittings of the Round Table Conference (1930-32) in which a federal structure of India was discussed and approved by the participants resulting in the Act of 1935, which served as the Constitution of India till 1947.

Rahmat Ali was witnessing this political drama with 'poignant anxiety'. Mohammad Iqbal's presidential address at the Muslim League session of 1930 had thrown up an idea of a separate Muslim region in the north-west of India. This appealed to Rahmat Ali as it diluted the hegemony of 'Indianness'. But that was forgotten and the delegates had unanimously agreed to the federal structure for India. Rahmat Ali claimed that he met the Muslim delegates at the first two sittings of the conference and tried to convince them of their folly of agreeing to an Indian federation, which would be perpetually dominated by the Hindus. "I knew that their action had obliterated the twelve centuries of our history, destroyed the very foundations of our heritage, and crippled all hopes of the fulfilment of our mission".[2] But he failed to convince them. He went back to Cambridge and published a four page pamphlet in January 1933, signed by three other students besides himself. The pamphlet was titled *Now or Never: Are we to live or perish forever?* He appealed for "sympathy and support for our grim and fateful struggle against political crucifixion and complete annihilation". The homeland of thirty million Muslims was defined in the first sentence as Pakistan, "by which we mean the five northern units of India viz: Punjab, North-West Frontier Province (Afghan), Kashmir, Sind and Baluchistan". It was further argued that India was neither a country nor a nation. "It is in fact, the designation of a state, created for the first time in history, by the British. The heterogeneity of its people was a proven fact. Our religion, culture, history, tradition, economic system, laws of inheritance, succession and marriage are basically and fundamentally different from those of the people living in the rest of India. These differencs are not confined to the broad basic principles — far from it. They extend to the minutest details of our lives. We do not inter-dine, we do not inter-marry. Our national customs and calendars, even our diet and dress are different". Although these ideas did not carry much weight at the time, it must be admitted that all the subsequent arguments in support of Pakistan proceeded from the thesis of Rahmat

Ali, and did not cover much new ground.[3] In fact Jinnah in his speech in the 1940 session of the Muslim League, while demanding a separate homeland for Muslims for the first time copied extensively, almost word for word, from Rahmat Ali's pamphlet. When later the Muslim League came to advocate its own Pakistan plan, it could not think of any new arguments and repeated and elaborated Rahmat Ali's points.

That pamphlet was sent to all the delegates of the Round Table Conference and several political leaders, both in England and India. But the pamphlet attracted little attention and was ignored by the Muslim League and Muslim Conference. When the representatives of these two organisations appeared before the Joint Select Committee of the Parliament in August 1933 they were asked "whether there is a scheme for a federation of Provinces under the name Pakistan?" Zafrulla Khan (the future foreign minister of Pakistan) replied, "It was a students' scheme and there is nothing in it." Another member Yusuf Ali replied, "We have considered, it is chimerical and impracticable." The only support which Rahmat Ali's scheme got was from the notorious Sir Michael O'Dwyer, who ruled Punjab during the Jallianwala Bagh massacre, Amritsar (1919), and its martial law aftermath. While testifying before the Committee, he argued against the all-India federation on the lines of Rahmat Ali, saying if the federal government, with a Hindu majority, endeavours to force its will on provinces with a Muslim majority, what is to prevent a breakaway of the Punjab, Sind, Baluchistan and the NWF as already foreshadowed and their possibility of forming a Muslim Federation of their own. "He did not explain the source of the word 'foreshadowed' but he appears to have received a copy of Rahmat Ali's pamphlet. Or could he perhaps have helped inspire it".[4] Obviously the British hand in the whole affair could not be ruled out.

To give an impetus to his theory, the 'shadowy' Rahmat Ali identified himself as "Founder of the Pakistan National Movement". This movement, in his own words, was "a centre of members to work for Pakistan, for the Pak Plan, and for the Pak ideology". He published another eight page pamphlet soon after, titled *What Does the Pakistan National Movement Stand For?* This was a virulent attack on 'Indianness', which he described as Hindu imperialism. A minor but significant change was the spelling of the word 'Pakstan' to 'Pakistan.' He continued issuing and distributing pamphlets widely in which he went on extending the boundaries of the Muslim state or the creation of other Muslim states like Bangistan, Usmanistan or Haideristan comprising Bengal plus Assam and Hyderabad respectively. These will be two independent 'nations' forming a triple alliance, he argued. Still later, he proposed setting up seven more states as Muslim pockets not only in India but even in Ceylon (Sri Lanka). All these pamphlets bore the address, 16 Montague Road, Cambridge and the later pamphlets of various sizes bore the signature of only one man, Rahmat Ali. The increasing number of 'stans' touched the limits of absurdity, but the impact of his Pakistan movement gathered momentum, and in the hands of a great strategist, Jinnah, became a reality in August 1947.

Rahmat Ali eventually decided to see the Shangrila of his dreams, towards which he had contributed his bit and spent many years of his adult life. He reached Lahore on 6 April 1948, met his friends and traced his family, who were now *muhajirs* (refugees) and found them in a pitiable condition. He found unbearable the partition of Punjab and Bengal and the loss of Assam, and blamed Jinnah for his 'treachery' and 'betrayal'. To get back the 'lost territories' of Pakistan of his conception, he planned to start a 'Pakistan National Liberation Movement.' He started calling Pakistan as 'Pastan' (a defeated country). He declared, "all our hopes reduced to dust and ashes by the folly and foulplay of one man and one man alone — *Quisling-i-Azam-Jinnah*". This outspokenness cost him dearly. The few old friends who had welcomed him as a 'hero' now deserted him. The government was soon after him. He was declared *persona non grata;* was refused a Pakistani passport; was condemned as a danger to the security and tranquillity of the country. The government did not remember, or even let it be known, that he had named the country over which they ruled, but it could not forget that he had criticised Jinnah, the Quaid-i-Azam for accepting an incomplete Pakistan. He was ordered to leave the country. He left on 1 October 1948 for England, and died in Cambridge on 3 January 1951, a lonely and dejected man. He is buried in Cambridge City Cemetry at New Market Road. His grave is flat earth. The hospital and burial expenses were paid by Welbourne, his tutor during his Emmanuel College days. "I am glad that I was able to prevent him dying as an unclaimed beggar in poverty and avert the disposal of his body as an unclaimed person," said Welbourne. During his lifetime, Jinnah did not show any consideration for Rahmat Ali from whom he had borrowed his ideal, his nomenclature, his arguments, even his words and phrases. Jinnah owed such a large debt to Rahmat Ali who had played a pivotal role in the creation of Pakistan.[5]

# References

1.  Aziz, K.K. *Rahmat Ali: A Biography*. Lahore, Vanguard. 1987, p.21.
2.  Ibid p.79.
3.  Majumdar, R.C. *History of the Freedom Movement in India*. Vol. 3. 2nd ed. Calcutta, Firma KLM, 1988, p.474.
4.  Wolpert, Stanley. *Jinnah of Pakistan*. OUP. 1984, p.132.
5.  Aziz, K.K. op. cit. p.338.

# Rash Behari Bose

## (1880-1945)

Rash Behari was one of those freedom fighters and revolutionaries who spent a major part of their lives in self-exile working for the freedom of the country from distant lands, braving innumerable sufferings and privations. Some such forgotten heroes are Ajit Singh (uncle of Sardar Bhagat Singh), Madam Cama, Raja Mahendra Pratap and Shyamji Krishna Varma. Among all these freedom fighters the name of Rash Behari stands out as the founder of the Indian Independence League and the Indian National Army, which later under the leadership of Subhas Chandra Bose, fought the British army and shook the foundations of the British Empire, forcing them to leave India in a hurry.

Rash Behari was born in 1886 in Subaldaha, Burdwan district. His parents, Binode Behari Bose and Bhavaneshwari Devi, formed an average middle-class family. His father was employed in Government Press, Shimla, as assistant. His mother died when Rash Behari was barely two. Binod Behari remarried soonafter, but Rash Behari seems to have good relations with his stepmother, who often came to his help whenever he was in difficulty. He had his early education at Subaldaha under the guidance of his grandfather Kalicharan. Later, he joined Dupleix College at Chandernagore, a French enclave. But Rash Behari was not interested in studies and stopped going to school after class II. He was more interested in physical culture. As Bengalis were debarred from joining the army, he tried to enlist in the army under a false name; was detected and punished. Seeing the waywardness of his son, his father Binode Behari took him to Shimla and somehow got him a job as a copyholder in the press. There he learnt English as well as typewriting. But soon he returned to Chandernagore, leaving Shimla and his job. There for the first time he came in contact with the revolutionaries of the Jugantar Party operating in Chandernagore, and decided to devote his life for the emancipation of the country. But soon after, he left Chandernagore and went back to Shimla. With the help of his father's acquaintances, he got a clerical job at the Pasteur Institute, Kasauli and later at the Forest Research Institute, Dehra Dun. In spite of being a government servant, Rash Behari started taking active part in revolutionary activities. He was in touch with the members of the Anushilan Samiti of Bengal and had formed a small group of devoted revolutionaries under his leadership. The first daring act of this group was throwing of a bomb on the procession of Lord Hardinge, the viceroy, on 23 December 1912, on the occasion of his state entry into Delhi riding on an elephant. The bomb was thrown by Basanta Kumar Biswas from the Punjab National Bank building in Chandni Chawk at the signal of Rash Behari Bose. The entire planning was done by Rash Behari. Lord Hardinge was badly wounded, the man holding his umbrella was killed, and another servant was seriously injured. Most of the members of this group were caught after the incident. Avadh Behari, Bal Mukand and Master Amir Chand (who used to give shelter to the revolutionaries) were executed in Delhi jail and Basanta Kumar Biswas was hanged in Ambala jail. But Rash Behari escaped because he had mastered the art of disguise to conceal his identity. Undaunted by the setback, Rash Behari continued his revolutionary activities, enlisting the support of several other revolutionaries from Punjab, Bengal and other parts of India. He felt that stray incidents of daredevilry were not of much help in weakening the hold of foreign power on the country. He felt that an attempt should be made to plan a general uprising by the Indian army on the lines of the 1857 uprising. Rash Behari started working towards that end. By that time he had formed a larger group of revolutionaries under his leadership. The First World War, which started in July 1914 provided them an opportunity to execute their plan.

"Rash Behari directed his main attention to propaganda work among the Indian soldiers with a view to inducing them to join in the general rebellion against the British, which was planned to take place simultaneously all over North India".[1] Rash Behari sent his most trusted lieutenants to work among soldiers in the various cantonments: Allahabad, Ramnagar, Banaras, Ambala, Ferozepur, Jalandhar, Lahore, Meerut and as far as Rawalpindi. According to the plan, sepoys were to revolt on a particular day overpowering or killing the English troops, whose number had been considerably reduced due to the War in Europe and the Middle East. The date of the uprising was fixed as 21 February 1915 throughout north India. But a police informer, Kirpal Singh, who had managed to enrol as a member of the Rash Behari group, conveyed the information to the authorities who took adequate measures to defeat the plan. Many revolutionaries were arrested and executed. So also many soldiers. Rash Behari once again escaped. As the police was after him, he decided to leave India. He applied for a passport under the assumed name of Raja P.N. Thakur. The declared purpose was to make arrangements for Rabindranath Tagore's ensuing visit to Japan. It is believed that Tagore had come to know about the impersonation but he kept quiet. The famous Bengali writer Sarat Chandra Chatterjee is believed to have contributed money for Rash Behari's passage to Japan. Rash Behari left for Japan on 12 May 1915 by S.S. *Sanuki Maru*, reaching the port of Kobe on 5 June. From there he travelled to Tokyo. From various sources the British secret agents in Japan learnt that P.N. Thakur was actually Rash Behari Bose who was wanted in India for attempt to murder the viceroy Lord Hardinge. Once the identity was established, the British would apply for his extradition. In 1915, Britain and Japan had very friendly relations and there would not have been any difficulty in getting him back in India as he was declared as the 'most dangerous criminal'. As Rash Behari suspected that the British secret police was after him he continuously changed his residence to avoid arrest. One Japanese family couple, Mr. and Mrs. Soma, moved by Rash Behari's hardships and deprivations let him stay in their house for sometime, which ended with Rash Behari marrying their daughter, Tosiko, in July, 1918. Still the sufferings of the couple did not end. They continued to change their residence at short intervals. Rash

Behari became a naturalised Japanese citizen in July 1923. Consequently, he could not be deported.[2] However, the health of his wife deteriorated due to the hardships she had to bear. She died in March 1925, at the age of twenty-eight, leaving behind a son Masahide (who was killed fighting the British during the War) and a daughter Tetuke.

Rash Behari kept himself busy playing host to revolutionaries, especially of the Gadar party who came to Japan from Canada and America. He had established a dormatory 'Ajio-Go' (Centre of Asia) for the convenience of visitors. In 1933 he established 'Villa Asians' in Tokyo for Asian students, which he managed till 1941. He also formed an 'Indo-Japanese Friends Society' and undertook extensive tour in Japan explaining the Indian viewpoint. He could speak Japanese fluently. In 1924, he had formed the Indian Independence League, which played an important role during the War, especially its military wing, Indian National Army (Azad Hind Fauj).

While in Japan, Rash Behari wrote several books, some of which are: *Panoramic Views of Asian Revolution (*1929), *Wit and Humour of India* (1930), *India Oppressed* (1933), *Stories of Indian People* (1935), *India in Revolution* (1936), *Victories of Young Asia* (1937), *India Crying* (1938), *The Bhagwat Gita* (1940), *Tragic History of India* (1942), *The Ramayana* (1942), *India of Indians* (1943), *Last Song* (1943) and *Bose Appeals* (1944). He also started a journal *New Asia* with himself as editor. Because of its attacks on the British policy, its entry into India was banned. He was also on the staff of the *Asian Review*.

The entry of Japan in the Second World War ignited in Rash Behari the revolutionary instinct which was lying dormant all these years and he organised a conference in Tokyo on 28 March 1942, under the auspices of the Indian Independence League with himself in the chair. General Tojo sent a message to the conference saying that, "The Japanese government is fully sympathetic towards your efforts and will not hesitate to render all possible help in this respect". But no formal declaration by the government of Japan was made, which created some consternation in the Indian camp. The conference passed several resolutions including the one requesting the Japanese authorities to declare their full support for the Indian cause and clarify their stand on the issue without delay. The conference also resolved to have an elected Council of Action and appointed Rash Behari Bose as interim president. These resolutions were to be ratified by a conference of the League representatives from all over east Asia to be held at Bangkok. The Bangkok conference was held for a week from 15 June 1942 in which delegates from various countries of east Asia participated. The Bangkok Conference ratified all the resolutions passed by the Tokyo Conference. The council was invested with powers of control over the Indian Independence League in all the territories and over the Indian National Army. It also invited Subhas Chandra Bose, who was in Germany to come to east Asia.

Immediately after the Bangkok conference, both the League organization and the INA plunged into action, with Bangkok as headquarters of the Council of Action and Singapore as headquarters of the INA. Over twenty thousand Indian Prisoners of War had deserted by this time and joined the Indian National Army headed by Gen. Mohan Singh.

An unfortunate development occurred when the Japanese replaced the popular Fujiwara as liaison officer with Iwakuro, who was not as understanding and sympathetic to the Indian cause as the former. The fact that the Japanese government was not committing anything officially, undermined the position of Rash Behari as the president of the Council of Action. Doubts were being expressed about his ability to lead the movement. "His thirty years stay in Japan, his advancing age, frail health and mild manners made some Indians doubt whether he could withstand the strain of an uncompromising stand vis-à-vis the Japanese". The schism between the Council of Action, the INA headed by Gen. Mohan Singh and the Japanese widened. Members of the Council of Action barring its president, resigned. Gen. Singh was peeved at the interference by the Japanese, who were issuing orders of movements to the INA troops without consulting the Council of Action or their commander. Gen. Singh protested and was arrested on 29 December 1942 in Singapore and was released only after the War was over. With the arrest of Gen. Singh, the INA ceased to exist, leaving Rash Behari as president of the Council of Action in quandry. "Six months of mounting suspicion, distrust, misgivings, tactlessness and lack of faith in Japanese sincerity culminated in the dissolution of the Council of Action and disbandonment of the first INA. Chaos and confusion prevailed for some time".

Rash Behari then set about the task of rebuilding the League as well as the INA. Dr. Lakshumiyah joined him on the civil side and Lt.Col. J.K. Bhonsle on the military side i.e. INA. He shifted the headquarters of the League from Bangkok to Singapore in March 1943 and tried to build up the two organizations, working day and night to the amazement of his colleagues. Rash Behari knew that it was a matter of time before Subhas Chandra Bose reached east Asia and assumed leadership of the movement.

Rash Behari called another conference of Indians in Singapore from 27-30 April 1943 and passed the resolution that "the Indian National Army is the army of the Indian Independence League and all officers and men of the INA as well as all members of the I.I.L. shall owe allegiance to the League". The constitution of the League was amended by another resolution investing Rash Behari with almost dictatorial powers.[3] Rash Behari had saved the IIL and the INA from an ignominious end with his foresight and devotion to the national cause. After resurrecting both the organizations to his satisfaction, he left for Tokyo in June 1943.

Subhas Chandra Bose's journey from Germany to east Asia in a submarine is a part of the romantic saga in the annals of the freedom movement. He reached Tokyo on 16 May 1943. The Japanese authorities gave assurance of full support to Subhas Bose. Even before Subhas Bose was brought to east Asia, the Japanese were concerned about the presence of the two Boses, who may not work in tandem and thus create problems. But when General Arisue of the Intelligence Bureau broached this question, Rash Behari's categorical reply, "I will step down" relieved the anxiety of the Japanese. Rash Behari Bose, accompanied by Subhas Bose, landed at the Sambawant aerodrome, Singapore, from Tokyo on the morning of 2 July 1943. Two days later on 4 July, before an enthusiastic gathering of five thousand Indians at the Cathey Cinema Hall, Rash Behari handed over the leadership to the 'younger and dynamic hands of Subhas'. Rash Behari voluntarily receded to the background as 'adviser', and let Subhas lead the INA, and left for Japan.

Rash Behari died in Tokyo on 21 January 1945. The news was announced by a Royal proclamation over the radio and his body was carried to the Yojoji Temple the next morning by the decorated Imperial bier sent from the Imperial Palace, for last rites. Hours before his death, the Japanese emperor decorated him with the Second Order-of-Merit of the Rising Sun. However, no honour has been bestowed on him by our country for the emancipication of which he worked throughout his life and suffered.

## References

1.  Majumdar, R.C. *History of the Freedom Movement in India*. Vol. 2. Calcutta, Firma KLM. 1988, p.425.
2.  Dharamvir. *I Threw the Bomb; The Revolutionary Life of Rash Behari Bose*. New Delhi, Orient Paperbacks, 1979, pp.111-12.
3.  Ayer, S.A. *Story of the INA*, New Delhi, National Book Trust, 1997 (Rev. ed.), pp.34-37.

# Subhas Chandra Bose

## (1897-1945)

Subhas Chandra Bose was the only soldier-statesman India has produced during the recent past. By alienating thousands of Indian soldiers in the British army from the Crown, he shook the foundations of the British Empire, compelling the British to leave India in a hurry. Thus, his role in the freedom movement is unique and paramount.

He was born on 23 January 1897 at Cuttack, Orissa, ninth of the fourteen children of his parents; father Janakinath Bose and mother Prabhabati. Janakinath was a lawyer by profession and had earned a name at the Cuttack Bar. He was elected chairman of the Cuttack Municipality in 1901; was later appointed government pleader and public prosecutor, the post which he resigned in 1917 due to differences with the district magistrate. He also served as a member of the Bengal Legislative Council (1912). "Ours was not a rich but what might be regarded as a well-to-do middle-class family", wrote Subhas in his *Autobiography*. But it was a 'healthy, disciplined home' where Subhas grew up.

Before he was five, Subhas was sent to the Baptist Missionary school in Cuttack where his brothers also studied. He was good at studies, learnt English well but did not take part in school sports. For seven years he studied in this school and then at the age of twelve he joined Ravenshaw Collegiate School and became proficient in Bengali also. He passed the Matriculation examination in 1913, standing second in the Calcutta

University. While studying in school, he was influenced by the teachings of Vivekananda who taught him that only service of humanity can bring about one's salvation. This inspired young Subhas to do social work in the nearby villages at the time of calamities like floods and epidemics. For further education, he was sent to Calcutta, where he joined Presidency College and a new chapter in his life began. Since his younger days, Subhas was influenced by sadhus and ascetics. During the college vacations in 1914 he, along with a friend, went out in search of a guru, visiting religious places like Hardwar, Rishikesh, Mathura, Vrindaban, Varanasi and Gaya, without informing his family. But after a few weeks they returned to Calcutta, greatly disappointed at not finding a guru, who could guide them in life.

Subhas found studies and lectures in the college quite boring and meaningless but he continued attending classes. He passed the Intermediate examination in 1915 with credit. For the degree course he opted for philosophy and had started taking interest in studies because philosophy was his favourite subject. Then the famous Oaten episode happened in 1916. Edward Farley Oaten was a young British teacher at the Presidency College, who, it is alleged, used to denigrade Indians and Indian culture while teaching. Once he manhandled some students who were making a noise in the corridors while his class was on. He came out and thrashed those students. As a reaction to that, some students assaulted Oaten after a few days. As the representative of the class, Subhas Bose was held responsible for this incident of indiscipline. "Bose, you are the most troublesome man in the college," the principal shouted at him. "I suspend you." Subhas was rusticated and had to discontinue his studies as he could not join any other college affiliated to the Calcutta University. That proved to be a turning point in his turbulent life. In a paper presented about the incident at a seminar in 1973. Oaten (who was eighty-eight at the time) tells a different version of the incident and denies that he had assaulted any student. He wrote, "It seems that I led the students to the office, but to do so violently could have been contrary to my nature; I was merely enforcing discipline. Next day I was assaulted from the rear by a body of students. Subhas Chandra Bose was supposed to have been connected with the affair, although I never had any proof of this. I suffered no injury except for a few bruises, and I bore the assailents no malice and refused to prosecute". He ended by saying, "I have been privileged in a long life to see India obtain her freedom in 1947. Netaji contributed towards obtaining that freedom, although not everybody approved of his method. I do not regret the fact that in the beginning of his career my name was linked with his. Both of us, each in his own way, helped to make modern India".[1] Oaten also wrote a poem on Subhas Bose (1947) the first two lines of which read; 'Did I once suffer, Subhas at your hand; Your patriot heart is still'd! I would forget!" About the incident Subhas wrote in his *Autobiography*, "I had stood up with courage and composure in a crisis and fulfilled my duty. I had developed self-confidence as well as initiative, which was to stand me in good stead in future. I had a foretaste of leadership — though in very restricted sphere — and of the martyrdom that it involves. In short, I had acquired character and could face the future with equanimity".[2]

After his suspension from college, Subhas went to his home at Cuttack and busied himself doing social work. For two years he had to discontinue his studies. He went back to Calcutta and with the help of Ashutosh Mukherjee, vice-chancellor of the Calcutta University, he was able to join the Scottish Church College in third year class in July 1917. He now took studies quite seriously and passed B.A. honours in philosophy, procuring a first class. Along with studies, he had joined, the University Training Corps (India's Territorial Army) and for four months received military training in a camp near Fort William, where the students received training like drilling with rifles. This brief military training was very helpful for him while organizing the Indian National Army.

At the suggestion of his father and elder brother Sarat (for whom he had great respect and affection) Subhas left for England in September 1919 to appear in the Indian Civil Service examination. There he joined the Cambridge University to prepare for the examination. He studied at the Cambridge University for only eight months. He must have worked hard because when the result of the examination was announced his name was fourth on the list. While undergoing his probationary training he started having second thoughts about becoming an ICS officer. He wanted to serve the motherland in a different capacity, working towards her freedom and not as a bureaucrat. He wrote to his father and elder brother Sarat, explaining the reasons why he wanted to resign from the Indian Civil Service. He also wrote a letter on 16 February 1921 to C.R. Das, the most important Congress leader in Bengal. Subhas wrote: "I would like to know what work you may be able to allot to me in this great programme of national service". Subhas also suggested in the letter what type of work he would be able to do as well as the ways to reorganize the Congress. On receiving an encouraging reply from C.R. Das, his mind was made up. He resigned from the ICS and left for India. On reaching Bombay on 16 July 1921, he met Mahatma Gandhi and had discussions with him about his programme of achieving 'swaraj in one year'. The replies which Gandhi gave to his searching questions did not satisfy Subhas. As already decided through correspondence, Subhas met C.R. Das in Calcutta and at once found the political guide he was pining for. At Das's suggestion, Subhas joined the Congress party; he joined the Calcutta National College started by the Congress as principal; became the publicity officer of the Bengal Provincial Congress Committee and captain of the National Volunteer Corps. When the Prince of Wales visited India (November, 1921), the Congress high command decided to boycott the visit. Subhas Bose was put in charge of the campaign. The government arrested thousands of volunteers including C.R. Das and Subhas in December. This was Subhas' first imprisonment; ten had yet to follow. C.R. Das and Subhas were imprisoned for six months. Much of the imprisonment of the two was spent together, bringing the guru and his disciple even closer. They had plenty of time to discuss the national problems and the strategy which the Congress should adopt. Then came the most disturbing news: Gandhi had withdrawn the Non-Cooperation Movement in February 1922. Non-cooperation had failed. An alternative strategy had to be evolved. C.R. Das proposed, supported by Motilal Nehru, that they should enter the legislatures and wreck the government from within. When the no-changers (the ardent followers of Gandhi) did not agree, C.R. Das resigned from the Congress and formed the Swaraj Party. They fought the 1924 elections under the newly formed party and won a thumping victory in the Central Legislature as well as in the states. C.R. Das was elected Mayor of Calcutta and Subhas Bose was elected chief executive officer in March 1924. He was twenty-seven by now but nature in his outlook. Both of them worked hard to provide better civic facilities for the people of Calcutta. But Bengal was once again in the grip of terrorism. Swarajists were suspected for abetting terrorism. Subhas was arrested in October 1924 under the Emergency ordinance. For two months, he performed his municipal duties in Alipur jail; then in January 1925 he was removed to Mandalay, the prison in which Lajpat Rai and Tilak had spent their prison sentences earlier. The rigours of prison life affected his health. The government offered to release him on condition that he should go to Europe without entering India. He contemptuously rejected the offer. 'I am not a shopkeeper, I do not bargain", he said. He was released unconditionally on 16 May 1927 on grounds of ill-health. He had spent two years in Mandalay jail. By that time, C.R. Das had died in June 1925. It was a 'cataclysmic loss' for Subhas as never before was he on his own. But during the two years of contemplation in prison, he had matured further. He came to be regarded by the masses as the natural leader of Bengal. He was elected chairman of the Bengal Provincial Congress Committee soon after. His health improved and he was again actively taking part in political developments. He became the general secretary of the Congress along with Jawaharlal Nehru. When the Motilal Nehru Report on the proposed constitution of India was released, both Subhas and Jawaharlal protested against the acceptance of Dominion Status. They wanted *purna swaraj* (complete independence). He shared with Nehru the formation of short lived India Independence League. Subhas toured the whole country explaining to the masses the need for *purna swaraj*. "His eloquence became more practised, his rhetoric more skillful, his stature as a leader greater and more widely accepted". The Congress fell in line with his thinking, when in 1929, during the Lahore session, under the presidentship of Jawaharlal, it was declared that Independence was the goal of the Congress.

Once again, a full-scale Disobedience Movement commenced in 1930 and Subhas was arrested on his birthday, 23 January. When he emerged from prison on 25 September 1930, he was elected mayor of Calcutta. The following year he was elected chairman of All India Trade Union Congress (AITUC). As a result of the Gandhi-Irwin Pact, the Disobedience Movement was suspended in March 1931. After Gandhi returned from the Second Round Table Conference on 28 December 1931, Civil Disobedience was resumed on 1 January and Subhas was once again arrested on 2 January 1932, along with other Congress leaders. But by the end of 1932, he was gravely ill and he was released on 22 February 1933 'on the condition that he would go to Europe for treatment'. He was suffering from tuberculosis and this time went to Europe. He was admitted to Dr. Furth's sanitorium in Vienna. There he met Vithalbhai Patel (elder brother of Sardar Patel), and both started enjoying each other's company and discussing political developments in India. They were stunned when Gandhi suspended the Civil Disobedience Movement on 8 May 1933. "This was an abject surrender", they cried and issued the famous joint manifesto on 9 May 1933: "We are clearly of opinion that as a political leader Mahatma Gandhi has failed. The time has therefore come for a radical reorganization of the Congress on a new principle and with a new method. For bringing about this reorganization a change of leadership is necessary". Vithalbhai died on 22 October 1933 in a sanitorium near Geneva, with Subhas by his side. Vithalbhai shared the view of Subhas that it was impossible for India to achieve independence without foreign help. For that, systematic propaganda was necessary. Vithalbhai left a hundred thousand rupees to organize such propaganda in Europe and England, making Subhas the trustee of the money. However, Subhas did not get the money due to legal wranglings in a Bombay court. Subhas spent the next two years in Europe, visiting several countries, addressing select audiences and meeting important persons including Hitler and explaining India's case to the world.

He returned to India on 8 April 1936 and was immediately arrested but released on 17 March 1937. During Gandhi's visit to Calcutta, Subhas conferred with him and agreed to be president of the 1938 session of the Congress. "Bose now was a man of more than national stature. Abroad he ranked after Gandhi and Jawaharlal Nehru as an Indian politician. Within India, his personality had proved to many the most attractive of the three. In some places his reputation rivalled that of Gandhi himself, and his nomination as president of the Congress at the early age of forty-one was without doubt an attempt by the Mahatma to consolidate with the orthodox Congress, those considerable left-wing elements in Bengal and elsewhere, which actually preferred Bose's leadership".[4] To Gandhi's chagrin, Subhas did not tow Gandhi's line of thinking as president of the Congress. In his presidential address at Haripura, though he did not attack Gandhi, his socialistic thinking was quite evident. He talked of the need for industrial revolution and the need for a national reconstruction programme through the National Planning Committee. Against the advice of Gandhi, Subhas wanted to be the president second time. Gandhi put up Pattabhi Sitaramayya against him. Election ensued and Bose won by 1580 to 1375 votes. Gandhi felt humiliated and declared that 'it was his own defeat'. When the Congress met at Tripuri (1939), Subhas was too ill to participate actively in the proceedings. At the instance of Gandhi, the entire Congress Working Committee resigned, leaving Subhas and his brother Sarat in the Committee. Subhas as president could have nominated the members of the Working Committee but he did not. He tried a compromise and pleaded with Gandhi, meeting with him personally and through correspondence. But Gandhi was adamant. Bose was left with no choice but to resign, and formed a new party, the Forward Bloc, which had to work within the Congress fold. In September 1939, war broke out and Subhas wanted the Congress to make the best of this opportunity to start a movement to oust the British. When the Congress wavered, the Forward Bloc, under his leadership, launched a bitter anti-British propaganda campaign without the approval of the Congress high command. He and his brother Sarat Chandra were expelled from the Congress for three years. He was arrested for his anti-government stance in July 1940, along with hundreds of his followers. He was released in November and interned in his house, guarded by police and the CID. For forty days he did not stir out of his room. But one day in the third week of January 1941, he disappeared in the guise of a Muslim priest and appeared in Germany in April, 1941, making a hazardous journey through Afghanistan and Russia. This is one of most daring and romantic episodes, not only of Indian history but that of the world. His presence in Germany was kept secret but after nine months he started broadcasting anti-British propaganda from a secret radio station from Rome and Germany under the name Azad Hind Radio. Free India Centres were established at Rome and Paris (October 1941) as anti-British centres. Many Indians in Europe started cooperating with Bose in this venture and started calling him *Netaji* (leader) and saluting him with 'Jai Hind'. Subhas also raised 'Indian Legion' of a regimental strength, comprising Indian Prisoners of War brought from North Africa camps for the purpose. But Bose was not sure how to use the Indian Legion to oust the British from India. From the beginning, Italians were more sympathetic towards Bose than the Germans. Bose had an interview with Adolf Hitler on 29 May 1942. The views expressed by Hitler were not very encouraging. Hitler said, "India was endlessly remote from Germany. The real route to India would have to be over Russia's dead body". Bose was very sceptical about this 'route.'

While Bose was still pondering over what to do in Europe, news came that the Japanese had attacked the American naval base at Pearl Harbour in December 1941 and had run through the British possessions in Southeast Asia. That area was much nearer to India than Europe and had many more Indian prisoners of war than Europe; the number of Indians living there was also much larger. Moreover, Rash Behari Bose had already been working in Japan and Asia for India's freedom under the banner of Indian Independence League. General Mohan Singh and others had also formed the Azad Hind Fauj, which was later taken over by Rash Behari Bose. A conference was held in Bangkok in June 1942 presided over by Rash Behari, in which delegates from several east Asian countries participated. One of the resolutions passed in the conference was to invite Subhas Chandra Bose to east Asia. On receiving the message, Subhas decided to leave Europe. A U-Boat (submarine) was arranged by the Germans for the purpose. Subhas left Germany along with Abid Hassan on 8 February 1942. They arrived in Tokyo on 13 June 1943, and reached Singapore on 2 July 1943. He was received enthusiastically by an immense surging crowd. On 4 July, Rash Behari Bose handed over the leadership of the Indian Independence League and its armed wing, Indian National Army, to the younger Bose. Subhas went on a whirlwind tour of several countries in the region and was received with warmth and expectation everywhere. Satisfied, he proclaimed Provisional Government of Free India in the Town Hall of Singapore on 21 October 1943 and took a salute of twenty thousand INA soldiers recruited from the Indian prisoners of war. Several departments of the new government were created, headed by trusted followers. INA men were given proper training. A march towards India, along with Japanese forces, commenced. Subhas shifted his headquarters from Singapore to Rangoon in January 1944, Burma sharing a border with India. Subhas set foot on Andaman and Nicobar islands, the first free Indian territory which were handed over by the Japanese to the INA. The INA opened campaign on the Arakan front on 4 February 1944. On 18 March, they had crossed over to Indian soil and had reached the plains of Imphal and were in the neighbourhood of Kohima. Then followed the retreat. American air forces helped the British army, which now had superior arms. Worst still, the monsoon had submerged the supply line of INA. Hundreds of INA men died from hunger, disease and wounds. Japanese forces were on the run too. The British had reoccupied country after country, starting with Burma. With the dropping of atom bombs on Hiroshima and Nagasaki, Japan had surrendered on 15 August 1945. All was over. But there can be little doubt that the Indian National Army, not in its unhappy career on the battlefield, but in its thunderous disintegration, hastened the end of the British rule in India, thus the bringing the life's struggle and sacrifces of Subhas to fruition. Subhas along with Col. Habibur-Rahman left Saigon on 17 August 1945 for Tokyo. On 22 August, Tokyo Radio announced the death of Subhas Chandra Bose in an aircrash over Formosa. Indians have consistently refused to believe that Subhas died in an air crash. Three enquiry commissions appointed by the Government of India have not been able to solve the mystery of the death of Subhas. His ashes are kept at Renkoji temple, Tokyo, but the Government of India is reluctant to bring these ashes to India because millions of Indians believe that those are not that of Subhas. Recent research has revealed that Subhas was alive at least till 1946.

While in Europe, Subhas had written to his brother that he had married a German girl, Emilie Schenkl. Subhas had known Emilie since 1934, when she served as his secretary and had helped him in writing his *Autobiography*. Formal records of his marriage do not exist, but Bose's biographer Hugh Toye wrote that Emilie had 'secretly' become his wife. In September 1942 she delivered a baby girl, Anita, who later visited India and was received with love and affection. But at that time, this relationship with Emilie had caused Subhas much mental stress because his high moral reputation was at stake — he had vowed to be a celebate till India got her freedom.[5]

Thousands of INA men were taken prisoner by the British after the surrender of Japan. Some were executed in Rangoon and Bangkok; thousands of others were brought to India to be tried 'for waging war against the Crown'. But the whole nation stood up to cheer them as freedom fighters, which staggered the British bureaucracy and the army. Many leading lawyers in the Congress offered their services to defend the INA men during their trial in the Red Fort, Nehru among them — the same Nehru who had said in April 1942: "I shall fight Subhas Bose and his party along with Japan if he comes to India." Such are the compulsions of politics. The fact is that "the attitude of the Congress both to Bose and the INA has been lukewarm throughout. It was not anxious to publicize their exploits. After all, Bose and the INA actually fought for India's freedom while the Congress leaders had merely gone to jail".[6] In spite of the attitude of the Congress, Subhas outshines others among the martyrs of the freedom struggle. He has become a national hero, and legends have been woven around him. He disappeared at a time when the nation needed him most.

# References

1. Oaten, Edward Farley. *The Bengal Student As I Knew Him*, in *Netaji And India's Freedom*; *Proceedings of the International Netaji Seminar*, 1973. Calcutta, Netaji Research Bureau. 1975, pp.28-34.

2. Bose, Subhas Chandra. *An Indian Pilgrim; An Unfinished Autobiography*. OUP. 1997, p.80.

3. Mookerjee, Girija K. *Subhas Chandra Bose*. New Delhi, Publications Division, 1975, p.107.

4. Toye, Hugh. *Subhas Chandra Bose; The Springing Tiger*. First pub. 1957, Jaico Reprint 2001, p.43.

5. Ibid p.77.

6. Edwards, Michael. *Nehru, A Political Biography*. New Delhi, Vikas, 1971, p.162.

# Syed Ahmad Brelvi

## (1786-1831)

Syed Ahmad was the founder of the Wahabi Movement in India. Wahabism had earlier started in Arabia by the efforts of Abdul Wahab (1703-92). He aimed at restoring Islam to the exact form it had in the days of the Prophet, rejecting the impurities which had crept among his followers. In India, the source of inspiration for Syed Ahmad was Shah Waliullah (1704-1763) who wanted to re-establish the Muslim rule in India with the help of Muslim rulers, like the Nizam of Hyderabad and Afghan ruler Ahmad Shah Abdali. Abdali did invade India, defeated the Marathas at Panipat (1761), killed and looted at will and soon left for Afghanistan, without strengthening the tottering Mughal empire, to the chagrin of Walliullah, who died soon after.

Learning from this experience, Syed Ahmad had come to believe that Muslims in India must take upon themselves the amelioration of their condition which was getting worse after the death of Aurangzeb. A greater part of the country had come under the control of Marathas, Sikhs, Rajputs and Jats. The Mughal ruler was reduced to a destitute, tituler head. "When in 1803 Lord Lake entered Delhi, he was shown a miserable blind old imbecile, sitting under a tattered canopy. It was Shah Alam 'King of the World', but captive of the Marathas, a wretched travesty of the Emperor of India".[1] Such was the condition to which the great Mughal empire had been reduced to. With the change of rulers, Muslims had lost all the privileges which were bestowed by the Mughal emperors on them. Syed Ahmad believed that Muslims must get organized to fight the infidel rulers, to bring back the 'glory of Islam' to India again.

Syed Ahmad was born at Rai Bareilly in Uttar Pradesh in 1786. He studied in a school in Delhi run by Shah Abdul Aziz, son of Shah Walliullah. His teacher had already issued a 'fatwa' declaring India as a 'dar-ul-harb' (enemy country) and was no more 'dar-ul-Islam' as it was ruled by non-Muslims. Abdul Aziz had begun to organize militant centres in north-western provinces (present Uttar Pradesh) and Bihar for the purpose of launching 'jehad'. He selected Syed Ahmad as his principal 'jehadi'. To learn the art of warfare, Syed Ahmad joined the army of Amir Khan, a Pathan pindari leader in 1809 in Rajasthan. His military training was cut short in 1817 when the pathan leader submitted to the British. Ahmad was back in Delhi. Shah Abdul Aziz then declared Ahmad as his successor, handing over his white robe and black turban to him as a ritual of succession. He also deputed two of his own relatives, Shah Abdul Hai and Shah Ismail, to render all possible help and to work under Ahmad's guidance.[2]

Thereafter, Ahmad started in earnest the work of organizing and preaching — organizing volunteers for 'jehad' and preaching to remove the evils which had crept in the Muslim society. He asked Muslims to shun Hindus and not to adopt their manners in dress and eating; not to join in their festivities like Holi and Diwali; shun idolatory by worshipping at mazars, veneration of 'pirs' and other places not sanctified by Islam and its Prophet. He was worried that Muslims were losing their identity. For the first time Islam was on the defensive in India. In Uttar Pradesh and Bihar, Ahmad started enrolling volunteers for jehad and collecting funds for the purpose. After reaching Calcutta, Syed Ahmad left for Mecca (1821). At the holy city, he came in contact with the Wahabis and his ideas about social reform and political struggle got crystallised. He was now convinced that it was only by overthrowing non-Muslim rule that the reformed faith could be enforced on the lines of Arabia. Thus, the immediate task before the Wahabis was the conversion of India from a 'dar-ul-harb' into a 'dar-ul-Islam'.

On his return journey, Syed Ahmad landed at Bombay in October 1823 and proceeded to Delhi with the same fanfare as his earlier journey from Delhi to Calcutta. Wherever he went, he continued enrolling volunteers and the number of volunteers (*jehadis*) continued to grow. His followers started weaving several myths around him and on this basis carried on vigorous propaganda among Muslims to prepare themselves for jehad. Even some Muslim rulers, like the Nawab of Tonk, became his followers. The sight of such devoted following, who had taken an oath of allegiance to him, emboldened Syed Ahmad. With eight thousand armed followers, he proceeded via Gwalior, Tonk, the desert of Rajasthan, Sind, Baluchistan, Kandahar, Ghazni, and Kabul reaching Peshawar in November of the same year. This circuitous route was chosen apparently to avoid passage through Sikh territory. He established his headquarters at Sittane near Peshawar. He appealed to the Pathan tribes to join him, and many of them did, giving further strength to his jehadi army. The selection of this region to start jehad against the infidel rulers was an astute one. The area was populated almost exclusively by Muslims, who resented the authority of the Sikh rule. It was not accessible to large armies; the barren hills stood as an excellent barrier against outsiders.

Under the Islamic law, the election of an Khalifa or Caliph was necessary to provide a leader to direct the 'jehad'. There was no difficulty in Ahmad getting elected as Khalifa by his followers. The news of his election and an explanation of this measure were communicated to the Muslims in different parts of India through circular letters. Coins were minted bearing the legend 'Ahmad the Just, the Defender of the Faith, the Glitter of whose Scimitar Scatters Destruction Among the Infidels', and were put in circulation among his followers.[3] The Khilafat was, however, shortlived. Ranjit Singh, who had annexed Peshawar earlier (1930), became concerned about the hostile activities of Syed Ahmed and sent his army to contain his activities and ambition. A battle ensued at Balakot in May 1931 and Syed Ahmad and his second in command Muhammad Ismail were killed. Alexander Gardner, who later became a colonel in the Punjab army and was with the crusaders at the time, gave an account of this skirmish in the following words:

"Syed Ahmed and the Maulvi (Abdul Haye), surrounded by his surviving Indian followers, were fighting desperately hand to hand with the equally fanatical Akalis of the Sikh army. They had been taken by surprise and isolated from the main body of the Syed's forces, which fought very badly without their leader. Even as I caught sight of the Syed and Maulvi, they fell pierced by a hundred weapons. Those around them were slain to a man, and the main body dispersed in every direction.... I was literally within a few hundred yards of the Syed when he fell, but I did not see the angel descend and carry him off to paradise, although many of his followers remembered afterwards that they had seen it distinctly enough."[4]

But this was not the end of Wahabism. His followers continued the jehad for another four decades. "Syed Ahmad had set-up a regular organization. He had appointed a number of *Khalifas* or spiritual vice-regents, who not only kept alive the movement after the death of their leader, but even made it more vigorous within a short time. Taking advantage of the political chaos in Punjab after the death of Ranjit Singh in 1939, the Wahabis established their authority over a large tract of territory along the left bank of Sindhu (Indus)".[5] When Punjab was annexed by Lord Dalhousie in 1849, the problem of Wahabis was transferred from the Sikhs to the British. Thereafter, the Sittana camp was a source of chronic anxiety to the British for two decades. Upto the late 1860s several expeditions, involving thousands of regular troops were made to North-West Frontier to destroy the rebels but withut much success. Then the British government changed their strategy. Instead of fighting the rebels in their stronghold situated in a difficult terrain, they started taking action against the ring-leaders in Bihar and present Uttar Pradesh and at other places, who were sending *jehadis* and money to Sittana. Thousands of them were imprisoned and the Wahabi movement died down in the early 1870s.

The importance of the Wahabi movement lies in the fact that it created a permanent schism between Hindus and Muslims and did not allow the composite culture to develop. The seeds of two-nation theory were thus sown. It is rather surprising that the Wahabis did not take part in the 1857 uprising and kept completely aloof from it, though both the revolts were directed against the British. The only explanation could be that the Wahabis wanted a purely Islamic uprising and did not want to join the one which comprised Hindus. At the same time it cannot be denied that the Wahabi jehad against the infidels was much better planned and organized than the outbreak of 1857, which was disjoined without effective coordination and leadership. The Wahabis had created a highly developed organization to which there is no parallel in the history of the revolutionary movements against the British during the nineteenth century and are regarded by some historians as having waged the first War of Independence in India, and the credit for this goes mainly to Syed Ahmad Brelvi.

It is interesting to note the reaction of Sir Syed Ahmad, who was trying to construct a bridge between Indian Muslims and the British rulers, to this anti-British movement by Muslims. He was afraid that his efforts towards reconciliation would suffer due to the jehad undertaken by the Wahabis. As in the case of the 1857 uprising, which was considered by the British as a rebellion mainly inspired by the Muslims, so also in this case Syed Ahmad tried to contain the damage to the Muslim cause by declaring that the Wahabi movement was the work of some misguided youth and it was not really based on true Wahabism. In a letter to *The Pioneer* (14 April, 1871), he wrote, "Wahabism, as exemplified by certain misguided men in India, is not Wahabism at all; and those who are really guilty of conspiring against Government are not acting upon the principles of their religious tenets".[6] Syed Ahmed's views on Wahabism were expressed in greater detail in articles published in *The Pioneer*, while reviewing W.W. Hunter's 'Indian Musalmans' (1871), in which Hunter had concluded that Wahabism was a rebellion against the British government whom they considered as an infidel government. Due to the efforts of Syed Ahmad and others, the hostility generated by the Wahabi movement and 1857 uprising was gradually neutralised and Muslims became the favoured community, especially after the formation of Indian National Congress.

## References

1. Lane-Poole, Stanley. *Aurangzeb and the Decay of the Mughal Empire*. First pub. 1989. Reprinted, Delhi, Low Price Publications, 1990, p.206.

2. Banerjee, A.C. *Two Nations; the Philosophy of Muslim Nationalism*. New Delhi, Concept, 1981, p.58.

3. Nagarkar, *V.V. Genesis of Pakistan*. New Delhi, Allied, 1975, p.20.

4. Gardner, Alexander. *Memoirs*, p.171-72. Quoted by Khushwant Singh. *Ranjit Singh; Maharaja of the Punjab*, Bombay, George Allen & Unwin (India) Reprint. 1973. P.164-65. First pub. in London, 1962.

5. Majumdar, R.C. *History of the Freedom Movement in India*. Vol. 1, Calcutta, Firma K.L.M. 2nd ed. 1971, p.247.

6. Malik, Hafeez, ed. *Political Profile of Sir Syed Ahmed Khan; A Documentary Record*, Delhi, Adams, 1933, p.310.

# Bhikhaji Rustam Cama

## (1861-1936)

Among the Parsi national leaders Madame Cama was the only one who sided with the revolutionaries; took active part to propagate their cause, supplied revolutionary literature and arms to them and acted as a 'mother figure' to them for thirty-five years, while living in self-exile in England and France.

Cama was born on 24 September 1861 in Bombay, in a wealthy Parsi family of businessmen. She was one of the nine children of Sohrabji Framji Patel and Jijibai. Very little is known of this affluent family of Bombay besides the fact that one daughter of the family was the first woman revolutionary to fight for India's freedom. She was educated at Alexandra Girls' School, Bombay and later learnt to speak several Indian and foreign languages, including French.

She was married on 3 August 1885 to Rustomji Cama, a barrister belonging to one of Bombay's prominent Parsi families. He was the son of K.R. Cama, a scholar and an illustrous Orientalist. The same year, the Indian National Congress was formed in Bombay and a new spirit of political consciousness swept the country and Bhikhaji could not remain unaffected. She was already twenty-four years old and had developed a strong independent mind. She started doing social work during the plague epidemic of 1896 in Bombay, nursing the sick patients in hospitals, which at the time was unusual for a lady coming from a respectable affluent family. The treatment received by Indians at the hands of some British officials during the plague epidemic created anti-British feelings in her, and she decided to work for the country's freedom. Her husband did not share her views, nor was he supportive of her activities. Bhikhaji was a lady of strong character. She did not yield to her husband's protestations. The schism between the two kept on widening, which resulted in separation in 1901. In 1902, she left for London for medical treatment. As her father had created a trust for his eight daughters she was not short of funds. Her mother had also given her ample jewellery as her share of the wealth which they possessed. She lived frugally while in Europe and spent a major part of her money for the nationalist cause. After the surgery which she had to undergo in London, she did not return to India. She had met Dadabhai Naoroji in London and worked with him for sometime for the Indian National Congress. But soon, she moved away from Dadabhai's moderate politics and was attracted towards more militant and revolutionary ideas. She was so excited to work as a revolutionary for the country that she decided to stay on in England.

In 1905 Shyamji Krishnaverma, a nationalist who was in England for sometime, opened India House, which became the headquarters of the revolutionaries in London, and the abode of famous revolutionaries like Sardar Singh Rana, Veer Savarkar, Har Dayal, Birendranath Chattopadhaya and others. It was also in 1905 that these revolutionaries formed the Indian Home Rule Society (modelled on the Irish Home Rule League). Shyamji also started the *Indian Sociologist*, an English monthly, which became the mouthpiece of revolutionary propaganda. Bhikhaji regularly wrote for it. She also addressed meetings at Hyde Park in London, explaining the need for freeing India of foreign domination. Though India House was founded by Shyamji, Savarkar had become the undisputed leader of the group and Cama was very much impressed with his dedication as a patriot and by his intellectual brilliance. Savarkar had written a book *The History of the War of Indian Independence (1857)*. Madam Cama helped translate it into French, as the book was banned in India. Savarkar was twenty-two years younger than Bhikhaji and she played the part of mother figure for Savarkar, trying to help him in all possible ways.

The year 1907 was memorable one for her and the country when in August she, along with S.S. Rana, was invited to attend the International

Socialist Congress at Stuttgart (Germany). There were about hundred delegates from several countries of Europe, Asia, Americas and Africa. In a brief but stirring speech she talked about conditions in India. She began: "Friends, Comrades and Socialists, I have come here to speak for the dumb millions of Hindustan, who are going through terrible tyranny under the English capitalists and the British government". At the end of the speech she dramatically unfurled the Indian flag. It was a tricolour with green, yellow and red with *Bande Matram* written on the middle band. It also had eight stars representing eight provinces. It was precursor to our national flag of free India, and was designed jointly by Madam Cama and Savarkar. This flag became a permanent companion of Cama; she always carried it in her suitcase and after every speech she used to unfurl it. It is now displayed in the Library Hall of the *Kesari* and the *Mahratta* in Pune.

Soon after the International Socialist Congress, she made a very successful tour of the United States. She visited several cities, addressing meetings and small gatherings, explaining the British oppression and the causes of India's poverty. Though not a powerful speaker, her sincerity and passion for India's cause impressed all. Like Annie Besant, Cama was also proud of India's cultural heritage and always highlighted the glorious past of India. "People of India have culture," she would say, "the poorest peasants had stored in their memories, all the spiritual truths of the *Mahabharata* and the *Ramayana*". Her visit to America was a great success and had become a media event there. She returned to Europe in October 1908 to meet Bipin Chandra Pal. The texts of her speeches were in great demand. In one of her famous speeches, which were later printed and circulated as a pamphlet titled *Bande Matram*, she said, "Friends let us put aside all hindrances, doubts, and fears. In Mazzini's words, I appeal to you, 'let us stop arguing with people who know our arguments by heart and do not heed them.' If our people appear degraded, it is an added reason to endeavour at all risks to make them better. A handful of foreigners, a few Englishmen, have declared war on us. Who can wonder if we millions accept challenge and declare war on them? The price of Liberty must be paid. Which nation has got it without paying for it". She concluded by reminding Indians of their own culture. "We want back our own country. No English oak is wanted in India. We have our own noble banyan tree and our beautiful lotus flowers. We do not want to imitate British civilization; we will have our own which is higher and nobler".[1]

Her activities were being watched by the British government and they banned entry of her post and other material sent by her into India. But such restrictions did not deter her from sending revolutionary literature, arms and explosives to Indian revolutionaries, which were now being sent through Pondicherry, a French enclave. In this, other revolutionaries like Savarkar and Rana were cooperating with her. Madam Cama and Shyamji were said to have been named in the British Intelligence Department reports to be financing the revolutionary movement in India. They suspected that both of them would be deported to India. Before that could be done, both Cama and Shyamji moved to Paris in 1909 to thwart the British move to deport them. Cama lived in Paris for thirty years. Her residence, which came to be called 'Paris India House' became a meeting place for the revolutionaries and she did everything in her power to help them. She started a paper *Bande Matram* from Paris in September, 1909 with Lala Har Dyal as editor. This monthly paper, appeared for nine years without break. Through this paper Cama carried on her attack on British imperialism. The *Talwar* (sword) 'an organ of Indian Independence' was also published by Madam Cama some time later, with Birendranath Chattopadhayaya as editor. This paper joined the *Bande Matram* in the attack on British misrule in India.

In June 1909, Veer Savarkar's brother, Ganesh Damodar Savarkar was sentenced to transportation for life in the Andamans on the pretext of writing a provocative poem. In retaliation A.M.T. Jackson, the collector and district magistrate of Nasik, was assassins. Veer Savarkar was accused of sending arms to the assassinators and was arrested in London in March 1910, and was ordered to be sent to India. While his ship docked at the French port of Marseilles, Savarkar jumped from the ship and reached ashore. However, he was arrested and sent to India. Madam Cama did everything to get Savarkar released, spending a good amount of money, but did not succeed. Savarkar, like his brother, was sent to the Andaman Cellular Jail where he languished for ten years. Cama was very upset and used to write to the two brothers while they were in prison. She also used to send money to the Savarkar family regularly.

When the First World War broke out in 1914, Cama along with Rana visited those theatres of war where Indian troops were operating, inciting them to lay down arms, as it was not their war. When on such a mission she visited Marseilles, she was interned by the French authorities under British pressure and was kept at Vichy and later at Bordeaux. She was released after three years, when the war was over. Because of her radical views and revolutionary activities, she was repeatedly refused permission to return to India until 1935, when she was seventy-four and in failing health and severely suffering from facial paralysis. On her return to Bombay she directly went to Parsi General Hospital, where she died on 13 August 1936, unwept, unsung and unhonoured. Madam Cama certainly deserved better treatment at the hands of her countrymen. She had written her own epitaph, "He who loses his liberty loses his virtue. Resistence to tyranny is obedience to God". Her vision of a free India was a republic with Hindi as the common language and Devanagri as the comon script. She firmly believed in the idea of 'one nation, one language, one people', though she remained a devout Parsi throughout her life.

Belatedly and even reluctantly, she was remembered during her centenary year (1961). A street was named after her in Bombay, and a postage stamp in her honour was issued in 1962, after much haggling. A commercial complex in Delhi has been recently named after her. But not much has been written about her in the annals of the freedom movement in the country.

## References

1. Agarwal, Deepa. *Bhikhaji Cama,* in our *Leaders.* Vol. 1, New Delhi, CBT. 1989, p.56.

# William Carey

## (1761-1834)

Christian missionaries who came to India have contributed greatly towards education, journalism, linguistics and allied fields. One such missionary was William Carey.

William was born on 17 August 1761 in Northamptonshire. His father, Edmund Carey, was a school teacher. William was an extremely adventurous boy and loved sports, travel, nature (which later developed in the study of plants) and reading in his spare time. At an early age he was apprenticed to a shoemaker at Hacleton and soon became a skillful shoemaker. As a hobby, he studied languages and became proficient in Greek, Latin and Hebrew, besides some modern European languages. Later in life, learning several Indian and Southeast Asian languages became a passion with him.

He joined the congregation of Baptists in 1783 and the same year he was publicly baptized. Baptists form a major denomination of Protestants; their faith was founded in the seventeenth century in Holland but soon spread to other countries including England and the United States. After baptism, Carey started taking a greater interest in religion by organizing prayer groups. By 1789, he was put in charge of congregation at Leicester. In 1791, he was ordained (became a clergyman) and helped in forming the Baptist Missionary Society (1792) at Kettering. In this society, he came in contact with Dr. John Thomas, who had earlier visited India. Carey was greatly influenced by the zeal of this man and decided to come to India for missionary work. The team left for India on 13 June 1793. Carey came with his wife, four children and his sister-in-law. They arrived at Calcutta on 13 November 1793. During this five month journey, Carey had begun studying the Bengali language. Later, he picked up Hindi, Marathi, Sanskrit and Persian — such was his facility in learning languages.

When Carey landed in Calcutta, the officials of East India Company would not allow any missionary work in their territory, fearing local backlash. (This restriction was removed only in 1813). To earn a living and support his family, he had to take up 'secular' jobs. He accepted work as an indigo planter at Madnabati in Malda district, North Bengal. During their first year in India, his whole family fell ill, and his five year old son, Peter, died. His wife was very deeply affected by this. He bore these calamities stoically. In 1799, two other missionaries, Joshua Marshman and William Ward, arrived from England and the three of them decided to establish a mission. As it was not possible to start any mission in Calcutta, it being a territory of the East India Company, the trio, along with their families moved to Serampore in 1800, which is about fifteen miles upstream from Calcutta, and was a Danish settlement. Thus, began the famous Serampore Mission started by Carey and his two associates, Marshman and Ward. A 'mission' in Christian parlance refers to 'a body of persons sent by a church to carry on religious work especially evangelization in foreign lands'.

Carey started translating the Bible in vernacular languages, including the tribal languages, but ended up contributing greatly towards education, health care, printing and journalism. While translating the Bible into Indian languages, he had to study their grammar, vocabulary and connotation. In the process, he compiled dictionaries and grammars of at least twenty-six languages, many of them for the first time by any person. Carey also edited the *Ramayana*. Carey's knowledge of Indian languages attracted the attention of authorities of the Fort William College, Calcutta, which Lord Wellesley, the Governor-General, founded in 1801 for training officials of the East India Company. He was initially appointed professor of Bengali in the College but later Marathi and Sanskrit were added. He served this College as professor till 1830 and had to commute between Serampore and Calcutta. While translating the Bible into Indian languages, Carey had been taking help from several pandits who were working in Fort William College.

Soon after his arrival in Serampore, Carey had brought a large house surrounded by an equally large compound near the river. Here, the community which Carey had planned, took shape and as the years rolled by, they undertook an astonishing range of activities. Among his two companions, Marshman and his wife, were schoolmasters and William Ward was a printer. Marshman and his wife started a boarding school for Anglo-Indian boys and girls. Soon, they added new schools, where children of local residents could be taught. These were elementary schools and by 1818 their number increased to 126. Subsequently, they felt the need of higher education and planned a college "for the instruction of Asiatic, Christian and other youth in Eastern literature and European sciences." Their aim was to produce a class of enlightened men, conversant with both the classical literature of India and the best Western learning of the day. From their own resources, they bought land and built the buildings and named it Serampore College. The building was begun in 1818 and classes opened in 1819, with thirty-seven students. Included in the curriculum were Sanskrit, Arabic, Bengali, English, natural sciences and medicine. In the early years, most of the subjects were taught in Bengali. In 1827, the King of Denmark granted the college a charter, empowering it to confer degrees.[1] This was one of the pioneering colleges in India teaching modern subjects along with theology. In 1910, the arts and science departments were affiliated to the Calcutta University, leaving out the theology department to be run by Christian bodies.

The Bible, translated in various languages, was printed in a press which was to be the first modern press in north-India and supervised by Carey's companion, Ward. Gradually they got typefaces of many languages designed and cast in their huge type-foundry; Arabic, Persian, Nagari, Telugu, Punjabi, Marathi, Chinese, Oriya, Burmese, Kanarese (Kannad), Greek, Hebrew and of course, English. The press was housed in a hall, 170 feet long and with scores of people employed. As this was the only press in the area, they undertook printing of secular books and journals from Calcutta and other nearby areas too. It was a self-contained press, having departments of paper and ink making as well as binding. Soon, the Serampore Mission Press became famous and for years the types produced in this foundry were used throughout the country. So also the press-ink and paper. As a result, the press not only became self-supporting but started earning handsome profits. Many important Bengali, Hindi and English works of the time were printed in this press. During the initial thirty-one years, the press had printed 2,12,000 books in forty different languages.[2] The press helped to spread education and literacy in the country.

The Serampore Mission also contributed towards journalism. In 1818, the trio started two journals: *Samachar Darpan*, a weekly newspaper in Bengali, edited by Marshman and his son, which is believed to be the first newspaper printed in any Oriental language. Another English monthly, *The Friends of India*, started the same year. Both these papers played a valuable part in enlightening the public on social questions and did not contain much of religious preaching. The first issue carried an article on sati. The paper continued to bring the horrible custom before the public by reporting actual cases. Some socially conscious officials, many Carey's former pupils, prohibited the practice in their districts on their own. Even the governor-general, Lord William Bentinck was moved and, helped by Hindu social reformers like Ram Mohan Roy, banned sati in the Company's territories in 1829 making it a criminal offence. Along with others, Carey deserves credit for the abolition of this inhuman practice of sati. Carey is also credited with the abrogation of the child sacrifice at Sagar Island in the Ganges. This was done by Lord Wellesley after Carey submitted a report on the practice in the first decade of the nineteenth century. Besides his other activities, Carey was instrumental in founding an asylum for lepers in Calcutta. The care of those suffering from leprosy has been a special field of Christian service, and Carey was a pioneering missionary who contributed towards helping the lepers who were shunned by society. Caring for the lepers by Christians goes back to the times of Jesus Christ.

Carey had a lifelong interest in botany and had developed his own botanical garden in Serampore. He was the founder of the Agricultural and Horticultural Society of Bengal, a purely 'secular' activity.

He died on 9 June 1834 at Serampore and was buried in the Serampore College premises. Carey lived in India for forty-one years and never visited England during all these years.

## References

1.  Firth, C.B. *An Introduction to Indian Church History*. Serampore, Senate of the Serampore College. Rev. ed. 1976, pp.153-54.
2.  Kesavan, B.S. *History of Printing and Publishing in India*. New Delhi, National Book Trust, 1985, p.191.

# Bankim Chandra Chattopadhyaya

## (1838-1894)

Bankim Chandra Chattopadhyaya (or Chatterjee) was born on 26 June 1838 at Kantalpara in 24 Pargana district. His father Jadabchandra was in government service and was a deputy collector when Bankim was born. In fact, it was a family of deputy magistrates and deputy collectors. Bankim's two elder brothers, Shyama and Sanjib, were deputy magistrates. His younger brother, Purna Chandra, also became a deputy collector in due course. Bankim's early education started in 1844 at Midnapore, where his father was posted at the time. His English education began there under the care of the English headmaster, F. Teed. This good start helped Bankim to master the English language in later life. But his father was transferred from Midnapore and Bankim was sent to Hooghly and he took admission in the Hooghly College, in 1849. He was a brilliant student and successfully got through the Junior and Senior Scholarship Examinations, in the year 1854 and 1856 respectively. While still a student at the Hooghly College, he took part and won a cash prize in a poetry competition (1853), organized by *Sambad Prabhakar* of Ishwar Chandra Gupta. In 1856, Bankim joined Presidency College, Calcutta, for studying law. But in 1858, the Calcutta University introduced the B.A. examination. Ten students took the examination in the first batch. Only two passed; Bankim was one of them, thus becoming the first graduate of the Calcutta University. His law studies were discontinued as a result, which he completed later in 1869. As Sanskrit was not taught in the college, he studied Sanskrit privately from a pandit.

His career as a government servant started immediately after graduation. He was appointed deputy magistrate and deputy collector and was posted at Jessore, now in Bangladesh. He had been married at the age of eleven to a five year old girl, who died while he was serving at Jessore. His second marriage in 1860, to Rajlakshmi Devi was a long and happy one. They had three daughters.

During his government service lasting for thirty-three years, Bankim Chandra travelled and worked in thirteen districts of the old province of Bengal. Some of these districts are now in Orissa and some in Bangladesh. As an officer, Bankim showed considerable ability and independence. His aristocrat demeanour, strong personality, wide reading and high intellectual attainments left a mark wherever he was posted. At the same time, because of his frank and fearless disposition, he often came into conflict with his immediate British superiors like collector Buckland in 1881, Westmacott in 1883 and collector Baker in 1888. His controversy with Christian missionary Rev. Hastie, principal of the General Assemblies Institution (now Scottish Church College), showed his 'undaunted argumentative, combative and debating powers'. By this time, Bankim had written several novels and other works and had become famous. He obviously lost interest in government service and resigned in 1891 at the age of fifty-three, serving the British government for thirty-three years. He was awarded the title of Rai Bahadur in 1892 and C.I.E. in 1894.

His government service did not seem to be a hindrance in his literary exploits, as he continued to write and publish books, one after another, and his literary genius flowered as time passed. He started writing in English and his story *Rai Mohan's Wife* appeared serially in the *Indian Field*, edited by Peary Chand Mitra, in 1864. He wrote English with facility and was a voracious reader of English fiction. Earlier, he had written poetry too. Gradually, he started writing prose. He also realised that he could express himself better in his mother tongue, Bengali. This realisation was most fortunate for Bengali literature, and his writings mark the dawn of a new era. His first novel in Bengali, *Durgeshnandini*, came out in 1865 and a new vista opened up in Bengali creative literature, though the influence of English romances was clearly discernible in it. His second novel *Kapalkundla*, published in 1866, describing the tragedy of a girl brought up in the company of a *kapalika* and later married to the wayworn Nabakumar, at once captured the imagination of the Bengali readers. The third novel, *Mrinalini* (1969), based on the Minhajuddin story of the conquest of Bengal by Bakhtiar Khilji with the help of only seventeen horsemen, 'gave the first sign of his patriotism which later developed into militant nationalism'. Novels and other prose works continued in an uninterrupted stream: *Bish Briksh* (1873, novel), *Indira* (1873, novel), *Yugalanguriya* (1874, novel), *Lokarahasya* (1874), *Chandrasekhar* (1875, novel), *Kamalakanter Daptar* (1875), *Rajani*, (1877, novel), *Kabita-Pustak* (1878), *Kamalakanter Will* (1878, novel), *Prabandha Pustak* (1879), *Samya* (1879), *Rajsinha* (1882, novel), *Anand Math* (1882, novel), *Devi Chaudhurani* (1884, Novel), *Muchiram Gurer Jivancharit* (1884), *Devatattva O Hindu Dharma* (1884), *Kamalakanta*, incorporating *Kamalakanter Dapter* (1885), *Radharani* (1886), *Krishnacharitra*, Part I (1886), *Sitaram* (1887), *Vividha Prabandha*, Part 1 (1887), *Dharamatattva*, Part 1 (1988), *Gadya, Padya ba Kabita Pustak* (1891), *Vividha Prabandha*, Part II (1892), *Rajsinha*, revised edition (1893). As can be seen from the list, Bankim in the later stages of his literary output had started writing on religious and spiritual themes.

Bankim Chandra started a literary magazine *Banga Darshan* in 1872 and edited it for four years. Later, he handed it over to his brother Sanjib Chandra in 1877, who revived it and continued it till March 1883. In *Banga Darshan* his novels appeared serially as also many of his famous essays on history, sociology, religion literature and philosophy were first published in in it. After the demise of *Banga Darshan*, Bankim Chandra sponsored another journal, *Prachar*, in July 1884 with Rakhal Das Banerji, his son-in-law, as incharge. His tracts on Hindu religion like *Dharmatattva-Anushilan*, *Krishnacharitra* and *Devatattva O Hindu Dharma* (being essays on Hinduism and Hindu gods and goddesses) were first published in it. He also wrote a commentary on the *Bhagwat Gita*, which remained incomplete.

Although in government service, Bankim was a bitter critic of the way British administration was being carried on, and his caustic and satirical remarks are clearly evident in his writings — *Bangla Shasaner Kal* and *Muchiram Gurer Jibancharit*. He had deep sympathy for the poor peasants and cursed the Permanent Settlement for their poverty in *Bangadesher Krishak*.

The greatest contribution of Bankim Chandra was to inculcate the sense of nationalism and patriotism among the masses through his novels and essays. He converted patriotism into religion and religion into patriotism. His famous novel *Anandmath*, contains the hymn *Bande Matram*, which had become a rallying cry of the patriotic sons of India, and thousands of them succumed to the *lathi* blows of British police and many mounted the scaffold with *Bande Matram* on their lips. The central plot of the novel moves round a band of *sanyasis,* called *santanas* or children, who left their hearth and home and dedicated their lives for the cause of the country. The imagery of the Goddess Kali in the novel, leaves no doubt that Bankim Chandra's nationalism was Hindu rather than Indian. This is made crystal clear from his other writings, which contain passionate outbursts against the subjugation of India by the Muslims. ' "From that day set the sun of our glory" is the refrain of his essays and novels which not unoften contain adverse, and sometime even irreverent remarks against the Muslims'.[1]

The hymn *Bande Matram* has made Bankim Chandra one of the most remembered writers of any age in India. Programme on the All India Radio begin in the early morning with the recitation of *Bande Matram*, which is in easy Sanskrit. It is officially recognized as the national song and has equal status with the national anthem *Jana Gana Mana*, composed by Rabindranath Tagore. The English rendering of *Bande Matram* by Aurobindo Ghose is as follows:

I bow to thee Mother
Richly watered, richly fruited
Cool with the winds of the South
Dark with the crops of the harvests
The Mother
Her nights rejoicing in the glory of the moonlight
Her hands clothed beautifully, with her trees
In flowering bloom, sweet of laughter, sweet speech
The Mother, giver of boons, giver of bliss.

"What is it for which we worship the name of Bankim today, what was his message to us or what the vision which he saw and has helped us to see? He was a great poet, a master of beautiful language and a creator of fair and gracious dream-figures in the world of imagination; but it is not as a poet, stylist or novelist that Bengal does honour to him today. It is probable that the literary critic of the future will reckon *Kapalakundla, Bish Briksh* and *Krishnakanter Will* as his artistic masterpieces and speak with qualified praise of *Devi Chaudhurani, Anand Math, Krishnacharit* or *Dharmatattva*. Yet, it is Bankim of these latter works and not the Bankim of the great creative masterpieces, who will rank among the 'Makers of Modern India'. The earlier Bankim was only a poet and stylist — the later Bankim was a seer and nation builder".[2]

# References

1.  Majumdar, R.C. *History of the Freedom Movement in India*. Calcutta, Firma K.L.M. Vol. 1. 1988, pp.302-03.
2.  Sri Aurobindo. *Collected Works* (Birth Centenary Library). Pondicherry, Sri Aurobindo Ashram Trust. Vol. 7. p.345.

# Alexander Cunningham

## (1814-1893)

Alexander Cunningham is considered to be the father of Indian archaeology. He made some important and startling discoveries through untiring excavations and the study of coins to fill gaps in the history of India. His successors like John Marshall and Robert Mortimer Wheeler, carried further the work started by him and were able to discover the Indus Valley Civilization.

Alexander was born on 23 January 1814 at Westminster, London, and was educated at Christ's Hospital and Addiscombe. That was the end of his formal education. He obtained an Indian cadetship as the age of fourteen on the recommendation of the famous novelist Sir Walter Scott. After training, he was appointed as second lieutenant in the Engineering division of the Bengal Army, when he came to Calcutta in 1833. There he came in contact with James Prinsep and got interested in the study of Indian numismatics and archaeology, in which he soon developed proficiency and started contributing articles in journals. For this hobby, he could find time even while serving as an engineer in the army.

In the army, he had quite a varied set of assignments. He served as bodyguard to Lord Auckland, governor-general (1836-40). In 1840, he became executive engineer to the Nawab of Oudh and was responsible for the construction of a highway from Lucknow to Kanpur. He was on military duty in Central India and later executive engineer in the Gwalior state (1844-45). During the First Anglo-Sikh War (1846), he was in Punjab on military duty and was responsible for the annexation of the Kullu and Kangra Valley. He was also responsible for demarcation of boundary between Ladakh and Tibet and also between Bikaner and Bahawalpur states. After the Second Anglo-Sikh War (1848-49), he came back to Gwalior as executive engineer. Then followed a series of transfers to distant places: Multan (1853), Burma (1856) and the North-West Frontier Province (1858), where he served as chief engineer. After he was promoted to the rank of major-general in 1861, he retired from the army and a new and important phase in his life commenced, for which he is remembered and has earned the gratitude of Indians for revealing their past.

However, he did not wait to indulge in his exciting hobby. "From his arrival in India in 1831, Cunningham devoted every minute he could spare from his military duties to the study of the material remains of ancient India, until, in 1862, the Indian Government established the post of Archaeological Surveyor, to which he was appointed".[1] While he was serving as a bodyguard to the governor-general, he found time to come to Varanasi, where his preceptor, James Prinsep, had earlier lived for ten years and had done some excavations, especially of temples turned into mosques. However, Cunningham's area of excavation was Sarnath, about six miles from Banaras. The mystery about the ruins of Sarnath had excited the curiosity of many scholars of Indian history, especially because both Fa Hian and Huan Tsang had described a great monastery and a huge pillar (stupa) at Sarnath, where the great Buddha delivered his first sermon to his five followers. There had been irregular and half-hearted excavations at this site, but "the most extensive excavations which have been made were affected under the personal superintendence of Major-General Cunningham and Major Kittoe, who dug out of the ruins an immense number of statues, bas-reliefs and other curious objects. The former alone, in 1835, found about a hundred statues and bass-reliefs, all of which worth preserving, were sent to the Museum of the Asiatic Society in Calcutta".[2] Cunningham studied in detail the great stupa, called *Dhamek* (presumably built by Asoka), at Sarnath and even got prepared a scaffold 110 ft. high and went up all the way to study the details of the uppermost end of the stupa. He wrote a detailed report of his findings in the *Journal of the Asiatic Society of Bengal* (Vol. xxxii), which remains the most detailed description to this day. After Sarnath, he excavated Buddhist mounds at Sanchi in Madhya Pradesh and at other places. He published the reports of these excavations in the *Journal of the Royal Asiatic Society*, London (1850) and later published them in a book, *Bhilsa Topes or Buddhist Monuments of Central India* (1854). He deciphered the inscriptions on the pillars and railings of the Buddhist ruins and gave their English renderings in the book. During his mission to Ladakh and Tibet in the 1840s, while in military service, he wrote a book on Ladakh which is still useful.

Cunningham made a great deal of contribution in the field of Indian numismatics also and had written several articles on the subject since 1834, in the *Journal of the Asiatic Society,* Calcutta, *Royal Asiatic Society,* London and in the *Journal of the Numismatic Society,* London. As a result of his study in Indian numismatics, Cunningham declared that coins were in use in India even before the invasion of Alexander (326 BC) and that there was no import of coins from Greece. All these years, this important work in Indian archaeology and numismatics was done by Cunningham as a hobby while he was serving as an engineer in the British army.

In 1846, Cunningham sent a proposal to the Asiatic Society, Calcutta and later submitted a petition (1860) to Lord Canning, governor-general, for the establishment of a department for a systematic exploration of historical relics spread over a vast area of the country and their proper preservation. Due to his efforts, the Archaeological Survey of India was set up in 1861 with Cunningham as its head (surveyor general). Now he worked full time, exploring the ruins and analysing and writing in detail about them. For the first time, he visited historical sites in Punjab as well as the river basin in northern India between Jamuna and Narbada. The findings of these explorations (1861-65) were published in two volumes under the title *The Ancient Geography of India* (London, 1871). In this work, Cunningham had identified all the historical places of India on the basis of Alexander's invasion and the Chinese travellers down to the seventh century AD.

In 1866, Cunningham had to return to England as the Archaeology Department had closed down due to paucity of funds. However, in 1870, the department was revived by Lord Mayo, governor general, and Cunningham was called back and put in charge of the department. He worked in the department as surveyor general for another fifteen years, 1871-85. During this period, he travelled from Taxila in the North-West Frontier Province to Gaur Pandua in Bengal in search of historical sites and recorded his findings meticulously. Of course, he was helped by several able assistants. Findings of these visits were published in twenty-four volumes as the *Archaeological Survey of India Reports*. Of these, Cunningham wrote the first thirteen volumes on the basis of his own visits. The remaining eleven volumes were prepared by his assistants under his guidance. In the thirteen volumes of his own reports, Cunningham had dealt with five hundred historical sites and also gives a description of the coins of various periods. An index for all the volumes was prepared by V.A. Smith under the title *General Index to Cunningham's Archaeological Survey Reports (1887)*.

It was Cunningham who, during his tours of the Harappa region (1872-73), came across some rare kind of seals, and he gave some indication about Harappa in his report of 1875 as being "a very ancient site and the likely storehouse of rich antiquities". This must have provided a 'hint' to his eminent successors, John Marshall and Robert Mortimer Wheeler and others, who were able to discover the Indus Valley Civilization during the twenties and thirties of the twentieth century.

In 1877, Cunningham collected and compiled all the Asokan edicts and published them, with photographs, in his *Corpus Inscriptionum Indiacarum* (Calcutta, 1877). In 1879, he brought out his work *The Stupa of Barhut* (London, 1879). And in 1883, was published his important work *The Book of Indian Eras* (Calcutta). In 1892, he published his great work *Mahabodhi or the Great Buddhist Temple; Under the Bodhi Tree at Gaya* (London). It was this work of Cunningham through which the modern world learnt about the glories of Buddha Gaya, Sarnath, Sanchi, Sraasti and Kausambi.[3]

In 1885, Cunningham retired from the Archaeological Survey of India and returned to England. Out of seventy-nine years of his life

Cunningham spent fifty in India, most of the time trying to unravel the hidden secrets of India's past. He donated a large number of historical relics and some old coins he had collected during his stay in India to the Indian Museum, which included city gate pillars and railings of Barhut and Sanchi. After retirement, he paid much attention to numismatics as he had carried with him a large collection of old Indian coins to England. He is considered an eminent authority on numismatics. This collection are now in the British Museum. He was knighted in 1867. He died in South Kensington on 28 November 1893. "Though he made no startling discoveries, and though his technique was, by modern standards, crude and primitive, there is no doubt that after Sir William Jones, Indology owes more to General Sir Alexander Cunningham than to any other worker in the field".[4]

# References

1.  Basham, A.L. *The Wonder that was India*. New Delhi. Rupa Paperback, 1981, p.7 (First pub. 1954).
2.  Sherring, M.A. *Benares; The Sacred City of the Hindus*. Delhi, Low Price Publications, 1990, pp.235-36. (First pub. 1868).
3.  Sengupta, G.G. *Indology and its Eminent Savants; Collections of Biographics of Western Indologists*. Calcutta, Pundhi, 1966, p.80.
4.  Basham, A.L. Ibid.

# Chitta Ranjan Das

## (1870-1925)

Chitta Ranjan Das was born on 5 November 1870 at Calcutta as the eldest son and the second child of Bhuban Mohan Das and Nastarini Devi. His father was a solicitor of the Calcutta High Court with a handsome income. Bhuban Mohan was a strong supporter of the Brahmo Samaj and edited the monthly *Brahmo Public Opinion* (later changed to *Bengal Public Opinion*) and was also the author of some books. Bhuban Mohan was of a very generous disposition and could not help spending money on the poor and people in distress. In the process he incurred debt which he could not clear and was declared insolvent by the court. It was for his son Chitta Ranjan to clear the debt later in life.

Chitta Ranjan received his early education in the London Missionary Society's Institution at Bhawanipur, and passed the entrance examination in 1885, as a private candidate. He graduated from Presidency College in 1890. The same year, he left for England to study law and to sit for the Indian Civil Service examination. He missed clearing the ICS by a narrow margin. He had joined the Inner Temple and was called to the Bar in 1894. Returning to India, he started practicing as a barrister in the Calcutta High Court. However, when he was still trying to establish himself at the Bar, pressure was brought to bear upon him by his father's creditors to clear the debt and finding it difficult for him to redeem the liability, he too was declared insolvent.

In 1897, he was married to Basanti Devi at the age of seventeen and led a happy married life. The couple had two daughters and a son: Aparna (1898), son Chira Ranja (1899) and daughter, Kalyani (1901).

Before he was involved in law and later politics, his genius was revealing itself in poetry and literature. He inherited the literary trait from his father and was also inspired by Bankim Chandra. His first literary work was *Malancha* (1895), a collection of poems. Then followed *Mala*, also an anthology of his poems published in 1902; *Sagar Sangeet* (1911); *Antaryami* (1914) and *Kishore-Kishori* (1915). Some of these verses were rendered into English by Chitta Ranjan himself with the help of Aurobindo Ghose. In 1914, Chitta Ranjan started a literary journal, *Narayan*, with which were asociated a number of eminent literary persons. He kept in constant touch with important literary organizations and people in the country, including Rabindranath Tagore and Bankim Chandra. He presided over the Bengal Literary Conference in 1915. He was one of the founders and a member of the editorial board of *Bande Matram* started by Bipin Chandra Pal.

Like many other leaders Das took part in the *Swadeshi* movement started after the partition of Bengal by Lord Curzon in 1905. He had also become member of the Anushilan Samiti, a secret society working under the guidance of Aurobindo, Sister Nivedita, P. Mitra and Jatindranath Banerji.

As a lawyer, success came gradually. The turning point in his legal career came when he was called upon to defend Sri Aurobindo in the famous Alipore Bomb Case in which Aurobindo was implicated for waging war against the King. This is the historic case during the freedom movement and Chitta Ranjan encountered with courage all obstacles and established himself as a barrister par excellence. His elocution originated, as if from Divine Essence, his vast learning, wisdom and foresight were amply vivid in the concluding remarks of his arguments; "Long after this turmoil, this agitation ceases, long after he is dead and gone, he will be looked upon as a poet of patriotism, as the prophet of nationalism, and the lover of humanity. Long after he is dead and gone, his words will be echoed and re-echoed not only in India but across the distant seas and lands. Therefore, I say that the man in his position is not only standing before the Bar of this court but before the Bar of the High Court of history".[1] Never has such eloquence been matched in Indian courts. It has become a classic and has been repeatedly quoted. Das pleaded for eight days, and Aurobindo was acquitted by the Court of Appeal in May 1909. This elevated Das to the rank of a legal luminary and paved the way for a roaring practice. Success followed success and many were the sensational cases in which he served as a counsel, even outside Bengal, including the Dumraon Adoption Case in 1910. Consequently, he built up a large and lucrative practice and started living like a 'prince'. In 1913, he followed the unusual procedure of applying for the annulment of the insolvency order and cleared his father's and his debts. This is only one of the instances of the magnanimity and large-heartedness which he showed during his life. The other most conspicuous court cases were those of revolutionaries and freedom fighters: Maniktola Bomb Case, Decca Conspiracy Case, Delhi Conspiracy Case (1914). He did not charge any fee in pleading these cases. He would even bear the travelling and other expenses, while going to plead for such cases.

His entry in active politics began in 1917, when he presided over the Bengal Provincial Conference held in April that year in Calcutta. Soon, Das became the leader of the Extremist group of the Congress in Bengal. When the Montagu-Chelmsford Reforms were announced in August, 1917, the Moderates hailed the reforms and wanted to give them a trial but the Extremists opposed. At both the Special Congress session (Bombay, August 1918) and AICC session (Delhi, December, 1918), C.R. Das took the lead in moving the resolution, denouncing the reforms as 'inadequate, unsatisfactory and disappointing', demanding full Provincial Autonomy instead. In the autumn of 1919, Das went to Punjab as a member of the Enquiry Committee appointed by the Congress to investigate into the Jallianwala Bagh tragedy and the working of martial law in Punjab. Das stayed in Punjab for three months, bearing all the expenses himself.

When Gandhi announced his historic Non-Cooperation Movement at the Special Session of the Congress at Calcutta in September 1920, where Lajpat Rai presided, C.R. Das led those who opposed Gandhi's proposal. He was supported by Bipin Chandra Pal, Madan Mohan Malaviya and Annie Besant. He was particularly opposed to the boycott of the

Councils. Three months later, at the annual session of the Congress held in December, 1920 at Nagpur, C.R. Das "made up his differences and endorsed Gandhi's standpoint, after his heart to heart talk with him". Das also declared at the session that he would give up his practice at the Bar. Returning to Calcutta, he did give up his roaring legal practice and renounced all comforts and luxuries. The whole country was moved at this supreme act of sacrifice and his reward was the title which his admirers gave him, Deshbandhu (friend of the country). Das's example in giving up legal practice was followed by some other lawyers in the country. Das now put his heart and soul to making the Non-Cooperation Movement a success. He toured East Bengal to arouse people for non-cooperation. He helped organize district Congress Committees throughout Bengal. In February 1921, he set up a National College at Calcutta, which was inaugurated by Gandhi. Thousands of miles away from home, a young man was inspired by the sacrifice made by C.R. Das and wanted to work with him, resigning from ICS apprenticeship. He was Subhas Chandra Bose, who wrote to Das from Cambridge on 16 February 1921. After introducing himself and his family, Subhas wrote, "I should like to know what work you may be able to allot to me in this great programme of national service". Subhas Bose came back to India and started working under the leadership of C.R. Das. They formed a formidable team and would have given an alternative leadership to the country had Das not prematurely died after four years.

During the visit of the Prince of Wales in November 1921, which was boycotted by the Congress, C.R. Das organized a volunteer corps to protest against the visit and to court arrest for violating the ban on demonstrations. In the first batch of volunteers, his only son Chira Ranjan, was arrested on 4 December 1921, and was sentenced to six month's imprisonment. This was followed by the arrest of C.R. Das's wife Basanti Devi and sister Urmila on 7 December. Other arrests included those of Subhas Chandra Bose and his own arrest on 10 December. His wife and sister were released soon after but Subhas and C.R. Das were imprisoned for six months. These arrests were made by the government in a bid to avert the general hartal proposed for 24 December 1921, the day of the visit of Prince of Wales. Incidentally, Lord Mountbatten, the last viceroy and governor-general of India, was ADC of the Prince of Wales on his visit to India. While still in prison, C.R. Das was elected president of the Ahmedabad session of the Congress to be held in December, 1921. The government did not allow him to attend the session. His presidential address was read by Sarojini Naidu, while Hakeem Ajmal Khan presided.

Gandhi had started the Non-Cooperation Movement formally on 1 August 1920 and suspended it on 24 February 1922 without consulting any one. After the Ahmedabad Congress session, Gandhi had announced mass civil disobedience in Bardoli, a taluka in Gujarat. But before it could be started Gandhi withdrew it, again without consulting anyone. C.R. Das was upset. So were many Congress leaders. Subhas Bose, who was in the same jail with C.R. Das describes how his mentor was upset with Gandhi's sudden decision and was beside himself with sorrow and anger at the way Mahatma was repeatedly bungling.[2]

On release from jail in August 1922, Das was unanimously elected president of the Gaya Congress (December 1922), where he sought to change the strategy of the non-cooperation movement and pleaded for 'Council entry' as a tactical measure. It was evident to everyone that the programme of boycott of Councils, courts and educational institutions had failed. All these bodies continued to run as before. Gandhi could not win freedom for the country in one year. Still, when C.R. Das moved a resolution for council entry in the Congress session, it was defeated by the followers of Gandhi, now called 'no-changers'. C.R. Das resigned in disgust from the Congress and along with Motilal Nehru, formed the Swaraj Party. C.R. Das went around the country, starting with Bengal, propagating the reason for entering the councils to thwart the government from within. More and more people were turning towards the Swaraj Party as an alternative to the Congress, which had miserably failed. Ultimately, seeing the writing on the wall, Gandhi yielded and in the special session of the Congress at Delhi in September 1923, the Swaraj Party was declared as the 'parliamentary wing' of the Congress.

During the November 1923 elections, the Swaraj Party swept the elections in Bengal and in some other provinces, as well as in the Central Legislative Council. By mutual agreement, it was decided that Motilal

Nehru will lead the Swarajists in the Central Assembly and C.R. Das in the Bengal Legislative Council. The obstructive tactics of the Swaraj Party were a great embarrassment for the government and in many instances, the viceroy had to use his powers to get things done. In the field of journalism too, the Swarajists made much progress. Das launched a daily paper, *Forward*, in October 1923. Subhas was asked to look after the affairs of the paper. "Within a short time *Forward* came to hold a leading position among the nationalist journals in the country. Its articles were forceful, its news service varied and up-to-date and the paper developed a special skill in the art of discovering and exposing official secrets".[3]

In 1924, Das was elected the first mayor of Calcutta with Subhas Bose as the executive officer of the Calcutta Corporation. Das was elected mayor for the second time in April 1925. The last AICC session attended by Das was the Belgaum session in December 1924, which Gandhi presided. There was complete reconciliation between the Swarajists, led by C.R. Das and Motilal Nehru and Gandhi. Later, C.R. Das presided over the Bengal Provincial Conference held at Faridpur on 2 May 1925.

C.R. Das donated his palatial house at Bhawanipur, Calcutta, to the nation and it was turned into a charitable hospital for women, known as Chitaranjan Seva Sadan.

Since the early months of 1925, Das was suffering from a poor state of health and while trying to recuperate at Darjeeling, he suddenly died on 16 June 1925. His body was brought to Calcutta for the last rites, attended by hundreds of thousands of wailing Indians, including Gandhi. The whole country plunged into grief. "Though his active political career consisted of barely five years, his rise had been phenomenal. With a reckless abandon of a Vaishnava devotee, he had plunged into the political movement with heart and soul and he had given not only himself but his all in the fight for Swaraj. When he died, whatever wordly possessions he still had, were left to the nation. He was clear headed, his political instinct was sound and unerring and unlike the Mahatma, he was fully conscious of the role he was to play in Indian politics".[4] Subhas Bose had lost his mentor. In future he had to fight his political battles single-handed against powerful foes.

## References

1.  Agarwala, B.R. *Trials of Independence*. New Delhi, National Book Trust, 1991, p.69.
2.  Bose, Subhas Chandra. *The Indian Struggle*, 1920-1942, New Delhi, OUP. 1997, p.82.
3.  Ibid p.97.
4.  Ibid pp.122-23.

# Dayanand Saraswati

## (1824-1883)

Among all the reformers of the nineteenth century, Dayanand was unique in the sense that he was not influenced by western education and philosophy; in fact, he did not even know English. In spite of that, he has left a more lasting impact on Indian society than any other reformer. The Arya Samaj, founded by him, is still active, not only in India but also in other countries where Indians have settled in considerable numbers like South Africa, Mauritius, Fiji, Trinidad, and England. The educational wing of the Arya Samaj in the form of Dayanand Anglo-Vedic (D.A.V.) schools and colleges, is the largest educational network in the country. In addition to these modern institutions there are gurukuls, established on the ancient pattern of education, for both boys and girls. Such was the impact of the gurukuls that when Gandhi returned from South Africa in 1915, he sent his sons and about one hundred other children, who were with him in the Phoenix Ashram, Durban, to Gurukul Kangri, Hardwar for some time. These institutions are keeping alive the name and message of Dayanand.

Dayanand's *Autobiography* does not throw light on his place of birth, nor about his family. But his biographers Lekhram and Devendranath Mukhopadhyaya, who went to Gujarat to find out the truth about his birth and family, have revealed that Dayanand was born at Tankara village in Morvi state of Kathiawar, in 1824. He was given the name Mulshankar or Mulji by his family, who were Brahmins. His father was a small landholder-cum-moneylender and commanded respect in the area. Mulji's family was orthodox Shaivites. Dayanand spent the first twenty years of his life in the village and got the education which such an environment could offer. He committed to memory *Yajurveda* and parts of other Vedas as well as *Rudradhyaya*, the scripture for Vaishnavas.[1] He learnt the Devanagari script at the age of five and was also taught Sanskrit. His father also taught him the rituals which a Shaivite family had to perform. Two events had a great impact on his life the death of his younger sister from cholera and that of his uncle soonafter whom he loved and respected. The second event was on a Shivratri night, when the young Mulji saw a mouse climbing on the Shivlinga and devouring the offerings, while other members of the family were asleep. These two events were the turning point in the life of the young Mulshankar. He began to ponder on the meaning of life and death and the true form of God as he was now convinced that the symbols of God, as represented in idols of various shapes and forms, could not be true God. When his parents came to know about his state of mind they decided that Mulji should get married. Before that could happen, Mulji left his home and family, never to return. He was initiated into *sanyas* by Swami Parmanand Saraswati, who changed his name to Dayanand Saraswati. He learned yoga from Jawalanand Puri and Sivanand Giri at Dudeshwar, near Ahmedabad. He traversed all of north-west India for many years in search of a guru and yogi who could clear his doubts and teach him true religion but could find none, till he met Swami Virjananda at Mathura. Here, his real education in Sanskrit and the Vedas started in 1860. He was already thirty-six years old. He stayed for three years in Virjananda's ashram. His guru found in Dayanand an extraordinary personality eager to do something for the Hindu society. At the command of his guru, Dayanand took a solemn vow to devote his life to spreading the Vedic message and for removing superstitions and ignorance from the Hindu society.

He started preaching about the true religion of the Vedas and condemning idol-worship, meaningless rituals and the evils inherent in the caste system. His slogan was 'back to the Vedas', the sacred books of the Hindus which should be read by all Hindus irrespective of the caste to which they belonged. For several years, he confined his efforts to lectures and *shastrarths* (debates) with orthodox Hindus to spread his message. He preached at the Kumbh Mela in 1867 at Hardwar and while preaching, he met with stiff resistance from the orthodox Hindus. His famous *shastrarth* in Varanasi (1869) with three hundred traditional *pandits* of Kashi did not bring any fruitful result.

His visit to Calcutta in 1872-73 was a turning point in the reforming mission of Dayanand. He had gone to Calcutta at the invitation of the Adi Brahmo Samaj and stayed at the house belonging to the Tagore family. There, he met several leaders of the Adi Brahmo Samaj, including Keshab Chandra Sen, Hemchandra Chakravarti and others. He studied the working of the Brahmo Samaj and learnt many lessons, being receptive to new ideas. Consequently, a major shift in his methods of preaching came about. Instead of preaching in Sanskrit, which only a few persons could understand, he decided to preach in Hindi in future, thus reaching a wider audience. He also changed his dress from a loincloth to a long gown, *dhoti* and a turban, all in ochre colour — the colour of the Indian sadhus. He also learnt that by merely giving lectures and holding debates, he would not be able to achieve much. To associate willing persons and to give some kind of permanency to his endeavours, he needed an organization on the lines of the Brahmo Samaj. He realized he would also have to write his views to convey his message to people living in different parts of the country and even outside. He learnt Hindi and gave his first lecture in Hindi in 1874, a year after his return from Calcutta.

The urge to start an organization fructified when in January 1875 the first Arya Samaj was established in Rajkot. But it did not survive for long. The second Arya Samaj in April of the same year was founded at Bombay, with one hundred founding members, and proved to be an important landmark in the history of the Arya Samaj movement. A committee was formed to supervise the activities and rules (twenty-eight in number) were framed for the initiation and guidance of its members.

But for Dayanand, real success came when he visited Punjab in March 1877. He went to Lahore at the invitation of the Brahmo Samajis, who had established some branches in Punjab earlier. But soon differences in ideology cropped up and the Brahmo Samaj people disassociated themselves from the Swami. However, his lectures attracted quite a few influential people, who were impressed by the personality and teaching of the Swami. There was hardly any debate there as Punjab did not have Brahmin orthodoxy. Hindus there had been facing foreign onslaughts for centuries. They were ready to try social transformation and wanted to get organized for their emancipation. The first Arya Samaj in Punjab was established in June 1877, at Lahore. From the very start, it was better organized than the one in Bombay. They elected a committee to run the affairs; reduced the number of principles from twenty-eight to ten, which are still followed by the Arya Samaj everywhere. They also formulated by-laws. Arya Samajs sprang up in all major cities of Punjab, except in the princely states, where Dayanand did not preach.

It was in Punjab, while the Swami was preaching, that a new concept emerged, that of '*shuddhi*' (purification). Christian missionaries and Muslim *mullahs* were very active at that time in Punjab, converting Hindus to their religions. Through *shuddhi*, a person who was converted to another religion could be 'purified' and brought back to the fold of Hinduism. Arya Samaj in Punjab had taken the work of *shuddhi* in earnest, facing the ire of both Muslims and Christians, especially of the former. Many Aryas were martyred while doing *shuddhi* work including leaders like Lekhram (biographer of Swami Dayanand) and later Shraddhanand. The *Shuddhi* movement has been criticized by a group of historians, forgetting that it was an ancient custom approved by scriptures like *Vratyastoma* and *Devalasmritii*.[2] One of the most famous cases of *shuddhi* was that of Harilal Gandhi, the eldest son of Mahatma Gandhi. Harilal had become a Muslim to avoid paying back the money borrowed by him from some Muslim moneylenders and also to spite his father, whom he held responsible for his troubles. He was converted to Islam in Jama Masjid, Bombay on 14 May 1936, in front of a cheering crowd of Muslims. This created a stir in the country and was a great embarrassment for the elder Gandhi and Kasturba. It was the Arya Samaj which came to their rescue and Aryas, showing great daring, brought back Harilal to the Hindu fold through *shuddhi* after six months.[3]

Another development which contributed to Swami's success in Punjab, was the publication of *Vedabhashya* in fascicules starting, in 1878. The response was overwhelming and the subscription for the book ran into hundreds. While in Punjab, Swamiji had written a small book earlier (1877) *Aryaddheshya Ratnavali*, containing a hundred definitions and descriptions of key terms of Hindu religion and philosophy, to help people in understanding his discourses and writings. "Swami spent only sixteen months in the Punjab and was never to pay a return visit, yet, when he left the land of five rivers, a new force had clearly been set in motion in Punjab society, a force that had decisive influence in the history of the province for many years to come".[4] Lahore had become the unofficial headquarters of the Arya Samaj and gave a lead to Arya Samajs around the world. Lahore, becoming part of Pakistan after the partition of the country in 1947, proved a great setback for the Arya Samaj, from which it has not been able to recover fully even to this day.

By the time Dayanand left Punjab, he had become famous and his following had increased considerably. Soon, the number of Arya Samajs multiplied and when Swamiji died, there were seventy-nine Arya Samajs functioning mostly in Punjab and U.P. Today the number runs into thousands. Of the five years and three months of his remaining life, the Swami spent in hectic activity visiting Uttar Pradesh and lastly Rajputana, where he died on 30 October 1883. According to his biographer J.T.F. Jordens, an Australian, the cause of Swami's death was acute dysentery, double pneumonia and mismanagement of his treatment by his followers, who had brought him from Jodhpur to Ajmer while he was seriously ill.[5] However, Arya Samaj people believe that Dayanand was poisoned by his enemies, especially a favourite concubine of the Maharaja of Jodhpur.

Dayanand has left a considerable number of books and pamphlets, which he wrote laborously. His *magnum opus*, of course, is *Satyarth Prakash*. The first edition of this seminal work was published in 1875 in Hindi, when Dayanand was not quite proficient in the language and thus was not satisfied with the end result. A second and final edition of *Satyarth Prakash* was published in 1882-83, a part of it after his death. Some other important works of his are: *Sanskarvidhi*, first edition 1877, second edition after his death in 1884; *Rigvedadibhashyabhumika*, published in fascicules from 1877 onwards; *Rigvedabhshya* and *Yajurvedabhashya*, published in fascicules from 1877 to 1880. His *Autobiography* written in Hindi by the

Swami and subsequently its English translation was published in *The Theophist*, a monthly of the Theosophical Society, 1879-80, at the time when the Swami had a brief association with the society and its founder, Blavatsky.

Besides preaching Vedic lore, Dayanand preached against idolatory, meaningless rituals and the caste system. He was one of the first reformers to advocate *swadeshi* and *swaraj* (self-rule). For the integrity of the country, he favoured Hindi as the national language and set an example himself. Though he did not know English, he encouraged Indians to learn English to understand the modern scientific advancement of the West. The name Dayanand Anglo-Vedic given to educational institutions run by Arya Samaj, implies just that.

Arya Samaj has attracted many luminaries during Dayanand's life time and since his death. Some of them have taken active part not only as social reformers but also as freedom fighters like M.G. Ranade, Lajpat Rai, Bhai Parmanand, Shyamji Krishnaverma, Shraddhanand and many others.

Jawaharlal Nehru sums up the contribution of Arya Samaj thus:

"The Arya Samaj was a reaction to the influence of Islam and Christianity; more especially the former. It introduced proselytization into Hinduism and thus tended to come into conflict with other proselytizing religions. The Arya Samaj, which had been a close approach to Islam, tended to become defender of everything Hindu, against what it considered as the encroachments of other faiths. At onetime, it was considered by the government as a politically revolutionary movement, but the large numbers of government servants in it made it thoroughly respectable. It has done very good work in the spread of education both among boys and girls, in improving the condition of women and in raising the status and standards of the depressed classes".[6]

# References

1.  Sarda, Har Bilas. *Life of Dayanand Saraswati*. Ajmer, Vedic Yantralaya, 1946, p.4.
2.  Jordens, J.T.F. *Dayanand Saraswati; His Life and Ideas*, OUP. 1997, p.170.
3.  Kulkarni, Sumitra Gandhi. *Mahatma Gandhi, Mere Pitamah* (Hindi), New Delhi, Diamond Pocket Books. 1997, pp.217-17. And Bhagubhai Chandulal Dalal. *Harilal Gandhi* (Hindi) Varanasi, Sarva Seva Sangh.
4.  Jordens, J.T.F. op.cit. p.160.
5.  Jordens, J.T.F. op.cit. p.242.
6.  Nehru, Jawaharlal. *Discovery of India*. New Delhi, Jawaharlal Nehru Memorial Fund, 1946. pp.335-36.

# Henry Louis Vivian Derozio

## (1809-1831)

Derozio was one of the earliest Indo-English poets. Besides being a poet of rare quality, he was an educationist, a journalist and a reformer, which made him a controversial figure in the educated circles of Calcutta in early nineteenth century. Henry Derozio was born on 10 April 1809 of Eurasian parentage; his father Francis Derozio being an Indian of Portuguese descent and his mother, Sophia Johnson, British. As a Christian, he was baptised in the same cathedral where three years later William Makepeace Thackeray, the famous British novelist, was baptised. The house on the Lower Circular Road, where Henry was born, was the property of the Derozio family. It is no longer there but the cemetry on Park Street, where he was buried, still remains.

At the age of six, Henry was admitted in the Drammond's Academy at Dharamtallah, the school run by David Drummond, 'a man of great force of character as well as something of a metaphysician and poet'. In the academy, Drummond helped young Henry to sharpen his splendid power of intellect and imagination. During the period of eight years at the Academy, Henry developed a taste for literature and philosophy and read widely the works of British and European thinkers. He did extremely well at school, wrote verses for several events and received prizes for his achievements. He left the Academy in 1822, at the age of fourteen. He joined the mercantile firm of James Scott & Co., in which his father was the chief accountant. The work at the commercial establishment was not to Derozio's liking, 'a mere drudgery', and after enduring it for two years, he left it and went to Bhagalpur (in present Bihar) to stay with Arthur Johnson, his uncle (the husband of his mother's sister), who was looking after an indigo plantation at nearby Tarapur. Derozio spent almost three years there, lending a helping hand to Johnson and at the same time enjoying the country scenery — the luscious paddy fields, the ripping river, and enjoying the company of rustic people around him. These serene surroundings kindled young Derozio's imagination and he began to write verses describing what he saw and imagined. Derozio started sending his poems to John Grant, editor *India Gazette*, regularly for publication under the assumed name of 'Juvenis.' Grant liked his poems and encouraged him to continue writing. When Derozio came back to Calcutta in 1826, Grant persuaded him to get his poems published in a book. Thus, came out the first volume of Derozio's poems which were appreciated in literary circles. This was when Derozio was still in his teens. Grant also offered Derozio the post of an assistant editor of *Indian Gazette*. Later, he edited the *Calcutta Literary Gazette* for some time. He also contributed poems to the *Calcutta Magazine, Indian Magazine,* the *Bengal Annual* and the *Kaleidoscope*, which widened his readership. In 1827 the second volume of his poems was published which included one of his most famous poems, '*The Fakir of Jungheera*'. This raised him to fame as a poet of considerable merit, with considerable interest being shown in his writing by literary circles in London too.

On his arrival in Calcutta in 1826, Derozio was also appointed assistant teacher of English literature and history in the Hindu College. Soon he was acclaimed by H.H. Wilson, Visitor of the College, as one of the best teachers of the institution "who possessed the rare power of weaving interest around any subject that he taught". Apart from the subject content, the distinctive feature of Derozio's teaching was to awaken in his pupil's mind a love for truth and a spirit of enquiry. Being a free thinker himself, he encouraged his students to do likewise. He had a genuine love and sympathy for his students which he expressed in a poem:

*Expanding like the petals of young flowers*
*I watch the gentle opening of your minds.*

By his method of teaching, Derozio helped his students to develop a sprit of enquiry and rationality and encouraged them to express their views and opinions without any inhibition or restraint. After college hours, the students used to meet Derozio either in the college premises or in his house at Lower Circular Road. These informal meetings took a formal shape of an Academic Association. Initially, the meetings were held in Derozio's house but later were shifted to the garden house of Srikrishna Singh. During the weekly meetings, discussions were held on varied subjects like free will, fate, faith, cultivating virtue, patriotism, God and idolatory. Some meetings were attended by a few leading intellectuals of the city.

Assisted by Derozio, his students started a weekly, the *Parthenon*. The first issue contained criticism of some of the actions of the government as well as highlighted the depraved and perverse practices of Hinduism. The authorities of Hindu College took a serious view of the kind of articles published and the paper had to stop publication. Apart from such unorthodox expressions, the students also indulged in activities which horrified their parents, like eating beef and pork and drinking beer and alcohol. The parents started blaming the kind of instruction which was given in the college. They collectively complained to the college authorities and even threatened to withdraw their wards from the college. The very existence of the college was at stake, the management believed. They blamed the teachings of Derozio for the waywardness of their wards. The authorities of the soon took steps to remove Derozio from the service of the college. Derozio was charged with atheism and immorality, which he allegedly taught to the students. It was decided that "Derozio being the root cause of all the evils and cause of public alarm should be removed from the College". In his reply, Derozio vindicated his stand and repudiated all the allegations. After doing that, he resigned from the college in April 1831.

After quitting Hindu College, Derozio started *The East Indian*, an evening daily on 1 June 1831. He was the editor as well as the proprietor of the paper. He turned it into an organ of the Anglo-Indian community, projecting their travails and disabilities and suggesting remedies. It was rather strange that a free thinker·and a rationalist should be reduced to a communal crusader. However, his life was cut short and he died of cholera on 26 December 1831 in Calcutta. He was hardly twenty-three. While he taught rational thinking and virtues of truth and duty, all borrowed from Western philosophers and thinkers, he had not delved into Indian philosophical and religious works like *Bhagwat Gita* and *Upanishads*, as his contemporary reformer Rammohan Roy had done. As a result, Rammohan had a much greater impact on society with wider ramifications. Derozio was never accepted as a role model for social reformers who followed him. But nobody could doubt his patriotism. In one of his poems, *To India — My Native Land*, he wrote:

*My country! in thy day of glory past*
*A beautious halo circled round thy brow,*
*And worshipped as a deity thou wast,*
*Where is that glory, where that reverence now?*

Derozio was one of the early Indo-English poets who has left a mark on the literary horizon. He wielded a powerful pen, his imagery and power of description were of a high quality. There is a music in his words and a rare depth of feeling. However, he lacked originality of style and he tried to copy Byron and Thomas Moore. But it was perhaps inevitable. Those were different days and to cut a new line for a youthful writer would probably have been a catastrophe. In spite of his limitations, he has an honoured place among the early Indo-English poets.[1]

"Derozio is remembered most for the influence he exerted on his students and followers, popularly known as Derozians or 'Young Bengal'. They were the harbingers of radical thought which contributed to the Bengal Renaissance of the nineteenth century. In that context, he was coadjutor of Rammohan Roy. Some of the Derozians who became famous and carried on the message of Derozio were; Krishna Mohan Banerjee, Ram Gopal Ghosh, Peary Chand, Rashik Krishna Mallick, Dekshinaranjan Mukherjee".[2]

# References

1. Sinha, R.P.N. *The Birth and Development of Indo-English Verse*. New Delhi, Dev Publishing House, 1971, p.147.
2. Sinha, Nirmal, ed. *Freedom Movement in Bengal* (1818-1914); *Who's Who*. Calcutta, Academic Publishers. 1991, pp.92-93.

# Morarji Desai

## (1896-1995)

Morarji was born on the intercalary day of 29 February 1896, in a Brahmin family in a village in Surat district. He was one of the six children of his parents, father Ranchhodji and mother Vajiben. His father was a teacher in a village school. The early childhood of Morarji, however, was spent in his maternal grandfather's place, Bhadeli. He received his primary education in this village and for secondary education, he was sent to Bulsar. When he was a boy of fifteen, his father committed suicide by jumping into a well, just three days before Morarji's arranged marriage to an eleven-year old Gajraben. However, Morarji went through with the marriage on the appointed day and became the head of the family, which included, besides the child bride, his grandmother, mother, three brothers and two sisters.[1] On his passing matriculation examination in 1912 he won a scholarship which enabled him to join Wilson College, Bombay, where he studied from 1913 to 1917. After graduation, he joined Bombay Provincial Civil Service in 1918 and spent the next twelve years in service there, working mostly as a revenue officer or a magistrate.

In 1930, Morarji resigned from government service and joined the Indian National Congress. The same year, Gandhi had started the Civil Disobedience Movement and Morarji took part in it and was imprisoned. But all the satyagrahis were set free after the Gandhi-Irwin Pact in March 1931. Morarji had become a member of the local Gujarat Congress

Committee and came to the notice of Sardar Patel, who was president
of the committee. He was appointed its secretary. During the next four
years Morarji was imprisoned thrice for participating in the anti-
government movement led by the Congress party. In 1931, he was
nominated as a member of the All-India Congress Committee (AICC).

In 1937, the Congress party fought elections for the provincial
Assemblies. Desai was elected from his home district and was appointed
minister for revenue and forests in the Congress ministry, headed by
Chief Minister B.G. Kher. In 1939, all the Congress ministries resigned
against the British government's decision to involve India in the World
War without her consent. After relinquishing office, Morarji participated
in the individual satyagraha and was imprisoned. During the Quit India
Movement, he was detained for three years. After the War, elections for
provincial assemblies were held in 1946 and Morarji was elected to the
Bombay Legislative Assembly and became home and revenue minister
(1946-52) again in B.G. Kher's ministry. During these six years, Morarji
earned the reputation 'as a puritan zealot', who would put even Mrs.
Grundy to shame. The most important of such puritanic measures was
the introduction of total prohibition, which led to bootlegging and
ultimately gave birth to criminals. Like some of his other measures, this
measure also proved unsuccessful. Because of the unpopularity of his
puritanical crusade, he lost the election to the Provincial Assembly in
1952. But B.G. Kher retired and made Morarji his successor, being the
seniormost member of his cabinet. Morarji later got himself elected in
a byelection and served as the chief minister of Bombay state from 1952-
56. As chief minister, he is remembered for ruthlessly putting down the
agitation for Samyukta Maharashtra, in which about eighty persons, mostly
students, were killed in police firing. In the words of the *Illustrated Weekly*,
Desai became 'the most hated person' in the province. Apart from this
notoriety, which he earned partly because of the vacillating policy of the
Nehru government with regard to the re-organisation of provinces on
the linguistic basis, Desai had proved himself a good administrator, a no-
nonsense man. He was instrumental in introducing far-reaching reforms
in the land revenue administration and also in police and jail re-
organisation. He thought of the peasant and tenant both, and enacted

progressive legislation for them, much before any Indian province did anything in this direction. His experience as a government official during the British Raj did help him in administering the Bombay province, which came to be known for its efficiency, progress and integrity.

In November 1956, Morarji joined Nehru's Union Cabinet, as minister for commerce and industry. He was elected to the Lok Sabha in 1962 elections and thus continued as finance minister, a portfolio he held from 1958 to 1963. In 1958, at the age of sixty-two, he went out of the country for the first time, visiting Europe, United States and Canada. As finance minister, he led the Indian delegation to the annual meetings of the Board of Governors of the International Monetary Fund and the International Bank for Reconstruction and Development in New Delhi in 1958 and in Washington in 1959, 1960 and 1961. He also attended the Commonwealth Finance Minister's Conference in London in 1960 and 1961. He was quite successful as a finance minister. "Defence through development, creation of a climate of confidence and initiative, export promotion and austerity in government administration, public corporations and companies in the private sector and in the personal lives of the privileged segments of the society, formed the main theme of his economic and fiscal policies". But as finance minister he is remembered most for promulgating the Gold Control Order as an ordinance in January 1963, which prohibited the production of any gold jewellery purer than fourteen carats, thus antagonizing many persons. "The main purpose of gold control was to prevent the smuggling of gold worth crores of rupees into India from outside. As long as the attraction of gold was not lessened and the demand for gold was not reduced, it would be difficult to control the smuggling of gold. It was, therefore, necessary to take steps to lessen the attraction of gold in the public mind", he contended.[2]

In 1963, he was forced out of the Nehru Cabinet under the Kamraj Plan which had called on the senior leaders of the Congress to resign from ministerial posts and to work for strengthening the party. Many believe, Morarji included, that the Kamraj Plan was essentially to oust Morarji from the Cabinet.

After the death of Nehru in May 1964, the question of his successor arose. By this time, Kamraj, his *bete noire*, had become the president of the Congress, who saw to it that Morarji did not become the prime minister. He put up the name of Lal Bahadur Shastri and managed to get him elected 'unanimously' as the prime minister. When Lal Bahadur died suddenly in 1966, Desai wasted no time in making a second bid for the prime ministership. Though Desai was the most prominent Congress leader, he had antagonized many members in the party. His advocacy of Hindi as the national language had made the entire South block against him. Kamraj rallied all his forces and proposed the name of Indira Gandhi as a candidate for prime ministership. This time Morarji did not quit and a contest became inevitable. The Congress parliamentary party met on 19 January 1966 to decide the issue. Indira Gandhi polled 355 votes against Morarji's 189. Indira Gandhi initially did not include Morarji in her cabinet. In the 1967 Lok Sabha elections, Morarji was again elected from Surat constituency and Indira Gandhi again became the prime minister, without any opposition. She wanted Morarji to join her cabinet because the Congress had suffered reverses in the 1967 elections and she thought that including Morarji in her cabinet would strengthen the Congress party. After some haggling, it was decided that Morarji would be the finance minister and also would be designated the deputy prime minister. 'His performance both in Parliament and in councils of the Party was so skilful and the force of his will and personality so evident that he almost came to exert decisive influence in the making of policy'. That made Mrs. Gandhi somewhat jittery as she did not want to be upstaged and was looking to undermine his position. Controversy cropped up in 1969 on the issue of nationalisation of banks and on the selection of a candidate for presidentship of the Congress. The old guard, including Morarji, opposed Mrs. Gandhi on these and on some other issues. She gambled and split the Congress party into two. Her wing of the Congress came later to be known as Congress(I) and the other faction as Congress (O). Morarji opted for the latter, and was asked by the prime minister to resign from the posts held by him (16 July 1969). From 1969 to the advent of the Emergency (1975), Morarji sat with the insignificant opposition in the Parliament, as leader of the Congress(O). Mrs. Gandhi used Emergency to remain in power after the verdict of the Allahabad High Court against the validity of her election of 1971. Morarji Desai was arrested along with thousands others whom Mrs. Gandhi considered her adversaries. He remained in prison for nineteen months. Emergency rules were relaxed in January, 1977, in preparation for parliamentary elections to be held in March 1977. Various political parties formed a coalition under the name Janata Party, Morarji heading the faction Congress(O). The other parties which joined hands to oppose Mrs. Gandhi's Congress were Bharatiya Lok Dal, Jana Sangh, the Socialists and a splinter group of Congress, led by Jagjivan Ram. Congress(I) was routed and the Janata Party formed the government with Morarji as the prime minister. He was eighty-one at the time but still active. One of the first acts of his government was to repeal laws imposing internal Emergency. It also initiated an economic strategy based on labour-intensive private industry and voluntary groups in rural areas. But the policy did not shift radically, and there was a rising tide of strikes, communal violence and general frustration in the country. Morarji was riding a chariot of twenty horses, each pulling in a different direction. There were ego clashes and factional disputes. The Janata government collapsed in July 1979, making way for Indira Gandhi to come to power again. Morarji's public career came to an end. He led a retired life for another sixteen years and died in Bombay on 10 April 1995.

After the 1930s Morarji led the life of a true Gandhian — wearing khadi, spinning regularly, being a strict vegetarian and a teetotaller. He even tried to copy Gandhi's technique of undergoing a fast to win over his opponents. But surprisingly he was never one of those close to Gandhi. In the most comprehensive and official eight volume biography of Gandhi by Tendulkar, titled *Mahatma*, the name of Morarji Desai does not appear even once. His outspokenness could be one of the reasons.

Morarji Desai was a tall, handsome man. A man of fixed habits and equally fixed ideas, he did not change with the times. However, he was an extremely good administrator and a man of courage. He was also a man of integrity, though it came under question during his prime ministership when charges of corruption were levelled against his son Kantilal, who was his private secretary. He wrote his autobiography, *The Story of My Life* in three volumes, which is prosaic and tiresome, and in which he devotes one full chapter to defending Kantilal and his relations with him. In the preface of the book, he says: "He felt that he had to write the book, because it was my duty to write about my experiences so that the reader might get some guidance from them when he is confused". Modesty was certainly not one of his virtues.

## References

1. Mehta, Ved. *A Family Affair; India Under Three Prime Ministers*. Madras, Sangam Books. 1982, p.71.
2. Desai, Morarji. *The Story of My Life*. Macmillan. Vol. 2, p.190.

# Romesh Chunder Dutt

## (1848-1909)

The Dutts were a respectable and literary family of Calcutta. Toru Dutt, who had become famous as a poet in young age, was a cousin of Romesh Chander. In fact a collection of poems by members of the Dutt clan was published as *Dutt Family Album* in 1870. It was natural for Romesh to inherit this literary taste and aspirations. A few members of the family embraced Christianity in 1862, led by Govind Dutt, father of Toru, which was criticized by other family members.

Romesh Chander was born on 13 August 1848. His father, Ishan Chander Dutt, was a deputy collector in the revenue department of the government. His early education was in district schools, wherever his father got posted. Unfortunately, his father died due to drowning in 1861. His mother had died two years earlier. The four brothers and two sisters came under the guardianship of their uncle, Soshee Chunder. Romesh was admitted to Hare School, from where he passed the Entrance Examination in 1864. The same year he was married to Matangini (Mohini) Bose, daughter of Nabagopal Bose of Calcutta, at the age of sixteen. However, the marriage does not seem to have affected his studies. He joined Presidency College and passed the First Arts Examination in 1866, and obtained a scholarship. In March 1868, he left for England to compete for the ICS. He passed and stood third in the order of merit. During this period, he also undertook legal studies and was called to the Bar. He returned to India in 1871 and his career in the Indian Civil Service began.

From 1871 to 1897, he served the Indian Civil Service in various capacities in districts of Bengal and Orissa, beginning as probationer assistant magistrate of Alipore and rose to the position of divisional commissioner of Burdwan and officiating commissioner of Orissa (1895). Realising that he had no scope of further promotion as permanent commissioner, he took premature retirement in 1897, at a relatively early age of forty-nine. His work as a civil servant earned him praise from official quarters as well as from the public. He was one of the early administrators who showed that Indians could administer as well as any British officer.

As a free man, he started on a very fruitful and exciting career as a public person and as a writer. Before retirement, he took leave preparatory to retirement and for months he visited several countries in Europe. Soon after, he was appointed a lecturer in Indian history at the University College, London, where he stayed till 1904. Those seven years in England was his most productive period as a writer. In 1898, appeared the English translation of the *Ramayana* and next year (1899) that of *Mahabharata*, which helped the west to appreciate and understand the great Indian epics better. Max Muller wrote the introduction to the *Ramayana* while *Mahabharata* was dedicated to him. In 1899, another book of his titled *England and India: A Record of Progress During 100 Years*, appeared. Next came his *Famines in India*, which included his five open letters to Lord Curzon. His classical work and perhaps the most important one, *The Economic History of India*, in two volumes, was published in 1902 and 1904 respectively. Apart from other aspects of Indian economic history, he highlighted the causes of famines in India and their remedy. He graphically traced the decline of Indian industries during the early British rule, under a deliberate policy of harming and discouraging Indian industries so that India might not offer competition to British products. He also highlighted the drain on the Indian economy in the form of 'Home Charges.' Another great Indian, Dadabhai Naoroji, was also writing on the same subject at the time and his well-known book *Poverty and Un-British Rule in India* was published in 1901. They were contemporaries and as nationalists, were concerned with the pathetic situation into which the British rule, with its colonial economic policies, was pushing the Indian masses.

However, Romesh Dutt's *Economic History* is more detailed and he wrote with the background of his administrative experience in the Indian Civil Service. But, in spite of his criticism of the British administration, Romesh Dutt was a 'loyal' Indian and did not believe that the British rule was wrong by itself. It must be remembered that during the second half of the nineteenth century, British rule was accepted as a necessity. Even the Indian National Congress used to pass a resolution of 'loyalty' in every session from its inception in 1885. Romesh Dutt believed that the British connection was basically good and that the future of India lay in advancing within the framework of the British Empire. Because of his 'moderate' attitude towards the British, he was invited to preside over the 1899 session of the Congress at Lucknow. In his address, he concentrated on the economic problems faced by the Indians, and did not touch the political aspirations of the people. The idea of swadeshi was still another six years away, when Lord Curzon partitioned Bengal.

Even before his retirement, while serving in the Indian Civil Service, he had written books on various topics. His first book was *Bengal Peasantry* (1875), in which he pleaded the cause of the peasants against the government and landlords. In 1889-90, he had published *History of Civilization in Ancient India*, in which he tried to place before the inquisitive student of Indian culture a book in a handy form, the aspects of Indian culture which until then were known only to scholars and Orientalists. In 1894, he had published *Lays of Ancient India* in verse form in English. This was the translation of some of the best known passages from the *Upanishads*, from the edicts of Ashoka and from the short epic, *Bhairavi*.

In the field of social reform, except for his two Bengali novels *Sansar* and *Samaj*, Dutt made no active contribution, unlike Ranade, who was also a government servant like Romesh Dutt, though in the judicial service.

Romesh Dutt made substantial contribution to Bengali literature, which at that stage was passing through a phase of revolutionary innovation, both in form and content. Romesh Chander's first homage to Bengali literature was a book *Literature of Bengal* (1877), which was in English. This was perhaps the first scientific attempt to write a history of Bengali literature, from the twelfth century down to his time — the nineteenth century. He tried to join the galaxy of Bengali fiction writers led by Bankim Chandra. He wrote four historical and two social novels, all of which were well-received by the reading public. *Banga Bijeta* (or the Conquerer of Bengal) and *Madhabi Kankan* (or bracelet of flowers) depicted the conquest of Bengal by Akbar. The other two historical novels were *Maharashtra Jiban Prabhat* and *Rajput Jiban Sandhya*. All four were published in 1879 — an amazing output by any standard, especially by a high official in government service. His two other novels, *Samaj* (1885) and *Sansar* (1893), were written with a social purpose in mind: the first one advocating widow re-marriage and the second one, inter-caste marriage. Another contribution of Romesh Dutt to Bengali was his translation of the *Rig Veda* (1885).

He left London in 1904, came to India and in August of the same year joined as revenue minister of the state of Baroda, a state which was ruled by a very progressive and enlightened Maharaja Sayaji Rao Gaekwad, who gave him a free hand to handle the reforms in the state. Romesh Dutt did his job diligently and earned the praise of everyone. In an article published in *India* magazine, London, Sir William Wedderburn praised his work on several fronts: lessening the burden of revenue on the royals by rationalizing the revenue structure; for giving great fillip to education in the state, by spending 6.5% of the state revenue on education as compared to one per cent in British India. He also revived panchayat system in the state.[1]

His departure from London saw the end of his career as a writer. After 1904, he did not write any books though he continued to deliver speeches and write articles in papers and journals.

In 1903, during the annual session of the Congress, an exhibition of Indian products was held for the first time as an adjunct to the Congress session. Romesh Dutt was requested to preside over the Industrial Conference. In his presidential address, he made a masterly analysis, in simple language, of the current economic and industrial situation in the country and the role which swadeshi could play in helping Indian industries, both small scale and large scale, to develop.

He was appointed a member of the Royal Commission on decentralization which visited India in 1907, and had to leave Baroda service. The commission was set up to formulate ways and means to involve an increasing number of Indians in the administration. He was the only Indian member of the commission and signed its report with dissent notes on several points.

Romesh Dutt spent another year in London from April 1908 to March 1909, where he 'freely placed his counsel and criticism at the disposal of John Morley, Secretary of State, for India, on the impending scheme of constitutional reforms'.

In June 1909, Dutt returned again to Baroda service as Diwan. However, this time he could not do much as his health started deteriorating. He died on 30 November 1909 in Baroda.

Romesh Dutt was one of the early Indians who as administrator showed that Indians could administer as well as any British or European official. He was perhaps no pioneer, but his interests were spread over many areas and his contribution in many of these were significant. "If a comparative assessment has to be made, however, his work in the economic field would probably stand out as his most outstanding contribution to the future of the country. His contribution to Bengali literature and his researches in ancient Indian history were substantial, but his two volumes of *Economic History* and his *Famines in India* undoubtedly influenced more than any of his other works the future course of the national movement in the country".[2]

# References

1. *Collected Works of Mahatma Gandhi*. Vol. 4, pp.456-7.
2. Dutt, R.C. *Romesh Chunder Dutt*, New Delhi, Publications Division, 1981, p.171.

# Indira Gandhi

## (1917-1984)

Indira Priyadarshini was born on 19 November 1917 at Allahabad. She was the only child of Jawaharlal and Kamala Nehru. A son was born to Kamala in 1924 but unfortunately he died after a few days, leaving Indira without any sibling. Indira later described her childhood as 'lonely' and 'insecure.' Soon after Indira's birth, her mother became sick. Later the sickness was diagnosed as tuberculosis and the family was engrossed with her treatment for the rest of her life. At the same time, Indira's grandfather, Motilal Nehru, and her father Jawaharlal, joined the Congress party and were greatly involved in the freedom movement led by Gandhi. Both of them were often in and out of prison. As a result, Indira's formal education was peripatetic and unsystematic. When she was six years old, she was admitted to Cecilia High School at Allahabad, but because of the protestation of Jawaharlal, who was against Anglo-Indian education as prevelant in India, she did not continue her studies there for any length of time. In March 1926, Indira accompanied her parents to Europe, where Kamala had to undergo treatment for tuberculosis. Indira was admitted to L'Ecole Nouvelle at Bex, Switzerland, where she picked up French and learnt to speak fluently. Later, she studied at the International School in Geneva. In December 1927, the family returned to India as Kamala's health had improved, as a result of which Indira's education in Europe was interrupted. In 1931, she was admitted to Pupil's Own School at

Poona run by a devoted couple, Coonverbai J. Vakil and her husband Jehangir, an Oxford educated confirmed socialist. It was a school with a difference and gave full scope to students to develop individual thinking at their own pace. At the age of sixteen, Indira passed the matriculation examination of the Bombay University. Soonafter, she was admitted to Santiniketan as a student of Siksha Bhavan and came under the benign influence of Rabindranath Tagore. But in April 1935, Indira had to leave Santiniketan as her mother's health had worsened and she had to accompany her to Europe. Dr. Madan Atal, a cousin of Kamala, had accompanied them. Jawaharlal was in Almora jail at the time and could not go but was released on 4 September 1935 and joined his wife and daughter at Badenweiler, Germany, where Kamala was admitted in a sanatorium. In January 1936, Kamala was shifted to a sanatorium near Lausanne in Switzerland. Indira was admitted to her old school at Bex nearby but had come to Lausanne to be with her mother during her last days. Feroze, who had been a family friend also joined them, uninvited. Kamala died on 28 February 1936 with Indira, Jawaharlal, Dr. Madan Atal, and Feroze Gandhi at her bedside. After studying for sometime at Bex, Indira left for London and got herself admitted to Badminton School in Bristol to appear for the matriculation examination of London University. Feroze Gandhi was also in London, as a student at the London School of Economics. Indira often met Feroze and together they used to sightsee or go to the theatre. A recent biography of Indira Gandhi, in which the author has described their relationship during their stay in London, has raised quite a controversy. Indira was in London for one year. After finishing studies at Bristol, Indira went to Oxford and joined Somerville College on the recommendation of Prof. Harold Laski, a friend of Nehru. At Oxford, she fell ill and had to go to Switzerland for treatment of pleurisy. When she recovered, she went back to Oxford but had to leave for India soon after as war clouds gathered over Europe. She sailed in a steamer via Cape of Good Hope, along with Feroze Gandhi. After a long and tortuous journey, they reached Bombay in June 1941. Soon after, Indira announced that she wanted to marry Feroze. Kamala had been very much against Indira marrying Feroze. Before her death Kamala had told Nehru that "she was worried about Indira's relationship with Feroze because she was sure he was unstable".[1] Nor did she think Feroze would enter any profession and be in a position to support Indira. It is not certain if Kamala knew that Feroze came from a doubtful parentage. After an initial reluctance, the Nehru family agreed and Indira and Feroze got married on 26 March 1942 at Allahabad. She changed her name to Indira Gandhi. The couple went to Bombay to attend the historic Congress session on 9 August 1942, where the 'Quit India' resolution was passed. After some time both of them were arrested. Indira was sent to Naini jail, and was given 'A' class in prison. On 13 May 1943, nine months after her arrest, Indira was released. Three months later, Feroze was also released from Faizabad jail. They set up home in Allahabad, in a small house on Fort Road. Rajiv was born on 20 August 1944. The second son, Sanjay, was born on 14 December 1946 in New Delhi, where Nehru was heading the interim government at the time. Feroze was appointed managing editor of *National Herald*, Lucknow, an English daily founded by Jawaharlal Nehru. He moved to Lucknow while Indira lived with her father in New Delhi, in the prime minister's official residence. She not only looked after her father but accompanied him on foreign tours, taking on the responsibilities of a hostess. She also started taking active interest in the Congress affairs and was nominated a member of the Congress Working Committee (1955) and of Central Parliamentary Board (1958). In 1959, she was elected president of the Indian National Congress, and held this office till January 1960. Obviously she was being groomed by Nehru as his successor.

Indira's domestic life during the years of Nehru's prime ministership was not a happy one. Feroze did not relish being referred to as Nehru's son-in-law, which phrase was acquiring the overtones of a taunt. He found the whole business of protocol galling, because it relegated him to a humble position at social functions.[2] In course of time, he was elected a member of Parliament. Resigning his post of managing editor of the *National Herald,* he moved from Lucknow to Delhi, where he was allotted a house as a member of the Parliament. But Indira did not stay with him. She continued staying with her father along with her two sons in Teen Murti House, as his official hostess. There were rumours that the relations between Feroze and Indira had reached a breaking point. Indira denied the rumours unconvincingly. "When Indira assumed office as Congress president (1959), they were hardly on talking terms. He often used to write letters to her addressing sarcastically as 'Comrade Congress president' and ending with 'Yours fraternally.'"[3] Feroze led a lonely and reckless life though he had emerged as a very successful parliamentarian, embarassing Nehru in the Parliament, exposing some serious corruption cases. But due to strain of public life and an unhappy married life leading to indulgences, his health deteriorated and he died on 8 September 1960. He was only forty-seven.

The war with China in 1962 affected the prestige of Nehru as well as his health. He died in May 1964. Though he had groomed Indira for the prime ministership through the Congress Working Committee and Congress presidentship, and tried to compensate her lack of formal education by writing over two hundred odd letters, mainly on history (which did not interest her), the time was not ripe for her to head the government. She was only forty-seven when Nehru died. Lal Bahadur Shastri was elected 'unanimously' as prime minister, Kamraj playing a leading role in this decision. Indira was inducted by Shastri in his cabinet as information and broadcasting minister. In August 1964, she was elected unopposed to the Rajya Sabha. The sudden demise of Shastri in January 1966 necessitated the selection of a prime minister once again. The weighty Congress leadership, known as 'the Syndicate', backed her candidacy as the successor to Shastri, reportedly because they considered her pliable *'goongi gudia'* (dumb doll). As Morarji Desai was also an aspirant, an election ensued. Indira won by 355 to 169 votes. She was sworn in as prime minister on 24 January 1966. Mrs. Gandhi received a challenging inheritance. The country had to face two wars in four years and an insurgency in the northeast. On the economic front successive monsoon failures had affected food grain production, resulting in scarcity. She was handicapped by her own administrative inexperience and awkwardness in Parliament. Her decision to devalue the rupee in 1966 by a whopping 57.7 per cent, without adequate preparation at home and financial assistance from abroad, had disastrous consequences. The prestige of the Congress was on the wane. When the election to Parliament was held in 1967, the party won only 283 seats of the 520 seats of the Lok

Sabha and lost power in eight states. Many Congress stalwarts including Kamraj and several ministers were defeated. However, she herself won from the Rae Bareli constituency and was sworn in as prime minister for the second time in March 1967 without opposition. As an act of prudence and as a gesture of goodwill, she invited Morarji Desai to become deputy prime minister holding the Finance portfolio. She herself took over the External Affairs portfolio in September and made an extensive tour of East European countries and Russia in October 1967 and of South America and Caribbean countries in 1968. She addressed the UN General Assembly on 14 October 1968. She was trying to emerge on the international scene as the prime minister of the largest democracy in the world.

In India, she also toured extensively, first as Congress president and later as prime minister and became quite popular among the masses, earning the sobriquet 'Mother India.' She directly appealed to the people to look to her for their emancipation from poverty and hunger over the heads of the party bosses. Her penchant for populism deepened as her dislike grew for the pressures put on her by the party bosses. The Syndicate had been weakened as many of the leaders had been humbled in the 1967 election. After the death of President Zakir Hussain in May 1969, she came in direct confrontation with the Syndicate over the choice of the new president. V.V. Giri won with the support of Indira Gandhi, defeating the Syndicate candidate Sanjiva Reddy and the Congress party split into two. The majority of members of Parliament joined the Indira camp and the rump called themselves Congress Old (O). Morarji had opted for Congress (O) and resigned, to the delight of Indira Gandhi. The former 'meek and shy' young lady was transformed into a great political strategist.

She had won the battle against the Syndicate but she did not have a majority in the Parliament, which irked her and she felt that she was vulnerable. By now, she had learnt the art of being popular with the masses. To everyone's surprise, she put on the garb of a socialist, though as late as 1962 she had told an interviewer. "I really don't have a political philosophy. I can't say I believe in any 'ism'." She was forty-five then and had never evinced interest in socialism, never talked of it, until the expediency of office forced her to.[4] She initiated several populist (leftist) measures like nationalisation of fourteen major banks (July 1969), abolition of privy purses of the princes (November 1969) which Sardar Patel had certified at the time of Independence. Such measures had transformed her personal fight into an ideological one. Her ten point programme aimed at a 'socialist pattern of society'. She thus acquired an image of a leader who felt deeply for the poor. Armed with such an image, she decided to hold the election in February 1971 instead of 1972, which would have been the normal course. The battle at the hustings was fought under the slogans *Indira hatao* (remove Indira) by the opposition against *Garibi hatao* (remove poverty) by her party. Throughout January and February, Indira Gandhi campaigned even more strenuously and relentlessly than she had done in 1967. She won a landslide victory; her Congress winning 325 seats, a two-third majority in the Lok Sabha. It was her personal victory. She was sworn in as prime minister for the third time in March 1971 and 'she became the most powerful Indian prime minister since independence'. While Nehru first gained power and then office Indira Gandhi first gained office, then power. Her socialist agenda now encompassed several other spheres: she constituted a commission to regulate future expansion of industry and trade, abolished the old managing agency system, nationalised general insurance.

The year 1971 was one which threw up immense problems for Indira's government and ultimately brought unrivalled glory to her. Trouble had been brewing in East Pakistan (now Bangladesh) from the very birth of Pakistan because of the cultural differences between the Eastern and Western wings. Early in 1971, elections were held in Pakistan and Mujibur Rehman's Awami League won with an overwhelming majority in the state assembly and a majority in the national assembly. But he was not allowed to head the government and was arrested. The army let loose a reign of terror in East Pakistan. Ten million refugees from there entered India, which affected India, politically and economically. For India, it was no more a domestic matter of Pakistan. Indira Gandhi's government signed a Treaty of Peace, Cooperation and Friendship with the Soviet Union in August 1971. This treaty strengthened India's position vis-à-vis China and to some extent the USA. India started training and helping the Bengali guerilla force, named Mukti Bahini (freedom force). Pakistan retaliated by bombing Indian airfields. There is a view that Pakistan offered a lifetime opportunity to India to dismember Pakistan. On 4 December, India declared war on Pakistan and the Indian Army, supported by the Air Force, entered East Pakistan and Pakistan army surrendered on 16 December. Bangladesh was born. Indira had become Goddess Durga for the masses, to the chagrin of her enemies. Her popularity was confirmed in the March 1972 state assembly elections, in which the Congress captured seventy per cent of the seats contested. The president conferred the Bharat Ratna on her on 26 January 1972. On 2 July 1972, the Simla Agreement was signed by Mrs. Gandhi and the Pakistan president, Zulfiqar Ali Bhutto, India agreeing to return the conquered territories and to release ninety-one thousand Pakistani Prisoners of War. Her prestige and popularity was further enhanced when India conducted a nuclear explosion for peaceful purposes on 18 May 1974. By now, Mrs. Gandhi had established complete dominance over the party, parliament and the country. When the Supreme Court invalidated the nationalisation of banks and abolition of privy purses of the princes, she tampered with the independence of the judiciary, making it subordinate to the Parliament. She started depending on the advice of her younger son Sanjay, a school dropout. He was issued a licence to produce a small car and got alloted a huge plot of land near Delhi for the factory, bypassing all bureaucratic norms. Gradually, he became as powerful as Mrs. Gandhi herself and was surrounded by a score of young sycophants. The mother-son duo was now destroying the very pillars of democratic government. In 1973, she appointed A.N. Ray as chief justice of India, superceding three judges senior to him. A new slogan was concocted, that the country required a 'committed judiciary' and 'committed bureaucracy'. It was argued that these were essential for the progress of the country and for implementing the 'progressive' policies of the government. Actually, it was to snuff out any oppositon and to get away with illegal and corrupt dealings. Nationalisation of banks and general insurance had enlarged the scope of corruption by Mrs. Gandhi and Sanjay. The episode of Nagarwala, a bizarre scandal involving sixty lakh rupees in 1972, was only a tip of the iceberg. The government treasury was no longer safe.

In 1975, came a bombshell. Justice Jagmohan Sinha of the Allahabad High Court set aside Mrs. Gandhi's election to Lok Sabha on grounds of corruption and debarred her from contesting polls for six years. While she consulted her lawyers to appeal to the Supreme Court she encouraged her son Sanjay and his associates to organise mass rallies by hired hoodlums in her favour. To add to her woes, her party lost elections in Gujarat. She was also confronted by Jayaprakash Narayan's mass rallies, which were swelling in number by the day. The fact of Congress(I) losing the support of the people, rankled in her mind. Moreover, the decision of the Supreme Court regarding her appeal did not help her either — a stay order against depriving her right to vote was all she got. She did not want to lose power and took a drastic step of proclaiming internal emergency and made President Fakhruddin Ali Ahmed sign the proclamation on 26 June 1975, in the dead of the night. All the opposition leaders, including Jayaprakash and Morarji, were arrested; censorship of the worst type was enforced and courts were closed. Indians did not get newspapers on that day. According to Amnesty International, during the first year of Emergency more than 1,10,000 people were arrested and detained without trial. Some were tortured and a few defiant ones were even killed. The Constitution was tampered with. Presidential orders were issued suspending articles 14, 21 and 22 of the Constitution. Sanjay Gandhi, became the *de facto* ruler of the country, an extra-constitutional authority. He aggressively tried to implement his 'five point programme' which included forced sterilisation and slum clearance, along with his mother's twenty point programme. The rule of law was being replaced by the rule of Sanjay Gandhi. Everything was being done to save their rule. Election to Lok Sabha was postponed, which was due in 1976. However, there were some advantages of Emergency for the common man: trains were running on time, offices were working punctually and efficiently, there was less of crime on the streets. Emergency, at least outwardly, seemed to be a success. But on the whole there was fear and disgust among the people.

On 18 January 1977 Indira did a U-turn and announced the general election to be held in March of the following year. Most of the detainees were released and press censorship was relaxed. The opposition parties joined hands and formed the Janata Party. The results of the election stunned Indira and Sanjay. Both of them lost. The Congress(I) could win only 153 as against 299 by Janata including Jagjivan Ram's Congress for Democracy. The Janata Party formed a government, headed by Morarji Desai. The Janata Party had come to power on a negative vote — a protest vote against the Emergency. It had neither a history nor an organisation; neither an ideology nor a programme of its own. The Janata conglomerate had several inner contradictions and the leaders did not work as a team. Their clumsy efforts to punish Indira Gandhi for Emergency excesses, especially arresting her twice, proved counter-productive. It did not come as a surprise to the nation when the Janata government fell in July 1979. Fresh election was held for the Lok Sabha and Indira Gandhi became the prime minister again, for the fourth time, on 14 January 1980. Her party had won 351 seats in a house of 542, trouncing all other parties. She herself had won the Rai Bareli seat with a record margin. Sanjay Gandhi won from neighbouring Amethi. Using undemocratic methods, she dismissed nine Janata state governments, imposing President's Rule. Fresh elections were held. Indira's party won all but one of them. Sanjay once again came to his own element along with his coterie, most of whom were now members of Parliament. However, Sanjay died in an air crash on 23 June 1980 in Delhi. Indira was heart-broken but regained her balance and started working almost immediately. Many people felt that Sanjay's death was 'the best thing that could happen to India'.

The concentration of power, almost dictatorial, at the centre had resulted in the neglect of the states. The Congress lost in Andhra, Tamil Nadu and Karnataka. There was trouble in Assam, Kashmir and above all in Panjab, where the Akali Dal was challenging the supremacy of the Congress and had wrested power in the 1977 election. To meet their challenge, Sanjay Gandhi when alive, with a nod from his mother, had cultivated a demagogue named Bhindrawala. Bhindrawala, who was a fundamentalist at heart, soon gained a large following, which was armed by the Pakistan secret service. As his strength grew, Bhindrawala began to demand a separate, autonomous Sikh state — Khalistan. He moved into the Golden Temple, made the Akal Takht his headquarters and converted it into a fortress. His military adviser, a retired major general

Subheg Singh, who had trained the Mukti Bahini in Bangladesh, gave regular training in arms to the followers of Bhindrawala. They had become terrorists and had spread all over Panjab, killing people at will, mostly Hindus. Even the police was afraid of them. Indira Gandhi watched the tragic drama for sometime with patience but then decided to strike. On 6 June 1984, the army entered the Harmandir Sahib (Golden Temple). It was called 'Operation Blue Star'. There was fierce fighting between the Indian Army and well-entrenched Bhindrawala and his armed followers. Tanks and artillery had to be used. The Akal Takht, where Bhindrawala was hiding with his men, was heavily damaged and had to be rebuilt later. More than three hundred army men had died in the confrontation. That was the end of Bhindrawala along with many of his followers who had become a terror in Panjab.

Indira Gandhi now feared her assassination, and even wrote out instructions for her funeral. Her security was beefed up. But she refused to be protected by the army. She was assassinated by two of her own Sikh security guards, on the morning of 31 October 1984 in her own residence, 1 Safdarjung Road.

Indira Gandhi did not aspire to be a world leader as her father did but she was active in the Non-Alignment Movement, founded at the initiative of Nehru at Belgrade in 1961. She attended the fourth Non-Aligned Conference at Algiers and in March 1983 chaired the seventh Non-Aligned Conference held at New Delhi. Mrs. Gandhi was not an intellectual like Jawaharlal Nehru and did not write much. Her speeches and reminiscences have been published in several volumes by the Publications Division, Government of India. Some other volumes have been published by the Indira Gandhi Memorial Trust.

Indira's character was summed up by her father, Jawaharlal Nehru in a letter to his sister, Vijaya Lakshmi Pandit, in 1934, which is in the nature of a complaint. He wrote: 'She (Indira) scarcely writes to her parents, she ignores us completely. Her behaviour is extraordinarily self-centred, remarkably selfish.' In another letter, he complained that "she is remarkably casual and indifferent to others. Indu revolves around herself, self-centred, she hardly thinks of others".[5] In the light of her behaviour as prime minister, it seemed as if Indira never lost her sense of solitariness in a hostile world, always sought security in ways that made her intolerant of criticism and identified herself so completely with India that she made little distinction between her person, her family and her government. There was always lurking authoritarianism behind her cultivated charisma.

## References

1.  Frank, Katherine. *Indira; The Life of Indira Nehru Gandhi*. London, Harper Collins, 2001, p.111.
2.  Pande, B.N. *Indira Gandhi*. New Delhi Publications Division. 1989, p.107.
3.  Harvani, Ansar. *Gandhi to Gandhi; Private Faces of Public Figures*. New Delhi, Gyan, 1966, p.211-12.
4.  Ram Gopal. *Indian Freedom; Rhetorics & Reality*. Vol.2, Ghaziabad, Vimal Prakashan, p.114.
5.  Frank, Katherine. Indira op. cit., p.84.

# Mohandas Karamchand Gandhi

## (1869-1948)

An astounding volume of Gandhian hagiology has come into existence
which is noted for its ornate redundancy, its petrified Victorian Indian-
English, its grandiloquent claims, and its reverent lore.

— *Ved Mehta*

Mohandas Karamchand Gandhi was born on 2 October 1869 at
Porbandar, also known as Sudamapuri, in Gujarat. His father Karamchand
was diwan (prime minister) of Porbandar. His grandfather, Uttamchand,
also had been diwan of Porbandar and later of Junagadh. Earlier, his
ancestors had been grocers, a common occupation of the *Vaish* (bania)
community to which Mohandas belonged. Mohan's mother, Putlibai,
was an extremely religious lady who devoted much of her time in worship,
trips to the temples and fasting. The family belonged to *Vaishnava* sect
which has much in common with Jainism  Gandhi was greatly influenced
by the preachings of this sect and his belief in non-violence and the
efficacy of fasting in later life could be traced to this early influence. It
may be noted that Jainism venerates extreme forms of asceticism, like
slow starvation, and many Jain spiritual leaders have died in this way. But
Gandhi used fasts as a moral force as well as a coercive tactic to achieve
his ends.

When he was seven years old, his family moved to Rajkot, another state in Kathiawar, where his father, Karamchand, had become a diwan. There Mohandas joined a primary school and later a high school. He was a mediocre student and was very shy and timid. He hardly took part in sports or gymnastics but was fond of walking, a hobby which he adhered to till the last days of his life. While still in high school, he was married at the age of thirteen (1887), to Kasturba, daughter of a merchant of Porbandar, who was of the same age or a year older than her husband. A baby was born to the couple within a year of marriage, who died after a few days. Mohandas did not care to know the sex of the baby, nor do we know to this day. But later, four sons were born to the couple: Harilal (1888), Manilal (1892), Ramdas (1897) and the youngest, Devdas (1900). Then in 1906, at the age of thirty-seven, Gandhi claims that he became a *brahmachari*, a celibate.

While still struggling with studies in school, his father died in 1885. Gandhi has devoted a full chapter in his Autobiography describing in poignant detail the death of his father which had moved him. After passing the Matriculation examination in 1887, he joined Samaldas College in Bhavnagar, where the shy and introvert found studies difficult and the atmosphere in the college uncongenial. Someone suggested to him that it was much easier to get a barrister's degree in England than getting a law degree in India. Mohandas jumped at the ideas and with the support of his family, sailed for England on 4 September 1888. He had already become a father. His eldest son Harilal was born in June 1888. Kasturba and the baby boy thus became the responsibility of Mohandas' mother, Putlibai, and other members of the joint family. Mohandas spent almost three years in England and was called to the Bar in June 1891. A few days later, he left for India. During these three years, he had tried to live like an Englishman and had bought expensive clothes and a silk hat. He learnt ballroom dancing, keeping to himself the fact that he was a married man. He had managed to remain a vegetarian and had even joined the London Vegetarian Society. He was five feet five inches tall, with an unimpressive personality but there was something in his character and bearing, which attracted people to him. During all these years, Mohandas never wrote to his wife Kasturba. She was illiterate.

On his return to India, Gandhi decided to set up his legal practice in Bombay but he did not succeed. Frustrated, he returned to Rajkot and tried his luck there without much success. While he was wrestling with the problem of his career as a lawyer, help came from an unexpected quarter. An offer came from the firm Dada Abdulla & Co. with headquarters at Durban, South Africa, to advise the firm in a law suit. Mohandas wanted to leave India, where he had not succeeded and was happy to accept the offer. Since his return to India, his wife had given birth to another son, Manilal (1892). "Mohandas felt no pangs at the thought of leaving his young sons, and because he had been spending less and less time with his wife, he was not distressed by the thought of abandoning her either".[1] Gandhi sailed for South Africa in April 1893. On reaching Durban, Gandhi started studying the case and also started looking after the correspondence of the company. He was also helping the lawyers who were already fighting the case. After studying the case in detail he advised the litigants to settle the matter through arbitration, which to his delight, Gandhi was accepted by the parties. This exercise had taken one year. The task done, was ready to go back to India. During this period he had observed the pitiable condition of the Indians in Transvaal and Natal and had some humiliating experiences himself. When he learnt that the situation for Indians was going to be worse through a proposed legislation to disenfranchise all the Indians in the Crown colony of Natal, he decided to stay on and fight for the rights of the Indians. Most of the Indians there were illiterate. They had come there as indentured labourers to work on sugar plantations and mines. Gradually, some of them had become businessmen, most of whom were Muslims like Dada Abdulla. But all of them remained almost illiterate, and ignorant of their rights. The Indians were called coolies, whatever their profession. Gandhi started with writing petitions to the Natal government, making speeches and demanding interviews with government officials. To provide Indians with an organisation, he founded the Natal Indian Congress. He enrolled himself as an advocate in the Supreme Court of Natal. His legal practice flourished and gradually, he was able to employ a large staff in his office. He rented a big house in Beach Grove, where the elite of Durban lived. His efforts to fight for the rights of Indians were only partially successful.

The Bill for disenfranchisement of Indians was passed, though it was finally agreed that Indians already on the voters list would not be excluded. The £25 tax on Indians (a sort of *Jazia* of Mughal vintage), was reduced to £3. In June 1896, Gandhi decided to visit India, to bring his family to South Africa. During his six months stay in India he met several Indian leaders like Pherozeshah Mehta, Tilak and Gokhale but was impressed most by the gentle, soft spoken, Gokhale. One thing he realised during his visit to India was that while in South Africa he was among intellectual inferiors; in India he will be among intellectual giants. He sailed back for South Africa with his wife, two sons and a nephew in December. In his absence, his clerks had been working for him in his office and his legal practice had not suffered. By now, he had become a prosperous barrister. 'His tone became more authoritative and more unyielding'. Besides being a successful barrister, he had become a political representative of the Indians, through his social work. The iron of ambition had entered him. He had set up his home in that big, beautiful house facing the sea in Durban, with wife, children and quite a few 'friends' who worked for him. The Natal government was determined to restrict the number of Indians and were implementing laws towards that end. Gandhi continued the fight against injustice but it was an unequal struggle, which he rarely won and often lost. But when the Boer War broke out in October 1899, he at once offered his services to the Natal government, because he felt a great sense of loyalty to the Empire. To help the British army, he raised an Indian Ambulence Corps. For their services Gandhi, and thirty-seven other Indian volunteers, were awarded the War Medal after the war was won. When Queen Victoria died (January 1901), he led a procession of Indian mourners through the streets of Durban. But, to his chagrin, all his effort to show his loyalty to the Empire proved counterproductive and after the war, the discrimination and harassment of Indians continued. He felt frustrated. "On my relief from war-duty, I felt that my work was no longer in South Africa but in India", he wrote in his autobiography. He left for India with his wife and children, telling his friends in Natal that he would return if they needed him. The family reached India in December 1901. Leaving his family at Rajkot, he hurried to Calcutta to attend the Congress session. Gokhale took him under his wings and got

Gandhi's resolution on South African Indians passed in the Subject Committee.

Gandhi reached Rajkot and tried to practice law once again but without confidence and consequently without success. "The memory of past failures oppressed him. The man who spoke so boldly in Durban, was tongue-tied in his own country". Once again South Africa came to his rescue. A telegram from Durban summoning him back. He sailed for South Africa in the middle of November 1902, along with his family. He had been in India for about a year. On his return to South Africa, he found that after Britain's victory in the Boer War, the condition of Indians was becoming worse. Consequently, the challenge he had to face was the worst he had so far faced, especially in Transvaal. He, therefore, decided to stay in Johannesburg and enrolled as an advocate of the supreme court of Transvaal. In the meanwhile, Gandhi wanted to live a different kind of life — community life where everyone would work with his or her own hands and earn his living. In this, he was influenced by the Trappist monastry near Durban, which he had visited earlier and books like *Unto This Last* by John Ruskin, and Leo Tostoy's *The Kingdom of God is Within You*. He bought a hundred acre farm in 1904, fourteen miles from Durban, and established the famous Phoenix settlement. His family and several other persons started living at the Phoenix Farm. Such acts and experiments marks him apart from ordinary men. Even some Britishers like Henry Polak and Albert West joined him. Now, Gandhi had to commute between Phoenix Farm and Johannesburg, where he was practicing as a barrister. In spite of the deteriorating condition of Indians under British rule, he once again wanted the Indians to show their loyalty to the British Empire during the Zulu uprising (1906). He exhorted the Indians not to be afraid of war. "Wars were relatively harmless. They (Indians) would prove their patriotism by killing Zulus (the local inhabitants)", he argued. This was a strange and perverse arguement, which ran counter to his religious beliefs. "To the generation accustomed to remembering Gandhi as an apostle of peace, these arguments may startle them. It is strange that not only Gandhi approved of war during Zulu uprising but whenever war broke out he was in the forefront, calling upon Indians to volunteer".[2] The Zulu uprising was suppressed brutally by the British in a few months. Gandhi had no remorse in giving a token help to the British in this unequal conflict.

The situation in Transvaal continued to get worse. To plead the Indian case to the government in London, the Indians decided to send a delegation to England. They financed it through contributions. The two member delegation comprised Gandhi and H.O. Ally. They sailed for England in October 1906, travelling first class and stayed at the Hotel Cecil, one of the more expensive hotels in London. A similar delegation was sent in 1909, comprising Gandhi and Hajee Habib. Again, they had travelled first class and stayed at Cecil Hotel. The two delegations did not achieve anything. But the indomitable Gandhi continued to fight the Black Acts of Transvaal and Natal governments and exhorted the Indians to violate the unjust laws non-violently. This he called Satyagraha, in which even some whites participated. He spread his ideas through the paper *Indian Opinion*, which was published in English, Gujarati, Tamil and Hindi, from his Phoenix Farm from 1904 onwards. Thus, he had prepared himself and the Indians well for the forthcoming battle. They agitated against the £3 tax on Indians; against compulsory registration and giving fingerprints, and against annulment of all marriages not solemnised according to Christian rites. The fight through satyagraha continued for several years. Gandhi and hundreds of Indians were arrested for violating the law, time and again. In 1910, Gandhi had established another settlement named Tolstoy Farm near Johannesburg to accommodate and feed the satyagrahis. In 1912, Gokhale visited South Africa to argue the case for the Indians. General Smuts agreed to dilute some of the harsh measures but went back on his promise, after Gokhale left. Ultimately, a provisional agreement was arrived at between General Smuts and Gandhi in which some minor demands of Indians were conceded, but the government did not change the policy of apartheid and Indians there continued to suffer discrimination. In July 1914, Gandhi sailed for India via England, where he spent several months for the treatment of pleurisy which he had developed. "Though the limited gains Gandhi realised for the Indian community in South Africa were later nullified by the racialist policies of successive white governments, his *satyagraha* movement did reveal the effectiveness of organised non-violent resistance against the more powerful opponent".[3] In fact, the experiences of Gandhi in South Africa left a permanent imprint on Gandhi's thinking and we find him referring to these experiences time and again during his innumerable discourses in India. According to Jawaharlal Nehru, "Gandhiji underwent a tremendous conversion during his early days in South Africa, and this shook him up greatly and altered his whole outlook on life. Since then, he has had a fixed basis for all his ideas, and his mind is hardly an open mind".[4]

In South Africa, Gandhi also had some very unpleasant experiences. One such happened in February 1908. In that year he had led an agitation against the 'Black Act' which required every Indian to get himself registered, after giving ten finger-prints. He and some other satyagrahis were imprisoned for refusing to give fingerprints. But soonafter, he without consulting any of his colleagues, agreed to register after giving fingerprints "voluntarily". He was released. This infuriated some of his followers. When he came out of prison some Pathans questioned him. "It was you who told us that fingerprints were required only from criminals. How does that fit in with your present attitude"? The Pathan bluntly told Gandhi, "We have heard that you have betrayed the community and sold it to General Smuts for £15,000. We will never give fingerprints nor will let others do so". When Gandhi went to the Registration Office to give fingerprints a group of Pathans confronted him and a burly Pathan, Mir Alam, hit him with a heavy stick. Others gave him more blows and kicks. He fell unconscious. A Christian missionary, Joseph Doke, who was passing by, took pity on him, brought him home and nursed him back to health.[5] Gandhi appealed to the government not to take any action against those who had assaulted him. Doke was so impressed by Gandhi and his philosophy of life (which was similar to that of Jesus Christ) that he wrote a biography of Gandhi, the first one among hundreds which were to follow. The incident shows two sides of Gandhi: his inconsistency and whimsical attitute to the problems at hand, and secondly, his winning ways through gentleness and what came to be called 'charisma', sowing the seeds of greatness in the man. Gandhi was so excited on seeing his biography in print that he bought all the copies of the book and distributed them to his friends, acquaintances and to people in power, free of cost. The blow inflicted by Mir Alam seems to have changed the attitude of Gandhi towards Muslims, resulting in the appeasement of Muslims during the remaining years of his life. We find him writing a letter (21 June 1909) to a Muslim friend Habib Motan, which was in reply to a letter in which Motan had asked Gandhi's opinion about the demands of the Muslim delegation presented to Lord Minto (1906) and the latter conceding to all the demands. Gandhi wrote, "My personal view is that, since numerically Hindus are in a great majority, and are, as they themselves believe, better placed educationally, they should cheerfully concede to their Muslim brethren the utmost they can. As a *satyagrahi*, I am emphatically of the view that the Hindus should give to the Muslims whatever they ask for, and willingly accept whatever sacrifice this may involve".[6] It is evident that the policy of Muslim appeasement was enunciated by Gandhi while still in South Africa. In this, he was neither influenced by Tilak nor Gokhale. He was his own guru.

Gandhi also had some other enemies in South Africa, besides Pathans. In a letter to Chhaganlal (11 March 1914) from Cape Town he wrote, "Medh (Surendra) writes to say that they are plotting again in Johannesburg to take my life. That would indeed be welcome and a fit end of my work. In case I die suddenly, by the reason this of any other, I want to set down here certain ideas which I have thought out".[7] The remainder of the letter is somewhat like a testament, giving details of how different members of his extended family were to be provided for. It is not clear who was after Gandhi's life.

Gandhi reached Bombay on 9 January 1915. He had already sent his apostles to India, before leaving South Africa. They arranged a hero's welcome for their mentor, as Gandhi was not yet known to the Indian masses. As advised by Gokhale, Gandhi toured India for one year, 'keeping his eyes open and mouth shut', but he could hardly follow the latter part of Gokhale's advice. He made several speeches during the year. He had become a compulsive speechmaker or rather sermoniser, his weekly 'silence day' in later life, notwithstanding.

After the stipulated year of wandering, he settled down at Ahmedabad, where he founded an ashram on 25 May 1915. The beginning was actually made at the suburb Kochrab, in a bungalow. But soon the bungalow proved too small for the projected ashram. He then bought 1130 acres of land on the bank of the Sabarmati river and moved the ashram there. He appealed for funds and donations came pouring. Gujaratis are a rich community and have a tendency towards philanthropy. Gandhi had no dearth of money for his ashram. He named it 'Satyagraha Ashram'. This was the third ashram he had founded. The number of inmates grew from thirty to about two hundred, as Gandhi's fame spread. Each member of the ashram had to take some vows; of truth, ahimsa (non-violence), celibacy, non-stealing, non-possession, and control of palate. But the vows were often broken, especially that of celibacy by both male and female inmates, some of whom were married couples. In spite of the vows, Gandhi attracted social workers, scholars, minor politicians, students and cranks. Later, his secretary Mahadev Desai remarked that "the Ashram to me looks like a mad house". This was a cynical exaggeration. The ashram had developed into a small village with its own farming, dairying and tannery. It also had a school and a small workshop. On 12 February 1926, the Satyagraha Ashram was registered in the name of Mohandas Karamchand Gandhi and Maganlal Khushalchand Gandhi, his cousin, and the value of the property was assessed at Rs. 2,75,000. For fifteen years (1915-1930), this ashram served as the headquarters of Gandhi.

Soon the time came for Gandhi to launch his political career in India, for which he had done preparatory work in South Africa and later in India. He had studied the psychology of the Indian masses, which helped him to create a mass following. He knew that Hindus were a people who adored sacrifice and identified leaders with what they gave up and less by what they had. He changed his dress to give him a look of a poor Indian farmer. If politics is to be compared with marketing, Gandhi was a marketing genius. He used his appearance to communicate. The communicative power of costume transcended the limitations of language in a multilingual and illiterate India. His apostles, based in his ashram at Ahmedabad, augmented his own efforts and strategy by spreading myths about him and soon he earned the reverent title of the *Mahatma*. The illiterate, superstitious masses now looked to him for miracles. Small miracles did follow. The first one was in Champaran, Bihar in 1917 where he went to look into the problems of peasants working in indigo plantations owned by white planters. Through his efforts, the condition of farmers was ameliorated to some extent and the Mahatma earned the gratitude of thousands of poor farmers. The next satyagraha was for solving the dispute between workers and mill owners at Ahmedabad, which was solved partially through arbitration (1918). Immediately afterwards, he launched a satyagraha at Kheda district, Gujarat, where farmers were heavily taxed, even when their crops had failed. After four months of 'no-tax campaign', the government agreed to suspend the assessment of tax for the poor farmers. Gandhi was emerging as a miracle man.

However, during the war (1914-1918) while freedom fighters like Rash Behari Bose and others were trying to inspire the Indian soldiers in cantonments in various parts of the country to stage a revolt against the British, Gandhi acted as a recruiting agent for the British army, and earned a medal for his services. Then came the Jallianwala Bagh tragedy (13 April 1919) at Amritsar, in which hundreds of innocent, unarmed Indians were shot dead and wounded. The ghastly and inhuman act of the British shook the nation and Gandhi was quick to sense the mood of the masses and intellectuals alike. He started an anti-British movement. In the meanwhile, the Muslims in India were angry with the British for the treatment meted out to Turkey and the Khalifa (based in Turkey), who was the head of the Muslim *umma* (faithful). They had formed a Khilifat Conference, which decided to start non-cooperation with the British government. The movement was led by Ali brothers (Mohammad and the burly, Shaukat) and Maulana Abul Kalam Azad. They invited Hindus to join in their anti-government, and obviously a Pan-Islamic movement. Gandhi not only joined the Khilafat Conference but started acting as their guide and friend. "Thus, the truth is that the non-cooperation had its origin in the Khilafat agitation and not in the Congress movement for Swaraj; that it was started by the Khilafatists to help Turkey and adopted by the Congress only to help the Khilafatists; that Swaraj was not its primary object, but its primary object was Khilafat and that Swaraj was added as a secondary object to induce the Hindus to join it".[8] According to Annie Besant; "As the Khilafat was not sufficiently attractive to Hindus, the Punjab atrocities and the deficiencies of Reforms Act were added to the list of provocative causes".[9] Gandhi himself wrote in his autobiography that, "the adoption of non-cooperation for the sake of the Khilafat was itself a great practical attempt made by the Congress to bring about Hindu-Muslim unity". Many Indian leaders like Madan Mohan Malaviya, Annie Besant, B.C. Pal, C.R. Das and others tried to dissuade Gandhi from fighting for a cause which did not concern India at all. But Gandhi ignored their protests and convinced himself that he was fighting for a sacred cause. He could not see that the Khilafat movement was "oddly unreal, for the Muslims in India had not previously felt any great bond with the Caliph nor was there any concerted movement in any of the Muslim countries for the restoration of the authority of the Caliph. It was an essentially an Indian Muslim movement and drew its strength from imaginery grievances". Gandhi gambled dangerously and unwisely. But he felt that he was in a strong position now, Muslim support adding to his strength. He formally inaugurated the non-cooperation movement on 1 August 1920 (the very day Tilak died), by returning three medals the government had awarded him for his services to the Empire. Gandhi then reached Calcutta, on 4 September, to attend the special session of the Congress, accompanied by an army of enthusiastic khilafatists. There he moved his resolution on non-violent, non-cooperation, which stipulated every Indian to surrender all the titles and honours conferred by the government; lawyers to boycott the courts; teachers and students to walk out from government aided schools and colleges and all government employees to leave their offices, culminating in a no-tax campaign. The idea was to bring the government machinery to a grinding halt. Gandhi did not explain how lawyers and government employees would live and support their families if they left their jobs. There was strong opposition to the proposal, coming from leaders like C.R. Das, Annie Besant, B.C. Paul. However, Gandhi and the Khilafatists had got a crowd assembled at the venue of the Congress as Congress delegates. Train load of 'delegates', hired by Bombay's merchant prince Mian Mohemed Chotani, arrived and packed the *panaal*, to vote for the resolution of Gandhi. All Muslims, except Jinnah, voted for, and almost all leading Hindus, except Motilal, voted against the resolution. When put to vote the verdict was 1855 votes for and 873 against the resolution. The Calcutta Congress gave Gandhi his first major victory. Emboldened by this, he reached Nagpur for the regular session of the Congress in December 1920, where the resolution on non-violent, non-cooperation passed at Calcutta had to be ratified. By this time, leaders like C.R. Das and Lajpat Rai were won over by Gandhi to his side. Like the Congress session at Calcutta, the Nagpur session was also dominated by the Muslim presence. According to a leading Muslim League leader, Khaliquzzaman, "The Congress session in Nagpur was almost a Muslim session of the Congress for I believe that the number of Muslims was so large as to give it a Muslim colour".[10] The only strong voice against the resolution was that of Jinnah. When he stood up to oppose the resolution and addressed Gandhi as 'Mr.' he was shouted down, 'Say Mahatma,' the unruly crowd demanded and didn't let him proceed. Jinnah walked away never to return to the Congress. Many believe that it was the turning point in the history of the Congress, and that of India. Gandhi's resolution was passed with overwhelming majority of votes once again.

Immediately after the Nagpur session of the Congress, Gandhi declared that he would now get swaraj (self-rule) within one year through non-violent non-cooperation and he went around the country accompanied by the Ali brothers propagating his proposed miracle. But while the Muslim leaders were making violent speeches, inciting the religious fervour of the Muslims, Gandhi was speaking on an entirely different level of non-violence and non-cooperation. As nothing startling was happening, Muslims were getting impatient and they unleashed their fury in Malabar, spearheaded by Moplas. Murder, rape, pillage and forcible conversion of Hindus followed. Annie Besant wrote in anguish in her weekly *New India*. "It would be well if Mr. Gandhi could be taken into Malabar to see with his own eyes the ghastly horrors which have been the result of his preachings and his loved Ali brothers, Mohammed and Shaukat. The slaughter in Malabar cries out his responsibility". But Gandhi not only remained unmoved by the plight of thousands of Hindus but tried to defend the Moplas by saying that, "the brave, God-fearing Moplas are fighting for what they consider as religion, and in the manner they consider as religious". The Congress, under his guidance, suppressed all reports about the atrocities and started blaming the authorities for suppressing the riots and started a relief fund for the Moplas. The Congress government in free India even went a step further by classifying Mopla rioters as freedom fighters and made them eligible for pension.

The year 1921 ended without swaraj. By this time, leading Congressmen like C.R. Das, Subhas Bose, Lajpat Rai had been imprisoned. To the dismay of Gandhi, the massive boycott which he had expected did not take place: a large number of students continued to study (even universities like Banaras Hindu University and Aligarh University were not closed); there were long queues in front of government recruiting offices; lawyers did not stop attending courts except a few like C.R. Das, Motilal Nehru and Rajagopalachari, who had amassed wealth and were secure. Fearing dismal failure of the non-cooperation movement, Gandhi, without consulting any one, suspended the movement on 24 February, 1922, giving the Chauri Chaura incident, in which some policemen were burnt alive as reason for suspension. The nation was stunned. Lajpat Rai wrote a seventeen page letter from prison addressed to Congressmen in which he blamed himself and other Congress leaders for "surrendering our better judgement to his (Gandhi's) decision". Along with this, mass 'civil disobedience' as planned by Gandhi in Bardoli taluka in Gujarat, was also abandoned, for which hectic preparations had been made earlier.

Congress leaders like C.R. Das, Motilal Nehru and Lajpat Rai lost faith in the infallibility of Gandhi and his methods and formed the Swaraj Party; contested in the forthcoming elections and entered the Councils. The declining popularity of Gandhi emboldened the government to arrest him (10 March 1922). He was sentenced to six years imprisonment but was released after two years due to his illness. He went to his ashram, spending his time spinning and learning Urdu. He asked his followers to do 'constructive work'. But his hold on the masses did not completely vanish. His charisma remained. The reason was that Gandhi had carried out his propaganda among the masses rather than at the Congress sessions. His activity was not confined to the podium but was conducted among the people in the streets of rural and urban India. He was a great and asute organiser. When he took over the Congress party in 1920, he made it into a mass movement. Earlier it was a sort of discussion club of the elite, who passed resolutions during the annual sessions. Now the Congress had committees comprising committed members from the taluka, district, state and culminating into the All India Congress Committee and, its executive smaller wing, the Congress Working Committee. He also ensured that Congressmen should demonstrate allegiance to him, and him alone. The spinning wheel was the first item on Gandhi's economic agenda and it served as a barometer to judge the loyalty of the Congress workers to him. He had politicised it by making regular spinning incumbent on every Congressman; failing which his membership would cease. The other criterion was non-violence, absolute non-violence. This was to check the glory earned by revolutionaries for their daring deeds. (Muslims were, however, exempt from these two norms). The hold on the Congress machinery was evident when he was elected to preside over the Congress session at Belgaum in 1924.

Failure of the non-cooperation movement provoked the Muslims to indulge in large scale rioting, though the Khilafat question was solved by the Turks themselves by ousting the Sultan (Kaliph) from Turkey. The most serious riot took place in Kohat, West Punjab and Gulburga in the Nizam's territory, both in 1924, The communal riots continued in subsequent years, proving the dangers of dubious methods adopted by Gandhi to bring unity among Hindus and Muslims. Gandhi went on a twenty-one-day fast after the Kohat tragedy, in which almost the whole Hindu and Sikh population of the town was shifted to Rawalpindi. The fast did not bring any change in the communal situation and the riots continued at different places. Frustrated, he lived quietly in the Sabarmati Ashram after that. Though he continued to make speeches, he didn't have anything new to say. People were tired of hearing his familiar sermons on *charkha* and untouchability. However, he watched the political developments in the country and waited patiently for the comeback. By 1928, top leaders of the Congress were dead: Tilak (1920) C.R. Das (1925) Lajpat Rai (1928). Motilal Nehru was a sick man and was worried about the future of his son, Jawaharlal. Gandhi placated the Nehrus, by offering presidentship of the Congress to Jawaharlal in 1929. Once again Gandhi had no rival. He occupied centre stage. Then he burst on the political scene of India like a tornado. On 1 January 1930, the Congress declared complete independence (*purna swaraj*) as its political objective and authorised the Working Committee to launch a Civil Disobedience Movement. Gandhi, the great strategist and publicist, started the movement in a most dramatic manner. He was to break Salt Laws. On 12 March

1930, Gandhi, followed by seventy-eight members of his Sabarmati Ashram, started a march heading towards Dandi, a small village on the sea coast of Gujarat. The party took twenty-four days to reach Dandi, passing through scores of villages. It was a well-thought out publicity gimmick. The march became world news. On 6 April, after reaching Dandi, Gandhi picked up a little lump of salt left by the waves. The whole of India was electrified. Salt laws were being violated at thousands of places in the country. The Civil Disobedience Movement had begun. Gandhi was arrested on 4 May. Always ready to compromise, he wrote a letter from prison to the viceroy, seeking an interview which was granted. This resulted in the famous Gandhi-Irwin Pact, the details of which were announced on 5 March 1931. The Congress agreed to suspend Civil Disobedience. The government agreed to release all prisoners, restore the forfeited lands, and allow villagers living near the coast to collect salt for personal use (which they had been doing for centuries anyway). But the government monopoly on salt remained. The Salt Laws were not changed. Gandhi also agreed to attend the Second Round Table Conference in London (for the first one, the Congress did not send its representative), to be held later in 1931. He elected himself as the sole representative of the Congress. The Conference was a complete failure and the parties did not reach a consensus. It was left to the prime minister to give his verdict. On his return, Gandhi renewed Civil Disobedience and was arrested, along with thousands of Congress workers. While he was still in Yervada Jail, the Communal Award was announced in August 1932 by the government, which allowed separate electorates for the Depressed Classes (Scheduled Castes). Gandhi saw in it, the bifurcation of the Hindu society and went on a fast unto death to get it annulled. The fast was broken when a pact known as the Poona Pact was signed between B.R. Ambedkar (representing the Scheduled Castes) and Madan Mohan Malaviya, on behalf of the caste Hindus. Separate electorates were withdrawn but a larger number of seats were allotted to Scheduled Castes in the assemblies. This was one of the greatest achievements of Gandhi, saving the Hindu society from a great catastrophe.

While starting on the Dandi March, Gandhi had abandoned the Sabarmati Ashram and sometime later established another ashram,

Sevagram, near Wardha. He severed his formal connection with the Congress in September 1934 but remained the undisputed leader of the Congress, taking important decisions till almost the very end. In March 1940, the Muslim League passed what has come to be known as the 'Pakistan Resolution'. Gandhi was the first Congress leader to support the Muslim league contention of an 'autonomous and sovereign Muslim nation'. Under the title 'A Baffling Situation', Gandhi wrote in *Harijan* (6 April 1940), "Muslims will be entitled to dictate their own terms. Unless the rest of India wishes to engage in internal fratricide, the others will have to submit to Muslim dictation if Muslims will resort to it".[11] This view he reiterated again and again in subsequent years.

On 9 August 1942, the 'Quit India' resolution was passed by the Congress Working Committee, drafted like many others resolutions, by Gandhi. But the government swiftly acted and arrested him and other Congress leaders during the night of 9/10 August. Gandhi, with twenty-three of his colleagues, including Kasturba, were kept in the Aga Khan Palace, Poona, where Kasturba and Mahadev Desai, died during internment. He was released on 6 May 1944, as usual, on health grounds. Then happened one of the most humiliating incidents in his life when he went to Bombay to meet Jinnah, offering him the Rajaji Formula which contained the 'essence' of Pakistan. For eighteen days, 9 to 27 September 1944, Gandhi trudged to Jinnah's palatial house on Malabar Hill. The two met daily, discussed and then exchanged letters summarising their discussions. Gandhi addressed Jinnah as 'Dear Quaid-e Azam' and Jinnah address his adversary as 'Mr. Gandhi' in the letters. How things had changed! In 1920, at Nagpur, Jinnah addressed Gandhi as 'Mr. Gandhi' and he was heckled and humiliated. But in 1944 not a single Gandhite came forward to protest. On the last day, Jinnah dismissed Gandhi by writing, "No responsible organisation can entertain any proposal from any individual, however great he may be, unless it is backed up with the authority of a recognised organisation, and comes from its fully accredited representative". Gandhi never again boasted that he was not even a four anna member of the Congress. Gandhi had been warned for undertaking this misadventure by leaders like M.R. Jayakar. After the failure of the talks, K.M. Munshi wrote to Gandhi, "Your formula is now in Mr. Jinnah's hands and he will use the formula as a bargaining counter with the British government and also as the starting point in future negotiations with Indian leaders". About the Gandhi-Jinnah meeting, Lord Wavell wrote in his *Journal*, "Anything so barren as their exchange of letters is a deplorable exposure of Indian leadership. This surely must blast Gandhi's reputation as a leader. Jinnah had an easy task; he merely had to keep on telling Gandhi he was talking nonsense, which was true and he did so rather rudely."[12] Indeed, this mistake of Gandhi had weakened his position and that of the Congress, and had brought Pakistan several steps nearer. In July 1946, when his biographer, Louis Fischer, asked Gandhi what he had learned from his eighteen days with Jinnah, he replied. "I learned that he (Jinnah) was a maniac. I could not make any headway with Jinnah because he is a maniac". It took Gandhi three decades to understand Jinnah, while Mountbatten reached the same conclusion in his first meeting with Jinnah in March 1947. Gandhi returned to his Wardha Ashram, a dejected man. He became ill, suffering from "bad cold, a bronchitic cough and pain in the chest". Soon he had his fourth nervous breakdown. "He felt so spiritually isolated from his flock and from all India that there were many who wondered whether he would ever resume his political life".[13]

As the withdrawal of the British approached and the top leaders saw power coming in their hands, differences between Gandhi and his colleagues began to crop up and during the talks with the Cabinet Mission (March–June 1946), they became serious. Pyarelal, his secretary, writes, "In that hour of decision they had no use of Bapu. The Cabinet Mission invited the members of the Working Committee to meet them. Bapu, not being a member, was not sent for and did not go. On their return, nobody told Bapu a word about what had happened in the meeting". In a note to G.D. Birla in 1946 Gandhi wrote, "My voice carries no weight in the Working Committee. Today I feel like *Trishanku*. Is it really time for me to retire to the Himalayas"? He felt that he was not wanted in Delhi and left for Noakhali in November 1946, and later, went to Bihar, where serious communal riots had broken out. He came to Delhi at the end of March 1947 at the invitation, not of his colleagues, but of the new viceroy, Mountbatten. The new viceroy had a one line brief: 'Hand over India to the Indians'. It had become dangerous for the British to hold on. As the Muslim League was adamant to have Pakistan and was resorting to large scale rioting and killings, for which the Congress, wedded to non-violence, had to answer for, it was decided by the British to partition the country.

Gandhi attended the meeting of the All India Congress Committee, in which the resolution about accepting the partition of the country was to be discussed and passed. He had already made known his views about the partition of the country. The burden of his speeches and writings during 1940-47 was: Partition of the country on religious basis is an untruth; the only solution to deal with this untruth is to yield to it; if we do not yield, there will be bloodshed and destruction (civil war); there was no other, violent or non-violent method, to solve this problem. In his speech in the AICC (14 June 1947), he forcefully advocated the partition of the country and silenced the opposition led by Puroshotam Das Tandon, J.B. Kriplani and others. The resolution accepting partition was passed by an overwhelming majority. It is travesty of truth to claim that Gandhi was opposed to partition till the very end. Facts do not support that claim. India was partitioned and became independent on 15 August 1947. Two independent dominions were created: India (Bharat) and Pakistan. Gandhi stayed on in Delhi, residing in the Birla House.

The winter of Gandhi's life was a winter of despair. His charisma ceased to work. The masses who used to come for his *darshan*, more often came now to abuse him. his unsympathetic attitude towards the unfortunate millions of Hindus and Sikh refugees (who believed that Gandhi was mainly responsible for their misery) antagonised them. Several of his prayer meetings were disturbed by angry refugees. Nearly ninety-five percent of his mail was full of abuse in those post-Partition days. For millions of Indians, he had become a dangerous man. The worst had yet to come. Late in 1947, war between India and Pakistan broke out over Kashmir. Gandhi went on a fast, forcing the Government of India to release fifty crore rupees to Pakistan, which were held up by the Indian government 'until the Kashmir affair was settled'. This upset many people. He was assassinated on 30 January 1948, while he was coming out to address a prayer meeting in the Birla House garden. His funeral procession was organised as a military operation by the

British commander-in-chief. His body went on its last journey in an army vehicle.

The aftermath of the assassination was horrible, but the details were suppressed by the government. Chitpawan Brahmins (to which caste Nathuram Godse, his assassin, belonged) were the target of the fury of the followers of Gandhi. Nobody knows how many innocent people were killed, their houses burnt down, their property looted in Poona, Bombay, Nagpur, Satara, Belgaum and Kolhapur. One of the rare studies of the post-assassination violence was made by Maureen Patterson who ruefully reported that she was not given access to relevant police files even decades after the incident. She estimated that the death toll may run into hundreds.[14]

After the death of Gandhi, a vast hagiography appeared. Miracles were assigned to him; things he had never done, words he had never spoken, were credited to him. He became a government institution, with his portrait on the walls of Indian embassies abroad and government offices and courts inside India. Across the Raj Ghat in Delhi, where Gandhi was cremated, stands a museum and library to perpetuate the memory of the great man. His few possessions are carefully exhibited there, including the Australian woollen shawl he was wearing at the time of his death.

"There is something in Mahatma Gandhi which appeals to the mass of Indian people. Born in another country, he might have been a complete misfit. What, for instance, would he have done in country like Russia or Germany or Italy. His doctrine of non-violence would have led him to the cross or to the mental hospital", wrote Subhas Chandra Bose.'[15] In an unguarded moment, Gandhi said about himself in a prayer meeting (10 June 1947). "In India, public opinion is not as vigilant as in England. Had it been so, a worthless fellow like me should not have presumed to become a mahatma. And even after I became a mahatma, everything that I did would not have been put-up with. As it is, in India everyone who is called a mahatma ceases to be answerable to the public, whatever — right or wrong — he might do".[16] Gokhale had remarked, while living with Gandhi in South Africa that, "there is arrogance even in Gandhi's humility".

The real tragedy of Gandhi was his family life. He did not care to bring up his four sons like a loving and caring father. As head of the family,

Gandhi was a bully. His wife and children feared him. None of his sons could be called educated in the real sense. The most tragic life was led by his eldest son, Harilal, who became an alcoholic and a pervert and spent last two decades of his life abusing his father whom he believed was responsible for his plight. By his behaviour, Gandhi almost alienated the feelings of his wife Kasturba. No one ever saw her laughing or even smiling. Her spirit was crushed by an autocratic and eccentric husband. But Gandhi had no idea that he was tormenting his wife and sons. "Ba often wondered why her husband acted like God because he was but a mortal like herself. She remembered how he had groaned and moaned when his first molar was extracted". Her being illiterate was a boon for Gandhi. Many secrets and truths about his life were cremated with her in 1944.

In spite of his concern about his health and about preaching others how to keep oneself healthy, Gandhi was not a healthy man. He had been suffering from high blood pressure almost all his adult life. He had pleurisy, piles, appendicitis (1924) and chronic constipation, followed by acute dysentery, which was made worse by frequent fasting. He had bleeding gums and all his teeth had to be extracted before he was fifty. Mentally also he had problems and suffered nervous breakdown four times, the worst collapse being in 1937. "Gandhi's collapses were rarely due solely to overwork. The undoubted physical and mental strain to which he constantly exposed himself was often overlaid with emotional tension or distress which precipated a 'physical collapse'. Although the aging Mahatma seemed to the public a tranquil spirit, he was often moody, and experienced a turbulent anger with himself, his family and his close colleagues".[17]

Those who believe that Gandhi lived the life of a poor Indian farmer will be surprised to learn the kind of diet he used to take. In a letter to Satis Chandra Das Gupta (20 June 1933) Gandhi wrote: "I am taking nearly four lbs of milk and plenty of oranges, pomegranate, juice and grapes. That is my staple food". In his early life, Gandhi was fanatically opposed to taking milk. In a letter to Chhaganlal, (11 March 1914), Gandhi wrote, "The idea of it (milk) is pure flesh, and not in keeping with the way of non-violence, will never leave my mind. I do not think that I shall ever be able to consume milk, *ghee* etc. while I inhabit this body". Gandhi's whole life is full of such contradictions. He could work as recruiting agent for the British army during the war and keep intact his faith in the creed of ahimsa (non-violence). He justified his inconsistencies by quoting Emerson, 'Foolish consistency is the hobgoblin of little minds'. My aim is not to be consistent with the previous statements on a given question, but to be consistent with the truth as it may present itself to me at a given moment. The result has been that I have grown from truth to truth. My words and deeds are dictated by prevailing conditions. There has been a gradual evolution in my environment and I react to it as a satyagrahi. What I am concerned with is my readiness to obey the call of Truth, my God, from moment to moment, and, therefore, when anybody finds any inconsistency between any two writings of mine, if he has still faith in my sanity, he would do well to choose the later of the two on the same subjects".[18]

Gandhi was not only a compulsive speaker and preacher but also a compulsive writer. He believed in the power of the written word. He did not write many books but three of them stand out. A small booklet *Hind Swaraj* (1896) which contains criticism of modern civilisation and machinery. Times have made it outdated and Utopian. *Satyagraha in South Africa* (1928) describes his experiences in South Africa. His best-selling work has been *An Autobiography or The Story of My Experiments with Truth* which was initially written in Gujarati but later translated by him in English (1927). It ends with the Nagpur session of the Congress (1920) but has been the major source of information for his biographers, especially British and American. It has been translated into every Indian language and many foreign languages as well. "Inevitably it omits much that is important and the accounts of the later years is sketchy and disorderly. He occupies the centre of the stage, and has not gift for bringing any other character to life". However, the autobiography does provide a peep into the fascinating character of Gandhi.

As a journalist he has edited, or has been associated with, at least five journals. Most of his journalistic writings are either in Gujarati or in English. In South Africa, he took charge of the *Indian Opinion*, a weekly in Gujarati and English in 1903. In India, he was responsible for bringing out *Navajivan* (Gujarati). *Young India* (English) a weekly started by the Home Rule party of Bombay was taken over by Gandhi in 1919 (ceased publication in 1932). *Harijan* (English), *Harijan Bandhu* (Gujarati) and *Harijan Sevak* (Hindi), started in 1933. Most of his letters, speeches, addresses and miscellanies appeared in these journals, which have been published, meticulously edited, in the hundred volumes of *Collected Works of Mahatma Gandhi*. He had an army of secretaries who recorded for posterity almost every word uttered by Gandhi in speeches or during personal interviews. "No public figure has written so much over such a long period. For the greater part of his adult life we know what he was doing and thinking at every hour of the day".

In spite of his mistakes and failings, he rode like a colossus on the political horizon of India during the first half of the twentieth century. This period is rightly called the Gandhian era. He awakened the masses and moulded them into an army of freedom fighters almost single-handedly. He had mastered the technique of winning over his enemies which added to his greatness. At the same time, Gandhi was a very complex personality. He combined in himself, the dual role of a saint and an active politician. Thus, he tried to ride two horses at the same time. "Unfortunately Gandhi's followers did not make this distinction and gave unto the political leader what was really due to the saint". Even Jawaharlal Nehru, the rationalist, fell into this trap. He wrote, "Gandhi was a unique personality and it was impossible to judge him by the usual standards or even to apply the ordinary canons of logic to him". But history must apply to him the same standards of judgement and criticism as have been applied to all other personalities, great or small, who have played any role in public affairs".[19] The most serious mistake which the followers and admirers of Gandhi make, is when they attribute to him the sole credit for freeing the country from foreign rule. This does great injustice to thousands of freedom fighters and revolutionaries who sacrificed their lives to see India a free country. The most notable name among those freedom fighters is that of Subhas Chandra Bose whom the British feared most and whose exploits in Southeast Asia were the main reason of the hasty retreat of Britain from India, at a time when the Congress leaders, including Gandhi, were an exhausted and harmless lot. When the Bill on 'Granting Freedom to India' came up before the British Parliament, the leader of the opposition, Winston Churchill, took the government to task and demanded reasons for doing so. Prime Minister Attlee gave two reasons:

1. The Indian mercenary army was no more loyal to the British Crown; (obviously referring to the raising of Indian National Army by Subhas Bose);
2. England was not in a position to organise and equip its army on so large a scale as to control India.

   Gandhi was nowhere in the picture.

However, Gandhi did not need any certificate from the British Government confirming his unique services to the nation. There could be no doubt that none in the Freedom Movement played as large a part as Gandhi did. At the same time it must be conceded that he did not work on a virgin soil and did not work alone. There were thousands who sacrificed their very lives for the national cause. But Gandhi certainly walked like a colossus among millions others for more than thirty years.

## References

1. Payne, Robert. *Life and Death of Mahatma Gandhi*. New York, E.P. Dutton. 1969, Rupa Paperback. 1997, p.86.
2. Ibid p.121-22.
3. Thomson, Mark, *Gandhi and his Ashrams*. Bombay. Popular Prakashan.1993, p.38.
4. Nehru, Jawaharlal. *An Autobiography*. London, John Lane. 1936, p.516 Several reprints. Dist. OUP).
5. Tendulkar, D.G. *Mahatma*. New Delhi, Publications Division. Vol.1. (Rev. ed.) 1960, p.90-91.
6. *Collected Works of Mahatma Gandhi*. Vol. 9, p.265.
7. Ibid. Vol.12, p.380.
8. Ambedkar, B.R. *Pakistan or the Partition of India*. Bombay, Thacker & Co. 1946, p.148. (Reprint by Education Dept., Govt. of Maharashtra, 1990).

9. Besant, Annie. *Future of Indian Politics*. Madras Theosophical Publishing House. 1922, p.250.
10. Khaliquzzaman, C. *Pathway to Pakistan*. Lahore, 1961, p.57.
11. *Collected Works of Mahatma Gandhi*. Vol.71, p.388.
12. Payne, Rabert. op. cit. p.512.
13. Moon, Penderel, ed. *Wavell, the Viceroy's Journal* OUP, 1973, p.91.
14. Elst, Koenraad. *Gandhi and Godse*. New Delhi, Voice of India, 2001, p.12-13.
15. Bose, Subhas Chandra. *The Indian Struggle, 1920-1942*. OUP. 1997, p.327-28.
16. *Collected Works of Mahatma Gandhi*. Vol. 88, p.124.
17. Brown, Judith. *Gandhi, Prisoner of Hope*. OUP. p.284.
18. *Collected Works of Mahatma Gandhi*. Vol. 55, p.61.
19. Majumdar, R.C. *History of the Freedom Movement in India*. Calcutta, Firma KLM. Vol. 3, end. ed. 1977., p.XVII.

# Asadullah Khan Ghalib

## (1797-1869)

Ghalib's *shairs* (couplets) are recited and quoted by persons who do not even know the Urdu language. He is the only Urdu poet for whom a research academy has been formed by the Government of India in Delhi. There seems to be no decline in his popularity with the passage of time. Even Nehru used to quote Ghalib's couplets in his letters to friends and relatives. In his *Discovery of India* Nehru writes, "The leading poet in Urdu and one of the outstanding literary figures of the century (nineteenth) in India, was Ghalib, who was in his prime before the Mutiny".[1] There must have been something unique which other Urdu poets lacked.

Ghalib was born on 27 December 1797, at Agra, where his father Abdullah Beg was living with his wife's parents. His father had taken service with the Raja of Alwar, Bhakhtawar Singh and was killed in a battle in 1802. Thereafter, Ghalib and his siblings were taken care of by his uncle Nasrullah Beg Khan. His uncle, who was under the service of the British, also died in 1806. The British gave his family pension, out of which Ghalib's share came to Rs. 750.50 annually and which he continued to receive upto 1857 when the Mutiny broke out.

Ghalib himself wrote about his ancestry in one of his letters to a friend on 15 February 1866; 'I am of Seljuk, Turkish stock. My grandfather came to India from beyond the river (Transoxiana), in Shah Alam's time". The most detailed and authoritative biography of Ghalib is *Yadgar-i-Ghalib* by

Altaf Husain Hali, who was his contemporary and himself a poet of standing. So unlike many other Urdu poets, the life of Ghalib is quite well documented. His own letters to his innumerable friends in Persian as well as in Urdu, are another authentic source of his life and times.

Ghalib's full name was Mirza Asadullah Khan. Ghalib was his *takhallus*, (i.e. an assumed one-word name which Urdu poets use for their works.) Earlier, he also wrote some poetry under the penname 'Asad'. His childhood was spent in Agra in the home of his maternal grandparents, who were quite well-off. Ghalib's father had married into one of the most distinguished families of Agra, and lived most of his life in his in-laws' house. So did his children. Early in life, Ghalib was sent to a *maktab* (school) run by one Muhammad Mu'azzam, a reputed scholar of his time, and Ghalib studied classical Persian prose and poetry under him. Around 1810, there arrived in Agra a Persian traveller, Abdul Samad, who stayed with Ghalib's family for two years. Ghalib learned the intricacies of the Persian language from him. Though Ghalib had no formal *ustad* (guide) as most of the poets of his time used to have, he remained grateful to Abdul Samad throughout his life and often boasted in his letters to his friends that he had learned Persian from an Iranian.

In 1810, at the age of thirteen, he was married to eleven-year-old Umrao Begum, daughter of Nawab Ilahi Bux Ma'aroof, brother of Ahmad Baksh Khan of Loharu. Soon after their marriage, around 1812, Ghalib came to Delhi and settled permanently there, though he frequently visited Agra. Umrao Begum gave birth to at least seven children, but unfortunately none of them survived more than a few months. Even otherwise, it could not be called a happy marriage because the couple had not much in common. According to Hali, his biographer, "Ghalib's wife was an exceedingly pious and sober lady, meticulous in keeping the fasts and in saying her prayers. She was as strict in her religious observations as Ghalib was lax in these matters — so much so that she even kept her own eating and drinking utensils apart from her husband's".[2] Ghalib seems always to have felt that a wife was an encumbrance and he could very well have done without one. He was a frequent visitor to courtesans and even fell in love with at least one of them. Ghalib was tall, handsome with broad shoulders and dressed like an aristocrat, even when he was in financial troubles, which he was during most of his adult life. His pecuniary troubles, to some extent, were of his own making because he lived beyond his means. At no time Ghalib had fewer than five servants, including a maid who helped the ladies with their chores. While going out, he never walked but travelled in a palanquin carried on the shoulders of four men. The total wages of these servants came to about twenty-five rupees per month.[3] He was also fond of rich food and expensive drinks like whiskey and drank daily. He was very proud of his insignificant ancestry, which tempted him to lead a lavish lifestyle, and instilled in him a certain unreasonable pride. When he was offered a job to teach Persian in the newly founded Delhi College, he went there in a palanquin and expected the principal of the College to come out and receive him. When the principal refused to oblige him, Ghalib spurned the offer and never went back.

Due to these habits, Ghalib was always in financial troubles and spent much of his time pursuing his cases of pension from the British and appealing and accepting largesse from Nawabs of Rampur and Lucknow, and later from Bahadur Shah Zafar. Much of his time and energy was wasted 'fighting his pension battles'. His trip to Calcutta, to appeal to the governor-general, took one year and in all, three years to fight his pension case. After all the trouble which he took, he lost the case. Often his friends and disciples, both Muslim and Hindu, who loved him, came to his rescue. He had also started gambling, perhaps to overcome his financial difficulties. At one time his house had become a gambling den, and was raided in 1841 for this unlawful activity. He was fined Rs.100 and let off by the British authorities. But he did not desist from gambling. In 1847, he was caught again. This time he was fined Rs.200 and sentenced to six month rigorous imprisonment, but was released after three months. This must be one of the most distressing experiences of his life. Most of his friends deserted him; only Nawab Mustafa Khan Shefta stood by him and used to visit him regularly in prison.

Ghalib did not believe in religious rituals. He never prayed or fasted, and was accustomed to drinking daily. According to Hali, Ghalib believed that "the long and respectable pedigree of a particular doctrine did not guarantee its correctness; that human fallibility was as evident in former days as now, and that a man must use his own judgement to decide on the correctness or otherwise of an accepted belief. His whole temperament drove him to reject any idea of the absolute finality of anything that had happened in the past".[4] In modern parlance, he was a rationalist. Ghalib came from Sunni stock, but at some stage of his life became a Shia, or if not actually a Shia, one closely sympathetic to the Shia belief. In fact, when he died, there was a dispute between Sunnis and Shias regarding his burial ceremony. But at the end, Sunnis prevailed and he was buried as a Sunni.

He had little respect for the *maulvis* who preached in the mosques and made fun of them in his poetry:

*Ham ko maloom hai jannat ki haqiqat lekin*
*Dil ko khush rakhne ko Ghalib ye khayal achha hai.*

(We know the reality about Paradise but it is a good idea to keep oneself happy.)

Again:

*Kahan maikhane ka darwaza Ghalib aur kahan waiz*
*Par itna jante hain, kal woh jata tha ki hum nikle*

(Ghalib cannot think of the preacher entering the doors of the bar but he knows this much that yesterday he was going in while he (Ghalib) was coming out.)

Muslims accepted these barbs in good humour and took these as poetic licence.

Ghalib was thus completely devoid of religious bigotry or racial prejudices. He had as many Hindu friends as Muslims. In a letter to Tafta he says, "I hold all human beings, whether Musalman, Hindu or Christian, dear to me and regard them as my brothers". One of his servants was a Hindu, who served him throughout his life.

Ghalib started composing Urdu and Persian poetry at a very young age but he concentrated the next twenty-five or thirty years on writing Persian poetry. He even wrote letters to his friends in Persian during this early period. Thus, his output in Persian far exceeds that of Urdu. While his '*Dewan*' (collection) of Persian poetry has over eleven thousand verses, his Urdu collection has only two thousand verses which were selected by Ghalib himself, discarding another three thousand which he considered not upto the mark. Two compilations of Ghalib's Persian poems were published in his life time: *Mekhana-i-Arzoo Saranjam* (1845) and *Kulyat-i-Nazm-i-Farsi* (1862). His prose works in Persian are: *Panjahang, Mehri-i-Neemroz* and *Dastanba. Panjhand* consists of five parts and contains his Persian letters which he wrote to his friends before the Mutiny. *Mehr-i-Neemroz* is the story of the Timur dynasty, which Ghalib was commissioned to write in 1850 by Bahadur Shah Zafar. Ghalib was getting a stipend of Rs.600 annually for writing this. Only the first volume could be completed which ends with Humayun's return to the throne. *Dastanbo* was written during 1857-58, when Ghalib was holed up in his house and describes what happened during those days in Delhi. It is mostly in praise of the British. Six out of its eighty pages are devoted to a 'qasida' of Queen Victoria. It must have helped Ghalib to get his pension restored by the British, which had been stopped in 1857. Ghalib also wrote a critique of a Persian dictionary *Burhan-i-Qateh*, under the title *Qateh-i-Burhan*, which raised a lot of controversy among the literary circles of the day.

Ghalib was proud of his Persian poetry and dismissed his Urdu poetry as of no consequence. He wrote:

*Farsi bin ta babini naqsh-hai rangarang*
*Bigyzar az majmua-i-Urdu ki be rang-i-manast.*

(Read my Persian verses if you want to see pictures of various hues.
Overlook my Urdu collection for it is devoid of my true colour.)

Ironically, it is the Urdu poetry which has made him famous and popular with the masses. Very few are familiar with his Persian poetry. Later, Iqbal's Persian poetry and writings also met the same fate.

As stated above, Ghalib wrote much less in Urdu. Several versions of his '*Dewan*' were published in his lifetime spanning several years. He himself had selected two thousand verses out of five thousand and called it the real 'dewan' of Ghalib. But after his death, these three thousand discarded verses have also been included in his later 'Dewan'. One consolidated 'Dewan' was published in 1951, by Panna Lal Bhargava, proprietor Munshi Publishers, Lucknow. By the time Ghalib's first 'Dewan' was published in the 1830s he had already become famous and was participating in *mushairas* held in the Red Fort by Bahadur Shah Zafar and other places like Lucknow, Rampur etc. Several Nawabs and rulers of states had become his *shagird* (disciples) and used to get their verses corrected or improved by him. This correction work of various disciples and admirers, who used to send their poetry to him in a continuous stream, he did till his last days and seemed to have enjoyed doing so. Ghalib's prestige was considerably enhanced when in 1854, 'Zauq', the court poet died and Badshah Zafar appointed Ghalib as the court poet and his own *ustad* (guru). Two of the princes also became his disciples.

Ghalib is remembered as an Urdu poet because he transformed the entire spirit of ghazal writing. "He broadened its spire from a mere love prattle to encompass the whole gamut of man's life and experiences. The thought contained in Ghalib's verses is for the most part expressed in strikingly original manner".[5] Besides the subtle style of presentation of his thoughts, he added humour into his writings, often tongue-in-cheek, which set him apart making him a rage for a century and a half. Some of his verses are so subtle that scholars and critics have been arguing for decades about their deeper meanings. However, Hali's interpretation, given in *Yadgar-i-Ghalib* are considered most authentic because he had discussed the interpretations of many of such verses with Ghalib himself. But Hali does not cover all such controversial verses.

Ghalib's prose is mainly represented in his letters, which he wrote to his friends, disciples and benefactors, during the last two decades of his life. Earlier, he used to correspond in Persian. The language of Ghalib's letters has a unique flavour. He addresses the person as if he was sitting in front of him. He had cut down the flabbiness and superfluous elements from Urdu prose. His prose sparkles with wit and drollery. Even his barbs are good-humoured, incapable of offending the person towards whom they are directed. Ghalib enjoyed repartee and people flocked to him to hear his witticism, *à la* Voltaire. Ghalib had genuine love for his friends and disciples whom he tried to help in all possible ways. Of course, he had his enemies and critics but their number was insignificant as compared to the overwhelming number of his admirers.

Ghalib's letters throw a flood of light on his times, especially on the events during the Mutiny. He was distressed, which is evident from his letters, because many of his relatives and friends were hanged or imprisoned by the British. Two collections of his letters *Ud-i-Hindi* (1868) and *Urdu-i-Mualla* (1869), were compiled during his lifetime, though the latter was published a month after his death. Many other letters have been discovered and published since. Through these letters, Ghalib "initiated a simple, natural and fascinating style of prose, which became a model for other writes and laid the foundation of chaste modern Urdu". But Ghalib, among the multitude is remembered for his verses only.

Ghalib never built a house and spent all his life in rented houses, but remained mostly in Gali Qasim Jan of Mohalla Ballimaran, near Chandni Chowk in Delhi. The last house which he occupied was near a mosque. Ghalib writes:

*Masjid ke zer-i-saya ik ghar bana liya hai*
*Ye banda-i-kameena hamsaya-i-khuda hai*

(Ghalib has taken residence under the shadow of a mosque. This mean person is now a neighbour of God.)

Wit and humour did not desert him till the end.

During the last years of his life he had lost the ability to hear and his vision too failed him. After a long illness he died on 15 February 1869, and was buried in Hazrat Nizamuddin, beside Amir Khusro.

## References

1. Nehru, Jawaharlal. *Discovery of India*, New Delhi, Jawaharlal Nehru Memorial Fund. 1946, p.346.

2.  Quoted by Ralph Russell and Khurshidul Islam: *Ghalib: 1797-1869, Vol.1; Life and Letters*. London, George Allen & Unwin, 1969, p.104.
3.  Sud, K.N. *Eternal Flame; Aspects of Ghalib's Life and Works*. New Delhi, Sterling, 1969, p.20.
4.  Russell op.cit. p.34.
5.  Sud, K.N. op.cit. p.61.

# Aurobindo Ghose

## (1872-1950)

Aurobindo was born in Calcutta on 13 August 1872. His father, Krishnadhan Ghose, a civil surgeon, had a medical degree from Aberdeen University (Scotland), and had come back fully westernized. His mother Swaranlata was the daughter of Rajnarain Bose, a Brahmo and a distinguished Bengali of the nineteenth century. Aurobindo was the third son of five children of his parents.

Aurobindo's father was so influenced by Western culture that he wanted his children to have 'an entirely European upbringing.' The three brothers were sent to Loreto Convent in Darjeeling, an English medium school. Their father also had arranged an English nurse to train his children in English customs and manners. At home, the family spoke only English and Hindustani. Aurobindo learnt Bengali late in life.

When Aurobindo was seven, his father took the three brothers to England for their education. Aurobindo studied privately from 1879 to 1884, under Mr. and Mrs. Drewett. But in 1884, he was sent to St. Paul School in London, where during his five years stay he learnt Greek and Latin. He also learnt Italian, some German and a little Spanish. It was during this time that he started writing poetry — a hobby and a passion which he carried to Cambridge and indeed continued throughout his life. He excelled academically and won a scholarship to the King's College, Cambridge. While in the final year at St. Paul's, he got through the ICS open competition getting a good position but managed to fail in the riding test and was disqualified much to the chagrin of his father.

From St. Paul, Aurobindo came to King's College, Cambridge, where he studied from 1890 to 1892; passed the first part of the Tripos but did not graduate. After staying for nearly fourteen years in England, he sailed back to India and joined the Baroda State Service. From 1893 to 1906, he was serving in Baroda; first as a probationary officer in the Revenue Settlement Department and later as a lecturer in French and then shifting to English language and literature in the Baroda College. When he left the College, he was the vice-principal, getting a salary of Rs. 750 per month. During his stay in Baroda, he learnt Sanskrit, Marathi and Gujarati and copiously wrote prose and verse in the English language. He also contributed a series of articles in the *Indu Prakash*, Bombay, during August 1893 and February 1894, under the title *New Lamps for Old*. But the publication of his articles was stopped after only two articles (out of the proposed nine) as the publishers feared that it may result in a sedition charge. Thereafter, Aurobindo 'drew back in silence' and worked surreptitiously till 1905.

In 1901, Aurobindo married Mrinalini Devi, daughter of Bhupalchandra. When Aurobindo left for Pondicherry, he did not take her with him. Mrinalini passed her days in religious pursuits and died in 1918, a forlorn lady.

The partition of Bengal by Viceroy Lord Curzon, resulted in the awakening of Bengal and a movement for the annulment of partition was launched, culminating in an outburst of revolt against the government. Aurobindo had been visiting Bengal during vacations in his college and had come in contact with revolutionaries like P. Mitra, president of the Anusilan Samiti, Sister Nivedita and other revolutionary leaders and had even joined a splinter group of revolutionaries for some time.

The *Swadeshi* movement ushered in by the partition of Bengal brought out the sense of nationalism in the masses of India. Aurobindo could not resist the temptation to jump in and contribute his share in the national struggle. When the National Council of Education set up National College and School in August 1906, in Calcutta, Aurbindo resigned from the Baroda service and became its first principal, on a nominal salary. But soon he veered round to active politics. He started writing inflammatory articles in *Yuganter*, a Bengali daily started by the revolutionaries in 1906. He joined the daily newspaper *Bandematram*, started by Bipin Chandra Pal in 1906, as its editor. As *Bandematram* demanded his full-time attention Aurobindo resigned from the National College. Sometime in December 1906, Bipin Chandra separated from *Bandematram*, leaving Aurobindo in control of the paper. In article after article in the *Bandematram*, Aurobindo spelled out the programme and agenda of the Nationalist party and advocated complete independence through *swadeshi*, boycott, national education, non-cooperation and passive-resistance. In his articles he also developed a political philosophy of revolution and wrote that many leaders 'aimed at destroying the shibboleths and superstitions of the Moderate party such as the belief in British justice and benefits bestowed by foreign government in India'. Because of this aggressive publicity (in the *Bandematram*), the ideas of the nationalists gained ground everywhere. The *Bandematram* was almost unique in journalistic history in the influence it 'exercised in converting the mind of a people and preparing it for revolution'.[1] Soon Aurobindo emerged as a great nationalist along with national leaders like Tilak and Lajpat Rai. People started looking to him as the new messiah, who would deliver the nation from foreign bondage.

In 1907, the government began taking repressive measures against the press. *Bandematram* was the first one to be charged for sedition. On 16 August 1907, an arrest warrant was issued against Aurobindo for publishing a letter titled *'Politics for Indians'*. However, he was acquitted on 23 September. "The arrest and the nonchalant attitude of Aurobindo inspired Rabindranath Tagore to write a beautiful poem which begins with 'Arabinda Rabindrer laha namaskar' (Rabindranath, Oh! Aurobindo, bows to thee). The *Bandematram* case added to the fame and stature of Aurobindo in national politics.

On 30 April 1908, a bomb was thrown at a carriage in Muzaffarpur (Bihar) which killed two British ladies, Mrs. Kennedy and her daughter, mistaking the carriage as that of Kingsford, who, as chief presidency magistrate, had pronounced hard sentences on the revolutionaries while posted at Calcutta. The bomb was thrown by Khudiram Bose and Prafulla Chaki who met a martyr's death. A wave of shock and consternation shook India, followed by unprecedented repression. In May 1908, thirty-seven persons were arrested for the crime which included Aurobindo and his brother Barindra, who was active as a revolutionary. All of them were put on trial. Consequently, Aurobindo spent one year in jail. The defence council for Aurobindo was C.R. Das who argued for eight days. He concluded with the statement: "Long after this controversy is hushed in silence, long after the turmoil, this agitation ceases, long after he is dead and gone, he will be looked upon as the poet of partriotism, as the prophet of nationalism, and the lover of humanity. Long after he is dead and gone, his words will be echoed and re-echoed not only in India but across distant seas and lands. Therefore, I say that the man in his position is not only standing before the Bar of this court but before the Bar of the High Court of history".[2] Aurobindo was released after the trial but he had already spent one year in Alipore jail.

When he came out of the jail on 6 May 1909, Aurobindo was a completely changed man. Though he had been practicing yoga since 1904, in the seclusion of the prison cell he reached much higher in the realm of yoga and had deep spiritual experiences. But he did not quit politics immediately. After the closure of *Bandematram*, he had started two magazines, a weekly *Karamyogin* (19 June 1909) in English and *Dharma* a weekly in Bengali, in collaboration with Sister Nivedita and some others. In these two journals, he wrote articles on the 'deeper significance of Indian nationalism'. He still seemed to exert great influence on the younger generation and even the elder statesmen listened to him. His motto 'No compromise' rankled the government and they were busy finding an excuse to nab him once again. He got an inkling of that and wrote 'An Open Letter to My Countrymen' published in *Karamyogin* on 31 July 1909 in which he affirmed the nationalist political programme. This letter is considered as his last political will and testament. The government got even more apprehensive about his activities. In February 1910, Aurobindo received information that the office of the *Karamyogin* would be searched and he would be arrested. To avoid another arrest and jail term, he left for Chandernagore, a French enclave. After staying there for sometime he reached Pondicherry on 4 April 1910, another French settlement in India. He spent the rest of his life there.

Soon after his arrival in Pondicherry he was joined there by a French couple Paul Richard and his wife Mirra, who later became famous as the Mother. Jointly they started an English monthly the *Arya*, a philosophical review, in August 1914 in which were revealed new truths about man's divine destiny and the path for its realisation. It also contained the inner meaning of the *Vedas*, the *Upanishads* and the *Gita* as well as the significance of Indian culture and civilization. It also contained a French section. The *Arya* ceased publication in 1921 but its contents were later published in several books authored by Aurobindo: *The Life Divine, Synthesis of Yoga, The Human Cycle, The Ideal of Human Unity, The Future Poetry, On the Vedas, The Upanishad, Essays on the Gita* and *Foundations of Indian Culture*.

Aurobindo's life in Pondicherry is a closed book, though off and on he reacted to the political situation developing in the country and the world at large. For example, in 1940, he advised the Congress to accept the Cripps proposals which the Congress rejected. During the Second World War, he expressed his sympathies with the British and the Allied powers, notwithstanding his anatagonism to the British rule earlier. He even wrote a poem about Hitler's triumphant march through the countries of Europe titled *The Children of Wotan* (Wotan is a Germanic god), a few lines of which read:

Where is the end of your armourmed march,
O Children of Wotan?
Earth shudders with fear at your tread,
The death flame laughs in your eyes.

In Pondicherry, several ex-revolutionaries and other seekers of truth and salvation joined Aurobindo. He called them *sadhaks* (seekers). Gradually, an ashram developed with strict rules of conduct. But in 1926, Aurobindo retired into seclusion, which he maintained till his death, handing over the management of the ashram to the Mother. For forty years he shut himself up in his ashram and refused to see people from outside. In December 1933, Gandhi expressed a desire to see Aurobindo and the Mother. When Gandhi's letter was shown to Aurobindo by a disciple he wrote on it in pencil: "You will have to write that I am unable to see him (Gandhi) because for a long time past I have made it an absolute rule not to have any interview with anyone—that I even do not speak with my disciples and only give silent blessings to them three times a year. All requests for an interview from others I have been obliged to refuse. The rule has been imposed on me by the necessity of my *sadhana* (spiritual pursuit) and is not at all a matter of convenience or anything else. The time has not come when I can depart from it".[3] That gives a glimpse of Aurobindo's life in his ashram in Pondicherry.

Aurobindo died of kidney trouble on 26 November 1950 leaving behind the ashram where over two thousand of his followers (*sadhaks*) live today as a well-knit community. There is also a Sri Aurobindo International Centre of Education, which runs several educational institutions on principles taught by Aurobindo. Auroville, an international commune, is where nationals of various countries reside.

Aurobindo's role in the freedom movement and later as a yogi and philosopher has dwarfed his talent as a poet. "Sri Arvind's original verses as well as translations of portions of the *Mahabharat* and the *Ramayan*, devotional songs of Chandidasa and Vidyapati and Bhartrihari bespeak of his poetic talents; his writings are refulgent with rich imagery, buoyancy, mysticism, originality of approach and refineness of style. And even in his sardonic poems he could weave good poetic garlands".[4] The culmination of Aurobindo's poetic genius is reflected 'in his supreme spiritual work' in blank verse, *Savitri*, perhaps the longest epic poem in the English language: An American critic called it 'a great cosmic poem'. It is in three parts. The first part was published in 1950 just before Aurobindo's death, while part two and three were published in 1951.

Thus, with his few golden utterances and many silences, Aurobindo left his indelible marks on the hearts of his people, and on the sands of history.

## References

1. *Sri Aurobindo On Himself*. (His Collected Works) Pondicherry, Sri Aurobindo Ashram, vol. 26, 1972, p.29-30.

2. Agarwal, B.R. *Trials of Independence*. New Delhi, National Book Trust. 1991, p.69.
3. *Collected Works of Mahatma Gandhi*. New Delhi, Publications Division. Vol. 56, 1973, p.499.
4. Sinha, R.P.N. *The Birth and Development of Indo-English Verse*. New Delhi, Dev Publishing House, 1971, p.167.

# Gopal Krishna Gokhale

## (1866-1915)

Gopal Krishna Gokhale, son of Krishna Rao Shridhar and Satyabhama, was born in Ratnagiri district of Maharashtra on 6 May 1866. They were poor but respectable Chitpawan Brahmins. Gopal had no difficulty in getting a formal education though his father had died when he was only thirteen. After finishing primary education in a village school, he studied at Rajaram College, Kolhapur, Deccan College, Poona and Elphinston College, Bombay, from where he graduated in 1884. He also joined a law course there but left the college without completing it.

Gokhale was married at the age of fourteen to Savitribai, who soon developed some chronic disease. Consequently he was married a second time in 1887. Unfortunately, his second wife died in 1900, while giving birth to her second daughter. Soon after, the first wife also died. Gokhale remained a widower for the rest of his life.

Soon after his graduation, Gokhale joined the Deccan Education Society founded in 1884 by Tilak, Agarkar and others. When Fergusson College was opened by the society in 1885, Gokhale was invited teach English literature and mathematics. He taught in the College for eighteen years, retiring in 1904. At different times he taught History, Economics, Political Science, besides English literature and Mathematics and was nicknamed 'professor-to-order', demonstrating his wide knowledge of subjects. However, gradually Economics became his favourite subject. He studied the economic conditions of the country in depth, enabling him to use this knowledge later in his political career, especially during Assembly debates on the budget.

In 1886, Gokhale was introduced to Mahadev Govind Ranade, an influential political leader and social reformer, and started his political apprenticeship under him. Though a high government official (he was a judge of the high court), Ranade devoted much of his time in political and social activities. Gokhale's later political life was largely shaped by his mentor's liberalism and moderate philosophy. Ranade also introduced Gokhale to journalism. To begin with, Gokhale started writing articles for *Mahratta*, an English weekly started by Chiplunkar, Tilak, Agarkar and other young men. When Agarkar left *Kesri* due to differences with Tilak, he had started *Sudharak*, an Anglo-Marathi weekly. Gokhale joined this venture and edited its English section for four years, while Agarkar looked after the Marathi section. From 1887 to 1896, under the inspiration of Ranade, Gokhale edited the *Quarterly*, a journal of the Poona Sarvajanik Sabha. In 1895, Gokhale started the *Rashtra Sabha Samachar* which, however, did not last long. As a journalist, Gokhale did not have the kind of impact which Tilak had with his earthy similies and bold editorials.

Gokhale joined the Indian National Congress in 1889. The following year he was made secretary of the Poona Sarvajanik Sabha, the leading political and social organisation of Maharashtra. In 1893, he was elected secretary of the Bombay Provincial Conference and two years later (1895), he became joint secretary of the Indian National Congress along with Tilak. In 1896, he collaborated with Ranade to form the Deccan Sabha to counter the Sarvajanik Sabha which Tilak and his orthodox followers had captured earlier.

In 1897, Gokhale was among the four Indians invited to London to give evidence before the Royal Commission on Indian Expenditure, popularly known as Welby Commission (after the name of its chairman Lord Welby). Gokhale's written and oral evidence before the commission was universally appreciated, reflecting his deep knowledge of Indian economic problems. This first visit to England gave Gokhale a chance to meet the liberal minded British statesmen and thinkers, including John Morley who later became secretary of state for India and developed a lasting friendship with Gokhale. Gokhale, thereafter, became a familiar figure in London circles, visiting that country seven times from 1897 to 1914.

Gokhale was elected to the Bombay Legislative Council in 1900, from the constituency earlier represented by Tilak. But only after two years he was elected to the Imperial Legislative Council on the seat vacated by Pherozshah Mehta. He was a member of this august body till 1911, being elected successively for three terms. In these councils, he was virtually the leader of the opposition. In the Imperial Council he was particularly noted for his 'impressive participation' in the annual debate on the budget. In 1904, he was awarded a C.I.E. (Companion of the Order of the Indian Empire).

The most important year in Gokhale's life was perhaps 1905. In June 1905, he founded the Servants of India Society in Poona "with the object of training men to devote themselves to the service of India as national missionaries and to promote by all constitutional means the national interests of the Indian people". Gandhi, in one of his letters to his nephew in 1910, criticised the working of the society saying that "it was simply an indifferent imitation of the West. Is it proper for the 'servants' to have servants? I do feel that the aims of Phoenix (his settlement in South Africa) as well as the way of life there surpasses those of the Society".[1] Ironically, when Gandhi returned from South Africa early in 1915, he wanted to join the xociety but his application was rejected with the remarks that "his (Gandhi's) ideals and methods of work and those of the Society were different and it would not be proper for him to join".[2] Gokhale considered the founding of the society as his greatest achievement and the future of the society was on his mind even at the time of his death. The Society attracted important persons who devoted their lives for its work: Srinivasa Sastri, Thakhar Bapa, N.M. Joshi, H.N. Kunzru and others.

In 1905, Gokhale went to England a second time as a delegate of the Congress, along with Lajpat Rai, to enlighten the British public opinion about conditions in India on the eve of the general elections there.

It was also in 1905 that Gokhale was elected president of the Indian National Congress for the Banaras session and emerged as one of the leaders of the 'moderate' group along with Pherozeshah Mehta and Dinshaw Wacha. This was the year when militant nationalism took root in Bengal, and later in India, as a result of the partition of Bengal by Lord Curzon. The movement for the annulment of partition was led by a section of Congressmen, Tilak, Lajpat Rai, B.C. Pal (Bal, Lal and Pal) and others, who came to be known as 'extremist'. Thousands of youths joined the movement and terrorist activities were resorted to. The government used repressive meansures but the movement could not be crushed. In the Calcutta session of the Congress (1906), resolutions were passed advocating self-rule, swadeshi, boycott and national education. While Gokhale and other moderates were opposed to the partition of Bengal and favoured swadeshi as an economic measure to ameliorate the condition of the masses, they were against self-rule, boycott and national education. Gokhale considered the British rule as an 'irrevocable necessity' which had done immense good to India. He wanted to depend on the generosity and democratic traditions of the British people to get instalments of reforms. Extremists called it the 'policy of mendicancy' and thus humiliating. Gokhale also believed that Western learning was a 'liberating force' for India and should not be replaced by national education. Gokhale was also opposed to boycott and believed that "boycott has a sinister meaning and it implies a vindictive desire to injure another". In short, Gokhale and other moderates did not want to offend the British in any way. Consequently, moderates criticised both the ultimate goal set up by the extremists as well as their methods to achieve it.

The conflict between the two factions of the Congress came in the open in the Surat Session of the Congress in 1907. The session was controlled by the moderates, Surat being the stronghold of Pherozeshah Mehta. They manoeuvered not to get the resolutions passed in Calcutta confirmed, going against the usual practice after each session. When Tilak went up the rostrum to move an amendment about the Calcutta resolutions, hell was let lose. Chairs were thrown at the rival group and a shoe was hurled at Tilak who ducked and the shoe landed on the face of Pherozeshah Mehta. This was a most disgraceful incident in the history of the Congress. Tilak and other extremists were expelled from the Congress. The Surat split not only weakened the Congress, it virtually destroyed its effectiveness till the Lucknow reunion in 1916. The extremists (nationalists) were persecuted by the government; the moderates were abandoned by its own people.

Soon followed Tilak's conviction in a sedition case in 1908 and he was sentenced to six years internment in Mandalay jail. This had a grave consequences for Gokhale and his party. Gokhale was accused of being an instigator for Tilak's conviction through Secretary of State Morley while in London. He was subjected to continuous sniping in the local Marathi press. He was lampooned by cartoonists and vilified in malicious verses sung in the Ganpati festival processions in Poona.[3] To add to the dilemma of moderates, Congress sessions had become increasingly dull and insipid. Gokhale wanted the extremists to come back and revitalise the Congress but in the absence of Tilak it could not be possible.

Gokhale visited England thrice during 1905 to 1908. In 1905, he went in a delegation of the Congress along with Lajpat Rai to enlighten British public opinion about the conditions in India on the eve of general elections in that country, as stated earlier. In 1906, he went again to plead for reforms with British liberal leaders and parliamentarians. The visit in 1908 was essentially to meet Lord Morley, secretary of state for India. He had several meetings with Morley about the proposed reforms, later known as Morley-Minto Reforms under the Act of 1909. Gokhale was kept in the dark by Morley about the true nature of reforms. Gokhale evidently failed to distinguish between Morley the writer and philosopher and Morley the bureaucrat. The reforms were much below the expectations of the Indian people. The worst part was the ominous clause which gave Muslims separate electorate and other concessions. Gokhale agreeing to separate electorates for the Muslims showed his meekness and lack of farsightedness. The Reforms gave "statutory recognition at the highest legislative level to the communal separateness which had plagued Indian society with its divisive influence since the mass Muslim invasions of the Hindu subcontinent at the start of the eleventh century. Perhaps it would have been asking too much of him to have been able to anticipate how the mushrooming of this communal representational demand was to result within four decades in the tragic partition of the sub-continent. Just as the nationalist party reviled Gokhale for cooperating with the government so now many of his own Congress supporters accused him of showing excessive favouratism towards Muslims".[4]

Gokhale's speeches and letters are replete with criticism of the British economic policies which had resulted in India's poverty and distress of the masses. He criticised heavy taxation including salt-tax and unreasonably high land revenue which had ruined the farmers. He was an advocate of swadeshi along with industrialisation. But his criticism of the government had hardly any effect on their policies. They just ignored what he said or wrote because they knew that it was not backed by mass agitation. His was benign criticism, they believed. Gokhale was even ready to support the government when they resorted to high handedness. When the Indian Press Act was passed in 1910 to throttle the Indian press and was rightly condemned by public opinion throughout the country, Gokhale supported the Act in the Imperial Legislative Council saying, "My Lord, in ordinary times I should have deemed it my duty to resist such proposals to the utmost of my power. The risks involved in them are grave and obvious. But in view of the situation that exists in several parts of the country today, I have reluctantly come, after a careful and obvious consideration, to the conclusion, that I should not be justified in opposing the principle of the Bill".[5] It seems Gokhale was unconscious of his unpopularity.

As a social reformer he was against caste system, untouchability, child marriage and other ills of the society which invited the ire of the orthodoxy as was experienced by Ram Mohan Roy, Swami Dayanand and other reformers including his 'guru' Ranade, before him.

In 1912, Gokhale was nominated as a member of the Islington Commission on Public Service. He visited England in 1912, 1913 and 1914 in connection with the interrogation work of the commission which sapped his energy. He became quite weak and a tired man and during the later stages he had lost interest in the commission's work. By the time the commission's work was completed and its report submitted, Gokhale was dead.

In 1912, Gokhale went to South Africa from England at the invitation of Gandhi who needed his support for his satyagraha work. He was well-received there and drew appreciative crowds. Gandhi was with him all the time during his visits to various places in South Africa. He was in South Africa for twenty-six days, almost the whole of October.

Gokhale started having indifferent health even before his old age. His frequent visits to England certainly affected his health. He died when he was hardly forty-nine years old in Poona, in February, 1915. When he saw that his end was near he called the members of the Servants of India Society to his bedside and said, "Do not occupy yourself with writing my biography or spend your time in putting up my statues. If you are true *servants* of India, dedicate your lives to the fulfillment of our aims, to the service of India".

Tilak, who had gone to Sinhgad, a health resort for rest, rushed to Poona hearing the news of Gokhale's death. At the cremation ground Tilak made a brief speech, "This is time for shedding tears. This diamond of India, this jewel of Maharashtra, the prince of workers is laid to eternal rest on the funeral ground. Look at him and try to emulate him".

# References

1.  *Collected Works of Mahatma Gandhi* Vol. 10, p.138-139.
2.  Deogirikar, T.R. *Gopal Krishna Gokhale*. New Delhi, Publication Division, 1964, p.173.
3.  Nanda, B.R. *Gokhale and the Indian Moderates and the British Raj*. New Delhi, OUP. 1979, p.474.
4.  Wolpert, Stanley A. *Tilak and Gokhale*. OUP. 1961, p.234-35.
5.  Ibid. p.243.

# Lala Har Dayal

## (1884-1939)

Har Dayal was born on 14 October 1884 at Delhi, to Bholi Rani and Gauri Dayal Mathur, who was a reader in the district court of Delhi. The couple had seven children; four sons and three daughters. Har Dayal was the sixth child. Gauri Dayal was a scholar of Persian and Urdu and Har Dayal inherited the love of the two languages from his father. In later life he learnt several other languages including Sanskrit, Hindi, and almost all the European languages.

Har Dayal's formal education started at the age of four when he joined the primary section of the Cambridge Mission School, Delhi. He was a very bright student, with a phenomenal memory. He always stood first in class. He passed his middle school examination at the age of twelve and the matriculation examination at fourteen. He earned Bachelor of Arts degree from St. Stephen's College, Delhi and joined Government College, Lahore from where he passed M.A. examination in English literature in 1903 and obtained another M.A. degree in History the following year, standing first in both the examinations. What set him apart from other students was not only the marks obtained in the examinations but his love for reading. He was a voracious reader, often finishing a book in a day, retaining in memory what he had read. He was selected for a state scholarship by the Government of India which provided him two hundred pounds annually for a three-year study in England. It also provided a round trip passage. He left India in 1905, at the age of twenty-one, to join Oxford University. Before, he left for England, he had already been married at the age of seventeen (1901) to Sundar Rani, daughter of wealthy Lala Gopal Chand. A son was born to the couple after two years of marriage but the child lived only for ten months. A daughter Shanti was born five years later in 1908.

At Oxford, he joined St. John's College and proposed to read for the Honour School in Modern History. At the university of Punjab, Lahore, he had been an Aitchison-Ramrattan Sanskrit Scholar, and he continued his studies in Sanskrit at Oxford, and was made a Boden Sanskrit Scholar. He was also designated Cashered Exhibitioner in History. These honours carried with them stipends amounting to £130. There seems to be little doubt that Har Dayal made his mark in academics at Oxford. But it seems that he was feeling extremely homesick and at the end of his first term at Oxford, he left for Delhi and brought back his wife with him in spite of stiff opposition from his family as well as from that of his wife. That was in the summer of 1906. In England, Har Dayal had a wider range of friends and acquaintances than most Indian students studying there. He met G.B. Shaw and the poet laureate Robert Bridges, who spoke of Har Dayal "in the highest terms, both of his character and his intellectual attainments". He also made the 'pilgrimage' to see Alexander Kropotkin, the Russian anarchist who was living in England at that time. He also visited London frequently and met Shyamaji Krishna Verma, the Indian nationalist who had established the India House in London and was editor and publisher of *Indian Sociologist*. In the India House, Har Dayal also met V.D. Savarkar who was the acknowledged leader of the revolutionaries connected with the India House. Har Dayal was greatly impressed by Savarkar's nationalistic views and was initiated into the Abhinav Bharat, a party founded by Savarkar, and took the required oath. Har Dayal was now in the company of great nationalists and revolutionaries. This was the time when Savarkar was distributing the *Bomb Manual* to revolutionaries and trying to send arms to India. Har Dayal's association with Savarkar was noticed by the British secret agents, "though Har Dayal was never personally identified with violence, his career was both directly or indirectly influenced by the cult of the bomb". The arrest of Lala Lajpat

Rai and Ajit Singh and their deportation to Mandalay (1907) affected Har Dayal's sensitive mind. He decided to discontinue his studies at Oxford in the fall of 1907 and decided not to accept any money in future as scholarship from the British government. He wrote to Oxford: "I am unable to continue my studies for the Final Examination. I request the favour of your allowing me to withdraw from the College. I am sincerely sorry that I find myself unable to finish my course of studies". He had already put in two and a half years at the College and was to finish his studies after six months. He did not give any reason for his action. Neither had the university nor the government found any "political misconduct or indiscretion" on his part.

During the interim, between the resignation of his government scholarship and his return to India, Har Dayal started wearing a kurta (long shirt) and *dhoti*, discarding Western clothes and became a strict vegetarian. Actually Har Dayal's nationalism became an overriding commitment during his Oxford days which included his visits to the India House and meeting with revolutionaries like Shyamaji Krishna Varma, Savarkar and Madame Cama. His identification with extremism was evident not only in his political views but also in his conduct. "His almost total rejection of everything Western was more than just eccentricity".

Har Dayal returned to India in January 1908. He wanted to be a 'political missionary' or a 'wandering friar of freedom' to the chagrin of his relatives, especially his father-in-law who saw his daughter's life being ruined. Har Dayal, however, put aside affection for his wife, their little daughter, and his brothers and sisters to become 'a mendicant agitator'. During his brief stay in India, he wrote articles in various papers including Lajpat Rai's *Panjabee* on different subjects. In these articles he attacked the British educational system, which he thought was the cause of many ills of the country. These articles were later published in a book titled *Our Educational Problem*. Har Dayal returned to England in September 1908. The reason for his leaving India was that "repressive laws and spies were making further work impossible within the country". He never set foot on Indian soil again and spent the remaining thirty years of his life in exile. On his return to England, he started living at Oxford. It is difficult to know exactly what Har Dayal was doing during his stay in Oxford (September

1908 to February 1909) beyond continuing "to contribute his diatribes to the Lahore newspapers". According to Madame Cama, Har Dayal lived during this period in the "direst poverty". "This lifestyle", she said "rendered him neurasthenic" and friends in Paris finally pursuaded him to join them, which included Krishna Varma, S.R. Rana and Cama. He regained his health. As Krishna Varma's *The Indian Sociologist* writings were getting 'tepid and tentative' after the assassination of Sir William Curzon Wyllie by Madan Lal Dhingra in London, Cama and Rana wanted to start a newspaper "which would reflect a vigorous revolutionary policy". The paper was called *Bande Matram* and was, in a way, a continuation of the one, with the same name, started in Calcutta by B.C. Pal in 1905 and edited later by Aurobindo Ghose, which had ceased publication in 1908 under the Newspapers Act of 1908. Har Dayal was the obvious choice for its editor. Cama provided the financial support. The first issue of *Bande Matram* appeared on 10 September 1909. *Bande Matram* was almost wholly written by Har Dayal for several months. It was published from Geneva. With *Bande Matram*, Har Dayal identified himself as an advocate of open rebellion. The arrest and deportation of Savarkar, his closest political colleague, if not his *guru* and his impending fate, affected him very much. He left Paris and spent a few months in Algiers but found it difficult to live in a Muslim country. He returned to Paris in July 1910 and resumed the editorial work. He was living with S.R. Rana but was restless. Without consulting any of his friends, he left Paris in October 1910 for Martinique, an island in E. West Indies, which was also part of the French Empire. The only account of Har Dayal's stay in Martinique has been given by Bhai Parmanand, an Arya Samaj missionary, in his autobiography *The Story of My Life*. The two friends lived together in Martinique for a month. Parmanand found that Har Dayal was living the life of an ascetic and spent his time in meditation and study. Har Dayal told Parmanand that he wanted to give a new religion to the world like Buddha did. Parmanand claims that he dissuaded him doing anything like that and suggested that he should go to the United States to preach the ancient culture and philosophy of the Aryan race. After days of discussion, Har Dayal agreed.

Har Dayal arrived in the United States in February, 1911 and went to Harvard University to carry on his study on Buddhism. But hardly had he started, when he was informed by a fellow Punjabi that there were thousands of Sikhs and Punjabi labourers working in fields or factories on the West Coast, who lacked leadership in their struggle for social acceptance and economic equality. Har Dayal agreed to go to California to do something for the unfortunate Indians. He established himself in Berkeley by the end of April 1911. At Berkeley, he did not pursue any academic course but he did associate himself with campus radicals and intellectuals and introduced himself to select members of the faculty. He also met some literary personalities like the famous novelist Jack London who immortalised Har Dayal introducing a character like Har Dayal, calling him Dayal Har, in his novel *The Little Lady of the Big House*. At Berkeley, he was asked to speak on Indian philosophy at private gatherings. He was a powerful and enchanting orator as he was considered an intellectual giant. His fame spread and the University of Berkeley invited him to give a series of lectures on philosophy. His lectures at Berkeley had attracted attention and he was offered to join the faculty of Stanford University. Har Dayal refused to draw any salary. Soon after, Har Dayal started writing on subjects which the university did not approve of. He had become a Marxian, and took a step still further preaching anarchism. He advocated 'free love'. Several parents of female students objected and Har Dayal was removed from the Stanford University faculty panel.

By 1912, Har Dayal was a devout communist, nay an anarchist. To spread his gospel, he founded 'The Radical Club' during his days in Stanford and served as its secretary. He defined its members "as dissenters from the establishment in any social, political, or intellectual area". It was like a clearing house for anyone and everyone to come and vent his feelings, somewhat like London's Hyde Park. It started attracting people, especially the young. The authorities of the university as well as of the government were concerned. The club could be one of the reasons for the university to have dissuaded Har Dayal to leave the university. By the end of 1912, Har Dayal was a figure to be reckoned with, as well-known in "Washington as he had been in official circles in London, Delhi, Calcutta and Simla. His literary production (mainly articles in newspapers and journals) had made him one of the most 'avidly' read young Indians of his time. Wherever Har Dayal went, there was excitement. His energy and enthusiasm seemed inexhaustible, and the variety of his interests and commitments left both Indian informers and British agents bewildered and worn out".[1]

A crucial event occurred in 1912 in Delhi which brought Har Dayal back to nationalist activities. This was the assassination attempt on the viceroy, Lord Hardinge. The event was celebrated in Berkeley, in which Har Dayal took a leading part. He also wrote an article titled 'Salute to the Bomb Thrower', and sent it for publication. He was now again lambasting the British in his writings. To bring Indians on a common platform, he founded the Hindu Association of the Pacific Coast in May 1913. (In the America of those days all Indians were called Hindus). It was decided that the association would sponsor the publication of a revolutionary newspaper. The journal was called *Gadar* (revolution) and Har Dayal announced the formation of Gadar Party on 1 November 1913. The first issue of *Gadar* was also brought out on that day in several Indian languages like Punjabi, Hindi, Urdu etc. Har Dayal was the editor and was helped by some members who knew these languages. A house at 436, Hill Street, San Francisco was purchased and was named as 'Yugantar Ashram', which was to be the headquarters of Gadar Party and from where the journal *Gadar* was to be published. In the first formal meeting of the party, Baba Sohan Singh was elected as president and Har Dayal as secretary and editor of *Gadar*. The fame of Har Dayal rests more as the founder of Gadar Party than on anything else. A majority of the members of the party were Sikhs, working on agricultural farms and factories, who were treated shabbily by the white overlords. The recurring theme of the Gadar was, "*Chalo chaliye desh nun yudh karan/Eho akhari vachan farman ho gaye*" (Let us go to the motherland to fight the enemy/ These words (of Har Dayal) are last words and order).[2] But before the orders could be implemented by Gadarites, Har Dayal was arrested by the U.S. Immigration Department with the connivance of British Embassy on 25 March 1914 in San Francisco. He was, however, released after signing a bond of $1000. Har Dayal left the country and after about five weeks appeared in Lausanne, Switzerland. In the Yugantar Ashram in San Francisco, the Gadar movement and the propaganda machine had been turned over to Ram Chandra, a Punjabi, who edited the party organ.

From Switzerland, Har Dayal moved to Germany where he opened an Oriental Bureau and sought German help for armed revolution in India. He was in Germany all through the war years. During the first year of his stay in Germany, he got close to the Germans but later on he was completely disillusioned. In an article on 4 December 1918 which was published in the *San Francisco Call* he wrote, "My residence in Germany has convinced me that German imperialism is a very great menace to the progress of humanity, and I rejoice to see that American arms bid fair to humble this arrogant nation". From Germany he crossed over to Sweden in November 1918, just before the War ended. That was also the end of Har Dayal the revolutionary. He was now an adherent of the Home Rule instead of the old revolutionary party. He now advocated that India should remain a part of the great British Empire. Har Dayal lived in Sweden for almost a decade. "He earned his rather precarious living by lecturing on Indian philosophy, art and literature". This miserable financial condition was changed when in November, 1926 Har Dayal met agda Erikson, "a Swedish social worker and philanthropist of significant accomplishment. She was to become his companion from then on and his acknowledged wife from the summer of 1932".[3] She bought a cottage at Edgware when the couple moved to London later, which became their home for the rest of their lives. Egda gave him company, inspiration, financial support and much more. She was with him when he died.

Har Dayal applied to the British government for amnesty which was refused. However, the British ambassador in Stockholm issued a passport to Har Dayal for Great Britain *only*. Har Dayal reached London on 10 October 1927, accompanied by Egda Erikson. He was admitted to the doctoral programme at the School of Oriental and African Studies and submitted a dissertation, *The Bodhisattva Doctrine in Buddhist Sanskrit Literature*. He was awarded the Doctor of Philosophy degree in 1930 and was published in book the form of a in 1932. It is still considered as an authoritative work in its field. Two years later, in 1934, Har Dayal's second book, and by far the most famous of his works, *Hints For Self-Culture* was published. "The scope of the book is almost overwhelming". In the brief preface he wrote, "In this little book (it has 363 pages) I have tried to indicate and explain some aspects of the message of Rationalism for the Young men and women of all countries". In it, the later stage of 'Hardayalism' gets manifested, "a free, united and humanly perfect India" has given way to "a free, united, and humanly perfect world, having one state, one flag, one language, one ethic, one ideal, one love, one life". From it emerges Har Dayal, as the man without a country, finding his identification as a world citizen.

On 30 December 1935, Har Dayal renewed his request for amnesty because he wanted to return to his motherland. By the time the permission was dispatched to their Edgware address, the couple had left for the United States. They started residing in Philadelphia where Har Dayal was invited to deliver a series of lectures under the auspices of the Society for Ethical Culture. However, life ended for Har Dayal on 4 March 1939. He was only fifty-four. His sudden death remains a mystery. He was cremated at a simple service at which tributes were paid to him by the devotees of the twelve religions he had singled out in his book *Hints*. The only music at the funeral service was the singing of *Bande Matram*. Egda Erikson left for Sweden. She was heartbroken to discover that Har Dayal's first wife was still alive and she had married a man who was neither a divorcee nor a widower. She died on 11 January 1940 in Sweden. For the relatives of Har Dayal, Egda never existed. So also for many Indian biographers of Har Dayal. She had lived with him for thirteen years, first as a friend and later as his wife.

When the news of Har Dayal's death reached India almost after a month, it did not go unnoticed. Most of the major newspapers devoted considerable space recounting his career. But the most memorable tribute came from the aged and ailing C.F. Andrews: "He (Har Dayal) was one of India's noblest children and in happier times would have done wonders with his gigantic intellectual powers. For his mind was one of the greatest I have ever known and his character also was true and pure". However, as a personality Har Dayal is elusive. "What has intrigued most of those who knew him were the seemingly abrupt changes in his actions and attitudes which occurred as he moved from a militant nationalist to a pacifist and internationalist who embraced not only the ideals but the homilies of the society he had once scorned and reviled".[4]

# References

1. Brown, Emily C. *Har Dayal; Hindu Revolutionary and Rationalist.* 1975, University of Arizona Press. (Indian reprint Manohar, New Delhi), p.127.
2. Dharamvira. *Lala Har Dayal and Revolutionary Movements of His Time.* New Delhi, Indian Book Co. 1970, p.193.
3. Brown Emily C. op.cit. p.238.
4. Ibid p.7.

# David Hare

## (1775-1842)

The East India Company had little in common with the long line of India's traditional invaders from West Asia. Revolutionary changes were gradually introduced in administration as well as in the socio-economic structure. The important agent for these changes was the new educational system; first in Bengal and gradually in other parts of the country. The Company did not make any conscious efforts as such to spread English education and western sciences. But the Christian missionary schools taught these subjects and gained popularity among the middle-classes. The advantages of learning English and western sciences was becoming apparent to the Indian intelligentsia. The first decade of the nineteenth century saw a number of schools, apart from missionary schools, coming up, teaching English and western sciences. It culminated in the establishment of the famous Hindu College in Calcutta. David Hare was the founder of this great institution. He was supported by men like Ram Mohan Roy, who became his lifelong friend. Besides Hindu College, Hare was instrumental in the establishment of several other educational institutions in Calcutta. With the de-recognition of Persian as an official language in 1835 by the Company and giving the status of official languages to English and vernacular languages of each province, the spread of English and Bengali was accelerated. David Hare, along with Ram Mohan Roy, played a leading role in making these languages popular.

David Hare was born in Scotland on 17 February 1775. He did not have a college education and adopted the profession of his father — watch-making. He came to India in 1800 and spent the remaining forty-two years of his life in Calcutta. He compensated for his lack of good education by reading widely and had even built his own small library. But he was no intellectual like Ram Mohan.

Within a short time of his arrival in Calcutta, he built up a prosperous watch-making business. Though he had become a successful businessman, his heart was not in this profession. After making a small fortune, he voluntarily transferred his business to his assistant E. Gray, who was perhaps his relative, early in 1820, and devoted the rest of his life doing social work mainly in the sphere of education in Calcutta.

He soon earned the friendship of Ram Mohan Roy, as both of them believed in the diffusion of English education and western sciences among Indians if India had to progress. When Ram Mohan Roy visited England in 1830-33, David had written to his relatives in England to look after him and Ram Mohan stayed with them for some time. A niece of David Hare attended to the needs of Ram Mohan during his last illness at Stapleton Grove where he died. All the members of the Hare family were present during Ram Mohan's last rites. David himself was, however, a lifelong bachelor.

Even before David Hare said good-bye to his watch-making business, he was active in spreading English education. In 1814, he proposed to his friend Ram Mohan for the establishment of an English school in Calcutta. Consequently, the first English school by a native came into existence. The establishment of the Hindu College on 20 January 1817 was the result of the proposal Hare had sent to Justice Sir Edward Hyde East of the Supreme Court. The college is located on a piece of land owned by David Hare on the north side of College Square. Thus David is considered to be the founder of Hindu College. Whether as a superintendent of the School Society's meritorious boys studying in the Hindu College or as a director of the College Managing Committee from 1925, he was a constant source of inspiration for the teachers and students. When in 1818 the School Society was formed to look after vernacular and English schools, Hare was the European secretary. Apart from taking special interest in the activities of the students at Arpuli Vernacular School and the Pataldanga English School, he kept a close watch on the progress of the poor but meritorious students selected for study at the Hindu College by the School Society. Due to financial stringency the two schools had to be merged and are now called Hare School and are still "perpetuating the hallowed memory of the Scottish pioneer".

From the beginning Hare stressed the importance of Bengali education in his schools, along with English. In the fitness of things, he was asked to lay the foundation of the Bengali pathshala (Hindu College Pathshala) near the Hindu College on 14 June 1839.

Hare played a leading role in the establishment of the first medical college in India on 1 June 1835. He was asked by the principal to be the secretary to the Calcutta Medical College, a post he held from 1837 to 1842, "because of his influence over Hindu homes". Hindu families were reluctant to send their children to the medical college because of the deep-rooted prejudice against dissecting dead human bodies. Hare had succeeded in convincing the friendly families of the necessity of knowing the human body for doctors and thus helping them to overcome the prejudice. "When in January 1836 some students mustered enough courage to shake off their prejudice to dissect dead bodies, guns boomed from the Fort William, virtually welcoming the opening of a new chapter in the history of renascent Bengal".[1]

Though a Christian himself, Hare abhorred the proselytisation activities of the missionaries who were active in the educational institutions in his schools 'who will spoil my boys', he used to say. He was termed as an atheist by the orthodox Christians. His inveterate hostility to the Gospel cost him the goodwill of orthodox Christians and he was denied burial in a consecrated Christian cemetry and was buried near his beloved Hindu College in his own land.

As there was a dearth of books in English as well as Bengali, Hare founded the Calcutta School Book Society in 1818, for printing and publishing English and Bengali books. These books were distributed free to the needy students. "The Young Bengal Address (1831) spoke of Hare as the man who has breathed a new life in Hindu society, who has voluntarily become the friend of a friendless people, and set an example to his own countrymen and ours".[2]

Hare worked hard, along with Ram Mohan Roy, for the repeal of regulations against the press which ultimately led to the restoration of the freedom of the Press by Act XI of 1835. He also took active part to secure trial by jury in civil cases in the Supreme Court. He was at the forefront of the agitation against the British practice of collecting Indian coolies (indentured labour) for emigration to Mauritius, British Guyana, Trinidad and Ceylon.

Hare's many generous benefactions, small and large, put him in financial difficulties towards the end of his life. To help him in his distress, Lord Auckland appointed him as the third commissioner in the Court of Requests in March 1840, in recognition of his services for the cause of native education, on a salary of Rs.1000 per month. His appointment to this post was not liked by many. The *Friend of India* paper commented, "He has laid the country under a debt of gratitude by his labours in the cause of education, which even the salary of a Commissioner does not repay. By the present appointment the cause of education has lost much, while the cause of justice has gained nothing".[3]

But he did not live long to serve as commissioner and died on 1 June 1842, of cholera at the age of sixty-seven. His funeral, on a soggy day, was attended by at least two thousand grateful students and staff of Hindu College and Medical College along with many European dignitaries. His memory is cherished and is kept alive to this day. The street on which he lived with his relative Mr. Gray, is called Hare Street. The Government of India has put a memorial tablet at his residence; a full-sized marble statue was erected by public subscription between Presidency College and the Hare School; and in the Hare School a beautiful portrait of his, which was commissioned by his students, adorns the wall of the room used by him.

## References

1. Sinha, Nirmal, ed. *Freedom Movement in Bengal, 1818-1904, Who's Who*. Calcutta, Academic Publishers, 1991, p.19.
2. Sarkar, Susobhan. In *Dictionary of National Biography*, ed. by S.P. Sen. Calcutta, Institute of Historical Studies. Vol. 2, 1973, p.145-47.
3. Sinha op.cit. p.22.

# Keshavrao Baliram Hedgewar

## (1889-1940)

Hedgewar was a nation builder who tried to unite Hindu society, working silently, almost imperceptibly, and created an organisation which is still alive and working for the national cause without seeking any reward. What Vivekananda preached and tried to implement about unity and strength, was what Hedgewar succeeded in doing during the last fifteen years of his life. In one of his speeches, Vivekananda had said, "I want a band of workers who would, as Brahmcharins, educate the people and revitalise the country". This is also what Hedgewar believed and worked for the creation of such a band of workers.

Keshavrao was born on 1 April 1889 at Nagpur, in an orthodox Brahmin family. The family had migrated from Kundukurti in Andhra Pradesh to Nagpur at the turn of the nineteenth century. They were by no means rich and Keshavrao had experienced poverty right from infancy. His father Balirampant and mother Revtibai died of plague in 1902 when Keshav was twelve years old. Keshav was the youngest of the three brothers. He also had three sisters. The passing away of the parents put the family further in financial trouble but the eldest son Mahadev was able to steer the family out of difficulties.

While Baliram was still alive, he had put Keshav in a modern school, as from his childhood, Keshav had shown no interest in the traditional priesthood which was the profession of the family. From the beginning,

Keshav was interested in history and politics, "particularly the life and deeds of Shivaji". He had developed a hatred of British rule while still a boy and expressed it in several ways. When the Diamond Jubilee of the Coronation of the British Empress Victoria was celebrated in his school in 1896, he threw away the sweets which were given to every child. He also took part in the *Vande Matram* agitation and was expelled from the school. He continued anti-British activities and was expelled from school after school. He passed the matriculation examination as a private candidate from Nagpur in 1910. By this time, Keshav came in contact with Dr. B.S. Moonje, a militant nationalist and an admirer of Tilak. Keshav lived during much of his adolescence with Dr. Moonje who was a major influence on his life. Hedgewar went to Calcutta in 1910 to qualify as a doctor. According to one source 'Moonje sent Keshav to Calcutta to study medicine at the National Medical College because he wanted Hedgewar to establish contacts with the revolutionaries of Bengal". No wonder Hedgewar joined Anushilan Samiti, the revolutionary society of Bengal, and "rose to its highest membership category". In the Samiti he handled many risky jobs with the pseudonym 'Koken'. He also identified himself with Bengali way of life and participated in varied student movements and social service activities. He returned to Nagpur in 1916, after getting LM&S degree. He did not practice medicine, however, which would have enabled him to earn money and respect in society. To the dismay of his family members, he announced that he would not marry nor would he practice as a doctor. And he never did. He resolved to devote his life to the revolutionary struggle. Very little is known of his revolutionary activities during the years 1916-1920. The *Nagpur District Gazetteer*, however, reports that he was the brain behind the revolutionary movement in Nagpur.

In 1921, Hedgewar joined the Indian National Congress and participated in its non-cooperation movement. He was arrested on 14 August 1921 and was sentenced to one year rigorous imprisonment, and was released on 12 July 1922. But he was not an ardent member of the Congress. He was equally at home with revolutionaries, Congress party and the Hindu Mahasabha and had friends and well-wishers in all these organisations. When Gandhi suddenly called off the Non-Cooperation

Movement in 1922, Hedgewar became increasingly disenchanted with Gandhi and his politics but did not sever ties with the Congress.

The communal riots of 1923 in Nagpur made Hedgewar think about the causes of the riots and about the timidness shown by the Hindus though they were 150,000 as against twenty thousand Muslims in Nagpur. When the government banned the Dindi procession in Nagpur on 30 October 1923 more than twenty thousand Hindus marched in defiance of the order. This was done for the first time. Hedgewar had found lack of unity as the cause of the timidness of the Hindu. And the remedy — unity. Out of this incident emerged the Nagpur Hindus Sabha, with Dr. Moonje as vice-president and Hedgewar as secretary. The Sabha organised more protest marches. Hindus in Nagpur were not slow to appreciate the influence they could exert if they were organised. The intellectual basis of the birth of Rashtriya Swayamsewak Sangh was found. Hedgewar was now convinced that our nation's malady did not lie in foreign slavery but in its disunity. Even foreign domination was a direct result of this national failing. To overcome this, a cadre of dedicated and disciplined persons was required. This was actually the task of character building.

After great thought Hedgewar launched his new movement on *Vijaydashmi* day in 1925 at Nagpur. He gave it the name Rashtriya Swayamsevak Sangh. According to him "it is a body of those persons who have voluntarily dedicated themselves to the service of the Motherland", which results in national consciousness, brotherhood, discipline and self-sacrifice. He had come to believe that only "such a patriotic and disciplined society alone could be expected not only to throw off its foreign shackles but also offer an unfailing guarantee for the protection of the nation's freedom in future also and form the inevitable base for all future national reconstruction as well".[1] A small group of persons gathered in an *akhara* (gymnasium). Soon they started meeting daily. Mohitewada grounds, near the *akhara* in Nagpur, was the place where the first *shakha* (group) meetings were held. Gradually, the other features which distinguish the RSS from other bodies were added: the *bhagwa dhwaj* (saffron flag) which became the *guru*; a uniform of white shirt, khaki shorts and black cap; a stick for protection. A prayer in Sanskrit was recited every day by the *shakha*. The number of *shakhas* increased, first in Nagpur and then in other cities nearby. During the 1927 riots, the *swayamsewaks* organised defence in the Hindu localities, demonstrating the utility of unity leading to strength. A bugle and a band was added, which was used during processions in the city. They had no newspaper or journal to publicse their activities or to do propaganda. However, a *swayamsevak* now stood apart from the ordinary public, the result of 'character building' process introduced by Hedgewar. The behaviour and the conduct of swayamsevaks among the public was the only source of publicity. Gradually the RSS came to be noticed. During the religious functions the RSS volunteers started disciplining the crowd, getting appreciation from the public. The organisers of the December 1927 Hindu Mahasabha session to be held at Ahmedabad invited Hedgewar to send RSS volunteers in uniform to maintain order. The political parties saw in the RSS a disciplined core for their party. V.D. Savarkar approached Hedgewar to let his volunteers join the Hindu Mahasabha. Hedgewar politely declined. Savarkar then frequently denounced RSS for its purely 'cultural' orientation. Savarkar once publicly taunted the RSS saying that "The epitaph for the RSS voluntter will be that he was born, he joined the RSS and he died without accomplishing anything". Dr. Hardikar, the leader of the Hindustan Seva Dal (a wing of the Congress), criticised the RSS for its refusal to get politically involved.[2] But Hedgewar was quite clear in his mind that the RSS would remain an apolitical organisation devoted to the service of the Motherland. He wanted to create a nationally conscious society through discipline and patriotism and by placing the interest of the society above self. This, he felt, was not possible in politics.

In spite of the initial success of his venture, Hedgewar continued to be a member of the Congress party 'in his individual capacity'. He took part in the Civil Disobedience Movement and was imprisoned for nine months in 1930. But after his release from prison in 1931, Hedgewar devoted all his energies to the building up of RSS and set out to make it a national organisation. He toured several states in the early 1930s, starting with Sind, Panjab and Uttar Pradesh, founding 'shakhas' wherever he went. He got good response in areas where Hindus were in a minority "Gopal (Babarao) Savarkar, elder brother of V.D. Savarkar helped the RSS. He merged his own Tarun Hindu Sabha as well as Mukteshwar Dal into the RSS". He accompanied Hedgewar on trips to Western Maharashtra, introducing him to Hindu nationalists. Some of them later became prominent RSS workers. The number of *shakhas* went on increasing; as also the membership. But RSS did not keep any written record about its branches or its members. The other unique feature of the RSS was that it was a self-supporting organisation. The members contributed their share to the organisation on Dussehra in the form of 'Guru dakshina' — Guru was the *dhwaj* (flag) of saffron colour. It is unfurled in every *shakha* daily and every member saluted it. The other feature of the RSS was that it did not admit ladies in its çadre; it was an all-male organisation. The greatest contribution of Hedgewar to Hindu society and the RSS was that it abolished caste identities and distinctions in its cadres. It is amazing how this could be achieved without consciously trying when stalwarts like Gandhi and others before him had failed. It was part of the 'discipline' and the devotion to the Motherland dinned daily in the minds of the *swayamsevaks* which created this miracle. Dr. Ambedkar in his address to the Sangh Camp at Pune in 1939 particularly noted the spirit of social equality and harmony in the Sangh. He said, "This is the first time that I am visiting a camp of Sangh volunteers. I am happy to find here absolute equality between the *savarnas* (high castes) and Harijans, without anyone being even aware of such a difference existed". So was Gandhi, when he visited the Sangh Camp at Wardha in 1934.

Till his last days, Hedgewar continued to work ceaselessly without caring for his health. He died of high blood pressure on 21 June 1940, in the home of Babasahab Ghatate in Nagpur. The wide roads of Nagpur saw a traffic jam for the first time as thousands of his admirers wanted to pay homage to the man who shunned publicity but built an organisation of devoted and well-disciplined members. Even after six decades of Hedgewar's death, whenever there is a catastrophe in the country — a cyclone in Andhra Pradesh; an earthquake in Kutch or an air-crash in Haryana, volunteers in khaki half-pants and white shirts are the first to reach there to provide relief to the victims. And on every such occasion, the nation-builder Hedgewar is remembered with gratitude. The future historian will have to decide his place in modern Indian history, because, so far, he has received more brickbats than bouquets at the hands of some Indian historians.

# References

1.  *RSS; Spearheading National Renaissance*. Bangalore, Prakashan Vibhag, Rashtreeya Swayamsevak Sangh, 1985, p.11.
2.  Andersen, W.K. and Shridhar D. Damle. *The Brotherhood in Saffron*. New Delhi, Vistaar, 1987, p.36.

# Allan Octavian Hume

## (1829-1912)

Though the British rule is remembered more for economic exploitation, for inflicting atrocities on innocent people and keeping thousands of them in the Cellular jail in the Andaman, there were several Britishers who spent the major part of their lives in India helping people to lead a better life. One such Englishman was Allan Octavian Hume. He was born in London in 1829 of Scottish descent. His father Joseph Hume (1777-1855) was a qualified doctor and had served in India for ten years in the service of the East India Company before he went back to England; became a 'radical of the deepest dye' and for thirty years was recognised as the leader of the Radical Party in the British Parliament. Allan inherited these traits of "independent thinking and swimming against the stream" from his father. He was educated at Haileybury and intended to join the navy. With that aim in mind, he joined the training college at Haileybury. But he changed his mind and did not join the Royal Navy. Instead, he studied medicine and surgery at the University College Hospital. He had a scientific bent of mind and on his own cultivated deep interest in plants and birds.

In 1849, at the age of twenty he left for India to join the Bengal Civil Service and served as district officer at Etawah, a district of North-West Provinces (present Uttar Pradesh). Here, he started his social reforms along with his official duties, unlike other district officers. He started with education and opened several free schools and libraries. He instituted scholarships for deserving students to go in for higher education. He started juvenile reformatories for disturbed children instead of throwing them in prison. He also encouraged female education. The first medical institute in Etawah was built in 1856 with his efforts. He built a commercial complex in the centre of the town, which local people called Humeganj.

He was also preaching against alchohol and alchoholism to the chagrin of the revenue officials who wanted to increase the *abkaree* revenue and which Hume openly called 'wages of sin'. While at Etawah, he studied the agricultural situation in the district including the soil composition and weather conditions and tried to help farmers in increasing the yield of their crops by adopting better methods of cultivation based on the nature of the soil and vagaries of weather. During the 1857 uprising, he managed to ward off the rebels with the help of local population and was awarded C.B. (Commander of the Bath) by the government for his services. The uprising only temporarily affected Hume's social work. For another nine years, he continued to expand and consolidate his work of reforms. This was the most productive and happiest period of his life. His wife Mary Grindal, whom he married in 1853, was there to share his work and add to his happiness.

For the next three years (1867-70), Hume worked as commissioner of customs for the North-Western Provinces. In this capacity, his principal achievement was the gradual abolition of the vast customs barriers which had hitherto been kept up to protect the government salt monopoly by excluding the cheap salt produced in the Rajputana states. From 1870, Hume was secretary, department of Agriculture, Revenue and Commerce at Simla. In this important position he tried to change the policy of the department towards poor Indian farmers, the policy which was earlier concentrated "on shearing the sheep than to feeding it". Utilising his knowledge of Indian agriculture gained at Etawah, he published in 1879 a pamphlet, *'Agricultural Reforms in India'*, with suggestions to the government to implement the reforms so that the poor Indian farmers could lead a better life. But the Simla mandarins and the secretary of state in London wanted revenue to be the main concern of the department. Even Lord Mayo, the viceroy, could not convince the authorities in London about the need for reform in Indian agriculture. Hume was getting too difficult for the imperialists in India and London which resulted in his being shifting from Simla secretariat to the Revenue Board at Allahabad. He was also removed from the ICS cadre without being given any reason. This was a severe blow to Hume. His demotion and degradation was noted by the Anglo-Indian press. *The Pioneer* termed it as "the greatest jobbery ever perpetuated" and *The Statesman* commented that "undoubtedly he (Hume) had been treated shamefully and cruelly". Almost all the leading journalists of the time believed that his offence was that he was "too honest and too independent".

Apart from the setback to his official career, the transfer to Allahabad dealt a disastrous blow to his scientific studies in ornithology and botany which he was pursuing at Simla. His interest in ornithology was such that he had spent thousands of pounds in collecting bird skins and eggs and had studied them in detail. He also started an ornithological quarterly journal *Stray Feathers* in 1872 and published it till 1899. He also published in joint-authorship with C.H.T. Marshal, *The Game Birds of India, Burma and Ceylon* in three volumes which till today is a standard work on the subject. He had built an extensive ornithological museum in his beautiful home, Rothney Castle, at Simla, which was later transferred to the British Museum of Natural History as a gift. His collection of plants was transferred to South London Botanical Institute. This was the largest collection of its kind in the world.[1] It is reported that Hume was offered the lieutenant governorship of North-West Provinces by the viceroy Lord Lytton but he declined and suggested he rather be home member which was declined by the secretary of state, Lord Salisbury. Helena P. Blavatsky, the founder of Theosophical society, gives a different version of this episode. In a letter to her friend in Moscow dated 5 December 1881 she wrote, "This year I was invited to Rothney Castle 10,000 feet above the level of sea by Mr. Hume who had just been made Lieutenant Governor of the N.W. Provinces. He (Mr. Hume) gathered some fifty people from the Society and after they had all become members of the Theosophical Society, he founded a collateral branch called 'Simla Eclectic Theosophical Society'; was elected president and under the pretext that the Society needed all his time and services, sent his resignation to the viceroy declaring that he preferred Theosophy to the services of Her Majesty."[2] What Blavatsky writes must be taken with a pinch of salt as modesty was not one of her virtues.

Hume retired from service in 1882 and embarked upon an equally important phase of his life for which he is remembered to this day. He devoted himself to the formation of an all-India organisation representing various parts of the country "that would afford a legitimate vent to the seething discontent then rife among the people, and direct it along constitutional channels". From well-wishers in different parts of the country and from C.I.D. records, he received warnings of the danger to the government, and to the future welfare of India and if steps were not taken to meet the challenge posed by the discontent of the people the situation may lead to a catastrophe. The happenings of the 1857 uprising, in which he had taken an active part in thwarting the rebels in his area, were still fresh in his mind. He feared "a terrible outbreak, destructive to India's future". He believed that unless men like him did something to remove the general feeling of despair and thus avert a catastrophe, the result could be disastrous. He believed that the intelligentsia of a country, however small in number, were after all, the natural leaders of the people. He wanted such people to get together on a common platform to discuss and find solutions for the problems facing the country. He addressed an open letter to the graduates of the Calcutta University on 1 March 1883, appealing them to take the initiative in establishing an Association "having for its object to promote the mental, moral, social and political regeneration of the people of India". There was a good response to this appeal and the 'Indian National Union' was formed with Hume as general secretary, the preamble of which read, "The union is prepared, when necessary, to oppose, by all constitutional methods, all authorities, high or low here or in England, whose acts or omissions are opposed to those principles of the Government of India laid down for them by the British Parliament and endorsed by the British Sovereign, but it holds the continued affiliation of India to Great Britain, at any rate for a period far exceeding the range of any practical political forecast, to be essential to the interests of our own national development".[3]

Thus, the seed for the Indian National Congress was sown by Hume. The next meeting of the Union was held in Bombay on 27 December

1885. The name of the Union was changed to Indian National Congress, which has survived to this day with various ups and downs and with noble and ignoble deeds. Seventy-two delegates coming from different parts of the country attended the meeting. Hume continued to be the general secretary till 1893, painstakingly noting down the proceedings of each session.

There was strong opposition to the Congress by Sir Syed Ahmed Khan who was quite vehement in condemning the formation of the Congress calling it Bengali Hindu conspiracy to grab power and advised Muslims not to join it and was quite successful in doing so. Very few Muslims sought membership of the Congress. Hume considered this opposition unimportant, and held that, "excluding an inappreciable fraction, the whole culture and intelligence of the country was favourable to Congress." The number of delegates went on increasing every year attracting almost all the stalwarts of the country like Dadabhai Naoroji, Justice Ranade, Pherozshah Mehta, W.C. Bonnerjea, Gokhale, Krishna Swami Iyer, Tilak and others, increasing Hume's work, as general secretary which he continued to do diligently. The activities of the Congress were confined to meeting once a year and passing resolutions for the consideration of the government. But it did help the government in understanding the sentiments and aspirations of the intelligentsia and through them, of the nation. After putting the Congress on a firm footing, Hume left for England in 1894, but even while in England, was elected secretary year after year till he relinquished the post in 1906, at the age of seventy-seven. In England also he went on doing propaganda for India and had started a journal *India* in 1892, to put before the British public and Parliament, information about India and grievances of Indians. During the last eighteen years of his life he carried on the work of the Congress from England, though he had retired to a 'quiet little home', a few miles from London, where he spent most of his time with his first love — plants. In 1910, he established 'The South London Botanical Institute'.

On 31 July 1912 in his eighty-fourth year, Allan Octavian Hume died peacefully. There were more mourners in India than in England. "No one could have had mourners more multitudinous, or more sincere". Even after forty-five years, people of Etawa remembered him; shops in the town were closed in his memory. At the Bankipore session in December 1912, the Congress party placed on record that Allan Octavian Hume was the father and founder of the Indian National Congress. "He taught us how to fight bloodless battles of constitutional reform. Well may we, our children and our children's children remember the name of Mr. Allan Hume through succeeding generations with gratitude and reverence".

# References

1.  Wedderburn, William. *Allan Octavian Hume; Father of the Indian National Congress*. London, 1913, Reprint, New Delhi, Pegasus, 1974, pp.39-41.
2.  Jinarajadsa, C. Ed. *H.P.B. Speaks*, Vol. 2. Madras, Theosophical Publishing House. 1951, pp.33-4.
3.  Pradhan, R.G. *India's Struggle for Swaraj*. First pub. 1930 Reprint, Delhi, Low Price Publications, 1993, p.20.

# Muhammad Iqbal

## (1877-1938)

Iqbal is an important member of the fraternity of Muslim leaders who preached Muslim separatism after the collapse of the Muslim rule in India. The earlier protagonists were Shah Waliullah (1704-1763), Syed Ahmad Barelvi (1786-1831), Jamaluddin Afghani (1838-1897) and Sir Syed Ahmed (1817-1898). In Pakistan, all these leaders are considered as freedom fighters who laid the foundations of Pakistan. Mohammed Ali Jinnah only completed the work which these leaders had started. It must be added that Iqbal, besides creating a schism between Muslims and non-Muslims, contributed greatly in some other fields also. He was one of the greatest Urdu and Persian poets after Ghalib. He also wrote treatises attempting to construct a philosophy out of Islamic scriptures and was an intellectual *per se*.

Muhammad Iqbal was born on 9 November 1877 at Sialkot, West Panjab. His ancestors were Kashmiri Brahmins who had been converted to Islam some generations earlier due to unknown reasons. Iqbal's grandfather, Sheikh Muhammad Rafiq, migrated to Sialkot from Srinagar early in the nineteenth century. Iqbal's parents, father Sheikh Noor Muhammad and mother Imam Bibi, were almost illiterate but had a religious bent of mind. Iqbal had one brother Ata Muhammad. It was a middle-class family devoid of any intellectual pursuits.

Iqbal's initial education was in the traditional *maktab* (school). One of his teachers was Sayyid Mir Hasan, the famous Oriental scholar. Iqbal learnt Urdu, Persian and Arabic there. He started composing Urdu poems while still studying at the *maktab*. After completing his education at the *maktab*, Iqbal joined the Sialkot Mission School from where he passed matriculation examination. For higher studies, he joined the Government College, Lahore, from where he passed B.A. in 1897 and then Master's degree in philosophy in 1899, topping the list of successful candidates, thus demonstrating his intellectual acumen. He was appointed as a lecturer in Arabic at the local Oriental College. But soon he shifted to Government College, his *alma mater*, as assistant professor of Philosophy. Here he was influenced by Thomas Arnold, who was working as professor of Philosophy in the College. All these years till 1905, he had been writing beautiful Urdu poetry without any trace of fanatacism or pan-Islamism which is reflected in his later poetry. His *Tran-e-Hindi* (*Sare Jahan se achha Hindustan hamara*), *Naya Shiwala* and *Aftab* (translation of Gayatri) were all composed by him before 1905. He also wrote beautiful Urdu poems for children, which remain unrivalled to this day.[1]

Professor Arnold, impressed by the talents of Iqbal, advised him to go to England for higher studies. He joined the Trinity College, Cambridge and did research under Mac Taggart and James Ward, and was greatly influenced by these two thinkers. He also studied law and was called to the Bar in 1908. He must have worked very hard those three years in Europe because besides getting a degree from Cambridge and qualifying as a barrister, he also got a Ph.D. from Munich University, Germany in 1907. The topic of his dissertation was, *The Development of Metaphysics in Persia*.

He came back to Lahore in 1908 and was appointed a part-time lecturer of Philosophy and English literature at the Government College. He was allowed to practice as a barrister as well. However, Iqbal's heart was not in the legal practice and thus he could not be a successful lawyer. After his return from Europe, there was a complete transformation in his thinking. He was deeply concerned with the fate of Islam in the world and almost all his writings during this period are devoted to that sentiment. He now stopped singing praises of 'Hindustan' and instead wrote on pan-

Islamism. He also condemned nationalism. His *Tran-e-Milli*, starts with *Chino-Arab Hamara, Hindustan hamara; Muslim hain hum watan hai sara jahan hamara* (China and Arabia are ours and India is ours; for we Muslims the whole world is our country). Was he the same Iqbal who wrote *Taran-e-Hindi* only four years earlier? About nationalism, he expressed his views in a short poem *Vasniyat*. He wrote: "Among the newly discovered gods, the greatest is the country; But the apparel of this god is the shroud of religion". Was he referring to *Bande Matram*? His two poems *Shikwa* and *Jwab-e-Shikwa* depicts the sorry state of Muslims who had drawn sword in the name of true God and spread His message (Quran) in the world. The second poem *Jwab-e-Shikwa* is the reply of God who tells the Muslims that they had forgotten the message of Muhammad the Prophet. Iqbal exhorts the Muslims to go back to early Islam and shed timidness. In his famous *mathnvi Asrar-e-Khudi* (The secrets of self), he tells the Muslims to have confidence in themselves and know their intrinsic powers. It was translated by Prof. R.A. Nicholson, the famous Orientalist of Cambridge. As a result, Iqbal came to be discussed in the Western academic circles. He was conferred knighthood in 1922, 'for his literary eminence'. By 1928, he had earned a reputation as a great Muslim philosopher and was invited to deliver lectures at Hyderabad, Aligarh and Madras. These lectures were later published as *The Reconstruction of Religious Thought in Islam*, which is his major prose work. In it, he makes an attempt, as he himself says, "to construct Muslim religious philosophy with due regard to the philosophical traditions of Islam and the more recent developments in the various domains of human knowledge".

As his legal practice dwindled, which had never been lucrative any way, Iqbal decided to try his luck in politics. In the 1926 elections, he stood as a candidate and was elected to the Punjab Legislative Council. After that he became an active member of the Muslim League and in a way its policy maker. He joined Aga Khan and Jinnah to denounce the Nehru Report (1928), putting forward 'demands' for the safeguards of Muslim interests. In that year he was elected as secretary of the All India Muslim League. He presided at the 1930 session of the Muslim League at Allahabad. His presidential address marks the formal beginning of the demand for a separate home for the Muslims and deserve quoting:

"Communalism, in its higher aspects, is indispensable to the formation of a harmonious whole in a country like India. The units of Indian society are not territorial as in European countries. India is a continent of human groups belonging to different races, speaking different languages, and professing different religions. The principle of European democracy cannot be applied to India without recognizing the presence of communal groups. The Muslim demand for the creation of a Muslim India within India is, therefore, perfectly justified. — I would like to see Punjab, the North-West Frontier Province, Sind and Baluchistan amalgamated into a single state, self-governing within the British Empire, or without the British Empire. The formation of a consolidated North-West Indian Muslim state appears to me to be the final destiny of the Muslims, at least in Northwest India".[2] Iqbal's selection of the north-west as the most appropriate region for the establishment of a Muslim state had an interesting history behind it. Apart from its being a compact Muslim majority area, it was the geographical link between India and the Muslim world of Central and Western Asia. The memory of the Wahabi state founded in this region by the advocates of *Dar-ul-Islam* like Syed Ahmed Breilvi, was still fresh in the minds of the fanatical Muslims.[3]

Iqbal attended the Second and Third Round Table Conferences (London) in 1931 and 1932, "where his only contribution was to oppose every suggestion for the introduction of joint-electorates and the formation of federation in India".

Iqbal's last years were not happy. He was keeping indifferent health and two deaths in the family shattered his equanimity. Still, his mind was active. He was worried about the future of Islam and of Muslims in India. Daily, his admirers gathered at his residence and he discussed with them what was foremost in his mind. During these sittings Iqbal censured territorial nationalism and the doctrine of separation of Church and State. He categorically asserted that narrow nationalism was the antithesis of Islam, which believed in an international brotherhood of Muslims (Pan-Islamism). He criticised the concept of a common Indian nationality.[4] Iqbal believed that Islam was perfect and eternal as a guide for social and political life. Thus the 'philosophy' of Iqbal comes down almost to the level of a fundamentalist clergy.

He remained as the president of the Provincial Muslim League of Punjab, though he could not take active part in its activities. He regularly corresponded with M.A. Jinnah, expressing his views about the political developments in India vis-à-vis Muslims. In a letter to Jinnah in 1937, Iqbal wrote, "The construction of a polity on Indian national lines, if it means the displacement of the Islamic principle of solidarity, is simply unthinkable to a Muslim".

He died in Lahore on 21 April 1938 at the age of sixty-one, and was buried in the backyard of Badshahi mosque, built by Aurangzeb.

It is difficult to assess Iqbal. "He was too contradictory and unsystematic to permit a systematic assessment". The fact that he put forth his philosophy in poetic form, adds to the confusion. "He was very far from being a mass leader; he was a poet, an intellectual and a philosopher with affiliations to the old feudal order. He supplied in fine poetry, which was written both in Persian and Urdu, a philosophic background to the Moslem intelligentsia and thus diverted its mind in a separatist direction. His popularity was, no doubt, due to the quality of his poetry, but even more so, it was due to his having fulfilled a need when the Moslem mind was searching for some anchor to hold on to".[5]

## References

1. Iqbal, Muhammad. *Bange Dara* (Urdu). Lahore, Shaikh Mubark Ali, 1924.
2. Zaidi, A.M. *Evolution of Muslim Political Thought in India*. Vol. 4, New Delhi, S. Chand, 1978, pp.60-70.
3. Banerjee, A.C. *Two Nations; The Philosophy of Muslim Nationalism*. New Delhi, Concept, 1981, p.203.
4. Khairi, Saad R. *Jinnah Reinterpreted*. Karachi, OUP. 1966, p.341.
5. Nehru, Jawaharlal. *The Discovery of India*. OUP. 1946, pp.350-51.

# Kasturi Ranga Iyengar

## (1859-1923)

During the freedom struggle some newspapers and their editors, with nationalistic leanings played an important role in the formation of public opinion. One such editor was Kasturi Ranga Iyengar of *The Hindu*.

Kasturi Ranga was born on 15 December 1859 in an orthodox Brahmin family. His father Sesha Iyengar was a revenue official under the district collector of Tanjore. Kasturi Ranga started his education in village schools in Innambur and Kapisthalam where his father got posted. But at the age of twelve, he was sent to Provincial School and College at Kumbakonam, where his elder brother was studying. After completing his matriculation at Kumbakonam, Kasturi Ranga joined Presidency College, Madras, from where he took his Arts degree in 1879. While he was still in school at Kumbakonam, Kasturi Ranga was married to a ten-year-old girl Kanakammal. When he was seventeen, his father Sesha Iyengar died (1876). However, Kasturi Ranga continued his studies and joined the law course in Presidency College but he failed in the first attempt. He joined the post of a sub-registrar in the Registration Department in 1881, which did not carry any salary but he earned commission on the stamp value of registered documents which came to about rupees forty per month. After serving as sub-registrar for three years, he again appeared for law degree and this time got through (1884). He started his apprenticeship under. V. Bashyam Ayyangar, a leading lawyer of Madras. After his apprenticeship, Kasturi Ranga was enrolled as a *vakil* (lawyer) in March 1885. Instead of setting up his legal practice at Madras he opted for Coimbatore, a smaller place. In a short time, he had a lucrative practice. He was also motivated to play an active role in the public life of the town. He was elected to the Municipal Council; was appointed honorary magistrate as well as a jail visitor. Later, he was nominated to Coimbatore District Board. After nine years of practice at Coimbatore, Kasturi Ranga moved to Madras city (1894), hoping to augment his practice and to play a greater role in public affairs. His calculation about increasing his legal practice did not fructify but he started taking greater interest in politics as well as in journalism. His public activities naturally brought him in close touch with *The Hindu*, the upcoming newspaper in Madras, and its manager and editor. He also took great interest in the activities of Madras Mahajan Sabha, a leading social and political society of Madras, whose office was located in the premises of *The Hindu*. In 1895, Kasturi Ranga became legal adviser to *The Hindu* which was then edited and managed by two of its founders, G. Subramania Iyer and M. Veeraraghavachariar respectively. As the two did not devote much time to the monetary aspect, *The Hindu* had run into financial difficulties. In addition to being the legal adviser, Kasturi Ranga was a regular contributor to the columns of *The Hindu* on legal, political and social issues.

In 1905, Kasturi Ranga took the most important decision of his life. He purchased *The Hindu*. His first concern after the take-over was to reorganise the business set-up of the paper. And within a month, he had to take up the entire burden of editorial responsibilities also. Simultaneously, he started strengthening its news services. He subscribed to a fuller service from Reuters which was the sole news agency covering Indian and foreign affairs. He also appointed correspondents in a number of places. He expanded the 'Letters to the Editor' columns to know the reaction of the readers and introduced several other features to make *The Hindu* a popular newspaper.

Even when Kasturi Ranga was preoccupied with the affairs of *The Hindu*, he took active part in politics. He was in sympathy with the policies of Bal Gangadhar Tilak and was critical of 'Moderate' leaders. When after the Surat Congress in 1907 the Moderate faction took over the Congress, Kasturi Ranga practically retired from active politics for nearly ten years. He returned to politics when in 1916 there was rapprochment between the two adversaries in the Congress after Tilak's release from prison. He played an important role in formulating the Congress-League Pact of 1916 (Lucknow Pact), along with other important leaders of the Congress including Tilak. He also supported the Home Rule movement of Annie Besant and Tilak (1916). During the First World War, Kasturi Ranga gave cautious support to the Allies headed by Britain. In August 1918, the British government invited a small team of five journalists from India to visit Britain and even witness the goings-on in the battlefield on the Western Front. Kasturi Ranga was one of those five journalists. Writing on the invitation to Britain, Annie Besant wrote in her paper *New India* "Mr. Kasturi Ranga Iyengar holds easily a very high place among the Indian journalists who have contributed not a little to the public life and the formation of influential public opinion in the country".[1] The visit lasted for five months and he learnt a great deal from the visit which was reflected in the despatches he sent from the War Front for *The Hindu*. When Mahatma Gandhi started the Non-Cooperation Movement in 1920, he gave selective support to the movement but was an ardent supporter of the freedom movement as such. During the critical years of 1920-22, the support of *The Hindu* was a great asset for the freedom struggle. Kasturi Ranga used his position as editor from behind the scenes to influence the views and decisions of men in power as well as in the Indian National Congress. When the Non-Cooperation Movement was suspended in February 1922 after the Chauri Chaura incident and Gandhi was arrested the following month, a committee was constituted, headed by Hakim Ajmal Khan, by the All India Congress Committee to review the situation. The other members of the committee were Motilal Nehru, C. Rajagopalacharier, V.J. Patel and Kasturi Ranga Iyengar. The committee members were divided among those who wanted to change the nature of the movement and enter legislatures and those was wanted no-change, opposed the Council entry proposal and recommended doing 'constructive work' as advised by Gandhi. Kasturi Ranga was among those who opposed the Council entry proposal. Though he supported the Congress party and its policies through the editorials and write-ups in *The Hindu*, he never courted arrest.

From the very beginning when he took over *The Hindu*, Kasturi Ranga did not hesitate to risk the displeasure of the authorities. For instance, highlighting the failure of the banking firm of Arbuthnot and Company, and the misdeeds of its proprietor Sir George Arbuthnot who was found guilty of misappropriation of public funds in the paper, resulted in his getting eighteen months rigorous imprisonment. By taking up such public causes *The Hindu's* circulation increased and within a few years it became self-supporting and stopped accepting donations. In eighteen years (1905-1923) Kasturi Ranga made *The Hindu* one of the best produced and most influential newspapers in India.

Late in his life Kasturi Ranga emerged as a labour leader. In March 1920, he helped to organise the South Indian Railway Employees Association at Tiruchi. The inaugural meeting was held under his presidentship and he was elected the association's first president. In 1921, when ten thousand labourers were locked out of the Buckingham and Carnatic Mills, it was *The Hindu* under the editorship of Kasturi Ranga, that came forward and defended their cause. During the strike Kasturi Ranga, in spite of poor health, attended a public meeting of the citizens at the Triplicane beach to express sympathy for the workers. Kasturi Ranga donated five hundred rupees for the 'Strikers Relief Fund' and was elected a member of the committee that was formed to help the strikers. Thus he helped the striking workers both with his pen and his money.[2]

At the end of 1922, Kasturi Ranga fell ill. He was suffering from liver trouble and also had to be operated upon for hernia. For one full year he was in bed and died on 12 December 1923 in Madras.

Kasturi Ranga Iyengar was a leading journalist and a nationalist of the twentieth century. "His single minded patriotism and strict adherence to truth in the publication of news and features and freedom from malice or personal prejudices in dealing with those with whom he did not agree, entitle him to respect and gratitude and a high place among the builders of modern India".[3] The *London Times* in an obituary described him as 'one of the most influential of extremist journalists in India". A more detailed tribute was paid by Mahatma Gandhi when he was invited to unveil a portrait of Kasturi Ranga at the Hindu office, Madras (22 March 1925). Gandhi said, "I believe that Kasturi Ranga Iyengar represented some of the best that is to be found in Indian journalism. He had a style of his own. He commanded a sarcasm which was also peculiarly his own. Whenever he wrote as an opponent or as a friend, you could not fail to admire his style in which he wrote. I think it can be fairly claimed for him that he never wavered in his faith in his own country. And although he was always a courteous critic, he was also one of the most fearless critic of the Government.

"I had on many an occasion to differ from him. But I always valued his decision because I understood thereby wherein lay the weakness of my argument or my position. Very often it appeared to me that he occupied, if I may take such a parallel, about the same position in this Presidency, that the editor of the London *Times* occupies in England".[4]

Kasturi Ranga Iyengar had three daughters and two sons. When Kasturi Ranga died in 1923 his two sons Kasturi Srinivasan and K. Gopalan inherited the paper. Kasturi Srinivasan (1887-1959) was more talented and was a worthy son of a worthy father. *The Hindu* under his direction became highly respected and internationally known. The paper, even after a century and a quarter maintains the same position successfully.

# References

1.  Narasimhan, V.K. *Kasturi Ranga Iyengar*. New Delhi, Publication Division, 1963, p.138. (Quoted in).
2.  Ibid, pp.197-98.
3.  Santhanam, K. *Dictionary of National Biography*. Calcutta, Institute of Historical Studies. Vol.2. 1973.
4.  *Collected Works of Mahatma Gandhi* Vol. 26, pp.368-69.

# M.R. Jayakar

## (1873-1959)

Mukund Ramrao Jayakar was born on 13 November 1873 in Bombay in a middle-class family. His father Ramrao was a junior official in the Bombay secretariat. His mother, Sonabai, was able to create a religious atmosphere in the family. Mukund was brought up by his grandfather, Vasudeo Jagannath Kirtikar, after the early and untimely death of his father. Vasudeo was a reputed scholar, philosopher and lawyer and greatly influenced Jayakar. Thus Mukund was brought up in an ambience of scholastic studies, religiocity and sobriety resulting in his becoming a multifaceted personality. He was educated in the Elphinstone High School and St. Xavier College, Bombay. He graduated in 1895, and passed M.A. in 1897 and LL.B. in 1902. In 1903, he left for England, joined law and was called to the Bar in 1905. Returning to India the same year, he started practising at the Bombay high court. In 1907, he joined the Bombay Law school as a professor but resigned in 1912, when a junior person, who was an Englishman, was appointed principal. He started practising at the Bombay high court again and became one of the leading barristers of Bombay. M.C. Chagla, who at the time was working as assistant to Jinnah, writes, "Jayakar was an erudite lawyer and argued his cases with words which were carefully chosen, and which bore the impress of a scholar. He rose to great eminence and eventually became a member of the Privy Council".[1] Before becoming a member of the Privy Council, London, he had accepted an appointment as judge of the Federal Court of India in 1937.

At the age of twenty-six Jayakar married Sushilabai in 1899. They had one son and three daughters.

Jayakar had become keenly interested in politics but he did not join any political party formally, though his inclinations were towards Hindu Mahasabha, like those of Madan Mohan Malaviya, as he was deeply imbued in Hinduism. However, he played an important role, along with Tej Bahadur Sapru, as a Liberal and moderate leader, political negotiator and peacemaker. In 1918, the Poona District Conference at Lonavala was held under the chairmanship of Jayakar. "This Conference", he said, "was an assertion of the political tenets of Maharashtra, professed since the days of Ranade, Tilak and Gokhale." At this time, Jayakar was a follower of Annie Besant. He was a member of the Home Rule League deputation led by Mrs. Besant that waited upon Viceroy Lord Chelmsford and Secretary of State Montagu in November 1918. Later Jayakar was drawn towards Gandhi but never did he become a Gandhian. The deportation of B.G. Horniman (1919) editor of *Bombay Chronicle* brought them nearer, as Gandhi had taken up the Horniman's illigal deportation case and closure of his paper. Jayakar revived *Bombay Chronicle* spending considerable time and money. He became the chairman of the Board of Directors of the paper.

The Congress Punjab Enquiry Committee (formed after the Jallianwala Bagh tragedy) brought Gandhi and Jayakar still closer when Jayakar replaced Motilal Nehru as a member of the Committee. The Congress had assigned Jayakar the work of writing the report and seeing it through the press. Gandhi collaborated with him in scrutinising the final proofs. When the Report was ready it was decided to send someone with to London to inform the British public what really had happened in Jallianwala Bagh and about the atrocities committed on the innocent public under Marshal Law. In a letter to Jayakar, Gandhi wrote on 28 March 1920, "I consider that I am the fittest to go, but my going is a virtual impossibility. You come next in my view, because you are student like me and we want a man of application and studious habits and possessing a level head".[2] However, the idea of sending someone to England with the report was dropped because of Jayakar's illness. In July 1921, Gandhi came to Poona in connection with the Tilak anniversary and visited Jayakar, who was still ill and in bed. Jayakar gave twenty-five thousand rupees to Gandhi for the Tilak Swaraj Fund.

Jayakar was a powerful speaker both in the assemblies and outside. He was leader of the Swaraj Party in the Bombay Legislative Council (1923-26). His speeches were informative, thought-provoking, backed by statistical data. In 1926, he was elected to the Central Legislature, where he acted as deputy leader of the Nationalist Party (1926-30).

Along with Tej Bahadur Sapru, his role as a mediator and peacemaker gave a turn to history. The Gandhi-Irwin Pact (March 1931) was the outcome of ceaseless efforts of Jayakar-Sapru duo. He was mainly instrumental in effecting the Poona or Yerwada Pact between Gandhi and B.R. Ambedkar (1932). Great was his work, along with Sapru, in a silent and unobstrusive manner. "Their non-alignment with the Congress and Gandhi gave them a stature and they often struck a line of rapprochement when dark clouds were ominous". Jayakar participated in the three Round Table Conferences in London (1930-32) and took active part in the negotiations between the Indian leaders and the representatives of the British government. He was a keen observer of the political developments in the country and unhesitatingly warned the leaders when he thought, some wrong step was being taken which was not in the interest of the country. He wrote a strong letter on 21 January 1942, to Rajagopalachari, who was going to meet Jinnah, for a settlement of Hindu-Muslim question conceding to the Muslims fifty per cent share in central and state legislatures as well as in government services. He wrote, "You have publicly spoken of the fifty-fifty basis being acceptable to you with Jinnah as Prime Minister. I am not worried about the Prime Ministership, which may go to Jinnah or anyone else. But it is my duty to warn you that the fifty-fifty basis at the Centre or in the Provinces or in the Services or administration will not be acceptable to the Hindus".[3] He had written a similar letter to Gandhi before he went to meet Jinnah in his Malabar Hill residence in Bombay (September 1944) to offer him the Rajaji Formula which was virtual acceptance of Pakistan. Jayakar was a very upright man and a nationalist to the core.

Apart from his interest in politics he was an eminent educationist. He had set-up the Aryan Education Society and was its chairman for several years. He was a member of the Bombay University Reforms Committee (1924-25). In 1941, he was appointed chairman of the committee set-up to consider the establishment of Maharashtra University, which materialised in the establishment of Poona University, Jayakar becoming its first vice-chancellor. He ably performed his duties for two terms (1948-56). He was instrumental in securing, and being generous in donating funds, to the Bhandarkar Oriental Research Institute, enabling the publication of a critical edition of *Mahabharata*. He was an extremely erudite Sanskrit scholar. In 1924, he edited *Studies in Vedanta* written by his grandfather, V.J. Kritikar. His contributions on Hindu law were widely acclaimed. As an educationist, he was invited by several universities to deliver convocation addresses.

Jayakar was a great lover of art and music and had spent several years in studying classical music and fine arts. His presidential address at the Gandharva Mahavidyalaya, Bombay, is considered an outstanding and original contribution to modern music.

Jayakar was also greatly interested in social activities. He was the president of the Social Conference (founded by Ranade) held at Nasik in 1917. He also worked for the eradication of untouchability. In 1924, Jayakar, as a member of the Depressed Classes Mission, sought Gandhi's help in assisting the Harijans build their own temples, schools and hostels in Bombay. A number of letters were exchanged between Gandhi and Jayakar on this issue.

Jayakar lived a very fruitful and varied life but patriotism and liberality were reflected in whatever he did. In spite of being a devout Hindu and close to several Hindu Mahasabha leaders, he was considered a liberal by even his enemies.

After a prolonged illness, he died on 10 March 1959 at Bombay at the ripe age of eight-six. His autobiography *The Story of My Life*, in two volumes, describes the events and personalities of the time in an objective and unobtrusive manner.

## References

1.  Chagla, M.C. *Roses in December; An Autobiography*. Bombay, Bharatiya Vidya Bhavan. 1973, p.92.
2.  Jayakar, M.R. *The Story of My Life*. Vol. 1, Bombay, 1959, p.366.
3.  Pandey, B.N. ed. *The Indian National Movement, 1885-1947; Select Documents*. London, Macmillan, 1979, pp.167-69.

# Mohammad Ali Jinnah

## (1876-1948)

"Few individuals significantly alter the course of history. Fewer still modify the map of the world. Hardly anyone can be credited with creating a nationstate. Mohammad Ali Jinnah did all three".

*– Stanley Wolpert*

Mohammad Ali Jinnah was born in Karachi to Jinnahbhai Poonja and Mithibai. The family had moved to Karachi from Rajkot in Gujarat a generation before. Jinnah's grandfather was a Hindu (of Bhatia caste) who got converted to Islam for unknown reasons. They were now Khoja Muslims, a business community among Muslims who are followers of Aga Khan. Mohammad Ali was the first of six children of his parents. Surprisingly, his date of birth is still under dispute. But according to his own assertion, he was born on Christmas day (25 December) in 1876, and that is the day officially celebrated in Pakistan. His father was a hide merchant and had prospered since the arrival of the family in Karachi. When Mohammad was about six, his father arranged a tutor for him but the boy was not interested in studies. His aunt (father's sister) Manbai tempted him to visit her in Bombay and put him in a school there. In Bombay, he studied for an uncertain but brief period at the Gokul Das Tej Primary School. Returning to Karachi in 1887, he was enrolled in Sind *madarsa* in December 1887 but he studied there only for a few years. Later, he studied in Christian Missionary High School. He was fond of horse riding; his father owned several horses. Reading bored him. He was not easy to control even as a child. It is doubtful if he learnt enough of Gujarati (his mother tongue), Hindi or Urdu because we find Gandhi writing to him on 28 June 1919: "I have your promise that you would take up Gujarati and Hindi as quickly as possible".[1]

Jinnah's father's firm was closely associated with a British firm Douglas Graham & Co. The company's general manager, Leigh Croft, developed a liking for the young energetic lad and suggested to his father that his son should be sent for an apprenticeship in the company's head office in London. Jinnah's father agreed but his mother insisted that her son should marry before he left for England. So in 1892 the sixteen-year-old Jinnah was married to a Khoja girl, Emibai, two years his junior. In January 1893, Jinnah left for England. Not long after arriving in London, he abandoned business for law. He shortened his name to M.A. Jinnah for the convenience of his British friends and acquaintances. He was called to the Bar from the Lincoln's Inn in 1896. While in London he used to visit the House of Commons and listened to the debates there. He also fell in love with theatre. After three and a half years in England, Jinnah sailed back to his country, reaching Karachi in 1896. "His home-coming was grim. His mother and wife had died and his father's business was on the verge of collapse". Instead of settling in Karachi, he decided to seek his fortune in Bombay. He had to struggle hard for some years but his law practice soon picked up. In time, he had earned a name as a brilliant barrister; his income soared and he started living in luxury and was always immaculately dressed. He lived more like a British than an Indian; wee bit a dandy.

Jinnah had two brothers and three sisters but the only sibling with whom he established a close, continuing relationship till the end was sister Fatima, seventeen years younger than him. Jinnah defied Muslim conventions by sending Fatima to a Catholic boarding school and later encouraged her to study dentistry. But Jinnah never tried to usher in any reform movement among the Muslim community as such.

Besides his legal practice, Jinnah developed an interest in politics. He was influenced by Dadabhai Naoroji, Gokhale and Ferozeshah Mehta (in whose chambers he worked for some time when he was trying to establish himself). It was at the Calcutta session of the Congress in 1906 that Jinnah made his debut in politics. Dadabhai presided over the session and Jinnah served as his secretary. Jinnah formally joined the Congress party in that year. Gradually his flirtations with the Muslim League (which was founded in 1906 at Dhaka) started. Though not a member of the Muslim League, he addressed their sessions in 1910 and 1911. In 1910, he was elected to the Imperial Legislative Council from the Muslim constituency of Bombay. The separate constituencies for Muslims had been created under the 1909 Act. Except for 1913 when he was nominated, he was elected, often unopposed, from Muslim constituencies in 1915, 1923, 1926 and 1934. During his election in 1910 and again in 1915, he was still a member of the Congress. He had a long and brilliant career as a legislator and vied for prominence with stalwarts like Motilal Nehru, Lajpat Rai, Madan Mohan Malaviya and M.R. Jayakar. He started enjoying his political outings, and along with law, politics became his second passion. In fact, apart from law and politics, he had no other interests. "He seldom, if ever, read a serious book in all his life. His staple food was newspapers, briefs and law books".

In 1913, he formally joined the Muslim League and the interest of the Muslim community became the prime concern of his life. It is true that he did not believe in Islamic taboos like eating pork and in rituals like going to the mosque for prayers and to Mecca for salvation. For him these were non-essential things. What he did during the rest of his life was to get the maximum benefits for the Muslim community, so that they could become a power to reckon with. His brilliant legal brain produced the document called Lucknow Pact in 1916, as he presided over the Lucknow session of the Muslim League at Kaisar Bagh, Lucknow. Nobody else but Jinnah could get for the Muslims what he got under the Lucknow Pact. Separate electorates for Muslims were retained; Muslims got heavy weightage in legislatures: one-third at the centre and in Bombay, one-half in the Punjab, forty per cent in Bengal, thirty per cent in the United Provinces, twenty-five per cent in Bihar and Orissa and fifteen per cent in Central Provinces and in Madras. Except for Punjab and Bengal, it was quite heavy weightage in the centre and other states. Muslims also got virtual veto during the enactment of new legislation in the assemblies. In return, the Muslim

League promised to work with the Congress in their fight for *swaraj*. In spite of these concessions to the Muslims in the Lucknow Pact, the loss of majority in the Punjab and Bengal rankled Jinnah for years, and he wanted to annul that clause which went against the interest of the Muslims. In 1924, he said, "As a party to the Lucknow Pact, I can say that it was never intended to be permanent. I suggest that in Bengal and Punjab, Muslims should be restored to their majority."[2]

Jinnah was a widower for more than two decades when he thought of marrying again. His choice was a beautiful, young, vivacious Parsi girl Ratanbai or Ruttie, daughter of one of the wealthiest Parsis in Bombay, Sir Dinshaw M. Petit. Jinnah was forty-two and she nineteen when they got married on 19 April 1918 against the wishes of her father. Three days earlier Jinnah got her converted to Islam. "Sir Dinshaw never forgave her daughter, never saw her again and even when she died, he refused to attend the funeral or even to see her body". The couple had only one daughter Dina, born in 1919. The marriage proved a disaster. Apart from the age factor, the nature of husband and wife were distinctly different. "Ruttie had married Jinnah because of the glamour of his personality, and there was nothing in common between them. Jinnah used to pore over his briefs every day, and what little time he had to spare was given to politics. Ruttie was a young woman, fond of life and frivolities of the young. They gradually drifted apart".[3] While Jinnah found solace in his briefs and politics, Ruttie had nothing to fall back on. She became a mental wreck and tried to find solace in drugs, in Theosophy, séance, and her pets. But nothing seemed to work for her and she died in the prime of her youth in February 1929. Before she died, she had confided to her dear Parsi friend Kanji Dwarkadas that she would like to be cremated. But Jinnah ignored her last wish and got her buried under Muslim rites. Ruttie was a true nationalist and "kept Jinnah on the right track so long as she was alive. After her death, Jinnah's sole companion at home was his sister Fatima, who was even more communal minded and partly responsible for the transformation brought about in Jinnah subsequently. There is reason to believe that Jinnah rehearsed his speeches before her. She enjoyed Jinnah's diatribes against the Hindus, and if anything, injected an extra dose of venom into them".[4]

The year 1920 proved to be a turning point in the life of Jinnah, and that of India. It was the year when Gandhi promised *swaraj* in one year and got his non-cooperation resolution passed by the Congress. When Jinnah stood up to oppose 'Mr. Gandhi's resolution' at the Nagpur session of the Congress he was "howled down with cries of shame, shame. "Not 'Mr.' but say 'Mahatma'," the unwieldy crowd yelled. Jinnah taken aback, tried to argue but was shouted down. He left the stage in disgust and the Congress for good, "the searing memory of his defeat at Nagpur permanently emblazoned on his mind". He waited for revenge. The importance of Jinnah remained outside the Congress. In 1923 and 1926, he was elected to the Central Legislature from Muslim constituencies. His community still believed in him, and he decided to serve the Muslim community with renewed vigour, as president of the Muslim League.

In 1924, he was appointed a member of the Maddiman Committee, which was to examine the working of India Act of 1919. He was also nominated a member of the Skeen Committee, along with Motilal Nehru, which was to examine the problem of Indianisation of army officers. It was evident that the government considered him as one of the most important members of the Central Assembly. When in 1928, the All-White Simon Commission visited India, the Jinnah faction of the Muslim League joined the Congress in boycotting the commission which was appointed to assess the working of the 1919 Act and to propose further legislation leading towards self-government. Simultaneously, the All-Parties Conference appointed a committee headed by Motilal Nehru in February 1928 "to report on the principle of a constitution for independent India". The committee submitted its report (later called Nehru Report) at the Lucknow meeting in August 1928. The main recommendations were: dominion status; joint electorates; weightage to minorities etc. The parties agreed to the proposals. But the agreement did not last long and when the conference met on 22 December 1928, Muslims under the leadership of Jinnah, made four new demands in the form of amendments. These were thirty-three and a half percent representation for the Muslims in the Central Legislature; reservation of seats on population basis in Punjab and Bengal; residuary powers with the provincial governments and separation of Sind from Bombay. The amendments were turned down and Jinnah left the Conference disappointed calling it 'parting of ways'. From Calcutta after wrecking the All-Parties Convention, he reached Delhi, to attend the All-Parties Muslim Conference. Aga Khan, who presided over the meeting, welcomed the prodigal to the Islamic fold. Jinnah's four points in Calcutta swelled to fourteen by the time he reached Delhi. The elaborate demands put forward in Jinnah's famous 'fourteen points' were not yet Pakistan, "but almost its early embryo, within a weak federal womb." He threw away his nationalist and secular mask which he was wearing since the Lucknow Pact days. "I have no future in any Hindu dominated body," he declared. The Muslim League elected him life-long president.

Jinnah sailed for England on 4 October 1930, along with his sister Fatima and daughter Dina, to attend the Round Table Conference as a Muslim nominee. There he put forward a wide range of demands of special Muslim interests contained in his fourteen points adding a few more to it. The vision of Pakistan was getting clearer in his mind. It will remain a mystery why Jinnah was not invited to attend the Second and Third Round Table Conferences. But according to his own admission, "I was not invited to the later sittings of the Conference because I was the strongest opponent of the Federal Scheme". Disappointed, Jinnah decided to stay on in England to practice before the Privy Council but without much success. However, when the Communal Award was announced in 1932, all his fourteen points had been conceded by the British government and actually more concessions to the Muslims were given than what they had asked for.

At the request of several Muslim friends and well-wishers like Iqbal and Liaqat Ali, Jinnah returned to India in 1934 to lead the Muslim community. Muslims were in need of a dynamic and cunning leader. Between 1928 and 1936 many Muslim leaders of national stature died: Ajmal Khan, Mohammad Ali, M.A.Ansari, Shafi and Fazli Hussain. Sikandar Hyat Khan in Punjab and Fazlul Haq in Bengal were busy in provincial politics. The burden of rejuvenating the moribund Muslim League fell on Jinnah's shoulders and he seemed to like the role assigned to him. The Communal Award had given a new orientation to the communal politics in the country and Jinnah emerged as the saviour of the Muslim community. In the Bombay session of the Muslim League (April 1936), a resolution was adopted rejecting the Federal Scheme of the 1935 Act while recommending the Provincial Scheme to be tried 'for what it is worth'. Elections to the provincial legislatures were held in 1937 under the 1935 Act. The results of the elections were extremely disappointing from Jinnah's point of view. Of the 485 Muslim seats, the League could win only 108 seats in all the eleven provinces; the remaining Muslim seats went to other Muslim groups. Congress won almost all the 'general seats' and formed ministries in seven out of eleven provinces. The defeated Jinnah started vicious propaganda against the Congress ministries charging that inequities and injustices were being inflicted on the Muslims in the 'Hindu Raj'. To add weight to the accusations, a committee headed by Raja of Pirpur was formed to "look into the grievances of Muslims under Congress rule". Another committee was formed in Bihar to go into the details of Muslim suffering under Congress rule which was even more intemperate. "At this distance of time their truth or untruth matters little. What was important is the technique adopted by Jinnah to incite the Muslim masses by making them believe that 'Islam was in danger.'" The Muslim masses flocked to the League, the membership jumping from a few thousand to over hundred thousand in United Provinces alone. Jinnah had become a mass leader, tens of thousands of people greeting him with cries of *Allah-hu-Akbar* and *Quaid-e-Azam Zindabad*. To Jinnah's delight, the Congress ministries decided to resign in November, 1939, after the War broke out. This, not a very wise act of Congress, left the political field entirely to be exploited by the Muslim League. Under Jinnah's orders the Muslims observed 22 December 1939 as the 'Day of Deliverance'. Only a few months later, Jinnah was bold enough to demand a separate area of the country for the 'Muslim nation' in the Lahore session of the Muslim League (March 1940). Pakistan had arrived. Henceforth, Pakistan became a passion and a mania with Jinnah. He evolved a strategy to deal with the Congress, which puzzled and bewildered the Congress leaders and to a lesser degree the government. Every Congress error was irreversibly exploited by Jinnah and the Congress led by Gandhi managed to commit many such errors during 1940-1947. "Never was the Gandhian leadership less relevant to practical politics; never did the Congress need more to recognise its own shortcoming".[5] Gandhi's launching the Quit India campaign (1942) without proper planning and the government, putting almost all the Congress leaders behind the bars, left the political arena open for Jinnah to exploit to achieve his end. The repeated contradictory announcements by Gandhi that Muslims have a right to ask for the division did help Jinnah to be adamant in demanding division of the country. The worst thing Gandhi did was to go to Jinnah's house in Bombay daily for eighteen days in September 1944 with the offer of Pakistan contained in the Rajaji Formula. Jinnah, the superb tactician, humbled Gandhi on the last day of their meeting by pointing out that he (Gandhi) did not represent any political organization. Jinnah emerged as the most important leader to decide the destiny of the country. Even before Gandhi's disastrous journey to Jinnah's residence in 1944, several Congress leaders including Jawaharlal Nehru, Rajendra Prasad and Subhas Chandra Bose had tried to convince Jinnah about his unreasonable attitude, through correspondence and personal meetings. But Jinnah was adamant and wanted that the Congress recognize Muslim League as the sole representative of the Muslims. Congress could not accept that because it claimed to represent all Indians irrespective of caste and creed. Jinnah's technique of getting the other man to make an offer so that he could turn it down and ask for more was difficult to counter and paid him rich dividends. His intransigence became a rewarding strategy and his obstinacy his great asset. Through these tactics he almost got the Hindu majority reduced to a minority in legislature and services during the Simla Conference (1945) and Cabinet mission (1946) discussions. His greatest triumph came during the December 1945 elections for the Central Assembly in which Muslim League won all the Muslim seats in the Central Assembly securing eighty-seven percent of Muslim votes. There was a chance for India to remain united when the Congress and the Muslim League agreed to the proposals of the Cabinet Mission (March-June, 1946). There was some dispute about the 'grouping' of provinces but that was almost resolved. However, a statement by Nehru on 10 July 1946 immediately after taking over as president of the Congress, that Constituent Assembly was a sovereign body and was capable of changing the accepted plan, gave Jinnah an excuse to reject the Cabinet Mission proposals. Sensing that the vast majority of Muslims were with him he changed his strategy. In the last week of July, the Muslim League Council met at Bombay and pased a resolution, the significant sentence of which was, "the time has come for the Muslim nation to resort to Direct Action to achieve Pakistan". When a corespondent asked Jinnah if the Direct Action would be violent or non-violent, Jinnah retorted: "I am not going to discuss ethics." Direct Action was launched in Calcutta on 16 August 1946 as planned. An orgy of violence, killings, stabbing, looting, arson and rape continued for three days, leaving five thousand dead. Gandhi's reaction to the Calcutta carnage was typical of him: "If through deliberate courage the Hindus had died to a man that would have been deliverance of Hinduism and India and purification of Islam in this land." The riots spread to East Bengal and then to several parts of India. When Hindus retaliated in Bihar, Jinnah was unnerved and on 20 November 1946 he pleaded for complete exchange of population. But the Congress leadership ignored his proposal.

Though the Cabinet Mission proposals were rejected, formation of an Interim government and the Constituent Assembly were implemented by the Government. After initial reluctance, the Muslim League joined the Interim Government headed by Nehru but with more Muslim members than the Hindus. The League never participated in the Constituent Assembly of united India. While the Bihar riots were ruthlessly suppressed under Nehru's guidance, riots in other parts of the country continued and Jinnah looked the other way. The worst affected area was now Punjab. By March 1947, the riots became more serious and Hindus and Sikhs started leaving many parts of Panjab. Gandhi and his creed of non-violence had made the task of Muslim League easier. Jinnah was speaking the language of Hitler. "The riots were a sufficient indication that gangsterism had become a settled part of their strategy in politics. They seem to be consciously and deliberately imitating the Sudetan Germans in the means employed by them against the Czecks".[6] Congress leaders were utterly shaken and on 8 March 1947 they passed a resolution asking for the partition of Punjab and Bengal. This was virtually accepting partition of the country. At the same time the British were in a hurry to leave the country as after the War they were in no position to hold on to India. Things moved fast after that. The British prime minister, Attlee, announced in Parliament that the British will be leaving India by June 1948. They sent Lord Mountbatten as viceroy in March 1947 to wind up. He advanced the date to 14/15 August 1947. The country was divided on that day and two dominions, Bharat and Pakistan emerged, Jinnah accepting the 'mutilated and motheaten' Pakistan. The last meeting of the Muslim League was held in Delhi on 9-10 June 1947 in which Jinnah had a difficult time for the first time. He was accused of 'betrayal' for accepting partition of Punjab and Bengal. *Khaksars* tried to lynch him; the Muslim League National Guards coming to his rescue. But the most intriguing aspect about the creation of Pakistan is: How Jinnah could delude his co-religionists in Hindu majority provinces into believing that Pakistan was good for them. Jinnah flew to Karachi along with his sister Fatima on 7 August 1947. His daughter Dina refused to accompany him as she had married a Parsi converted to Christianity, Neville Wadia owner of commercial and textile empire Bombay Dyeing. According to M.C. Chagla, when Jinnah learnt about his daughter's intention to marry a non-Muslim, he was furious said: "There are thousands of Muslim boys to choose from. Why you want to marry a non-Muslim?" The girl retorted, "Father: there were thousands of Muslim girls who would have liked to marry you, why did you marry a Parsi girl?" Jinnah had no answer to that. But he disowned his daughter and left most of his property to his sister Fatima. In poetic exuberance Sarojini Naidu had described Jinnah as an ambassador of Hindu-Muslim unity during the earlier decades of the last century but the label deserves scrutiny. Jinnah's actions and his concern for Muslim interests from the very beginning of his political career cast a doubt about his ever being a nationalist or a secularist.

Jinnah had appointed himself as governor-general of Pakistan. But he was a dying man and he knew that. Doctors had told him some years earlier that tuberculosis had devoured his lungs, and he did not have many years to live. During his thirteen months as Pakistan's governor-general, he was fighting ill-health most of the time. He died on 11 September 1948 at Karachi.

What kind of man was Jinnah? People who came to know him have assessed him in different ways. In July 1946, when Gandhi's biographer

Louis Fischer asked Gandhi, "What did you learn from your eighteen days with Jinnah?" (in September 1944). Gandhi replied, "I learned that he was a maniac. I could not make any headway with Jinnah because he is a maniac." Mountbatten, after a series of meetings with Jinnah reported to his staff that he considered, "Mr. Jinnah was a psychopathic case." And later added that "Until he had met Mr. Jinnah, he had not thought it possible that a man with such a complete lack of sense of responsibility could hold the power which he did". The reaction of Lord Ismay, Mountbatten's chief of staff, was, "the dominating feature in Mr. Jinnah's mental structure was his loathing and contempt of the Hindus. He apparently thought that all Hindus were sub-human creatures with whom it was impossible for the Muslims to live". Paying a left-handed compliment to Jinnah, V.D. Savarkar said in one of his speeches, "Jinnah is a true representative and custodian of Muslim rights. Hindus needed a leader like Jinnah." B.R. Ambedkar gave a detailed assessment of Jinnah, "He (Jinnah) may be too self-opinionated, an egotist without the mask and has perhaps a degree of arrogance which is not compensated by any extraordinary intellect or equipment. It may be on that account he is unable to reconcile himself to a second place and work with others in that capacity for a public cause. He may not be overflowing with ideas although he is not, as his critics make him out to be, an empty headed dandy living upon the ideas of others. It may be that his fame is built up more upon art and less on substance. At the same time, it is doubtful if there is a politician in India to whom the adjective incorruptible can be more fittingly applied. No one can buy him".[9]

Jinnah was single-handedly pitted against Indian leaders whom we call 'great' like Gandhi, Nehru, Patel and Rajaji. All of them felt defeated against him.

## References

1. *Collected Works of Mahatma Gandhi*. Vol. 15, p.399.
2. Nagarkar, V.V. *Genesis of Pakistan*, Allied, 1975, p.172.
3. Chagla, M.C. *Roses in December*, Bombay, Bharatiya Vidya Bhavan, 1973, p.120.

4. Ibid p.119.

5. Hodson, H.V. *The Great Divide*. Karachi, OUP. 1985, p.526 (First Pub. Hutchinson, London, 1969).

6. Ambedkar, B.R. *Pakistan or the Partition of India*. Bombay, Thacker & Co. 3rd, ed. 1946, p.269.

7. *Collected Works of Mahatma Gandhi*, Vol. 85, p.514.

8. Wolpert, Stanley. *Jinnah of Pakistan*, OUP. 1984, p.319.

9. Ambedkar op. cit. p.328.

# Kumaraswami Kamaraj

## (1903-1975)

Kumaraswami Kamaraj was born on 15 July 1903 at Virudhunagar in the district of Ramnad in Tamil Nadu to Kumaraswami Nadar and Sivakami Ammal. He had a sister called Nagammal. The family belonged to Nadar caste. His father had a small coconut shop and died when Kamaraj was only six years old. An uncle came to the rescue of the family and supported the family for sometime. Kamaraj had very rudimentary education and even during school days, he often played truant. Throughout his life he could learn no other language other than his mother tongue, Tamil, At twelve, he started assisting his uncle in his cloth shop. While sitting in the shop he used to read newspapers and started taking an interest in political developments around the world and in India. The First World War was in progress and exciting things were happening. Then came the Jallianwala tragedy (1919) which proved to be a turning point in his life. Freedom from foreign rule became the passion of his life. Gandhi had emerged as the national leader by 1919 and Congress as the national party. Kamaraj joined the Congress party and became a devoted follower of Gandhi. But for years he was content to remain a rank and file and nameless Congress worker. He had a brief stint in the insurance business but gave it up after a few months. Then on, political activity became his sole occupation. Another important decision which he made during this time was to remain a bachelor throughout his life.

The Nadar community, to which he belonged, was relatively affluent among the low-castes; were upwardly mobile and considered themselves as *kshatriya*. They were largely pro-British, and it was hard to work as a Congress volunteer among them. During the Con-Cooperation Movement, he worked for the propagation of *khadi* and prohibition but somehow was not arrested. After the withdrawal of the Non-Cooperation Movement in 1922, the Congress party was divided between no-changers (still believing in non-cooperation) led by Rajagopalachari in Madras and those who wanted to enter the legislative bodies 'to wreck their working from within'. The latter group in the south was led by S. Satyamurthi and S. Srinivasa Iyengar. Kamraj joined this group of pro-changers. Satyamurthi became his political guru and Kamaraj started working closely with him, though he was a Brahmin. It required some courage because the anti-Brahmin Justice Party had emerged as a powerful political force in Madras and had even formed the first ministry in Madras under the 1919 Act in the 1920s. Kamaraj remained in the Congress party and worked for the emancipation of the poor masses of Madras irrespective of caste or language. He had a few domestic responsibilities and led a semi-bohemian life roaming about villages of the *taluka* selling khadi and preaching freedom from foreign rule. He was still a silent worker, partly because he was not a good speaker and rabble-rouser.

However, he was gradually being drawn more and more into the political arena. In 1925, he was elected to the Tamil Nadu Congress Committee from Cuddalore. In 1930, he took part in the Salt Satyagraha in his taluka; was arrested and sentenced to two years imprisonment, which he spent in Bellary jail. However, he was released in March 1931 under the Gandhi-Irwin Pact. He came back to his native place Virudhunagar and received a hero's welcome. During the Civil Disobedience movement, he was again arrested in 1932 and lodged in Vellore jail.

In the 1936 assembly elections, the Justice Party was routed and the Congress Party formed ministry under Rajagopalachari in 1937. Kamaraj was elected to the Madras Assembly from Sathur. However, he kept himself almost completely in the background and hardly took part in the debates. He was not cut out for parliamentary work. Another reason was that the Assembly was completely dominated by Rajaji and his men and Kamaraj, as everyone knew, was a Satyamurthi man, who was a *bete noire* for Rajagopalachari.

In 1940, Kamaraj fought the election for the presidentship of Tamil Nadu Congress against Rajaji's candidate C.P. Subbaiah and won by a narrow margin. This election marked, in a very real sense, a turning point in the political career of Kamaraj. But he was arrested during individual satyagraha in December 1940; was kept in Vellore jail and released in November 1941. He was arrested again during the Quit India Movement on 16 August 1942 and sent to Vellore jail again and later to the Amravati jail. He was released in June 1945. After his release, he continued as president of the Tamil Nadu Congress Committee, as during the War years, fresh elections could not be held. During this time, several things happened. Kamaraj's mentor Satyamurthi had died in 1943. Rajagopalachari rejoined the Congress with the blessings of Gandhi and without the knowledge of the TNCC president, Kamaraj, which irked him. Further friction was caused when during a tour of the south, Gandhi pleaded for Rajaji's resumption of leadership of the Congress in Tamil Nadu. In an article in the *Harijan* (10 February 1946) Gandhi paid tribute to Rajaji and wrote that he was "pained to find a 'clique' against him. It is a clique that evidently counts in the official Congress in Madras, but the masses are devoted to Rajaji".[1] Kamaraj felt that Gandhi's accusation was a reflection on him and his colleagues and resigned from the Tamil Nadu Congress Parliamentary Board. However, there was no doubt that there was a strong feeling among Congressmen in Tamil Nadu against Rajaji for his Pakistan resolution and for leaving the Congress party in 1942. However, in the election of 1946 the Congress party swept the polls. Kamaraj was elected from the Sattur-Aruppukkottai constituency. He was also elected to the Constituent Assembly in 1946. He also served as a member of the All India Congress Committee from 1947 to 1969. In the 1952 election, Kamaraj was elected as a member of the Lok Sabha from Srivilliputtar constituency. In his absence, Rajagopalachari was sworn in as chief minister of Tamil Nadu in April 1952. However, opposition to his education policy grew and he had to resign in April 1954. Kamaraj was then elected as the leader of Congress Legislative Party and was sworn in as chief minister a week later, and consequently resigned from the Lok Sabha. He remained chief minister of Tamil Nadu for nine years, (1954-63) and was elected to the Assembly for three terms in 1954, 1957 and 1962 consecutively. His long tenure as chief minister is "generally regarded as an outstanding success for laying the infrastructure of economic development, for accessible, firm, and impartial administration, and for striking at caste hierarchy without undue confrontation or rhetoric". By the time he resigned as chief minister in 1963, Madras state had made notable progress on all fronts — food, agriculture, industry, education, power, irrigation and roads.

Then happened a political event which catapulted Kamaraj to the national scene. It was what has come to be known as Kamraj Plan, for which he is remembered most. In June 1963, Kamaraj had met Jawaharlal Nehru at Hyderabad and had showed his anxiety for the decline in the prestige of the Congress and suggested that all the senior leaders should resign their executive posts as cabinet ministers and chief ministers and devote their time for the rejuvenation of the party. Then the prime minister should decide whom to retain as Cabinet ministers and chief ministers. Kamaraj himself offered to resign. Nehru quickly realized what a powerful weapon Kamaraj had put into his hands. On 21 August 1963, Kamaraj was urgently called to Delhi to decide with the prime minister who should be axed. An understanding was soon reached. While all the Union ministers and all the chief ministers submitted their resignations; only those of six Cabinet ministers and six chief ministers were accepted. Those Cabinet ministers who had to go were — Morarji Desai, S.K. Patil, Jagjivan Ram, Lal Bahadur Shastri, K.L. Shrimali and Gopala Reddi. Among the chief ministers to go were, Kamaraj, C.B. Gupta, Biju Patnaik, Ghulam Mohammed, B. Jha of Bihar, and B.A. Mandloi of Madhya Pradesh. The 'purge' at the highest level neatly dispensed with some of the 'less desirable' candidates in the run-up to Nehru's succession, prominent among them, of course, was Morarji Desai. Soon after Lal Bahadur was brought in as minister-without-portfolio 'to lessen the burden of the prime minister.' Kamaraj, on the other hand, got elected as president of the Congress party, the office which he held till 1969. Kamaraj, as Congress president, became a crucial figure during months before Nehru's death and even after his passing away.

He was an astute politician who came to the fore when twice in as many years, he succeeded in the selection of prime minister. After the death of Nehru he manoeuvred to get Lal Bahadur Shastri 'unanimously' elected as the leader of the Parliamentary Party. After Shastri's death in 1966, Kamaraj saw to it, with the help of his coterie, (which had come to be known as the 'Syndicate') that Morarji Desai was defeated in the quest for prime ministership by Indira Gandhi. Earlier, when his well-wishers had suggested that he should put his claim for prime ministership, Kamaraj's reaction was: "No English, no Hindi, How, How?" using the few words of English which he had learnt.[2] Later on, his relations with Indira Gandhi became strained, especially after Indira Gandhi devalued the rupee by 57.5 per cent under American pressure without consulting Kamaraj, who was party president. She did not consult Kamaraj because she knew that he was vehemently against devaluation. Kamaraj who had ensured that Indira, rather than Desai, became prime minister, reportedly moaned 'a big man's daughter, a small man's mistake'. Kamaraj, alongwith the 'Syndicate' and also Desai wanted Indira to be out. But she out-manoeuvred them all by splitting the Congress party into two, the old guard naming their party as Congress (O). Mrs. Gandhi's faction was called Congress (R) and later it was to be Congress (I).

The glorious days of Kamaraj were now behind him. He lost the Parliamentary election in 1967 to a twenty-six year old student leader of the Dravida Munnetra Kazhagam (DMK). His popularity and his power slided downwards. There was some respite when he won the by-election in 1968. But he never regained the position which he enjoyed during the early 1960s. The 1967 election brought DMK to power in Tamil Nadu and pushed the Congress into opposition. Kamaraj went to the villages to meet the rural folk — his first love and his strength. But he was a spent force now and died without much notice in 1975. He was awarded Bharat Ratna in 1976 posthumously.

The rise of Kamaraj as a shrewd Congress leader guiding the destiny of the country during a crucial decade is nothing short of a phenomenon. Coming from a poor family, belonging to a low caste, without much of schooling, not knowing Hindi or English, he overcame all these hurdles through his humility, hard work and subtle manoeuvering and sheer grit. He is remembered for his work as chief minister of Madras, for his Kamraj Plan and as 'king maker' to this day.

## References

1. Narasimhan, V.K. *Kamaraj; A Study*, Bombay, Manaktalas, 1967, p.34.
2. Frank, Katherine. *Indira; The Life of Indira Nehru Gandhi*. London, Harper Collins. 2001, p.299.

# Dhondo Keshav Karve (Maharishi)

## (1858-1962)

Karve was the foremost social reformer and educationist of Maharashtra who devoted his life for the emancipation of widows and for female education.

Dhondo Keshav Karve was born in Murud, a small village in the Konkan region of Maharashtra, in a middle-class family. His father, Keshav Bappunna Karve, was manager of a small estate in Ratnagiri district, getting a meagre salary.

Dhondo (later known as Annasaheb) had his primary education in his village Murud. Later he went to Bombay and joined Robert Money School and passed the Matriculation examination rather late in 1881 at the age of twenty-three, due to certain personal and family circumstances. He, however, obtained good marks and was able to join the prestigious Elphinston College, Bombay, from where he passed B.A. examination in 1884. Mathematics was his favourite subject.

While still a student, Dhondo was married at the age of fifteen (1873) to a nine-year-old girl Radhabai. Ten years after marriage their first son Raghunath was born. Two more sons were born later.

After graduation, Dhondo settled in Bombay and started his career as a teacher. From 1888 to 1891, he taught mathematics in the Cathedral Girl's High School, the Alexandra High School and the Maratha High School, Bombay. In September 1891, Karve joined Fergusson College,

Poona, as professor of mathematics. There he came in close contact with Gokhale who had a very high opinion of Karve. Unfortunately, the same year (1891) his wife Radhabai died. Karve was heartbroken but busied himself with his teaching work. In April 1892, he was elected a Life Member of the Deccan Education Society. He taught in Fergusson College for twenty-one years and retired in 1914.

While still teaching at the Fergusson College, Karve had been devoting his time for social work. He was much influenced by the work done by Ram Mohan Roy and Ishwar Chandra Vidyasagar, for the emancipation of Hindu widows in Bengal. In Maharashtra also, Pandita Ramabai had opened Sharda Sadan in 1889 for giving education to widows in Poona. Ramabai had been converted to Christianity and was getting money from foreign missions. Karve wanted to help widows while remaining in the fold of Hinduism. To set an example, Karve married Godubai, a widow, in March 1893. The couple was ex-communicated by the orthodox Brahmin community to which Karve belonged. But both of them showed examplary courage and weathered the storm. He was now determined to change social opinion about widow marriage. He founded a society in 1893, *Vidhva Vivahottejak Mandali* (Society for the Promotion of Widow Marriages). In 1895, the name of the society was changed to '*Vidhva Vivah Pratibandh Nivarak Mandali*' (Society for the Removal of Obstacles to Widow Marriages). Karve toured all over Maharashtra to popularize widow marriage. He also collected donations for the 'Mandali'. Karve's efforts for the emancipation of widows was bearing fruit. Gradually people began to appreciate the need to help these unfortunate women rejected by society for no fault of theirs. In 1898, he started the *Mahila Ashram* (Widows Home) in Poona, a home for destitute women where they could live safely and with dignity. In 1900, the ashram was shifted to Hingne, a village ten kilometres from Poona, where it still functions.

Karve soon realized that unless women, including widows, were educated, their condition and status could not be improved, nor would they be able to fend for themselves. With great foresight he reasoned that if girls were sent to school, their marriages could be postponed thus reducing the possibility of child marriage and early widowhood. Karve was convinced that education was the key to the emancipation of women.

With this object in mind, he started *Mahila Vidyalaya*, a residential school for girls in 1907. The school not only taught the three 'Rs' but also imparted training in different skills to make women self-reliant and self-confident. The ashram and the school became the centre of social reform. Here widows did not lead a life of misery and helplessness. They looked forward to a meaningful and exciting future. Educated widows were trained to take up teaching and administrative jobs in the school and the ashram. Some students even took up jobs outside the ashram. The success of the ashram and the unique school earned the admiration of several important personalities. The renowned Indologist R.G. Bhandarkar became the honorary president of the Ashram.[1] The news about the work being done for women, especially the widows, reached the far shores of South Africa. Gandhi, who was in South Africa at that time, wrote in the *Indian Opinion*, "Thousands of widows, mostly among Hindus, spend their whole life to no purpose. To that extent the wealth of India is being wasted. To prevent this waste, the benevolent Prof. Karve of Poona has dedicated his life to the country. He has been running, for several years, an institution in Poona for the education of widows. There, women are given training in midwifery and nursing. The work of the institution has been expanding. Because he is rendering honorary service himself, he is able to get similar assistance from others too. Moreover, he goes about from place to place collecting funds. There are so many things which can be done through sheer self help and without Government aid".[2]

In 1908, Karve started *'Nishkam Karma Math'*, a self-sacrificing institution to train workers for the ashram and *Mahila Vidyalaya*. In 1914, Karve, who was now endearingly being addressed as 'Annasaheb' by his admirers, retired from Fergusson College. Now he was free to devote all his time to the working and development of the institutions which, almost single-handed, he had established. Inspired by the Women's University of Tokyo, Annasaheb founded the Indian Women's University in Poona (later it was shifted to Bombay) in 1916. The following year, a training college for primary school teachers was added. Karve became its first principal. To run a university required more money than what Annasaheb had imagined. But a huge donation came from an unexpected source, which gave the university a stable base. The donation was from

Seth Vithaldas Thackersey. While giving the donation, he had requested that the university should be known as Shrimati Nathibai Damodar Thackersey and should be located in Bombay. Thus S.N.D.T. Women's University came about and is one of the leading universities in the country financed now by the University Grants Commission. Recently it has moved to its new campus in Bombay.

Annasaheb's name as a social worker and as an educationist was now known outside India. He was invited by several social and educational organizations in England and Europe to address select gatherings. He left for England in March, 1929. He attended the Primary Teacher's Conference and later spoke on 'Education for Women in India', at a meeting of the East India Association at Caxton Hall, London. From July to August, he was in Europe and spoke on 'The Indian Experiment in Higher Education for Women' in Geneva and Elsinor, Denmark. From Europe he went to America and delivered lectures and exchanged views at several places on women's education and social reform in general with particular reference to India. He returned to India via Japan, where he visited Women's University in Tokyo which had inspired him to start a similar university in India resulting in the establishment of S.N.D.T. He had been collecting money for his Women's University wherever he went. He returned to India in April 1930. In December the same year Karve left for Africa. He visited Kenya, Uganda, Tanganayika, Zanzibar and South Africa, collecting money for his institutions as usual. He was back in India in March 1932.

He was in his seventies now, an age at which most people ideally retire. But Annasaheb was still very active, planning to do still more for widows, for women and for society at large. With the funds which he had collected during his foreign tours, he started the Maharashtra Gram Prathmic Shikshan Mandal in 1936. The Mandal took up the task of opening schools in villages, — a field which Karve felt, he had neglected because he had been busy with widows' problems and women's education. Another important organization was established by him in 1944, the Samata Sangh. The aim of the Samata Sangh was to preach equality among men and inculcate the feeling of oneness in society. This was essentially a fight against caste distinctions and untouchability which was prevalent in Maharashtra in extreme form. Soon three hundred like-minded persons joined the Samata Sangh to spread its message of equality and fellow-feeling.

Many honours were bestowed upon Annasaheb during his long life. Banaras Hindu University awarded him a D. Litt. So did S.N.D.T. University and Bombay University. On his ninety-first birthday, Dr. Rajendra Prasad, president of India, presented him a purse of rupees one lakh which he distributed among the institutions founded by him. He was awarded the Padma Vibhushan in 1955 and Bharat Ratna in 1958. On the occasion Jawaharlal Nehru attended the main function in Bombay. Nehru in a brief speech observed, "Who am I in front of his personality? I have come to seek his blessings. We will be lucky if we can inculcate even a small bit of his great qualities — dedication and simplicity." Doordarshan made a film on his life and achievements. He was called a Maharishi (the great sage) by his admirers and fellow workers.

Karve did not write much, he being a doer. However, he started a monthly bulletin *Manavisamata* in 1947 to popularize the message of the 'Samata Sangh'. He wrote only two small books: *Atmavritta* (an autobiography) (1928) and *Looking Back* (1936).

He died on 9 November 1962 at the age of 104 leaving behind him a chain of memorabilia in the form of ashrams, schools and a university. Not many persons in India have done so much for widows and female education as Karve did in his long life.

## References

1.  Panandikar, Surekha. *Annasaheb Karve*, in *Remembering Our Leaders*, New Delhi, C.B.T. 1989, pp.38-39.
2.  *Indian Opinion*, 8-6-1907, included in the *Collected Works of Mahatma Gandhi*. Vol. 7, p.29.

# Abdul Ghaffar Khan

## (1890-1988)

Abdul Ghaffar was born in 1890 (exact date not known) in the village Utmanzai in Peshawar district of North West Frontier Province (NWFP) in an aristocratic family. He belonged to the Pathan tribe of Mohamadzai. His father, Khan Sahib Bahram Khan, was the headman of the village and commanded respect among his tribe, and surrounding villages.

At the age of five, Ghaffar Khan was sent by his parents to a *maktab* (school) attached to a mosque. There the sole teacher was a *mullah* (priest) who made the students learn by heart the Holy Quran. He continued his education at the Municipal Board High School in Peshawar and later went to the Edward Memorial Mission High School. It is difficult to explain why he changed so many schools: from Peshawar to Campbellpur, to Quadian and finally to Aligarh. However, he could not pass the Matriculation examination and returned home. That was the end of his formal education. Obviously Ghaffar Khan was not a good student and even in later life he could not communicate in the English language which was somewhat a handicap during his political career. That made some British officials like Lord Wavell pass snide remarks about him. It is believed that he had been selected as a commissioned officer in the army while still in school but did not join after he saw an Indian officer being insulted by a British officer who was his junior.

During his school days, Ghaffar Khan was influenced by one Haji of Turangzai, who was a pioneer educationist in NWFP. On his return from Aligarh in 1911, he associated with Haji of Turangzai in opening several schools, both for boys and girls in NWFP. He believed that the emancipation of the Pathans lay in getting educated. During this period, he began to subscribe to Urdu papers like *Al Hilal* (1912-14), edited by Maulana Azad and *Zamindar* edited by Zaffar Ali Khan. That was his initiation into political thinking.

In 1912, at the age of twenty-two, he was married to a Pathan girl. The following year his son, Abdul Ghani Khan, was born.

Ghaffar Khan was soon drawn into active politics. When the Khilafat movement, in support of the Khalifa of Turkey, was started in 1919-20, he attended a big political meeting at his village Utmanzai and was arrested along with his father, but both were soon released. He met Gandhi for the first time at the Khilafat Conference in Delhi in early 1920 and was drawn to him and his philosophy of non-violence. He also attended the Nagpur session of the Congress in which the resolution of non-cooperation was passed. Then on, he took active part in the activities of the Congress. To begin with, he organized the Khilafat movement in the North West Frontier Province which was spearheaded by the Congress. He was arrested and sentenced to three years rigorous imprisonment and was transferred to various prisons in Punjab where he came into contact with Hindu and Sikh prisoners and found that there was so much common in Hinduism, Islam and Sikhism. He studied the *Gita* and the *Granth Sahib* with them and taught them the essence of the *Quran*. He was released in 1924 and started doing social and constructive work among his people as advised by Gandhi after the Khilafat movement had failed. Later, he took part in Bardoli satyagraha (1928) and gave impressive speeches. But his main area of work remained NWFP. To organize the work he was doing, he started a movement called *Khudai Khitmatgars* (God's Servants). It was not just a political movement. It taught the Pathans love and brotherhood that inspired them with a sense of unity. It also inculcated in them the virtues of non-violence, 'thus harnessing the martial spirit of the Frontiermen in constructive channels'. "The Khudai Khitmatgars (also known as Red Shirts, because of the colour of their uniform) became shock brigade of every non-cooperation movement and were proving a bogy to successive Governments".[1] The British had a tough time during the nineteenth century in the NWFP and were very much concerned about the potential danger of Pathans getting organized. The government, therefore, unleashed a reign of terror of the worse kind, imprisoning and torturing thousands of Khudai Khitmatgars including Abdul Ghaffar Khan, under the Frontier Crimes Regulation Act. But he and his followers remained disciplined and bore all the punishments and atrocities stoically, something rare for the warlike Pathans. In spite of the government's reprisal, the number of Red Shirts went on increasing and at one time the number had crossed one hundred thousand. His followers started calling him Badshah Khan. Badshah Khan attended the Karachi session of the Congress in 1931, and brought with him thousands of Khudai Khidmatgars in their red uniforms. Badshah Khan's presence at the Karachi session gave the entire Congress leadership a greater dimension, proving that it was not a party of the Hindus only. After this, Badshah Khan emerged as a national leader. He was a member of the Congress Working Committee between 1930 and 1946. He was arrested in 1930 and was in prison for one year. Again he was arrested in 1934 for taking part in the Congress satyagraha. In fact he was in and out of British jails for about fourteen years between 1920 to 1947. At one time his entry into NWFP and Punjab was banned and he used to spend months with Gandhi in his Sabarmati Ashram or Wardha Ashram when Sabarmati Ashram was abandoned in 1933. During Gandhi's prayer meetings, he used to recite verses from Quran.

To spread his message to larger number of Pakhtuns, Badshah Khan started a Pashtu monthly *Pakhtun*, the first issue of which appeared in May 1930. Unfortunately, it had to be closed down in 1930 after Badshah Khan's arrest. It was revived the following year but had to be closed down again. After a few years it was again brought out as *Das Roza* in April 1938 but was closed down in 1941. It was revived in 1945 as a weekly but was closed down finally after the partition of the country in 1947.

Elections to the provincial assemblies were held in 1937 under the 1935 Act. The Congress party, led by Ghaffar Khan and his elder brother Dr. Khan Sahib, won a majority of seats in the NWFP Assembly and formed the ministry with Dr. Khan Sahib as chief minister. The Muslim League did not win a single seat. Badshah Khan never held any office throughout his life. Even when in 1934 he was offered presidentship of the Congress, he declined saying that he would rather be an ordinary worker. Of course, his brother Khan Sahib was certainly better suited for a highly important job of chief minister. He was a qualified doctor and had studied in India as well as in England, and was an able administrator.

In October-November 1938, Gandhi toured the NWFP accompanied by Badshah Khan starting from Utmanzai and ending at Taxila. They ran into an embarassing situation when Hindus of Bannu complained that their life and property were not safe in the NWFP because tribes like the Waziris raided their houses regularly, looting and burning their homes and property. After hearing them Gandhi remarked, "After studying all the facts I have gained the impression that the situation in respect of border raids has grown worse since the inauguration of the Congress Government. I therefore feel that unless Dr. Khan Sahib can cope with the question of the raids it might be better for him to tender his resignation."[3] It was a great embarassment for the host Badshah Khan, but he kept quiet. It was evident that the Khan brothers did not hold influence on all the Pathan tribes. However, Dr. Khan Sahib did not resign, ignoring Gandhi's advice.

Badshah Khan took part in the Quit India Movement of 1942 and was imprisoned along with other Congress leaders. He was released in 1945. By that time the British had made up their mind to leave India. Partition was in the air and the Congress leadership was yielding to the unreasonable demands of the Muslim League. In this atmosphere, elections were held in December 1945. While the Muslim League won all the Muslim seats in the Central Assembly, it could not win majority in any of the Muslim-majority provinces. In the NWFP, the Congress-Khudai Khidmatgar ministry was formed, headed by Dr. Khan Sahib. Badshah Khan and Abdul Kalam Azad were elected members of the Constituent Assembly in 1946 from NWFP, which also served as the Indian Parliament.

A bolt from the blue came for Badshah Khan when the Congress party accepted the partition of the country in the Working Committee meeting on 3 June 1947, without consulting NWFP leaders. Badshah Khan was present in the meeting and "he was completely stunned and for several minutes could not utter a word". His fate and that of the NWFP was sealed. As per agreement, a plebiscite was to be held, giving the electorate the option of joining India or Pakistan. The Khudai Khidmatgars wanted another option — an independent Pakhtunastan. The demand was rejected even by India. Khudai Khidmatgars boycotted the plebiscite. Consequently, the Muslim League won by an overwhelming majority. NWFP became part of Pakistan. "They (the Congress) have thrown us to the wolves," Badshah Khan lamented. Undaunted, he started an agitation for the creation of Pakhtunastan. He was pitted against a powerful and remorseless enemy. He was put in jail by the Pakistan authorities while his brother Dr. Khan Sahib had reconciled to his fate and accepted Pakistan. He was made a minister for sometime. But his younger brother Badshah Khan rotted in Pakistan prisons for sixteen long years. In 1969, Badshah Khan came to India at the invitation of Indian prime minister Indira Gandhi, to attend the Gandhi centenary celebrations. To the correspondents who wanted him to say something, he repeated what he had said in 1947 *'Aap ne to hamen bhedion ke samne phaink diya.'* (You had thrown us to the wolves). He went back to Jalalabad in Afghanistan where he had settled to live a peaceful life, taking with him his shattered dreams. He could come back to his village only in 1972. He was awarded the Bharat Ratna by the Indian government in 1987 to atone for their sins. He died on 21 January 1988 at Jalalabad, at the ripe age of ninety-eight. Thus ended the long journey of a man who was honest, fearless, a devout Muslim and a great nationalist. He has left behind his memoirs *My Life and Struggle*, published in 1969.

## References

1.   Hodson, H.V. *The Great Divide: Britain, India, Pakistan*, OUP. 1985, p.227-78.
2.   Nagarkar, V.V. *Gennesis of Pakistan*. Allied, 1975, p.277.
3.   *Collected Works of Mahatma Gandhi*. Vol. 68, pp.55-56.

# Syed Ahmed Khan

## (1817-1898)

Syed Ahmed Khan was born to Syed Muttaqi and Azim-un-Nisa on 17 October 1817. His ancestors had come to India from Persia during the reign of Shah Jahan and enjoyed the patronage of the Mughal emperors. Ancestors from his wife's side of the family had held important posts under the Mughal kings; Azim's grandfather, Khwaja Fareed-ud-din Ahmed, was prime minister of Emperor Akbar II for sometime. He also enjoyed the patronage of the East India Company and was sent on a diplomatic mission to Persia (Iran) and later to Burma. Among his ancestors, Syed Ahmed was influenced more by his maternal grandfather than by anyone else, as he had spent his childhood in his house.

Syed Ahmed had no formal education but learnt Arabic, Persian, Urdu and some mathematics from private tutors, besides the study of Quran. But it must go to the credit of Syed Ahmed that in spite of his rather unsystematic education he developed a taste not only for reading but also for writing and was able to author some quite significant books and tracts. However, he picked up only a smattering of the English language and could not master the language even in later life. Almost all his written works are in the Urdu language.

His father died when Syed was twenty-one years old and the family was hard pressed for money. Through the good offices of his uncle Maulvi Khaliullah, he succeeded in securing a job in the employment of the East India Company, that of a petty judicial officer, or *serishtedar*. In 1839, he was promoted to the post of *Naib Mir Munshi* or assistant to the commissioner of Agra division. Privately he studied law and qualified in 1841 for the post of *Munsif*. In this capacity he worked for many years: in Delhi (1846-54) and in different towns in Uttar Pradesh: Bijnor (1855-60); Moradabad (1860); Ghazipur (1862); Aligarh (1864); Banaras (1867); Aligarh again (1877). He retired as a subordinate judge in 1878.

During these long years of service under the British government he had come to believe that it would not be possible to dislodge the British from India. The atrocities committed by the British on the Indians after the Mutiny also convinced Syed Ahmed that it would be better for the Muslim community not to antagonize the British in future. While he was posted at Bijnor, Syed Ahmed had saved the lives of about twenty Europeans from the wrath of the mutineers. The role played by Syed Ahmed in Bijnor earned him a distinguished position in the official circles and he utilized it fully for the upliftment of the Muslim community. Even while in service, he set before himself the twofold task of bringing about a rapprochement between the British government and the Muslims and to introduce the modern type of education among the Muslims to compete with the Hindus. Through his writings he tried to convince the British that Muslims were not against the British rule. He started with a pamphlet *Tarikh-I-Sarkashi Bijnor* followed by *Risalah Khairkhwahan Musalman* (The Loyal Muslims of India) in two parts (1860) and *Asbah-i-Baghawat-i-Hind*, which he got translated into English as *The Causes of Indian Revolt*. In it, Syed Ahmed tried to prove that the main cause of the revolt was lack of communication between the rulers and the ruled. Copies of it were sent to members of the British Parliament in London.

He also wanted the Muslims to shed their antagonism to Christianity. While at Ghazipur (1862), Syed Ahmed started writing *Tab'inulkalam*, a commentary in Urdu on the Old and New Testament, emphasizing in it the points of similarity between Islam and Christianity and the fundamental unity that ran through the two faiths and among the 'People of the Book'.

To achieve his second objective, of educating the Muslims about Western science and literature, he founded in 1864, while posted at Ghazipur, Translation Society for the translation of important English books into Urdu. Soon after, he was transferred to Aligarh and he took the office of the Society with him to Aligarh. The name of the society was changed to Scientific Society. There he got several important English works translated into Urdu. In 1866, the society started a weekly paper *The Aligarh Institute Gazette* to put the views of Muslims before the government on various issues. In 1869, his son Syed Mahmud was awarded a scholarship to study in the Cambridge University. Syed Ahmed accompanied his son to England, taking with him the second son Syed Hamid also. Syed Ahmed stayed in England for seventeen months. There he met several British officials and literary men including Carlyle. While in London, he wrote *Khutbat-e-Ahmadiya* (Essays on the Life of Mohammed), in which he refuted the charges against Islam in William Muir's *Life of Mahomet*. His visit to England inspired him to propagate the English system of education for the Muslim community in India with even greater zeal. In fact, "he had been much impressed by what he had seen of European civilization, and indeed some of his letters from Europe indicate that he was so dazed that he had rather lost his balance".[1] After his return from England in late 1870, Syed Ahmed settled in Aligarh and started to implement his plans of educating the Muslim community, on the lines of British schools and colleges. He could foresee the antagonism of the Muslim orthodoxy. To explain his ideas about modern education and culture, he started another Urdu weekly, *Tahzibul-akhlaq* (December, 1870). Through the columns of this weekly, he started vigorous propaganda against the fanatical *ullema* and in favour of social reform. He immediately became a controversial figure. The *ullema* sharply reacted to his unorthodox ideas and issued *fatwas*, condemning him as a *kafir*. To meet the challenge of the orthodoxy, he wrote a commentary on the Quran, *Tafsir*, (which he could not complete in his lifetime), giving a liberal interpretation and a rapproachment between religion and science which further infuriated the *mullahs* accusing him of making sacred religious beliefs subordinate to science. All this opposition by the orthodoxy could not shake his conviction that the emancipation and progress of the Muslims was impossible without higher education on the western pattern.

Undaunted, he succeeded in establishing the Mohammadan Anglo-Oriental College in 1875 at Aligarh. (The college was raised to the status of a university, Aligarh Muslim University, in 1920). The foundation of the college was laid by the viceroy Lord Lytton in January 1877. In the address presented to the Viceroy, Syed Ahmed explained that the aim of the College was: "to educate the students so that they might be able to appreciate the blessings of the British rule; to reconcile Oriental learning with Western literature and sciences; to make the Muslims worthy and useful subjects of the Crown and to inspire in them that loyalty which springs not from servile submission to foreign rule, but from genuine appreciation of the blessings of the good government".[2] By making such 'faithful exhortations' he could easily win the favour of the government. It is surprising that even Syed Ahmed could not rid himself completely of Muslim orthodox beliefs and practices. In the M.A.O. College, The history of India commenced from the medieval period and students were given instruction in the traditional Shia and Sunni theology and religious laws. Even the religious instruction was based on the traditional interpretation of Quran and the Sunnah. The students were thoroughly indoctrinated through the columns of the *Aligarh Institute Gazette*. *Namaz* was compulsory for both Shia and Sunni students. There was a prescribed uniform for students, a black *achkan* (gown) and red fez. There was no sign of liberalism in the college.

Morris Dembo, an American, (scholar of Indic Islam and Urdu literature) opines that "The puritan rational (or shall we say 'Wahabi) steak is, quite clearly evident in Syed Ahmed's character. It was not in jest that Sir Syed once answered a question about his religion from an English official by saying 'I am a Wahabi'". Sir Syed's sympathy for the militant anti-British movements of his day is most strikingly seen in his great work on the monuments of Delhi, the *Athar a-Sanadid*.[3] The book was translated into French in 1861 by Gracin de Tassy. The pro-British preaching of Syed Ahmed got a big jolt when Wahabi *jehad* against the British government continued even after the 1857 revolt. In September 1871, John Norman, judge of the Calcutta Supreme Court, was assassinated during a Wahabi trial in the court itself. This was followed by the murder of the viceroy, Lord Mayo, in February, 1872 by a Wahabi prisoner in the Andamans. W.W. Hunter in his book *The Indian Musalman* (1871) devotes three of the four chapters of his book on the Wahabi movement and the *jehad* against the

British government. The 'Wahabi streak' in Syed Ahmed impelled him to come forward in the defence of the Wahabis. In a letter to *The Pioneer* dated 14 April 1871 Syed Ahmed argues that the Wahabi *jehadis* were not true Wahabis therefore "false charges have been laid against innocent men". The forceful and persistent pro-British stance of Syed Ahmed prevailed upon the British to accept his pleadings in good faith. The Wahabi Movement was completely crushed by the early seventies, any way. It is surprising how the British Government gradually changed their attitude from anti-Muslim to pro-Muslim within two decades after the Mutiny. The whole credit for this change must go to Sir Syed Ahmed and the resultant benefits he got from the government for his community.

Syed Ahmed had to face anew the wrath of the Muslim orthodoxy because of his decision to include English and Western sciences and philosophy in M.A.O. College curriculum. They had started a virulent attack on Syed Ahmed once again. Many *fatwas* were circulated, declaring Syed a *kafir*. Maulvi Ali Baksh Khan even went to Mecca to get a *fatwa* against Syed Ahmed and his college. A part of the fatwa read: "No assistance is allowable to the institution. May God destroy it and its founder. No Mohammedan is allowed to give assistance to or countenance the establishment of such an institution."[4] Consequently, Syed Ahmed was obliged to seek financial assistance from the non-Muslims, especially in Punjab and North-West Province (U.P.) for his College. His oft quoted speech in which he has metaphorically compared Hindus and Muslims as the two beautiful eyes of a bride, belongs to this period. However, soon the landed gentry of Uttar Pradesh, Punjab and other Muslim dominated areas started sending their wards to the college and started giving it financial support. Syed Ahmed did not need the monetary help of non-Muslims. Gradually a sea change came in his thinking especially after the formation of the All India Congress in 1885. In this he was supported and even guided by Theodore Beck, who had joined the M.A.O. College in 1883 as principal. Beck was only twenty-four years old when he joined the college. Inexperienced and amateur as he was, Syed Ahmed started depending on Beck and he became an important member of the team which guided the destiny of the college and the political movement started by it which came to be called as the Aligarh Movement.

From the very birth of the Indian National Congress, Syed Ahmed started a campaign against it and in speech after speech he advised the Muslims not to join the Congress. It is not difficult to understand the antagonism of Syed Ahmed towards the Congress. The Congress, from its very inception, demanded a representative government on British lines. This meant rule of the majority community. As the Muslim formed only one-fourth of the total population of the country they would always be dominated and ruled by the Hindus in a democratic set-up, he argued. He felt this was not in the interest of the Muslim community. Hence, his virulent attack on the Congress. Thus, Syed Ahmed gave a distinctly new turn to Muslim politics which became anti-Congress and also anti-Hindu, because he looked upon the Indian National Congress as a Hindu organization. In a speech at Meerut on 16 March 1888 Syed Ahmed said, "Suppose that the English community and the army were to leave India, taking with them all their cannons and their splendid weapons and all else, who then would be the rulers of India? Is it possible that under these circumstances, two nations — the Mohammedans and the Hindus — could sit on the same throne and remain equal in power? Most certainly not. It is necessary that one of them should conquer the other. To hope that both could remain equal is to desire the impossible and the inconceivable. At the same time, you must remember that although the number of Mohammedans is less than that of the Hindus, and although they contain far fewer people who have received a higher English education, yet they must not be considered insignificant or weak. — This thing — who after the departure of the English would be conquerors would rest on God's will. But until one nation has conquered the other and made it obedient, peace cannot reign in the land".[5] So explicitly, Syed Ahmed had sown the seeds of the two-nation theory. He gave similar speeches at Lucknow and other places, with only minor variations.

When Badruddin Tyabji presided over the Congress session in 1887 at Madras, he was reprimanded by Syed Ahmed through letters to the press and also through personal letters addressed to Tyabji. Tyabji was so unnerved that he wrote to Hume, secretary of the Congress, that "the main object of the Congress to unite different communities and provinces have miserably failed; that the Mohammedans were divided from the

Hindus in manner they were never before, that the gulf was becoming wider day by day". He suggested that the Congress should be prorogued for five years. Of course, his suggestion was not accepted.

The last ten years of Syed Ahmed's life were devoted mainly to political awakening of the Muslims against the Indian National Congress and the Hindus. In August 1888, Syed Ahmed formed the Indian Patriotic Association. The nomenclature was changed to United Indian Patriotic Association, with himself as secretary and Principal Beck as treasurer. He told that the association was formed as a rival to the Congress. Initially, both Muslim and Hindu landed gentry, who were opposed to the Congress, had joined the association. But after the Council Bill of 1892 was passsed, the association was wound up in December 1893 and a purely Muslim organization called Muhammedan Anglo-Oriental Defence Association was established. In 1896, this association prepared a memorandum highlighting the Muslim demands for separate communal electrorate, weightages in local bodies etc. Syed Ahmed in a speech broadly hinted that if the demands were not conceded the Muslim minority might be forced to take up sword to prevent the tyranny of the majority. (This is actually what the Muslim League did in 1946 through 'Direct Action'). The memorandum formed the basis of the Simla Deputation to Lord Minto in 1906. In 1886, Syed Ahmed founded the All India Muhammadan Educational Congress (the world 'Congress' was changed to 'Conference' in 1890) to 'propagate the idea of the Aligarh Movement throughout the country by holding annual conferences at various places.

The role of Principal Beck in directing the activities of Syed Ahmed during the last fifteen years of latter's life cannot be over-emphasized. Soon after he joined as principal of M.A.O. College, he had become the right-hand man of Syed Ahmed; indeed his friend, philosopher and guide. Syed Ahmed's lack of mastery over English made him depend on Beck for many crucial decisions. Beck made a systematic effort to alienate the Muslims from the Hindus and thus contributed considerably towards anti-Hindu bias in the Aligarh Movement. The personal influence exerted by Beck upon Syed Ahmed was believed to be so great that one Muslim writer humorously remarked that 'the College is of Syed Ahmed but the order is of Beck'. Mr. Morrison, who succeeded Beck after the latter's death in 1899, followed the same policy as that of Beck. "Thanks to the efforts of the founder and the first two Principals of Aligarh College, an open manifestation of uncompromising hostility against the Indian National Congress formed the basic creed of the Aligarh Movement". It is interesting that one Britisher (Hume) was guiding the destiny of the Congress, while another Britisher (Beck) was attacking it through the Aligarh Movement.

To be fair to Syed Ahmed, one must try to understand the reasons for his pro-British and anti-Congress policy. "The Aligarh Movement was to the Muslims what the Renaissance and National Movement of the nineteenth century was to the Hindus. It raised the Muslim community from the slough of despondency in which it had sunk after the Mutiny and transformed it from the Medieval into the modern age. Syed Ahmed, who ushered in this movement, deserves the highest praise for his love of Muslim community and the far-sighted vision which he displayed regarding the problems of the Muslims".[7] At the same time, it must be admitted that in the process he created a schism between the Hindus and Muslims which ultimately resulted in the division of the country. Aga Khan in his *Memoirs* wrote that "the independent sovereign nation of Pakistan was born in the Muslim University of Aligarh". The famous Pakistani historian G. Allana wrote, "Pakistan owes as much to Aligarh, as Aligarh owes to Sir Syed Ahmed Khan for its conception, establishment and development. In other words, Sir Syed Ahmed's contribution in the cause of the Pakistan Movement has been a spectacular one and deserves honourable mention in the annals of our freedom movement".[8]

Syed Ahmed received many well-deserved honours and positions in life. In 1878, he was nominated a member of the Viceroy's Council. In 1887, he was made a member of the Public Service Commission. In 1888, he was decorated with KCSI and in 1889 an honorary doctorate was conferred on him by the University of Edinburgh. But his greatest reward was when in 1920 his M.A.O. College became Aligarh Muslim University.

In February 1938, Jinnah visited Aligarh. "I have from you today the greatest message of hope", he told the students of Syed Ahmed Khan's University. "Henceforth Aligarh was to be the 'arsenal of Muslim India' ".[9] Even after four decades the message of Syed Ahmed was reverberating in the corridors of his College. No educational institution ever played such a decisive role in the fortunes of any nation as Aligarh did in the case of Indian Muslims.

Syed Ahmed died on 27 May 1898 in Aligarh at the age of eighty-one after an eventful life, and is revered in both India and Pakistan.

## References

1. Nehru, Jawaharlal. *The Discovery of India*, New Delhi, Jawaharlal Nehru Memorial Fund, 1946, p.345.
2. Nagarkar, V.V. *Genesis of Pakistan*, New Delhi, Allied, 1975, p.37.
3. Dembo, Morris. *Introduction in 'Political Profile of Sir Sayyid Ahmad Khan* ed. by Hafeez Malik, Delhi, Adam Publishers, 1993, p.vi-vii.
4. Shan Muhammad. *Sir Syed Ahmad Khan; A Political Biography*, Meerut, Meenakshi. 1969, pp.71-72.
5. Zaidi, A.M. ed. *Evolution of Muslim Political Thought in India*. New Delhi, Michika & Panjathan, 1975, p.48.
6. Nagarkar op. cit. p.52.
7. Majumdar, R.C. *History of the Freedom Movement in India*, Calcutta, Firma KLM. Vol.1, 1988, p.434.
8. Allana, G. *Eminent Muslim Freedom Fighters*. Delhi, Low Price Publications. (Reprint). 1993, p.111.
9. Khairi, Saad R. *Jinnah Reinterpreted*, Karachi, OUP. 1996.

# Khuda Bakhsh

## (1842-1908)

Rarely does a person devote his life and spend his fortune for the building of a library for public use; that too a man of modest means. Khuda Bakhsh was one of the greatest bibliophiles this country has produced, and an authority on Islamic bibliography, covering Arabic and Perian manuscripts and books.

Khuda Bakhsh was born at Chapra in Bihar on 2 August 1842. His father, Muhammad Bakhsh, was a pleader and a devoted bibliophile. Khuda Bakhsh's education started at the Patna High School and he studied there till 1859. The school was, however, closed after the uprising of 1857-58; and the boy was sent to Calcutta for further studies. He passed the Entrance examination from Calcutta University in 1861. Soon after, his father fell ill and the responsibility of supporting the family fell on Khuda Bakhsh. He came back to Patna and worked as *peshkar* of the district judge. After sometime, he resigned and got the post of a Deputy Inspector of Schools. In 1869, Khuda Bakhsh passed the Pleadership examination and started practicing at the Patna Bar. He soon had a lucrative practice and earned a name in the local courts as a pleader.

Khuda Bakhsh was married early in life but his wife died childless. He married twice thereafter. From the two wives he had five sons and two daughters. At least two of his sons, the eldest Salahuddin and the second Shihabuddin, have made their mark as Orientalists. One of his wives, Razia Khatun, was an Urdu poetess of some merit.

Khuda Bakhsh's reputation as a pleader and as a forensic expert came to the notice of the government and he was made a Government Pleader in 1881. Besides his professional activities, he ungrudgingly gave time to public causes, for which he was rewarded. For his work on the School Committee, he got a Certificate of Honour at the Delhi Durbar of 1877. He was the first vice-chairman of the Patna Municipality and the Patna District Board, when these self-governing bodies were created by Lord Ripon. Khan Bahadurship was conferred on him in January, 1883 and a C.I.E. in 1903. He was also a Fellow of the Calcutta University, thanks to his academic interests. He was appointed chief justice of the Nizam's High Court, Hyderabad in 1896 for a term of three years. He returned to Patna in 1898 and again started his practice at the Bar. But unfortunately, the same year he had a paralytic stroke (the disease which also killed his father) and did not fully recover from its ill effects. He was, however, appointed secretary of the library on a monthly salary of Rs.200. He had stopped earning at the Bar and was in deep financial trouble. The government made him a grant of Rs. 8000 for the liquidation of his debts so that he could die in peace.

All the honours which were conferred on him pale into insignificance before his magnificent library which he built and which is now called the Khuda Bakhsh Oriental Public Library at Patna. His father Muhammad Bakhsh must share part of the credit for its inception, for while on his deathbed in 1876, Muhammad Bakhsh handed over 1400 manuscripts to his son and asked him to enlarge the collection and build a library for public use. Khuda Bakhsh endeavoured throughout his life to give a concrete shape to the wish of his father and started collecting rare manuscripts from various parts of India and also from various Islamic countries. In this, he found a powerful rival in Nawab of Rampur, who was also collecting manuscripts for his library. However, Khuda Bakhsh was able to entice a collector in Rampur's service, an Arab Mohamed Maqi, and employed him at a regular salary of Rs. 50 a month besides commission. For eighteen years, Maqi worked for Khuda Bakhsh hunting and procuring rare manuscripts (mostly Arabic) from Syria, Arabia, Egypt and Persia. It was also Khuda Bakhsh's practice to pay double railway fare to every manuscript seller who visited him offering manuscripts. Thus, he became famous as a collector and was given the first choice by every manuscript seller.

Not all the manuscripts were collected by honest means. "The founder's sons relate with a dash of pride not unmixed with humour, that many of the manuscripts were stolen. The love of letters, it is said, carried both the founder and the Library and his emissaries with an impetus that was stayed with no scruples, over the fine — and shall we say the trivial — line that divides one man's property from that of another".[1] Khuda Bakhsh and his collectors did not allow the Penal Code to come in the way of their adventure of acquiring manuscripts legally or otherwise. Khuda Bakhsh used to tell his friends, with a mischievous twinkle in his eyes; "There are three classes of blind men: those who were bereft of sight; those who lent valuable books even to a friend; and those who returned such volumes, once they had passed into their hands".

As the years rolled by, the number of manuscripts increased and his own house proved insufficient in keeping them in some order. Khuda Bakhsh started thinking of a separate building to house his valuable collection. He also remembered the promise given to his father on his deathbed. He started getting the building for the library constructed in 1886, which was completed in 1888. By the time the building was completed, Khuda Bakhsh had spent eighty thousand rupees on it — several millions at the current price level. The library was soon came to the notice of the government of Bengal and they became its patron and sponsor. The library was formally opened to the public after the opening ceremony performed by the then lieutenant governor, Sir Charles Elliot, in 1891, under the name Khuda Bakhsh Oriental Public, Library. The importance of the library and its building can be gauged from the fact that when the chief architect Sir Edwin Lutyen planned New Delhi in the thirties of the last centrury, he did not include a public library in his extensive plans for the new Imperial city. The main branch of the Delhi Public Library is still housed in a canteen built during the Second World War for American soldiers. After more than five decades of Independence it is still functioning from that canteen building. Even the Indian National

Library at Calcutta is functioning in a building which was once the residence of the governor general and viceroy. And here was a man Khuda Bakhsh (gift of God) who, with his own efforts, not only acquired a valuable collection, but built a magnificent building to keep the books and manuscripts properly along with reading halls for the users. Khuda Bakhsh also had a taste for binding and hundreds of volumes in the collection have excellent binding, many in leather.

Khuda Bakhsh loved his library and its valuable collection more than anything else in the world. The British Museum made him a magnificent offer for his collection, but he declined it. "I am a poor man and the sum they offered me was a princely fortune, but could I part for money with that to which my father and I have dedicated our lives," and as he said this, his clean-cut features betrayed a singular emotion; his large luminous eyes welled up with tears. "No, he said, the collection is for Patna, and the gift shall be laid at the feet of the Patna public."[2]

Khuda Bakhsh was not just a collector of books; he was also a scholar. He knew his books; not only their titles, authors and their rarity but also the content. The famous historian, Jadunath Sarkar visited the Khuda Bakhsh library several times while he was doing research on medieval India and had a chance to meet and discuss his projects with Khuda Bakhsh. Prof. Sarkar wrote, "I remember how one day he (Khuda Bakhsh) poured out the copious store of his memory, full list of Arabic biographers and critics from the first century of the Hijra to the eighth, with running comments on the value of each. Most of these manuscripts he had himself collected. Next to the acquisition of a rare manuscript, what gave him most delight was to see anybody using his library in carrying on research".[3] His scholarship is quite evident in a detailed article which he wrote in the *Nineteenth Century*. He translated in Persian Bacon's essays which shows his mastery over Persian prose.

Not only scholars but some British bureaucrats also visited the library to see the rare and beautiful collection. Sir Antony Macdonnel, acting lieutenant governor, visited the Library in 1903 and wrote that, "I had not expected to see anything so fine". In the same year, Lord Curzon, the viceroy, also visited the library. "The sanction for the construction of the reading-hall and the preparation of the descriptive catalogue, under the supervision of Dr. Denison Ross, were the direct outcome of the Viceroy's visit".

In the rare collection one finds manuscripts which were once the property of Mughal emperors like Akbar, Shahjahan, Jahangir and Adalshahi and Kutab Shahi Sultans. There are charming and matchless specimens of Eastern painting and Persian caligraphy. There are numerous rare manuscripts on Islamic law, history, philosophy, theology, science and medicine. The importance of the Khuda Bakhsh Public Library was recognized by the Government of India and in December, 1969 the library was declared as an Institution of National Importance and the management of the library was completely passed on to the Government of India.

Khuda Bakhsh was a man of striking personality, of average height and was rather slim, 'cast in the mould of the old Moslem'. He was a devout Moslem saying his prayers five times daily. The Muslim community and its welfare was always taxing his mind, but he was not a bigot. The last two years of his life were spent in misery. The paralytic attack had immobilized him and he was penniless. He died on 3 August 1908 and is buried in the precincts of the library which he built almost single-handed.

Since 1969, when the Indian government took the library under its wings, the library has progressed and is better managed than most of the manuscript libraries in the country. The number of manuscripts has gone up to over twenty thousand and the number of printed books to two hundred and fifty thousand. A staff of sixty persons, both trained and untrained, look after the upkeep of the library. Thirty-six printed volumes of the *Descriptive Catalogue* of manuscripts have been published which, however, cover only one-third of the collection. The compilation, editing and publishing the remaining volumes of the *Descriptive Catalogue* will take several decades, it seems. In the absence of a catalogue, the full use of the rare manuscripts, is not possible. However, the dream of its founder has come to fruition beyond his expectations and the future of the library is secure under government patronage.

# References

1. O'Connor, V.C. Scott. *An Eastern Library; An Introduction to the Khuda Bakhsh Oriental Public Library*, 2nd ed. Patna, Khuda Bakhsh Library, 1977, pp.6-7.
2. Ibid, p.8.
3. Sarkar Jadunath, *Khuda Bakhsh, the Indian Bodley*, Modern Review, September, 1908.

# J.B. Kriplani

## (1888-1982)

Jiwatram Bhagwandas (J.B.) Kriplani was born in Hyderabad, Sind (now in Pakistan), in 1888 in an upper middle-class family. His father, Bhagwandas Kriplani, was a *tehsildar* (revenue and judicial officer) in the British government. Jiwatram had six brothers and one sister, he being the sixth child.

Kriplani went to school in Hyderabad and passed the Matriculation examination in 1906. He was an intelligent boy, spirited and mischievous and not very fond of studies, having a healthy contempt for book-learning. In 1906, he joined Wilson College, Bombay. Those were the days of the Bengal partition and consequent agitation. The turmoil had spread to other parts of the country, including Bombay. Wilson College students agitated against the partition of Bengal, with Kriplani taking a leading part. He was expelled from the college and joined D.J. Sind College, Karachi. Here too, he got himself involved in a strike by college students against the principal of the college who had denigrated Indians in one of his speeches, and was rusticated. He went to Poona and joined Fergusson College, run by Indian nationalists. He graduated in 1908 and went on to get a Master's degree in history and economics in 1911.

Surprisingly, he chose teaching as his profession in spite of his dislike for books. From 1912 to 1917, he taught English and history at Muzaffarpur College in Bihar. There he met Gandhi for the first time and joined him in his fight against the indigo planters, who were exploiting the poor farmers of Champaran villages. He accompanied Gandhi during his travels around the villages of Champaran. There was something about Kriplani that appealed to Gandhi; his sincerity, his simple way of living, his passionate concern for the poor peasants and downtrodden villagers. It did not take much time for Gandhi to realize that he had found a new and powerful disciple. On his part, Kriplani felt that he had found a great guru and was ready to follow his footsteps. It must be pointed out that though Kriplani never became a devotee of Gandhi's religious beliefs and he could say sharp and bitter things about Gandhi's fads and eccentricities, he never wavered in his faith in Gandhi as such.[1] From then onwards, Kriplani was completely devoted to Gandhi, his differences with him on certain points notwithstanding, as long as Gandhi lived. He became a firm believer in non-violence and *swadeshi* as preached by Gandhi. Writing about the Champaran days, Gandhi wrote, "Professor Kriplani could not but cast his lot with us. He was my gatekeeper-in-chief. For the time being he made it the end and aim of his life to save me from *darshan*-seekers. He warded off people, calling to his aid his unfailing humour, now his non-violent threats. At nightfall he would take up his occupation of a teacher and regale his companions with his historical studies and observation, and quicken any timid visitor into bravery".[2]

In 1918, Kriplani joined Banaras Hindu University, first as the secretary of Madan Mohan Malaviya, and later started teaching political science. When in 1920, Gandhi started the Non-Cooperation Movement and asked students and teachers to leave the universities and colleges aided by the government (which Banaras Hindu University was), Kriplani was the only lecturer serving in the University who quit his job. He founded an *ashram* in 1920 in Banaras and named it Gandhi Ashram. Some students who had quit the University along with Kriplani, started living in the ashram. The main purpose of the ashram was to produce khadi and to propagate its use among the city folks and villagers alike. Among all the ashrams started with the same purpose, Kriplani's ashram was one of the best and was being managed professionally It had several departments: production, dyeing, printing, washing, calendering and sales. The ashram had become a profit making body and when it was shifted to Meerut later, they had saved enough money to purchase a building of their own.

In 1922, Gandhi asked him to join Gujarat Vidyapith. There he served as Principal for five years (1922-1927). About his stay at the Vidyapith, Gandhi wrote, "Acharya Kriplani was borrowed from the Kashi Ashram, which is his own creation. I relieved him as I had promised to do so. Under his leadership, too, the Vidyapith has not taken a retrograde step. At the time of the student's strike, we saw that he had stolen the heart of the students. Acharya Kriplani was a second gift that Sind gave to Gujarat'.[3] Gandhi used to address Kriplani as professor or acharya. After leaving the Vidyapith, Kriplani came back to his ashram and started propogating Rhadi work once again. But from the early thirties, Kriplani had started devoting himself completely to Congress party work. He served as general secretary of the Congress from 1934 to 1942 when he was arrested, along with other Congress leaders, during the Quit India movement and was kept in Ahmednagar jail. During the rift between Subhas Chandra Bose and Gandhi on the issue of the election of Congress president, Kriplani was wholly with Gandhi.

An event of great significance happened in 1936. Kriplani decided to marry at the age of forty-eight. He had met Sucheta Mazumdar, who was teaching at the Women's College of Banaras Hindu University. Though there was a difference of twenty years in their ages, they were attracted to each other and got married with the blessings of Gandhi. Sucheta also played a significant role in the freedom movement and after Independence served as chief minister of Uttar Pradesh. They were married for almost forty years but had no children.

In 1946, Kriplani was elected president of the Congress party and steered the organization through the critical days of the transfer of power. During the A.I.C.C. meeting held on 14-15 June 1947, in which the June 3 Plan for the division of the country was to be discussed and approved (which had already been accepted by the Congress Working Committee two days earlier), Kriplani, as the president, made a most memorable speech at the conclusion of the discussion, describing graphically what was happening in some parts of the country, especially in Punjab. Concluding his speech he observed, "The Hindus and Moslem communities have vied with each other in the worst orgies of violence. I have seen a well where women with their children, 107 in all, threw themselves to save their honour. In another place, a place of worship, fifty young women were killed by their menfolk for the same reason. I have seen heaps of bones in a house where 307 persons, mainly women and children, were driven, locked up and then burnt alive by the invading mob. These ghastly experiences have no doubt affected my approach to the question. Some members have accused us that we have taken this decision out of fear. I must admit the truth of this charge but not in the sense in which it is made".[4] To avoid such bloodshed in future it had become imperative to accept the partition of the country as laid down in June 3 Statement of the viceroy, he argued. Nehru, Patel and Gandhi had already spoken for the partition of the country but Kriplani's speech was more graphic. The resolution when put to vote was carried by 157 votes for, and 29 against while 32 members remaining neutral. After Independence, Kriplani found that the Congress president was not part of the decision-making process of the government. On the other hand, Nehru and Patel felt that the government cannot, and need not consult the party president while taking important decisions. In protest Kriplani resigned from the party presidentship in 1947. After his resignation, he was offered the governership of Bihar but he declined. He wanted to be free of official duties in order to express publically his disagreement with the government's policies. In 1950, he started a political weekly *The Vigil* to express his own views as well as those of like minded people. In 1951, he resigned from the Congress party. He formed the Kisan Praja Party in 1952 but soon merged it with the Socialist Party, giving it the new name the Praja Socialist Party (PSP), of which he was elected chairman. During the 1952 general elections, PSP polled the largest number of votes after the Indian National Congress. Soon differences cropped up in the party not only on ideological issues, but also about the relationship to be maintained with the Congress on the one hand, and the Communist party, on the other. The discord resulted in the resignation of Kriplani from the Praja Socialist Party in 1954. He became an 'independent' for the rest of his parliamentary career. He was elected to Parliament for four consecutive terms. His parliamentary life came to an end in 1971. During his parliamentary career, Kriplani was very popular for his forceful and fearless speeches. In 1977, Kriplani, along with Jayaprakash Narayan, helped in the formation of the Janata Party and in getting Morarji Desai elected as the prime minister. He was, however, disillusioned when the Janata Party split and when it had to quit office before completing its term.

Kriplani wrote a number of books mainly on Gandhi and Gandhism. Some of these are: *Non-violent Revolution; The Gandhian Way; The Indian National Congress; The Fateful Years; The Politics of Charkha; The Future of the Congress; The Gandhian Critique; Where Are We Going?; Gandhi the Statesman;* and *Freedom in Peril*. He also regularly contributed to leading Indian newspapers and journals. Some of these articles were published under the title *Some Stray Thoughts* (1979), by Navajivan, Ahmedabad, He had a distinct style of his own — simple, crisp but forceful. "Kriplani was a tall, elegant, somewhat saturnine man with a gift for sharp humour and a passionate concern for the peasants and the poor". He was loving and kind at heart but at times showed quick temper which eclipsed many of his virtues. Although he did not wield power, his contribution to the national upliftment will be long remembered.

When his wife Sucheta died in 1974 he said, "Mysterious are the ways of God. I was to go first, but instead she, much younger than myself, preceded me." He died on 1 December 1982 at the Harijan Ashram, Ahmedabad. He willed his assets, worth about four lakh rupees, to various public institutions. He was cremated on the banks of the Sabarmati river.

## References

1. Payne, Robert. *Life and Death of Mahatma Gandhi*. First Pub. Dutton & Co. New York, 1969, (Rupa reprint 1997), p.307.
2. Gandhi, M.K. *An Autobiography*. Ahmedabad, Navajivan, 1927, p.349.
3. *Collected Works of Mahatma Gandhi*. Vol. 42, p.328.
4. Majumdar, R.C. ed. *Struggle for Freedom*, Bombay, Bharatiya Vidya Bhavan, 2nd, ed. 1988, p.781. (Vol. 11 of *The History and Culture of the Indian People*).

# Lakshmi Bai

## (1835-1858)

Rani Lakshmi Bai of Jhansi is perhaps the best remembered freedom fighter in India. Her heroic tale has inspired generations and is still a role model for millions of girls. She has become a legend; it is now difficult to distinguish between the myths and facts that surround her.

Lakshmibai's maiden name was Manikarnika, abbreviated as 'Manu', and she was also affectionately called 'Chabili' in her in-laws' household. She was born in Varanasi to Moropant Tambe and Bhagirathi Bai, who were Karad Brahmins from Satara district. Her date of birth remains uncertain. Some Indian historians put the date of her birth as 19 November 1835 while British sources believe that the Rani was twenty-nine or thirty years of age during the mutiny, which means that she was born around 1827.

Her mother died when Lakshmi was still a small child. Her father, Moropant, was a member of the retinue of one Chimnaji Appa, brother of Peshwa Baji Rao II, at Benaras. After the death of Chimnaji Appa, Moropant took employment with the last Peshwa Baji Rao II at Bithur, near Kanpur, where the Peshwa had settled. Manu was three years old at the time.

At Bithur, Manu grew up alongwith the Peshwa's sons Nana Saheb and Bala Rao (better known as Rao Saheb), and Tatya Tope, whose father was a retainer of Baji Rao. She had hardly any female playmates and while playing with somewhat older boys in the palace, she became skilled in horse-riding, shooting and swordplay. She also became a good judge of horses. There she also learned to read and write.

In 1842, at the age of seven (or fifteen whichever date of birth we accept), she was married to Gangadhar Rao, the ruler of Jhansi, a man in his forties. She was given the name Lakshmibai by her in-laws. Moropant, Rani's father, accompanied her to her new home in Jhansi against the established Hindu custom. In 1851, Lakshmibai gave birth to a son who unfortunately died after three months.

Gangadhar, never a healthy man, died on 21 November 1853, leaving the Rani a teenage widow. By that time she had developed a magnetic personality, high-spirited resolve and enchanting demeanour. The dying raja, just two days before his death, adopted as his heir, Damodar Rao alias Anand Rao, a five-year-old relative in the presence of two English officers, Major Ellis and Captain Martin, whom he had invited to officially witness the adoption. They were both given copies of the Raja's will.

After the death of Gangadhar Rao, the Rani sent her petition (3 December 1853) to the governor-general seeking confirmation of the adoption, followed by a number of petitions. The governor-general, Lord Dalhousie turned down Rani's pleas and did not recognize the adoption, and decided to annex Jhansi under his 'Doctrine of Lapse'. After Dalhousie's proclamation of the annexation, the Rani continued to send appeals, at times through her counsel, John Lang, who was a British barrister practicing in Calcutta. But the governor general was adamant and did not recognize the adoption.

Lord Dalhousie, a church going Presbyterian, the most unscrupulous and wily of all governor-generals who were sent to India, was obsessive about extending the territories of the Empire and filling the coffers of East India Company. He applied the 'Doctrine of Lapse' to at least eight Indian states during his stay of eight years in India. He was a sick man, when he was to leave India at the age of thirty-five. He left Calcutta in 1856 on a stretcher. It is believed that his illness was the cause his behaviour and obsessions. It is also believed that his dealings with Indian rulers was the main cause of the uprising of 1857. The *Hindu Patriot* wrote on 18 May 1854, "Lord Dalhousie is determined to shame the devil and beat even Nicholas hollow in the matter of forcible appropriation of neighbouring states, without the shadow of a pretext to colour his grasping policy".[1] But nothing moved Dalhousie to change his mind.

Consequently, in May 1854, Jhansi came under British administration, with Alexander Skene as superintendent of police, Captain Gordon as deputy commissioner, and Captain Dunlop in the command of the troops in Jhansi. Under the new arrangement, the Rani was to leave the fort and the palace within, while keeping her smaller palace in the town as her residence. A paltry amount of rupees five thousand per month (or £6000 a year) was settled as pension for the support of the Rani and her retinue, which she refused to accept, and decided to live on her deceased husband's private estate. She believed that the acceptance of pension would mean acknowledging the 'lapse' of Jhansi, something she could never do.

Several official measures taken after the 'lapse' offended the religious feelings of the Rani and her people. Refusal to allow Lakshmi to draw on the maharaja's trust for her adopted son Damodar Rao's sacred-thread ceremony, was one of them. Other insulting measures followed: lifting the ban on cow slaughter; resumption of two villages whose revenue used to support the temple of Mahalakshmi, a temple, east of the townwall, which was associated with the Newalkar (Gangadhar's) family and regularly visited by the Rani; and Maharaja's debt being deducted from the Rani's pension. As if that was not enough, the Jhansi grasslands, which used to be the private property of the Maharaja, were taken over, as well as the state buildings, from the Rani's control. The government's deliberate acts to humiliate the Rani must have hurt her sentiments. But she was helpless. The only recourse was to send appeals and petitions to Fort William, Calcutta, the seat of British government in India at the time.

In May 1857, sepoys at Meerut rose in rebellion and occupied Delhi. The news rapidly spread to Jhansi where tension among the sepoys was already brewing. On 5 June the sepoys in Jhansi rose in rebellion and occupied the Star Fort in the cantonment area where the treasury and the munitions were stored by the British officials. The next day the entire garrison at Jhansi rebelled and killed Captain Dunlop and a few other British officers. Captain Skene and Gordon took all the Europeans from the city to the main fort, which was also soon attacked by the rebels. On the 7 June, three English officers: Andrews, Scott and Purcell left the fort for seeking Rani's help, but they were intercepted on the way and killed. In the meantime, Captain Gordon was also killed by the mutineers' bullets. On the fourth day of the siege, i.e. the afternoon of 8 June, Captain Skene, baffled as he was at the death of Captain Gordon and other officers, hung out a flag of truce. The rebel leaders promised safe conduct of the besieged English if they would vacate the fort and lay down arms. Accepting the terms, Captain Skene led the besieged and came out of the fort, when they were "seized, bound and taken to Jokhun Bagh outside the city wall where all men, women and children were massacred".

There is nothing to indicate that the Rani was involved in the mutiny or the massacre that followed. It is certain that the insurgents, prior to the mutiny, did not consult the Rani; on the contrary they all went to the palace of the Rani with loaded guns and demanded assistance and supplies. She was obliged to yield and to furnish guns, ammunition and supplies to save her life and honour. The same treatment was administered to Bahadur Shah Zafar at Delhi by the mutineers who had arrived from Meerut.

After the departure of the rebels on 11 June 1857, for Delhi the Rani wrote to Captain Erskene, the commissioner at Sagar, under whose jurisdiction Jhansi was, narrating the events that took place and deplored the massacre. Erskene, while forwarding the Rani's letters to the Fort William, Calcutta, remarked about the Rani having had no complicity with the mutineers.

Erskene in the meantime, in response to the Rani's letters to him, authorized her to manage the state of Jhansi till a new arrangement was made and issued a proclamation to this effect. When Lakshmibai assumed charge of Jhansi (June 1857), she devoted herself to manage the state with the help of her chief minister Lakshman Rao Bande, efficiently and with all sincerity. However, the British officials including Dalhousie, suspected her of connivance with the mutineers, Commissioner Erskene views to the contrary notwithstanding.

Ever since June 1857, when Lakshmibai was authorized by Erskene to manage Jhansi, she kept on writing and appealing to the British officers at Jabalpore, Agra, Jalaon and Gwalior till January-February of 1858, seeking help as she was facing trouble from neighbouring satraps. But there was no response from the English. "Rani gradually became disillusioned and disappointed with British failure to respond. She felt a growing apprehension that the British might capture and try her, even hang her. She was faced with two alternatives, namely death by hangman's rope or a heroic death in the battlefield. She chose the more honourable course".[2]

As soon as Lakshmibai decided to fight the British, she began recruiting troops and sought help from Tatya Tope, her childhood friend and a general of Nana Sahib. Help also came from other sources. The rajas of Banpur and Nurwar arrived with their troops by 15 March 1858 to help her. The Rani moved from the city palace into the fort with all her troops. She personally supervised the defence. Soon she was face to face with British forces. The British force under Hugh Rose, commander of the Central India Field Forces, arrived at Jhansi on 21 March 1858 and the following day, his forces invaded the city. Rani and her troops took shelter in the fort. They put up stiff resistance under the spirited leadership of the Rani and faced the British for ten days. Then, Tatya Tope arrived with his twenty thousand men and a fierce battle took place near Jhansi. But the powerful British army defeated Tatya Tope, who retreated with his army to Kalpi. Rani, to the anguish of the British, slipped from the fort on 4 April taking her adopted son and a few loyal soldiers with her and galloped to Kalpi to join Tatya Tope. Rose's army pursued them. Battles were fought at Koonch and Kalpi and the British proved superior. Rao Sahib, adopted son of the last Peshwa, joined them. They proceeded to Gopalpur, forty-six miles from Gwalior. Jointly, they conceived a daring plan to invade Gwalior. When their combined forces reached Gwalior, almost the entire army of Maharaja Scindia joined the rebels and Scindia fled to Agra. The rebel forces entered Gwalior in triumph and Rao Sahib was proclaimed Peshwa. However, their triumph was shortlived and Rose's forces soon encircled Gwalior. Rani faced the British forces at Kota-ki-Sarai, about four miles from Gwalior, attired in battle dress and mounted on horseback. A squadron of 8 Hussars charged through the rebel lines. While fighting on horseback, the Rani was struck by a Hussar; she fell from the horse and the wounds proved fatal. So died Rani

Lakshmibai on 16 June 1858 fighting heroically against the British, when she was in her twenties. Commander Rose, when he learnt about her death described her as "the best and bravest of the rebel leaders".

This is the commonly held narrative of her exploits and death, mostly written by British historians. But there are other versions. Here the myth gets mingled with facts and it's difficult to distinguish. While the British blame her for the killing of sixty-six British officers, women and children, calling her "the Jezebel of India",[3] her story has become a legend in India. "Her courage against her adversaries and her martyrdom in battle stimulated the growth of an epic and transformed her from a woman who lived and died into a legend that is immortal. There is no doubt that her heroism has left an indelible imprint on the Indian imagination. But the Rani of Jhansi has taken a significant part in the historiography of the rebellion as well. While questions remain about aspects of her historical role, the actions she took in battle make her place in history secure".[4]

## References

1. *Freedom Struggle in Uttar Pradesh*; Source Material. Vol. 1. Publication Bureau, Uttar Pradesh, 1957, p.33.
2. Majumdar, R.C. *History of Freedom Movement*. Vol. 1. Calcutta, Firma K.L.M. 1988, p.147.
3. Jezebel, in the Bible, was the wife of Ahab, the king of Israel, who killed the Prophets. Now it is used to connote wickedness.
4. Lebra-Chapman, Joyce. *Rani of Jhansi*, Bombay, Jaico, p.165.

# Madan Mohan Malaviya

## (1861-1946)

A great nationalist and educationist, Madan Mohan Malaviya was born in an orthodox and devout Brahmin family of Allahabad on 25 December 1861. He was the fifth son and eighth child of Pandit Brajnath Vyas. His ancestors hailed from Malwa in Madhya Pradsh and thus the family was called Mallais, which gradually changed to Malaviyas. Madan Mohan's grandfather, Premdhar, as well as his father Brajnath were learned Sanskrit scholars. Madan Mohan inherited their scholarship. He had his early education in Sanskrit at home under the guidance of his grandfather and father. Later, he was sent to Haradevaji Dharmopadesh Pathshala and then to the Vidyadharma Vardhini Sabha Pathshala. At the age of eight, he joined the local government zila school and passed the entrance examination in 1879, after which he took admission in the Muir Central College, Allahabad affiliated to Calcutta University. He graduated in 1884. In college, Malaviya was a favourite student of Pandit Aditya Ram Bhattacharya, who had a great hand in moulding his life and character. When the Banaras Hindu University started functioning in 1921, Malaviya requested Bhattacharya to be the pro-vice-chancellor of the university, the post from which he resigned after two years due to ill-health.

While still a student, Malaviya was married in 1879 to Kundan Devi. They had five sons and three daughters.

After graduation, Malaviya joined M.A. classes but was compelled to leave studies due to financial difficulties. He accepted an appointment as a teacher in the Government High School at Allahabad. There were no restrictions imposed by the government on its employees joining political parties at the time. Malaviya attended the second session of the Indian National Congress at Calcutta in December 1886, and made his maiden political speech there, which was highly appreciated by everyone including A.O. Hume, secretary of the Congress. In fact, Malaviya had started public speaking while still a child and used to give discourses at religious gatherings. He had also taken part in dramatics as a student. In later life, became a forceful speaker both in Hindi and English. In his school days, Malaviya had also composed poems and written stories and essays on various topics which were published in magazines. Raja Ram Pal Singh of Kalakankar (Rampur) heard about Malaviya's and offered him the editorship of the Hindi weekly paper *Hindustan*, of which he was the proprietor. Malaviya accepted the offer and worked there from July 1887 to the end of 1889, converting it to a daily paper. The success of Malaviya as an editor brought him fame in journalistic circles, and in later life, emboldened him to launch a number of papers of his own.

At the persuasion of friends, Malaviya took up the law course at the newly established Allahabad University and passed the LLB examination in 1892 and entered the Bar as a junior to Beni Ram Kanyakubja. Soon he set up a lucrative practice of his own, and came to the rank immediately after Sir Sunder Lal and Motilal Nehru. However, Malaviya was not interested in amassing wealth in the legal profession because his heart was in social work and upliftment of the Hindus, for which he devoted all his energies during his life time. He was actively associated with 'Hindu Samaj', a social service organization set up in 1880, largely through the efforts of Aditya Ram Bhattacharya, Malaviya's Sanskrit teacher in the Muir Central College. When in 1884 the Kendriya Hindu Samaj (Central Hindu Samaj) was formed, Malaviya took active part in it. The Samaj had its annual functions held from 1884 to 1891 at different places. Malaviya continued serving the Hindu interests and tried organizing the community during this period. He founded the Hindu Dharma Pravardhini Sabha at Prayag in 1888. On the occasion of the Kumbh Mela at Prayag in January 1906, Malaviya called a grand assembly of the Sanatan Dharma Mahasabha, where he advocated Hindus to follow the ideals of Sanatan Dharma and for the first time revealed his scheme for founding a Hindu University at Banaras. The Sanatan Dharma Sabha became the All India Sanatan Dharma Mahasabha in 1928 and under its auspices two weekly journals were brought out in 1933, *Sanatan Dharma* edited by Malaviya from Banaras and *Vishwabandhu* from Lahore (the office and the library of which was shifted to Hoshiarpur, Panjab, after partition in 1947).

By 1909, Malaviya had almost given up practice at the Bar and was devoting all his energies for social welfare of the community. However, he made an exception when he accepted the brief in the lawsuit of 225 accused in the Chauri Chaura incident of 1922 near Gorakhpur, and by his brilliant defence saved 170 accused from the gallows or transportation for life. He did not charge any fee. In 1912 Malaviya founded the Seva Dal to look after the comfort of pilgrims who came to have a dip in the Sangam in Prayag. The Dal under the presidentship of Malaviya did commendable work during *Ardhkumbh Mela* in 1912 and Kumbh Mela in 1918. Malaviya was a very popular leader in the Panjab along with Lajpat Rai and did much to promote the welfare of the Hindus and safeguarding their religious beliefs. After the Jallianwala Bagh tragedy in April 1919, he, along with Swami Shraddhanand, toured Panjab and after locating the affected Hindu and Sikh families, provided monetary and other help to the families of the deceased. Both of them collected funds for the purpose, people responding enthusiastically. Malaviya had no inhibition in joining the Arya Samaj leaders in making the Shuddhi movement a success, their differences notwithstanding. Though a believer in Sanatan Dharma, he was against untouchability and took active part in opening the doors of temples for all Hindus. He treated B.R. Ambedkar as his son and Ambedkar on his part, had great respect for Malaviya. As one of the founders of the All India Hindu Mahasabha, Malaviya figured prominently in it, presiding consecutively over its annual functions from 1922-24, and again in 1935.

Malaviya, from his early years, took active part in promoting the cause of Hindi in Devnagari script. Along with some other Hindu leaders, Malaviya played an important role in securing the order of the government in April 1900 for the use of Devnagari script, along with the Persian script, in the courts. When in 1910 the first Hindi Sahitya Sammelan was convened in Varanasi, Malaviya presided. He continued to take active part in the promotion of Hindi.

After his early journalistic stint in *Hindustan* as an editor, Malaviya launched his own papers. He started *Abhudaya*, a Hindi weekly in 1907, which was converted to a daily in 1915. He also started *Maryada*, a Hindi monthly in 1910. He also started another Hindi monthly, *Kisaan*, in 1921 to fight for the cause of poor peasants of Oudh. His greatest journalistic venture, however, was *Leader*, an English daily, started on 24 October 1909. Both *Abhudaya* and *Leader* played an important role in the cause of national movement as envisaged by Malaviya and his associates. He also edited *Sanatan Dharma* from 1933 as stated earlier.

Malaviya had joined the Congress party way back in 1886 and attended almost every session during his lifetime. He was elected president for the 1909, 1918, 1932 and 1933 sessions, though he could not be present during the 1932 and 1933 sessions as he was undergoing a jail term. However, Malaviya did not always approve of the Congress policies, especially after it came to be controlled by Gandhi, his respect for Gandhi notwithstanding. Because of his independent views, he was never elected a member of the Congress Working Committee. In politics, Malaviya was essentially a Moderate or a 'Responsivist' or 'Responsive Cooperator' — responding positively for those actions of the government which he thought were good for the country. When Gandhi started the Non-Cooperation Movement, Malaviya opposed it strongly. He openly preached against Gandhi's move for the closing down of educational institutions, boycott of legislative assemblies and burning of foreign clothes. He defied Gandhi on the question of closing of schools, colleges and universities, because Malaviya believed that the existing educational system could be made to serve the aim of national regeneration and questioned the wisdom of Gandhi's policies.

When Gandhi visited Banaras in November 1920 to preach Non-Cooperation, Malaviya invited Gandhi to address the students and staff of Banaras Hindu University on 27 November 1920. Malaviya himself presided over the meeting and let Gandhi have his say. Gandhi told the students, "Advantages are dangled before us. There are a number of facilities in this University. There is instruction in engineering and various other facilities. For the good of India these things must be sacrificed'.[1] Malaviya did not contradict Gandhi in the meeting because he was confident about the sanity of his students and teachers. Hardly any student or teacher left the university. Not only did Malaviya not close the university, he invited the Prince of Wales (later King Edward VIII) to declare the newly constructed buildings of the university open on 13 December 1921. The university also conferred on him the honorary degree of Doctor of Letters, to the chagrin of Gandhi and his followers, who had boycotted the visit of Prince of Wales to India.[2]

The Banaras Hindu University remains the greatest achievement of Madan Mohan Malaviya. With the joint efforts of Malaviya and Annie Besant, the Banaras Hindu University Act was passed by the government in 1915. Lord Hardinge, the viceroy, laid the foundation stone of the university in 1916. Malaviya had collected over a crore of rupees to build the campus. The Maharaja of Banaras donated hundreds of acres of land for the purpose. The University had started functioning in the buildings of the Central Hindu College, which Annie Besant had founded in 1898 at Banaras. The University moved to the new campus in 1921 and soon many subjects of science and technology, arts and commerce were introduced along with the study of Hindu religion and culture. Malaviya served as the vice-chancellor of the University from 1919 to 1938 when he resigned because of ill-health but remained as Rector till his death. Soon Banaras Hindu University became pre-eminent among the Indian universities and still retains that status. It is interesting to note that Gandhi, who wanted the university to be closed in 1921, was the chief guest during the silver jubilee of the university in January 1942.

Malaviya was a member of the Allahabad municipality for many years and was elected its vice-chairman twice. In consequence of the active work which he did for the Allahabad municipality, he was elected to the Provincial Legislative Assembly in 1902, and in 1909 to the Imperial Legislative Council. He remained a member till 1920 and again from 1923 to 1930. He was one of the most important members of the Council. When the Swaraj Party was formed in 1923 by C.R. Das and Motilal

Nehru, Malaviya joined the party because he was very much against the boycott of legislatures as advocated by Gandhi. But when he found that the Swaraj Party could not protect the interests of the Hindus who were suffering during communal riots in the country, he, along with Lajpat Rai, resigned from the Congress as well as from the Swaraj Party and founded the Indian Nationalist Party and fought the 1926 general elections under its banner. The Swaraj Party was completely routed in U.P. and Panjab and its number of seats depleted in other provinces. Again in 1932, after the announcement of the Communal Award, Malaviya was greatly upset. Malaviya had attended the Second Round Table Conference as a Hindu nominee of the government. Though the Round Table Conference ended in failure, Malaviya did not expect such an award from the British government. The award had recommended separate electorate, and heavy weightage, and much more for the Moslems at the expense of the Hindus. The Congress, while condemning the Award as 'intrinsically bad' and 'anti-national' decided neither to support nor oppose it. Malaviya, along with M.S. Aney, M.R. Jayakar, Ramanand Chatterjee and others, once again resigned from the Congress and floated the Congress Nationalist Party. During 1935 elections to the Legislative Assemblies, they won all the general seats in Bengal and all but one in Panjab. Again and again Malaviya was upset with the Muslim appeasement policies of the Congress and opposed it with remarkable success. In spite of his great regard for Gandhi, who was eight years his junior, he never succumbed to the gimmicks of Gandhi like spinning the *charkha* etc. He felt that he had more important things to do in life. Along with theology and Oriental learning, Malaviya advocated the use of western science and technology to build large-scale industries in the country. The Banaras Hindu University was one of the first universities to start departments like mining, metallurgy, geology and various branches of engineering. Graduates from these departments played not an insignificant role towards the industrialization of the country. Because of his interest in industrialization, he was appointed a member of the Indian Industrial Commission (or the Holland Commission) in 1916. In his minute of dissent he made some important suggestions.

During the last years of his life, Malaviya stopped taking active part in politics. He spent his days in the Banaras Hindu University's extensive campus and was mighty pleased to see his dream come true. He died on 12 November 1946 in Banaras at the ripe age of eighty-five, mourned by millions throughout the country. Nehru wrote in his *Autobiography*: "His (Malaviya's) long record of public service in various fields from early youth upwards, his success in establishing a great institution like the Banaras Hindu University, his manifest sincerity and earnestness, his impressive oratory, and his gentle nature and winning personality, have endeared him to the Indian public, particularly the Hindu public, and though many may not agree with him or follow him in politics, they yield him respect and affection. Both by his age and his long public record he is the Nestor of Indian politics"[3]

## References

1.  *Collected Works of Mahatma Gandhi*, Vol. 19, pp.35-36.
2.  Dar, S.L. and S. Somaskandan, *History of the Banaras Hindu University*. Varanasi, BHU Press, 1966, p.530.
3.  Nehru, Jawaharlal. *An Autobiography*, New Delhi, Jawaharlal Nehru Memorial Fund, 1980. (First published London, 1936), p.158.

# Pherozeshah Mehta

## (1845-1915)

Pherozeshah Mehta, son of Merwanji Mehta was born on 4 August 1845 in Bombay, where he spent most of his life. He belonged to a middle-class Parsi merchant family. His father was a partner of M/s. Cama and Company. Beginning his education in Ayrtons School, he passed the Matriculation examination in 1861 and graduated from Elphinston College, Bombay in 1864. He was married the same year, at the age of nineteen. A good student of history and English literature, he was awarded a scholarship at the recommendation of his college principal, Sir Alexander Grant, which enabled him to go to England for further studies. He left for England in December 1864, entered Lincoln's Inn, took three years to qualify and was called to the Bar in 1868 and left for home.

While in England, he used to meet Dadabhai Naoroji and was influenced by his liberal thinking, which resulted in his joining the liberal school of Indian politics, the important members of which were M.G. Ranade, W.C. Bonnerjee, Gopal Krishna Gokhale and Dinshaw Wacha. After the death of Ranade and Bonnerjee, Pherozeshah Mehta and Gokhale led this group of Congressmen which came to be known as Moderates as against the group led by Tilak, Lajpat Rai, B.C. Pal and Aurobindo, who were called Extremists.

After his return from England, Pherozeshah started legal practice in Bombay and soon became successful as a criminal lawyer. His services were requisitioned in almost all parts of Bombay Presidency including Gujarat and Kathiawar. He also acted as a legal consultant for some Indian rulers like those of Kathiawar and Junagarh.

While in England, Pherozeshah had joined the East India Association for which Dadabhai and Bonnerjee were working. On his return to India, he was selected as one of the secretaries of the Bombay branch of the East India Association and used to deliver lectures under its auspices.

Mehta's public life began with his involvement with Bombay Municipal Corporation, which he joined in 1872 and remained connected with for four decades. It was his speech in 1872 that paved the way for the introduction of principle of election in the municipality. The Municipal Laws of 1872 and the Municipal Act of 1888 were, to a large extent, the result of Pherozeshah's untiring efforts. He was chairman of the Bombay Municipal Corporation in 1884, 1885 and 1905. His involvement in the Bombay municipal affairs had actually reduced him to a provincial leader and he had hardly any following in large parts of India.

Along with K.T. Telang and Badruddin Tyabji, Pherozeshah formed the Bombay Presidency Association in 1885, of which he became honorary secretary. Under his stewardship it served as the organizational wing of the Indian National Congress in the metropolis for nearly thirty years (1885-1915). He continued to take part in the working of the Bombay branch of East India Association also. In 1886, Pherozeshah became a member of the Bombay Legislative Council, and when the Council was reconstituted in 1892, he was elected to it. He represented Bombay in the Imperial Legislative Council during 1894-95 but resigned in January 1896 because of poor health and left for England for treatment. He came back from England in February 1898, stood for election and got re-elected to the Imperial Legislative Council in 1898 itself and continued as member till 1901, when he finally resigned on health grounds once again. In the legislative bodies' he distinguished himself by his eloquent speeches criticizing the government's economic policies, as did most of the Moderates starting with Dadabhai Naoroji. But because they sang praises of the British rule and swore by constitutional methods, the government never took them seriously. In a way they were a contradiction in themselves. They were called mendicants by the Extremists.

Pherozeshah had some role in founding of the Indian National Congress and presided over its session of 1890 at Calcutta, and twice served as chairman of the reception committee at the Bombay sessions of 1889 and 1904. Gradually, he became a dominant figure in the Congress in the first decade of the twentieth century. His main endeavour in those days was to keep the Extremists, led by Tilak, from dominating the Congress and in this he was largely successful though the Congress suffered grievously under his autocratic control. His most unprincipled act was during the Surat session of the Congress in 1907. The session was scheduled to be held in Lahore; he got the venue changed to Nagpur and from Nagpur to Surat where he had influence. He realized that neither at Lahore (where Lajpat Rai was a dominant force) nor at Nagpur (where Tilakites had the sway) he could have his way. He, along with Gokhale, did not want to get the resolution about swadeshi, boycott, national education and swaraj, which was passed in 1906 at Calcutta, confirmed in 1907. The intention of the Moderates became clear when during the Provincial Conference in April, 1907 at Surat, the resolution about boycott etc. was omitted and also when they refused to accept Lajpat Rai as president of the Surat Congress to be held in December (Lajpat Rai later withdrew to avoid controversy and the Moderates elected Rash Behari Ghosh as president). Aurobindo wrote an article in the *Bande Matram* under the caption 'Phirozeshahi at Surat' castigating the autocratic nature of Pherozeshah.[1] Not heeding the criticism, he resorted to unethical and unparliamentary methods to teach the 'Extremists' a lession at Surat Congress in December, 1907. He is said to have kept ready in the pandal, in case of need, some hired men (Pathans) armed with sticks to forcibly expel the Extremists. The Surat session ended in pandemonium when Tilak went up the rostrum to move an amendment about the Calcutta resolution. The Extremists were expelled from the Congress and remained expelled as long as Pherozeshah was alive.

Pherozeshah behaved in the same autocratic manner when he was elected president of the Congress to be held at Lahore in 1910. He changed his mind not to be president at the eleventh hour as he feared that the session would not be a peaceful one and at Lahore he would not be able to repeat Surat. He refused to go to Lahore and the Reception

Committee was in a dilemma. Pherozeshah's biographer, Homy Mody, wrote about the incident: "The country was bewildered. Not even the closest friends of Pherozeshah suspected his intentions or could guess at the reasons that prompted this extraordinary step which threw the Congress into utter confusion. The President elect was as silent and mysterious as the Sphinx'. Whatever be the reasons, the whole episode was in bad taste. Madan Mohan Malaviya then presided over the Lahore session. Being so autocratic by nature, Pherozeshah could not have a mass following and actually remained a provincial leader.

However, his apolitical contribution to the nation was not insignificant. As a supporter of indigenous industries Mehta was one of the first to invest in cotton textile mills. He also raised an indigenous bank which later came to be known as the Central Bank of India, at present a leading Indian bank. Mehta had a deep interest in education, both primary and higher. Like so many other leaders of his time, he believed that western education was one of the most precious gifts of the British rule. He had been connected with the University of Bombay since 1868, when he was nominated a fellow of the senate. He took active interest in the university affairs, and in 1886 helped to promote the Graduate Association, along with Ranade, which did useful work in the educational field in Bombay. He was elected Dean of the Faculty of Arts at the Bombay University. In March 1915, he was appointed vice-chancellor but he died soon after. He was awarded the D.Litt degree by the Bombay University the same year.

The British government was always quick to honour the Moderates. Pherozeshah was honoured with C.I.E. (Companion of the Order of the Indian Empire), in 1894; and a knighthood in 1904.

Pherozeshah did not dabble in journalism nor did he write any book or tract. However, he was mainly responsible for the founding of an English newspaper, the *Bombay Chronicle* in 1913, which became an important source for expressing Indian opinion, under the editorship of B.G. Horniman.

"Majestic in appearance and stately in his manners Pherozeshah was endowed with wonderful intellectual powers. At the sittings of the Indian National Congress, in the Bombay Legislative Council and the Viceregal Legislative Council, Pherozeshah Mehta made contributions to debate all matters of public importance which were not only unsurpassed in brilliant phrasing but also in practical sagacity. Great as a speaker, he was the greatest debater that India ever produced. He had a rich and sonorous voice, when he was speaking to an audience, without effort, he could be heard in the most distant corner".[2] Pherozeshah was a born leader of men and those who came in contact with him, seemed to succumb under the charms of his personality. Gokhale was the best example, who always looked to Pherozeshah as his leader and had to do and say things which he did not believe in. Wacha, Setalvad, Jinnah, Paptista and Jayakar had their early lessons in public life in Pherozeshah's chambers.

In Western India, Pherozeshah is remembered mainly as the maker of the modern Bombay Municipal Corporation and the father of civic life in that city. His magnificent statue in front of the Bombay Corporation Building is a symbol of that contribution.

He died in Bombay in 1915, at the age of seventy.

# References

1. Aurobindo, *Collected Works*, Pondicherry, Sri Aurobindo Ashram. Vol. 1., 1972, p.246.
2. Parvate, T.V. *Portraits of Greatness*, New Delhi, Sterling, 1964, p.52-54.

# V.K. Krishna Menon

## (1896-1974)

"Reason and emotion, logic and passion, sarcasm and affection combined paradoxically in Krishna Menon's life to make him one of the most fascinating personalities of our time."

– *R. Venkataraman*

Vengalil Krishnan Krishna Menon was born on 3 May 1896, at Panniankara, a suburb of Calicut. His father, Komath Krishna Kurup, was a successful lawyer at the Calicut courts. His mother, Lakshmikutty Amma, was a gifted lady with high erudition in Sanskrit and was an accomplished musician. It was a respectable, wealthy and talented Nair family in which Krishna Menon was born.

Krishna Menon started his education at the Municipal Lower Secondary School and at Brennen High School, where he studied only for a year. In 1910, the family moved to Calicut and Krishna Menon was enrolled at the Native High School (now known as Ganpati High School) and passed the Matriculation examination in 1913. He passed the Intermediate examination from the Zamorin's College, Calicut in 1915 and B.A. from the Presidency College, Madras in 1918. After taking his B.A. degree, he joined the Law College, Madras but did not complete law studies and started taking an interest in politics. He was a voracious reader and tried to imbibe the writings of Western thinkers like John

Locke, John Stuart Mill and others. Later, he was influenced by the writings of Karl Marx and Engels. He had hardly any interest in Indian literature, religion, epics or philosophy.

While in Madras, Menon came under the influence of Annie Besant and joined the Theosophical Society. He moved into Adyar and into a new life. He was also a lecturer for sometime, at the National University founded by Annie Besant. He devoted his energies doing social and political work under the aegis of the Theosophical Society. He also joined and worked for the Indian National Boy Scout Association which was founded by Annie Besant and who was its chief scouts commissioner. Krishna Menon worked for the Scouts movement in Madras and later (1918) in his home district in Malabar. Impressed by the talent and devotion of the young Menon, Dr. Arundale and Besant decided to send him to England for a short course in education so that on returning to India, he could serve the National University better after exposure to a more enlightened atmosphere. Menon left for England in June 1924. His father, Kurup, agreed to his son's going to England, thinking that he could pursue law there and become a barrister and practice law on his return.

Krishna Menon got a teacher's job on his arrival in London, at St. Christopher School. Letchworth, Hertfordshire, run by the Theosophical Society. In July 1925, he joined the London School of Economics to study political science. He was a student of Professor Harold Laski who was greatly impressed by Menon's intellectual acumen. Menon passed B.Sc. from L.S.E. in 1928 with first class honours. He continued his studies and got an M.A. degree from University College, London and an M.Sc. degree from London School of Economics in 1934. In the same year he was called to the Bar from the Middle Temple. Menon was thirty-eight by the time he completed his formal education. However, he had been taking part in political activities also since his arrival in England. Annie Besant had founded Commonwealth of India League in 1923, which was an auxillary of her Home Rule League started in 1916 in India. Krishna Menon started working for the League as desired by Besant, and became its joint secretary. With his efforts, several branches of the League were opened at places like Manchester, Bristol and Liverpool.

The end of the Commonwealth of India League came with extreme suddenness. At the end of an unfinished annual meeting, (1930) the majority of members in support of outright independence, (in place of Dominion status) adjourned elsewhere. The same day they decided to form a new body, calling it India League with V.K. Krishna Menon as honorary secretary. Annie Besant resigned from the Commonwealth of India League, leaving the field for Krishna Menon to run the new India League, which he did, almost single-handedly for the next seventeen years. He managed to get an ideal premises for the office of the India League on Strand Street. The League was formally inaugurated on 11 November 1931. Its aim was "educating the British people on India, appealing to their conscience, lobbying among the Members of Parliament, making the India League platform available for all visiting national leaders, publishing pamphlets on India".[1] He also kept the Indian public informed about the activities of the India League and the political developments in England vis-à-vis India through his write-ups in Indian newspapers. Krishna Menon, at one stage, represented a dozen Indian newspapers in London. He was also regularly writing letters in British newspapers whenever he found misrepresentation of facts about India. The Indian National Congress tried to utilize the services of Krishna Menon. Though not formally affiliated to the Congress, the India League became an outpost of the Congress in England and Krishna Menon its unofficial representative.

Through his teacher, the socialist Harold Laski, Menon was able to befriend several socialists and Labour party leaders like Sidney and Beatrice Webb, Stafford Cripps, Bertrand Russell, Clement Attlee and others. In 1932, Menon succeeded in convincing some British Parliament members to visit India to see first hand what was happening in India. The India League Parliamentary Delegation, consisting of three Labour Members of Parliament with Krishna Menon as secretary, reached India in August 1932. They travelled to different parts of India, including its villages. During their eighty-three days sojourn, the delegates were shocked by the atrocities committed by the government on innocent people who participated in the Civil Disobedience campaign. The 536 page report when submitted to the government sent shock waves in Britain among people interested in Indian affairs, and the Congress led by Gandhi got powerful support for their campaign. The report became a landmark in the history of the India League and was considered as a personal triumph of Krishna Menon. This also resulted in closer association with the Labour Party, his socialist leanings helping him greatly. Krishna Menon joined the West Pancras Labour Party in 1934, which is in the east end of London. He was elected councillor repeatedly for thirteen years until he became Indian high commissioner in the U.K. in 1947. Another achievement of Krishna Menon in England was in the publishing industry. He is credited with the launching of 'paperback revolution'. Along with Allen Lane of Bodley Head, they started the publishing company, Penguin. Later the Pelican series, with Krishna Menon as its general editor, was started.

In 1939, Krishna Menon was selected by the Labour Party as a candidate for the Dundee Constituency Parliamentary seat. But his participation in the 'Daily Bazar', a People's War platform, revealed his leanings towards communism. He was declared a communist among Labour circles and his candidature was cancelled. The repercussion of this in America was even stronger. He came to be regarded as a mouthpiece of the Soviet Union. He was shunned by the Labour Party and the socialists henceforth. His communist leanings came to the surface even when he was the Indian high commissioner in London. In a letter to Jawaharlal Nehru, Sardar Patel (6 January 1949) wrote, pointing out the accusations made by Krishan Menon in an interview with T.G. Sanjivi, director, Intelligence Bureau, against the Government of India. Menon was perturbed by the action taken by the Government of India against the communists who had committed atrocities in Hyderabad, Madras, Bengal and other parts of the country, and indulged in murders, pillage, arson and loot, and were planning an armed insurrection. Menon was not convinced and shouted at Sanjivi: 'It is you who are murdering the communists.' In reply, Nehru wrote to Patel (6 January 1949) "I can only explain and excuse it to some extent by imagining that he (Menon) was under some deep mental strain and consequently completely upset. He is often rather ill and sometimes his nerves give way when he is unwell'. The views held by Menon about communism and communists are of consequence because Nehru as prime minister was guided by Krishna

Menon on foreign and economic affairs for years, resulting in Nehru making some grievous mistakes.

Menon and Nehru maintained their intellectual and emotional links ever since they met in London in 1935. Of course, socialism was the common link. But Nehru was obliged to Menon for projecting him as 'one of the greatest men of our time'. Perhaps Menon sincerely believed that only Nehru could lead free India. After Independence, Menon was appointed as the Indian high commissioner in London, in which capacity he worked for five years and retired on 13 June 1952. During his tenure there was, the famous Jeep Scandal coinciding with the 'Police Action' in Hyderabad (1948). He was charged "with having entered into a business deal with persons of no substance for the purchase of defence equipment in order to oblige friends'. Prime Minister Nehru had a hard time defending his friend in the Parliament. Nothing could be definitely found against Krishna Menon, and the matter was eventually dropped.

Soon after, Nehru sent him to the U.N. as a member of the Indian delegation. Vijayalakshmi Pandit was the leader. Following her election as president of the U.N. General Assembly, Krishna Menon became the leader of the Indian delegation. When the Kashmir question came up for discussion, Krishan Menon is believed to have made the longest speech in the history of the U.N.O. He was successful in converting a lost case to one of complexity to the chagrin of Britain and America who wanted to see Kashmir independent as well as disarmed. Menon also suggested solutions for many controversial international issues including Korea and Vietnam, which the great powers did not relish.

Menon returned to India in 1956 and was taken in the Union Cabinet as minister without portfolio. He was elected a member of the Lok Sabha in 1957 and again in 1962. In 1957, he was appointed the Defence minister. Two major events attracted global attention during Krishna Menon's term of office as Defence minister. One was the integration of Goa in December 1961 and the other was the conflict with China in 1962. The Goa affair was a smooth operation but invited strong reaction from the Western block who were eyeing Goa as a naval base. Even Mountbatten, a friend and admirer of Krishna Menon, lamented, "Krishna Menon — got this invasion of Goa linked up without Nehru understanding or knowing about it. In doing so, he destroyed Nehru. Nehru was the great idealist, who had always said that force must never be used. In forcing Nehru to bless the invasion of Goa he destroyed him, not only his credibility, his prestige, his reputation, but he destroyed his faith in himself, for he felt that he had been betrayed. And he later killed him with the disastrous Chinese war".[3] The debacle during the war with China in 1962 will go down in history as the blackest spot in the political career of Krishna Menon as well as that of Nehru. Before his death in 1950, Sardar Patel, in a detailed letter to Jawaharlal Nehru, had warned him about the intentions of China. Nehru had ignored the warning. Krishna Menon perhaps never cared to read that letter. Worse, when the army chief, General Thimayya, informed Nehru and Defence Minister Krishna Menon about Chinese forces' incursions into Indian territory, Menon blew up and accused Thimayya of "lapping up CIA agent provocateur propaganda'. It is believed that General Thimayya submitted his resignation after the incident. "Fearing that it might be used further to criticize the Government and in particular the Defence Minister, who were already under heavy attack for neglecting border defence, Nehru persuaded Thimayya to withdraw his resignation, but news of it leaked out".[4] Krishna Menon's perception of Chinese policy was coloured by his communist leanings and he believed that China would never attack India. He and Nehru had convinced themselves that China, under Communist regime, was a friend of India and as a co-sponsor of *Panchsheel*, was morally bound to be friendly towards India. They seemed to have never learnt the basic precept of statesmanship that in politics there are no permanent friends, only permanent national interests. The arrogant Krishna Menon would not listen to the plea of the army generals for upgradation of the army to face the challenge of the Chinese. The Chinese knew that the Indian army was 'ill-clothed, ill-armed and much smaller in number". The voices against Krishna Menon started getting louder in the media, among general public and even in the Congress circles. Nehru continued to shield his friend but after the debacle in the India-China War in 1962, when the Chinese force almost reached the Indian plains without much resistance by the Indian army, Nehru found it difficult to protect Krishna Menon. Menon had to resign as Defence minister. The prestige of Nehru as a world leader also came under a cloud. Krishna Menon's political career almost came to an end. He had no following in the Congress party and was denied a Congress ticket in the 1967 Parliamentary elections. He resigned from the Congress party. After the death of Nehru, he was almost pushed into oblivion. He started to practice at the Supreme Court as a 'progressive' lawyer, taking up cases of the leftist leaders like E.M.S. Namboodaripad. His health deteriorated and he was in and out of hospitals most of the time. He died on 6 October 1974 in Delhi.

An agnostic and a bachelor throughout his life, he had made few friends. With his haughty, arrogant and superstitious nature, it was easy for him to make enemies. No Indian politician faced more bitter criticism, both at home and abroad, than Krishna Menon did. People have forgotten his service to the nation through India League, fighting for Indian independence in a foreign land for more than two decades and only remember the humiliation which the country suffered at the hands of the Chinese in 1962 when he was Defence minister.

He did not write much about himself. 'I do not believe in what is called autobiography,' he once said. Whatever we know about him is through his friends and his enemies. He did not write any book of substance; only some pamphlets, though he was certainly a distinguished intellectual. Lord Greenwood, who knew Krishna Menon from his court days in London, paying a tribute to Krishna Menon after learning about his death said, "Vitriolic, intolerant, impatient, exigent — Yes! but generous, sensitive, considerate, a great teacher too. I doubt if I shall ever meet a great man or one who will leave behind him so many so deeply in debt to him for all the lessons he taught to those of us who will cherish his memory".[5]

## References

1. Madhavan Kutty. *V.K. Krishna Menon*, New Delhi, Publications Division, 1988, p.43.
2. Shankar, V. Ed. *Select Correspondence of Sardar Patel, 1945-50*. Vol.2. Ahmedabad, Navajivan, 1977, pp.371-375.

3.  Collins, Larry and Dominique Lapierre. *Mountbatten and the Partition of India*, New Delhi, Vikas, 1983, p.46.
4.  Edwards, Michael. *Nehru; A Political Biography*. New Delhi, Vikas, 1971, p.290. (First pub. London, Allen Lane).
5.  Madhavan Kutty op. cit. p.166.

# Syama Prasad Mookerjee

## (1901-1953)

Syama Prasad was born in one of the most illustrious families of Bengal on 6 July 1901. His father, Asutosh Mookerjee, had become a legend in his own time and had occupied a unique position as vice-chancellor of the Calcutta University and a judge of the Calcutta high court. Syama Prasad's mother, Jogamaya Devi (who outlived him), possessed a strong character and played a character-forming role while bringing up her three sons, eldest Rama Prasad and youngest Bama Prasad. His father's scholarship, which was reflected in the huge collection of books on various subjects, attracted the intelligentsia of Calcutta to their *bari* (house) in Bhavanipur. (Ashutosh's personal library is now a part of the National Library, Calcutta, forming an important section). The Mookerjees also were devout Hindus and puja celebrations in their house were well-attended. Such was the atmosphere, a blend of religious and scholastic, in which Syama Prasad grew up.

He started his education at the Mitra Institution, from where he passed the Matriculation examination at the age of sixteen, winning a scholarship. For college education, he joined Presidency College, Calcutta, getting a Bachelor's degree in 1921, securing a first class first. For his M.A. he opted for Bengali rather than English or any other subject. While studying for M.A., Syama Prasad got married to Sudha Devi in 1922. They had four children; two sons and two daughters. However, they could lead a happy married life only for twelve years. Sudha Devi died in 1934. Syama Prasad, though only thirty-three at the time, did not remarry.

Asutosh Mookerjee died in 1924, creating a void in the educational circles of Calcutta, which was later filled by Syama Prasad. He was elected to the Senate and Syndicate of the University in 1924 itself. He enrolled as an advocate in the Calcutta high court and did legal practice for sometime. In 1926, he left for England to study for the Bar and joined the Lincoln's Inn and was called to the Bar in 1927. On his return, he did not practice at the High Court as he was drawn to the University work as a member of the Senate and Syndicate. In 1934, he was appointed vice-chancellor of the Calcutta university for two successive terms, 1934-38, the youngest vice-chancellor at the time. As vice-chancellor, he brought innovative changes in the university. Even after 1938, he remained the most important member in the Syndicate and continued to guide the affairs of the university. His involvement in education was not restricted to Calcutta University. He actively participated in the affairs of the Asiatic Society of Calcutta; was a member of the Court and Council of the Indian Institute of Science, Bangalore, where C.V. Raman and Bhabha were working at the time. He was also chairman of the Inter-University Board. Thus, for thirteen years education was his main activity.

Thereafter, he entered the sphere of politics. He was elected to the Bengal Legislative Council as a Congress candidate in 1939, representing Calcutta University. But the following year (1940), he resigned when the Congress party decided to boycott the legislatures. The following year, Syama Prasad was elected as an independent candidate from the same constituency. Thereafter, he was actively involved in politics.

In August 1939, Veer Savarkar visited Bengal, bringing with him his new ideology of the Hindu Mahasabha. Syama Prasad met him and was impressed by his concern for the Hindus. "Being then greatly perturbed at the helpless position of Hindus — whom the Congress failed to rouse and protect — some of us were drawn to Savarkar's influence and it gradually took root. My tour in eastern Bengal in September 1939, further made me realise how desperate the position of Hindus had become, and I saw how the spirit of resistance against an outrageously communal aggression was dying out — slowly but surely".[1] He joined the Hindu Mahasabha and became its acting president. As a member of the Bengal Legislative Council, he quickly learnt a few lessons. He found that no political party cared to look after the interests of the Hindus. The Communal Award had crushed the Hindus politically. The number of Hindu seats had been drastically reduced. Initially, he was attracted towards the Congress because "it was the most organized and representative political body and depended mainly on Hindu support". However, he soon found that the high command of the Congress did not assess properly the ground realities in Bengal. In the 1939 elections, Krishak Praja Party, headed by Fazlul Haq, had emerged as the largest party in the Council, while the Congress had won almost all the Hindu seats. Fazlul Haq wanted to form a coalition ministry with the Congress. However, the Congress refused to cooperate with him, compelling Fazlul Haq to form coalition ministry with the Muslim League. Thus, Bengal Hindus had a taste of Muslim League ministry (1939-41) in the form of communal riots in Dacca and other places. Syama Prasad worked hard to topple the ministry before further damage was done. He rallied round non-Congress and non-League members and succeeded in forming a Progressive Coalition ministry headed by Fazlul Haq. He joined the Ministry as finance minister. New and dangerous developments were taking place in the country. Japan had joined the War on the side of the Axis powers; had run through most of East-Asia and was knocking at the doors of India. British had adopted the 'scorched earth' policy, destroying crops, stocks and means of communication in east Bengal without taking the Bengal ministry into confidence. "The Governor, John Herbert, was interfering in the day-to-day working of the ministry thus rendering so-called provincial autonomy into a meaningless farce'. Exasperated by the attitude of the governor, Mookerjee resigned on 16 November 1942. While he was still in the Ministry, the Congress led by Gandhi had started the Quit India movement, resulting in the imprisonment of all the Congress leaders. The nationalism of Syama Prasad came to the fore and he addressed a letter to the viceroy, Lord Linlithgow, on 12 August 1942, three days after the arrest of Gandhi and other Congress leaders. Though he was acting president of the Hindu Mahasabha at the time, in the letter he defended the Congress saying that

"The demand of the Congress, as embodied in its last resolution, virtually constitutes the national demand of India as a whole'. He further wrote that "What is regarded as the most unfortunate decision on the part of the British government was its refusal to negotiate with Mahatma Gandhi". That shows that Syama Prasad was not anti-Congress *per se* but a true nationalist.

The 'scorched earth' and 'denial' policy of the British government resulted in a terrible famine in Bengal in 1943, in which more than a million and a half people lost their lives. Syama Prasad organized relief measures in Calcutta, saving thousands of lives, heading the Bengal Relief Committee and Hindu Mahasabha Relief Committee. Famine over, he worked to strengthen the Hindu Mahasabha, of which he was elected president in 1943 after Veer Savarkar relinquished office in 1942. He presided over the Silver Jubilee Session of the Hindu Mahasabha at Amritsar in December 1943. In the speech he revealed that the Hindu Mahasabha volunteers had urged the Hindu and Sikh youth to join the army, navy and air force in large numbers. As a result of their efforts, the proportion of Hindus and Sikhs in the armed forces had increased from one-third to three-forth. Free India will need their services, he asserted. Prophetic words! Under his leadership, the Hindu Mahasabha tried to avoid the vivisection of the country. However, the Congress, as the largest party in the country had already conceded Pakistan under what has come to be known as the Rajaji Formula. When Pakistan became a reality, Syama Prasad concentrated his efforts to get Bengal and Panjab also divided on the same basis on which India was divided. On 11 May 1947, Syama Prasad wrote to Sardar Patel that "We demand the creation of two provinces out of the present boundaries of Bengal — Pakistan or no Pakistan". Congress also passed a resolution demanding partition of Bengal and Panjab. In the meanwhile, a new situation had arisen when Sarat Chandra Bose and Suhrawardy of the Muslim League jointly pleaded for a sovereign Bengal. Syama Prasad, in speech after speech delivered in various places in Bengal, denounced this effort of Sarat Bose, at the same time demanding partition of Bengal and Punjab. He succeeded in his efforts. It used to be said that "Jinnah partitioned India and Syama Prasad partitioned Pakistan".

In 1946, he was elected to the Constituent Assembly, which was also serving as the Parliament of India. In August 1947, he was invited by Jawaharlal Nehru to join his Cabinet. He became the minister of Industry and Supply. India was passing through a period of acute scarcity of goods of every kind and Syama Prasad did a commendable job as a minister, establishing industries and looking after the proper distribution of the scarce goods. However, in 1950, differences cropped up between Nehru and Syama Prasad, when the former signed the Nehru-Liaqat Ali Pact, under which Pakistan could interfere with the internal affairs of India regarding minorities (Muslims). Syama Prasad gave the reasons for his resignation in a comprehensive statement before the Parliament. He gave seven reasons, besides tracing the pitiable condition of Hindu minority in Pakistan. Sardar Patel, in a letter to Syama Prasad, dated 15 April 1950, appealed to Syama Prasad to retrace his steps "in obedience to the call of both of us, the demand of the Party and the interest of your province and country."[3] But Syama Prasad had already made up his mind and did not withdraw his resignation. Along with him K.C. Neogy, Union minister, Refugee Rehabilitation, had also resigned.

Syama Prasad resigned from the moribund Hindu Mahasabha and founded a new party, Jan Sangh, whose membership, unlike Hindu Mahasabha, was open to all. He was returned to the Lok Sabha from North Calcutta in the 1952 elections. Only two other Jan Sangh candidates could win. Even then, Syama Prasad became the virtual leader of the opposition in Parliament by bringing together a few smaller parties under the banner of National Democratic Party. As a parliamentarian he earned respect even from the prime minister.

Soon after he entered Parliament, the situation in Kashmir drew his attention. He found it strange that though Kashmir was an "integral part of India" it had its own prime minister, separate flag, separate constitution — virtually a sovereign state within the Republic of India. The Jammu and Kashmir Praja Parishad was agitating, demanding that Jammu and Kashmir be integrated with India like other states. Indians had to seek a permit from the Kashmir government even to enter the state. He had a lengthy correspondence with Sheikh Abdullah and Jawaharlal Nehru on the Kashmir question, pointing out the dangerous implications of the situation but to no avail. Nehru had full confidence in Sheikh Abdullah at that time, which he had to regret later on. To know the ground realities in Jammu and Kashmir at first hand, Syama Prasad entered Jammu on 11 May 1953 and was immediately arrested, and taken to Srinagar. He died in detention on 23 June, 1953. Several leaders, crossing party lines, including M.R. Jayakar, Jayaprakash Narayan, M.V. Kamath, Purushotamdas Tandon, suspected foul play. Syama Prasad's mother Lady Mookerji, wrote to Nehru requesting him to hold an enquiry into the circumstances of her son's death in detention but Nehru did not agree to that and tended to believe what Sheikh Abdullah told him. Many feel that Syama Prasad Mookerjee died a martyr's death. He was cremated on Calcutta in 24 June.

Even while being involved in politics Syama Prasad was interested in cultural and religious activities. From 1947, he was president of the Mahabodhi Society, Calcutta. He presided over the Banga Sahitya Sammelan at Cuttack in 1952. He was actively associated with the Asiatic Society of Calcutta for many years.

## References

1. Mookerjee, Syama Prasad. *Leaves From a Diary*. OUP. 1993, p.29.
2. Ibid pp.191-93.
3. Patel, Vallabhbhai. *Sardar's Letters — Mostly Unknown, The Year 1950*. Ahmedabad, Sardar Vallabhbhai Patel Samarak Bhavan, 1983, p.35.

# Lord Louis Mountbatten

## (1900-1979)

Mountbatten was the last viceroy and the first governor general of free India. He was born on 25 June 1900, and was the youngest child of Prince Louis of Battenberg and Princess Victoria of Hesse (Germany). He was christened as Louis Francis Albert Victor Nicholas of Battenberg but the exceedingly complicated name remained only in official records. In the family and among friends he came to be known as Dickie. He had one brother, George and two sisters, Princess Louis (married to King Gustavus VI of Sweden) and Princess Alice (married to Prince Andrews of Greece), whose son Philips, now Duke of Windsor, is married to Queen Elizabeth II of Britain. Dickie was related to at least six royal houses of Europe including the Czars of Russia. And to top it he was great-grandson of Queen Victoria whose daughter Alice was married to Grand Duke Louis IV of Hesse. Dickie was proud of his ancestry and tracing his lineage was his most absorbing hobby.

His father, Prince Louis, had come to Britain from Germany, and joined the British navy. In due course he became a naturalized citizen. Due to the anti-German mania of the British public during the First World War, he changed his name from Battenberg to Mountbatten in 1917, renouncing his German titles and became the first Marquess of Milford Haven. Henceforth, the family came to be known as Mountbatten. Following the example of his father, Dickie joined the British navy at an early age. He loved the navy more than anything else in the world. He came to India in 1921, as ADC to Prince of Wales, his cousin, who was on a tour of South Asia. They were guests of Lord Reading, the viceroy. Here Dickie proposed to Edwina Ashley, with whom he had fallen in love earlier and who had followed him to Delhi. The room where Dickie proposed to Edwina is now room number 13 of the registrar's office, Delhi University. Both of them developed a sentimental attachment with India, which played some part in their coming to India later as viceroy and vicereine. They were married in 1922; he was twenty-two, and she twenty-one. Edwina inherited fabulous wealth in 1921 after the death of her maternal grandfather, Ernest Cassel, a German Jew, the richest man in the world at the time. On the other hand, Dickie had very a limited source of income, besides his salary in the navy. This disparity in income played a significant role in their discordant married life. Soon after marriage, the couple found that there was a serious lack of compatibility in their characters. Dickie was not a reflective type and had not studied much beyond technical manuals and P.G. Wodehouse. Thus, his intellectual resources were limited. The gadgets which he used to design and invent for the navy, the hours he spent on his geneology, did not interest Edwina. There was nothing which could excite or interest her. Most of his friends agreed that Dickie was dull, 'naturally dull'. There were strains and to overcome the ennui, the couple indulged in infidelities started by Edwina as early as 1924. Both of them opted for lovers; Edwina more than Dickie. Their physical intimacy had ended by 1929 and had arrived at a pact that their marriage would not come in the way of having lovers. They both adhered to it till Edwina's death in 1960. Thus, their marriage was more of an alliance than a union. Even then, two daughters were born to Edwina; Patricia (1924) and Pamela (1928), who came to India along with her parents in March 1947. The relationship which the couple developed with Jawaharlal Nehru during their viceroyalty and after, must be seen in the light of these early developments in their married life. That also explains why Dickie was such an extremely tolerant husband.

Mountbatten was a very handsome man, tall, athletic, full of energy and verve. He lived in style, made possible by his wife's millions. It was but natural that women fell for him. Even years later, when he kissed the famous writer of romantic novels Barbara Cartland on the cheek, she wrote. "A streak of fire ran through me as if I had been struck by lightning. From a woman's point of view the power was devastating'. Others less privileged than Cartland still found the impact of his personality almost overwhelming. He radiated ineffable self-confidence. The impact of his personality was not confined to women, as Indian leaders in 1947 found to their chagrin. It is rather strange that the personality which overwhelmed people did not enamour his wife. The treatment meted out to Dickie at the hands of his wife and the resultant sense of inferiority was perhaps partly responsible for his ambition to reach at the top of his career and he worked furiously to achieve that end. He wanted to show that though unsuccessful as a husband he was an exceptional and talented naval officer, respected and feared by men. This attitude helped Mountbatten to achieve great success as a distinguished leader of men for which he is remembered. Love for his career sustained Mountbatten through the rough patches of his married life. He meticulously planned to climb the professional ladder step by step, and put all his energies and used all his talents towards that end. The Second World War came as a blessing in disguise for Mountbatten. The harassed British were in search of a commander with dash and one who could take risks. Churchill surprised everyone when he appointed Mountbatten as chief of the Combined Operations in Europe. When the tide was turning in favour of the Allied and Japan was proving a greater menace, he was sent as supreme commander in South East Asia (1943) to tackle the Japanese. Japan was defeated with the help of Americans and Mountbatten emerged as a hero for the demoralized British public and establishment.

The British had won the war but were in no position to retain the Empire. Their economy was shattered, the best of their manpower had been killed. Their cities were in ruin. There was shortage of almost everything; food, petrol, clothes, coal. All of a sudden, Britain become a poor country. After two centuries, the British were worried about themselves. They had been ruling India with the help of the Indian army. The formation of INA and the navy mutiny in February 1946 had cast doubts about the reliability of the Indian army. The British were convinced that they could no longer hold on to India. They feared an uprising similar to the one in 1857, or worse. They wanted to get out of India before it was too late. They found to their chagrin that their man on the spot, the Viceroy Lord Wavell, was incapable of doing what was needed. Therefore, Prime Minister Attlee selected Mountbatten for the job. To the British Parliament he explained the reasons for his choice: "Mountbatten is an extremely lively, exciting personality." He has an extraordinary faculty for getting on with all kinds of people. He added after a pause, "He is also blessed with a very unusual wife." The Parliament agreed. According to Mountbatten, when Attlee told him about his plan to send him to India as viceroy, 'he was staggered'. He was not telling the truth. His close friends and those who knew him in official circles believe that his eyes were set on the viceroyalty while he was still in South-East Asia. "All this business about being surprised when he was offered the job of going away to India as viceroy — and then first refusing it — is all my eye".[2] It was part of the great plan. Feigning reluctance and by being difficult, he did manage to extract several concessions from the prime minister: taking with him some of his own trusted men, a private four-engine plane and a specific date for the withdrawal. He was given greater liberty in making his arrangements and writing his own instructions "than had traditionally been allowed to even the most magnificent of viceroys'. It is, however, doubtful if he enjoyed plenipotentiary powers, as he claimed later.

When everything was decided, he went around and met several persons. First his mother. She was eighty-four but still active. She warned her son that he was going to fail; Linlithgow failed, Wavell completely failed. What made him think that he would succeed. Dickie replied, "You have so little faith in your own son as to think I am not slyer than them. I'm going to tie them up in such knots that I shall succeed at their expense." When he met Churchill, the latter told him: "I am not going to tell you how to do it, but I will tell you one thing — whatever arrangements you may make, you must see that you don't harm a hair on the head of a single Muslim." Dickie promised and some of his actions must be seen in this light as a viceroy and governor general.

Mountbatten arrived in India on 22 March 1947 along with his wife Edwina and daughter Pamela. They were received at the Delhi airport by

Nehru, Liaquat Ali Khan and c-in-c, Auchinleck. He was officially sworn in on 24 March. His brief was precise: "Hand over India to the Indians by June 1948". Mountbatten's arrival had irked a great many civil servants who regarded Mountbatten as a jumped-up ex-playboy and Edwina as a spoilt Jewish playgirl of doubtful morals, in spite of what they had done during the War. Mountbatten started interviewing Indian leaders one by one — Nehru, Patel, Jinnah, Liaquat Ali, Gandhi and lesser mortals, giving one hour to each. The Indian leaders were at a disadvantage during these meetings. While Mountbatten had been briefed by his predecessors Linlithgow and Wavel as well as by the I.C.S. clique about the Indian leaders and their standing in their party, they were completely in the dark about the seamy side of Mountbatten's character. Most of the Indian leaders, including Gandhi, were dazzled by his personality; his royal connections, his informal affability. But those who had worked with Mountbatten knew that he delighted in intrigue. He would never give a straight answer to a straight question. "Dickie was a born intriguer. If there was a choice between open dealing and a corkscrew approach he always chose the latter,' a friend of his remarked. Field Marchal Temple once exploded across a dinner table, "Dickie, you are so crooked that if you swallowed a nail you would shit a corkscrew."[4] During his fifteen months of stay in India he indulged in intrigues of the worst kind. Mountbatten also indulged in double talk. According to Chaudhri Muhammad Ali, prime minister of Pakistan (1955-56): "Mountbatten won the confidence of both, the leaders of Congress and the Muslim League, by denouncing one to the other. At the very time when he was wooing Congress leaders day and night, he was portraying them to Jinnah as unreasonable men".[5]

In spite of Dickie's friendship with Nehru, he had a fondness and admiration for the Muslims and hardly any sympathy for the Hindus and much less for the Sikhs. According to his own admission, "Muslims were mostly the people from the officer's class of the Indian Army — much more than the Hindus. I wasn't pro-anybody, but I really did like the Muslims. I had so many friends. I think you'll find this one of the things that's not completely understood. The British out there were naturally more easily friends with Muslims because they played polo, they went out shooting, they mixed freely, they didn't have any sort of inhibitions.

The Hindus didn't get along so well with the British. Frankly, no Muslim ever took part in any plotting against the British. They wanted the British to remain; it secured their position. The last thing that Jinnah wanted was that we should go. But the Hindus wanted us to go".[6] This affinity of Mountbatten towards Muslims was not only shared by Churchill but by almost all the British officials of any consequence in India. It did not come as a surprise to anyone when three Governors and scores of I.C.S. officials decided to serve Pakistan after Partition; and hardly any for India. Many of the actions of Mountbatten also must be seen in this background: his advice to Maharaja Hari Singh of Kashmir to opt for Pakistan; his exaggerated description of the sufferings of Muslim refugees in Delhi while ignoring those of Hindu and Sikh refugees who were in much greater number and in much worse condtion; of his exploitation of naïvety of Gandhi to go on fast to coerce the government to release fifty-five crore rupees to Pakistan, a country at war with India.

After consultations with Indian leaders, Mountbatten set to work "to hand over India to the Indians". By this time he was convinced that the partition of the country could not be avoided. It was not difficult to convince the Congress leaders about the inevitability of Partition, harassed as they were by the tactics of the Muslim League members in the Interim Government. In the meeting of the Congress Working Committee of 8 March 1947 a resolution for the partition of Punjab was passed (later Bengal was added to it), thus accepting the partition of the country by implication. That made things easier for Mountbatten. He had started with the Cabinet Mission Plan but soon abandoned it. Next, he with the help of his aides, prepared a plan what has come to be known as 'Plan Balkan'. His 'hunch' deceived him when he showed this plan to Nehru who was with him in Simla. Nehru rejected the plan, as it presented "a picture of fragmentation, conflict and disorder". A new plan was hurriedly drafted with the help of V.P. Menon, reforms commissioner. Mountbatten flew to London on 18 May with the new Plan, and was able to convince the authorities about its viability. He, along with Ismay, returned to Delhi on 31 May. Any apprehension about the rejection of the revised plan by Indian leaders was taken care of. "I will drive them forward at a pace which would make it impossible for anyone to have second thoughts or fuss overmuch about the details," he told his staff on his return. On June 3, he announced that the power would be handed over to Indians on 15 August 1947, instead of June 1948 as had been announced by Attlee earlier in the British Parliament. The reason given by Mountbatten was that 15 August was the first anniversary of the Japanese surrender. Within seventy-three days of his arrival in India, the partition plan had been announced. In a further seventy-two days, two independent countries would emerge on the corpse of the Empire.

Mountbatten was a hustler. He often took decisions without caring for the consequences. This was one such decision. Seventy-two days were such a short time to bifurcate a country of India's size, especially when communal riots were becoming uncontrollable. The whole of north India was in the grip of communal frenzy, from Peshawar to Noakhali. The deadline of 15 August 1947 did not allow time for proper precautions and arrangements to be made. It took three years to separate Burma from India and two years to separate Sind from Bombay but only seventy-two days to divide India Maurice Zinkin, formerly of the Indian Civil Service, says, "Wavell represented the Indian point of view in England. Mountbatten was not basically interested in India but represented British interests. He did the job with dash and deftness but without compassion."[7] The British were in such a haste to leave the country that the Indian Independence Bill was hurried through the British Parliament in unprecedented haste and got the Royal assent on 18 July 1947, clearing the deck for the transfer of power.

It did not take much time through voting in the legislatures or through refrendum as to which states would form a part of Pakistan; the whole of North-West Frontier Province, Baluchistan, Sind and the district of Sylhet in Assam were to go to Pakistan. The most serious problem was the bifurcation of Punjab and Bengal on the basis of Muslim and non-Muslim majority areas. Such areas were not distinctly clear. To decide the issue, a Boundary Commission was formed under the chairmanship of Sir Cyril Radcliffe. Radcliffe arrived in India on 8 July and submitted his report in a sealed envelop on 13 August to the viceroy. In less than five weeks two lines were drawn, dividing the two provinces of Punjab and Bengal on the basis of contiguous majority areas. To control the communal riots in Punjab, where thousands of innocent people were being massacred, their houses burnt, their property looted, their women molested and even the children killed before the eyes of their parents, a Boundary Force was raised on 1 August 1947 with 55,000 army personnel under Major-General T.W. Rees. A major segment of the force was stationed in East Punjab while the worst carnage was being enacted in West Punjab. The riots and killings continued unabated. The Boundary Force came under fire and was disbanded on 29 August.

Most of the Indian states in the Indian territory were integrated with the Indian Dominion by 15 August due to the deft handling of the princes by Sardar Patel as head of the States Department. It must go to the credit of Mountbatten that not only did he reiterate on 25 July, while addressing the Chamber of Princes, what Patel had told them on 5 July, but as the Crown Representative, advised them to join either of the proposed two Dominions because Paramountcy would lapse on 15 August. After hearing Mountbatten, all the princes, who were still reluctant, signed the Instrument of Accession, except Kashmir, Hyderabad and Junagarh.

As the time of the transfer of power approached, the intensity of the communal riots increased. Uncertainty about the Boundary Commission's award made things worse. Though Radcliffe had sent the details of the Award on 13 August, Mountbatten did not make it public. On 14 August, Mountbatten and Edwina flew to Karachi to participate in the celebrations of the birth of Pakistan, leaving the envelope sent by Radcliffe unopened on the table. To dramatise the event, a canard went around that there was a plan to assassinate Mountbatten and Jinnah by the Sikhs and the RSS men. That was just like Mountbatten. There was hardly any presence of Sikhs in Karachi, or of the RSS men. There was no way for them to execute such a plan. But it did add to the drama. At times it was difficult for Mountbatten to distinguish between truth and untruth. "The truth in his hands was swifty converted from what it was to what it should have been. He sought to rewrite history with cavalier indifference to the facts to magnify his own achievements".[8]

Back in India, Mountbatten participated in the Independence celebrations in Delhi. The fate of millions of Indians still lay sealed in that envelope sent by Radcliffe, millions still not knowing to which

Dominion they would belong. "Let the Indians have the joy of their Independence Day," he said nonchalantly, "they can face the misery of the situation after." When the details of the Boundary Commission's report was made public on 17 August, hell was let loose. Almost the whole of West Pakistan was cleansed of Hindu and Sikhs by September. So was east Punjab of Muslims. In the eastern part of Pakistan, there were riots but of lesser intensity. Nobody is sure how many people were killed in this carnage, the worst in the history of the world. Nobody is sure. Estimates vary from two million to a quarter of a million. When Mountbatten relinquished the office of governor general, returned to England and met Churchill, the first thing Churchill said was, 'So you got two million Indians killed.'

Mountbatten emerged as the saviour of the British residents in India and at the same time a 'true friend' of India. Indians were so obliged to him for handing over India to them that he was asked to be the first governor-general of free India. Jinnah had refused him this honour and appointed himself as governor-general of Pakistan, to the great disappointment of Mountbatten who wanted to be governor-general of both the Dominions. Mountbatten remained governor-general of India till 21 June 1948 after which C. Rajagopalachari took over. Indians trusted Mountbatten but true to his character he deceived India, creating the 'Kashmir problem'. While accepting the accession of Kashmir to India, as proposed by Maharaja Hari Singh, Mountbatten as head of the Dominion added a sentence, "It is my Government's wish that as soon as law and order have been restored in Kashmir and her soil cleared of the raiders, the question of State's accession should be settled by reference to the People'. Not only that, Mountbatten advised Nehru to stop fighting and refer the matter to the UNO in November 1947. The Kashmir problem, thus created by Mountbatten, remains unsolved to this day and has cost India dearly in terms of men, money and material. Another act of treachery on the part of Mountbatten was talking Gandhi into a fast to give fifty-five crore rupees to Pakistan. On 12 January 1948, Sardar Patel in a press statement had said categorically that, 'we would not agree to any payment until the Kashmir affair was settled'. Gandhi started his fast the next day on 13 January. Mountbatten later boasted that it was he who convinced

Gandhi. Later he admitted, "I acted as a kind of forwarding agent for Pakistan because I felt, to some extent, they'd been pushed and I therefore had to remain to see it." Mountbatten must share the blame for the assassination of Gandhi.

"Nehru's motives in the Kashmir affair remain opaque. Why did he promise a plebiscite? Why was the issue taken to the United Nations and the offer repeated? It seems clear that the initiative both for the holding of a plebiscite and referring Kashmir to the United Nations came from Mountbatten". Did Edwina influence Nehru to take these decisions? It cannot be accepted with certainty. However, it is true that Edwina had played an important role, which none of the earlier vicereines had done. Her relationship with Nehru added a new demension to the policy-making process in India. When Edwina died in February 1960 and was buried at sea, as she had willed, Nehru ordered the Indian frigate *Trishule* to escort the British frigate *Wakeful* which carried her body to the south coast of England.

Mountbatten returned to the navy in October 1948 to command a cruiser squadron in Malta. His career in the navy was on expected lines. He became the First Sea Lord in 1955 and chief of the Defence Staff in 1958. He retired from active service in 1965. He was a lonely man and after Edwina's death his share of her wealth came to a shilling for every pound and he was worried about his financial position. On 27 August 1979, he died when his boat was blown to pieces by Irish revolutionaries. Along with him died two of his companions and a child. His assassination became world news. Though he did not serve India well during his stay of fifteen months as viceroy and governor-general, he served his country well.

## References

1.  Ziegler, Philip. *Mountbatten, the Official Biography*. London, Collins. 1985, p.483.
2.  Hough, Richard, *Edwina, Countess Mountbatten of Burma*. London, Weidenfeld of Nicolson, 1983, p.179.
3.  Ibid, pp.188-89.

4. Ziegler op. cit. p.528.

5. Quoted by Rajmohan Gandhi in *Eight Lives*, New Delhi, Roli, 1986, p.174.

6. Collins, Larry and Dominique Lapierre. *Mountbatten and the Partition of India*, New Delhi, Vikas, 1983, pp.59-60.

7. Hatch, Alden. *The Mountbatten*. London, W.H. Allen, 1966, p.359.

8. Ziegler op. cit. p.701.

# Kanaiyalal Maneklal Munshi

## (1887-1971)

K.M. Munshi was a very complex personality. He has been called a 'genius', an 'iconoclast', 'an embodiment of Indian culture'.

Kanaiyalal Maneklal Munshi (K.M. Munshi) was born on 30 December 1887, at Broach, south Gujarat, in a Bhargava Brahmin family. He was the only son of his parents, father Maneklal and mother Tapiben. It was a higher middle-class family, his father being a *mamlatdar* at Mandvi in Surat district. Maneklal had a literary bent of mind and wrote a drama in verse as a child. His mother, Tapiben, in spite of having little formal education, composed poems and wrote moral discourses in Gujarati. She was extremely religious and told her son stories from the *Ramayana*, *Mahabharat* and *Puranas*, which Munshi used in his literary works when he grew up. Maneklal died when Kanaiya was a teenager, leaving the mother to look after her growing son. Munshi had his early education at home and then joined Khan Bahadur Dalal High School, Broach. Before he passed the matriculation examination in 1901, he was married to a nine-year-old girl Atilakshmi. He was thirteen. After passing his matriculation he joined Baroda College in 1902. In 1905, he passed the first year of LL.B, getting a first class and the following year, he completed his B.A., winning the Eliot Memorial Prize. In Baroda College, he came under the influence of Aurobinda Ghose, his professor, who instilled in him the spirit of nationalism. He even tried to associate with some terrorist group but did not join it as described in his autobiography. In 1910, Munshi passed the final year of LL.B. and decided to settle in Bombay. He enrolled as a pleader on the Appellate side of Bombay high court. Soon he became a successful lawyer. It is said that, as a lawyer, he dramatized his cases, and his briefs read like novels. Munshi's legal knowledge and perception were praised by members of his profession and the judiciary alike. He was very pleasant in manners and behaviour to his clients, and never lost his temper while arguing a legal case. Success as a lawyer brought affluence and he used to live in an aristocratic style.

Munshi's career as a lawyer and a creative writer dovetailed. His first book, a collection of short stories, came out in 1912. This was the modest start of a prolific writer which left a lasting imprint on Gujarati literature through his novels and plays. "That Munshi acquired a great name for himself both as a lawyer and as a literary artist is nothing short of a feat. But between the two, law and literature, I think his first and more abiding love was for the Muses. He gave to law and politics much of the time, energy and enthusiasm which the gods intended he should give to the service of literature. But the artist in him was always peeping from behind the lawyer and the politician".[1]

His first outing in the political arena was attending the turbulent 1907 session of the Congress party at Surat where the Extremists led by Tilak and the Moderates led by Gokhale and Pherozeshah Mehta clashed, and the Extremists were expelled from the Congress party. Munshi's sympathies lay with the Extremists, Tilak and Aurobindo. Though Munshi continued to produce literary works of merit in Gujarati and devoted much of his time to his legal practice, he was able to associate himself with several political as well as social and educational bodies. In 1915, he joined the Home Rule League founded by Annie Besant and in 1919, he was elected secretary of its Bombay Branch, while M.A. Jinnah was elected as president. In 1917, he became member of the Subjects Committee of the Indian National Congress. In the same year, he was elected secretary of the Bombay Presidency Association, then the premium political association of Western India. In 1920, he resigned from the Home Rule League when Gandhi took over and changed its constitution. It was followed by resignation from the Indian National Congress when it passed the non-cooperation resolution moved by Gandhi. In 1923, he visited Europe to acquire firsthand knowledge of Western culture.

The years 1922-1926 were full of vicissitudes in the personal life of Munshi. In 1922, he started *Gujarat*, an illustrated Gujarati monthly. In this venture he sought the collaboration of Lilavati Sheth, wife of a rich Jain businessman and fell in love with her. Her marriage was on the rocks and the couple had almost separated. As willed by destiny, Munshi's wife Atilakshmi died in 1924 during childbirth. Two years later, Lilavati's husband died of heart attack. The same year (1926), Lilavati and Munshi got married and they bore the criticism caused by intercast and widow marriage nonchalantly. Lilavati was thirteen years his junior but they led a very happy and fruitful married life, Munshi calling her 'my undivided soul'.

In 1927, Munshi was elected to the Bombay Legislative Council from the University Constituency and continued to represent the university till 1945, when he did not contest. He had resigned from the Bombay Legislative Council during the Bardoli satyagraha led by Sardar Patel (1928), but was re-elected. He was appointed chairman of the Bardoli Committee of Inquiry. He rejoined the Congress which he had left in 1920. This was the time when he and Lilavati came close to Gandhi, though he never became his 'blind follower'. He and Lilavati participated in the salt satyagraha movement started by Gandhi. Munshi was sentenced to six months simple imprisonment for offering salt satyagraha at Bhatia Wadi opposite Victoria Terminus. Lilavati's sentence was for a three months only. After the Gandhi-Irwin Pact (1931), he restarted practicing at the Bombay Bar. The same year he was elected member of Bombay Pradesh Congress Committee as well as of the All India Congress Committee. In January 1932, he was again arrested in the anti-Congress campaign launched by the government and was sentenced to two years simple imprisonment, which he spent in Bijapur jail. On his release in December 1933, he, along with some others, revived the Swaraj Party (founded in 1922 by C.R. Das and Motilal Nehru) as the parliamentary wing of the Congress. He contested the election to the Central Legislative Assembly and lost. But in 1937, he was elected to the Bombay Legislative Assembly (elections held under the 1935 Act) and became Home minister in the Congress ministry, headed by B.G. Kher. The Congress ministries resigned in November 1939. In December 1940, Munshi took part in the individual satyagraha and was arrested; but was released in March 1941 because of illness.

In 1941, happened the now famous clash between Gandhi and Munshi. The latter had advised the Hindus to join *akharas* (gymnasiums) to get strength and face the challenge of Muslim *goondas* (ruffians). Gandhi took it as an attack on his philosophy of non-violence. Munshi has described this episode in detail in his book *Pilgrimage to Freedom*. When Munshi stood his ground, Gandhi ordered him to leave the Congress party; which he did. Along with Munshi, several others left Congress, including Dr. Satyapal of Punjab, and Bhulabhai Desai. Munshi then founded an organization, *'Akhand Hindustan'* (united India), and went on an all-India tour, propagating the idea of unity of India to meet the challenge of Muslim League's devisive politics. In 1944, Munshi again crossed swords with Gandhi when Gandhi pleaded for the acceptance of Rajaji Formula which, in fact, was like accepting Pakistan. Gandhi was so annoyed with Munshi that he sent him a note (12 August 1944) through Munshi's son Jagdish, a part of which read: "Munshi has raised a new cry ('Akhand Hindustan') and I cannot stop him. Munshi very much loves to dominate everywhere and become a leader. I know that everybody hates him for that reason. Everybody believes that even in the Congress he wants to set up his own protagonists. But how can one prevent a person if he is capable of spreading his influence because of his own power".[2] Munshi kept his cool to the annoyance of Gandhi.

Munshi also criticized Gandhi for his advocacy of Hindustani. Gandhi had been in favour of Hindi as national language. However, in the mid-thirties, he started to preach in favour of Hindustani for the sake of the chimera — Hindu-Muslim unity. Even bodies like Hindustani Prachar Sabha were founded by him. Munshi wrote to Gandhi on 12 October 1944 expressing his disagreement with Gandhi's language policy: "Sanskrit is our most valuable treasure. With its help alone we can make our language as powerful as English and French. The Congress aims to make the colloquial Hindustani a common medium for the whole country. But how can the colloquial Hindustani be the medium of thought or literature.

The moment it attempts to be any such thing, it has to seek the help of Sanskrit or Perso-Arabic words. Nothing else is possible."[3]

Munshi rejoined the Congress party in 1946 as advised by Gandhi and was elected member of the Constituent Assembly and played an important role in draftng the Constitution. Early in 1948, however, he was appointed agent-general of the Government of India in Hyderabad and kept the government informed, about the developments in the Hyderabad state especially Sardar Patel. "He had an advocate's capacity to analyse facts and figures and present them in a logical form. He had also organized a reasonable amount of intelligence in the state. As Agent-General, he had to undergo considerable hardships. He was isolated; he was spied upon; he was looked down upon as a foreigner by a large number of Muslims of Hyderabad. Nizam in one of his telegrams to Monckton (legal and constitutional adviser to the Nizam) has called him a 'notorious character' and a 'dignified blackguard".[4] The despatches from Munshi convinced Sardar Patel of the necessity of 'Police Action' which was undertaken in September 1948. The role of Munshi in this important historical episode has not been given due recognition by his biographers and historians. Munshi has recorded his experiences in Hyderabad in his book *The End of an Era* (1957). After the Hyderabad 'Police Action', Munshi returned to Delhi and continued his participation in the drafting of the Constitution.

During 1950-52, Munshi served as food and agriculture minister in the Nehru Cabinet and tried to reduce the deficit in foodgrains which the country was experiencing at that time through his project 'Grow More Food". He is also credited with the launching of *Vanamohatsava* (grow more trees), which is still celebrated annually. From 1952 to 1957, he served as the governor of Uttar Pradesh. In 1959, he resigned once again from the Congress party and joined the newly formed Swantra Party and was elected its vice-president. His political life had come to an end soon after. In 1969, he was felicitated by the president of India, Dr. Zakir Hussain, at the *Abhinandan Samaroha* (felicitation ceremony) and was presented a souvenir.

Munshi was such a multifaceted personality that it will not be possible to document all his activities. But some of his contributions stand out.

As an educationist, his contribution is quite significant. In 1924, he was elected president of the Panchgani Hindu Education Society, which he, in association with the Pandit brothers, had founded. The society was responsible for starting several educational institutions. In 1926, he was elected Fellow of the Bombay University as well as a member of its Senate. In the same year, he founded the Gujarat University Society in association with K.G. Naik and K.T. Shah and became its secretary. He was also appointed a member of the Baroda University Commission. In 1928, he was appointed chairman of the Physical Culture Committee by the Bombay government. In 1938, he founded (with Sardar Patel) the Institute of Agriculture at Anand and was elected its vice-chairman, and later in 1951 became its chairman. In 1946, he founded Meghji Mathradas Arts College and Narrondass Manordass Institute of Science in Bombay. In 1956, he was elected president of the Charotar Education Society which ran colleges in arts, sciences, commerce and engineering. In 1957, he was elected executive chairman of the Indian Law Institute. But the most important, and the one for which he is remembered the most, is the Bharatiya Vidya Bhavan which he founded in 1938 in Bombay. He wanted it to be "a symbol of the intellectual, literary, educational, ethical, cultural and spiritual life of India". It is a comprehensive national institution with an international outlook. Today it encompasses 355 constituent institutions imparting education in various subjects including languages, journalism *et al;* it has 120 centres in India and seven centres abroad. Its publication wing has published over 1500 titles on Indian religion and culture. Several journals in English, Gujarati and Hindi are also published. Munshi sponsored a project for writing Indian history by Indian authors, under the generic title *History & Culture of the Indian People*, in eleven volumes, under the general editorship of renowned historian R.C. Majumdar. It is the most comprehensive Indian history available to this day, and is as unbiased as history can be.

Munshi developed a taste for journalism early in life. As early as 1907, he started writing articles which were published in *East & West* and the *Hindustan Review*, journals of all-India repute. In 1912, he promoted the monthly *Bhargava*, a caste magazine. In 1915, started *Young India*, jointly with Jamnadas Dwarkadas, but resigned shortly afterwards. In 1922, he started *Gujarat*, an illustrated Gujarati monthly, and became its joint editor. In 1936, he established 'Hans Ltd.' and took over the Hindi magazine *Hans* and became its joint-editor with the famous Hindi writer, Prem Chand. It remained a leading Hindi journal for years. He started yet another journal, *Social Welfare,* an English weekly, in 1940 and served as its editor. In 1954, he founded the *Bhavan's Journal*, an English fortnightly, devoted to life, literature and culture. It is one of the most widely read English monthlies in the country and abroad today.

Munshi founded, or was associated with, several literary and social welfare societies or associations. In 1910, he joined Gurjar Sabha and became its secretary. In 1922, he founded Sahitya Sansad (literary society) and became its president. In 1924, he worked for framing the constitution of Gujarat Sahitya Parishad, and was elected its president in 1926. During 1938-39 he was elected vice-president of Children's Aid Society and worked for its re-organization. Under its aegis, he founded the Children's Home, and Home for Mentally Deficient Children in Bombay. In 1944, he founded the Bharatiya Itihas Samiti (Indian History Society). In 1946, he was elected president of the Hindu Deen Daya Sangh (Association for Mercy to the Hindu Poor). In the same year he was elected president of the All India Hindi Sahitya Parishad. In 1951, he founded the Sanskrit Vishwa Parishad (International Sanskrit Convention). In 1966, he was elected chairman of the All India Colloquium on Ethical and Spiritual Values. He also acted as chairman of several trusts, too numerous to list here.

Above all, Munshi manifested his total self in his literary writings in Gujarati. He is primarily known as a novelist and a dramatist, though he wrote in all genres of literature except poetry. "Since the spirit of nationalism motivated him to generate cultural revitalization of contemporary society, Munshi's ideology is best represented in his historical and mythological works that recast India's past traditions in their modern relevance".[5] Munshi wrote fifty-six literary works in Gujarati but his best works are considered to be his historical novels: *Patan-ni-rabhuta* (1916), *Gujarat-no-Nath* (1917), *Prithvi Vallabh* (1920), *Jai Somnath* (1940). They are all marked by "romantic setting, lively characters and dramatic movement of action". His autobiographical writings, *Shishu ane Sakhi, Aadhe Raste* and *Sidhan Chadhan* reveal the man. He wrote thirty-eight books in English, (all non-fiction) starting with *Follow the Mahatma* (1940) in which he records his personal convictions and experiences. Some other English writings are *Foundations of Indian Culture* (1962), *The Saga of Indian Sculpture* (1957) and *Pilgrimage of Freedom* (1968), which is autobiographical.

Munshi was a man of taste and lived in style but never shed his 'Indianness'. He was active till almost his eighty-fourth year. Regular yogic exercise kept him fit. It is difficult to believe how a man could achieve so much in one lifetime. He died on 8 February, 1971 in Bombay.

Munshi represented the spirit of India's national awakening. His activities had several dimensions. He emerged as a lawyer, literary artist, journalist, politician, statesman, historian and an educationist. His individualism and non-traditionalism were combined with his urge for revitalization of Indian culture which is manifested in the Bharatiya Vidya Bhavan. His contribution to the advancement of Indian culture made him a 'man of the era'.

# References

1. Chagla, M.C. *Roses in December*, Bombay, Bharatiya Vidya Bhavan, 1973, pp.58-59.
2. *Collected Works of Mahatma Gandhi*. Vol. 78, pp.23-24.
3. Ibid, pp.419-20.
4. Shankar, V. Ed. *Selected Correspondence of Sardar Patel, 1945-50*, Vol. 2, Ahmedabad, Navajivan, 1977, p.15.
5. Sheth, Jayana. *Munshi, Self-Sculptor*, Bombay, Bharatiya Vidya Bhavan, 1979, p.xv.

# E.V. Ramaswamy Naicker

## (1879-1973)

Ramaswamy Naicker was undoubtedly one of the most colourful and important leaders of the anti-Brahmin, Dravidian movement in south India. He was born on 17 September 1879 at Erode, Tamil Nadu, in a well-to-do artisan family. His father, Venkatapa Naicker, and mother, Chinnaathai Ammal, were pious Hindus with an orthodox bent of mind and wanted their son to grow up in the orthodox tradition. Instead, their son, when he grew up, tried to destroy all the 'tradition' which was so dear to his parents.

Ramaswamy attended a local school only for three years. His teachers found that the boy was unfit for school education and advised his parents to withdraw their son from school. Ramaswamy never entered a school again. His parents put him into business, where he did not do too well either. His orthodox parents used to invite preachers, priests and pandits to deliver religious discourses, which motivated the young boy to study the scriptures in Tamil. The more he studied, the more critical he became about some of the tenets of Hinduism, especially its caste structure. While he was still struggling to decide about his future, he was married off at the age of nineteen to his thirteen-year-old cousin, Nagammai.

His critical study of the religious texts did not satisfactorily answer his queries about caste distinctions, untouchability and other ills of the Hindu society. At the age of twenty-five, Ramaswamy left his family, without even telling his parents and wandered about like a recluse, visiting religious places in the north, including Kashi, in search of the ultimate truth and spirituality. He had no idea how cold it would be in winter, in north India. Exposed to the chill and the rain, he suffered terribly. Exhausted and not much wiser, he returned home. However, his hatred towards Hindu orthodoxy was gradually taking shape.

But Ramaswamy's protestations against the ills of Hindu society were somewhat subdued when he joined the Indian National Congress in 1907. For eighteen years, 1907-1925, he was in the thick of Congress politics in Tamil Nadu, and was also very active in public life, in and around Erode. He was an honorary magistrate for twelve years, and served as chairman of Erode Municipality in 1917 and was known for his efficiency and dynamism. He played active role in removing encroachments on public roads. He also got the sanitation system of the town considerably improved. This drew the attention of C. Rajagopalachari who was, at the time, chairman of the municipality of a nearby town, Salem. Rajagopalachari requested E.V.R. to lend the services of a trained sanitary inspector for Salem municipality. Several items in the agenda of the Congress appealed to Ramaswamy, like the eradication of untouchability, enforcement of prohibition, *swadeshi* and above all, their fight for the freedom of the country. In 1920, he joined the Non-Cooperation Movement under the guidance of Gandhi. E.V.R. courted arrest while picketing the toddy shops. After his arrest, his wife Nagammai and sister Kannamma continued the picketing. On his release, as a true satyagrahi, he resigned from all the honorary posts held by him. He even closed down the lucrative wholesale business of the family and destroyed all the promissory notes and documents of mortgages and ledgers. However, for E.V.R., his days in the Congress ended abruptly in 1925. Several incidents happened during 1924-25 which left a deep impression on the sensitive and rational E.V.R. In 1924, he took an active part in the Vaikom Satyagraha (Travancore state), which was organized for opening of roads leading to the Mahadevar temple, for all castes. Earlier, the low caste people were not allowed to use the roads. E.V. Ramaswamy emerged as the 'Vaikom Hero' for the depressed classes. A large number of depressed class people, led by Ramaswamy and his wife Nagammai, walked along the newly opened roads amidst great rejoicing.[1] When Ramaswamy returned to Tamil Nadu, some orthodox Brahmins belonging to the Congress party, resented his participation in the Vaikom agitation. He was hurt and could not understand the reason for their negative reaction.

Another incident which added to his resentment against the Brahmin orthodoxy in the Congress was observance of *Varnashrama Dharma* in the Chiranmadevi Gurukula run by the Congress. This was a national volunteer training school getting Rs.10,000 from the Tamil Nadu Congress party. To the surprise of Ramaswamy, Brahmin and non-Brahmin volunteers were served food in separate halls. The quality of food served was also different for different castes—Brahmins getting much better food. The proverbial last straw came when the resolution moved by him in the Kanchipuram Congress in 1925, seeking justice for the non-Brahmins in the form of proper representation in the Congress bodies in Tamil Nadu, was defeated by the strong Brahmin lobby. He walked out of the Congress with a vow to take revenge. 'I will destroy the Congress in Tamil Nadu,' E.V.R. told his followers, who had also walked out with him. He almost succeeded.

After leaving Congress in 1925, Ramaswami launched the Self-Respect movement to fight for the cause of downtrodden, low caste communities. He vociferously, and somewhat crudely, attacked Brahmanism, *Manusmriti* and various rituals and institutions of Hinduism. He attacked their gods and goddesses and ridiculed various 'inhuman' instruments of Brahmanic and Aryan culture. He aspired to create a Dravidian state based on Tamil culture. In 1931-32, Ramaswamy visited several countries in Africa, Asia and Europe. He also visited the Soviet Union, where he was well-received as the leader of the atheist movement. The Soviet Union visit led him to believe that materialism, and not spiritualism, was the answer to the problems of the starving millions of this country. He asked his followers to address him as 'Comrade E.V. Ramaswamy'. He dropped his caste name 'Naicker'.

He came to prominence in 1937, when the Rajaji-led Congress government in Madras presidency made Hindi a compulsory subject in schools. Ramaswamy led the first anti-Hindi agitation in the south. He termed the 'imposition of Hindi' an insult to Tamil culture. The anti-

Hindi agitation soon gathered momentum throughout the Tamil speaking areas and the regulation had to be changed. When the Constitution of India made Hindi the national language, Ramaswamy refused to recognize Hindi as such. His Hindi phobia made Ramaswamy do some very eccentric, and even comic things. His followers would go round the cities and towns of Tamil Nadu tarring and erasing Hindi letters on the billboards at the railway stations and at other places. Since then, anti-Hindi sentiments have carved a niche in the minds of the Tamil speaking people. The credit or discredit for this must go to Ramaswamy. In 1937, Ramaswamy was arrested for such activities. While still in prison, he was elected president of the Justice Party. This party was formed in 1916 to fight for the rights of the intermediate castes and its official organ was *Justice*. The party did extremely well during the 1920s, but was routed during the 1937 elections. When Naicker took over, the party was moribund. He tried to breathe life into the party with his anti-Hindi and anti-Brahmin slogans. In 1944, Naicker reorganized the Justice Party as the Dravida Kazhagam. A new rival to the Congress had emerged and the politics of Tamil Nadu took a new turn.

Since the late thirties, Naicker had also launched a separatist movement similar to the Muslim League's 'two-nation' concept. He had started demanding a separate state for the Tamil, Telugu, Kannada and Malayalam speaking areas calling it Dravidistan. At the Madras session of the Muslim League in April 1941, Naicker and some other non-Brahmin leaders were present as special invitees. Jinnah gave his blessings for their separatist demand and promised support for the creation of an independent, sovereign state in the south. He assured the non-Brahmin invitees that "seven per cent Muslim population will stretch its hands of friendship and live with you on lines of security, justice and fair play".[2] But when in 1944, Naicker reminded Jinnah of his promise through a letter (9 August 1944), the reply of Jinnah was non-committal. Jinnah wrote, "I have always had much sympathy for the people of Madras, ninety per cent of whom are non-Brahmins, and if they desire to establish their Dravidistan it is entirely for your people to decide on this matter".[3]

On 30 March 1942, a Justice Party delegation led by Ramaswamy Naicker met Stafford Cripps and told him that their party "owing to lack of education and of wealth and opportunity was unable to win any election and to stand up against the more wealthy and powerful Brahmin population. In view of this they demanded that Madras should be separated from the Indian Union. The Cripps proposals had provided for non-accession of provinces either through a vote of the legislature or by a plebiscite. The delegation argued that non-accession of Madras was not feasible by either of these methods. Hence they demanded separate electorate for non-Brahmins to achieve that end. Cripps replied that it was 'a wholly impracticable suggestion".[4]

Later Naicker's anti-Brahmin movement took an ugly turn when he and his followers started destroying Hindu idols, hitting the deities with shoes and chappals, blackening the faces of the idols and the priests, cutting the tufts of the Brahmins, breaking their rosaries, burning their scriptures, especially the *Manusmriti*, and insulting Brahmins in several other ways. He had built up a formidable anti-Brahmin cadre. Thousands of black flags with a red dot in the centre (the party flag) fluttered on house tops of party workers. They claimed to be the saviours of Tamil and Dravidian culture.

Then came a setback for Ramaswamy from an unexpected quarter. In 1949, at the age of seventy, Naicker married a twenty-eight year old party worker Maniammai. Thousands of party workers led by Annadurai left Ramaswamy's Dravida Kazhagam. They formed a new party Dravida Munnetra Kazhagam (DMK). The new party gradually became more popular and powerful. In the election of 1967 they won majority of seats in the legislature and formed the ministry with Annadurai as chief minister. This, however, was indirectly the victory of Naicker against the Brahminism, because the party was completely dominated by non-Brahmins.

The anti-national and secessionist activities of Ramaswamy continued even after Independence. When India declared itself a Republic under the Constitution, it did not deter him from spewing venom. He openly said that he would prefer any alien rule to the Brahmanical rule. He declared Republic Day (January 26) as a day of mourning for the Sudras and the Dravidians. He had no hesitation in burning the national flag and the map of India. Till his last days, he stood for a sovereign independent

Tamil Nadu. His questionable tactics, a disregard for other's sentiments, made him unpopular even among the low-caste people. But his impact on the political scenario of Tamil Nadu is quite visible. However, to the chagrin of Ramaswamy, anti-national sentiment did not spread to other southern states. The tri-language formula adopted by India in 1965 defused and weakened the anti-Hindi forces. "Dravidian pride and cultural-linguistic assertiveness remained lively but was conducted within the political boundaries of the Indian Union".

To propagate his views, Ramaswamy wrote several pamphlets and started several journals. In 1925, along with Thangaperumal Pillai, he started a Tamil weekly *Kudiarasu. Revolt*, an English weekly was started in 1928. *Purachi* in Tamil was started in 1933 to propagate socialism, and *Pakutharivu* in Tamil in 1934, which was started as a daily but was later converted to a monthly. Naicker initiated a Tamil script reform and used it in *Pakutharivu*. This reform is adopted by the Tamil Nadu state government, educational institutions and by Tamil journals.[5] The last important conference in which Ramaswamy took active part, was the Superstition Eradication Conference in January 1971 at Salem. Age was catching up with him and his robust body was showing signs of decay after he crossed the ninth decade of his life. He addressed his last meeting in Madras on 19 December 1973. After that, he suddenly fell ill and died on 24 December 1973. His body was not cremated accordings to Hindu rites but was buried at, what is now called Periyar Thidal in Madras (Chennai). While the demand for a separate sovereign state of Dravidistan has died down, anti-Hindi and anti-Brahmin sentiments are very much alive in Tamil Nadu even today and the political equation has changed in favour of non-Brahmins. After centuries of dominance, Brahmins are at the receiving end in Tamil Nadu today. The credit for this goes largely to E.V. Ramaswamy Naicker, *Periyar* (great soul) to the millions.

## References

1. Subramanian, M.K. Periyar *E.V. Ramaswamy; His Life and Mission*. Chennai, Periyar E.V. Ramaswamy-Nagammai Education and Research Trust. 2004, p.9.

2. Nagarkar, V.V. Genesis of Pakistan, Allied, 1975, pp.333-34.
3. Pirzada, S.S. *Quaid-e-Azam Jinnah's Correspondence*. New Delhi, Metropolitan, Reprint, 1981, p.233.
4. Mansergh, Nicholas. *The Transfer of Power*, London, Her Majesty's Stationery Office. Vol. I, p.555.
5. Subramanian, M.K. op. cit. p.12.

# Sarojini Naidu

## (1879-1949)

Sarojini, born in Hyderabad on 13 February 1879, was the eldest of the five children of Aghorenath Chattopadhyay and Baradasundari. Aghorenath was a multifaceted personality; a scientist, philosopher, poet, linguist and an educationist. He had a Ph.D. in Chemistry from Edinburgh. He also wrote verse. Sarojini's mother, Baradasundari, wrote poetry in Bengali. Sarojini inherited her love for poetry from her parents, though she was more attracted towards Urdu and English poetry than Bengali. In 1878, Aghorenath established the Nizam College in Hyderabad, a pioneering institution in English and women's education, with the encouragement of the Nizam. Aghorenath served as principal of the college for many years.

Sarojini passed the matriculation examination at the age of twelve in 1891, standing first in the Madras Presidency. For the next three years, 1892-95, she stayed at home, reading widely and writing English poetry. When she was thirteen, she wrote a narrative poem of about two thousand lines. During this time, she also wrote a little Persian play (in English) called *Meher Munner*, a copy of which she sent to the Nizam, who was so impressed with this attempt by a teenage girl, that he endowed her in 1895 with a scholarship granting her passage to England and three hundred pounds a year for support.[1] Thus she went to England at the age of sixteen in 1895, and joined King's College, London, as she was too young for

Cambridge. Later, she was able to get admission at Girton College, Cambridge. The cold climate, as well as the rigours of college discipline, did not suit her and she did not complete any course to get a degree. The climate of England, (about which even the diehard imperialist Rudyard Kipling has said, "accursed bucket-shop of a refrigerator called England,') had affected the health of many Indians who had gone there, like Ram Mohan Roy, Devendranath Tagore (both of whom died there) and Ramanujan, the great mathematician. Sarojini had to return to India in 1898 without earning a degree. But during these two years she moved in literary circles and developed some valuable friendships. The famous poet and critic Sir Edmond Gosse (1849-1929), whom she met at Cambridge was one of them. 'I implored her to consider,' wrote Gosse, "that from an Indian of extreme sensibility, who had mastered not merely the language but the prosody of the West, what we wished to receive was not a rechauffe of Anglo-Saxon sentiment in an Anglo-Saxon setting, but some revelation of the heart of India, some sincere penetrating analysis of native passion, of the principles of antique religion and of such mysterious intimations as stirred the soul of the East long before the West had begun to dream that it had a soul'.[2] She readily took to his counsel and the real poet in her emerged, depicting everything Indian and revealing her soul. She received similar advice from the famous critic Arthur Symons, who became a lifelong friend. Outside poetic circles, she developed a friendship with one Maudie Cassel, daughter of Sir Ernest Cassel, reputed to be the richest man in the world. Maudie was charmed by the lively personality of Sarojini who became her confidante and used to discuss everything with her including the choice of a husband.[3] Fifty years later, Maudie's daughter, Edwina Mountbatten, the last vicereine of India, sought Sarojini's friendship and loved to hear anecdotes about her mother's youth. Edwina however, became a rival of Sarojini's daughter, Padmaja, in seeking the friendship of Prime Minister Nehru, to the chagrin of the mother-daughter duo.

On her return to India, Sarojini got married to Dr. Govindarajulu Naidu, with whom she had fallen in love before leaving for England. He was then a major, incharge of the medical services in Hyderabad. After initial reluctance, her parents agreed to her marriage to a non-Brahmin. It was performed in Madras according to Brahmo Samaj rites. Four children were born to the couple in quick succession: Jayasurya (1899), Padmaja (1900), Randhira (1902), and Lilamani (1903). Their house in Hyderabad was the famous 'Golden Threshold', and she lived a very happy married life there for sometime.

By 1905, she had composed a number of poems. The collection was published in 1905 itself, by William Heinman, London, under the title *The Golden Threshold*. Arthur Symons wrote the preface, introducing her to the English speaking world. It got rave reviews. The *London Times* wrote, "Her poetry seems to sing itself as if her swift thoughts and strong emotions sprang into lyrics of themselves'. The second anthology of her poems, *The Bird of Time*, followed in 1912. *The Broken Wing* (1917), also published by Heinman, was the culmination of her poetic flights. Sarojini's poems had the scents of all that was Indian 'in all its freshness, glory and romanticism'. "They are mellifluous and catching and disclose a depth of feeling that is rare in the works of most of her contemporary writers of English verse".[4] She lived for thirty-two years after the publication of *The Broken Wing* but wrote very little after that and was lost in the whirlwind of politics, the feminist movement and the wings of poetry in her were really broken.

She simultaneously entered the political and women's emancipation movements, when she attended the annual session of the Indian National Congress at Bombay in 1904. A large part of the deliberations were devoted to problems faced by women which were led by Ramabai Ranade and others. Sarojini was very moved and she composed *Ode to India* there and then and recited it in her melodious voice: "Oh young through all the immemorial years! Rise Mother, rise, regenerate from thy gloom; And like a bride high-mated with the spheres; Beget new glories from thine ageless womb." Sarojini had arrived in a new world of politics and women's movement. She made a fiery speech at the 1906 annual session of the Congress at Calcutta and met Gokhale for the first time who saw in her oratory and brilliance, a leader of the future. Her presence in the Congress agitations and social reform gatherings became almost a routine. She worked with Gokhale and his Servants of India Society for some time. She was also attracted towards Annie Besant and her social activities, especially for the cause of women. The period between May 1912 and

October 1914 was her London interlude once again, in spite of her ill-health, when that country was in the throes of great suffrage campaign. She threw herself into the campaign, propagating women's cause, and at the same time dispelling wrong notions about women in India. She met Gandhi in 1914 in London while he was returning from South Africa on his way to India. Soon she became one of his devoted followers. Gandhi's advocacy of Hindu-Muslim unity appealed to her greatly and became almost an obsession with her. She had been brought up in Hyderabad amidst Muslim culture. She could read and write Urdu and loved Urdu poetry. She had also befriended many Muslims, one of whom was Mohammad Ali Jinnah. Jinnah first met Sarojini at the Calcutta Congress (1906) when he was "already accounted a rising lawyer and a coming politician, fired by a virile patriotism," according to her. She was instantly captivated by his stunning appearance and "rare and complex temperament and she has left a most insightful portrait of young Jinnah".[5] She remained charmed by his personality for many years to come, calling him "ambassador of Hindu-Muslim unity" even when he was instrumental in getting separate electorates for the Muslims in the Lucknow Pact of 1916. Her intimacy with Muslims was well known in Congress circles. Gandhi wrote in one of his letters, "I believe that I can contribute my humble share in the promotion of Hindu-Muslim unity, in many respects she (Sarojini) can do much better. She intimately knows more Mussalmans, than I do. She has access to their hearts, which I cannot pretend to. Add to these, qualifications of her sex, which is her strongest qualification".[6]

By 1917, she was completely influenced by Gandhi and soon became one of his chief confidantes. Along with politics, she was drawn to the women's movement in India and retained her interest in it to the last. Sarojini was in fact one of the pioneers of women's emancipation movement in India. In spite of her ill-health (she had developed heart problem early in life) she went around the country spreading the message of freedom and women's emancipation. She made herself available wherever and whenever she was wanted. She also worked on several committees of the Indian National Congress and was a member of the Congress Working Committee in the early twenties. She was sent to South Africa in March 1924, to oppose the proposed Class Areas Bill which was to segregate Asians in the urban areas. She toured South Africa for two months, addressing mixed gatherings, speaking against the policy of Apartheid in Johannesburg, Maritzburg, Durban etc. She initially met with hostility but her eloquence, personality and tact left a sobering impact. Her speeches gave some confidence to the demoralized Indian community, and they showered her with gifts which she carried back in six boxes. On her way back, she visited Kenya, Uganda and Tanganyika, addressing gatherings of Indian immigrants.

In the early twenties, she had shifted to Bombay and often lived at the Taj Hotel. It will ever remain a mystery how she could afford such a luxury. On her return from her African trip, her name was proposed for the 1925 annual session of the Congress for presidentship to be held at Kanpur. Her name was proposed by Gandhi himself. G.D. Birla, in a letter to Gandhi, did not see much virtue in Sarojini whom Gandhi had extolled, and differed with the choice of Gandhi for presidentship. In his reply, Gandhi wrote to Birla on 3 July 1924, "I do not think any praise of Mrs. Sarojini Naidu is overdone. I do not consider her an ideal Indian woman, but she was an ideal ambassador for the work in Africa".[7] She did preside over the Kanpur session of the Congress. Her brief poetic speech as Congress president was applauded by all. However, she was not a real politician and never could be counted as a front rank leader of the Congress who took part in policy and decision making.

She had her admirers outside political circles also. M.C. Chagla writes in his autobiography, "For many years, whenever she was in Bombay she lived at the Taj, always in the same room; and for me, it was a sort of Mecca to which I turned, whenever I was in difficulty, or whenever I wanted solace or comfort. There were innumerable days and evenings spent in her room talking to her".[8] He was not the only one who found comfort and solace in her company though; she herself was often miserable from within.

In 1928, she was asked to visit United States and Canada to undo the damage done to India's image in the West by the publication of *Mother India* by Katherine Mayo. Sarojini visited several cities of both countries, addressing select gatherings from the East to the West coast. Charles Andrews, who was in America at the time wrote, 'Sarojini Naidu's visit has been amazing. She has won all hearts, and I have been hearing nothing but praise about her visit everywhere I have gone, both in Canada and the United States'. An American who heard her speak in New York remarked, "I have never heard either from man or from woman the equal of her platform performance, for the beauty and flow of English diction and for the structure and sequences of English sentences. However, more beautiful and significant than the grammatical structure of English sentences, were the beauty and goodness and truth of her utterances." It was a great triumph for Sarojini and for India.

On her return, she was active in the 'Salt March' undertaken by Gandhi as a part of the Civil Disobedience movement (1930). Gandhi had announced that after his arrest Abbas Tyabji would take over as leader and after Tyabji, Sarojini Naidu would lead the satyagrahis, which she did. She was arrested on 21 May 1930 while leading a batch of volunteers towards Dharasana salt depot to break the salt laws. She was released after the Gandhi-Irwin Pact, along with others. In 1931, she was invited to attend the Round Table Conference in London, not as a Congress representative but as a representative of Indian women. However, there was not much discussion on the problems of women; politics and the shape of the future Indian constitution was the main agenda. She did address several gatherings outside. She seemed to have learnt to face the inclement weather of England, this being her third trip of England after her student days at Cambridge.

In 1942, she was again arrested along with Congress leaders and was kept in Aga Khan Palace in Poona where Gandhi, Kasturba, Mira and twenty others were also kept. In those grim days which saw the passing away of Mahadev Desai (Gandhi's secretary) and Kasturba, she lightened the atmosphere with her wit and laughter. After the end of war in 1945, the British realized that it was not possible to hold on to India any longer, and were eager to quit. The Cabinet Mission, which visited India in 1946, tried to resolve the differences between the Congress and the Muslim League. Their proposals included the formation of an Interim Government and setting up of a Constituent Assembly. There was a stalemate, and the Muslim League led by Jinnah, was not willing to join the Interim Government or the Constituent Assembly. The viceroy, Lord Wavell, was at a loss. It seems the friendship between Jinnah and Sarojini was known even among British circles. Lord Wavell tried to seek the help of Sarojini to resolve the crisis. An entry in his *Diary* reads, "Dined with Jinnah's old friend, Sarojini Naidu on September 10 (1946) and we had a long talk on politics and the necessity of getting Jinnah and the M.L. (Muslim League) in the Interim Government and the difficulties of Jinnah's character".[9] After the meeting, Muslim League did join the Interim Government though it is difficult to say how much Sarojini's friendship with Jinnah helped in this. But nobody could avoid the partition of the country, along with freedom, on 15 August 1947. In free India, Sarojini was appointed governor of Uttar Pradesh. During the remaining eighteen months of her life, she relaxed reading detective novels. She was never in good health but by sheer will-power, she lived for almost seventy years. She died on 2 March 1949 in Lucknow.

Even as an important member of the Congress party, she maintained a distinct character. She loved life in all its varied aspects. "Unlike the grim-faced khadi-clad leaders and volunteers of those days, she dressed herself in colourful, sparkling silks. She wore heavy necklaces and dangling ear-rings". The austerity of ashram life was not for her. She felt at ease in a five-star hotel. Her wit and laughter became proverbial. She had the audacity to call Gandhi Mickey-Mouse (because of his large ears) at his face and telling him how much the country had to spend on him to keep him poor, without offending him. She was one of the most talented daughters of India, and one whose spirit never submitted to bodily pain and even in suffering she would burst into peels of laughter and keep the atmosphere enlivened. Many still lament that the great poet in her was sacrificed at the alter of politics and feminism. A posthumous collection of her later poems was published under the title *Feather of the Dawn*.

## References

1. Baig, Tara Ali. *Sarojini Naidu*. New Delhi, Publications Division. 1974, p.16.
2. Sinha, R.P.N. *The Birth and Development of Indo-English Verse*, New Delhi, Dev Pub. House, 1971, p.179.

3.  Morgan, Jenet. *Edwina Mountbatten*, Macmillan, 1991, p.9.
4.  Sinha op. cit., p.180.
5.  Wolpert, Stanley. *Jinnah of Pakistan*. OUP, 984, p.27.
6.  *Collected Works of Mahatma Gandhi* Vol.24, p.386.
7.  Ibid, p.351.
8.  Chagla, M.C. *Roses in December*, Bombay, Bharatiya Vidya Bhavan; 1994, p.89.
9.  Wavell, Archibald. *The Viceroy's Journal* Ed. by Penderel Moon, OUP, 1974, pp.348-49.

# Dadabhai Naoroji

## (1825-1917)

Dadabhai Naoroji was born on 4 September 1825 in a priestly Parsi family of Bombay. His father, Naoroji Palanji, died when his son was only four years old and Dadabhai was brought up by his mother, who though uneducated, had boundless courage and fortitude, and managed to give a good education to her son. Dadabhai was educated at the Elphinstone Institute and later graduated from Elphinstone College, Bombay, in 1845. He was the product of pre-university English education but was in no way inferior to the university era. His mother was eager to get her son married. Thus, Dadabhai was married at the age of eleven to a seven-year-old Parsi girl Gulabi, thus revealing that child marriage was not the monopoly of the Hindu society. They had three children; one son and two daughters.

After his graduation, Dadabhai was appointed head assistant at his alma mater, the Elphinstone Institute, and in 1850, he shifted to Elphinstone College as assistant professor of mathematics and natural philosophy. In 1855, he went to England to join as a representative of Cama & Co., the first Indian firm to open a branch in London. But soon differences cropped up between the company's management and himself because he did not want to be party to their 'fraudulent and deceitful conduct'. He parted company with Cama & Company in 1859. In the meantime, he was appointed professor of Gujarati at the University College, London.

He held that post for ten years till 1865-66. In 1859, he started his own firm Dadabhai Naoroji & Co., which flourished for a while and then ran into bad days. After that, Dadabhai concentrated more on political and economic issues facing India and educating the people in England through speeches and writings about the plight of Indians under the British Rule.

During 1865 to 1876, Naoroji travelled back and forth between India and England. He was an admirer of the Western system of education like a number of his contemporaries. Thus, he was active in the field of education during his sojourns in India, establishing several schools including those for girls, and also worked towards improving the teaching methods and efficiency of the existing schools. He was also active in the social reform movement concerning the Parsi and Hindu communities. Back in London, Dadabhai gradually became the most distinguished member of the small band of Indians who made England their centre of activity for political advancement of India by awakening the consciousness of the English towards their sense of duty and awakening their democratic instinct and liberal principles about which they were noted in the world. In order to carry out this work more effectively, he, in collaboration with W.C. Bonnerjee, started a society in 1865 called London Indian Society. Dadabhai was the president and Bonnerjee its secretary. The society was amalgamated within a year with another society known as the 'East India Association' which was formed in 1866. This society became very popular and counted among its members patrons and sympathizers, a large number of Englishmen.[1] It also had branches in India at several places. In 1869, Naoroji came to India for a brief period during which he started a branch of the East India Association in Bombay and undertook a lecturing tour to educate the Indian people about the objectives of the association.

In 1874, Naoroji was appointed Dewan of Baroda state, but resigned after a year due to differences with the Maharaja and the British Agent stationed there. In July 1875, he was elected member of the Bombay Municipal Corporation and to the Town Council but the following year, he resigned from both and left for England. In 1883, he was nominated as Justice of Peace and was elected to the corporation for the second time. In January 1885, when the Bombay Presidency Association was formed, he was made one of its vice-presidents. In August the same year, he was nominated to the Bombay Legislative Council. Then, in December, the Indian National Congress was formed in Bombay. He took active part in its formation; he was made its president thrice, in 1886, 1893 and 1906.

Early in 1886, he went to England to contest the election to the British Parliament, but did not succeed. In fact, he contested four times and succeeded only once in 1893 from Central Finsbury constituency in London. He sat as a Gladstonian Liberal, the party which stood for Home Rule for Ireland. He was the first Indian to become a member of the British Parliament. However, his speeches outside the Parliament proved more effective than those he delivered inside, which were not many anyway. The British public heard him as he was a liberal and a moderate, who believed that India had benefited greatly from the British rule and advocated the continuation of the British connection. Like other 'moderates' he had full faith in the sense of justice and fair play of the British people. At the same time, in line with other moderates like Gokhale and R.C. Dutt, he was very critical of the economic policies of the British administration — the administration which was fully supported by Whitehall, London.

He made significant contribution to Indian economic thought, especially finance. He brought home before the British public, the fact that Indian capital and wealth was being depleted year after year, to enrich England. His famous observation that the streets of London were paved with the wealth of India, was repeated from hundreds of platforms in India for years. He wrote a series of papers on the appalling poverty of the Indian people and on Indian finance. He made a concerted effort in enquiring about the causes of Indian poverty and wrote a paper, *Poverty in India*, in 1870, which he read before the East India Association. Later he developed this subject and published a pamphlet, *Conditions of India*. Continued research into the subject during his stay in England, was undertaken with the help of official files and documents in the India Office Library. He also entered into voluminous correspondence with public figures there, to propound his now famous 'Drain Theory' i.e. drain of India's wealth to England. His finding resulted in his most famous book, *Poverty and Un-British Rule in India*, published in London in 1901. He was also the first

Indian to have estimated the per capita income of India. Naoroji vigorously pleaded for readjustment of Indo-British financial relations. The appointment, in 1873, of a Parliamentary Select Committee on Indian Finance, known as the Fawcett Committee, was largely the result of his efforts and he gave evidence before it. Not much came out of the Committee but, undaunted, he continued his efforts, which resulted in the appointment, in 1896, of the Royal Commission on Indian Expenditure (better known as Welby Commission) of which he was the only Indian member. Not satisfied with the findings of the commission, Naoroji, along with Wedderburn and Thomas Caine, submitted a minority report. In 1898, he also gave evidence before the Indian Currency Commission.

Naoroji was a powerful speaker and for years he continued to express his views through his well-attended lectures. Perhaps the most memorable, was the one which he delivered on 6 July 1900 in the aid of Indian Famine Relief Fund in which he sarcastically admired Lord Salisbury, secretary of state, for revealing the truth that 'India must be bled'. He said, 'You have formed this great British Empire at our expense, and you will hear what reward we have received from you. The European army in India at any time was comparatively insignificant. During the Indian Mutiny you had only forty thousand troops there. It was two hundred thousand Indian troops that shed their blood and fought your battles which gave you (your) magnificent Empire. It is at India's cost and blood this Empire has been formed and maintained up to the present day. It is in consequence of the tremendous cost of these wars and because of the millions you draw from us every year that India is so completely exhausted and bled — You impose upon us an immense European military and civil service; you draw from us a heavy taxation. But in the disbursement and the disposal of that taxation we have not the slightest voice. I ask anyone here to stand up and say that he would be satisfied, if after having to pay heavy taxation, he was given no voice in governance. I ask any one of you whether there is any great mystery in these famines and plagues? No other country, exhausted as India has been exhausted by an evil system of government, would have taken it for even half the time.'[2]

Apart from publishing tracts and books on the Indian problem, he also ventured into journalism. In 1883, he started the *Voice of India* in

Bombay which was later incorporated in the *Indian Spectator*. He regularly contributed articles in papers like *India, Manchester Guardian* and other British papers. He wrote hundreds of 'Letters to the Editor' in those papers. In 1889, he started the *Rast Guftar*, (Path of Truth) a Gujarati weekly concentrating on social reform. It lasted for only two years.

Naoroji was an ardent social reformer and also promoter of education in the Bombay Presidency, endowing schools for the poor and women, especially for the Parsi community. For that purpose, he founded many important organizations like Framji Institute, Irani Fund, Parsi Gymnasium, Widow Re-marriage Association. He also helped in establishing the Victoria & Albert Museum and the Royal Asiatic Society in Bombay.

He played a memorable role in the Indian National Congress, presiding over its session in 1886 and 1893. But the most memorable one was that of 1906 at Calcutta, when he was asked to preside and patch up the differences between the 'moderates' led by Gokhale and 'extremists' led by Tilak. Naoroji had stayed above internal quarrels in the Congress, thus earning the respect of both the factions. The conflict between the two factions thus did not come out in the open at Calcutta but resulted in ugly scenes and a split at Surat next year. There was no Naoroji in 1907 to serve as a peacemaker. The 1906 session of the Congress is also significant because the idea of swaraj was propounded by Naoroji from the Congress platform for the first time, though it meant self-rule within the Empire at that time.

Dadabhai came to India for good in 1913 and was welcomed back as a triumphant hero by the people of India. His active life was over. He died on 30 June 1917 at the age of ninety-one in Bombay. Thousands of his admirers joined in the funeral procession. It is given to but few to live so full and complete a life as Dadabhai Naoroji did.

## References

1. Majumdar, R.C. *History of the Freedom Movement in India*. Calcutta, Firma K.L.M. Vol. 1, 1988, pp.339-40.
2. Quoted in H.D. Sharma ed. *100 Best Pre-Independence Speeches*. New Delhi, HarperCollins, 1998, pp.51-52.

# Jayaprakash Narayan

## (1902-79)

Jayaprakash Narayan was one of the last outstanding moral and political figures in India who never aspired for any office. Unlike Gandhi, he did not 'control' any organization. He was a great protagonist of socialism, the definition of which he kept on changing trying to bring 'total revolution' through it. In a way, he belonged to the long tradition of radical utopians.

Jayaprakash Narayan (or J.P. for short) was born on 11 October 1902 in a small village Sitabdiara (or Sitab Diyara) in Saran district of Bihar. He was the fourth child of Harsu Dayal and Phul Rani. His father was a government servant in the Canal Department. As the first two children of his parents had died soon after birth, Jayaprakash's parents were indulgent towards him, and he spent a somewhat lonely childhood. At the age of six, his education started in the village primary school. After completing primary education, he was sent to Patna and joined the Patna Collegiate School in the seventh standard. His success in the matriculation examination earned him a scholarship. But while he was studying in the Intermediate class, Gandhi started the Non-Cooperation movement and asked students to shun government-aided schools. That made him join Bihar Vidyapeeth, a non-aided institution started a short while earlier, by the Congress. But there were no classes beyond I.Sc. in the Vidyapeeth. It was not very well managed due to a paucity of funds. Jayaprakash was facing a dilemma and once thought of joining the Banaras Hindu University, founded by Madan

Mohan Malaviya. Jayaprakash came to realize that he had sacrificed his education and career for nothing, when Gandhi suspended the Non-Cooperation movement early in 1922. Most of the students had rejoined government-aided schools and colleges. But not Jayaprakash.

While still in college, the young, tall and handsome Jayaprakash was married in October 1920 at Darbhanga to Prabhavati, daughter of Brij Kishore Prasad, a lawyer of some repute, who had met Gandhi during the Champaran campaign for the cause of indigo farmers. Prabhavati was fourteen and Jayaprakash eighteen. After only a month of her marriage, she was sent to Gandhi's ashram at Ahmedabad on the continuous pleading of Gandhi with her father and father-in-law. She lived there for many long years.

An unexpected opportunity came Jayaprakash's way when his friend Bhola Pant, who had gone to the USA for higher studies, invited him there to continue his studies, and even offered him hospitality. Jayaprakash obtained a passport and visa and wrote to Prabhavati in Gandhi's ashram to accompany him. She refused. Prabhavati was 'completely overawed and dominated by Gandhi's personality'. Himself the father of four sons, Gandhi made her undertake the vow of celibacy, and she died childless. Jayaprakash left for America in May 1922, without Prabhavati, and landed at San Francisco on 8 October 1922. As the semester had already started, he had to wait for the next semester, doing odd jobs to support himself. He stayed in America for eight years changing universities frequently — Iowa, Chicago, Wisconsin, California and Ohio. He had also changed his subject from science to social sciences and did his M.A. from Ohio University, majoring in sociology in August 1929. The topic of his thesis was 'Societal Variation', which won him high praise from his teachers. During his stay in America, he had come in contact with Leftist groups and had studied indepth the works by and about Karl Marx, Lenin, Trotsky and others. He was also inspired by the writings of M.N. Roy. Seeing his interest in communism, he received an invitation to study in the Soviet Union. He wrote to Prabhavati that she accompany him. 'This was in one sense, his bid to begin their marriage, to start building a deep personal relationship through shared purposes. Prabhavati once again refused to go with him'.[1]

Jayaprakash returned to India in October 1929. M.N. Roy's writings had convinced him that Gandhi was against the social revolution but the 'Marxian science of revolution seemed to him to offer a surer and quicker road than civil disobedience. Lenin's success seemed immeasurably more thrilling than Gandhi's failures'. But before taking the plunge in any direction, he went to Sabarmati Ashram to see his wife. There he met Gandhi and Nehru. They travelled together to Lahore where a significant session of the Congress was to be held under Nehru's presidentship. There, *Sampurna Swaraj* (complete independence), as the aim of the Congress, was announced amidst a lot of fanfare. To Jayaprakash, it seemed that freedom was round the corner. He joined the Congress party. Nehru, as president, had set up the Congress office in their family house and Jayaprakash was made secretary of the labour wing. Nehru and Jayaprakash became close friends. Jayaprakash joined the Civil Disobedience movement of 1930, was arrested and detained in Nasik Jail. Here, he met Achyut Patwardhan and Minoo Masani and formed a socialist group. After their release, he along with Acharya Narendra Dev, organized the All India Congress Socialist Party (1934) working within the Congress party. He became the secretary with Narendra Dev as its president. To explain the purpose of this splinter group he wrote a booklet *Why Socialism* (1936). Later, in his book *Towards Struggle* (1946), he claimed: 'The Congress Socialist Party played a notable part in giving shape to the socio-economic content of the Congress Party and a keener edge to the struggle for freedom'. By this time, his love for Marxism had completely waned. He was greatly disturbed by the numerous trials and purges in the Soviet Union in the 1930s. He also found that the Indian communists were a tool for Moscow and had no free will. Consequently, he had drifted towards democratic socialism.

Then came the War, and the British government forced India to participate in the war effort. Jayaprakash was a strong critic of this high-handedness on part of the British, and toured the country telling the people, especially the labour class, to revolt and not cooperate with the government. He was arrested at Jamshedpur after he had addressed the workers, on 18 February 1940, and was sentenced to nine months rigorous imprisonment in Jamshedpur jail. He was released towards the end of

1940. After his release, he tried to convince the Congress party, unsuccessfully, that the country was ready for a revolution to oust the British. Then, on his own, he toured India urging people for a 'socialist revolt'. He also set up secret organizations in Bihar, U.P. and Gujarat as well as in Calcutta and Bombay. He was arrested in Bombay on 1 January 1941 and sent to the Deoli Detention Camp. Due to miserable conditions in the Deoli Camp, Jayaprakash and several others went on a hunger strike. For thirty-one days, he was almost without food. The government ultimately yielded, and he was transferred to the Hazaribagh Prison in Bihar. But he, along with five other prisoners, escaped from the prison scaling a fifteen feet high wall on 9 November 1942. He secretly visited different parts of India, organizing a Central Action Committee. He openly repudiated Gandhi's policy of non-violence and brought in a strong element of armed struggle in the Quit India movement started by Gandhi in August 1942. He wrote two famous letters in December addressed to "All Fighters of Freedom". He dubbed 'non-violence of the brave' as cowardice clothed in *Shastric* subtleties to block the development of this revolution, He established a network of secret organizations to carry out his programme of the 'People's Revolution', and finally fixed his headquarters in Nepal, where he trained *Azad Dasta* (guerilla bands) to carry out the work of dislocating and paralyzing the alien administration. He stayed in Nepal for two months, and came back to India, where he was arrested in May 1943, and put in Hanumannagar jail. But one night a band of fifty revolutionaries raided the jail and rescued J.P. and six others. He left for Calcutta and tried to establish contact with the Azad Hind Fauj of Subhas Bose. But was arrested again on 18 December 1943.[2]

He had become a hero for his daredevil exploits during 1942-43. People idolize the brave and they did it to Jayaprakash in a big way. After his release in 1946, 'he bestrode the country like a colossus'. "*Jayaprakash ki Jai*" rent the air. Hundreds and thousands came to listen to him wherever he spoke. Trade unions invited him to be their president — All India Railwaymen's Federation, All-India Postal Employees and IV Grade Staff Union, All-India Ordnance Factories Union and the Defence Employees Union. These were the largest trade unions in India. His presidentships made him one of the most powerful and influential labour leaders in the world, potentially able to paralyze the government.

However, even in late 1946, he did not believe that the British were serious in relinquishing power. He still thought that only a 'people's revolution' could oust the British. He called the Constituent Assembly and the Interim Government a cruel joke played upon the Indians by the crafty British. He had misjudged the compulsions of the British after the World War. To his surprise, India was divided and two dominions emerged on 15 August 1947.

After Independence, Jayaprakash was very critical of the inflation and rampant corruption among Congress ministers and officials under the new government. When offered, he refused to join the Nehru ministry 'unless the present set-up was changed to give them (Socialists) an effective voice'. He came to believe that the stumbling block for such a change was Sardar Patel, whom he considered the leader of the bourgeois-reactionary forces. He was also critical of Patel for doling out huge pensions to the princes, the exploiters of the poor peasants. After Gandhi's assassination, J.P. openly attacked Patel 'for his laxity and his encouragement of the Hindu Mahasabha, declaring that he bore moral responsibility for the crime'. J.P. wrote to Nehru that he and his followers were ready to join Nehru's cabinet if Patel was dismissed. Nehru did not oblige him.[3] J.P. further criticized the handling of the Hyderabad problem by Patel, who was the head of the States Department. On 15 June 1948 (a week before Mountbatten left India), Patel wrote to Nehru: 'Some of the speeches of Jai Prakash have been filling me with misgiving. The one about Hyderabad in which he tried to put the entire blame on the State Ministry, and claimed that, if the Socialists had been allowed to function in their own way, things would have been settled long ago, was particularly vicious and mischievous. I would not have troubled you with this letter had it not been that you have been publicly praising him and been hailing him as the coming man. I feel that such irresponsible utterances and embarassing attitude on his part hardly justify any faith in him. I have all along been of the view that if the future of India is in the hands of men like Jai Prakash, it would probably be a most unfortunate circumstance'.[4]

Jayaprakash even criticized India's policy in Kashmir, pleading for plebiscite. He accused India of 'exhibiting the growing symptoms of chauvinism, jingoism and narrow nationalism'. He had the audacity to visit Pakistan in September 1964. Black-flags and demonstrations followed him wherever he went in India. Undaunted, he headed a four member 'Conciliation Group' and met General Ayub Khan, president of Pakistan twice in the latter's palace in Rawalpindi. The visit was fruitless and Jayaprakash was embarassed when Pakistan started a war with India soon after. The hero of yesterday had become a man of disrepute.

The schism between the Socialists and the Congress had widened after Independence and in April 1948, at the Nasik Conference, the Socialists decided to sever connection with the Congress and the Congress Socialist Party became simply the Socialist Party, under whose banner they fought the 1952 elections. J.P. was not a candidate but his party was trounced, winning only twelve seats. The Communist Party with twenty-seven seats, became the second largest party. By 1956, the Socialist Party fell apart altogether. Seeing no future in the political arena, he turned to Vinoba Bhave who had started the Bhoodan movement in 1951. He found Vinoba a man of 'incredible strength'. J.P. was prepared to submerge his ideas as well as his personality in Vinoba's. 'Vinoba's bigotry sat on his shoulders for many years.' Following Vinoba, J.P. started walking from village to village, asking for land from the rich landowners and distributing it among the poor. He enjoyed the work, forgetting his socialistic commitments, political or otherwise. During a certain week, nearly seven thousand acres were received as gifts. The experience was exhilarating for him in the initial stages. The concomitant organizations like Gramdan and Sarvodaya also fascinated him. During the Sarvodaya Sammelan in Bodhgaya on 18 April 1954, he concluded his speech with a vow of Jeevandan — to devote the rest of his life to Bhoodan and not to take part in party and power politics in future. J.P. set up an ashram in Sokhodeora village in 1954, with a grant from J.R.D. Tata and the gift of land from a local zamindar. He recruited a hundred-odd volunteers to help in the work of Bhoodan and Sarvodaya and paid them nominal salaries out of the money he had got from Indian and foreign philanthropists. He got government grants and financial help from Khadi Board. For ten years, he lived in this ashram though he often had to go out to give lectures, attend seminars and meet people. Overwork caused him a series of heart-attacks and he was treated at various hospitals —

in Vellore, Bombay and even in America. In April 1973, his wife Prabhadevi
died of cancer.

Differences cropped up between J.P. and Vinoba by 1972-73. He felt
that Vinoba's Bhoodan-Gramdan movement had failed to uplift villagers
and had become ineffectual because it lacked the atmosphere of struggle
which drives men to accept challenges and remake society. He was for
'total revolution'. (The word 'revolution' had fascinated him throughout
his life, in one form or the other). The differences were apparent to their
followers and the movement in Bihar had come to be known as J.P.
movement. But the drudgery of the movement now started to irk him.
Forgetting his vow, he once again jumped into the political cesspool. In
1974, the students' movement in Gujarat against corruption,
unemployment, high prices and shortage of essential commodities, was
launched under the leadership of Morarji Desai, who even went on a fast
unto death. The movement resulted in the dissolution of the Legislative
Assembly. J.P. started a similar movement in Bihar, resulting in police
firing and several deaths. J.P. wrote a booklet on this movement titled
*Total Revolution*. In mid-April 1974, J.P. inaugurated in New Delhi, a
forum called 'Citizens for Democracy'. J.P. declared that the party system
was the mother of corruption and pleaded for a partyless democracy. He
wrote *A Plea For Reconstruction of Indian Policy*, considered by some as his
magnum opus. He became a severe critic of Prime Minister Indira
Gandhi. Then came the Emergency on 26 June 1975. J.P. was arrested,
along with thousands of other leaders. By this time, his health was failing
him. Both his kidneys had failed and he had been put on dialysis. His
heart problem continued. In spite of ill health, he wrote a *Diary* during
the imprisonment. When in March 1977, the Emergency was lifted, he
became active again. Along with J.B. Kriplani, he urged all the opposition
parties to unite against Indira Gandhi's Congress. The Janata Party was
born and it swept the elections of 1977. Morarji Desai was elected as
prime minister on the recommendation of J.P. and Kriplani. But the years
1977-79 were a constant struggle for him against death. His efforts to act
as a moral mentor to the Janata government was interrupted by his visits
to hospitals in Bombay and America. The Janata Party betrayed his 'Total
Revolution'. He died a frustrated man in his small flat in the premises

of Mahila Charkha Samiti in Patna on 8 October, 1979. *The Indian Express* wrote in the obituary column: 'Not since Mahatma Gandhi, has a single individual without power of office exerted as much influence on India as J.P. did.'

# References

1. Scarfe, Allan and Wendy. *J.P.; His Biography*, Orient Longman, 1998, p.32.
2. Majumdar, R.C. *History of the Freedom Movement in India*, Vol. 3, Calcutta, Firma KLM. 1988, p.552.
3. Scarfe op. cit. p.123.
4. Patel, Vallabbhai. *Select Correspondence of Sardar Patel, 1945-1950*, Vol. 2, Ahmedabad, Navajivan, 1977, pp.107-08.

# Jawaharlal Nehru

## (1889-1964)

Jawaharlal Nehru was born to Swarup Rani and Motilal Nehru on 14 November 1889 at Allahabad in Uttar Pradesh. Their ancestors were Kashmiri Pandits who had migrated to the plains during the Mughal rule. Contrary to the general impression, Jawaharlal was not born with a silver spoon in his mouth. His father was only a *vakil*, neither a bar-at-law nor a law graduate, and the family lived in a dark and dingy house in the heart of Allahabad city, adjacent to the red light area. However, Motilal proved to be a quick-witted and an astute lawyer. His practice soared, and he became a very successful lawyer. The family first moved to the Civil Lines area, inhabited mostly by the Europeans. Soon Motilal bought a big colonial bungalow at Church Road, Allahabad, with an acre of land surrounding it. From Nishat Manzil its name was changed to Anand Bhavan. The house was extensively renovated and in time, became one of the most renowned houses in the country, because it played an important role during the freedom movement. Jawaharlal was eleven years old when the family moved to this house. Motilal's monthly income was now in five figures and he could afford to live in a lavish, western style. He had become an admirer of Western culture from his college days at the Muir Central College, where the principal and several teachers were British. His admiration for Western culture was fortified by his visit to Europe in 1899 and again in 1900. The family's life-style became completely westernized though Swarup Rani zealously guarded a separate 'Indian kitchen' with Brahmin cooks. A daughter Sarup (later Vijay Lakshmi Pandit) was born in 1900. A European governess was employed for her and a European tutor for Jawaharlal, because Motilal did not want to send his son to an Indian school to be 'polluted' in the company of riff-raff. Thus, in early life, Jawahar led a lonely life without the company of his peers. His tutor F.T. Brooks, a young man of twenty-six, left certain indelible imprints on Jawaharlal's mind. Brooks was a believer in Theosophy and he initiated his 'shy and intellectually receptive pupil' into the Theosophical Society. Annie Besant, its president, came all the way from Adyar to initiate the young boy. Brook also inspired Jawaharlal to acquire a taste for serious reading, which never left him. It was Brooks who created in Jawaharlal an interest in science. A small laboratory was set up in one of the rooms where simple experiments were carried out in elementary physics and chemistry by the tutor-pupil duo. Brooks left after three years. Motilal now wanted his son to be educated in a British public school. The family, Motilal, Swarup Rani, Jawaharlal, and four-year-old sister sailed for England on 13 May 1905. With the help of some English friends, Motilal succeeded in getting his son admitted to Harrow, a prestigious public school. Jawaharlal spent two uneventful years at Harrow. From Harrow he went to Cambridge University, joined Trinity College and studied the natural sciences, chemistry, botany and geology. However, he read widely and developed interest in other subjects like English literature, history, politics and economics. He took his degree in 1910, a second class honours in the natural sciences tripos. The same year, he joined the Inner Temple to read for the Bar as advised by his father. Here, he lived like the son of a rich father. Motilal gave into all the monetary demands made by his son. Nehru frequented the night clubs of London and its theatres. In his *Autobiography* Jawaharlal is silent about his relations with women which should have come naturally to a handsome, rich young man in the free society of London. It was two years of frivolous life for Jawaharlal. He never visited the India House, which had become the abode of freedom fighters like Savarkar, Madam Cama and others. He was called to the Bar in 1912 and sailed back to India, carrying several English traits in his character.

On his return, Jawaharlal joined the chamber of Tej Bahadur Sapru, one of the prominent lawyers of Allahabad. But Tej Bahadur found him wanting in the necessary qualities required for becoming a successful lawyer. He was not a good speaker and lacked the vibrant personality of his father. 'My profession did not fill me with a wholehearted enthusiasm,' Nehru writes in his *Autobiography*. Gradually, he was drawn to politics, aggressive politics. He joined the two Home Rule Leagues started by Annie Besant and Tilak, but worked especially for the former, who had started taking an ever increasing part in Indian politics. This was in 1916, the year which was important for Jawaharlal for another reason. He was married on 8 February 1916 at Delhi to Kamala Kaul who was barely seventeen, while Jawaharlal was twenty-seven. Jawaharlal had had no say in the choice of the girl and as a consequence, Jawaharlal was not, it seems, emotionally attached to his wife. After marriage, the couple went to Kashmir, along with some other members of the Nehru clan. Jawaharlal went on a long hiking trip, with one of his cousins, in the mountains up the Ladakh road. Kamala waited for her husband at Srinagar. When the couple returned to Allahabad, Kamala was a physical and mental wreck. Her father-in-law, who dabbled in homoeopathy, diagnosed her illness as 'nervousness and hysteria'. She never fully recovered. She was a misfit in a Westernized home, coming from a traditional middle-class Hindu family. Kamala gave birth to a girl, afterwards named Indira Priyadarshni.

Jawaharlal never practiced seriously at the Bar. Exciting and tragic things were happening elsewhere in the country. The most tragic was what happened at Jallianwala Bagh at Amritsar in April 1919. After the relaxation of marshal law in Punjab, many Congress leaders descended on Amritsar to get details about the tragedy. Among those leaders were Jawaharlal's father Motilal, C.R. Das, Gandhi, Malaviya and several others. Jawaharlal also joined them and worked as assistant to C.R. Das. Jawaharlal started getting involved in the political goings-on. The emergence of Gandhi in 1918 (Champaran campaign) and later as a guiding spirit of the Non-Cooperation movement (1920-22) attracted Nehru and he became the follower of this 'queer and saintly leader' of the Congress. He joined the Congress party and became a serious worker. He found the work much more exhilarating than working at the Bar. Though Gandhi could not get freedom in one year as promised by him in 1920, he had transformed the Congress party from an elite body into a mass movement. Nehru took active part in the Non-Cooperation movement. He went to villages with other Congress workers and learnt the first lesson of public speaking. By now Motilal had also joined the Congress and was constantly in touch with Gandhi. Later that year, the Prince of Wales visited India. The Congress party boycotted and staged demonstrations against the Royal visit. The government responded by arresting Congress workers. Among the thousands arrested were Motilal and Jawaharlal. They were arrested on 6 December 1921 at Anand Bhawan and sentenced to six months imprisonment. Jawaharlal was, however, released after three months. This was his first imprisonment. Several more were to follow, nine in all. He was arrested again after six weeks for picketing shops selling foreign goods and was sentenced to eighteen months in prison. The prison for people like Nehru and Gandhi and his close associates, was quite different from those of 'dangerous' freedom fighters like the Savarkar brothers, Bhai Parmanand, Bhagat Singh and his comrades and thousands others. The latter were kept in isolation on a killer diet. Many of them died unnoticed in prisons or in the Cellular jail in the Andamans. Those who survived, were complete physical and mental wrecks. But the 'safe' freedom fighters were treated differently in 'A' class prisons. Jail diet for them could be supplemented by home diet including fruits and other nourishing items. They could spend their time doing gardening, reading newspapers and books and even writing books. Nehru, in his *Autobiography*, has written in several places, that he liked prison life, where he could meditate and indulge in creative activities away from the humdrum of daily routine. The British were quick to realize — and retained that belief — that they had nothing to fear from Congressmen like Gandhi and Nehru and as long as they controlled the Congress they had an unofficial ally. 'As long as civil disobedience remained non-violent, the Government had little to worry about. Who was hurt by non-cooperation anyway'.[1] Therefore, not much should be read in Jawaharlal's going to prison.

By this time, it was clear to Motilal that unlike him his son was not going to be a success at the Bar. Motilal let him find his destiny in politics.

He himself became a follower of Gandhi; started wearing homespun clothes, reliquishing his western style of life. It did not take much time for Motilal and Jawaharlal to earn name and fame. Gandhi took them under his wings and became not only their political but also family adviser. Jawaharlal started climbing the political ladder. To begin with, he became general secretary of the United Provinces Provincial Congress Committee and conducted the official business, including visits to various places. Later, he became general secretary of the All India Congress Committee. But as the Congress work did not offer him any money, he was unable to support himself and his family — wife and daughter. He was living on the largesse of his rich father. He was distressed. In a state of despondency, he wrote to Gandhi in 1924 about his predicament. In reply, Gandhi wrote a letter to his father and another to Jawaharlal. To Motilal, Gandhi wrote (2 September 1924): 'This letter like the former is meant to be a plea for Jawaharlal. He is one of the loneliest young men of my acquaintance in India. The idea of your mental desertion of him hurts me'. To Jawaharlal, Gandhi wrote (15 September 1924): 'Shall I try to arrange for some money for you? Why you may not take up remunerative work? After all you must live by the sweat of your brow even though you may be under father's foot. Will you be correspondent to some newspapers? Or will you take up a professorship'.[2] Things did not change. However, Jawaharlal was elected chairman of the Allahabad Municipality in 1923 and he served there for almost two years. In the meanwhile, Motilal, along with C.R. Das, had founded the Swaraj Party, fought the elections, won and entered the Central Legislature. He was elected the leader of the opposition. Motilal had given up much of his law practice but by no means all of it.

Meanwhile, Kamala's health had begun to deteriorate. Doctors diagnosed her illness as tuberculosis and advised the family to get her treated in Switzerland. In March 1926, Jawaharlal, Kamala and their daughter Indira sailed for Europe. While Kamala battled with her illness in a sanatorium near Geneva, Jawaharlal found time to explore Europe. In February 1927, he attended, as a delegate of the Indian National Congress, the Congress of Oppressed Nationalities at Brussels. There he met leading communists and socialists from various countries. In

September 1927, Motilal arrived in Europe. Both father and son went on a tour of Europe staying at the very best hotels. The tour included a trip to the Soviet Union. They stayed there for only four days but it left a lasting impression upon Jawaharlal which came to the fore in the shape of the Five Year Plans when he became the prime minister. Kamala's health in the meanwhile, had been improving and the couple sailed back for India in December 1927. They had been away from India for nearly two years.

In 1929, Gandhi opened his political cards and showed his preference for Jawaharlal against everyone else. Although he himself and Sardar Patel had got more votes than Jawaharlal had, Gandhi insisted that Jawaharlal be made president of the Congress party for the 1929 session and lead the Congress during the crucial year of 1930. Those who objected to this undemocratic attitude, were silenced by Gandhi with the description of qualities which Jawaharlal possessed. 'Pandit Jawaharlal has everything to recommend him. He has for years discharged, with singular ability and devotion, the office of Secretary of the Congress. He has come in touch with labour and peasantry. His close acqaintance with European politics is a great asset to enabling him to assess others'. After two months, he again wrote in *Young India*, 'In bravery he is not to be surpassed. Who can excel him in the love of the country? He is rash and impetuous, say some. This quality is an additional qualification at the present moment. And if he has the dash and the rashness of a warrior, he has also the prudence of statesman. He is the knight *sans peur sans reproche* (without fear and without reproach). The nation is safe in his hands'.[3] To Nehru's detractors in the Congress, Gandhi assured that 'it would be like having himself in the chair' — a revealing statement. Gandhi went even a step further later by nominating Jawaharlal as his political heir, thus eliminating Vallabbhai Patel, who was favoured by more Congressmen, for the race of primacy.

The Congress session of 1929-30 at Lahore proved to be a historic one. January 26 was declared as Independence Day and a pledge to that effect was taken on the banks of the river Ravi and repeated at gatherings throughout the country. The freedom movement had entered a new phase and Jawaharlal had emerged as an important Congress leader next only to Gandhi. During his Congress presidentship several important events were witnessed. Among them were Gandhi's 'Salt March' (March-April 1930) and immediately afterwards, the Civil Disobedience movement. Jawaharlal took part in these political developments (though he was not one of the companions of Gandhi during his march). He was in and out of prison several times during the next five years. Motilal Nehru died on 6 February 1931, at the age of seventy. As long as his father was alive, Jawaharlal was frequently torn between the two dynamic figures of Motilal and Gandhi. Now he was entirely dependent on Gandhi. Not that their relationship was always cordial and smooth. Nehru criticized Gandhi several times for his medieval mindset and out-moded economic ideas. But soon there would be reconciliation and each time the sacrifice's were made by Nehru, who knew where his interest lay. 'His acceptance of Gandhi's leadership was without reservation. Nehru's entire political career was built on the basis of that enigmatic relationship between two personalities which apparently had so very little in common. Nehru was (a) man of modern education and culture, endowed with refinement and personal charm. But all the merits and assets might not have raised him to the high pedestal of the 'Tribune of the People' and subsequently to political power, but for his mystic and mysterious relations with Gandhi. It can reasonably be doubted if Nehru could become the hero of the Indian nationalism except as the spiritual son of Gandhi'.[4]

Nehru was undergoing one of his imprisonments when he was suddenly released on 4 September 1935 because his wife, Kamala, was seriously ill and was taken to Europe for treatment. Nehru flew and joined his wife who had been admitted in a sanatorium in Germany. In his absence, Nehru was elected as president of the Congress for the 1936 session. However, Kamala died on 28 February 1936 and Nehru returned to India with her ashes in an urn, which he kept in his room as long as he lived. As president of the Congress party, he sponsored the formation of the Left wing in the Congress which came to be known as the Congress Socialist Party but was careful not to join it formally. That would have annoyed Gandhi. In the 1937 elections to the provincial assemblies, the Congress had won absolute majority in five out of eleven provinces and was the largest single party in three others. Nehru is often blamed for not agreeing to the formation of a coalition government with the Muslim League as agreed upon before the elections. However, there was no such official written agreement. The whole story is based on the 'gentlemen's agreement' supposedly made by the Congress leaders with Khaliquzzaman, a senior Muslim League leader of U.P. It is difficult to prove the authenticity of that statement. Nehru is also blamed for his statement that 'there are only two parties in the country — the Congress and the British government'. After some haggling with the British, the Congress formed ministries in eight provinces and had emerged as a strong contender for the take-over after freedom was granted. However, in September 1939, Gandhi unwisely asked the Congress ministries to resign, because the British authorities did not consult the Indian representatives while dragging India into the war with Germany. The Churchill government sent Sir Stafford Cripps (March 1942) to negotiate with the Indian leaders to explore the possibility of participating in the war effort. The negotiations failed and Gandhi launched the Quit India movement in August 1942. The Congress leaders, including Gandhi and Nehru, were arrested. While Gandhi was kept in the Agha Khan Palace near Pune, Nehru was sent to the Ahmednagar Fort. This was his ninth and the longest period of imprisonment. He was released in June 1945.

By the time the Congress leaders came out of prison, things had changed. There was no need to continue the freedom struggle. The British were in a hurry to leave India. Though they had won the war, their country had almost been vanquished. Their finest manpower had been decimated, their industry had been crippled, their debt was running into billions and there was a shortage of almost everything in their country. In India, the number of civil servants (the steel-frame) was not even one-third of what it was before the war. Above all, they could not depend on the Indian army anymore, with the help of which they had been ruling India. Subhas Chandra Bose, by raising a formidable Indian National Army, had shown that the Indian soldiers could change sides and were no more loyal to the Crown. The British now could not govern India, they had enough problems at home. To wind up the Empire, the British sent the Cabinet Mission in March 1946 to negotiate the final settlement with Indian leaders. After long drawn discussions, two decisions were to be implemented without delay: there would be an Interim

Government to run the country till the final handover by the British; and a constituent assembly would draw up the constitution for free India. In September 1946, an Interim Government was formed, headed by Nehru, with an equal number of Congress and Muslim League ministers. But the Muslim League members saw to it that the government did not function properly. Large scale communal riots took place at several places, from Peshawar to Noakhali in east Bengal. The British feared a civil war. To hasten the exit, Wavell was replaced by Lord Mountbatten as the last viceroy of India. In June 1947, it was decided that the British would handover power to the Indians on 15 August 1947. It was also decided to partition the country into two dominions — Hindustan and Pakistan, forming the Muslim majority areas. Nehru became the first prime minister of India on the night of 14-15 August 1947 and a new chapter began in his life. Sardar Patel became the deputy prime minister. By this time, Mountbatten and his wife Edwina had befriended Nehru and some other Congress leaders. Mountbatten was requested to stay on as the first governor-general of independent India.

Independence and the partition of the country created several problems. The most serious one was the arrival of millions of refugees who were forced to leave their hearth and home in Pakistan. It took several years to rehabilitate those unfortunate families, taxing the scanty resources of the government. It is ironic that Nehru did not show any sympathy for the Hindu and Sikh refugees. He was more concerned and active in saving the Muslims in Delhi and surrounding areas. He is reported to have said, 'I think the major issue in this country today is to solve satisfactorily our own minority problems. What happens in Pakistan is not my primary concern'.[5] Such views of Nehru brought him in conflict with Sardar Patel who had heartfelt compassion for the refugees and took great pains towards their rehabilitation. Their conflict came into the open at the time of the election of the first president of India. Nehru's choice was Rajagopalachari, but the overwhelming majority of Congressmen including Patel, supported Rajendra Prasad whom Nehru considered an orthodox Hindu but who had been president of the Constituent Assembly. Rajendra Prasad became the first president of free India. Soonafter came another election, that of president of the Congress. Nehru's choice was

Kripalani (no friend of Nehru, but 'lesser evil') but Patel supported the candidacy of Purushotam Das Tandon, who won, to the extreme discomfiture of Nehru, and whom he had called 'a symbol of communal and revivalist outlook'. Nehru refused to cooperate with Tandon, and after the death of Patel in December 1950, forced him to resign, and himself took over the Congress presidentship.

The more serious problem was faced by India in Kashmir, which Nehru did not allow Patel to deal with, though he was incharge of the States Department. Pakistani tribals invaded Kashmir in October 1947. Maharaja Hari Singh's forces could not check their advance. He panicked, and in a hurry, acceded to India on 26 October. While accepting the accession, Governor General Mountbatten stipulated "that the Indian government's acceptance of the Maharaja's act of accession was conditional on the will of the people being ascertained as soon as law and order were restored". When the Indian army was advancing to clear the area of invaders, Nehru unwisely, on the advice of the Mountbattens, took the matter to the UNO where the matter still stands. In the meantime, Nehru's government did everything to make the whole world believe that Kashmir was not an integral part of India.

Another problem India faced was the annexation of Tibet by the Chinese in 1950, which had been a buffer state for centuries. Nehru quietly accepted the Chinese act to the surprise of the world. Nehru did not want to displease China and busied himself to emerge as the undisputed leader of the Asian and African countries neglecting the problems, both internal and external, which India faced. Even when important events were taking place in India, Nehru had organized the first Asian Relations Conference in March 1947 in Delhi. But he had yet to as emerge the leader of the developing countries. In 1954, he enunciated the principle of Panchsheel (five principles of peaceful coexistence) in conjunction with the Chinese. Panchsheel became the cornerstone of India's foreign policy. Soon after, came the Bandung Conference (April 1955) hosted by Indonesia with full cooperation of India, which was attended by twenty-nine countries. He advocated non-alignment, which meant not taking sides in the Cold War, in progress at that time between the two blocs led by Soviet Union and America. Nehru also attended almost every

Commonwealth Prime Ministers' Conference during his seventeen years of prime ministership. Thus, he became an important actor on the international stage bringing laurels for the country and its people, and his image as world leader was recognized by every country. However, in 1962, his image was tarnished when China attacked India, subdued NEFA and almost reached the plains of India. Earlier, China had already annexed Aksai Chin and thousands of square kilometres of area in Ladakh and south of the McMahon Line on the western front. Regarding the China policy, Nehru was guided by two leftists, V.K. Krishna Menon (who had joined Nehru's cabinet as Defence minister in 1957) and K.M. Panikkar, (who was India's ambassador in China). Both had sympathy with China and had convinced Nehru that China would never invade India and that there was no need to deploy army on the high mountains facing China 'where not a blade of grass grew'. But the great pragmatist, Sardar Patel, had warned Nehru in a letter from his deathbed (7 November 1950) that, 'Even though we regard ourselves as friends of China, the Chinese do not regard us as their friends.' With uncanny foresight Patel added. 'In our calculations we shall now have to reckon with Communist China in the north and in the north-east, a Communist China which has definite ambitions and aims and which does not, in any way, seem friendly disposed towards us'.[6] Nehru completely ignored Patel's friendly warning and had to suffer because of this lapse. To add to his agony, none of the non-aligned countries announced their support for India. The Chinese withdrew from Indian soil unilaterally, but left a deep scar on Nehru's mind. His image as world leader, to which he had devoted much of his time and effort, had been eroded. His health deteriorated, and the end came only after eighteen months.

On the home front, Nehru is justly admired as nation builder. He is credited with the establishment of heavy industry; a chain of national scientific laboratories and strengthening the democratic institutions in India. He also introduced the controversial planned development, which left only a small patch of economy for private enterprise. It was termed as 'mixed-economy'. However, his economic policies did not bear fruit as expected. India remained short of foodgrain and had to import wheat from U.S.A. The Planning Commission was set up in 1950 and during his life time two Five Year Plans were completed, and the third which was in progress, went awry and was followed by one year plans or no plans. Shortages of consumer goods led to quota and 'licence raj', which inevitably led to corruption. Critics point out that "Nehru's stubborn faith in socialism froze individual entrepreneurship and stunted economic growth", and the nation had to wait for four decades to undo the damage done by Nehruvian economics. As the years rolled by, the very foundations on which Nehru's prestige and reputation rested, began to weigh him down. 'At one time, he had a solution to every difficulty, later he faced difficulty in every solution'.[7]

In spite of his failures, Nehru has been recognized by many as a great man of world stature. He was the darling of the masses. At the same time, he was at ease with scientists like Einstein, literary giants like G.B. Shaw, pacifists and philosophers like Bertrand Russell, statesmen like Roosevelt and John F. Kennedy and historians like Arnold Toynbee. His confidence in himself is evident from the fact that he appointed in his cabinet antagonists like B.R. Ambedkar and S.P. Mukherjee. Nehru imparted dignity to the parliamentary proceedings by listening patiently to the opponent's viewpoint.

As a memento for the coming generations, Nehru has left two of his bestsellers *An Autobiography* and *Discovery of India*. His letters to his daughter Indira have also been published in a book titled *Glimpses of World History*.

When Nehru entered his seventy-fifth year, he had already ruled India for almost seventeen years. Now he was a tired man, his strength was failing, and he retained control "more by momentum of the past than by mastery of the present". He died in Delhi on 27 May 1964 and was cremated at the bank of Yamuna in the presence of several heads of states. The place is now called Shantivan. With Nehru's death an era came to an end.

## References

1. Edwardes, Michael. *Nehru; A Political Biography*, London, Allen Lane, 1971, p.47. (Reprint by Vikas, New Delhi).

2.  Nehru, Jawaharlal, ed. *A Bunch of Old Letters*, New Delhi, OUP. 1958, p.41-42.
3.  *Collected Works of Mahatma Gandhi*, Vol. 41, pp.240, 499.
4.  Roy, M.N. *Jawaharlal Nehru — An Enigma or a Tragedy, in Jawaharlal Nehru, A Critical Tribute* ed. By A.B. Shah, Bombay, Manaktalas, 1965, p.39.
5.  Shankar, V. ed. *Select Correspondence of Sardar Patel*, 1945-50. Vol. 2. Ahmedabad, Navajivan, 1977, pp.320-23.
6.  Laxman, R.K. in *A Study of Nehru* ed. by Rafiq Zakaria. New Delhi, Rupa, 1989, p.422.
7.  Ibid.

# Motilal Nehru

## (1861-1931)

Motilal was born at Agra on 6 May 1861. His ancestors were from Kashmir who finally settled in Delhi. His grandfather, Lakshmi Narayan, served as *vakil* of the East India Company at the Mughal Court of Delhi. His father, Gangadhar, was a police officer in Delhi during the 1857 uprising, and fled to Agra along with his family when the British forces re-occupied Delhi. Gangadhar died at Agra four years later and three months after his death, Motilal was born to Jeorani. Motilal spent his childhood at Khetri in Rajasthan, where his elder brother Nandlal, was a dewan. But in 1870, Nandlal left for Agra, where he began practising as a lawyer and after sometime the family settled in Allahabad when the high court was established there.

Motilal's early education was in a Mohammedan *maktab* (school) where he learnt Persian and Arabic and the Muslim culture left a deep influence on him. When he grew up, he was closer to the Muslim way of life than of a Hindu pundit. Motilal was the first rank Hindu political leader who showed no deep attachment or love for the ancient Hindu culture.[1] To some extent, this attitude towards Hindus and Hinduism was inherited by his son Jawaharlal Nehru. Motilal Nehru learnt English only in his teens. It is doubtful if he ever learnt Sanskrit or even Hindi. After matriculation from Kanpur, Motilal joined the Muir College at Allahabad. He did not complete his B.A. Instead, he took the lawyer's course (1883) in which he topped. He started practising law at Kanpur. Three years later, he moved to Allahabad where his elder brother, Nandlal had a lucrative practice. Unfortunately, Nandlal died soon after in 1887, and Motilal had to bear the responsibility of a large joint-family. He was only twenty-five at the time. Soon after, however, he was married to Swarup Rani and had one son, Jawaharlal (1889) and two daughters Sarup (Vijaylakshmi Pandit) and Krishna (1907), who was married to G. Hutheesingh.

Motilal soon became a leading lawyer at the Allahabad High Court 'by the dint of his forensic ability' and mastery over the legal procedures. It is said that, by the time he was forty, his income was in five figures. In 1900, he purchased a bungalow at Church Road, Allahabad, got it renovated and named it 'Anand Bhavan' (house of joy). The family started living lavishly in a westernized manner, a process which was accelerated by visits to Europe in 1899 and 1900. On his return, he was ex-communicated by his orthodox community for refusing to perform the religious ceremony of penance. Undaunted by the strictures, he again sailed for England in 1905, alongwith his family, to admit his son Jawaharlal at a school in Harrow.

Motilal's early political life was 'reluctant, brief and sporadic'. He attended several Congress sessions, beginning with the one in 1888. In 1903, he attended the Congress session at Madras along with his son Jawaharlal, a boy of fourteen. Initially, Motilal was 'immoderately moderate' in political views. Law was then his first love, and the discipline of the mind he acquired as a lawyer, made him a constitutionalist. During the tug-of-war between the Moderates and the Extremists in 1907, he was with the former. When he presided over the U.P. Provincial Conference at Allahabad later, he vigorously criticized the Extremists. In April 1909, he presided over the third U.P. Social Conference at Agra. In 1910, he was elected to the U.P. Provincial Legislative Council, of which he remained a member till 1919. Motilal attended the Delhi Durbar of 1911 held in honour of King George V. Gradually, he was drawn towards a political career. He became a member of the Allahabad Municipal Board, and in 1916, when he took an independent stance on what was known as the Jehangirabad amendment to the Municipal Bill, a step alleged to be a surrender to the Muslims, he was criticized by the Hindu press and politicians of U.P. He was increasingly taking part in the Congress party, and became a vice-president of the Seva Samiti; a member of the All-India Congress Committee and president of the U.P. Congress. However, it was still the family and professional matters which were his mainstay. When his son Jawaharlal returned from England in 1912 after qualifying as a barrister, he tried to induct him in the legal profession, but Jawaharlal did not succeed as a lawyer, and gradually drifted towards politics. Then on he had to plan things in a way that would help his son in his political career, besides his own.

When Annie Besant founded the Home Rule League in 1916, Motilal joined the League of which Jawaharlal was already a member. Motilal worked wholeheartedly for the League and became president of the Allahabad branch of the Home Rule League and criticized the government for arresting Annie Besant, which the Anglo-Indian press did not appreciate, including the *Pioneer* (Allahabad). After 1916, the Congress party came to be controlled by the Extremists. Motilal started shedding his 'moderate' image and joined the Extremist camp. The events in Panjab, the Jallianwala Bagh tragedy and the atrocities unleashed by the government under martial law, shook the nation. It gave Motilal an added reason to avoid being called a Moderate. Motilal openly parted company with the Moderates during the Bombay Congress of 1918 over the question of Mont-Ford reforms and sided with the Nationalists in demanding radical changes in the proposed reforms. In February 1919, he started a daily paper, the *Independent*, 'as a counter blast to Madan Mohan Malaviya's *Leader*' whose pro-Hindu policies Motilal did not approve of. However, the *Independent* was short-lived and had to close down in 1923 due to financial difficulties.

After the Jallianwala Bagh tragedy, the government had appointed a committee under the chairmanship of Lord Hunter to look into the tragic episode. The Congress party also appointed an unofficial committee to unearth the facts and record the grievances of the people of Panjab. Motilal was elected as its president with Gandhi and some others as members. Motilal, however, had to resign after he was elected president of the ensuing Congress session at Amritsar in December 1919 and was replaced by M.R. Jayakar. Now Motilal was actively involved in political developments in the country. When Gandhi's non-cooperation resolution came before the special Congress session in September 1920, at Calcutta, Motilal was the only front-rank leader to lend support to the resolution. 'Motilal's fateful decision to cash in his lot with Gandhiji was no doubt influenced by the tragic chain of events in 1919'. Apart from the compulsion of events, there was another vital factor, without which, he may not have made, in his sixtieth year, a clean break with his past and plunged into the unknown. This was the unshakable resolve of his son to go the way of satyagraha, in other words, the way of Gandhi.[2] Motilal was more concerned about Jawaharlal's political career at this stage, than his own. To show his solidarity with Gandhi and his movement, he resigned from the U.P. Council on his return from the Calcutta Congress, gave up his legal practice, curtailed the number of servants in Anand Bhavan, changed his life-style, consigned to flames all the foreign clothes the family had, and started wearing khadi. However, the Nehru family still had enough money to live like the upper strata of society. When Kamla Nehru fell ill, they took her to Europe twice, accompanied by some members of the family including Jawaharlal, and got her treated at the most expensive hospitals and sanitaria in Europe.

Motilal participated in the Non-Cooperation movement, and both father and son were arrested on 6 December 1921, and sentenced to six months' imprisonment. When Motilal came out of prison early in June, the Non-Cooperation movement had already been withdrawn by Gandhi in February 1922. The movement was obviously a failure and even Gandhi had been arrested in March the same year without any serious repercussions in the country. The 'constructive programme' which Gandhi substituted for Non-Cooperation, hardly evoked any response. Gandhi had left the Congress party in doldrums. Motilal, in cooperation with the Bengal leader C.R. Das, joined hands, modified the non-cooperation movement by taking out the boycott of assemblies from the ambit of non-cooperation. They decided to fight elections for the assembly seats under the Mont-Ford provisions and harass the government from within. As the Gandhi faithfuls (called 'no changers') resisted their move, C.R. Das and Motilal formed a new party, the Swaraj Party, after their move for Council entry was defeated at the Gaya Congress (December 1922) by the no-changers. The Swarajists fought the Assembly elections at the end of 1923 and succeeded in winning forty-five of the 145 seats in the Central Legislature, emerging as the largest party. In some states like Central Province, Bengal and U.P., they were in a dominant position. In the Central Legislature, Motilal emerged as the leader of the opposition and remained in that position for six years. His debating ability, knowledge of parliamentary procedure and accommodating attitude towards other political parties in the Assembly made him a formidable opponent of the government, which ruled mostly through the arbitrary use of the viceroy's powers of certification. He thoroughly enjoyed his leadership of the Swaraj Party in the Central Assembly. He came from a legal background and he relished fighting constitutional battles on the floor of the Assembly rather than participating in mass rallies in the streets. He initiated 'walk-outs' in the Councils as a protest against the arbitrary actions of the government, a method which the present day politicians are using in legislatures in free India with a vengeance. In 1925, Gandhi and his supporters (no-changers) had to yield and the Swaraj Party became the legislative wing of the Congress, adding to the stature of Motilal. However, after the 1926 elections, things became difficult for him in the Assembly, with the exit of stalwarts like Madan Mohan Malaviya and Lajpat Rai from the Swaraj Party. In fact, the elections of 1926 for the legislatures, proved the nemesis of Motilal. C.R. Das, the founder of Swaraj Party, was dead by that time. Malaviya and Lajpat Rai, after resigning from the Swaraj Party, had formed a new party, the Indian Nationalist Party, and fought the 1926 elections under its banner. The Swaraj Party was routed in states like U.P. and Panjab. In fact, in U.P., Motilal was the only Swarajist to win. In a letter to Jawaharlal Nehru, who was in Europe at the time where his wife Kamala was being treated, Motilal wrote on 2 December 1926, complaining bitterly against the 'Malaviya-Lala gang', 'Publicly I was denounced as an anti-Hindu and pro-Mohammedan but privately almost every individual voter was told that I was a beef-eater in league with the Mohammedans … I am thoroughly disgusted and am now seriously thinking of retiring from public life'.[3] But he did not retire, more for the sake of Jawaharlal than for himself.

In 1927, Lord Birkenhead, secretary of state for India, had almost thrown a challenge to Indian politicians to produce an agreed constitution for India. It was to meet that challenge, that an All-Party Conference was called in February 1928 and a committee of nine persons was constituted, with Motilal Nehru as chairman, to frame a constitution for India. The report which the committee submitted has come to be known as the 'Nehru Report' and Motilal is remembered more for this report carrying his name than for anything else in the history of the freedom movement. The two main features of this report were Dominion Status for India and a joint-electorate. The report was torpedoed by Muslims, led by Jinnah and Agha Khan, who were averse to the joint-electorates. It was time for Gandhi to enter the political arena once again, after a lapse of several years. He started the Civil Disobedience movement starting with the famous Salt March early in 1930. Motilal, after his initial reluctance, joined the movement; so did Jawaharlal and thousands others. Motilal was not in good health and had actually gone to Europe in August 1927 for treatment and had returned only in February 1928, without much relief. He was suffering from several diseases including acute asthma. He was interned and lodged in Naini prison near Allahabad. Jawaharlal was with him. Father and son were taken to Poona to meet Gandhi, who was in Yeravada jail, to discuss a compromise formula with the government. Nothing came out of the meeting and Motilal and Jawaharlal were sent back to Naini by a special train. As Motilal's condition was deteriorating, he was released on health grounds on 8 September 1930. He was in prison for only ten weeks. His health kept deteriorating and he died on 6 February 1931 in Lucknow, where he had been taken for treatment. His body was brought back to Allahabad where his last rites were performed. At the funeral, Gandhi made a speech, as was his wont, in which he asserted that Motilal's wife Swarup Rani had informed him (Gandhi) that a day before his death, her husband had uttered the name 'Rama' for the first time in his life and had even remembered miraculously the *Gayatri Mantra* which he (Motilal) had never recited in his life. Thus concluded Gandhi, 'Panditji departed a pure man.'[4]

# References

1. Kahairi, Saad R. *Jinnah Reinterpreted*, Karachi, OUP. 1995, p.224.
2. Nanda, B.R. in S.P. Sen, *Dictionary of National Biography* Vol. 3 Calcutta, Institute of Historical Studies, 1974.
3. Nehru, Jawaharlal, ed. *A Bunch of Old Letters*, OUP. 1958, p.52.
4. *Collected Works of Mahatma Gandhi*, Vol.45, p.158.

# Nivedita (Sister)
# Margaret E. Noble

## (1867-1911)

Sister Nivedita was born at Dunganon, a small place in Tyrone county, Ireland. Her original name was Margaret E. Noble. She was the eldest daughter of Samuel Richmond and Mary Isabel. She had a younger sister, May and a brother, Richmond. Her father had studied theology and was working as a priest in Great Torrington, Devonshire county in England. He was a friend of the poor and was loved by his parishioners. Margaret seems to have inherited from him, her religious zeal and her passion to serve people. Unfortnately, Samuel died at the young age of thirty-four. Mary, her mother, returned to Ireland with her three children. Margaret went to school there. After finishing her school, she went to Halifax College, run by the Congregational Church. She studied music, art and natural sciences. She completed her college education in 1884 at the age of seventeen and started teaching in a school at Keswick in England and then in 1886 at Wrexham and in 1889 at Chester. She was influenced by the educational theory of German educationist Friedrich Froebel, founder of the kindergarten system. Mrs De Leeuw invited her in 1890 to open a similar school in Wimbledon, a suburb of London, using the Froebel method of teaching. In 1892, she opened her own school in Wimbledon and named it Ruskin School. Due to her enthusiasm and intellectual gifts, she came to be known in the high society of London which met at the Sesame Club. She was a keen student of literature and religion. Since childhood, Christian doctrines were instilled in her mind as both her father and grandfather were priests. But by this time she had developed a rationalist way of thinking, resulting in her doubting the validity of Christian doctrines and dogmas. She set out in search of 'Truth'. Christianity did not provide her satisfactory answers to allay her doubts. She studied Buddhism for three years and found that those doctrines were 'decidedly more consistent with the Truth than the preachings of Christianity'. But her search for Truth did not end. Then something happened that changed her life; she met Vivekananda in London in a small group in 1895. She discussed with him several aspects of religion and the purpose of life. When Vivekananda returned from America in 1896, she attended many of his lectures and was impressed by what Vivekananda preached. It took her two years to make the final decision to follow him. She came to India, reaching Calcutta on 28 January 1898. Vivekananda was at the dock to receive her. After ascertaining that Margaret was serious in her search for Truth, and that she was willing to stay in India, Vivekananda initiated her into the Ramakrishna Order and gave her the name 'Nivedita', the dedicated one. While still in London, she had promised the swami that she would start a school in India as desired by him, whom she regarded as her guru. The time had come to redeem her promise. She started a kindergarten school for girls in her house at 17 Bosepara Lane, Baghbazar on 17 November 1898. Besides reading and writing, she taught the girls painting, clay work and sewing. Sister Christine, an American lady, helped her in this venture. At a time when singing *Bande Matram* in public was banned, she introduced it in her school's daily prayer. For voluntary teaching work, Nivedita succeeded in enlisting the honorary services of many ladies of position in Calcutta including Labanya Basu, sister of Sir J.C. Bose, and Amiya Devi, daughter of Bipin Chandra Pal. An adult section was also opened, and many widows joined in and began to earn their livelihood after receiving training from the school. The school still exists. Sister Nivedita's birth centenary was celebrated by the school by the publication of *Complete Works of Sister Nivedita* in 1967 in four volumes.

As an ordained member of the Ramakrishna Order, she started taking part in their welfare activities. In 1899, plague threatened once again to take the proportion of an epidemic in Calcutta. The Ramakrishna Mission began its relief work and Sister Nivedita joined the team of workers. 'About Sister Nivedita's part in the work, we have it on the authority of Sir Jadunath Sarkar, an eye-witness, that when the sweepers had fled away, he chanced about a white woman one day cleaning the streets with broom and basket in hand. This was none other than Nivedita, whose courage and sense of civic duty spurred the local youths to take up the cleaning of the lanes and streets following her example, and make their quarters free from the threat of pestilence'.[1]

After running the school for six months, Nivedita realized that she would need money to make it a success. She left for England and America to raise funds for the school. She returned to India in February 1902, and restarted her school in February 1902. 'The 17 Bosepara Lane was her home, her school and a meeting place of many great people of that time'. It was the house where Sister Nivedita lived till the end of her life. In 1963, the management of the school was taken over by Ramakrishna Mission and is now called, "The Ramakrishna Mission Sister Nivedita Girl's School".

Vivekananda died on 4 July 1902, and on 18 July she dissociated herself from the Ramakrishna Order. The reason was that she wanted to work in a much broader sphere than was possible while remaining in the Ramakrishna Mission which prohibited members from taking part in political activities. By now she had developed an interest in the political struggle for independence which was going on, especially in Bengal. She had completely identified herself with India and considered herself a Hindu. Her mission now was to rejuvenate her adopted country. With that purpose in mind, she went on a lecture tour during 1902-1904 to Indian states 'to rouse the national consciousness of the people'. She addressed women most of the time. In one of her lectures on 2 October 1902 at the Hindu Ladies Social Club in Bombay she spoke on 'Why I became a Hindu'. She said, 'I love India as the birthplace of the highest and the best of all religions; as the country that has the grandest mountains, the Himalayas; as the place where the sublimate of mountains are located. The country where the homes are simple; where domestic happiness is found most, where the woman unselfishly, unobtrusively, ungrudgingly serves the dear one from early morn to dewy eve; where the mother and the grandmother study, foresees and contribute to the comfort of their children regardless of their own happiness, and in the unselfishness raises womanhood to its highest status'.[2] She never criticized or questioned even a bad custom in Hinduism 'but rather looked below the surface to find out the original idea of which it had become a parody'. The genuine love and sympathy shown by her for India and the Indians, won the hearts of many, and even great men like Rabindra Nath Tagore, Aurobindo, B.C. Paul, Sir J.C. Bose and many others, became her friends and admirers. Several others: artists, scientists, historians, literary men, politicians and patriots were helped and inspired by her. When the great artist Abanindranath Tagore saw Nivedita for the first time in a white gown and *rudraksha* beads 'she appeared to him to be a *tapasvini* carved in marble, a meditating Uma'.

It did not take much time for her to realize that India would have to win political freedom before making advances in other spheres. She befriended political leaders of all shades of opinion like Gokhale, B.C. Pal, Surendra Nath Banerjee, Aurobindo Ghose, B.G. Tilak and others. In her native land Ireland, the Home Rule movement had gathered some force while she was there and 'she could be inferred to be instinctively predisposed to try those methods in India to oust the British'. She worked in close collaboration with P. Mitra, Aurobindo Ghose, C.R. Das and Surendranath Tagore, as member of the first Executive Committee of the Anusilan Samiti, the revolutionary society of Bengal. 'But whether Nivedita was an active member of the group who indulged in revolutionary activities, besides giving general advice and encouragement, it is difficult to say'.[3] Besides politics, she devoted herself to the cultural regeneration of India. Through her personal contacts as well as through her writings and speeches, she proved to be a source of great inspiration to writers, artists, scientists and historians. She was a friend of Rabindranath Tagore and both had great admiration for each other. Tagore wrote a beautiful character sketch of Nivedita in his book *Parichaya* in which he said, 'She is to be respected not because she was Hindu, but because she was great. She is to be honoured not because she was like us, but because she was greater than us'.[4] In turn, she admired Tagore whom she met for the first time in 1898.

Rabindranath's appearance, bearing, his sonorous voice and his intellectual prowess impressed her. This was before Tagore had won the Nobel prize. She also encouraged and blessed the young Subramania Bharati during his days of struggle. In gratitude, he dedicated his first two books of poems to her.

She had harboured many dreams about India and about her regeneration and glorious future. One such dream was the revival of Indian art. In one of her letters she wrote: 'This birth of national art is my dearest dream'. She felt that Indian artists followed the Western style of painting though they were so gifted. She exhorted them to depict Indian themes in their paintings in Indian style. Great artists like Abanindranath Tagore, and his pupils Nandlal Bose, Asit Haldar and others got inspiration from her. Her other dream was to encourage Indians in the pursuit of science. She saw in Jagdish Chandra Bose, a great scientist, and helped him to publish his important work *Plant Response* and some other works. She believed that J.C. Bose was a unique scientist who had a rare blend of philosophical outlook with scientific precision. She not only proved to be a trouble shooter for Bose, but even tried to understand his scientific researches, which is evident from her letter to Rabindranath Tagore dated 18 April 1903, in which she had explained in simple language, various research works of Bose at Tagore's request. She had become a true friend and a constant companion of Bose and his wife Abala, and shared many joys and sorrows with them. Bose's tribute to her memory is enshrined at the entrance of the Bose Research Institute which reads: 'Entering the Institute, the visitor finds to his left the lotus fountain with a bas-relief of a Woman Carrying Light to the Temple. Without her no light can be kindled in the sanctuary. She is the true light-bearer, and no plaything of man'.

Unfortunately for India and for her, the sultry climate of Calcutta did not suit her. She fell dangerously ill in 1905, and suffered repeatedly from malaria during the next year too, which permanently impaired her health. Again and again, she went to England and America to recuperate. The last three years of her life were mostly spent outside India. She returned to India in 1911 and went to Darjeeling for a change and had an attack of acute blood dysentery and died on 13 October 1911 at the house of Jagdish Chandra Bose, her dear friend. She had made her last will and left all her possessions and writings in the hands of the trustees of the Belur Math, 'to be used for her school to give national education to the women of the country'.

Nivedita was a versatile genius; a forceful writer, a persuasive speaker and a charming conversationalist. Nivedita's prose had the naturalness and freshness of poetry. She threw new light even on a hackneyed topic. She wrote several books during her less than ten years stay in India (excluding her foreign sojourns). Some of her books are: *The Master as I Saw Him* (about Vivekananda); *The Cradle Tales of Hinduism; Myths of the Hindus and Buddhists; The Web of Indian Life; Studies From an Eastern Home; An Indian Study of Love and Death; Footfalls of Indian History; Hints on National Education in India; Religion and Dharma; Lambs Among Wolfs*. She was born a Christian, became a Hindu and left her mark on her adopted country. Rash Behari Ghose said about her after her death, 'On one thing I can speak with confidence and that is this. If we are conscious of a budding national life at the present day, it is in no small measure due to the teachings of Sister Nivedita.' And Bipin Chandra Pal said, 'I doubt whether any Indian loved India the way Nivedita loved her.'

# References

1. Gambhiranand, Swami, *History of Ramakrishna Math and Ramakrishna Mission*, Calcutta, Advaita Ashram, 1983. (3rd ed.) p.105.
2. *Complete Works of Sister Nivedita*, Vol. 2, Calcutta, Sister Nivedita Girl's School. 1967, p.471.
3. Majumdar, R.C. *History of the Freedom Movement in India*. Vol.1, Calcutta, Firma KLM. 1988, p.409.
4. Atmaprana, P. *The Story of Sister Nivedita*, Calcutta, Ramakrishna Sarda Mission Sister Nivedita Girl's School. 1997, pp.62-63.
5. Mukherji, Visvapriya. *Jagdish Chandra Bose*, New Delhi, Publications Division., 1994 (2nd ed.), pp.57-58.

# Bipin Chandra Pal

## (1858-1932)

Bipin Chandra Pal's life is an example of vicissitudes and reversals; from an undisputed national hero he was reduced to a non-entity in later life. His is an inspiring tale; his is a tragic tale. In the *Swadeshi* days of Bengal (1905-1908), he was a fire spitting prophet. Alongwith Lajpat Rai and Bal Gangadhar Tilak, the trio led the nation and came to be known as 'Lal, Bal and Pal'. He gave shape to the political philosophy of India during the first decade of the twentieth century and awakened the nation through his impassioned patriotic writings and fiery speeches. The same militant nationalist, in later life, underwent a complete transformation and started singing praises of the British Empire. The people who worshipped him earlier, began to scoff at him and he died unsung and unhonoured. There have been very few Indian nationalists who have suffered as Bipin Chandra did in later life. His rise was meteoric; so was his downfall.

Bipin Chandra Pal was born in a village in Sylhet district (now in Bangladesh) on 7 November 1858. His family was quite well-off, his father being a zamindar. He was the only son of his parents but had a sister Kripa. Bipin learnt the three Rs from his father and was then sent to an English school in 1866 in Sylhet, followed by two missionary schools. He passed the entrance examination of the Calcutta University in 1874, at the age of sixteen. The following year, he went to Calcutta for higher studies, joining the prestigious Presidency College. He was not a good student and was not interested in studies and failed twice in the First Arts examination. This was the end of his formal education but his self-education continued. He had developed a taste for reading, thus acquiring notable literary competence, and equipping himself for his future tumultuous life.

In spite of his incomplete formal education, he started his career as a headmaster of a high school in Cuttack in 1879 as his grasp of various subjects was extraordinary. But he was a restless being and went on changing jobs, working as headmaster in several schools one after another: Sylhet (1880), Bangalore (1881) and Habiganj (1886). For a year and a half, he acted as librarian and secretary of the Calcutta Public Library (1890-91).

While studying in Calcutta, he had come in contact with Brahmos like Keshab Chandra Sen (whose biography he wrote in 1893). He was much influenced by the philosophy of Brahmo Samaj and joined the organization, antagonizing his orthodox father, and was temporarily alienated from his family. However, before his death in 1886, his father forgave him and reconciled with him. The philosophy and doctrines of Brahmo Samaj had influenced Bipin Chandra's personal life to a great extent. In December 1881, at the age of twenty-three, he married a widow out of his caste, and after the death of his first wife in 1890, he again married a widow out of his caste, which showed the strength of his character, as such marriages were quite rare at the time.

Bipin Chandra started using the power of his pen early in life as a journalist. He wrote articles for several journals published in Bengal and also worked for several of them and founded more than one. His first journalistic venture was a Bengali weekly *Paridarshak* which he published from Sylhet at the age of twenty-two in 1880. It did not survive for long. He worked in the *Tribune*, Lahore during 1887-88. Like in his teaching career, in journalism too, he did not stick to one place or to one journal for long. He started an English weekly, *New India*, in 1901. In 1906, he started his most significant journalistic enterprise *Bande Matram*, an English daily paper, with Aurobindo Ghose as its editor. These were the turbulent anti-partition agitation days and *Bande Matram* played a momentous role in spreading the message of swadeshi, boycott, passive resistance and swaraj in Bengal. 'The *Bande Matram* leaped into popular favour almost in a day, and soon achieved for itself a remarkable position in the field of Indian journalism—No newspaper that we know of, has ever evoked such passionate personal enthusiasm as the *Bande Matram* did during its short tenure of life'.[1]

To spread the message of swadeshi, passive resistance *et al* to wider audiences, Bipin Chandra undertook a tour of Bengal, Assam, U.P. and the most memorable one of Madras, in 1907, and emerged as a national hero. He was one of the most forceful speakers of the time and the government had begun to fear him. The report of the Intelligence Branch reported: 'He (Bipin Chandra Pal) is a good speaker and has the power of carrying his audiences with him, and the after-effects of this man's visits to different centres are nearly always more in evidence, than when other agitators have taken the lead'.[2] 'Oratory had never dreamed of such triumphs in India; the power of the spoken word had never been demonstrated on such a scale,' observed Srinivasa Sastri after listening to one of his speeches in Madras in 1907. Lord Minto, the viceroy acknowledged in his Confidential Minutes dated 3 May 1907, that, 'lecturing as practiced by Bipin Chandra was far more dangerous than any number of newspaper articles'.[3]

The year 1907 brought fresh laurels for Bipin Chandra when he voluntarily courted arrest and imprisonment in connection with the *Bande Matram* sedition case, in which Aurobindo Ghose, the editor of the paper, was being prosecuted. Bipin Chandra was summoned as a witness but he refused to give evidence. He was charged with contempt of court and sentenced to six months imprisonment. When Bipin Chandra was released from jail after six months on 9 March 1908, the day was widely celebrated throughout the country as a day of rejoicing. Meetings, processions, illuminations and fireworks were witnessed at several places. This gave a great impetus to the swadeshi movement and everything else for which Bipin Chandra stood for.

Bipin Chandra visited England thrice; each time with a different purpose. He went to England for the first time in 1898, for theological studies, on a scholarship granted by the British and Foreign Unitarian Association which was working in tandem with the Brahmos in India.

But he gave up the scholarship after a year and used his stay in England to preach Hindu theism and to carry out propaganda for his country. At the invitation of the national Temperance Association of New York, Bipin Chandra visited U.S.A. on a four month lecture tour. In 1900, he returned to India as a fiery nationalist; and for the next eight years, he led, along with Aurobindo Ghose and others, the national movement in Bengal which inspired the whole country, as stated above.

His second visit to England was in 1908. His trip was sponsored by Shyamaji Krishna Varma, a revolutionary working in England, and later in France. This time Bipin Chandra stayed in England for three years, making scores of speeches and writing articles for papers. The tenor of his speeches and writings underwent a sea change. He started condemning the cult of violence and terrorism, and was convinced that it was in the interest of India to be part of the British Empire. He often said that if a choice was to be made between absolute but isolated sovereign independent India; and an equal partnership with Great Britain and her colonies in the present association called British Empire, he would definitely prefer the second alternative. Krishna Varma who had sponsored his trip to England to join the band of revolutionaries, was deeply hurt by the change his thinking and called it a good example of 'Indian apostasy'. While in England, Bipin Chandra started at least three newspapers *India, Indian Sociologist* and *Indian Student* one after the other, but all these faded away for want of funds as all these were extremely moderate in tone. On his return to India in 1911, Bipin Chandra tried to propagate his views about the 'theory of the Empire' idea, and he even started a monthly journal the *Hindu Review* in 1913 for the same purpose, but without much success. Sensing the growing antagonism to him and his Empire Idea, he tried to retrieve the situation by joining the Home Rule League of Tilak and Annie Besant, and also rejoined the Congress which he had left after the arrest of Tilak in 1908.

The third time Bipin Chandra went to England was as a member of the Congress and Home Rule League delegation led by Tilak in 1918. During this visit, his views about the Empire idea notwithstanding, Bipin Chandra was very much concerned about the economic exploitation of India by the British and spoke on the subject while in Britain. He returned to India in 1919 and summed up his ideas in the book *The New Economic Menace to India* (1920).

When Gandhi started the Non-Cooperation movement in 1920, he, like Annie Besant, Madan Mohan Malaviya and others, opposed it and did not join the movement. Bipin Chandra's opposition was essentially due to the fact that the main plank of the movement was the Khilafat cause. He warned the nation that it had nothing to do with the freedom movement and that it would strengthen the cause of pan-Islamism which posed a grave danger for the future of India. He also believed that one reason for his advocating the Empire idea, was to meet the challenge of pan-Islamism. The Empire idea, he believed, could provide an effective remedy for this evil.[4]

In 1921, Bipin Chandra presided over the Bengal Provincial Conference held at Barisal. He spoke against the Non-Cooperation movement of Gandhi who had promised swaraj in one year. The erstwhile idol of the people was hooted out. His words that 'I do not know magic, but I know logic', implying that Gandhi did not have a logical programme, blew him up.[5] After that, he almost retired from public life. The last eleven years of his life were spent in poverty, isolation and misery. The change of tide overwhelmed the man and he died unsung and unhonoured on 20 May 1932. Gandhi did not write an obituary after his death, as was his wont, though he had borrowed much from his adversary, including the concept and philosophy of swadeshi and boycott.

Bipin Chandra was a prolific writer, besides being a compulsive journalist. Some of his books are: *The New Spirit* (1907), *The Spirit of Indian Nationalism* (1910), *The Soul of India* (1911), *The New Economic Menace to India* (1920) and *Memoirs of My Life and Times*, 2 vols. (1932).

## References

1. Banerji, J.L. *Modern Review*, Quoted by R.C. Majumdar in *History of the Freedom Movement in India*, Vol. 2, 1988, pp.184-85.
2. Vide file No. 634 of 1909 of the Eastern Bengal and Assam quoted by Haridas and Uma Mukherjee. *Bipin Chandra Pal*, Calcutta, Firma K.L. Mukhopadhya, 1958, p.71.

3. Ahluwalia, M.M. *Freedom Struggle in India*, 1858-1909, Delhi, Ranjit Printers and publishers, 1965, p.339.

4. Mukherjee, Amitabha in *Dictionary of National Biography* ed. by S.P. Sen, Calcutta, Institute of Historical Studies. Vol. 3, 1974, p.286.

5. Roy Chaudhury, P.C. *Gandhi and his Contemporaries*, New Delhi, Sterling, 1986, p.37.

# Vishnu Digambar Paluskar

## (1872-1931)

Vishnu Digambar was born on 18 August 1872 in the village Palus located in Kurundwad, a small state in present-day Maharashtra, to Digambar Gopal and Ganga Devi. His father was a well reputed *kirtan* singer (singer of religious songs at gatherings). The surname Paluskar is derived from the village Palus, where the family lived. His formal education was brief. He studied English upto sixth class. But he used to accompany his father and brother to *kirtan* gatherings and was thus introduced to musical rhythm early in life, which is essential for a good *kirtanist.* An unfortunate incident occurred when Vishnu was in his early teens. During Diwali festivities a cracker hit his face and his eyesight was severely affected. His parents took him to Miraj, a nearby town, for treatment. Dr Kishore Bhirbhire, who was the chief medical officer at Miraj, tried to restore his eyesight but without much success. But when the doctor heard the boy singing *bhajans* (religious songs) he was so impressed by the exquisite rendering of *bhajans* by the young boy, that he told his father that the boy had great talent and that if properly trained he would become a great musician some day. This incident was significant in deciding the career of young Vishnu Digambar, and from then on, there was no looking back. With the help of Dr Bhirbhire, Vishnu became a pupil of the court musician of Miraj, Bal Krishna Buwa Achaljikar. For nine years, from 1887 to 1896, Vishnu received training in music from Achaljikar who was a reputed musician of that time, and an exponent of the Gwalior *gharana*.

The *guru-shishya* (teacher-pupil) Indian tradition of education prevalant in India, requires the student to live with the teacher as a family member. It is a tradition which is centuries old but has some drawbacks. For one thing, it has no regular hours and the student has to perform many chores for the teacher's household. It also depends on the mood of the teacher to teach. Moreover, the teacher may not be versatile and may have some serious limitations, as music teachers were exponents of a particular *gharana* (style). Vishnu experienced all that during his stay with his guru. Then he started thinking of a better method of imparting music education. But several years passed before he could give practical shape to his thoughts. Vishnu was also concerned about the poor financial condition of the musicians, which resulted in their poor social standing. Except for the few lucky ones, who became court musicians, the others lived in rather deplorable conditions. Vishnu felt that musicians deserved better as they fulfilled a great cultural need of society. He left Miraj in search of an ideal place to settle and to give concrete shape to his ideas. This was in 1896, when he was only twenty-four years old. To support himself, he used to give musical performances, capping them with *bhajans* (devotional songs) as he was essentially a vocalist. These wanderings took him to many places, starting with Aundh. From Aundh, he went to Baroda, where he performed at the royal court and was suitably rewarded for his outstanding performance, which was appreciated more than those of the court musicians. From Baroda, Vishnu travelled to Saurashtra and then on to Gwalior, the seat of his guru's *gharana* and stayed there for about four months giving musical performances for music lovers of all classes and status. Maharaja Madho Rao invited him to his palace and was extremely pleased with the musical renderings of ragas and *bhajans* and bestowed on him several gifts. From Gwalior, Vishnu moved on to Mathura. There he studied Braj sangeet, learnt Hindi and Sanskrit and acquired the intricacies of the *dhrupad* style of music which was very popular in Mathura. There he stayed for nine months, a very fruitful stay. From Mathura he moved on to Delhi and gave performances and met the most talented of musicians there. While in Delhi, he was surprised to receive an invitation to perform at the famous

Hariballabh musical assembly at Jallandhar in Panjab, which is held in the memory of Sri Hariballabh Swami, a great saint and musician. It was a great honour for any musician to get invited to this function where musicians were respected and paid well. For several years, even musicians from Pakistan used to participate in this musical meet. The rendition of Vishnu was greatly appreciated and applauded there, and his fame as a great musician spread throughout Panjab. After visiting a few other places in Panjab, Vishnu Digambar reached Lahore, the capital of Panjab and a great seat of learning. Vishnu decided to put his ideas into practice there, encouraged by the response from the people. By this time, he was convinced that the *guru-shishya* traditional method of learning music was time consuming and did not always yield good results. He thought of starting a music school similar to the schools where subjects like science and literature are taught. As a result, the foundation of the first music school in the country was laid on 5 May 1901 by P.G. Chatterjee, the senior judge of the Panjab high court, and was named Gandharva Mahavidyalaya, (college). Thus, music was brought within easy reach of the common man who aspired to be a musician. The Mahavidyalaya started in a rented building with fifteen students. The students paid a nominal fee like in any other college. As the fees were not sufficient to run the institution, Vishnu used to give music performances to earn money. Another source of income was donations from music lovers. The Maharaja of Jammu and Kashmir bestowed a grant of Rs. 150 per month.

To learn the elements of music, the students needed books. Vishnu wrote many books like *Sangeet Bal Prakash* in two parts; eighteen books on each of the eighteen ragas containing full *gyaki* (melody) of each in *Rag Pravesh*. He wrote some other books on music also. For some years he also brought out a music monthly called *Sangeetmrit Pravah*. To publish his books and journal, he also established a press on the college premises. One of his most important contributions was the creation of notation for Indian music system, similar to the one used in Western music. The notation is called Vishnu Digambar Lipi (notation). He tried to find out the symbols for the notation which could serve for Indian music. The Indian notation system is classified in three octaves i.e. lower, medium and upper. He has used different symbols for notations of different octaves. He has also used symbols for representing the rhythm of tunes.[1] A similar notation was invented by one of his equally great contemporaries, Vishnu Narayan Bhatkhande, the founder of Bhatkhande schools of music, and is known as Bhatkhande Swar Lipi (notation).

In a short time the Gandharva Mahavidyalaya had earned great name as a respected centre of Indian music. When Prince of Wales (later King George V) visited Lahore in 1906, Pandit Vishnu Digambar was asked to give a performance of Indian vocal music (bhajan) for fifteen minutes. It was greatly appreciated and Vishnu Digamber got an invitation for the evening dinner along with the elite of Lahore. Later, Gopal Krishna Gokhale visited the Mahavidyalaya and spent sometime with its founder and was pleasantly surprised with the activities of the college. By then the college had prepared its own syllabus for a four-year course and an advanced nine-year course. Graded textbooks were published for each year and regular examinations were held for vocal as well as instrumental music. The four-year degree course was called *Sangeet Praveshika* and the nine-year course entitled the student to get *Sangeet Praveen*, the highest degree in music from Gandharva Mahavidyalaya. Vishnu Digambar thus prepared qualified teachers to teach in Gandharva Mahavidyalayas, the branches of which were started in various parts of the country. The greatest success came when a branch was opened in Bombay in 1908. The response was so good that Vishnu Digambar moved from Lahore to Bombay. Here, the number of students went on increasing and the number soon reached five hundred. About twenty-five teachers had to be appointed, who were mostly Vishnu Digambar's students. An important contribution of Gandharva Vidyalayas was that female students could also join the mahavidyalaya and become musicians, which was not possible in the *gharana* system. Vishnu Digambar trained his wife and two cousins to teach female students. As there was no provision for repairing musical instruments, a musical instruments repair shop was established under the name Musical Instrument Supply Company.

The mahavidyalayas in the country became so popular that the number of students getting degrees was large enough to necessitate holding of a convocation for the successful students. The first convocation was held in 1911. Lord Syndenham, governor of Bombay, awarded degrees to successful students. After that, convocations were held every four years.

For years, the mahavidyalaya had been running in rented premises. Vishnu Digambar decided to get a building constructed. Finances were arranged through fees, musical programmes, donations and loan from the government. The building was completed in 1915 and was inaugurated by the then governor of Bombay, Lord Wellington. A building for the hostel was added later on. National leaders like Gandhi, Tilak, C.R. Das and Madan Mohan Malaviya visited the mahavidyalaya and appreciated the contribution of its founder to Indian classical music. Unfortunately, the loans could not be paid back on time to the government and the two buildings had to be auctioned, causing great distress to Vishnu Digambar. The mahavidyalaya again had to move to a rented building.

Pandit Vishnu Digambar was a nationalist too and used to attend the All India Congress sessions, starting with the 1916 session at Lucknow. He was always requested to sing *Bande Matram* at the end of the session. The whole gathering used to standup and join Vishnu Digambar. At the Cocanada session of the Congress in 1923, President Mohammad Ali, raised objection to the singing of *Bande Matram*. Ignoring his ruling, Vishnu Digambar went up on the stage and started singing *Bande Matram*, getting a thunderous applause from the delegates. He also composed tunes for songs like *Sare Jahan Se Accha, Pagree Sambhal Jatta* and other nationalist songs which became very popular.

One of his greatest gifts to the music world was the crop of talented pupils he cultivated in his mahavidyalaya. These included B.A. Kalashkar, Omkar Nath Thakur, B.R. Devdhar, B.N. Patwardhan and others. In 1916, Mahatma Gandhi sent a messenger to Vishnu Digambar to recommend a music teacher for his ashram school. He sent his pupil, Pandit Narayan Khare, who served the ashram till his death in 1938.[2] His services to the ashram were very much appreciated by Mahatma Gandhi.

Vishnu Digambar had a paralytic attack in 1930. He did not recover fully and died on 21 August 1931, leaving the music world much poorer.

## References

1.  Veer, Ram Avtar. *The Torch Bearer of Indian Music; Maharshi Vishnu Digambar Paluskar.* New Delhi, Pankaj Publications, 1978, p.23-24.
2.  *Collected Works of Mahatma Gandhi* Vol. 49, pp.23-24.

# Govind Ballabh Pant

## (1887-1961)

Govind Ballabh Pant was born to Manorath Pant and Govindi on 30 August 1887 in village Khunt near Almora in the Kumaon hills. The Pants are believed to have come from the Konkan region of Maharashtra. Manorath Pant was a government official who was frequently transferred. Therefore Govind was sent to stay with his maternal grandfather, Badri Dutt Joshi, at Almora. Badri Dutt was an important person in Almora, being *sadar amin* or judicial officer of Kumaon. Govind did not feel the absence of his parents as his grandfather had a big three storied house, where about fifty relatives lived as a joint family — uncles, aunts, cousins. The children were tutored at home and were sent to school much later. Govind learnt the three Rs at home. He was sent to the primary section of the Ramsay Intermediate College in 1897, at the age of ten. He passed the lower middle (sixth class), getting a first class. In 1899, when Govind was in the seventh class and only twelve years old, he was married to Ganga Devi. The same year, his grandfather died leaving Govind without a mentor and a model. However, Govind continued his studies. He liked Sanskrit, mathematics and English and took part in debates while at college. He passed the matriculation examination in 1903, getting a first division. Though a brilliant student, he was always late for school because in the large family food could not be served in time for school and he became notorious as a latecomer. This habit of unpunctuality stayed with him throughout his life but surprisingly he was nonchalant about it. During his school, and later college days, he never took part in sports and always sat outside the field watching other boys play, which earned him the nickname 'Thapwa'.

In December 1904, while he was studying in the Intermediate class, he suffered from chest pain and difficulty in breathing. It was diagnosed as heart trouble and was treated by an ayurvedic doctor of Moradabad. After that, he was never fully fit. However, he passed the examination with good marks, getting a scholarship of rupees twenty per month. He joined the Allahabad University for higher studies in 1905 and was admitted to Muir Central College. After graduation, he joined law in 1907. Two years later, he was at the top of the first batch of law graduates, getting the Lumsden Gold Medal, which Motilal Nehru also had received earlier. "He had gone from Almora as a youth of uncertain aims and left Allahabad as complete a man as possible".

Govind Ballabh Pant started his legal practice in Almora in 1910. He was an immediate success. But one day a British magistrate insulted him and Pant decided to leave Almora. He practiced for sometime in Ranikhet and then moved on to Kashipur (1912). There he became a successful lawyer. He used to study his cases carefully and never took if he was convinced that his client was in the wrong. But he was sympathetic to the poor (there being no dearth of them in Kashipur and adjoining areas) and took up their cases without charging any fee. In summer, the courts moved to Nainital, so Pant was practicing there half the time. His practice flourished. But soon he was faced with a series of personal tragedies. His first wife, Ganga Devi, had died in 1899. In 1912, Pant had remarried but his second wife also died in 1914 while giving birth, a son, who died too. His father, Manorath Pant, died the same year. It followed with the death of his sister's husband. One severe blow after another shattered Pant but he managed to survive the tragic phase of his life. At the insistence of his relatives, especially that of his mother, Pant married a third time in 1917, when he was thirty, to Kaladevi. A son, K.C. Pant and two daughters were born from this marriage.

Govind Ballabh Pant had grown to be a giant of a man. He was over six feet tall, and heavy-set. He kept his moustache untrimmed and was quite careless about his appearance  a buttoned up khadi coat, Gandhi cap, *kurta* (long shirt) and a loose white pyjama. In winters, he would add a waistcoat. He was also careless about food and consequently suffered from indigestion throughout his life.

While still at Kashipur, he started taking interest in civic and public affairs. In 1914, through his efforts, the Prem Sabha was established, "to spread literature and introduce social reforms in Kashipur". It was first a branch of the Kashi Nagri Pracharni Sabha. Its members did social service in Kashipur and nearby areas. In 1914, through Pant's efforts the Udairaj Hindu Sabha School was established, which was the first high school in Kashipur. Pant served as its secretary for several years. He was nominated to the Notified Area Committee in 1916. Pant was responsible for introducing free and compulsory education for the first time in Kumaon. The founding and establishment of the Kumaon Parishad the same year, was one of the notable achievements of Pant. He was able to get the exploitative custom of *coolie begar* (unpaid labour) abolished and forced the British officials to pay to the labourers who carried their luggage during their tours, earning the gratitude of thousands of poor labourers. Next, he fought to have Kumaon included in the purview of the Montague-Chelmsford reforms of 1919 and the area gained the right to send representatives to the provincial assembly.

The Kumaon region was getting politically conscious and newspapers like *Almora Akhbar* were making efforts in that direction. Sensing danger, the government forcibly shut down this nationalist paper. Pant took the initiative to fill the gap and started the *Shakti* weekly in 1918, which has survived to this day. By this time, he had joined the Congress party and had attended the Lucknow session of the Congress in 1916 as a member from Kumaon. There he had his first meeting with Gandhi and Sarojini Naidu. The first elections to provincial assemblies under Mont-ford reforms were held in 1920. As the Congress had boycotted the elections under the Non-Cooperation movement, Pant stood as an independent candidate from Nainital, but lost. When the Swaraj party was formed in December 1922 by C.R. Das and Motilal Nehru to enter the legislatures, Pant joined it. He fought as a candidate from Nainital and won. He entered the U.P. Legislative Council as the member from Kumaon. A great parliamentary career had begun. The Swaraj party had thirty members in the council and Pant proved a strong spokesman of the party and spoke forcefully for social, economic and political reforms, especially on the forest problem which affected the Kumaon region. In 1926, Pant was re-elected to the U.P. legislative Council.

In 1928, Pant led a demonstration against the Simon Commission along with Jawaharlal Nehru in Lucknow. The procession was lathi-charged and both Nehru and Pant were beaten. Nehru writes about the incident in his *Autobiography:* "Govind Ballabh Pant, who stood by me, offered a much bigger target, being six foot odd in height, and the injuries he received then have resulted in a painful and persistent malady, which prevented him for a long time from straightening his back or leading an active life".

Pant had met Gandhi during the Lucknow session of the Congress in 1916 but got close to him when Gandhi visited Kumaon in 1929. Pant was his host at Nainital. When Gandhi started the salt satyagraha in 1930, Pant took part in it and led the movement in U.P. On 20 May, Pant was arrested and sent to the Dehra Dun jail. By now he was fully engrossed in political activity and had abandoned his legal practice. The government banned the provincial Congress session in U.P. under the leadership of Pant. He was arrested again in Haldwani on 18 February 1932 and was released in August.

In 1934, the Congress decided to contest the elections and Pant won a seat for the Central Assembly on Congress ticket but resigned later when he was elected to the U.P. Legislative Council under the Government of India Act of 1935. In 1937, when the Congress formed a ministry in U.P., Pant became the premier of the province, taking his oath on 17 July 1937. Pant took Home, Finance, General Administration and Forests, "a burden big enough for the broadest of shoulders". The province was faced with several problems. Communal strife was taking a serious turn, fanned by the disgruntled Muslim League. Other problems faced by the province were educational reforms, labour welfare and the condition of the peasantry. Pant, and his able team of ministers, tried to tackle these problems with tact and firmness. When the government refused to release the political prisoners in 1938 as promised, Pant tendered his resignation.

The governor had to relent and even started appreciating the working of Pant's ministry. The retiring governor, Sir Harry Haig, wrote to Viceroy Linlithgow about Pant on 10 January 1938. "He is essentially a conciliator and not a dictator, or even a strong democratic leader. With all his defects, he is the only possible right wing leader in this province and in fact stands out head and shoulders above the others'.[1] About the accusations of the Muslim League leaders regarding ill-treatment of Muslims under the Congress rule, the governor wrote: "In dealing with communal issues the ministers, in my judgement, normally acted with impartiality and a desire to do what was fair". U.P. Tenancy Act of 1939 was the most important piece of legislation of his ministry, paving the way for abolition of zamindari later on.

For a time, Congress party affairs assumed great significance when against the wishes of Gandhi, Subhas Chandra Bose defeated his candidate Dr Pattabhi Sitaramayya for the presidentship by over two hundred votes. It was one of the most serious crises in the long history of the Congress. Govind Ballabh Pant had to perform an unpleasant task of moving a resolution at the AICC Session on 12 March 1939. The last and significant lines of the resolution read. "In view of the fact that Mahatma Gandhi alone can lead the Congress and the country to victory during such crisis, the Congress regards it as imperative that the Congress Executive should command his implicit confidence and requests the President to nominate Working Committee in accordance with the wishes of Gandhiji'. The entire Congress Working Committee, except Sarat Bose, resigned, resulting in the resignation of the president, Subhas Bose. The passing of Pant's resolution 'made Gandhi a dictator *de jure*, and though he had long been one *de facto*, still the Resolution made a very serious difference. Henceforth, the Congress had not even any pretence of functioning as a democratic body'.[2] Admirers of Pant have wondered why he had to do something so undemocratic against one of the most charismatic Congress leaders who had won through a democratic process.

The Congress ministries resigned in October-November 1939 when the Second World War broke out in 1939 and the British dragged India into the war. Pant and his ministers also resigned. Pant took part in an individual satyagraha in 1940 and was imprisoned in Almora jail. He was again arrested during the Quit India movement in 1942, along with other senior leaders of the Congress and was kept in Ahmednagar Fort along with Nehru, Azad, Kriplani and others. Gandhi was kept in the Aga Khan Palace, Poona. After Independence, Pant again took oath as chief minister, Uttar Pradesh in 1947. During his second tenure as chief minister, 1947-54, Uttar Pradesh (the name was changed from United Provinces to Uttar Pradesh) made tremendous progress on all fronts. Zamindari was abolished in 1952, giving much relief to the peasants. He also introduced other measures to help the farmers. The irrigation system was improved by digging many new canals, and improved methods of farming were introduced. The industrial sector was not neglected either. Both heavy and cottage industries were established. Education, public health, Harijan upliftment and panchayats got a major boost. For nine long years, he guided the destiny of the largest state in the Union.

In 1954, Jawaharlal Nehru asked Pant to come to the Centre. People were stunned. Pant had become a sort of Peshwa of U.P. and it was difficult to think of U.P. without Pant. After he left, the situation in U.P. worsened; groupism and castism took over. The province and the people suffered. At the Centre, Pant was first sworn in as minister without portfolio. He took over as Home minister on 15 February 1955 and established a grip on the ministry as if a second Patel was again at work. In August 1956, he took over Heavy Industries in addition to Home. He had to handle certain difficult tasks such as state reorganisation, which had become a very sensitive and volatile issue. But Pant handled the difficult situation with great dexterity and tact. 'If Patel was an Indian Bismarck who brought about states' integration, Pant was the second Indian Bismarck who brought about states' reorganisation as Union Home Minister'.[3] Another sensitive, even dangerous issue, which Pant solved amicably was the language controversy. Concluding his speech in the Parliament while discussing the Report of the Committee of Parliament on Official Language on 2 September 1959, Pant, putting forward a compromise formula acceptable to both factions, resolved the controversy. He had made the non-Hindi speaking people accept the constitutional settlement. English would remain as the associate language as long as the non-Hindi speaking people wanted it, but Hindi was free to become the official language of the Union in all respects. It was one of Pant's main achievements of statesmanship. This remains the situation today as far as the language issue is concerned.

In 1957, the Bharat Ratna was conferred on him. In 1960, he suffered a heart attack. His health had never been good. He fell seriously ill in February 1961 and was in coma for several days. He died on 7 March 1961, and was cremated at Nigambodhghat in Delhi with full state honours. Nehru, who was attending the Commonwealth Ministers' Conference in London at the time, sent a condolence message which summed-up the man: 'We are left desolate and forlorn. Dear friend and comrade, great captain of our people during the days of our struggle for freedom, great in leadership after freedom came, wisest of counsellers, gentle and yet firm of purpose, with malice to none, child of our beloved Himalayan mountains carrying with him something of their calm and imperturbability, rock of stability and lighthouse to guide people's minds and paths, how shall we replace him or find his like again'. 'Pant indeed was a considerable figure in India's parliamentary life. In some ways he was the most considerable'.

Pant's assembly debates, letters and other communications were published as *Selected Works of Govind Ballabh Pant*, edited by B.R. Nanda.

# References

1.  Rau, M. Chalapathi. *Govind Ballabh Pant; His Life and Times*, Allied, 1981, p.184.
2.  Majumdar, R.C. ed. *Struggle for Freedom Bombay*, Bharatiya Vidya Bhavan, second ed. 1988, p.570.
3.  Rau op. cit. p.385.

# Bhai Parmanand

## (1874-1947)

Bhai Parmanand came from a family whose ancestor, Bhai Mati Das was sawed alive and martyred by the orders of Emperor Aurangzeb, along with his guru, Teg Bahadur, in 1675 in Chandni Chowk, where the gurdwara Sis Ganj stands today.

Parmanand was born in 1874 at Karyala, a village near Chakwal, district Jhelum (now in Pakistan). His father, Bhai Tara Chand, was serving in the British Indian army. Parmanand had his early education in a local school at Chakwal. While still a student, he was very impressed by the tenets of Arya Samaj. He even helped in the establishment of a branch of Arya Samaj at Chakwal while still in his teens. After passing the middle examination, he joined D.A.V. school at Lahore, from where he passed the entrance examination. Soon after, the Arya Samaj was split into D.A.V. wing and Gurukul wing. For two years, Parmanand worked for the cause of the D.A.V. movement at the bidding of Lala Hansraj, the principal. After passing F.A. (the First Arts examination), he went to Jodhpur and founded the Rajput School. After a year, he came back to Lahore and passed the B.A. examination. That was the year when Parmanand was married to Bhagi Sudhi. The following two years were spent as headmaster of the Anglo-Sanskrit School at Abbotabad. Thereafter, he left Abbotabad and went to Calcutta to study for an M.A. degree but came back to Lahore after one year and passed the M.A. examination from the Punjab University in 1902. The same year, he joined the Dayanand College as a professor. Along with teaching in the college, he used to lecture about Arya Samaj in different towns of Punjab during vacations, and had become a forceful speaker. After three years of teaching at the Dayanand College, a letter addressed to the Arya Samaj, Lahore, came from the Indian settlers in South Africa requesting the services of a preacher. The principal of the college suggested the name of Bhai Parmanand, who agreed. Parmanand left for South Africa in 1905. On the way, he gave lectures on Arya Samaj and Vedic religion at Bombay, Mambassa and Nairobi in East Africa.

Reaching South Africa, he toured Natal, Transvaal and Cape Colony, giving lectures. He was warmly received wherever he went and his lectures were even attended by a large number of Whites. The Indian residents collected about Rs. 8000 and sent it as donation to Dayanand College, Lahore. At Durban, Parmanand met Mahatma Gandhi. About Gandhi, Parmanand writes in his *The Story of My Life*: 'He (Gandhi) took the chair in one of these lectures. Subsequently, I stayed nearly a month at his house at Johannesburg (in Transvaal). His simple life and asceticism left a deep impression on me even then. He also wrote letters to England (where Parmanand planned to visit) on my behalf to his friend Shyamji Krishna Varma and two English friends'.[1] From South Africa he reached England after a three-week journey, where he stayed at the India House, established by Shyamji Krishna Verma, in London. He also visited Oxford and Cambridge. He came back to London and devoted much time in researching the history of India at the British Museum. He submitted a thesis for the M.A. degree at London University titled, *The Rise of British Power in India*, which was, however, rejected by the two Anglo-Indian experts. All his expenses in England were borne by the Dayanand College, Lahore. While he was still in England, Lajpat Rai and Ajit Singh were deported to Burma for organizing the agrarian movement in Punjab. Parmanand was close to Lajpat Rai and was very pained to hear the news of Lajpat Rai's deportation. Meetings were held in London against the high-handedness of the government in which Parmanand also took part and spoke. Lala Har Dayal (who later organized the Ghadar Party in USA) was then studying at Oxford and was a friend of Parmanand from his

Lahore days. They came close to each other and exchanged views on various problems that India was facing. This made Parmanand a suspect in the eyes of the Indian government officials later on.

In 1908, Parmanand returned to India and resumed the work of Arya Samaj. During the summer vacation, he went to Burma to spread the word of Arya Samaj and to collect funds for the college. Even after his release from Mandalay prison, Ajit Singh was under surveillance. To avoid arrest once again he left India for good. As luck would have it, Parmanand rented the same house where Ajit Singh was staying in Lahore. As a result, Parmanand became a suspect and his movements were watched day and night. During the vacation of 1909, Parmanand went on a lecture tour in the Madras Presidency and founded an Arya Samaj at Madras. The lecture tour lasted for five months. On his return, his house was searched; many letters and some written material was found, one of which contained hints on bomb making, about which Parmanand had no knowledge. How this found its way into his papers, he did not know. He was produced before a magistrate. The trial lasted for a few months. He was released on bail and had to give an undertaking of good behaviour for three years. It is unfortunate that the Arya Samaj did not show any interest in his case. On the other hand, he was dismissed from the college service. He once again left the country in 1910. He visited British Guiana, Trinidad and Martinique (a French colony), where he met Lala Har Dayal and spent some time with him. He lectured to the local audience consisting of Indians settled there, and was respected as a pandit. As most of the schools there were run by Christian missionaries, he opened a Hindu school for the Indians. From there he came to the United States, where he studied at the University of California and got a degree in 1913, and left for England. Meanwhile, Lala Har Dayal had founded the Ghadar Party, whose object was to overthrow the British Raj through revolution and who had brought out a journal, *Gadar*, for spreading the objectives of the party.

Though Parmanand never took any interest in the activities of Har Dayal and the Ghadar Party, his friendship with Har Dayal was known to the British Consul in New York and this information was passed on to the secret police in India. During his brief stay in England, he was put to much annoyance by the secret police. He returned to India in December 1913 as a suspect revolutionary, constantly being followed by C.I.D. (Criminal Investigation Department) men. As he had been discharged from the college, he opened a pharmacy on Mohan Lal Road. But this was the time when members of the Ghadar Party started coming to Punjab from America and Canada. They regularly visited Parmanand and he could not shun them, such was his character. Thus, suspicion about his participation in the revolutionary activities further deepened. He was arrested along with twenty-four other 'conspirators' in 1915. The trial was conducted under the Defence of India Act. It was alleged that a huge and terrible conspiracy was being hatched by Parmanand in the absence of the leader Har Dayal. His book *History of India* was also a charge against him. The trial lasted for several months. The verdict was death sentence, which was later commuted to life imprisonment. Bhai Parmanand was sent to the Andaman Cellular Jail, where he spent five years, along with hundreds of other political prisoners as well as some hard core criminals and he suffered terribly. His wife residing in Lahore, was an even greater sufferer. The property of the family had been confiscated. Each item from the house was auctioned. She lived in a small dark room, earning rupees seventeen from teaching in a private school. Their two daughters died of malnutrition and fever while Parmanand was in the Andaman jail. She met Madan Mohan Malaviya, Gandhi and C.F. Andrews. They all showed sympathy for her but it was Andrews who was moved greatly by her misery fought for her husband's release and wrote several articles in the *Tribune* about her case and about the innocence of her husband. Gandhi also wrote in *Young India* about Bhai Parmanand's imprisonment: "Bhai Parmanand belongs to the band of Indians daily growing in numbers who have set apart their lives for India's service and have accepted comparative poverty as their lot. During his visit to South Africa he was for nearly a month my honoured guest and left on my mind a deep impression as a man full of truth and nobility. The Government have grievously erred in treating an honourable man as a common felon".[2]

All these efforts bore fruit and Parmanand was released in 1920. He has given graphic details about the life of prisoners in the Andaman jail in his autobiography, *The Story of My Life*. There was great jubilation in the country, especially in Punjab, on his release. He became active again and attended the Calcutta session of the Congress along with Lala Lajpat Rai, in which the resolution recommending non-cooperation with the government, was passed. Though he did not approve of the Congress espousing the cause of the Khalifa of Turkey, he was all for national education which was very near to his heart. When the Congress party established Central National College or University (Vidya Pith) at Lahore he was put in charge of the National College and Vidya Pith. An industrial school and a National Medical College were also established and Bhai Parmanand was put in charge of these also. However, these two institutions were soon closed. The Vidya Pith functioned from 1921 to 1926. It had to be closed because hardly any student sought admission to it after that. Sometime earlier, Lala Lajpat Rai had founded the Tilak School of Politics. When Lajpat Rai went to jail in 1921, he made Bhai Parmanand the director of the Tilak School.

The purely political part of the Non-Cooperation movement did not interest Parmanand and he did not believe that swaraj could be won in a year, as claimed by Gandhi. When, after the suspension of the Non-Cooperation movement, communal riots took place in several parts of the country, starting with the Mopla riots in Kerala, Bhai Parmanand was greatly upset. In almost all these riots, Hindus were the sufferers, though they were in a majority. When serious riots took place in Saharanpur (U.P.), Lajpat Rai sent Bhai Parmanand to study the situation first hand. Parmanand wrote: "The misery and suffering of the Hindus there pained me deeply. And when I learnt that the office-bearers of the local Khilafat Committee were responsible for the riots and the destruction of the lives and property of the Hindus, I was forced to the conclusion that the Khilafat agitation was at the bottom of all Hindu-Muslim riots".[3] For the rest of his life he worked for Hindu Sanghatan (unity). He joined the Hindu Mahasabha and was elected its president for the 1933 session at Ajmer. To put forward the Hindu point of view in the Central Legislative Assembly, he fought the election on the National Party ticket and was elected in 1931 and again in 1934. He vehemently opposed the Nehru Report (1928), "and my strongest reason for this was that I felt sure that no amount of yielding on the part of the Hindus to the Muslim demands

could ever win them over to making common cause with the Hindus".
For the same reason he opposed the Communal Award (1932). In the
Central Legislative Assembly, he gave a powerful speech against the
Communal Award, which had specially harmed the interests of Bengal
and Punjab Hindus but the Congress leadership took a neutral stand.
Parmanand said, "The Communal Award is a great constitutional wrong,
and a serious political blunder". But the harm had been done and Muslims
had their way, supported as they were, by the government as well as by
the Congress. In 1933, he went to England to give evidence before the
Joint Select Committee on behalf of the Punjab Hindus. But his first and
last love was Arya Samaj and the propagation of its message. He wrote:
"To my mind the Arya Samaj had but one mission for the Universality
of mankind, to establish Truth in the place of untruth. But preparatory
to and side by side with this, it should resuscitate through spiritual power
the nation which had to this day kept alive the religion of the Vedas. The
question of the political unity of Hindus and Muslims would also find
solution only when the Hindus grew strong. Nobody cared to cultivate
friendship with the dead, nor is unity worth the price of self-government.
The Arya Samaj alone can vivify the Hindu nation".[4] Like Vivekananda
and Aurobindo before him, he was a votary of Hindu nationalism.

As a social reformer, he was again influenced by the Arya Samaj. He
strongly opposed the caste system among Hindus and founded an
organization, 'Jat Pat Todak Mandal', for breaking caste distinctions among
the Hindus, and was its first president. He preached against child marriage
and advocated widow remarriage. Like many Arya Samajists, he worked
for female education.

Bhai Parmanand was a prolific writer and wrote more than twenty
books, mostly in Hindi and Urdu. Some of these are: *Swarajya Sangram,*
*Bharat Nari Rattan, History of Europe* (Hindi and Urdu), *History of Maharashtra,*
*Kaum Ka Naya Janam, Bharat Varsh Ka Itihas* (which was banned), *Arya*
*Samaj and Congress, Hindustan Ki Rajniti* and of course, his autobiography
*The Story of My Life* (Urdu, Hindi and English).

The journalistic ventures of Bhai Parmanand included *Hindu Weekly*
(1927), *Akash Vani* (Hindi Weekly) and *Hindu* (Urdu). But the last two
weeklies had a very short life-span. Parmanand also wrote articles for
several newspapers.

Parmanand led a simple life and wore *khadi* all his adult life, made from the yarn spun by his wife. He had a robust constitution and suffered the tortures in the Andaman jail stoically. His noble physical presence reminded one of the Roman warriors of yore. The couple had four children, three daughters and a son. Their two daughters, had died very young due to malnutrition. Another daughter Sushila was born to them on Parmanand's return from the Andaman. As they did not have a son, they adopted a boy Dharm Vir as their son. But soon after Bhagi Sudhi, his wife, gave birth to a son who grew up as Bhai Mahavir. He served as governor of Madhya Pradesh for some time. Dharm Vir, however, continued to be a member of the family. Bhagi Sudhi died in 1932 of tuberculosis. Parmanand's last letter to his wife is one of the most moving and touching letters ever written by a husband to his dying wife. Gandhi wrote a condolence letter to Bhai Parmanand from Yervada Jail on the death of Parmanand's wife, which became a treasured possession for Parmanand. He bore the demise of his wife with great equanimity and continued to serve the cause of the Hindus and Arya Samaj while fighting the evils of Hindu society like caste distinctions, till the very end.

During the holocaust of the Partition, he left his beloved Lahore burning and in ruins, including the headquarters of Arya Samaj, for the building of which he had not played an insignificant role. He died on 18 December 1947 at Jalandhar, East Panjab.

## References

1. Parmanand, Bhai. *The Story of My Life*. New Delhi, Ocean Books. 2002, p.47. (Earlier published 1935 at Lahore).
2. Young India 19.11.1919. (*Collected Works of Mahatma Gandhi*. Vol. 16, p.303).
3. Parmanand, Bhai. *The Story of My Life*. op. cit. p.161.
4. Ibid, pp.92-93.

# Vallabhbhai Patel

## (1875-1950)

Vallabhbhai Patel, the 'Iron Man of India', was born in Nandiad, Gujarat, to Ladbai and Jhaverbhai Patel. He was one of their six children, five boys and a girl. There is no record of his date of birth. The generally accepted date, 31 October 1875, is taken from his matriculation certificate. It was an agriculturist family in which Vallabh was born and not a well-to-do one. His childhood was spent working on the family's ten acre farm at Karamsad, just like any other farmer's son, away from books. His education was thus erratic, though he was sent to the Middle School at Karamsad from where he passed in his late teens. To continue his education, he joined the High School at Nandiad and passed the matriculation examination in 1897 at the age of twenty-two. In the meanwhile, he was married at the age of sixteen to Javerbai, a girl from a nearby village. Javerbai died in 1909 when Vallabhbhai was thirty-three but he did not remarry. The couple had two children, a son, Dhyabhai and daughter, Maniben.

The family could not afford to send their son to Bombay for higher studies, so Vallabhbhai·sat for the District Pleader's examination. After passing the examination, he set up a legal practice at Godhra. He had to leave Godhra after two years due to an outbreak of plague in the town, and moved to Borsad. This was in 1902. Borsad was notorious as the criminal belt of Kheda district. Vallabhbhai specialized in criminal cases and soon became the foremost criminal lawyer at the Bar, earning a handsome fees. He could save enough money to aspire to go to England for qualifying as a barrister. But as his elder brother Vithalbhai also desired to go to England also to qualify as a barrister and so he let his brother proceed go first. On his brother's return, he sailed for England in 1910, and joined the Middle Temple. He worked hard and was called to the Bar at the end of two years instead of the usual three. He had also won a prize of fifty pounds in Roman Law. He returned to India in February 1913 and set up legal practice at Ahmedabad and made a great success of it. In less than six months he became the acknowledged leader on the criminal side. We are so used to see Patel in simple khadi that it is difficult to imagine that he dressed like an Englishman on his return from England. G.V. Mavlankar, a close friend of his, describes Patel of those days: "A smart young man, dressed in well-cut clothes, with felt hat worn slightly at an angle, stern and reserved, his eyes piercing and bright, not given to many words, receiving visitors with just a simple greeting but not entering into any conversation, and of a firm and pensive expression, almost as he looked down upon the world with a sort of superiority complex".[1] Except for the dress, this description of Patel could be applied to him during later years also. He joined Gujarat Club where the elite of Ahmedabad met, gossiped and played bridge. He first met Gandhi in the Gujarat Club during one of Gandhi's visits to the Club, a meeting which was somewhat inconsequential.

In 1917 Patel was elected for the first time as a municipal counsellor of Ahmedabad Municipality; from 1924 to 1928 he was its chairman. He devoted much of his time for the improvement of the civic amenities in Ahmedabad like water supply, sanitation and town planning. The municipality was transformed from a mere adjunct to the government department into a popular body 'with a will of its own' in which people's participation became an integral part of its working. During these years, Ahmedabad and its surrounding areas were affected by floods, famine and plague and Patel did a commendable job in organizing relief work for the affected people and earned their gratitude. In later life Patel considered his work in the municipality as one of his major achievements in life. Replying to the civic address presented to him by the Bombay Municipal

Corporation in 1948, he said, "I served Ahmedabad municipality to the best of my ability. I had unalloyed happiness in the task which I performed then. After all, to all of us, to serve our own city must give unmitigated pleasure and satisfaction which I cannot get in any other sphere. Further to cleanse the dirt of the city is quite different from cleaning the dirt of politics. From the former you get a good night's rest while the latter keeps you worried and lose your sleep".[2]

Patel became one of Gandhi's confidants when in 1917 Gandhi was elected the president and Patel, secretary, of the Gujarat Sabha, a political body which proved to be of great assistance to Gandhi in his campaigns. Then came the Kheda satyagraha (1918), which was launched to seek exemption from paying land revenue by the farmers as their crops had been washed away in floods. The government refused to reduce or remit the land revenue. Sardar Patel was responsible for organizing the satyagraha, which lasted for four months. Patel emerged as the chief organizer of the movement. "Discarding his Western dress, he wore a shirt and a *dhoti* as he walked from village to village, exhorting, encouraging, bullying good-humouredly when necessary. He sat down with the peasants and shared their meals, happy to be away from the courtroom. Gandhi, watching him closely, found so much to admire in him". The satyagraha ended when the government partially yielded and asked only those farmers to pay the land revenue who could afford to pay. For his contribution to the satyagraha, Patel received kudos from Gandhi and gratitude from the farmers.

The admiration between Gandhi and Patel was mutual. Patel was very impressed by the lifestyle and philosophy of Gandhi and decided to be his follower. During the Non-Cooperation movement, Patel decided to relinquish his legal career (1920). When the Congress was faced with a dilemma about joining the legislatures and the Swaraj Party was formed (1922) as a legislative wing of the Congress, Patel did not join the Swaraj Party and decided to undertake 'constructive work' as advised by Gandhi. Along with Rajendra Prasad, Patel was the most devoted constructive worker.

In 1928, Vallabhbhai Patel organized a 'no-tax' campaign in Bardoli, Gujarat. It was a repeat performance of the Kheda satyagraha of 1918, but on a much larger scale and was much better organized. One great achievement of Patel in this campaign was to inspire the illiterate rural women to take active part in it. The government had enhanced the land revenue arbitrarily to an extent which the poor farmers were in no position to pay. Patel appealed to the farmers not to pay the enhanced tax. The government in turn resorted to coercion, confiscating the lands and other property of the farmers. Hundreds of farmers were arrested. Patel once again moved from village to village on foot to comfort and cheer up the farmers and their families. The struggle lasted for six months. Ultimately, the government yielded. An enquiry committee was constituted; farmers were released; the lands restored to them and the tax was considerably reduced. It was a victory for Patel and he emerged as a leader of national stature. People started calling him *Sardar*, the unofficial title which he retained for the rest of his life.

Gandhi found in Sardar the best organizer in the Congress party. When in 1930, Gandhi decided to undertake the Dandi (Salt) March, Patel was sent a week earlier to arrange for food and lodging for the participants along the route of the 'March'. But Patel was arrested on 7 March, five days before the commencement of the journey to Dandi. This was Patel's first visit to a prison. He could not take part in the Dandi March as he was released only on 26 June. Then commenced Gandhi's Civil Disobedience movement. Patel took part in it and was arrested again on 31 July. He was released in March 1931, under the provisions of the Gandhi-Irwin Pact. Immediately after his release, Patel was elected president of the Congress session to be held at Karachi in March 1931. On reaching Karachi, he along with Gandhi, had to face the ire of the demonstrators who were blaming Gandhi for not doing enough to save the lives of Bhagat Singh, Sukhdev and Rajguru who were hanged a day earlier. Patel's presidential address was perhaps the briefest of all presidential addresses. Sardar's speeches were always brief and to the point. He was a man of action and seldom indulged in verbosity.

After the failure of the Round Table Conference, Gandhi returned and resumed the Civil Disobedience movement. Congress leaders, including Gandhi and Patel, were arrested. Both were lodged in Yervada jail where they were together for sixteen months from January 1932 to May 1933. While Gandhi was released on 8 May on health grounds, Patel spent another year in Nasik jail. While in prison, Patel learnt Sanskrit and was able to read the *Bhagwad Gita* in the original Sanskrit.[3]

The Congress fought elections for provincial assemblies in 1937, under 1935 Act. Patel played an important role, as the chairman of the Parliamentary Sub-Committee, in the success of the Congress in winning most of the 'general' seats and forming ministries in seven provinces. After the formation of ministries, he guided and controlled the activities of these ministries. After the resignation of Congress ministries in November 1939, Gandhi started Individual Civil Disobedience, opposing India's participation in the war without her consent. Patel was arrested on 17 November 1940 and was released on health grounds on 20 August 1941. Prison life had affected Patel's health and he had developed acute constipation and was suffering from piles. In later life, he became a heart patient. In August 1942 started the Quit India movement and the Sardar, along with other leaders, was arrested on 9 August 1942. He was in Ahmednagar jail for about three years this time.

"A study of Patel's biography and papers suggest that from 1936 he came into his own. Although he had the greatest respect and admiration for Gandhi, but the sense of reality that pervaded with the changing circumstances convinced Patel of the need for a more realistic approach to the problems of India. One has to concede that Gandhi was not directly concerned with the practical side of the adminstration".[4] Gandhi wanted to have power without responsibility. This came in the way of a pragmatic administrator like Patel, who did not want to mix religion with politics. Patel never believed that the state's decisions could be taken on the bidding of 'inner voice'. The schism between Gandhi and Patel was on a very subtle level but it was there and became quite evident in later years. Still, Patel remained a follower of Gandhi to the very end and this 'Iron man of India' had to carry the cross of non-violence around his neck, at times affecting adversely his administrative capabilities.

The War ended with the victory of Britain, with the help of America, but it emerged as a battered nation. Britain's finest manpower decimated, her economy shattered and bankrupt and the dependence on Indian army, with the help of which it was ruling India, now in doubt, Britain realized that it could not hold on to India and that the days of the Empire were numbered. In Britain the conservative government led by Winston Churchill was defeated in the 1945 elections and a Labour government headed by Clement Attlee was formed. He was inclined to see the reality of the situation and was prepared to abandon the idea of the Empire.

India was partitioned and gained Independence on 15 August 1947, after bloody riots engineered by the Muslim League which left hundreds of thousands of innocent persons killed and many more uprooted. Pakistan had been created, comprising Muslim majority areas on the Western and Eastern side. In free India, while Nehru became the prime minister, Patel was deputy prime minister, incharge of Home as well as Information and Broadcasting ministries. Free India was faced with several problems and it was left to Patel to solve some of these gigantic problems. One of these was the existence of about 562 Indian states of sizes varying from a few acres to thousands of square miles spread over the whole length and breadth of the country. Patel assumed charge of the Department of States on 3 July 1947. On 5 July he addressed the princes. His speech is a fine example of precision and clear thinking. In a friendly tone he showed concern for the princes and offered them privileges and status to compensate for the loss of their rule. He also tried to evoke their patriotism: "It is by accident that some (Indians) live in the states and some in British India, but all partake of its culture and character. We are all knit together by bonds of blood and feelings no less than of self-interest. None can segregate us into segments, no impassable barrier can be set up between us. I suggest that it is therefore, better for us to make laws sitting together as friends than to make treaties as aliens".[5] His appeal, mixed with a mild and subtle threat, worked, and by 15 August 1947 all the states except Hyderabad, Junagadh and Kashmir had been integrated with India. A limited use of force had to be used to discipline Junagadh and Hyderabad. Junagadh was annexed in October 1947 and Hyderabad in September 1948 while Nehru was away on a foreign tour. In October 1947, Maharaja Hari Singh of Jammu and Kashmir signed the Instrument of Accession but the Kashmir case was handled by Jawaharlal Nehru directly. How Kashmir became a problem is a long and tragic story. It is anybody's guess how Patel would have handled the Kashmir issue, if like other states, it had come under the jurisdiction of Department of States. Patel integrated over 560 states thus adding 800,000 square kilometres of land and a population of 86 million to the Indian Union. This 'mild colossus' changed the map of India in one stroke. No other leader could have done it. Patel is often compared with Chancellor Bismark (1815-98), who effected the German unification in the late nineteenth century. While Bismark achieved unification, often through war, Patel did it through persuasion and tact. When the Russian leader Khrushchev visited India in 1956, he expressed surprise that India had managed to liquidate the princely states without liquidating the princes. In USSR, in those days, the princes would have been liquidated first, and then the states.[6] Patel could never think, however, that the promises given to the princes would be broken later by Indian rulers.

Another contribution of Sardar Patel was the support given to the Indian Administrative Services, without the help of which, he believed, that the country could not be run efficiently. He gave an honoured place to the civil services and acknowledged their great contribution and inspired them to work for the nation. Speaking in the Parliament/Constituent Assembly on 10 October 1949, Patel warned those members who were pleading for the abolition of Indian Civil Services as a legacy of British rule. He said: "These people are the instruments. Remove them and I see nothing but a picture of chaos all over the country. I wish to place it on record in this House that if, during the last two or three years most of the members of the Services had not behaved patriotically and with loyalty, the Union would have collapsed".[7] He created the Indian Administrative Service (in place of the I.C.S.) and the Indian Police service and other departmental services. Various institutions were founded to train these officers and new recruits joining the services. It is unfortunate that several politicians have started to treat the civil servants as their chattel. The frequency with which these officers are being transferred by politicians has greatly affected their morale and their efficiency, which Sardar Patel had feared.

Patel also ridiculed those who wanted to do away with the armed forces. "If the Indian Government is to be run today on the basis of Gandhian philosophy without army, I am prepared to change the whole thing. You are today spending 160 to 170 crores of rupees on the army.

Are you going to change that set-up? Tomorrow the whole of India will be run over from one end to the other, if you have not a strong army".[8]

Patel did not believe in any 'ism'. His was a pragmatic approach to economic problems as towards all other problems. He was definitely against Socialism. He believed that Socialism put more emphasis on distribution, than on creating wealth. There must be wealth before it can be distributed, otherwise we would be distributing poverty, he felt. He was also against nationalization of industries. He said once: "Some people want us to nationalize all industry. How are we to run nationalized industries if we cannot run our ordinary administration? It is easy to take over any industry we want to, but we do not have the resources to run them, not enough experienced men, not enough men of expertise and integrity". As long as Patel was alive, he did not allow any industry to be nationalized. On the other hand, Nehru had an obsession for nationalization and several key industries were nationalized during his prime ministership. Now, we are struggling to de-nationalize those industries. Patel was not an economist. He was not even a well-read man but he made up this deficiency by a massive common sense by which he was able to comprehend the intricacies and complexities of various problems and was able to reduce them to remarkable simplicity. Gandhi, in an off-guarded moment, praised Patel in the following words, "Sardar has a marvellous capacity of separating wheat from chaff. He is no visionary like Jawaharlal and me. For bravery, he is not to be surpassed. If he had any sentiment in him, he has suppressed it. Once he makes up his mind, he steels it against all arguments. Even I do not argue with him, but of course he allows me to lay down the law".[9] Yet another great contribution of his was his role in the Constituent assembly (1947-49). As chairman of the Advisory Committee on Minorities, Sardar Patel very tactfully got the separate electorates for the Muslims and some other minorities abolished, which had been one of the major causes of the partition of the country. His role in the acceptance of Hindi as the national language, in spite of the opposition by secularists like Nehru, has gone unnoticed. Later on, he succeeded in making Purushotam Das Tandon as president of the Congress (1950) and Rajendra Prasad elected as the first president of India, to the chagrin of Nehru who considered both of these Congress leaders as 'reactionaries'.

Patel's role in the rehabilitation of Hindu and Sikh refugees from Pakistan is commendable. He was very pained when, at the instance of Gandhi and Nehru, thousands of refugees were evicted from unused mausoleums and other buildings occupied by them and thrown on the roads in severe winter, resulting in the death of many. The greatest humiliation for Patel came in January 1948 regarding the release of fifty crores of rupees to Pakistan, a country at war with India at the time. Patel made a statement to the press on 12 January 1948, in which he said: "I made it quite clear (to the prime minister and finance minister of Pakistan) that we would not agree to any payment until the Kashmir affair was settled". The following day, Gandhi went on a fast (one of his innumerable ones) on the instigation of Lord Mountbatten and Maulana Azad, demanding release of fifty crores to Pakistan. On the sixth day of the fast, after an emergency meeting of the Cabinet, it was decided to release the amount to Pakistan. This was one of the most painful decisions which Patel had to be a party to and he never fully recovered from the shock. His pain became more agonizing because these fifty crores were the major cause for the assassination of Gandhi. Patel was the last man to see Gandhi on that fateful day of 30 January, the day of Gandhi's assassination, and it is believed that Patel had put in his resignation letter. But Gandhi's assassination made him change his mind.

Normally, Patel did not interfere in foreign affairs, as Nehru considered these as his special preserve. But Patel kept a watchful eye on international developments, especially those which affected India's security. When China occupied Tibet and Nehru did not react as he should have, Patel wrote a long letter on 7 November 1950, almost from his deathbed, in which he warned Nehru against the Chinese danger and the measures to be taken to meet the possible threat from the Chinese dragon.[10] This letter is still very relevant even today and should be compulsory reading for all diplomats dealing with China.

Heavy workload and the problems faced by the country were taking its toll on Patel's health. He had his first heart attack in February 1948. He soon recovered after rest but the heart ailment was not fully cured. Even during the last years of his life, he continued to solve the country's problems. In March 1950, he had a massive heart-attack from which he did not recover fully.

Patel had another heart attack while recuperating in Bombay and died on 15 December 1950 and was cremated there. "Patel's death inspired Nehru to a private pettiness and public eulogy. Patel had died in Bombay and the funeral was to be held there. Nehru tried to prevent Prasad (president of India) from attending the obsequies on the grounds, he said, that it was a bad precedent for the head of a state to attend the funeral of a minister. Prasad took this as an attempt to blacken Patel's reputation and refused Nehru's advice".[11] However, in public, Nehru praised the character and deeds of Patel: a fine example of hypocrisy at high places.

The country owes much more to Patel than has been acknowledged by historians. The part which he played in shaping contemporary events and policies of the country have not been highlighted and justice has not been done to him. While millions of rupees have been spent to promote Gandhi and Nehru, almost none has been spent on Patel. He was a Dr. Johnson without Boswell. But he was a quintessential politician and often steered the country out of difficulties with his practical and pragmatic approach without caring for the rewards. Criticism of Patel by persons like Maulana Azad is almost shamed into silence by his achievements.

After forty-one years of his death, Patel was honoured with Bharat Ratna in 1991.

## References

1. Tahmankar, D.V. *Sardar Patel*. London, George Allen & Unwin, 1970, p.49.
2. Ibid p.63.
3. *Collected Works of Mahatma Gandhi*. Vol. 43, pp.50-51.
4. Roy Chaudhury, P.C. *Gandhi and His Contemporaries*. New Delhi, Sterling. Rev.ed. 1986, pp.248-49.
5. Patel, Vallabhbhai. *For a United India; Speeches of Sardar Patel, 1947-50*, New Delhi, Publications Division. 1967, p.4.
6. Palkhivala, N.A. *Enduring Relevance of Sardar Patel*, New Delhi, Publications Division, 1993, p.
7. *Constituent Assembly Debates*. Vol. 10, pp.50-51.
8. Ibid.
9. *Collected Works of Mahatma Gandhi*, Vol. 69, p.343.

10. Shankar, V. ed. *Sardar Patel: Select Correspondence, 1945-1950*. Vol. 2, Ahmedabad, Navjivan, 1976, pp.320-327.

11. Edwardes, Michael. *Nehru; A Political Biography*. New Delhi, Vikas, 1971, p.242 (First pub. London, Allen Lane).

# Jotirao Govindrao Phule

## (1827-1890)

Jotirao or Jotiba was born in Pune. Though the date of his birth is uncertain, 1827 is generally accepted as the year of his birth. The family belonged to the *mali* (gardener) caste. The original surname of the family was Gorhe, but as Govindrao, Jotirao's father, was engaged in the trade of florists and supplied flowers to the household of the Peshwa, the family came to be known as Phule.

Jotirao started his education in a local Marathi school from where he completed his primary education (1834-38). Later, he was admitted to Scottish Mission School, Poona, from where he passed the Middle School Examination in 1847. It would be erroneous to say that he passed the matriculation examination, as the Bombay University which conducted this examination was founded only in 1857. While still a student, he was married to Savitribai in 1840, at the age of thirteen. By the time Jotirao completed his education, his father had become a successful building contractor, earning a considerable amount of money. Thus, Jotirao did not need a job. In school he must have acquired a pretty good understanding of the English language because he had started reading books like *Rights of Man* by Thomas Paine on his own. These left a lasting impression on the young mind. With financial support from his father, he decided to devote his life for social work aimed at the upliftment of *shudras*. The first step towards that end, he thought, should be education. He rightly believed that Brahmins were controlling the Hindu society through their knowledge of the scriptures which they acquired through education. He looked upon education as a liberating and revolutionizing factor for the downtrodden in society. His first preference was educating the girls of the *shudras* — a very revolutionary idea at the time. As it was difficult to get women teachers, especially to teach *shudra* girls, Jotirao taught his wife, who was illiterate at the time of marriage, for several years. When she had learnt enough of the three Rs, they opened a school for *shudra* girls in the house of one Bhide in Budhwar Peth, Poona. His father Govindrao was shocked because he feared a backlash from the high caste people. There was a rift between father and son and Govindrao asked his son and daughter-in-law to leave his house. Jotiba was compelled to close the school and earn a living. But soon, he received encouragement and financial help from some prominent Indians and Europeans as well as from the Dakshina Prize Committee and he reopened the school. Soon, the school was well established. Encouraged by the response, Jotirao opened more schools, one in Budhwar Peth itself (1851), another at Rasta Peth (1851) and the third one at Vithal Peth (1852). The later schools were open to all castes as even the girls of high-castes did not have access to free education. Jotirao also believed that the girls *per se* were like the *shudras* as many customs like polygamy, child marriage, agonizing widowhood etc. made their lives miserable. Along with emancipation of the *shudras*, he also worked for the emancipation of women. Thus, he was one of the first reformers who thought of the gender question along with the emancipation of *shudras* and the untouchables. In 1852, he founded the first Native Library for the low-caste, neo-literate people so that they did not forget what they had learnt in school.

Enraged by his activities, many people, not only of high-castes but also of low-caste, were against him. An attempt was made on his life in 1856. Both the would-be assassins turned out to be of low caste. On the other hand, the British government publicly recognized the noble effort of Jotirao and he was presented a pair of shawls at a public function as a token of recognition for what he had been doing.

In 1854, he accepted a part-time job of a teacher in the Scottish Mission School, his alma mater. Here he came under the influence of Rev. Murray

Mitchell, a free thinker, who encouraged him to read widely, including the books which discussed the deplorable side of the Hindu religion. But Jotirao was never tempted to convert to Christianity or Islam, as both the religions were revealed religions, depending on a prophet for revelation. As a free-thinker and a rationalist, he could not wear such a strait-jacket.

In 1855, Jotirao started a night school for adults in his house. He and his wife imparted free education to farmers and their wives, majority of whom were low-caste, for two hours every night. It is difficult to say how successful the couple was in their new venture. But in 1857, the government granted Jotirao a plot of land measuring more than six acres for his school and other educational activities he had been undertaking with a missionary zeal. In 1860, Jotirao founded an orphanage, where widows of all castes could live with dignity and engage themselves in useful activities.

After the death of his father in 1868, Jotirao began to supervise the contractor business of his father which added to his income enabling him to undertake his social and educational activities on a better footing.

By 1873, he had gained enough confidence to start a new religion, Sarvajanik Satya Dharma, based on truth and equality, free from superstition, bigotry, exploitation by priesthood etc. He also founded the Satya Shodhak Samaj (Society for Finding Truth) for the propagation of this new religion. There were several such organizations or sabhas working towards the same end such as Prarthana Sabha, Brahmo Samaj, Sarvajanik Sabha and Arya Samaj. "Phule's achievement was that he widened the very idea of a social organization, which Bombay and Calcutta had restricted to an upper-caste *bhadralok*, or to use the Marathi word *pandharpesha*. Phule and the Samaj began their activity at the lower end of the social spectrum. Phule's vision, and the scope of the Samaj's activity, was broad and sweeping. There was virtually no aspect of social life that did not engage his attention".[2] It is, however, not true that Jotirao ridiculed or considered the efforts of the Brahmin social reformers like Ranade of little consequence. He was a friend of Ranade and had great respect for him, which was reciprocated by Ranade. Jotirao Phule also showed appreciation for Dayananda as a reformer by walking alongside Ranade in a procession in honour of the swami in Poona (1875). This procession was threatened, and in fact disrupted by a rival procession organized by the opponents (orthodox Hindus) causing some injuries to the participants. Jotirao's men had joined the procession in large numbers to give protection to the social reformers.[3]

To propagate his views, Jotirao started a Marathi weekly *Dinabandhu*, the editorship of which was later transferred to N.M. Lokhande, his close associate in the Satya Shodhak Samaj, who also worked among the labourers. Phule also visited villages in the Poona district and delivered speeches to the rustic audiences. Unlike his contemporaries, Phule used the Marathi dialect, the language of the people, to convey his ideas. At times, he did not care for decency and quite often he used inappropriate language. Even his close associates criticized him for using such offensive language. To cite an example, Phule's book, *Cultivator's Whipcord (Shetkaryacha Asud)*, was being serially published in *Dinabandhu*. After the second chapter, Lokhande refused to publish the remaining chapters, as he found the language as well as the contents, offensive. The reason for Phule's unbecoming language was that he had a scanty knowledge of Sanskrit and Maratha etymology. His understanding and appreciation of the scriptures must have suffered as a result. This led him to many unworthy and distorted conclusions. In fact, Phule had not prepared himself well for the task he had undertaken. His sense of history was also rather inadequate.

From 1876-1882, Jotirao was a member of the Poona Municipality. In 1882, he gave evidence before the Hunder Commission and pleaded for the education of women and people belonging to lower castes. In 1888, at a huge gathering of his followers in Bombay, Jotirao or Jotiba was honoured with the title 'Mahatma'. Phule wrote extensively mainly in Marathi. Some of his works are: *Tritiya Ratna* (The Third Eye), a play (1855); *Powada; Chhatrapati Shivajiraje Bhosala Yancha* (Ballad of Shivaji (1869); *Brahmanache Sasab* (The Craftiness of Brahmans) (1869); *Gulamgiri* (Slavery) (1873); *Shetkaryacha Asud* (Cultivators Whipcord) (1883); *On Infant Marriage and Enforced Widowhood* (Comments on Malabari's Notes (1884); *Satsar* (The Essence of Truth, No.1 and 2) (1885); *Ishara* (Warning) (1885); *Religious Rites for the Satyashodhaks* (1887); *Sarvajanik Satya Dharma Pustak* (The Book of the True Faith). The last was posthumously published in 1891 and gives the essence of his views on society, religion and political economy. Some of his works are in dialogue form. He also wrote some poetry of indifferent quality.

Phule did not take part in the freedom movement because he was an admirer of the British rule. He felt that the British had given protection to the shudras from the evil designs of the Brahmins and high caste Hindus.

Late in life Phule argued for the ban on cow-slaughter because the poor farmers were so economically, rather than religiously, dependent on the cows and oxen.

Early in 1890, Phule had a paralytic attack on his right side. He continued giving finishing touches to his book *Sarvajanik Satya Dharma Pustak*. But before he could finish, he died on 28 November 1890 in Pune.

## References

1.  Shinde, J.R. *Dynamics of Cultural Revolution; 19th Century Maharashtra*. Delhi, Ajanta Publications. 1985, p.65.
2.  Deshpande, G.P. ed. *Selected Writings of Jotirao Phule*. New Delhi, Left Word, 2002, p.5.
3.  Keer, Dhananjay. *Mahatma Jotirao Phooley: Father of Our Social Revolution*. Bombay, Popular Prakashan, 1964, pp.137-38.

# Rajendra Prasad

## (1884-1963)

Rajendra Prasad was a gentleman politician, a contradiction in terms in today's world. With his mild manners and affable nature he easily won friends and admirers. Due to these innate qualities he was elected chairman (president) of the Constituent Assembly in 1946 and the first president of free India in 1950.

Rajendra Prasad was born on 3 December 1884, in village Zeradei of Saran district of Bihar. His parents, Mahadev Sahai and mother Kamleshwari Devi, had two sons and three daughters, Rajendra Prasad being the youngest. Mahadev, a scholar of Persian and Sanskrit, was fond of wrestling and was a good rider. Rajendra Prasad, though tall, had a frail body and thus could not wrestling and riding. Rajen Babu's (as he came to be known later) first teacher in their village was a *maulvi* (Muslim cleric) who taught him Persian. He started his formal education in the Chapra Zila School and passed the matriculation examination in 1902, standing first in the district. In the meanwhile, he was married to Rajbanshi Devi in 1896, at the age of twelve. However, his education continued. He joined Presidency College, Calcutta, because his elder brother Mahendra Prasad was staying there. He passed his B.A. and joined M.A. (English) and B.L. classes in the same college. After doing his Bachelor of Law, he started practicing at the Calcutta high court. In the meanwhile, he also got his Master of Law degree. When Patna got a separate high court in 1916, he moved to Patna from Calcutta. In 1917, he was appointed one of the first members on the senate and syndicate of the newly established Patna University. He soon became a very successful lawyer, liked by his clients and colleagues at the Bar, and even by the judges. He was not a great orator but was erudite and painstaking. He also came to be known as a man of character and integrity.

The year 1917 was a turning point in his life. In that year, Gandhi had come to Champaran to experience first-hand the miseries of the indigo workers, and to fight for their cause if possible. Though Rajendra Prasad's role remained peripheral, as several others like Babu Brajkishore, J.B. Kriplani, N.P. Malkani, Mazharul Haq were there to help Gandhi in his campaign, the seeds of national service were sown in Rajendra Prasad's mind after this encounter with Gandhi in Champaran. When Gandhi started the Non-Cooperation movement in 1920 and promised swaraj in one year, Rajendra Prasad cast his lot completely with Gandhi and became his most devoted and trusted follower. He relinquished his legal practice and withdrew his two sons from government-aided schools, as advised by Gandhi under the Non-Cooperation movement. Coarse khadi was now his dress which he adhered to for the rest of his life. So did his family members. When the Non-Cooperation movement was suspended early in 1922, the Congress party was split. While Gandhi wanted Congress workers to do constructive work, many other leaders like C.R. Das and Motilal Nehru, wanted to enter the Assemblies, thus violating the code prescribed by Gandhi for non-cooperation. The rift between the two factions became public and when the Swaraj Party was formed by Das and Motilal Nehru, Gandhi was isolated. The group which still followed Gandhi, now called 'no-changers', was led by Rajendra Prasad. He devoted himself sincerely and with a genuine spirit of sacrifice to do constructive work, mostly in the villages. He even wrote a pamphlet titled *Constructive Programme: Some Suggestions*. The programme included working for Hindu-Muslim unity, removal of untouchability, prohibition, khadi, village sanitation, adult education etc. For years, Rajendra Prasad devoted his time and energy to this work. There was nothing original in it. The ideas were those of Gandhi which he tried to implement. It was during this time that he started a Hindi weekly, *Desh*, at Patna to propagate the Gandhian philosophy and ideas. He also wrote articles in the English bi-weekly (later a daily) *Searchlight*, started in Patna around 1920. In 1924, he was elected chairman of the Patna Municipality from which he resigned a year later.

In August 1928, Rajendra Prasad went to London, his first trip abroad, for an important legal engagement which came to be known as the Burma case. After finishing the legal assignment, he decided to visit Europe. While giving a speech on non-violence and peace in Vienna, a stronghold of the Nazi party, he was assaulted by a group of fascists. He was injured but not seriously.[1]

Rajendra Prasad was not a rabble-rouser like Gandhi and lacked the charisma of Nehru but he was a very sincere, hardworking and a devoted Gandhian. Sadaqat Ashram, which was built by Mazharul Haq in the early twenties, and which housed the Bihar Vidyapeeth for several years, became the headquarters of the Congress whose leading light for twenty-five years was Rajendra Prasad. Here he could inspire young workers to do constructive work and devote their lives for the national cause. In 1923, a meeting of the A.I.C.C. was held at Nagpur. The government had banned the volunteers to march with the Congress flag. A satyagraha ensued against the ban. Sardar Patel was given full powers to conduct the 'Flag Satyagraha'. One thousand volunteers took part but Rajendra Prasad out-shone them all with his quiet resolve. Patel was impressed, which resulted in a lifelong friendship and mutual admiration. The Patel factor decidedly helped Rajendra Prasad in future.

An earthquake devastated northern Bihar on 15 January 1934. Rajendra Prasad, who had been imprisoned, was released by the government on 17 January to help in the relief work. The government, it seems, knew that it was Rajendra Prasad who had the organizational acumen to carry out the rehabilitation work sincerely and honestly. He, along with his volunteers, did their best to rehabilitate the people affected by the earthquake. He appealed to the people for funds, food, clothes. Thirty-eight lakh rupees were collected in no time. Such was the faith reposed by people in him. The work done by Rajendra Prasad became national news and from a provincial leader he emerged as a national leader. It did not come as a surprise to anyone when he was elected President of the Congress party in 1934 for the Bombay session and again in 1935 for the

Lucknow session. In 1937, when Congress ministries were formed in majority of the provinces, it was the Parliamentary Board consisting of Sardar Patel, Rajendra Babu and Abul Kalam Azad which really and effectively provided guidance and control. In 1939, came some unfortunate developments in the Congress party which not only tarnished the image of the party but also of Gandhi. Subhas Bose was duly elected president of the Congress at the Tripuri session in 1939. Gandhi connived to oust Bose as president because the candidate put up by Gandhi was defeated. He directed the Congress Working Committee members not to cooperate with Bose. Consequently, Bose resigned. There was a search for a new president. Several CWC members declined, including Nehru and Azad. However, Rajendra Prasad could not dare to defy Gandhi and became the interim president of the Congress. Such was the hold of Gandhi on Rajendra Prasad. He was certainly the most devoted follower of Gandhi and remained so during the latter's lifetime.

When an Interim Government was formed in September 1946, Rajendra Prasad was inducted in it and was assigned the portfolio of Food and Agriculture. The country was facing acute shortage of every food item besides other necessities. Rajendra Prasad did his best to face the situation. In November 1946, the Indian Constitution Assembly started functioning, as recommended by the Cabinet Mission. The proceedings of the Assembly started on 9 December under the temporary chairmanship of Dr. Sachchdanand Sinha. On 10 December, Rajendra Prasad was elected unanimously as the permanent chairman (later called president). Prasad's popularity among political circles could be judged by the laudatory speeches made by the members, starting with S. Radhakrishnan, on his unanimous election. He presided over the Constituent Assembly proceedings for three years, till 24 January 1950. The tact, patience and impartiality with which he conducted the proceedings is a glorious chapter in our parliamentary democracy. He patiently heard the absurdities voiced time and again during the debates by Muslim League members like Hasrat Mohani who repeatedly said that, "We regard the constitution framed by you worthy of being consigned to the waste paper basket". Rajendra Prasad, as president, bore all this with praiseworthy equanimity. Incidentally, Hasrat Mohani was the only member who refused to sign the draft constitution. Before the motion moved by Dr. Ambedkar to pass the drafted Constitution, Rajendra Prasad, as president, summed up the history of the constitution making in India. It is a masterly piece of 'summing up' spanning five decades and shows his erudition.

Even before the adjournment of the Constituent Assembly, the president of the new republic had to be elected by the members of the Constituent Assembly. Nehru was against Rajendra Prasad's candidature and wanted Rajaji to be the first president of India. Sardar Patel, however, was in favour of Rajendra Prasad's candidature and there arose a mild rift between Nehru and Patel on this issue. "Nehru even unwisely wrote a letter to Rajendra Prasad that Rajaji should be proposed as the President, clearly implying that Rajendra Prasad should step down". Even the mild Rajendra Prasad reacted strongly. Nehru raised the issue against the Sardar's advice, in a meeting of the Congress members of the Assembly. "There was immediate reaction and a rather vociferous majority expressed its support to Rajendra Prasad. Nehru felt humiliated and even thought of resigning which, of course, he never did. Nehru was astonished to find how popular Rajendra Prasad was among the Congressmen and even non-Congress members".[2] Ultimately, Nehru proposed the name of Rajendra Prasad saying, "It is a comfort for us all to know that in these future tasks and struggles, we shall have you as the head of this Republic of India". It was a piece of startling political hypocrisy.

This was not the only occasion when Nehru showed antipathy to Rajendra Prasad. Earlier, on 7 August 1947, when Rajendra Prasad was presiding over the Constituent Assembly, he wrote to Nehru a personal letter drawing his attention that he had received a large number of letters and telegrams favouring a legislation banning cow slaughter. Nehru sent a lengthy reply the same day. It is worth quoting: "I have also received a large number of telegrams and post cards about stopping cow slaughter. Indeed, the number of telegrams and post cards, though impressive, is itself a sign of artificiality to some extent. Dalmia's money is flowing and Dalmia is not exactly a desirable man. As you know, there is a strong Hindu revivalist feeling in the country at the moment. I am greatly distressed by it because it represents the narrowest communalism. I find myself in total disagreement with this revivalist feeling, and in view of this difference of opinion I am a poor representative of many of our people today. I felt honestly that it might be better for a truer representative to take my place".[3] As Gandhi had used the weapon of 'fasts' to get his own way, Nehru used the weapon of 'resignation' again and again to silence his critics. Cow slaughter was not banned. Nehru did not have to resign. An uneasy alliance continued between President Rajendra Prasad and Nehru.

After the 1952 elections, Rajendra Prasad was elected president of the Indian Republic for a term of five years. As president, he addressed the first elected Parliament on 16 May 1952, reminding the members of their responsibility towards the people and the nation. After the second general elections of 1957, he was once again elected as president, opposition of Nehru, who wanted S. Radhakrishnan as president, notwithstanding. Such was the reputation of Rajendra Prasad, the unassuming gentleman of unimpeachable integrity. During both the presidential elections, he was without the support of his staunch supporter Vallabbhai Patel, who had died in 1950. In 1960, Rajendra Prasad made his intention, that he would not be a candidate for the third term, public. He had already served as the head of the state for twelve long years. As president, he made goodwill visits to various countries starting with Nepal (1956). Other countries visited were Japan, Malaya, Indonesia, Indo-China, Cambodia, North and South Vietnam, Laos, Ceylon and lastly Russia in 1960. On 13 May 1962, he retired as president of India and straightaway went to Sadaqat Ashram in Patna, 'his old hermitage', where he had spent twenty-five years of his life.

On 25 January 1960, his elder sister, who was elder to him by twelve years, and had been like a mother to him, died. After taking a salute at the Republic Day parade as president, he rushed to the cremation ground to perform the last rites. He had hardly recovered from the tragedy when another one struck. His wife, Rajbanshi Devi, died in September 1962. That shattered his frail body. He had been suffering from asthma for quite a few years. Now, loneliness engulfed him and he breathed his last on 28 February 1963 in Sadaqat Ashram.

Rajendra Prasad was a scholar in his own right. Though he had started his education by learning Persian, he gradually mastered the Hindi language and wrote several books in Hindi: *Atmakatha* (Autobiography), 1946; *Bapu Ke Kadmon Mein* (At the Feet of Gandhi) (1954). In English he wrote: *Satyagraha in Champaran* (1922); *India Divided* (1946); *Mahatma Gandhi and Bihar, Some Reminiscences* (1949); *Since Independence* (1960). His book *India Divided*, is a somewhat detailed analysis of the consequences of the proposed partition of India. He tried to prove, with the help of plenty of statistics, that Pakistan was not a viable proposition. The same year, the revised edition of B.R. Ambedkar's book *Pakistan or the Partition of India* appeared in which he had argued for the partition of India *along with complete transfer of population*. That book stole the limelight. Rajendra Prasad was not an original thinker. As long as Gandhi was alive, he worked under his shadow. While Gandhi was around, he would even write his presidential address for the Congress sessions in consultation with Gandhi. After the death of Gandhi, his personality flowered, as was evident in the way he conducted the proceedings of the Constituent Assembly as its president and the dignified way in which he acted as president of the Republic of India thrice.

Several honours were bestowed on Rajendra Prasad during his lifetime. Delhi University conferred on him an honorary Doctor of Philosophy in a special Convocation. The rare title of 'Rashtra Ratna' was conferred on him by Sri Abhinav Bharati Samaj by Jagadguru of Singeri Sharada Peetham in 1960. Bharat Ratna was conferred on him by the Indian government in 1962.

The former U.S. Ambassador, Chester Bowles, gave a brief pen-picture of Rajen Babu thus: "Rajendra Prasad was a simple-living follower of Gandhi who spent many years in British jails fighting non-violently for Indian freedom. He had a big walrus-like moustache and his magnificient face always seemed to be holding back a smile at the strange twist of history which took him from the British Viceroy's jail into the Viceroy's own palace with the Viceroy's own bodyguard. He was such a warm and unostentatious person that the great long halls and chambers (of the Rashtrapati Bhawan) must have seemed oppressive and unnatural".

# References

1. *Collected Works of Mahatma Gandhi*. Vol. 37, p.214.
2. Shankar, V. Editorial Note. *Selected Correspondence of Sardar Patel, 1945-1950*. Vol.2, Ahmedabad, Navajivan, 1977, p.506.
3. Nehru, Jawaharlal. *Selected Works*, 2nd Series, Vol.3, pp.189-92.

# Premchand

## (1880-1936)

Premchand is considered as the greatest Hindi writer of the twentieth century. As he started writing in Urdu and later switched over to Hindi, protagonists of both Urdu and Hindi claim him. His short stories and novels are read with great interest even today. He is still a model and an inspiration for aspiring writers.

Premchand was born in village Lamhi, a few miles from Varanasi on 31 July 1880 as Dhanpat Rai. He adopted the pen-name Premchand later in life. Even before using Premchand as a pen-name, he wrote under the name Nawab Rai. He was the only son of his parents, Munshi Ajaiblal and Anandi, though he had an elder sister, affectionately called Suggi. Two other daughters of Ajaiblal and Anandi had died in infancy. Ajaiblal was a postal clerk, drawing a paltry salary. Premchand's mother died when he was just seven years old. After about two years, his father re-married, but his step-mother was most unkind towards him. Fortunately, his elder sister was married by that time. His father's job being transferable posted him to different places, mostly in eastern Uttar Pradesh. He left the family at their village Lamhi most of the time. Premchand's education started in the village Lalpur, a mile from Lamhi. He was admitted to a madarasa run by a maulvi, who was a tailor by profession and taught Urdu and Persian to boys part-time. Premchand recounted his experiences in this make-shift madarasa in his story *Chori* (Theft), published in *Madhuri* in 1925. Later, Premchand joined his father at Gorakhpur, which happened to be the longest period of stay for his father at one place. Here, Premchand passed the eighth standard from Mission High School, Gorakhpur. However, he was not a bright student and did not devote much time studying textbooks. Instead, he read whichever Urdu novels he could find. Besides novels by Urdu writers, he read with delight the translations of English novels in Urdu, like those of Reynold. "In two or three years, I might have read some hundred of them", he wrote later. When his father was transferred from Gorakhpur, the family again came back to Lamhi and Premchand took admission in Queen's College, Varanasi, in ninth standard. He commuted three miles from his village on foot. He was now in his fifteenth year — old enough to get married and was married in 1895. But unfortunately the marriage turned out to be an unhappy one.

After a year and a half years of his first marriage, his father died. But Premchand continued his studies and passed the matriculation examination in 1897, in second division. To support his family, he started coaching children of rich parents but the money thus earned was not enough and he had to borrow money. "Debts somehow became a recurring problem with him throughout his life". Premchand started looking for a job. He succeeded in getting one as an assistant teacher in the district school Bahraich in 1900 on a monthly salary of twenty rupees. His mother and stepbrothers stayed in Lamhi and he used to send them money regularly. From Bahraich, he was transferred to Pratapgarh. Here he studied the life of the people closely and also came into contact with the Arya Samaj people, who were doing social work there. Premchand wanted to improve his prospects in the teaching profession. He took leave and joined Teachers Training College, Allahabad and passed out in 1904. After working for sometime at Allahabad, Premchand was transferred to Kanpur, where he stayed upto 1909. It was at Kanpur that he married a second time. That was in 1906. His wife Shivrani was a child-widow. Premchand did not tell her about his first marriage nor had he formally divorced the first wife, who was staying with her parents most of the time. Fortunately for both, this marriage turned out to be a happy one. Inspired by Premchand, Shivrani developed literary taste later in life and was also active in the freedom movement, to the delight of Premchand. She wrote a biography of Premchand, *Premchand Ghar Mein* (Premchand at Home), after his death. It throws much light on Premchand as a person.

During his stay at Kanpur, Premchand started writing stories and novels. He came into contact with Munshi Dayanarayan Nigam, editor of *Zamana*. A friendly relationship ensued, which lasted throughout their lives. Premchand had failed in the intermediate examination twice because he was very weak in mathematics. He finally cleared the exam in 1910, when mathematics was made optional. By this time he had been promoted as sub-deputy inspector of schools and was getting a salary of fifty rupees. He passed his B.A. in 1919, at the age of thirty-nine. It is surprising that even when he had become famous as a writer and was producing stories and novels of unquestioned merit, he continued to be concerned about his government job in the education department. It seems he wanted financial security which, however, remained elusive throughout his life. He was being transferred from place to place in his new job: Mahaba, Basti, Gorakhpur. It also entailed a lot of travelling on horseback or bullockcart. But somehow he continued writing stories.

In 1915, Premchand started writing in Hindi instead of Urdu because he had a bitter experience with Urdu journals and publishers. "Which Hindu writer has achieved success in Urdu that I shall attain", he wrote to a friend. However, the influence of Urdu was quite marked in his novels and stories even while he was writing in Hindi. By his switching over to Hindi, a new phase in Hindi fiction writing had started. For quite sometime he felt that the job was a hurdle in his creative writing. So, after serving for twenty years in the education department, he resigned from his job in 1921. He was to live for only fifteen more years. Not that he devoted all his time to writing after retiring from service. He had varied experiences during this time; some pleasant and others bitter and even agonizing. But whatever he did and wherever he lived, he continued to write. By this time, he had already published some half a dozen novels and over one hundred stories.

The problem of supporting his family forced him to take up a teaching job in a private school at Kanpur, where he worked only for about eight months. He came back to his village Lamhi and built a small house which still stands as a memorial to the great author. Then he came to Varanasi, and edited the journal *Maryada,* published by Gyan Mandal, whose editor, Dr. Sampoornanand, had gone to jail for participating in the Non-Cooperation movement. After the return of Sampoornanand, he taught in the Kashi Vidyapeeth, on a salary of Rs. 125, for sometime.

His experiences with the publishers were not happy. Neither did they pay him his due, nor did they publish his novels and stories promptly. He then decided to establish his own press. Saraswati Press was established in 1923 in Varanasi. This proved to be a big mistake as the press took up most of his time and there was hardly any profit. He had run into debt. To extricate himself from the unenviable situation, he accepted a job offered by Ganga Pustak Agency in Lucknow, where he worked for a year till September 1925. Back in Varanasi, he struggled to live on the earnings from the Saraswati Press but did not succeed. Debts, in the meanwhile, were piling up. Once again he was offered a job in Lucknow to edit the prestigious Hindi journal, *Madhuri*. He also worked with the Naval Kishore Press, the publishers of *Madhuri*. He stayed in Lucknow for five years (1927-1932), the longest period at any place after his retirement. Here, he wrote some of the best textbooks for children in Hindi and Urdu for Naval Kishore Press, which were included in the school syllabi.

While still serving in Lucknow as editor of *Madhuri*, he launched his own journal, *Hans*, from Varanasi, published in the Saraswati Press, on 6 March 1930. He wrote for *Hans* from Lucknow, in addition to his editorial work for *Madhuri* and writing stories and novels. Those two years (1930-32) must have been the most hectic in his life. They affected his health adversely, chronic patient as he was of dysentery. But *Hans* was a success and the subscribers increased in number with each issue. Besides publishing stories by the established authors like himself and Jai Shankar Prasad, it offered space for new emerging authors. It also published articles on economic and political topics supporting the freedom movement and criticising the 'danda-rule' (stick rule) of the government. This is why it ran into trouble with the government and was asked to deposit a security of one thousand rupees which Premchand somehow managed to pay. He continued to publish *Hans* from his Saraswati Press as long as he lived. The writings in support of the freedom movement launched by the Congress and the use of the Hindustani language, deftly using Hindi and Urdu words, got the Congress leaders like Gandhi and K.M. Munshi interested in *Hans*. A special issue of *Hans* was brought out, featuring the best of not only Hindi but also other Indian languages including Bengali, Gujarati, Marathi, Kannada, Tamil, Telugu and Malayalam. The issue bore the names of K.M. Munshi and Premchand as co-editors. There seems to be some difference of opinion between K.M. Munshi and Premchand because we find Gandhi writing to K.M. Munshi on 1 July 1935: "If for the goodwill a payment has to be made to Premchandji, then I personally would prefer to start an independent paper. We would be able to secure the services of some Hindi writer. We can afford to have Premchandji only if he takes up the work in a spirit of service".[1] Thereafter, K.M. Munshi ceased to be co-sponsor and co-editor of *Hans*. While *Hans* was creating problems for Premchand he took over a fortnightly journal, *Jagran*, in August 1932 (which Vinod Shankar Vyas had started) and converted it to a weekly. Now he had to support two losing ventures, *Hans* and *Jagran*. But even when he was facing financial crisis and was busy with editing *Hans* and *Jagran* and running the press, his creative urge did not slacken.

But the lure of money and the burden of debt dragged him to Bombay for writing films of Ajanta Cinetone. He stayed in Bombay from 1 June 1934 to April 1935; was disgusted with the atmosphere there and returned to Varanasi. During the last year of his life, Premchand was invited to address various conferences. From Bombay he had visited south India and was invited to address the Hindi Prachar Sabha in Madras in December 1934. In February 1936, he attended the Hindi Sahitya Sammelan convention in Purnia, Bihar. In March, he went to Delhi to inaugurate the Hindustani Sabha meet at Jamia Milia. Soon after, he went to Lucknow to preside over the Progressive Writers Conference. This was followed by his visit to Lahore to preside over the Arya Bhasha Sammelan organized by the Arya Samaj. Within a week of his return from Lahore, Premchand had to attend the Bhartiya Sahitya Parishad meeting at Nagpur which was presided over by Gandhi. All the senior leaders of the Congress like Nehru, Patel, Rajendra Prasad and Maulana Azad were there. In these conferences, Premchand expressed his views about literature and language which was the burning topic of the day. Some of these addresses have been published by Saraswati Press under the title *Kuchh Vichar* (1936). His ready acceptance to attend conferences at different places in spite of his ill-health is perhaps a pointer that he had a premonition about his end. In these meetings, he advised Hindi lovers to borrow and induct more and more words from other languages like what the English language had done. That was the only way to enrich a language. Borrowing from other Indian languages may help non-Hindi speaking people to accept Hindi or Hindustani (as he called it) as the common language of the country.

Premchand breathed his last on 8 October 1936, at the age of fifty-six. Not even thirty people accompanied the bier to the cremation *ghat*. Gandhi's secretary Mahadev Desai remined him to write an obituary in the *Harijan*. "We take no editorial notice of men of letters", replied Gandhi.

Premchand's writing career spanned over three decades. During his last twenty years, he used Hindi in Devanagari as his medium. He wrote some two hundred and fifty short stories, of which only two hundred and twenty-five are extant. Most of these stories are now included in the anthology *Mansarover* (eight volumes) in Devnagari. Earlier anthologies in Urdu were *Soz-e-Watan* and *Firdaus-e-Khyal* and in Hindi, *Prem Pachisi* and *Prem Battisi*. He wrote sixteen novels starting with *Asrar-e-Mauvid* (1903-05) in Urdu and ended with *Godan* (1936). His unfinished novel, *Mangal Sutra*, was published posthumously in 1948. Most of his novels had both Hindi and Urdu versions with different titles. For example, *Rangbhumi* (1925) became *Chaugan-e-Hasti* in Urdu; *Kayakalp* (1926) was rendered as *Parda-e-Mejaz* in Urdu and *Karambhumi* as *Maidan-e-Amal* and so on. "The remarkable feature of these novels is the splendid sweep and range of his subject matter and the extensive canvas on which he constructed the plots".[2] He wrote in simple language, mixing deftly Hindi and Urdu words in addition to the people's language, giving it a colloquial flavour wherever warranted. Premchand's major concern was social reform through his writings. He did not believe in 'art for art's sake'. "Literature must have a social purpose", he believed. He was concerned with the fate of the poor peasants, workers and women, especially widows. He takes the reader again and again into the heart of India, its villages, and makes him see the exploitation and agony of the poor farmer and labourer. He also describes the traumas faced by the urban middle-class families, as in *Ghaban*.

Premchand had read widely both Indian as well as foreign writers and being a gifted translator, he translated into Hindi many stories of authors of other languages, both Indian and foreign. Among Bengali writers he translated stories of Tagore and Bankim. The Urdu work, *Fasan-e-Azad* by Ratannath Sarshar, was translated in Hindi as *Azad Katha*. He translated many stories of Tolstoy, Dickens, Galsworthy and Anatole France.

Premchand belonged to no political party and he believed in no 'ism'. He did not like the writers to be categorized as 'progressive' or otherwise. "A writer or an artist is progressive by nature; if this was not his nature, he would not be writer at all", he wrote.

Premchand was not a religious man, and did not believe in rituals. On his deathbed he told a friend: "At such a time, people remember God. People also remind me about it. But so far I haven't felt necessity to bother God. Why now". But he lived a noble and saintly life without the props of religion or God.

# References

1. *Collected Works of Mahatma Gandhi*, Vol. 61, p.218.
2. Bandopadhya, Manohar. *Prem Chand; His Life and Work*, New Delhi, Publication Division, 1981, p.148.

# James Prinsep

## (1799-1840)

The Prinseps were a rare breed whose members served the East India Company and India in many ways since 1771. John Prinsep, father of James, came to India in 1771 in the service of the East India Company, and was noted for introducing indigo plantation and copper coinage in India. Several of John Prinsep's sons were connected with India, especially Calcutta, the seat of power and commerce during the Company's rule. But among all his brothers, James became more famous for his achievements in various fields and earned the gratitude of Indians.

James Prinsep, the seventh son of John Prinsep, was born on 20 August 1799 at Chelsea, Sussex, England. He hardly had any formal education except for the school he attended for two years in Bristol (1809-11). Thereafter, there was no regularity in his education. However, even as a child, he showed great aptitude for mechanical and other drawings and aspired to be an architect. With that in view, he was placed under Augustus Pugin to study architecture. But his ambition to be an architect received a setback when he had to discontinue it due to eye trouble. As an alternative, he took an apprenticeship at the Royal Mint at London (1817-18) and in 1819 he was appointed at the Calcutta Mint under the East India Company's service. He joined duty on 15 September 1919 at Calcutta, where he worked under Horace Hayman Wilson, then assay master of the mint, who later became famous as a great Sanskrit scholar.

Within a short time, James became well-acquainted with his job at the mint and while his chief, H.H. Wilson, left for Banaras to remodel the mint there, James conducted all the work at the Calcutta Mint efficiently by himself. On Wilson's return, James Prinsep was appointed the assay master in the Banaras Mint at Nadesar in the Cantonement area, and retained that office until the mint was abolished in 1830. He was re-appointed at the Calcutta Mint as deputy assay master under Wilson and on the retirement of Wilson in 1832, Prinsep succeeded him as assay master and secretary of the Mint Committee. He continued in the job until 1838, when illness forced him to return to England.

Out of the nineteen years in India, James Prinsep spent ten years in Banaras and nine years in Calcutta. He has left an enduring impact of his work in both the cities as well as on the writing of ancient Indian history. At Banaras, he had got constructed the building of the mint and also a church — though the mint had been closed in 1830, the magnificent building of the 'Mint House' still stands. So also the church. He also had a bridge built over the river Karamnassa, connecting Uttar Pradesh with Bihar. He was fascinated by the old city of Kashi; its temples and mosques, its ponds and wells and gardens and the winding narrow lanes. As the secretary of the 'Baneras Committee for Public Improvement', he devised a drainage system with detailed drawings, which remained, for decades, one of the best drainage systems in the country and only with some additions is essentially the drainage system of the city to this day. He prepared a survey map of the city and compiled its directory containing census data and other statistical information about the city, which is of great historical value. His book, *Views and Illustrations of Beneres* (1825), contains sketches of the important objects and places of the city. The book also contains an "excellent layout of the ancient Bindo-Madhav temple which was destroyed by the orders of Moghul king Aurangzeb, and was prepared from a minute examination of the extant remains of the temple".[1] Prinsep also formed the Benares Literary Society with which were associated Edward Fell, secretary of the Sanskrit College, Dr. Thomas Yeld, Monsieur Duvavcel and other scholars.[2]

While serving in Calcutta, James Prinsep offered to complete the construction of a navigational canal, which his brother Captain Thomas

Prinsep of Bengal Engineers had begun, but could not complete because of his sudden death due to a fall from his horse. This canal, completed by James, served to connect the river Hoogly with the Sunderbans. In 1835, he reformed the Indian weights and measures and introduced a uniform coinage system. As a numismatist, Prinsep's well-known contribution is his *Useful Tables Illustrative of Indian History*, which contains information about all coins of India (extant at the time) from the earliest times and also provides chronological and genealogical descriptions of ancient and modern India.

But the greatest contribution of James Prinsep was the deciphering of the inscriptions on the Ashokan pillars, which were in early Brahmi script, in 1837. He also ascertained their dates. Prinsep decoded the inscriptions which had baffled scholars like William Jones, Henry Colebrooke, and H.H. Wilson. "This revelation shed light on the pre-Gupta period of Indian history. A new and glorious period in the ancient past of India was thus made recognizable for the first time". On this, Prinsep modestly said, "Like most other inventions, when once found, it appears extremely simple, and as in most others, accident rather than study, has had the merit of solving the enigma which has so long baffled the learned".[3] This discovery made him world famous. Among Prinsep's colleagues was a young officer of the Royal Engineers, Alexander Cunningham (1814-1893), the father of Indian archaeology.

Prinsep continued his literary and scientific studies and frequently wrote articles in the journal *Gleanings in Science*, of which he later became editor. The title of the journal later on was changed to *Journal of the Asiatic Society of Bengal*. After Wilson's retirement, Prinsep became the secretary of the Asiatic Society (1832-38) and also the editor of its journal. During his stint at the Asiatic Society, he devoted much of his time to the study of Indian antiquities and in deciphering ancient inscriptions collected from all parts of India. In fact, deciphering ancient inscriptions was only one of his fields of study. His scope of studies and research covered areas of chemistry, mineralogy, meteorology, numismatics and antiquities. His researches earned him the Fellowship of the Royal Society, London. Subsequently, he became a corresponding member of the Institute of France and the Royal Academy of Berlin. Prinsep's articles on various fields of studies were included in his *Collected Works*, which was edited by Edward Thomas and published in two volumes in 1858 as *Essays on Indian Antiquities, Historic Numismatic and Paleography of the Late James Prinsep F.R.S.* with a memoir by Henry Thoby Prinsep (his brother).

James Prinsep had married Marriet, the youngest daughter of Colonel Aubert of the Bengal Army, in 1825. They had one daughter. In 1838, illness forced him to return to England. Overwork and the humid climate of Calcutta affected his health adversely. He died on 22 April 1840, in his forty-first year. The grateful citizens of Calcutta raised a memorial in the form of a *ghat* at the left bank of river Hoogly just below Fort William and named it as Prinsep Ghat which has a handsome building for the protection of passengers landing or embarking there.

## References

1. Sherring, M.A. *Benares; the Scred City of the Hindus,* 1868, Reprint, Delhi, Low Price Publications, 1990, p.317.
2. Nair, P. Thankappan. *James Prinsep: His Life and Work.* Calcutta, Firma KLM, 1999, p.108.
3. Jaggi, O.P. *Friends of Inda, Biographical Profiles.* New Delhi, Munshiram Manoharlal, 1973, p.130.

# Sarvepalli Radhakrishnan

## (1888-1975)

Dr. S. Radhakrishnan is considered as one of the greatest thinkers of modern India. He interpreted Indian philosophy to the Western world through his lectures and books. He was an excellent teacher and was connected with educational institutions for half a century. In recognition of his teaching talents, his birth date i.e. 5 September, is observed as Teacher's Day. In later life, he served the nation, holding important cultural and political posts successfully culminating in his being elected as president of India.

Radhakrishnan was born on 5 September 1888 at Tirutani, forty miles from Madras, in a middle-class Brahmin family. Sarvepalli is a small village in Andhra Pradesh from where his ancestors migrated to Tamil Nadu; hence, the prefix Sarvepalli in his name. He was the second son of Sarvepalli Veeraswami and Sitamma. Veeraswami was serving as a tehsildar in a zamindari on a moderate salary. Radhakrishnan had his early education upto the age of eight at Tirutani and the following twelve years in various Christian missionary institutions: Lutheran Mission High School Tirupati (1896-1900); Voorhees College, Vellore (1900-1904) and Madras Christian College (1904-1908) getting his M.A. in philosophy in 1908. Radhakrishnan wrote in his autobiographical essay that "my entire education was pursued in Christian missionary institutions which made me familiar with the New Testament as well as the criticism of the missionaries against the Hindu beliefs and customs. By this criticism of Indian thought they disturbed my faith and shook the traditional props on which I leaned. A critical study of Hindu religion was thus forced on me".[1] He started writing on Indian philosophy while still a student. His thesis for the M.A. degree was *The Ethics of the Vedanta and its Material Presupposition*. It was intended he said "to be a reply to the charge that the Vedanta system had no room for ethics". The thesis was published in the form of a book in 1908, his first book.

After doing his M.A. he qualified as a teacher in the Training College, Saidapet and joined the Madras Subordinate Education Service. He was married in 1904, at the age of sixteen, while still a student, to a ten-year-old girl, Sivakamuamma. In 1909, Radhakrishnan was appointed as assistant lecturer at the Madras Presidency College (1909-16) and later, as lecturer (1917-18). In 1918, Radhakrishnan was selected professor of philosophy at the University of Mysore. By that time he had become somewhat famous because of his teaching ability and his writings. Sir Ashutosh Mukerjee, vice-chancellor of the Calcutta University, while in search of talent offered him the prestigious post of George V professor of philosophy at the Calcutta University in 1921, the post which he held from 1921 to 1931 and again from 1937-1941. He had to leave Calcutta to serve as vice-chancellor of the Andhra University which was founded in 1926. In 1937, he again joined the Calcutta University but in 1939, Madan Mohan Malaviya, the founder and vice-chancellor of Banaras Hindu university requested him to be the vice-chancellor of his university. He agreed to work in an honorary capacity. He was already holding two positions: that of a professor at the Calcutta University and also a Spalding Professor of Eastern Religions and Ethics at the Oxford University, England, teaching for six months at each of the two universities. He managed to squeeze in the vice-chancellorship of Banaras Hindu University. He used to travel to Banaras over the weekends and return to Calcutta for teaching during the week. However, from 1941 to 1948, when his term for vice-chancellor was extended twice he served full-time at the Banaras Hindu University till 1948. In that year, his academic career came to an end and an important new phase in his life started.

During the four decades of his academic career (1909-48), he lectured as visiting professor not only in India but also in several foreign universities, spanning a period of almost a quarter of a century beginning with the 'Upton Lectures' at Manchester College, Oxford University, England. The topic of the lectures was *The Hindu View of Life* which was issued later in the form of a book (1927). In September of the same year, he lectured at the International Congress of Philosophy at the Harvard University and those lectures were later published as *Kalki or the Future of the Civilization* (1929). In 1929, he was invited as professor of comparative religion at the Manchester College, Oxford once again and delivered Hibbert Lectures on *An Idealist View of Life* published in 1932. Some of his occasional lectures delivered at Oxford were published as *East and West in Religion* (1933). Then from the years 1936 to 1952, Radhakrishnan served for sixteen long years as Spalding Professor of Eastern Religion and Ethics at Oxford University. All those years he travelled back and forth from England to India to perform his duties as a professor and a vice-chancellor at the Calcutta and Banaras Hindu University respectively.

Immediately after Independence the government was anxious to tone up the system of higher education in free India. For that purpose the University Education Commission was appointed in 1948 with Radhakrishnan as chairman. It recommended far reaching reforms in the educational system. Unfortunately, all of them could not be implemented. Radhakrishnan was also a member of the Constituent Assembly from 1947 to 1949. He led the Indian delegation to UNESCO from 1946 to 1952 and was elected chairman of the UNESCO Executive (1948-49).

From the academic to the political was a big, and risky jump but Radhakrishnan, to the surprise of many, came out winning laurels. An important assignment came his way when he was chosen as India's first envoy to Moscow in 1949. "The Iron-man Stalin was quietly charmed by the genial philosopher. And before Radhakrishnan left Moscow in 1952, he had successfully laid the foundation of firm, friendly understanding between India and the Soviet Union, holding good till this day".[2] On his return from Moscow, he was elected vice-president of India (1952-57) and again for a second term (1957-62). As vice-president he also held the position of the chancellor of the University of Delhi from 1953 to 1962.

On 11 May 1962, he was elected president of India and retired after five years in 1967. While as president, he continued his academic pursuits. M.C. Chagla, who was a minister in the Nehru Cabinet, describes the scene in Rashtrapati Bhavan when he went to meet President Radhakrishnan: "I often saw him in his residence, Rashtrapati Bhavan. He used to meet me in his large bedroom which he had converted into a real office. He would sit up in his bed with papers and books scattered all round. It was more like a scholar's room from Oxford than the majestic habitat of the president of India — Dr. Radhakrishnan was ideally suited to fill the role of the philosopher-king which Plato had described".[3] As president, he paid very successful official visits to U.S.A. and Britain in 1963. When he relinquished office of the president in 1967 he gave a parting advice to the nation, "The feeling should not be encouraged that no change can be brought except by violent disorders. As dishonesty creeps into every side of public life, we should be wise and bring about suitable alterations in our life." He left for Madras in May 1967 to lead a lonely retired life; lonely because his wife Sivakamuamma had died in 1956 and his children were busy in their own affairs and families.

During his lifetime Radhakrishnan was awarded several honours and distinctions: Knighthood (1931) and honourary doctrates from a number of universities situated in different countries, Oxford, Cambridge, Moscow, Rome, Tehran, Ireland, Pennsylvania and Kathmandu besides several Indian universities. He was awarded the Bharat Ratna by the Government of India, in 1954. He was also awarded, shortly before his death, the Templeton Foundation Prize for progress in religion, the first non-Christian to receive the £40,000 prize.

Radhakrishnan was very close to Jawaharlal Nehru and as prime minster, Nehru sought his advice on several state matters. He was also close to Rabindranath Tagore for thirty years. Their association began when Radhakrishnan wrote a book, *The Philosophy of Rabindranath Tagore* in 1918, which was highly appreciated by Tagore. In a letter to Radhakrishnan, Tagore wrote: "Your book delighted me. The earnestness of your endeavour and your penetration have amazed me. I am thankful to you for the literary grace of its language which is so beautiful and free from all technical jargons and a mere display of scholarship". Radhakrishnan revered Gandhi as "the greatest living person because of his spiritual ideals". But he had reservations about Gandhi's type of political campaign that automatically elevated its followers to be heroes. Radhakrishnan could not understand the logic of burning foreign clothes, boycotting schools and colleges and Gandhi's economic programme based on the archaic *charkha*.

Radhakrishnan wrote several outstanding books on philosophy, ethics and religion: *The Ethics of Vedanta and its Material Presupposition* (1908); *The Philosophy of Rabindranath Tagore* (1918); *The Reign of Religion in Contemporary Philosophy* (1920); *Indian Philosophy*, 2 vols. (1923-27); *The Hindu View of Life* (1927); *The Religion We Need* (1928); *Kalki, Or the Future of Civilization; An Idealist View of Life* (1932): *East and West in Religion* (1933); *The Heart of Hindustan* (1936); *My Search for Truth* (autobiographical) (137); *Gautama, the Buddha* (1939); *Eastern Religion and Western Thought* (1939); *Mahatma Gandhi* (1939); *Education, Politics and War* (1944); *Is This Peace?* (1945); *The Religion and Society* (1947); *The Bhagwatgita* (1948); *The Great Indians* (1949); *The Dhammapada* (1950); *The Religion of the Spirit and the World's Need* (autobiographical) (1952).

As already stated earlier, the texts of some of these books were delivered as a series of lectures. His magnum opus remains *The Indian Philosophy* in two volumes. The book was written in response to the invitation of Prof. J.H. Muirehead who asked him to write for the 'Library of Philosophy' series. It is an oft quoted book. Jawaharlal Nehru quotes from it extensively in his book *Discovery of India* while explaining Hinduism and Buddhism. His books earned him fame among the intelligentsia the world over, and he came to be regarded as one of the greatest philosophers of the world. As a mark of this recognition, the 'Library of Living Philosophers' published, in 1952, an exclusive volume on the *Philosophy of Sarvepalli Radhakrishnan* devoted to the critical evaluation of his philosophical views. Other philosophers in the series included Bertrand Russell, G.E. Moore and Karl Jaspers. This was a rare distinction for Radhakrishnan.

He died in Madras on 16 April 1975 at the age of eighty-seven.

# References

1. Radhakrishnan, S. *Fragments of a Confession* in *Radhakrishnan Reader*. Bombay, Bharatiya Vidya Bhavan. 1969, p.21.
2. Radhakrishnan, J. *Sarvepalli Radhakrishnan* in *Our Leaders*, New Delhi, C.B.T., 1990, p.118.
3. Chagla, M.C. *Roses in December, An Autobiography*, Bombay, Bhartiya Vidya Bhavan, 1973, pp.437-38.

# Lala Lajpat Rai

## (1865-1928)

Lajpat Rai, popularly known as 'Punjab Kesari' or 'Sher-e-Punjab' was born on 28 January 1865 in village Bhudika in the Ludhiana district of Punjab. His father, Radha Kishan, was a school teacher in government schools and worked at different places in Punjab. His mother, Gulab Devi (in whose name Lajpat Rai established a hospital), came from a Sikh family. As the family belonged to the Vaish (bania) caste, normally the prefix 'Lala' was used with their names which explains the prefix 'Lala' with Lajpat Rai's name.

Lajpat Rai received his primary education at a village school and passed the matriculation examination from Mission High School, Ludhiana. In February 1881, he joined Government College, Lahore, in intermediate arts and law. In 1883, he passed the first law examination thus enabling him to practice law which he started in Jagraon. In 1884, he moved to Rohtak. In 1886, he passed the Vakil's examination and moved to Hissar, practicing in the district court (1886-1892), where his practice flourished. In 1892, he moved to Lahore, the nerve-centre of Punjab, and soon became a leading lawyer there.

As a boy of thirteen he heard a lecture by Swami Dayanand, founder of the Arya Samaj, and was taken in by his personality and his nationalistic views. He joined Arya Samaj formally in 1882 and served its cause throughout his life. He, along with Arya Samaj leaders like Lala Hansraj, founded the first Dayanand Anglo-Vedic (DAV) College in 1889 at Lahore, which played a significant role in the freedom movement. Later, he also founded the National College during the Non-Cooperation movement. Bhagat Singh and Sukhdev were alumni of this college.

Apart from Swami Dayanand, Lajpat Rai was very much influenced by revolutionaries and leaders like Mazzini, Garibaldi, Shivaji and Sri Krishna, whose short biographies he wrote in Urdu during 1896-98. Later in life, especially during his sojourn in the United States, he wrote several other books, mainly in English.

Though Lajpat Rai's political career started in 1888 when he attended the Congress session at Allahabad and joined the party formally, his political career was marked by fits and starts. He was interested in the social and economic upliftment of the masses for which he devoted much of his time, energy and spent a large part of his income.

From 1888 to 1904, he did not take much interest in the Congress party activities except for the Lahore session of 1893, when he served as chairman of the Reception Committee. He was not at all impressed by the Congress and its annual sessions which he used to describe as 'the annual national festival of the educated Indians' and Congressmen as 'holiday patriots'. He considered the resolutions passed in the Congres sesions as 'constitutional verbiage', ineffective and meaningless. However, he was not sitting idle during this time and was devoting much of his time to the Arya Samaj and D.A.V. College activities and other philanthropic works which were his first priority. In 1895, he alongwith Lala Harkishan, promoted the Punjab National Bank, which is one of the leading banks of the country today. He was also one of the founders of the Lakshmi Insurance Company which was the leading indigenous insurance company in Punjab and adjoining areas for half a century. In 1897, he started the Hindu orphan relief movement under the auspices of the Arya Samaj and opened Hindu orphanages at Ferozepur, Lahore and Amritsar. Under the movement, by 1900 some two thousand Hindu orphans were rescued from being converted to Christianity. The centres at Ferozepur and Amritsar are still active.

Lajpat Rai had met Tilak during the Congress session at Lahore in 1893 and shared his political philosophy of mass agitation alongwith swadeshi and boycott against the British rule. From 1904, when he attended the Bombay session, he identified himself with the 'Extremist' group as against the 'Moderates'. Another famous member of this group was Bipin Chandra Pal and the trio came to be known as 'Lal, Bal and Pal' (Lajpat Rai, Bal Gangadhar Tilak and B.C. Pal). The Congress deputed Lajpat Rai and Gokhale in September 1905 to England to educate the British public about the conditions in India prior to the general elections in that country. Both of them toured the country delivering lectures and meeting important persons. While Gokhale came back singing praises of the British, Lajpat Rai returned disillusioned and was frank enough to tell the Congressmen during the 1905 session at Banaras that "Britain was too busy with their own affairs to do anything for India; that the British press was not willing to champion Indian aspirations; that it was hard to get a hearing in England and that Indians would have to depend on themselves to win their freedom". The message of Lajpat Rai went to the hearts of young Indians assembled there.[1]

In 1906, Lajpat Rai and Ajit Singh (uncle of Bhagat Singh) led a movement in Punjab against the Punjab Land Colonization Act and increase in irrigation rates. Both of them made fiery speeches against the government's high-handed policy which was ruining the farmers. The government considered their speeches as seditious and on 7 May 1907 deported both of them to Mandalay jail for six months. While in jail, Lajpat Rai wrote the book *The Story of My Deportation*. The news of his deportation shocked the whole nation and Lajpat Rai's popularity got an unprecedented boost. He was hailed as a national hero when he was released in November 1907. He filed a defamation case against an Anglo-Indian paper and won the case. The following month in December 1907 came the unfortunate Surat Congress. His name was proposed by the Extremists for presidentship but to avoid any controversy, he declined the offer. After the Surat session of the Congress, Moderates headed by Pherozshah Mehta and Gokhale took complete control of the Congress which had become almost an ally of the government. Soon after, Tilak was deported to Mandalay jail for six years. In disgust, Lajpat Rai withdrew from the Congress, questioning its representative character. He left for England in 1908, using his time there for propagating India's cause. He came back to India in 1909. He was elected to the Lahore Municipality in 1911, where he did much useful work for the residents.

Lajpat Rai rejoined the Congress party in 1912. The following year the Karachi Session deputed a delegation to visit England once again to plead for reforms. Lajpat Rai was one of the four delegates. He reached London in May 1914. Soon the World War broke out and Lajpat Rai decided to go to U.S.A. (November 1914) where he stayed for the next five years. He toured extensively in the U.S.A., speaking to select gatherings talking about the woes of the Indian people. He also devoted his time to writing his major works there: *Arya Samaj* (1914), *Young India* (1916), *England's Debt to India* (1917) and *Political Future of India* (1919). He also made a short trip to Japan (July–December 1915) in the midst of his American sojourn. In October 1915, Lajpat Rai founded the Indian Home Rule League of America, borrowing the term from the Irish revolutionaries. He also started publishing a monthly organ of the League, *Young India*. In 1916, Tilak and Annie Besant also started Home Rule Leagues with the same objective but the three Leagues did not merge. Lajpat Rai's Home Rule League did not last long.

Lajpat Rai returned to India and landed in Bombay on 20 February 1920. He was warmly received by enthusiastic crowds wherever he went. He was pained to learn that repression by the British government was more ruthless than before and the Jallianwala Bagh incident (April 1919) was one of its manifestations. He joined the Congress and presided over its Special Session at Calcutta, (September 1920) where Gandhi presented his programme of Non-Cooperation and Civil Disobedience, assuring his countrymen that he would get freedom for the country in one year. Lajpat Rai was sceptical about Gandhi's claims but was won over, like many others, by Gandhi at the Nagpur session of the Congress (December 1920). Lajpat Rai participated in the Non-Cooperation movement with full vigour and was imprisoned. He was shocked to learn that Gandhi, without consulting anyone, had called off the movement, citing the Chauri Chaura incident as an excuse. Lajpat Rai wrote a letter, addressed to all the members of the Congress Working Committee, from the prison cell describing his anguish over Gandhi's action. Though he praised Gandhi as a person in the letter, he lamented that "we had surrendered our better judgement to his (Gandhi's) decision". He told the members frankly that "he had lost faith in the political leadership of Gandhi", and did not change his mind during the remaining years of his life. In one of his most memorable speeches after coming out of the prison, delivered while presiding over Punjab Provincial Congress at Amritsar on 8 December 1923, he tried to analyze the causes of failure of the Non-Cooperation movement. He said, "If freedom could be won by going to jails in large numbers we should have won it by this time; if liberty could be achieved by showing contempt of British courts, British laws and British prisons, we should have been free by now. We must not fail to remember that in spite of our propaganda, government service continues to be the chief attraction of our educated youth, be they Hindus, Mohammedans or Sikhs. That fact alone explains our failure, the most important item of our programme".[2]

Lajpat Rai was greatly upset by the communal riots in Punjab in which Hindus suffered grievously. The attitude of the Congress leaders white-washing the role of the Muslims after every riot pained him. He was critical of Gandhi who had exhorted the Hindus to show complete trust in Muslims and adopt an attitude of complete surrender. "Hindus have declined to accept this", he announced. He warned those who followed Gandhi blindly: "We must not add to the numerous cults and sects of this country by adding one more under the name of Mahatma Gandhi".[3] Lajpat Rai genuinely felt that the Congress party was neglecting the interests of the Hindus and was not caring for their lives and property to appease the Muslims. He told the Congress leaders that the party should depend more and more on the Hindus because Hindu-Muslim unity was a chimera. These proved to be prophetic words. He then lent active support to the Hindu Sangathan movement and Hindu Mahasabha. He became a prominent member of the Hindu Mahasabha and presided over its session at Calcutta on 11 April 1925. He also presided over the Provincial Hindu Conference at Bombay in December 1925.

In January 1926, Lajpat Rai joined the Swaraj party in the hope that it would take care of Hindu interests but found it working on the same lines as the Congress party. He resigned from the Swaraj party after six months and formed the Indian National Party or the National Party in association with Madan Mohan Malaviya, M.R. Jayakar, N.C. Kelkar, and others. It was totally a Hindu party, working in collaboration with the Hindu Mahasabha. They fought the general elections under the banner of this party. Swarajists were routed. They could not win a single seat in Punjab. In fact, the president of the party forfeited his security deposit. In U.P., the Swarajists could win only one seat, that of Motilal Nehru. In other states also Swarajists did not fare well. Lajpat Rai was elected to the Central Legislative Assembly, where he became the leader of their newly formed party and made some memorable speeches, including the one on 16 February 1928 when he moved a resolution for boycotting the Simon Commission, which was carried by sixty-eight to sixty-two votes.

During later years Lajpat Rai devoted much of his time and energy for the amelioration of the condition of industrial labour and took part in the working class movement in general. He presided over the First Trade Union Congress in 1920. He was elected to represent Indian labour at the Eighth International Labour Congress at Geneva in 1926, where he made a forceful speech for the abolition of *begaar* (forced labour) in British India as well as in Indian states.

In his early youth, Lajpat Rai edited the monthly *DAV College Samachar, Bharat Sudhar* (Urdu) and *Arya Gazette.* In October 1904, he started the *Punjabee*, a weekly English newspaper with K.K. Athvale as editor, *Bande Matram*, an Urdu daily and the *People*, an English weekly, which was read widely in Punjab.

To live up to his opposition to the Simon Commission and the resolution which he had moved in the Central Legislative Assembly, he led a demonstration in Lahore on 30 October 1928 for boycotting the Simon Commission, the members of which had reached Lahore on that day. The demonstrators were lathi-charged and a British officer assaulted Lajpat Rai. He was hit on his head and chest with a baton. He died of the injuries on 17 November 1928. About the police assault he remarked, "Every blow aimed at me is a nail struck in the coffin of British imperialism in India."

Lajpat Rai is remembered more for his role as a social and economic reformer, as an educationist and as a philanthropist. He translated his patriotism and love for his countrymen in the shape of several institutions and welfare associations, more than those left by any other leader of his rank. Amongst several others, he was instrumental in establishing the Tilak School of Politics, Dwarkadas Library (which is functioning now in Delhi), Lakshmi Insurance Company, Gulabdevi Hospital in Jalandhar, Servants of People's Society; Lok Sewak Samiti and Achchut Uddhar Mandal. Still the list is not exhaustive.

Punjab has yet to produce a leader of the calibre and status of Lajpat Rai.

## References

1. Tendulkar, D.G. *Mahatma*, New Delhi, Publications Division, Vol. 1, Rev. ed., 1960, p.14.
2. Ravindra Kumar, ed. *Selected Documents of Lala Lajpat Rai*, New Delhi, Anmol, 1992, pp.107-08.
3. Ibid.

# Chakravarti Rajagopalachari

## (1879-1972)

Rajagopalachari was the most maverick of all the national leaders. Something of a rebel, he ended as a tragic hero. His political career was like a roller-coaster; from a chief-minister of a state to governor of a state, to governor general of India, to a minister in the Central Government and ending up again as the chief minister of Madras. He has been praised for his sharp intellect and power of analysis. However, his political career as well as the type of causes for which he worked during his life time, do not demonstrate the kind of intellect for which he has been praised. He was a divisive leader; revered by some and bitterly resented by others.

Chakravarti Rajagopalachari (C.R.) was born in a middle-class family on 10 December 1879 to Singarammal and Chakravarti Iyengar. His father was a village munsiff in Thorapolli in Salem district. The family was orthodox Vaishnav Brahmin. Rajagopalachari had two elder brothers. He went to school in their village Thorapolli; then to an English school at Hozur taluka. Later, he joined a high school at Bangalore and moved thereafter to Central Hindu College, Bangalore. However, he graduated from the Presidency College, Madras at the age of eighteen. He could not be outstanding in academics because he suffered from acute myopia. The blackboard was a blur in the distance and the teacher's writing on it was not visible at all. His father, a stern, self-willed person would not let the boy use glasses till he was thirteen.[1] It must go to the credit of

Rajagopalachari that in spite of this handicap he continued his studies and passed the matriculation examination only a year after he started wearing glasses and could read and write properly. In 1897, at the age of eighteen, he was married to Alarmalu Mangammal, a girl of thirteen. By 1912, they had five children, three sons and two daughters. Manga, his wife died in 1915, when C.R. was thirty-seven. When some relatives brought a proposal for a second marriage, he curtly replied: "I don't want a sixth child." C.R. remained a widower for the rest of his long life.

After graduation, he studied law for two years and started practicing as a lawyer at Salem. His practice flourished. "Larger amounts of money than the family had ever known brought unprecedented transformations in the family's standard of living. Thus progress from bicycle to horsedrawn cart to coach, and finally to car was matched by changes in residence. He moved from rental of a bare simple dwelling to purchase of ever larger houses, with trees around them and fine furnishing within. Before long his stiff-collared snow white shirts were being stitched in Madras. These worn under a buttoned-up black coat, with white dhoti, silver bordered *angvastaram* across his shoulders, and silver-laced white turban marked his rapid rise to prominence at the Bar".[2]

Then something happened in 1919 which changed not only the life-style but also C.R.'s life. In that year Gandhi visited Madras to explain the implications of the Rowlatt Bill and C.R. met him for the first time. He was, as if, hypnotized by Gandhi, who was ten years his senior. We find him addressing Gandhi as 'My Dearest Master'. C.R. joined the Satyagraha movement launched by Gandhi and later the Non-Cooperation movement for which he was sentenced to three months' simple imprisonment. He gave up his legal practice, like C.R. Das in Bengal and Motilal Nehru in Uttar Pradesh. He became a protagonist of khadi. He established an ashram in 1925 in Tiruchangode, which became one of the important centres for khadi production. When C.R. Das and Motilal Nehru founded the Swaraj party in 1922 to enter the legislative assemblies, C.R. remained faithful to Gandhi and played an important role among the 'no-changers'. During Gandhi's imprisonment in 1922 he edited *Young India* for some time. He was active during that time as a social reformer and was actively associated with the Vaikom Satyagraha (1924) and the Temple Entry Movement. He was a strong advocate of prohibition. Early in life he became the chairman of the Salem Municipality where he had practiced as a lawyer for some twenty years. He was secretary of the Prohibition League of India and worked actively during the Anti-Drink Campaign of the Congress. He wrote several pamphlets highlighting the evils of drinking. Outmanoeuvred by Swarajists in Madras politics, C.R. retreated into his ashram and started doing constructive work as advised by Gandhi. Through his dedication, he acquired a reputation of saintliness which proved to be of incalculable political advantage during his impending struggle for power. Twenty days after Gandhi's famous Dandi March, C.R. led another 'march' of his own. He walked 150 miles, along with ninety-eight satyagrahis, from Trichy, reaching Vedaranyam on 13 April 1930. However, it did not raise as much dust as Gandhi's 'march' did.

C.R. and Gandhi were brought in a close non-political relationship in 1933. Gandhi's youngest son Devdas, during his long stay in Madras, had fallen in love with C.R.'s daughter Lakshmi way back in 1927. It took six years for the two fathers to give their consent to the marriage. The couple was married in Bombay in a simple, brief ceremony at Lady Thackersay's house, where Gandhi was convalescing after one of his illnesses. It was an inter-caste marriage between a high caste Brahmin and a Bania and raised some eyebrows. Madan Mohan Malaviya, in reply to the invitation, sent a telegram: "Though I do not approve the *samband* (relation) I wish Devdas and his spouse all happiness". C.R., to avoid any future trouble, insisted that the marriage be registered in a court.

The image of saintliness and nearness to Gandhi helped C.R. become the premier of Madras in 1937, when Congressmen were allowed to accept offices under the 1935 Act. As a premier for two years, C.R. did a commendable job in scaling down rural indebtedness, enforcing prohibition and enacting the Temple Entry Act. He also held in check the leftist violence. When the Congress ministries were asked to resign by the high command in 1939, C.R. was opposed to this move of the Congress but he was the first Congress premier to resign. However, this decision rankled him for years and he tried again and again to get into the seat of power.

The war resulted in his estrangement with the Congress — and Gandhi. While the Congress's policy was not to cooperate with the British government in the war effort unless they promised full independence, C.R. was all for cooperating with the government to ward off the Japanese menace. When the Cripps Mission (March 1942) failed, he openly blamed the Congress for the failure. As soon as Cripps left, C.R. started a campaign against the Congress saying that the talks failed not because the British government had gone back on the concept of a responsible national government at the Centre, or because it refused to part with the defence portfolio, but because the Congress unreasonably opposed the right of non-accession to the provinces. On 22 April 1942, he called a meeting of the Congress legislators from the Madras Presidency. Only fifty-two of the ninety-one members attended the meeting. Of them, thirty-six voted in favour of a resolution exhorting the Congress to accept the Muslim League demand of secession of Muslim majority areas to facilitate the establishment of a national government. In another resolution, permission was sought to form a provincial government in Madras in coalition with the Muslim League.[3] The resolutions were rejected by the Congress Working Committee. But C.R. did not give up. Like a true fighter, he travelled throughout the country making speeches (May-June 1942) explaining his viewpoint. The followers of Gandhi took it as an insult to their idol and indulged in hooliganism.[4] This they had done earlier to leaders like Annie Besant, B.C. Pal. Surendra Nath Bannerji, Dinshaw Wacha who dared to differ with Gandhi. Rajaji faced all this stoically. But when in August 1942 the Congress launched the 'Quit India' movement, he resigned from the Congress. When the Quit India movement fizzled out by 1943, Rajaji became active again and tried to overcome the impasse by putting forward his views in the form of a formula which has come to be known as the 'Rajaji Formula'. This formula in essence accepts the principle of the 'two nation theory' and its concomitant Pakistan. In brief it proposed: (1) Muslim League to endorse the demand for Independence and provisional interim government; (2) After the war a commission would demarcate the contiguous Muslim majority area (3) A plebiscite would be held in those areas to know the opinion of the people. If they voted for separation, the country would be divided into Hindu and Muslim majority areas. C.R. met Gandhi in the Aga Khan Palace, where Gandhi had been detained, and discussed the 'Formula' with him and convinced Gandhi about the rationale of his proposals. Gandhi gave his consent. Encouraged, Rajaji wrote to Jinnah on 1 September 1943 enclosing the gist of the 'Formula'. Jinnah rejected it saying that it offered only "a shadow and husk, maimed, mutilated and moth-eaten Pakistan". In the meanwhile, Gandhi was released from the Aga Khan Palace on health grounds. C.R. once again discussed his formula with Gandhi. Gandhi thought that he would be able to sell the formula to Jinnah, which C.R. was unable to do. Gandhi trudged to Jinnah's house in Bombay for eighteen days in September 1944, meeting him daily and discussing with him the details of the Formula and telling him that the Formula conceded the 'essence of Pakistan'. Jinnah rejected the offer, tucked the Formula under his arm and concluded "now that Pakistan has been conceded, it only remains to be decided when and how it will come into being". Gandhi came back a defeated and humiliated man and felt that he had been tricked. When Louis Fisher during his interview asked Gandhi what he learnt from the eighteen days with Jinnah, Gandhi replied, "I learnt that he was a maniac." Both C.R. and Gandhi (the two *samdhis*, relatives) had helped to restore Jinnah's prestige at the All-India level and converted the concept of Pakistan into reality.

C.R. rejoined the Congress in 1945. He was inducted into the Interim Cabinet (1946-47) headed by Nehru and given the education portfolio. After Independence, he was made the governor of Bengal, (1947-48). He held the exalted position of the governor-general of India replacing Mountbatten — the only Indian to hold that post. He was a minister without portfolio (May-December 1950) in Nehru's Cabinet and then a minister for Home Affairs in November 1951. He went back to Madras as chief minister (1952-54). His zigzag political career surprised many and raised eyebrows. But the fact is that he was in his elements only when he was the premier or chief minister of Madras. It was there that he achieved his most significant achievements, grappling with regionalism, communalism and above all, casteism. At the same time he has been blamed for the creation of anti-Hindi sentiments among the

Tamils. Dharma Vira, a senior I.A.S. officer who worked with him, writes: "Earlier C.R. was a protagonist of Hindi as the link language 'to bind the country together and to prevent growth of separatism'". During the first stint as chief minister, Hindi was a compulsory language in the curriculum of the schools of Tamil Nadu. The people everywhere were learning Hindi. Now (during the second term) he turned around completely. Not only was the compulsory teaching of Hindi abolished but a total elimination of Hindi undertaken. Today in the state there are no signs of Hindi anywhere, thanks to Rajaji and the policy he laid down for his successors".[5]

Rajaji was never at ease in the new political dispensation headed by Nehru. He decried the government's policies of heavy taxation, controls, licenses, permits and voiced his disagreement through his mouthpiece *Swaraj*. In 1959, he founded his own party, the Swatantra Party to oppose the Congress and its policies. Industrialists, rich farmers (landlords) and former princes joined the new party in large numbers. However, after the initial good start, it could not provide a viable alternative to the Congress and by the early seventies it was defunct.

During the last decade of his life, C.R. became a pacifist. In 1962, at the age of eighty-four, he led a three member peace mission sponsored by the Gandhi Peace Foundation, New Delhi with R.R. Diwakar and B. Shiva Rao to meet President Kennedy and appeal to him to stop nuclear tests. This was the only time he left Indian shores. The mission, as expected, did not succeed but it was a pleasant and educative outing for him and his two companions.

Rajaji was a man of letters and a voracious reader. Some of his works are: *Jail Diary* (1922); *The Way out* (1944); *Ambedkar Refuted* (1946); *Mahabharata* (1951); *Ramayana* (1957); *Hinduism; Doctrine and Way of Life* (1959): *Stories for the Innocent* (1964); *Gandhi's Teaching and Philosophy* (1967). Of all these books his most famous and widely read are the *Ramayana* and the *Mahabharata*. He had a knack for presenting the most abstruse philosophy in simple and lucid language. He had a good sense of humour and felicity for biting sarcasm. However, like Bernard Shaw, C.R. never really believed in anything. Like most lawyers he was clever enough at rationalizing anything he happened to believe in at any time.

It is this reputation for craftiness that ultimately destroyed him and pushed him to the margins of India's recent history.

## References

1. Gandhi, Rajmohan. *The Rajaji Story*. Vol. 1, Madras, Baratam Publications. 1978, p.6.
2. Frykenberg, Robert. *Career of Chakravarti Rajagopalachari* in Antony Copley, C. Rajagopalachari: *Gandhi's Southern Commander*. Madras, Indo-British Historical Society, 1986, p.10.
3. Nagarkar, V.V. *Genesis of Pakistan*, New Delhi, Allied, 1975, pp.354-55.
4. *Collected Works of Mahatma Gandhi*, Vol. 76, p.255.
5. Dharma Vira. *My Recollections of Rajaji*, in Antony Copley op. cit., p.27.

# Ramakrishna Parmahansa

## (1836-1886)

"The story of Ramakrishna Parmahansa's life is a story of religion in practice. His life enables us to see God face to face. No one can read the story of his life without being convinced that God alone is real and that all else is an illusion. Ramakrishna was a living embodiment of godliness. His sayings are not those of a mere learned man, but they are pages from the Book of Life". So wrote Mahatma Gandhi in 1924.

Ramakrishna was born on 18 February 1836 in village Kamarpukur, district Hoogly in West Bengal. His parents, Khudiram Chattopadhyay and Chandramani, were orthodox Brahmins. The village in which Ramakrishna was born was inhabited chiefly by people of the lower castes, mostly blacksmiths and karmakars or kamars; hence the name of the village Kamarpukur. Theirs was the only Brahmin family in the village. Naturally, Ramakrishna had playmates from the lower caste families inculcating in him love and affection for every caste high or low. His family was poor but commanded respect in the village. They owned an acre of fertile land and subsisted on its produce, leading a simple, dignified and contented life. In his leisure time, Khudiram made garlands for the family deity Raghuvira. It is believed that Ramakrishna's parents, while on a pilgrimage to Gaya in Bihar, had a dream in which Lord Vishnu promised to be born as their son. This was to be their fourth child. When born, he was given the name Gadadhar, 'the bearer of the mace', an epithet for Vishnu.

As a boy Gadadhar was healthy and restless, full of fun and 'sweet mischief', with a feminine grace which he proudly preserved to the end of his life. He was intelligent and precocious and was endowed with an amazing memory, which helped him to remember whatever he heard from visiting pundits, religious men and story-tellers. They recited passages from the *Ramayana*, *Mahabharata*, *Bhagvat Gita* and other religious books. He was averse to school and did not learn to read or write any language, including his mother-tongue Bengali. Even in later life, he could barely write his name. Whatever he learnt was from word of mouth and whatever he communicated and preached throughout his life was through the spoken word. It is amazing how he could understand the essence of Hindu philosophy and religion without knowing Sanskrit. He was very fond of painting and the art of moulding images of gods and goddesses, which he learnt from the village potters. He had a beautiful voice and sang divinely 'the pastoral airs of Sri Krishna'. He led his village playmates in staging stories from the *Ramayana* and the *Mahabharata* on a makeshift stage.

At an early age he started undergoing ecstasies which did not leave him till the end of his life. The first one he experienced was when he was only six years old. In his own words: "I was following a narrow path between the rice fields. I raised my eyes to the sky as I munched my puffed rice. I saw a black cloud spreading rapidly until it covered the heavens. Suddenly at the edge of the cloud a flight of snow-white cranes passed over my head. The contrast was so beautiful that my spirit wandered far away. I lost consciousness and fell to the ground. An access of joy and emotion overcame me. This was the first time that I was seized with ecstasy".[1] Ecstasies and visions became a regular feature of his life.

Gadadhar's father died when he was seven years old. It brought a great change in the young Gadadhar. He became serious and often visited cremation grounds, staying there for long hours. At the age of nine, he was invested with the sacred thread and was formally initiated into the Brahmin caste.

In 1852, Gadadhar's eldest brother Ramkumar took him to Calcutta where he had opened a Sanskrit *pathshala* (school) hoping that his younger brother would be tempted to learn reading and writing. But Gadadhar showed no such inclination. Soon after, a rich woman, Rani Rasmoni, built a large Kali temple on the bank of Ganges at Dakshineswar, four miles from Calcutta in 1853. Ramkumar was appointed as the priest for performing rites and rituals for the deity in the temple. Gadadhar soon joined his brother as his assistant. Ramkumar died in 1856 and Gadadhar took over as the head priest. The Kali temple at Dakshineswar became his spiritual abode where he experimented with various modes of god-realization and later preached to thousands of seekers for the rest of his life from a small room which was his home in the temple. Soon, Gadadhar came to be known as Ramakrishna. Surprisingly no definite information is available about the origin of this name.[2]

The temple, and the whole estate around it, were supervised by Rani Rasmoni assisted by her son-in-law, Babu Mathuranath. Both had great respect and affection for Ramakrishna and did not interfere with the daily routine practiced by him. His close association with the deity brought a strange emotional attachment in him for the deity. He began to look upon the image of the goddess Kali as his mother and the mother of the universe. He believed it to be living and breathing and eating food out of his hand. After the regular forms of worship he would sit in front of the image for hours singing hymns and talking and praying to her as a child does to his mother, till he lost all consciousness of the physical world. Sometime he would weep for hours, and would not be comforted because he could not see the mother in a living form.[3] At times he forgot to perform the rituals. To help him the Rani appointed a young boy, Hariday, a distant nephew of Ramakrishna, who was 'destined to play an important role in Ramakrishna's life'.

About this time (1856), as his longing for a vision of the Divine Mother became more and more intense but he did not succeed, and out of despair and agony he tried to commit suicide. And lo! he was blessed with a marvellous vision of the Divine Mother engulfed in a flood of light and he fell unconscious. After this first vision Ramakrishna often remained in ecstasy. People considered him insane. Ramakrishna was called back to Kamarpukur in 1858. The doctors could not cure him so the family members decided to get him married, hoping that marriage would cure him. So he was married to a girl of five years when he was twenty-three years old. She was Sarda Devi, daughter of Ram Chandra of a nearby village, who became famous later in life as the Holy Mother. She supervised the working of the Ramakrishna Mission and the *math* till her death in 1920. Ramakrishna stayed at Kamarpukur for a year and a half and then returned to Dakshnineswar. His 'madness' for the Mother reappeared tenfold. But when the visions appeared again and again he was satiated and became calmer and was ready for further spiritual pursuits.

Around 1861 came to Dakshineswar a Brahmin lady called Bhairbi Brahmani. She was around fifty but very handsome with a kind of divine grace. She was a learned lady, adept in the trantric and Vaishnava methods of worship. Ramakrishna welcomed her and told her all about his experiences and that people called him mad. After observing his activities for several days she proclaimed that Sri Ramakrishna, like Sri Chaitanya, was an 'Incarnation of God'. She stayed at Dakshineswar for two years.

Several scholars and religious people started visiting Dakshnineswar to interact with Ramakrishna. One such man was Totapuri (the naked man), who arrived in 1864. He was an Advaita Vedantist and tried to preach Advaita (oneness of God) to Ramakrishna. But when he saw Ramakrishna in *samadhi* (uninterrupted meditation) for three days continuously he was convinced about his extraordinary power and exclaimed: "He (Ramakrishna) has attained in a single day what took me forty years of strenuous practice to achieve".

Several other famous persons were drawn to Ramakrishna as his fame spread. Swami Dayananda Saraswati, the founder of Arya Samaj, came to meet him when he visited Calcutta in 1872. There is no record of what transpired between the two. At that time Dayanand knew only Sanskrit and Ramakrishna knew only Bengali. The most rewarding exchange of views was between the Brahmos led by Keshab Chandra Sen, and Ramakrishna. The exchange of views influenced the thinking of both. While Brahmo's antagonism to idol-worship was diluted to some extent, Ramakrishna came to know what the educated Bengali was thinking about God and religion.

While the meeting with these elderly intellectuals was rewarding, Ramakrishna was waiting for young men who would become *sanyasis* and carry on his mission in life. Gradually, a band of young men came to him, promised to renounce the world and do his bidding. The most talented of them was Narendranath Dutta, who later became famous as Vivekananda. There were about sixteen of them at the time of Ramakrishna's death, who later led the life of a monk to spread his message.

Ramakrishna had come to believe that all religions, if followed in the right spirit, lead to the same God. He even led the life of a Muslim and a Christian, in turn, for a few days to know their gods, which he concluded were in no way different from Hindu and other gods.

Ramakrishna's wife Sarda Devi joined her husband after attaining puberty but their marriage was never consummated as Ramakrishna considered all women as mothers. That included his wife. Sarda Devi, after the death of her husband, played an important role as the 'Mother figure' to the monks of Ramakrishna Mission and *math* and they always looked to her for guidance.

During the last years of his life, Ramakrishna preached incessantly from his room in the Dakshineswar temple. Crowds came at all hours of the day to listen to this man who had realized God. "The Western educated, the egnostics, the sceptics, the orthodox, the Brahmos, and the believers flocked to him to hear and imbibe the Upanishadic truths that fell from his lips".[4] He welcomed them all in unsophisticated Bengali 'with a slight, delightful stammer': "Greetings to the feet of the Jnani! Greeting to the feet of the Bhakta! Greeting to the devout who believes in the formless God! Greeting to those who believe in God with form! Greeting to the men of old who know the Brahma! Greeting to the modern knower of truth"![5]

The continuous preaching began to tell on Ramakrishna's health. In the beginning of 1885, he suffered what is known as 'the clergyman's sore throat'. The situation worsened. Soonafter, he had a haemorrhage of the throat. The doctor now diagnosed the malady as cancer. Ramakrishna was taken to Calcutta for treatment. He died on 15 August 1886. Before, he died he had declared that Narendra (Vivekanand) would be his spiritual heir. It was Vivekananda who spread the message of the master in the world with significant modifications brought by him. It was he who founded the Ramakrishna Mission and *math*. Ramakrishna's other apostles also did a commendable job by converting themselves into a team of monks, serving humanity devotedly and selflessly and spreading the message of Vedanta throughout the world. Every year, new monks join the cadre to keep alive the mission of Ramakrishna. His (Ramakrishna's) contribution towards improving the social tone of society, at a time when the influence of English education and missionary proselytization had considerably undermined the faith of the English educated Hindus in their own religion and in the values of their own culture, is inestimable. "By presenting to the believers, waverers and scoffers, the highest wisdom of the ancient sages, together with the difficult teachings of the Upanishads and the Vedanta in a language which was simple and lucid in style as it was rich in telling similes and metaphors, he not only revived their faith in the cardinal values of Hindu culture, but also revivified Hinduism in such a way as to turn it into a huge magnet exercising an irresistible attraction for them all, including the Brahmos".[6]

# References

1. Rolland, Romain. *The Life of Ramakrishna*, Calcutta, Advaita Ashrama, 1929, Reprint, 1997, p.6.
2. Nikhillananda, Swami. *Sri Ramakrishna; A Biogaphy*, Madras, Sri Ramakrishna Math, 1953, p.13.
3. Max Muller, F. *Ramakrishna; His Life and Sayings*, Calcutta, Adavaita Ashrama, 1898, (Sixth impression, 1998), p.36.
4. Sinha, Nirmal, ed., *Freedom Movement in Bengal (1818-1904)*; Who's Who, Calcutta, Academic Publishers, 1991, p.296.
5. Rolland, Romain. op. cit., p.xiii.
6. Sinha, Nirmal. op. cit., p.297.

# C.V. Raman

## (1888-1970)

Chandrasekhara Venkata Raman is undoubtedly the best-known scientist of modern India. He was the first Asian to win the Nobel Prize, way back in 1930. He also inspired several younger scientists like K.S. Krishnan and Sisir Kumar Mitra.

Raman was born on 7 November 1888 in a village near Tiruchirapalli in Tamil Nadu. His father, R. Chandrasekhara Iyer, was a school teacher and his mother, Parvathi Ammal, came from a family of Sanskrit scholars. Raman was the second child of his parents; the first one was Subramanian, who became famous as the father of renowned astrophysicist and Nobel Prize winner (1983) Subramanian Chandrasekhara. Raman's father, though not quite well-off, loved books and had built up a small library in his house, mainly of science books and English classics. Thus, from his childhood, Raman was brought up in an intellectual atmosphere. His father was also a good veena player and little Raman would watch his father playing veena for hours. Later the veena became the subject of his scientific investigations.

Soon after Raman's birth, his father obtained a bachelor's degree in physical sciences and moved to the coastal town of Vishakhapatnam as a science lecturer in a local college. Raman was a bright student and passed his matriculation examination in 1900, at the age of twelve from Madras University. After passing the First Arts examination from Hindu

College, Vishakhapatnam, he joined Presidency College, Madras and passed the B.A. examination, standing first and sweeping all the prizes. He joined M.A., choosing physics as his subject. Raman was the youngest in his class but had become a minor celebrity in the college. His teacher, Professor Jones, gave him freedom to study and experiment on his own. Raman spent most of his time in reading classics of mathematics and physics and experimenting in the laboratory. Even while he was a student, he wrote a short paper *The Unsymmetrical Diffraction Bands due to a Rectangular Aperture;* which was published in the prestigious British journal, *The Philosophical Magazine* in 1906. Early the following year Raman got his M.A. degree standing first in the university and winning several prizes. Now he had to think about a career. His heart was in science but opportunities in India for research scientists were non-existent, so Raman took the Financial Civil Service examination. After passing it at the age of nineteen, he was posted as assistant accountant general at Calcutta. At the same time he got married to a young girl named Lokasundri, who later proved to be the proverbial woman behind the great man.

In Calcutta, Raman used to go to office by tram. One day, while going to work, Raman saw a signboard of 'Indian Association for the Cultivation of Science'. The association was founded in 1876 by Mahendra Lal Sircar but unfortunately not much research work had been done there till Raman stepped in. Raman got permission to work in the laboratories of the association. He worked there mornings and evenings, before and after office hours. For ten years Raman led this double life, not even resting on Sundays. He started his research with the problem of 'Surface Tension' followed by studying 'Propagation of Light'. Gradually he organized the laboratory of the Association to serve his needs. He had now started announcing his findings by publishing articles in important British journals like *Nature* and the *Philosophical Magazine* and *Physical Review* published from America. During this period, the study of vibration of different musical instruments also engaged his attention and his work in this area created a good deal of interest in foreign scientific circles. In Calcutta, Raman became popular in educated circles as he used to deliver popular lectures on science. Often these lectures were accompanied by interesting demonstrations. Thus, Raman toiled alone for ten years, 1907-1917, in the laboratory of the association during his spare time in addition to his work in the office of the accountant general.

In 1917, an opportunity came his way and his career took a new turn. The vice-chancellor of Calcutta University, Sir Ashutosh Mukherjee, had come to know about the research work done by Raman in the association. The Calcutta University did not have a science department and was only an examining body in science and the vice-chancellor was keen to start one. After collection of funds Ashutosh Mukherjee started a science college as part of the university and was looking teachers. Fortunately an endowment was created by Taraknath Palit and a professorship in physics in his name was established. Sir Mukherjee wanted Raman to fill that chair. Raman was getting a salary of eleven hundred rupees per month plus substantial perks. The professorship carried a salary of six hundred rupees only. When formally offered, Raman accepted the post of university professorship and resigned from the much lucrative government job in 1917.

Though teaching was not included in the contract for the professorship, Raman started taking classes in the Science College of the university and continued doing research at the association. Soon his fame spread and several talented young scientists were attracted to work with him not only from Bengal but also from other states. Raman was happy to work full-time for physics in such conducive surroundings. The association became the research arm of the University Science College. In 1919, Amrit Lal Sircar passed away and Raman became the honorary secretary of the association. His interest in acoustics and musical instruments kept him engaged for some time but he soon took up research in other subjects also, particularly optics. Under his guidance, the *Indian Journal of Physics* published by the association came to be recognized as a standard journal in which many of the research papers by him and his associates were published, thus bringing honour and recognition for Raman. In 1921, the Calcutta University conferred on him an honorary doctorate degree. That was also the year when Raman went abroad for the first time to attend the Universities Congress at Oxford. There he got an opportunity to meet face to face many of the eminent physicists of the day. The return journey was memorable because he had started wondering why the colour of the sea was blue. On his return to Calcutta this 'why' became the subject of his investigation. Raman knew that John Rayleigh (1842-1919; Nobel prize winner 1904) had attributed the blue of the sky to the light rays of the sun scattered by the molecules of nitrogen and oxygen in the air. Rayleigh had also claimed that the blue of the sea was a mere reflection of the blue sky. But on seeing the deep blue of the Mediterranean Sea, Raman was not convinced about Rayleigh's explanation. He took up the study of the scattering of light by molecules of sea water and also various types of liquids, solids and gases. In due course, he found that the blue of the sea was mainly due to the scattering of blue light by the molecules of sea water when sunlight fell on them. The rest of the colours of the spectrum were absorbed. His researches in optics brought him recognition from all over the world. By then he had built up a team of devoted research workers who were collaborating with him in his investigations. Raman was elected a Fellow of the Royal Society, London in 1924. In that year he went to Canada and America where he spent three months at the California Institute of Technology as a visiting professor.[1] The following year in 1925 he visited the Soviet Union and met many Russian scientists conversing with them in German. Back in Calcutta, he concentrated intensely on research and avoided going abroad for several years. He started his investigations in optics again. In 1927, the Nobel prize in physics was awarded to A.H. Compton of the University of Chicago for his discovery about X-rays, which was called the Compton Effect. The Compton Effect was produced owing to the particle nature of X-rays. Raman rightly thought that something similar was happening with the light beam, which was in fact, a stream of particles known as photons. The photons hit the molecules of the chemical liquid losing some of its energy. The same phenomenon occurs when light rays pass through a transparent medium, whether solid, liquid or gaseous. This is what in essence is the Raman Effect. From the minute changes observed in the energy of the photons, or nature of light, the internal molecular structure of the medium can be deduced. "Thus, Raman Effect is important in understanding the molecular structure of chemical compounds. In fact, within a decade of its discovery, the internal structures of some two thousand chemical compounds were determined".

With the invention of the 'laser', with its powerful light radiation, the 'Raman Effect' has become a powerful tool for scientists.[2] One consequence of the use of such molecular and atomic probing machines as the Raman spectroscope, electron microscope and ultracentrifuge is that the knowledge acquired through them has shown the way to synthesize more and more artificial molecules, many of them vital to industry and science. Indeed, a whole crop of new industries such as colour photography, plastics and synthetic rubber has sprouted during the past few decades from our deeper understanding of the interior build of molecules and atoms.[3] He announced his discovery in 1928 and the prestigious journal *Nature* published it. Honours started to pour on him. He was knighted in 1929, besides being bestowed several other honours by foreign universities and scientific bodies. Raman was awarded the Nobel prize for physics in 1930.

In 1933, Raman was appointed director of the Indian Institute of Science, Bangalore and he shifted from Calcutta, after working there for twenty-six years, to Bangalore where he worked for the remaining years of his life. Here he started a new Institute of Physics and again he built up a team of upcoming scientists. In 1934, he founded the Indian Academy of Science and remained its president till his death. In 1937, he stepped down as director of the Indian Institute of Science and opted for the post of a professor at the Physics Institute. The research work in these two institutes continued and in fifteen years, 1933-1948, as many as 491 original scientific papers were published in national and international journals. Raman collaborated with younger scientists like Nagendra Nath and published several original papers.

In 1948, Raman founded the Raman Research Institute at Bangalore, where he could work in an atmosphere more conducive to pure research. The institute became to him a haven where he could carry on his personal research work. Here, among beautiful surroundings, he built large library and "an extensive museum containing prize collection of butterflies, shells, snails, insects, and above all a large variety of gemstones including a very large number of diamonds". He was made a national professor in 1948 to facilitate his work and the highest national award, Bharat Ratna was conferred on him in 1954.

Raman breathed his last on 21 November 1970, at the age of eighty-two and according to his wishes was cremated on the lawns of the Raman Institute. A vegetarian and teetotaller, Raman was a man of simple habits and dignified manners. He wore a turban and a long coat. During his lifetime he published hundreds of original papers and wrote a few monographs and books which include: *Molecular Diffraction of Light, Mechanical Theory of Bowed Strings; Theory of Musical Instruments; Physics of Crystals and Diffraction of X-Rays* and *The Physiology of Vision.*

## References

1.  Venkataraman, G. *Raman and his Effect.* Hyderabad, Universities Press, 1995, pp.28-29.
2.  Salwi, Dilip M. *Scientists of India,* New Delhi, C.B.T. Rev. ed. 1995, p.43.
3.  Singh, Jagjit. *Some Eminent Indian Scientists,* New Delhi, Publications Division, 4th ed., 1991, p.129.

# Srinivasa Ramanujan

## (1887-1920)

Srinivasa Ramanujan was one of the greatest mathematicians India has produced. He was born at Erode in Tamil Nadu on 22 December 1887. His father was a petty clerk in a cloth shop at Kumbakonam. The family was not well-to-do. Ramanujan went to school at the age of five. Two years later (1894) he joined the Town High School at Kumbakonam, where he got a free studentship. He passed the matriculation examination in 1904 and won the Subrahmanyam Scholarship by topping in mathematics, which enabled him to join Government College at Kumbakonam. He had such a fascination for mathematics that he devoted all his time to the subject, neglecting others, including the English language. The result was that he failed twice in his first year arts examination and had to leave college. That was the end of his formal education.

But from his early childhood it was evident that he was a mathematical prodigy, and Nature had gifted him an uncanny memory which he put entirely at the service of numbers. As a result "he remembered the idiosyncrasies of every one of the first ten thousand integers". His talent for mathematics was sharpened while still in school. He borrowed from the school library G.S. Carr's the *Synopsis of Elementary Results in Pure and Applied Mathematics*. For a boy of fifteen, the title of the book can be frightening, but Ramanujan was delighted as if he had got a fascinating mystery story to read. He devoured the book and found delight in verifying some of the formulae given in it and began to make new theorems and formulae. It triggered the mathematical genius in him. Mathematical ideas came rushing to his mind with great speed. He started doing problems on loose sheets of paper. By the time he left for England, he had filled three big sized notebooks, which later were known as Ramanujan's *Frayed Notebooks*. Even today scientists at the Bhabha Atomic Research Centre and Tata Institute of Fundamental Research are trying to decipher his *Notebooks* and his other works to prove or disprove the results given in them, and to find out if any of them could help them in their atomic energy research.

But this mathematical genius did not have adequate qualifications for a job. He would visit offices, showing his *Frayed Notebooks*, trying to convince the officials that he knew mathematics and could do a clerical job. But people could not understand what was scribbled in the *Notebooks* until he met Francis Spring, director of the Madras Port Trust, who was impressed by his *Notebooks*. Spring offered Ramanujan a clerical job on a monthly salary of rupees twenty-five. Ramanujan desperately needed a job because his parents had got him married in 1909, at the age of twenty-two, to an eight-year-old girl Janaki.

Ramanujan had continued his mathematical work after leaving college. His earliest contribution to the *Journal of Indian Mathematical Society* was in the form of questions, which appeared in 1911. The same year was published his article '*Some Properties of Bernoulli's Numbers*'. But because of his scanty knowledge of the English language he could not express himself properly. At that time, Ramanujan was working on theorems of prime numbers. In Cambridge University, Professor G.H. Hardy, in his tract on '*Orders of Infinity*', had posed some problems which were yet to be solved. Ramanujan had found the solution to those problems. These were communicated to Professor Hardy. Thus started a very fruitful friendship which resulted in Ramanujan going to England and working in collaboration with Professor Hardy.

While working in the Port Trust, Ramanujan was introduced to Dr. G.T. Walker, director of Meteorology, Government of India, who at once recognized the quality of Ramanujan's work and succeeded in arranging a monthly scholarship of rupees seventy-five for Ramanujan from the

University of Madras in May, 1913. All that time Professor Hardy was trying to get him a research scholarship at Trinity College, Cambridge, which he succeed soon after. It was conveyed to Ramanujan and he left for England in April 1914. The scholarship was worth £250. In addition, he was also awarded an exhibition (scholarship) amounting to fifty pounds. As a scholar, Ramanujan had no assigned duties at Cambridge and was free to work as he pleased. He devoted himself wholeheartedly to his research work and in collaboration with Professor Hardy put his genius to work in number theory. Ramanujan played with numbers as a child plays with toys. In Ramanujan, Hardy found an unsystematic mathematician. The several discrepancies in his research could be due to his lack of formal education. His inadequate knowledge of English did not help matters either. But Hardy and their other collaborator, J.E. Littlewood, took care of his deficiencies. His achievements at Cambridge include the Hardy-Ramanujan-Littlewood circle method in number theory, Roger-Ramanujan identities in partition of integers, a long list of the highest composite numbers, besides work on the number theory and the algebra of inequalities. In algebra, his work on continued fractions is considered to be equal in importance to that of the great Swiss mathematician Leonard Euler (1707-83) and the German mathematician Karl Jacobi (1804-51).

Ramanujan was elected Fellow of the Royal Society on 18 February 1918 and in October the same year became the first Indian to be elected Fellow of Trinity College.

His stay in England was cut short due to his ill-health. The extreme cold of Cambridge for a south Indian used to tropical climate was not easy to bear. His orthodoxy with regard to diet further contributed to the deterioration of his health. He had developed tuberculosis which was incurable at that time. He was removed to a nursing home at Cambridge. As his condition did not improve, he was kept at different sanatoria at Wales, at Matlock and London. When in autumn 1918 he showed signs of improvement, he resumed his research work and discovered some of his most beautiful theorems. Fearing that he may again become bedridden, the university authorities sent him back to India. On his return to India, he resumed his research work but his health went on deteriorating and on 26 April 1920 he breathed his last in Madras.

Ramanujan was a pure mathematician of the highest order, whose prime interest was the theory of numbers. As a pure mathematician, he wanted to keep his work away from any kind of technological application. "But what, one may enquire is the use of all this ado about splitting numbers in various ways? If Ramanujan had to answer the question, he, like his mentor and discoverer, G.H. Hardy, would have been the first to agree that such work was completely useless. I have no doubt that he would have wholeheartedly endorsed the famous toast which Hardy is said to have proposed at Cambridge some years after Ramanujan's death 'To pure mathematics — and may it remain useless for ever'".[1]

However, to the chagrin of Ramanujan and Hardy, even pure mathematics may not remain 'useless' for all times to come. It is gradually being made use of in technology. Ramanujan's mock-theta functions, modular equations, identities, theories of continued fractions and elliptic functions or some other of his numerous creations are being extensively studied with a view to ascertaining the possibility of understanding and regulating atomic furnaces. Some other uses may be invented in course of time. For posterity, Hardy and others have edited Ramanujan's works in a volume which came out in 1927. Like the unknown inventor of zero centuries ago, Ramanujan has put India on the map of the world of mathematics. No greater tribute could be paid to Ramanujan than what his mentor Hardy said: "I still say to myself when I am depressed and find myself forced to listen to pompous and tiresome people: 'Well, I have done one thing you could never have done, and that is to have collaborated with both Littlewood and Ramanujan on something like equal terms'".[2]

Jawaharlal Nehru writes in his book *Discovery of India*: "Mathematics in India inevitably makes one think of one extraordinary figure in recent times. This was Srinivasa Rajanujam". And all that he achieved was in a short span of thirty-three years.

## References

1. Singh, Jagjit. *Some Eminent Indian Scientists*, New Delhi, Publications Division, 4th ed. 1991, p.135.
2. Chakraburty, A.K. in *Dictionary of National Biography*, Calcutta, Institute of Historical Studies, Vol.3, 1974, p.479.

# Mahadev Govind Ranade

## (1842-1901)

Mahadev Govind Ranade was born on 18 January 1842 at Niphad in Nasik district of Maharashtra, in a middle class Chitpawan Brahmin family. His father, Govind Rao Ranade, was a clerk in the office of the deputy collector at Ahmednagar but later joined Kolhapur state service as *karbhari* (administrator). Mahadev was a quiet child; nothing excited him, a trait which he carried throughout his life.

At the age of six, Mahadev was sent to a Marathi school in Kolhapur, but in 1851 he was transferred to an English school, also in Kolhapur. After studying there for six years, he was sent to Bombay to join the Elphinstone institution. His academic record in the Institution was so good that the following year he was admitted to Elphinstone College. In 1859, he passed the matriculation examination of the Bombay University. He graduated with first class honours in history and economics in 1862; passed M.A. in 1864, winning a gold medal. The same year he passed the L.L.B. examination with first class honours. Throughout his college career he was a scholarship holder.

After passing his L.L.B. Ranade decided to join government service in preference to his own legal practice. He began his service career as a Marathi translator in the Education Department, government of Bombay in 1866 at the age of twenty-four. His job included keeping the government informed about any new Marathi literature that was published. That gave him an opportunity to study modern Marathi literature. For sometime, in 1867, he served as *karbhari* and a few months later as *nyayaadhish* (judge) in Kolhapur state. But the following year he came back to Bombay as assistant professor of English literature and history in the Elphinstone College, and served there till 1871. At the same time he undertook some temporary assignments such as that of a judge in the Small Causes Court, police magistrate and high court Deputy. In 1871, he also passed the Advocates Examination; left the College service and joined as a magistrate in Bombay. Judicial service was to his liking it seems, and he went up the ladder, step by step. In November 1871 he was appointed subordinate judge in Poona. In 1873, he was confirmed as first grade sub-judge. In January 1881, he was appointed additional presidency magistrate, Bombay. He was also entrusted with inspection duty in Poona and Satara districts under the Deccan Agriculturists Relief Act. This gave him an opportunity to come in direct contact with the farmers and gain deep knowledge about their problems. In 1887, he was appointed special judge under the Deccan Ryot's Relief Act. In 1893, he was elevated to the bench of the Bombay high court as a judge, the post which he held till his death in January 1901.

In recognition of his knowledge of legal matters, he was nominated as law member of the Bombay Legislative Council (1885-86); was renominated again in 1890 and 1893. In 1886-87, he was nominated as a member of the Finance Commission. In February 1887, he was made a C.I.E.

His work in the judiciary left ample time for him to study and to participate in social activities. For that purpose he established many societies and even founded some journals. Like other Moderates, he believed that British rule in India was a boon for the country and it would be in the interest of the country to maintain the British connection. He was thus against agitational politics. He believed that social transformation must precede political reforms and worked towards that end throughout his life. When the Indian National Congress was formed in 1885, Ranade unofficially joined it, and attended its every session till the last years of his life. Though not a politician (his official position would not allow him to be) he was a profound student of politics and took part in the policy making of the Congress by offering his views and suggestions. But soon the Moderates, who believed in the constitutional means to achieve political reforms, came into conflict with the Extremists led by Tilak who wanted to free the country through agitation, and, if need be, through violence. As long as Ranade was alive, he did not allow the schism between the two wings of the Congress to come in the open and worked all the time for a compromise. But after Ranade's death the Moderates started manipulating the affairs of the Congress to their advantage and captured the Congress. Their hold on the Congress lasted till the death of the two leading Moderates, Gokhale and Pherozeshah Mehta.

As an educationist Ranade took keen interest in the education of girls. He started a girl's high school at Hazur Paga in Poona, and a girl's training college (1884). He also took active part in the Deccan Education Society started by Tilak and G.G. Agarkar (1884) and was one of the five patrons of the society. Ranade was also associated with the University of Bombay. As a member of the University Senate and Syndicate as well as dean of the Faculty of Arts, he advocated for the inclusion of Marathi in the university curriculum and succeeded in his efforts. To spread education beyond the classroom, he started several associations like Elocution Encouraging Association, the Poona Summer Lectures, Vernacular Literature Encouragement Association, Industrial Conference and Exhibition, Native General Library etc.

Besides being a social reformer, a moderate politician and an educationist, Ranade was a distinguished economist along with two of this contemporaries, Dadabhai Naoroji and R.C. Dutt. The views of these three were identical, hovering around the 'Drain Theory'. Ranade pointed out that the maxims and principles of British economic writers would not apply to the conditions of our country. He also emphasized the role which the government must play towards the economic development of the country. Ranade's role in the growth of the Indian Economic Conference was significant. Before writing on the economic history of India, he studied the conditions of agriculture and peasantry in detail and became an authority on questions of land revenue, land tenure and land improvement. Ranade's economic writings consist of twelve essays on Indian economics (1898), fifteen articles in the *Journal of Poona Sarvanajik Sabha* (1878-1894) together with his books, *Report on the Material Conditions in the Maratha Districts* (1872); *Currencies and Mints Under Maratha Rule, A Review Manual of the British Empire in India* (1878), which was a compilation of his articles he wrote from time to time in the *Indu Prakash.*

Ranade was a keen student of Maratha history. This subject occupied his attention almost till his last days, as his *Rise of the Maratha Power* was published in 1900, and his studies of the heyday and decline of that power remained incomplete which he had planned jointly with K.T. Telang. Ranade, in his writings on Maratha history, tried to rectify the mistakes and misrepresentations of British writers like Grant Duff, who had depended mainly on Persian sources. The tradition among the British writers of Indian history was to regard the part played by the Marathas of little consequence. Ranade pointed out that it was a serious error of judgement and a deliberate suppression of facts. He proved beyond doubt that the British had to defeat the Marathas to establish their rule in India

Ranade also found time for journalism. He was editor of the English columns of the *Indu Prakash*, Bombay, an Anglo-Marathi daily devoted to reforming the Indian society of its inherent evils. From 1878 to 1896, he regularly contributed to the *Quarterly Journal of the Sarvajanik Sabha*, Poona, which was edited by S.H. Chiplunkar. He wrote on many topics but the main emphasis was on social reform. In the first volume of the journal he contributed as many as forty-one articles.

But "his title to being a great man must rest upon the social purposes he served and on the way he served them. On that there can be no doubt. Ranade is known more as a social reformer than as a historian, economist or educationist. His whole life was nothing but a relentless campaign for social reform. Ranade had both the vision and the courage which the reformer needs".[1] His methods included meetings, missions, lectures, sermons, articles, interviews, letters, 'all carried with unrelenting zeal'. He worked mainly through organizations: Prarthana Sabha, Bombay; Sarvajanik Sabha, Poona. (It was captured by Tilakites in 1895 and the reformers led by Ranade formed another sabha, naming it the Deccan Sabha) and above all through National Social Conference which Ranade founded in 1887. Its annual sessions were held alongwith those of the Indian National Congress in the same venue. Ranade presided over most of its sessions, delivering scintilating speeches exhorting people to realize the importance of social reform. In one of his speeches he said, "You cannot be liberal by halves. You cannot be liberal in politics and conservative in religion. The heart and head must go together. It is an idle dream to expect men to remain enchained and enshakled in their own superstition and social evils, while they are struggling hard to win rights and privileges from their rulers. Before long these vain dreamers will find their dreams lost".

Ranade tried to cooperate and respect other social reformers of his time like Nana Sankarset, Vishnusastri Pandit, Jotirao Phule, Dadaba Pandurang and Balsastri Jabhekar. In 1875, Ranade organized Swami Dayanand's visits to Poona. He found much to support in Dayanand's programme. Both Ranade and Jotirao Phule walked in the procession in honour of the swami in Poona. This procession was disrupted by the orthodox section and some participants were injured. This shows the kind of antagonism the reformers had to face. Ranade was instrumental in publishing fifteen lectures which the swami delivered in Poona. Ranade continued to correspond with the swami even after he had left Poona. Swami, in turn, showed his admiration for and trust in Ranade by including his name among the trustees of his will.[2]

While still studying in school, Ranade had been married to Sakubai who died of consumption in 1876. His second marriage was with eleven-year-old girl Ramabai. He was thirty-three. Although he advocated widow marriage strongly and opposed child marriage with equal sincerity, it is ironic that he himself was unable to put his beliefs into practice. This was very much resented by his followers and supporters. Criticism was voiced even by *Indu Prakash*. However, it must be said in his defence that he educated his illiterate child-wife and groomed her to do social work, and in the process she became a famous social worker in her own right. She was president of the Bombay and Poona Sevasadans for a number of years and did commendable work. She died in 1924 — outliving her husband by twenty-three years.

Ranade was a dominant figure in Western India in the late nineteenth century and exerted tremendous influence in almost all fields; social, religious, economic, educational and even political. It is regretable that social reformers do not get the praise and honour which they deserve. The hard work began to tell on Ranade's health. In 1900, he was unable to attend the session of the Social Conference at Lahore — the only session which he missed since its inception in 1887. He was suffering from heart ailment. The end came on 16 January 1901. He was fifty-nine.

# References

1. Ambedkar, B.R. *Ranade, Gandhi and Jinnah*, 1943. In Dr. Babasaheb Ambedkar *Writings and Speeches*: Bombay, Education Dept. Vol. 1, p.216.
2. Jordens, J.T.F. *Dayanand Saraswati*, New Delhi, OUP, 1978, p. 136.

# Manabendra Nath Roy

## (1887-1954)

M.N. Roy was a genius who lost his way amidst the debris of 'isms'. He is generally acknowledged as the founder of the Communist Party of India but he died preaching Radical Humanism.

M.N. Roy was born as Narendra Nath Bhattacharya on 21 March 1887 in 24 Pargana district of Bengal. His father, Dinabandhu Bhattacharya, was a Sanskrit teacher in a local school. Roy went to school in his native village, Arbalia, where he was born and then in Kodalia, where his father had moved in 1898. He was sent to Calcutta, where he joined the National University of Aurobindo Ghosh and later, the Bengal Technical Institute. But it is doubtful if he attended any classes in these institutions. He was essentially a self-educated man; an intellectual without any degrees.

As a schoolboy he was an ardent admirer of V.D. Savarkar and was also influenced by the preachings of Swami Ram Tirth, Dayananda and Vivekananda. But soon he was inspired by Bankim's *Anand Math* and joined the Anushilan Samiti, founded on the lines of Anand Math and also the Yuganter Group, whose leader was Jatin Mukherjee (the famous *Bagha*). Bengal was in ferment due to the partition of Bengal. Roy joined the movement in a big way and was prosecuted in a political dacoity case in 1907, followed by the Howrah Conspiracy Case (1910) and the Garden Reach Dacoity case (1914). On the outbreak of war in 1914, the revolutionaries, spread over Europe and other countries as well as in

India, looked to the Germans for help in the shape of arms and money which the Germans promised. It was planned that the arms would be sent through the Dutch East-Indies. Roy was assigned the job of collecting arms by Jatin and left for East Asia. As the arms shipment did not arrive, he did not return to India. Rash Behari Bose had also left India in 1915 and had surfaced in Japan. Roy met Bose in Japan and also San Yat Sen, who had also taken refuge in Japan but their meetings were not fruitful. After visiting several countries in East Asia, Roy landed in San Francisco in America on 15 June 1916 as Father C.A. Martin, with a copy of the Bible in his hand. At Stanford University, he stayed with Dhan Gopal Mukherjee, a contact person for Bengali revolutionaries and changed his name to Manabendra Nath Roy, the name by which he came to be known. At Stanford, he met Evelyn Trent, fell in love and married her. She worked with him till their divorce in 1926. Life was becoming difficult for Indian revolutionaries in America after the latter entered the war against Germany. Roy was soon arrested in a consipiracy case but jumped bail and escaped to Mexico. During this period in America and Mexico a complete change in his thinking took place. He read Marxian and other leftist literature widely. He also came into contact with some Marxians in America. Perhaps Evelyn, whom he married, was one of them. The 1917 revolution in Russia had stirred up the entire world and had changed the thinking of millions the world over. On the other hand, the revolutionary activities in India had been crushed ruthlessly by the government. His mentor, Jatin Mukherjee, had been killed in a police encounter. There was no chance for the revolutionaries to overthrow the foreign yoke by such sporadic outbursts. The Russian Revolution, based on the teachings of Marx, was a much surer way, Roy thought, and was converted to Communist thinking. The world must be conquered through Marxian methods was now his firm belief. Mexico, at that time, was already witnessing a social revolution. He befriended Michael Borodin, who was sent to Mexico as the first emissary of the newly founded Communist International. Together they founded Mexico's Communist Party, the first such party outside Russia. Roy's exploits in Mexico soon drew the attention of Lenin, who invited him to attend the Second World Conference of the Communist International in Moscow.

Roy arrived in Moscow early in 1920 and the Second World Congress of the Communist International was held in July-August 1920. The Congress set out to formulate a policy on what was known as the 'National and Colonial Question'. The Congress found itself confronted with two sets of theses on the question, presented respectively by Lenin and Roy. According to Roy's thesis, the revolution in colonies like India should mainly depend on organizing workers and peasants independently while Lenin had advocated cooperation with national movements spearheaded by the bourgeoisie. In the Indian context that would have meant the Indian National Congress. These two theses are usually dubbed as 'revolution from below' and 'revolution from above'.[1] Both the theses were incorporated in the resolution and have been tried intermittently by Indian Communists. Roy elaborated his thesis in a book, *India in Transition* (1922). Interestingly, Roy tried Lenin's thesis rather than his own, after his arrival in India by joining the Congress party.

Immediately after the Second Congress, a provisional All-India Central Revolutionary Committee was formed in Moscow, with Roy as chairman. He was sent to Tashkent, where he formed the Communist Party of India on 17 October 1920 with M. Acharya as chairman and himself as secretary. Roy rose very rapidly to occupy almost all the important positions in the Communist International: membership of the Executive, the Secretariat, the Educational Board, chairmanship of the Eastern Commission and membership of the Chinese Commission. No Indian has ever such a sway in the Communist International as Roy had. He also edited three journals — *Vanguard*, *The Masses* and *Advanced Guard*, from 1922 to 1928. During this period Roy also wrote several books on the Indian theme. There was an attempt to smuggle copies of these journals into India and some of them must have been confiscated by the British secret service. Thus his activities in Russia and Europe were known to the police resulting in his implication in the Kanpur Communist Conspiracy Case (1924). It seems that he wanted to return to India and start the Communist movement in the country but apprehended that he would be arrested. To forestall such an eventuality, he wrote a letter to British Prime Minister Ramsay Macdonald, who was himself a Socialist, on 21 February 1924, beseeching him that he should not be arrested and persecuted on his return to India. He wrote: "The fact of my membership of the Communist International cannot reasonably deprive me of the right of living and working in India, when adherents of the same International are not deprived of identical rights in Great Britain".[2] Macdonald did not reply. Roy postponed his return to India and was tried in absentia in the Kanpur Communist Conspiracy Case (or Bolshevik Conspiracy Case). Roy was charged with conspiracy to establish a branch of the Comintern in India and to deprive 'the King of his sovereignty of British India'. Roy had come to know about the conspiracy charge and decided to stay on in Russia and Europe.

Lenin died in 1924 but Roy did not lose his foothold in the Comintern immediately. On the other hand, he was sent to China to put across the Leftist line adopted by the C.I. In the meanwhile, little progress was made in India by the Communist Party even after Satyabhakata had formally announced the formation of the Indian Communist Party at Kanpur in September 1924. To put life in the C.P.I., some British communists like George Allison and Phillip Spratt came to India and tried to organize the party. By that time the Communist International in Moscow began to doubt the organizational capabilities of Roy to deliver the goods. The visit of Soumendranath Tagore, leader of the Worker's and Peasant's Party, to Moscow in 1927 proved to be Roy's nemesis. Tagore alleged that the Comintern leader were being misguided by Roy regarding the work of the Communists in India. While Roy had boasted that there were hundreds of Communists in India, actually the number did not exceed a dozen. Tagore also alleged that although the Comintern had placed enormous sums at Roy's disposal, hardly any money had been received in India, and the movement was handicapped because of lack of funds.[3] Other charges also cropped up against Roy and he was expelled from the Comintern in 1929. Consequently, Roy returned to India in December 1930, incognito and even attended the Congress Session at Karachi in March 1931, where he met Jawaharlal Nehru and Subhas Bose. But he was arrested soon after, the Kanpur Communist Conspiracy Case was revived and he was sentenced to twelve years rigorous imprisonment, which was reduced to six years on appeal. He was released in 1937. Before leaving Europe for India he had met a German lady, Ellen Gottachaulk and they had fallen in love. After Roy's release from jail, she joined him in India and they got married. She remained his lifelong companion, sharing his joys and sorrows in his tumultuous life.

Shunned by the Communists, he joined the Indian National Congress and was elected to the A.I.C.C. By then, Roy had become a bitter critic of the Marxian philosophy. His idea of joining the Congress was to form a 'Left-Nationalist Front' inside the Congress. Then came the War in 1939 and differences cropped up with the Congress on the issue of supporting the war effort. Unlike the Congress leadership, he was a fervent supporter of the war effort against Fascism. In 1940, he broke away from the Congress and formed a separate party, the Radical Democratic Party. The Congress, he maintained, had all the characteristics of a multi-class party, but it was the reactionary Gandhian leadership which stood in the way of its becoming a revolutionary organization'. This was an additional reason for leaving the Congress. On the same issue of supporting the war effort Roy and his followers left the INTUC also in 1940, which had passed a resolution against supporting the British, and formed a new outfit, Indian Federation of Labour and declared that labour should shun strikes during the war. It is alleged that the government sanctioned monthly grant of Rs. 13,000 to this organization for its support. He became a virulent critic of the Congress, calling the Quit India movement as a 'sabotage movement'. As a result of his anti-national utterances, he suffered a great deal in terms of popularity, which was never of much consequence to him any way.

After the Gandhi-Jinnah talks failed in 1944, resulting in great embarassment for Gandhi and the Congress, Roy saw his chance for his political resurrection. He was the only non-Leaguer to support Jinnah and advised him to give up the idea of coming to terms with Hindu India which would never accept the Muslim demand of self-determination. He proposed to Jinnah a 'democratic coalition' composed of the Radical Democratic Party, Scheduled Castes Federation, the non-Brahmin organization of Southern India and many other elements outside the two Hindu organizations, Congress and the Hindu Mahasabha.[4] It was very naïve of Roy to put such a proposal to Jinnah, who was gaining strength as the unquestioned leader of Muslim League by preaching Muslim separatism. He did not want to dilute his source of strength by associating with such sundry outfits as proposed by Roy. Jinnah snubbed Roy by not replying. In the 1946 elections, the Radical Democratic Party was routed and could win only one seat in the Bombay Assembly. That made Roy realize that he had no future in national politics. He retired from active politics to live in Dehradun surrounded by books and natural scenery. Soon after, he wound up the Radical Democratic Party. His new thinking now led him to 'beyond Communism', 'beyond revolution', 'beyond traditional politics'. He termed the new *mantra* he developed as New Humanism or Radical Humanism. It marked the culmination of his manifold heresies, condensed in a full-fledged system of thought. To spread his message, he founded and edited two journals, *The Radical Humanist* and *The Humanist Way* and wrote several books on the subject. "Radical Humanism maintains that man is the archetype of society; cooperative social relationships contribute to develop individual potentialities; development of the individual is the measure of social progress. Thus, progress results from the basic human urges, namely, quest for freedom and search for truth. Revolution must go beyond the economic organization". Thus, he had discarded dialectical materialism of Marx as an incomplete philosophy. At the same time Roy was never enamoured of India's contribution to spiritualism as expounded by Dayananda, Vivekananda, Aurobindo and others. He denounced Vedantic idealism and never accepted India's claim to spiritual superiority over the West. A born heretic, he might have discarded Radical Humanism also had he lived longer.

To trace the evolution of his thinking and changing concepts one would have to wade through at least fifty volumes of his writings and hundreds of articles published in journals, some of which he himself edited. He was certainly a prolific writer. Some of his important books are: *Problems of India,* Zurich (1920); *India in Transition,* Geneva (1922); *What We Want,* Geneva (1922); *One Year of Non-Cooperation* (with Evelyn), Calcutta, 1923; *Aftermath of Non-Cooperation,* London (1926); *Future of Indian Politics,* London (1926); *Political Letters,* Zurich (1924); *The Russian Revolution* (1930); *Heresies of the Twentieth Century* (1939); *Materialism* (1940); *Scientific Politics,* Calcutta (1942), *Indian Labour and Post-War Reconstruction,*

Lucknow (1943); *Future of Socialism*, Calcutta (1943); *Revolution and Counter-Revolution in China*, Calcutta (1946); *Beyond Communism* (1947); *New Humanism* (1947); *Reason, Romanticism and Revolution;* 2 vols. (1952); *Politics, Power and Parties* (1960); *Memoirs*, Bombay, (1964). That is a tremendous output by any standard and reveals his intellectual calibre.

In June 1952, when he was preparing to visit Europe and America for participation in the conference of his International Humanists and Ethical Union, he met with an accident while walking in the outskirts of Mussoorie, falling several feet in a gorge. He developed cerebral thrombosis and died on 25 January 1954 at the age of sixty-seven. His Radical Humanist movement had attracted several young men and women who had become his followers. His widow Ellen Gottachaulk carried the torch lit by him for sometime and his writings and library remained in circulation due to her efforts. His widow and followers maintained his house in Dehra Dun as the 'Humanist House' for sometime.

## References

1. Ray, S. ed. *Selected Works of M.N. Roy*. Vol.1. OUP. 1987, pp.174-8.
2. Ibid p.254.
3. Chowdhuri, Satyabrata Rai. *Leftist Movements in India*, 1917-47, Calcutta, Minerva 1977, p.228.
4. Nagarkar, V.V. *Genesis of Pakistan*, Allied, 1975, p.381.

# Rammohun Roy

## (1772-1833)

Rammohun was born in 1772 (or 1774) at Radhanagar, district Hooghly, fifth of seven sons of Ramakant and Tarini Devi. His father was a zamindar and was quite well-to-do. After learning some Bengali in a village 'pathshala' (school), some Sanskrit from his mother and Persian from his father, he was sent to a *madarsa* in Patna in his ninth year to learn Persian and Arabic, (the former still being the court language). He stayed there for a little more than three years, became proficient in the two languages and could read and recite works of famous poets. Coming from a Brahmin family he was supposed to learn Sanskrit and was sent to Banaras (Kashi), the seat of Sanskrit learning. He stayed in Banaras till his sixteenth year and while studying the *shastras* was influenced by the monotheistic tenets of Vedanta and Upanishads which made him a determined enemy of idolatory. Thus, he returned home quite a transformed man, one who was destined to upset the traditions of his family.

He was outspoken in his views about idolatory and expressed these in a pamphlet *Tuhfatul Muuahhiddin* (A Gift to Monotheists) in Persian in 1803, which offended his orthodox father. A dispute arose in the family and Rammohun left home and started travelling to various places in the country reaching as far as Tibet where he studied doctrines of Buddhism and offended the Lamas by stating his views about monotheistic doctrines. This nomadic life lasted for four years. His father, disturbed by the separation of his son sent out men to trace him. They brought him home, where he was received with warmth. Soon after he was married, but it did not divert him from acquiring knowledge and learning languages.

Early in life he saw his sister-in-law perform sati after the death of his elder brother Jag Mohan, who had died young. This tragic event made a deep impression on him and in later years he devoted his energies for the abolition of *sati*. He continued preaching against several evils in Hindu society including idolatory, *sati*, caste system and once again he was expelled from his house in 1800. He came back home only after the death of his father. By then time he had become a father of a son and to support his family he got a job as a clerk in Rangpore collectorate. Due to his ability and diligence he soon rose to become dewan and wielded significant power. He served as dewan for ten years. He had saved enough money, which was supplemented by what his father had left for him, resigned from service and came and settled in Calcutta in 1814. He bought a garden house built in European style on Circular Road and another house at Chowringhee Road. This was when Rammohun was forty. He lived like an aristocrat, throwing parties for his European as well as Indian friends thus widening his social circle. He started studying English in his twenty-second year while his study of the Hindu *shastras* continued. He came into contact with some Europeans also and from them he started learning Hebrew, Greek and Latin, such was his knack for learning languages. While learning English, he had come in contact with several Englishmen especially one Mr. Digby under whom he worked for several years till 1814 and started admiring many equalities in the Britishers.

His reforming zeal now asserted itself and he decided to devote his life towards reforming the Hindu society and to remove the evils which had crept in. He believed that to remove superstitions and gross and meaningless rituals people must be taught Vedanta, and the Upanishads. As very few people knew Sanskrit, he started translating Vedas and Upanishads in Bengali and English. Within a year he had brought out an abridgement of Vedanta and had translated the *Kena* and *Isha* Upanishads with the help of some friends. These and other publications antagonized the orthodox Hindus. But he withstood the turmoil boldly and did not budge from the path of reform which he had undertaken. At the same time he established 'Atmiya Sabha' (Friendly Society) to preach the unity of God.

In Calcutta he also came in contact with Christian missionaries. He studied the Bible in original Greek and Hebrew and liked some of the precepts contained in it. He wrote a small book *The Precepts of Jesus; the Guide to Peace and Happiness* in Bengali and Sanskrit in 1820. It contained only the precepts and omitted other irrational concepts like Trinity (Father, Son and Holy Ghost) which brought upon him the ire of missionaries especially those of the Serampur Baptists. But his views were appreciated in Britain and America by liberal thinking people and he became famous for his learning, especially by the Unitarians, who also did not believe in Trinitarianism.

Rammohun Roy is generally known as a religious reformer, but he was a social reformer as well. Indeed, religious and social matters are so intermixed that it is difficult to determine where religion ends and social reform begins. This is especially true of *sati* which had been given a religious sanctity by selfish predators. The English initially, though horrified, did not want to interfere as the practice had religious overtones. Rammohun Roy published his first tract against *sati* in 1818, originally written in Bengali but later translated into English. A second essay on the subject was published in 1820. In these, Rammohun had proved that there was no sanctity for this horrible practice in the Vedas or *Manu Smriti*. Convinced of the argument, Governor General Lord William Bentinck passed a regulation in 1829 declaring the practice of *sati* as illegal, and declared that persons taking part in it were punishable in the criminal courts. It was a moral victory for Rammohun against the Hindu orthodoxy. Polygamy was rampant during the time of Rammohun. He wrote an essay on 'Rights of Females' as prescribed by the scriptures. Citing authorities, he revealed that a Hindu is not legally free to take any number of wives. However, he did not pursue the matter as vigorously as he did in the case of *sati* but the custom gradually died down, economic considerations being one of the reasons. He also advocated widow marriage but, as in the case of polygamy, did not hotly pursue the matter.

His contribution to Indian education is somewhat unique. Though a Sanskrit scholar of merit, he appealed to the Indians to study English so that they could learn the science, philosophy and literature of the West which had made them the leaders of the world. With the active cooperation of David Hare (who donated his land for the purpose) the Hindu College was established in 1817 in Calcutta, 'to spread English education among the natives of the country'. In a way, his views about English education were similar to those of the much maligned Thomas Babington Macaulay, the only difference being in the purpose of learning English. Rammohun also started an English school of his own in 1822.

His fight against idolatory and polytheism took a concrete shape when he established Brahmo Samaj in Calcutta on 20 August 1828. It was to be a cosmopolitan house of prayer without any idol. His fame as a religious and social reformer rests with the establishment of Brahmo Samaj. A house was built for it at Jorasanko, where it was shifted on 23 January 1830, and the first meeting was attended by five hundred Hindus. The main purpose of the Samaj was to revive monotheism in India on the basis of the Vedanta and Upanishads. He tried to reconcile individual reason with the ancient scriptures. The aim of his new church was described in the trust deed of 1830: "This new theism aimed at the calm worship of the Deity, the practice of virtue and charity, reverence for all that is sincere and helpful in every faith, and active participation in every movement for the bettering of mankind".[1] He looked upon idolatory as a degeneration from the pure monotheistic doctrine of Vedanta and the Upanishads. He also fought an extended battle with the Christian missionaries who were active in proselytizing Indians. The missionaries were already upset by his publishing *Precepts of Jesus* in which he had debunked the concept Trinity. Now they were faced with his opposition to conversion. Rammohun argued with the missionaries, quoting from the original Bible in Hebrew and Greek, baffling the ill-educated and dogmatic missionaries. He published three pamphlets: *'Appeal to the Christian Public'* one after another and finally, *'The Missionary and the Brahmin; Being a Vindication of the Hindoo Religion Against the Attacks of Christian Missionaries'*. His efforts to save Hinduism from the onslaught of Christian missionaries saved thousands of Hindus from being converted.

Through his writings and preachings Rammohun had was known all over the world. In all he had written two books in Persian, three in Hindi, thirty-two in Bengali and Sanskrit and forty-seven tracts and books in English. Rammohun also tried his hand at journalism. He started *Mira-tul-Akhbar* (1820) in Persian and *Sambad Kaumudi* (1826) in Bengali. However, none of these survived for long. But he fought for the freedom of the press and launched a spirited protest against the Press Ordinance of 1823. His chance to go abroad came in 1830 when the phantom Emperor Akbar II asked him to go to England to represent his case for the restoration of his authority on some villages around Delhi, and bestowed the title 'Raja' on him. Rammohun also wanted to plead with the people and the parliament not to accept the petition filed by orthodox Hindus in the Prime Council for the repeal of the ordinance passed by the Indian government declaring *sati* as a criminal act. Besides, he wanted to appear before the Select Committee of the House of Commons.

He left for England on 19 November 1830 and reached Liverpool on 8 April 1831. His name and fame had preceded him. His personality added to his scholarship, wisdom and concern for social upliftment. "The stately figure of Rammohun caught the eye of king and commoner alike. The Raja, in the outer man, was caste in nature's finest mould; his figure was manly and robust; his carriage dignified; the forhead towering, expansive and commanding. To ladies his politeness was marked by most delicate manner, and his felicitous mode of paying them a compliment gained him many admirers among the high-born beauties of Britain. In conversation with individuals of every rank and of various nations and professions, he passed with the utmost ease from one language to another, suiting his remarks to each and all in excellent taste, and commanding the astonishment and respect of his hearers".[2] The Unitarians awaited the arrival of the 'Apostle of the East' with eager anticipation. A meeting was arranged in his honour. After staying for a few days at Liverpool, he left for London.

An intellectual celebrity who called on him the very first night of his arrival in London was the venerable philosopher Jeremy Bentham. Another celebrated Londoner whom Rammohun engaged in discussion was Robert Owen, 'The father of British Socialism'. There was a steady stream of visitors at 125 Regent Street where Rammohun was staying and a 'constant state of excitement drove him to a state of exhaustion'. The highest honour paid to Rammohun was his presentation to the King of England, making him the first Indian to be received at the British Court. In 1832, he visited France and was received there by King Louis Phillippe. He returned to England after a few days. He was happy to see the petition against the abolition of *sati* being rejected, and passing of the India Bill by the House of Commons in 1833. The same year at the invitation of Dr. Carpenter he went to live at Bristol and soon after died of fever there on 27 September 1833 with the sacred syllable 'Om' on his lips; sacred thread of the Brahmins was also found on his body.[3] In spite of his criticism of the evils which had crept in Hindu society he was proud to be a Hindu. Rammohun was buried at Stapleton Grove. But later Dwarkanath Tagore, his disciple and companion made a pilgrimage to Bristol and built a beautiful mausoleum in the cemetery Arno's Vale. The mausoleum is shaped like a Hindu temple carrying the following description:

> Beneath this stone rests the remains of Raja Rammohun Roy Bahadoor. A conscientious and steadfast believer in the unity of the Godhead; He consecrated his life with entire devotion to the worship of the Divine Spirit alone. To great natural talents he united thorough mastery of many languages, and early distinguished himself as one of the greatest scholars of his day. His unwearied labours to promote the social, moral and physical condition of the people of India, his earnest endeavours to suppress idolatry and the rite to *suttee*, and his constant zealous advocacy of whatever tended to advance the glory of God and the welfare of man, live in the grateful remembrance of his countrymen. This tablet records the sorrow and pride with which his memory is cherished by his descendants. He was born in Radhanagore, in Bengal, in 1774, and died at Bristol, September 27th, 1833.[4]

Was Rammohun really the harbinger of renaissance in the country, especially in Bengal? Scholars have recently cast doubt on the advent of renaissance in India in the nineteenth century. There is nothing comparable to the renaissance of the fourteenth-seventeenth century of Europe. Rammohun seems to have succeeded only partially in what he tried to do through his writings and Brahmo Samaj. While *sati* and polygamy have been abolished, idolatory and even child marriage (though outlawed) are still rampant in the country. Idolatory has indeed increased manifold since the time of Rammohun. Even Dayanand, who later fought the idolators more vigorously, could not succeed. Miles long queues of worshippers, hoping to have a glimpse of the deity at the Tirupati temple in the south and Vaishno Devi in the north are ample proof of the failure of Rammohun in eradicating idolatory — the main plank of the Brahmo Samaj. When the 200th anniversary of the birth of Rammohun was celebrated in 1972, there was a growing disillusionment over the prospects of modernization, and frustrated scholars, unable to perpetuate the heroic view of history held by their forbears, challenged the so-called myth of the "Renaissance and "Rammohun's role in it as a moderniser".[5] This has been the fate of most of the reformers the world over in every age.

## References

1. Bucland, E.C. *Dictionary of Indian Biography*, 2 Vols. Reprint, New Delhi, Cosmo, 1999, Vol. 2, pp.366-67.
2. Martin, Robert Montgomery. *Court Journal*, October 5, 1833, quoted by Sophia Collet in *The Life and Letters of Rammohun Roy*, Calcutta, Sadharan Brahmo Samaj, 1962, p.324.
3. Crawford, S. Cromwell. *Rammohun Roy; His Era and Ethics*, New Delhi, Arnold Heinemann, 1984, p.168.
4. Ibid. p.171.
5. Ibid. Preface.

# Swami Sahajanand Saraswati

## (1889-1950)

Sahajanand was born in 1889 in the village Deva near Ghazipur, Uttar Pradesh, in a respectable peasant Bhumihar family, a caste which is found only in Bihar and eastern Uttar Pradesh. He was the youngest among four sons of Beni Rai, and was given the name Navrang Rai. His mother died when he was barely three years old. The responsibility of bringing up the children thus fell on Beni Rai. Navrang Rai's education started rather late in a *madarasa* in Jalalabad, when he was ten years old. But being an intelligent and studious child, he did very well in school and completed the lower and upper primary school education in three years, instead of the usual six. Two years later, in 1904, he passed the Middle School examination, standing sixth in the merit list in the entire province, getting a scholarship of rupees five per month. The scholarship enabled him to get admission in a German Missionary School (now known as Government City Inter College, Ghazipur), for English education. He passed the English Middle School examination in 1906. Before that he was married in 1905. Unfortunately, his wife died the following year. This brought a complete transformation in Navrang Rai's life. To avoid a second marriage, which his father was planning for him, he left home without informing any one. He went to Varanasi (Kashi). There he decided to become a sanyasi (ascetic) and was initiated by Swami Achyutanand Saraswati, who changed his name from Navrang Rai to Swami Sahajanand.

This was in 1907. During 1908, he visited several religious places in India. Coming back to Kashi next year, he was initiated by a *Dandi Swami*, Advaitanand Saraswati, resulting in the addition of Saraswati to his name. Henceforth, he was known as Swami Sahajanand Saraswati. He spent the following three years studying Sanskrit grammar, Hindu philosophy Vedanta and yoga. By that time he had lost contact with his family members, including his father.

It did not come as a surprise to those who knew Navrang Rai from childhood that he became a sanyasi, because from his early years he was a practitioner of meditation. In spite of his good physique he never took part in sports and games. Thus "Swami Sahajanand Saraswati had the makings of a sanyasi from his early childhood. The death of his mother and wife created a feeling of detachment and loneliness in him. Meditative and intrepid by nature, he was abstinent and austere in his habits and living. He would sit for hours together under a banyan tree and very often visited temples in and around his village".[1]

During his stay in Varanasi, he was not treated equal to Brahmins in spite of his knowledge of Sanskrit and the *shastras*. This hurt him. He remembered that his ancestors were Jujhutia Brahmins who had come from Bundelkhand, and settled near Ghazipur. They had married among Bhumihars and thus had a right to call themselves Bhumihar Brahmins. For almost ten years he worked for the Bhumihar-Brahmin movement, with the object of socially upgrading the Bhumihars to the status of Brahmins. He wrote two books on this topic, *Bhumihar Brahmin Prichay* and *Brahmin Samaj ki Stithi* (condition of Brahmin society) in Hindi. He also published and edited a Hindi magazine called *Bhumihar Brahmin* during 1915-16. He organized and led the Bhumihar Brahmin Mahasabha in Bihar and Uttar Pradesh.

In 1920, he happened to meet Gandhi in Patna and discussed various political issues with him. He soon realized that he was wasting his time for the upliftment of his caste while a great battle was being fought under the leadership of Gandhi to free the country from foreign rule. Sahajanand joined the Non-Cooperation movement which was then in progress. He developed into a true patriot and a militant nationalist while still wearing the ochre coloured robes of a swami. He took leading part in organizing the Non-Cooperation movement in Shahabad district of Bihar and the adjoining district of Ghazipur. In 1921, he was elected president of the Ghazipur district Congress. In that capacity he toured the countryside, rousing the public to participate fearlessly in the Non-Cooperation movement. He attended the 1921 session of the Congress at Ahmedabad and was arrested after his return (1922) and was sentenced to one year rigorous imprisonment.

After being released from prison, he continued to be a member of the Congress and participated in various activities sponsored by the Congress party especially the khadi work. But a few incidents witnessed by him soon after, changed his life. He has described these incidents in his autobiography *Mera Jeevan Sangharsh* (1942). He saw a dead farm labourer wearing only a loin-cloth in Bihar's winter, resulting in his premature death. In another case, he saw a farmer's family so poor that they could not buy enough wood to cremate their son. These and other pathetic scenes which Sahajanand witnessed compelled him to study the causes of the deplorable condition of those hardworking, simple and innocent people — small farmers and landless labourers. Sahajanand travelled on foot from village to village, shared their huts to spend the night, discussed with them their plight and concluded that the zamindari (absentee landlordism) system was the main cause of their poverty and all the concomitant ills. He found that while the zamindars wasted huge sums of money on drinking, prostitutes and living in ugly ostentation, they exploited the poor labourers and small farmers through forced labour, illegal exactions, fraudulent evictions and other methods of feudal oppression. Sahajanand vowed that during the rest of his life he would work for the emancipation of these *kisans* (farmers), the poorest of the poor. "Our holimen in their selfishness pray and meditate in seclusion for their own salvation, but I will work for the salvation of the kisan while still remaining a sanyasi". And so he did for the next thirty years of his life. He worked on two fronts: abolition of the zamindari system and uniting and organising the *kisans* through the Kisan Sabha movement. "From 1928 to the end of his life he fought relentlessly for the emancipation of the poor peasantry from feudal oppression, as an integral part of the freedom movement. He travelled throughout Bihar and eastern Uttar

Pradesh exhorting the peasants to get organized under the banner of Kisan Sabha and not to yield to the atrocities unleashed by the feudal lords. He came into conflict with the zamindars but his attire of a swami saved him and even elicited respect from some zamindars who promised him that they would not be unduly harsh to the peasants working for them. But not much was achieved through personal contacts with the zamindars. The solution lay, he believed, in organizing the farmers through Kisan Sabha. He founded the first Kisan Sabha in 1927. In 1928, he organized the West Patna Kisan Sabha 'as a fighting organ of the Kisan movement'. Soon, the Kisan Sabha spread to other parts of Bihar, culminating in the Bihar Provincial Kisan Sabha in 1929 under his leadership at Sonpur. By now, he had emerged as the undisputed leader of the peasantry in Bihar and had a considerable following. When under the auspices of the Congress and the Congress Socialist Party, the All India Kisan Sabha was formed at Lucknow, he was elected president of the first session. Later, he worked as secretary of this organization. In that session a manifesto was also issued wherein it was declared that the object of the Kisan Movement was to secure complete freedom from economic exploitation and the achievement of full economic and political power for the peasants and workers and other exploited classes. "The manifesto enumerated the minimum demands of the peasants as abolition of zamindari, cancellation of all arears of rent and revenue, reduction of rent and revenue by at least fifty percent, right of permanent cultivation for the peasants, minimum wage for agricultural workers".[2] This was a great triumph for Swami Sahajanand. As secretary of the Sabha he toured several parts of the country explaining the objectives of the Kisan Sabha. Sahajanand was a powerful speaker having a dynamic personality. He had become an all-India figure.

When in 1937, Congress ministries were formed in several provinces, including Bihar and Uttar Pradesh, there was hope that the Congress ministries would take some concrete steps to ameliorate the condition of the farmers and landless labourers. But all that the Congress governments did was to ease a few of more iniquitous burdens that the peasant was made to bear. But his condition was so miserable that the remaining burdens were proving irksome and heavy. What was needed were some revolutionary steps. Sahajanand was greatly disappointed with the attitude of the Congress leadership including that of Gandhi who had said earlier, that, "the kisan movement must be confined to the improvement of the status of the kisans and the betterment of the relations between the zamindars and them. The kisans must be advised scrupulously to abide by the agreement with the zamindars, whether the agreement is written or inferred from custom".[3] Obviously Gandhi was ignorant about the condition of peasants working for the cruel feudal lords, the zamindars, and the atrocities inflicted by them. When Subhas Chandra Bose became the president of the Congress (1938) he took great interest in the Kisan Sabha movement and Sahajanand came very close to Subhas Babu. When Subhas Bose was expelled from the Congress on the advice of Gandhi, Sahajanand was with Bose wherever the latter went to put up his point of view of the masses. When Bose visited Bihar, Sahajanand was the president of the Reception Committee at Patna where Subhas Bose had to speak. To the surprise of everyone "there was a black flag demonstration against Subhas' visit (September 1939). There was stone-throwing and hurling of shoes by the followers of Gandhi resulting in the injuries to Swami Sahajanand and others".[4] After such incidents and the lukewarm attitude of the Congress leaders towards emancipation of kisans, Swami Sahajanand left the Congress and became a Marxist. He came to believe that violent class-struggle was the only solution for improving the condition of the farmers. However, after the Comilla Conference (1938), the Leftists began to dominate the peasant movement and a little later started considering the Kisan Sabha as a subsidiary of the Communist Party of India. Sahajanand, along with Indulal Yajnik, resigned from the All India Kisan Sabha in 1945. Sahajanand, Yajnik, Rahul Sankritayan and others wanted Kisan Sabha to have an independent existence and not as an adjunct of any political party. Sahajanand started a weekly, *Hunkar*, from Patna to propagate his views. He wrote a number of books and pamphlets mostly on peasant problems: *Kisan Sabha ke Sansmran* (reminiscences of Kisan Sabha); *How the Kisan Fight; Gaya ke Kisan ki Karun Kahani;* (Tragic Story of Gaya's kisans); *Mera Jivan Sangharsh* (My Life's Struggle); *Kranti aur Sanyukt Morcha* (Revolution and the United Front). It was due to the efforts of Swami Sahajanand and the Kisan Sabha that zamindari was abolished by law in 1952 in Uttar Pradesh and Bihar.

He died of high blood pressure on 26 June 1950 at Muzaffarpur, Bihar. To this day 26 June is celebrated as Swami Sahajanand day in some parts of Bihar and Uttar Pradesh. There is a college, Sahajanand Vidyapith in Ghazipur and a small library-cum-museum in his native village Deva, where works by and on him are preserved along with his mementoes and photographs. He has done more for the abolition of zamindari and emancipation of poor farmers than any other political leader or social reformer.

# References

1. Sharma, Yogendra. *Sahajanand Saraswati*, Calcutta, *Dictionary of National Biography* ed. by S.P. Sen, Vol. IV, 1974.
2. Chowdhuri, Satyabrata Rai. *Leftist Movements in India; 1917-1947*. Calcutta, Minerva Associates, 1976, p.214.
3. *Collected Works of Mahatma Gandhi*, Vol.20, pp.105-6.
4. Ibid Vol. 70, p.150.

# V.S. Srinivasa Sastri

## (1869-1946)

Srinivasa Sastri was born on 22 September 1869 in a village near Kumbakonam in the Madras state. His parents, V. Sankaranarayana and Valambal Ammal, were poor. His father was a village priest and a Sanskrit scholar; scholarship which was inherited by his son. Sastri was the third of six children of his parents.

Sastri started his education in the Native High School, Kumbakonam, from where he passed the matriculation examination in 1883. He was a brilliant student and got a scholarship which enabled him to pursue higher education. He graduated in 1888, standing second in the Madras Presidency. He joined the Teachers Training College, Madras in 1891 after serving a couple of years as a teacher in Municipal High School, Mayavaram. Trained as a teacher, he joined Salem College as assistant teacher (1893-95) and then joined the Pachaiyappa's High School, Madras. In 1902, he became headmaster of the Hindu High School at Triplicane, Madras and earned laurels from both the students and administration. During this period he edited the *Education Review*, and also founded *Indian Review* with G. Natesan as editor.

He was married off by his parents when he was hardly fourteen years old, against his wishes, to Parvati Ammal who bore him a son, V.S. Sankaran. Parvati died in 1896 and Sastri was married a second time to Lakshmi Ammal in 1898. They had two daughters from this marriage and had a very happy married life for thirty-six years. Parvati died in 1934, when Sastri was sixty-five years old.

While he was working as headmaster in the Hindu High School, he came into contact with Gopal Krishna Gokhale. He was immediately drawn towards him; liked his views and demeanour and decided to follow him as a disciple. This proved to be a turning point in his life. He resigned as headmaster and joined as a full-time worker of the Servants of India Society, Poona, which was established by Gokhale in 1905. After the death of Gokhale in 1915, Sastri took over as the president of the society. In 1918, he started a weekly journal, *Servant of India*, the official organ of the Servants of India Society. It also served as a source of propaganda for the All-India Liberal Federation floated by the Moderates in 1918 after leaving the Congress party. The Moderates believed in India's emancipation through constitutional means and opposed agitation of any kind against the British government. The two leading Moderates who controlled the Congress party, Gokhale and Pherozeshah Mehta, died in 1915, passing on the leadership of the group to Surendranath Banerjee and Srinivasa Sastri.

Even before that, Sastri was the secretary of the Madras session (1908) of the Indian National Congress, being an active member of the party. He also played an important role, along with Motilal Nehru, Tilak and Jinnah in formulating the Lucknow Pact (1916) between the Congress and the Muslim League. He published *The Congress-League Scheme: An Exposition* (1917) to explain the details and implications of the Pact. He was very vocal in maintaining the British connection and wrote *Self-Government for India under the British Flag* in 1916, in which he argued that India could attain her highest political goal within the British Empire.

He had been nominated to the Madras Legislative Council in 1913 and was elected by it to the Imperial Legislative Council in 1915. The pro-government policy and statements issued by the Moderates helped them to become the favoured party. Their decision to try the implementation of the Montagu-Chelmsford Reforms in 1918, which had been rejected by the Congress, further endeared them to the government policy makers. Sastri, being the most eminent among the Moderates, was lionized. Responsibilities and honours came in quick succession.

He was elected to the Council of State (the upper chamber of the Legislature) in 1920. He was made member of the Imperial Council the following year (1921). The same year he was selected as a delegate of the Government of India to the Imperial Conference, London, where he succeeded in securing the passage of his resolution that British subjects of Indian origin, lawfully settled in the British Dominions, should not be denied political franchise. In 1922, Sastri attended the Limitation of Naval Armaments Conference held in Washington, D.C., U.S.A. as head of the Indian delegation, thus enhancing India's prestige in international circles, though India was still a subject nation.

Sastri did commendable work for the Indian diaspora settled in British colonies like South Africa, East Africa (Kenya, Uganda, Tanganika), Malaya and the dominions more than any Indian had done before or since. He undertook a tour of the dominions (Canada, Australia and New Zealand) in 1922 as a representative of India, to plead with their respective governments for equality of citizenship for Indians settled in those countries. In 1926, he went to South Africa as a member of a delegation headed by Habibullah and in 1927 he took active part as a delegate to the First Round Table Conference between India and South Africa, resulting in Cape Town Agreement which compelled the South African government to withdraw the Areas Reservation and Immigration Bill to segregate Indians. It was Sastri again whom the Government of India sent to South Africa as agent-general to implement the Cape Town Agreement. In that role he strove hard in removing the hostility of the whites towards Indians settled there and creating better relations between the two races, though the policy of apartheid continued when Sastri left South Africa after one-and-a-half years. During his stay, Sastri managed to obtain permission to build a school for Indians in Natal, to the jubilation of Indians residing there.

In 1929, Sastri was sent on deputation to East Africa for implementation of the proposals for closer union between Kenya, Uganda and Tanganyika, but there he was received with hostility and minimum courtesy was shown to him by the local Indians in Mombasa, and was called a 'Kings Man'. He was even condemned in a meeting of Indians in Nairobi on 7 April 1929.[1] In 1931, he gave evidence before the Joint Select Committee of

British Parliament on Closer Union of the East African colonies. In 1936, he was deputed by the Government of India to Malaya to enquire into the condition of Indian labour there. He submitted a detailed report about his findings. He was a member of the Second Round Table Conference between India and South Africa in 1932, when the Cape Town Agreement was renewed with some changes.

He was a nominated member of the Round Table Conferences between India and England in 1930 and 1931 to evolve a new constitution for India. He was critical of the role played by Gandhi in the Second Round Table Conference in 1931.

In 1935, Sastri came back to his first love — education — when he accepted the vice-chancellorship of the Annamalai University, the post he held for two terms (1935-40). "In the University his name remains adored, his oratory remembered. A rich library and a magnificent auditorium remains as homage to V.S. Srinivasa Sastri".

In his *Autobiography* Nehru devotes several pages to Sastri and is highly critical of his role as a 'Moderate', showing the importance of Sastri as a Liberal or 'Moderate' leader. Before passing the 1935 Act finally, the British government had issued a 'White Paper' to gauge the Indian opinion. Nehru writes, 'At the Liberal Federation meeting held in Calcutta in April, 1933, Mr. Srinivasa Sastri, the most eminent of the Liberal leaders, pleaded that however unsatisfactory the constitutional changes might be they should work them. "This is no time to stand by and let things pass,' he said. The only action that apparently was conceivable to him was to accept what was given and to try to work it. "Mr. Sastri is always eloquent, and has orator's love of fine words and their musical use. But he is apt to be carried away by his enthusiasm and the word magic that he creates, blurs his meaning to others and perhaps to himself". Nehru concludes that Sastri's advice to the Indians is, "Whatever happens, however we might be insulted, crushed, humiliated and exploited by the British Government, we must submit to it. A worm may turn, but not the Indian people if they followed Mr. Sastri's advice. It struck me how extraordinarily similar was Mr. Sastri's outlook in regard to Britain and India to that of the 'diehard' British Conservative when he (Sastri) in one of his speeches in 1933 pointed 'the danger in India if British influence were suddenly withdrawn.' Mr. Winston Churchill could have expressed himself in identical language without doing any violence to his convictions".[2]

Sastri's relations with Gandhi were on a different footing which could easily be termed as 'love and hate' relationship. Sastri was only ten days older than Gandhi but the latter considered him as an elder brother. Gandhi also addressed him as 'Gurubandhu' in his letters as both of them had declared Gokhale as their *guru*. They were poles apart in their political thinking but that did not affect their personal regard for each other. It was under the advice of Sastri that Gandhi's application for membership of the Servants of India Society was rejected in 1915. Sastri was critical of Gandhi's fad for khadi, village work and Hindu-Muslim unity. Regarding khadi, Sastri had said, "It is an illegitimate imposition in an organization purporting to comprehend all progressive politicians". Sastri was against the Non-Cooperation movement which Gandhi launched in 1920 promising the country freedom in one year. In speech after speech Sastri criticized Gandhi and his Non-Cooperation movement. And in almost every city where he spoke, the followers of Gandhi hooted him and did not let him finish his speech. This happened in Pune, Bombay and even in Kumbakonam, Sastri's native place. However, Sastri was not the only leader who met this treatment at the hands of the 'Gandhi Brigade'. B.C. Pal, Annie Besant and Jinnah were some of the respected leaders who were hooted out by the intolerant Gandhites.

Regarding Hindu-Muslim unity, Sastri was highly critical of Gandhi for his appeasement of the Muslims. At the time of Kohat (Punjab) riots when Gandhi did not openly condemn the Muslims for the atrocities against the Hindus and Lala Lajpat Rai did, Sastri defended Lala Lajpat Rai and criticized Gandhi for his Utopian outlook. In one of his letters to his friend Sivaswami Aiyer, Sastri wrote that: "the Constitution of the Congress (which was framed by Gandhi) has given a practical veto to Muslims, which cannot lead but to the enthronement of the Mohammedan community in a position of indisputable advantage".

Gandhi knew his power and his hold on the masses and was not perturbed by such criticism. They continued to be friends in spite of serious political differences. Sastri knew in 1946 that it was only Gandhi who could avoid the partition of India. From his deathbed in the General Hospital,

Madras, Sastri dictated a letter to Gandhi: "Rajaji is not sound in this matter. Do not let him lead you again (referring to Rajaji Formula). The Punjab and Bengal would be ruined and blast your memory, if you give them up. Do not let any part of India go out and become independent. It is bound to be a lasting enemy and a blistering sore of India". Prophetic words these!

Like a true friend, Gandhi visited General Hospital, Madras, where Sastri was awaiting death, on 22 January and again on 30 January 1946. Sastri passed away on 17 April 1946. Gandhi did not write an obituary in the *Harijan*, as was customary with him. He wrote only a brief note: "Death has removed not only from us but from the world one of India's best sons. That he loved India passionately, everyone who knew him could see. His Sanskrit learning was as great, if not greater, than his English. I must not permit myself to say more, save this that though we differed in politics, our hearts were one and I could never think that his patriotism was less than that of the tallest patriot".[3]

Sastri wore the conventional dhoti, closed coat, turban and slippers. The most conspicuous part of his dress, of course, was his white turban 'which gracefully poised above his serene head'. Like Nehru, he switched to a suit and a pair of shoes while in foreign lands, but he felt comfortable only in his native out fit.

Sastri wrote several books and tracts: *Self Government for India Under the British Flag* (1916); *Congress-League Scheme an Exposition* (1917); *Life and Times of Sir Pherozeshah Mehta; Life of Gopal Krishna Gokhale; My Master Gokhale; Lecture on the Ramayana; Future of Indian States; Rights and Status of Women in India*. T.N. Jagadisan has compiled a few books containing the speeches and writings of Sastri.

In the preface to his biography of Sastri, T.N. Jagadisan writes: "He was one of the first of our great men to raise India's esteem in the world by his unsurpassed eloquence, his noble bearing, his serene wisdom and generous understanding of the other man's point of view. He was looked upon as a scholar-statesman. Like Gokhale and Gandhi, he did the service of spiritualizing politics by bringing into practice the highest moral values. Sastri had the temper that gives him the strength to renounce approbation and reject the fear of being called weak. He belonged to the galaxy of the founders of India's freedom".

# References

1.  Kondanda Rao, V. *The Right Honourable V.S. Srinivasa Sastri, A Political Biography*, Bombay, Asia Publishing House, 1963, p.275.
2.  Nehru, Jawaharlal. *An Autobiography*, New Delhi, Jawaharlal Nehru Memorial Fund, 1936, pp.389-91.
3.  *Collected Works of Mahatma Gandhi*, Vol. 84, p.19.

# Vinayak Damodar Savarkar

## (1883-1966)

Savarkar was undoubtedly one of India's greatest freedom fighters. He was a born revolutionary and defender of Hindu faith. Not only he, but his entire family suffered at the hands of the British government and he and his brother Ganesh spent eleven years in solitary confinement in the cellular jail in the Andamans. Only by sheer will-power could they survive. Valentine Chirol, the notorious correspondent of *London Times*, described him as "the most brilliant of modern Indian revolutionaries".

Vinayak Damodar Savarkar was born on 28 May 1883 in a middle-class Chitpawan Brahmin family in the village of Bhagur near Nasik, Maharashtra. His ancestors had come from Savar-wadi in Ratnagiri district; hence the surname Savarkar adopted by the family. His parents, Damodarpant and Radhabai, had four children, three sons — Ganesh (Babarao), Vinayak and Narayan — and daughter Mainabai. Vinayak passed the Marathi fourth standard at the age of ten. To continue his studies he had to be sent to Nasik but this was not possible for another two years. His mother had died when Vinayak was nine years old and the responsibility of bringing up the children had fallen on their father Damodarpant. But during this period Vinayak completed the course of the first two English standards at home. He also acquired the habit of reading books and newspapers, something which he continued throughout his life. He joined Shivaji High School in Nasik in 1895 and passed the matriculation examination in 1901. Before that Vinayak was married of in March 1901 to Yamunabai, daughter of an old family friend, R.T. Chiplunkar, a minister in a small state Jawahar, near Nasik.

Vinayak exhibited his talent for writing, especially poetry, at a very young age. He had begun to compose poems when he was barely ten years old. He also could write good prose and won prizes for his essays, one of which was '*Who Was the Best of the Peshwas?*' Vinayak was also a powerful speaker and won prizes in elocution contests in school. The closing years of the nineteenth century saw great turmoil in Maharashtra. Ganpati and Shivaji festivals, inaugurated by Lokmanya Tilak, had brought a new nationalist consciousness among the masses. The murder, in 1897, of Mr. Rand, the plague officer of Poona, by Chapekar brothers, who went to the gallows reciting verses from the *Gita*, stirred young Vinayak's mind and he vowed to do something like the Chapekar brothers for his country. During the plague epidemic, Vinayak, with his small band of friends, did social work for the families of the deceased. To his horror he saw his father and uncle die during the epidemic. Undaunted by the tragedy, he started organizing an association with a small nucleus of friends and named it 'Mitra Mela'.

In 1902, Savarkar joined Fergusson College, Poona and started living in the residency. He made an instant impact in the college with 'his striking personality and natural qualities of leadership'. He collected around him a small group of students with similar views and aspirations. Soon, his group dominated the goings-on in the college campus. They started a handwritten magazine, *Arya Weekly* which included articles by Savarkar and his colleagues. During vacations he would visit several places in Maharashtra and deliver patriotic speeches. The partition of Bengal in 1905 had stirred up nationalistic feelings not only in Bengal but also in other parts of the country. The movement started against the partition had come to be known as *swadeshi* movement. Taking a hint from this movement, Savarkar and his group organized a big bonfire of foreign clothes and other articles of foreign origin. The gathering was addressed by Tilak, Paranjpe and the young Savarkar. The college authorities, however, did not take kindly to this audacious act of Savarkar, fined him ten rupees and expelled him from the residency of the College but allowed him to study. Bombay University allowed him to appear in the B.A. Examination and he graduated in 1905. After graduating, Savarkar toured extensively in Maharashtra, opening branches of 'Mitra Mela'. After opening several branches, he organized a conference of the members of 'Mitra Mela'. In his address he brought out the essential features of the organization and changed its name to 'Abhinav Bharat', after Mazzini's 'Young Italy'. The object of this society was the political independence of India, if need be by armed revolt. The society spread its network throughout India and overseas too. "It has been said that poets, speakers, propagandists, patriots and martyrs were produced by Mitra Mela and Abhinav Bharat in scores".[1]

In a short span of time Savarkar became quite popular in Maharashtra. His 'rousing oratory', often conveyed in inspiring verse, attracted hundreds of young men who became his followers. He went to Bombay to study law and continued his anti-government activities there. But he had to suspend his activities because he was offered a scholarship by Shyamji Krishnavarma, an Indian patriot who was residing in London and working for the Indian cause there. Savarkar left for England in June 1906. He decided to study law there. "The study of law", he remarked, "shows the vital points in the system of government, and its lacunae where to strike." Shyamji Krishnavarma had established the India House in London for Indian students and Savarkar started living there. He was admitted to Gray's Inn to qualify as a barrister. But his urge to free India of foreign rule was unabated. He founded the 'Free India Society' to recruit young men for Abhinav Bharat. "His spirited style, erudition, the force of his arguments and his passionate sincerity soon enabled him to carry the youthful and impressionable student-world with him. The Indian students at Cambridge, Oxford, Edinburgh, Manchester and other places were rapidly brought under the influence of the revolutionary tenets".[2] The group began to hold weekly meetings and celebrate Indian festivals like Dussehra and Diwali. In 1907, they observed the silver jubilee of the 1857 uprising. Later, while still in England he wrote a voluminous book titled *Indian War of Independence, 1857* which was proscribed by the government before publication in 1910. But a copy of it was smuggled out of India and was published by Hardayal in America, Sardar Bhagat Singh in Lahore and INA of Subhas Bose in Singapore. The book has been translated in many Indian languages besides French and German. During his sojourn at the India House, he also translated Mazzini's *Autobiography* into Marathi, with a detailed introduction. Savarkar and his group published pamphlets conveying the message of Abhinav Bharat. They even got hold of a bomb-making manual and its cyclostyled copies were sent secretly to India. Savarkar used to write articles for *Indian Socialist*, edited by Shyamji Krishnavarma, which were translated and published in the *Yuganter* of Calcutta and *Vihari* of Bombay.

By that time, the India House had become notorious as a centre of seditious activities. In 1907, a question was asked in the House of Commons enquiring whether the government proposed to take any action against Shyamji. Though no action was taken, Shyamji thought it prudent to leave England and settle in Paris. Sardar Singh Rana, who was the manager of India House, also left along with Shyamji. Madan Cama had already left and had settled in Paris. Now Savarkar was entrusted with the management of the India House. On 1 July 1909, Madan Lal Dhingra, an ardent follower of Savarkar, shot dead Sir Curzon Wylie, ADC of the secretary of state for India. This shocked not only the British but also Indians living in England. A meeting called by the Indians passed a resolution to condemn the killing but Savarkar stood up to oppose the resolution. This rather rash act of Savarkar further infuriated the government. Sensing trouble, Savarkar left for Paris, closing down the India House. In India, his elder brother Ganesh (Babarao) was arrested in connection with the Nasik Conspiracy Case and was sent for transportation for life to the Andamans. Savarkar's family was also being harassed and their property was confiscated. But all this did not deter Savarkar from pursuing revolutionary activities. Although Savarkar qualified from Gray's Inn, he was not called to the Bar because he refused to pledge loyalty to the Crown.

In Paris, he had moved to Madam Cama's residence, who had earlier left England and had settled in Paris to continue revolutionary activities. At the Jackson murder trial in India, Savarkar was charged with abetting the crime, because it was India House from where the gun, which was responsible for the murder, was sent. A warrant was issued against him. On his return to England, he was arrested, on 13 March 1910. 'Savarkar should be sent to India' was the verdict of the Court. On 1 July the ship S.S. *Morea* sailed for India with Savarkar as the heavily guarded prisoner. In spite of that, he jumped from the ship through a porthole in the lavatory when the ship docked at the French port Marseilles and swam five hundred metres to the shore. He was now in French territory and had a right to asylum. But he was arrested by the British guards of the ship who chased him; brought him back to the ship; put him in chains, and sailed again for India. Shyamji, S.S. Rana and Madam Cama later protested to the French authorities because Savarkar was arrested on French soil by the British in violation of international law. Consequently, the case was referred to the International Arbitration Tribunal at The Hague. The case made headlines in Indian and world press. For the first time, Indian's fight for freedom was discussed all over the world. The trial opened on 16 February 1911 and though expected to last for a month, was wound up after few hurried sittings under British pressure. Nothing came out of the case.[3]

Back in India, Savarkar was not tried in a regular court but by a Special Tribunal, denying him the right of appeal. He was sentenced to transportation for life twice over, which meant fifty years in jail. His property was confiscated. He was sent to the Andaman Cellular jail in chains where his brother Ganesh was already incarcerated undergoing a similar sentence. They were allowed one visitor and could write one letter in a year. He was put on hard labour and spent days and nights in solitary confinement. He spent his time composing poetry and memorizing it. After sometime, when he was allowed to go out, though still in chains, he taught Hindi to the prisoners, many of whom were hardened criminals. The two brothers were joined there by another highly respected freedom fighter, Bhai Parmanand in 1915. He kept them company till 1920, when he was released.

After the World War there was a clamour for the release of political prisoners. The Montford Reforms came into force in 1919 and many prisoners were released. But not the Savarkar brothers. Pressure was brought on Gandhi to do something for their release. Gandhi wrote in *Young India* (18.5.1921) under his column 'Notes': "I had the pleasure of meeting him (Savarkar) in London (in 1909). He is brave. He is clever. He is a patriot.

He was frankly a revolutionary. The evil in its hideous form of the present system of Government, he saw much earlier than I did. He is in the Andamans for his having loved India too well. Under a just Government, he would be occupying a high office".[4] Ultimately Savarkar was brought to the Indian mainland on 2 May 1921, not to be released but to continue his sentence in Ratnagiri jail. There he wrote his much controversial book, *Hindutva* under the pseudonym 'Mahratta'. From Ratnagiri, Savarkar was transferred to Yeravada Jail. He was released on 6 January 1924 on the condition that he would not indulge in any political activity, and would remain in Ratnagiri. Sarvarkar used his stay in Ratnagiri to do social and religious reforms like preaching against the caste system, untouchability, superstitions and other ills of the Hindu society. For that purpose he founded the Ratnagiri Hindu Sabha on 23 January 1924. His political restrictions were removed in 1937. He was only twenty-seven when he was sent to the Andman Cellular jail, and became a free man at the age of fifty-four. Even then he jumped into the political arena and was elected president of the Hindu Mahasabha for the 1937 Ahmedabad session. For five successive years he presided over the Hindu Mahasabha sessions. He believed in the Hindu *rashtra* where the rights of all minorities would be safeguarded. He was aghast at the Muslim appeasement policy of the Congress party. He wanted the Muslim community to join Hindus in their fight for freedom as equals. At the same time he told them: "if you come, with you; if you don't without you; if you oppose, in spite of you". The Congress party had to adopt this very policy in 1942 when they started the Quit India movement without Muslim support. But it was too late. The movement was crushed. Fortunately, the British came out a much weakened nation from the War. They wanted to get out of India. Freedom came along with partition. Savarkar was not a happy man. His dream of 'Akhand Bharat' (United India) was shattered.

During the war years, Savarkar and his followers did a great service to the nation by asking Hindus and Sikhs to join the army in large numbers so that when freedom came they could guard the frontiers of free India. None of the Congress leaders had that kind of vision, tied down as they were to the impractical 'non-violence creed'. The Indian army, which had seventy per cent Muslims in it at the start of the War had seventy per cent of Hindu and Sikhs by the time the War ended. Savarkar and his followers had toured the length and breadth of India prompting Hindus and Sikhs to join the army to achieve this miracle. In 1943, Poona University conferred on Savarkar D. Litt for his contribution to Marathi language and literature.

Savarkar's difficulties were not over even in free India, though he was now an old infirm man. The assassination of Gandhi on 30 January 1948 resulted in the mass arrests of Hindu Mahasabha and Rashtriya Swama Sevak Sangh (RSS) workers. Savarkar was not spared. He was arrested on 4 February 1948 on the charge of conspiring. Nathuram Godse, who had assassinated Gandhi, in his long statement to the court during the prosecution said, "I emphatically deny that we saw Savarkar on the 17 January 1948 or that Savarkar blessed us with the words, 'yashasvi houn ya (Be successful).'"[5] Savarkar was honourably acquitted on 10 February 1949.

The first part of his biography, *Mazya Athavani* (My Reminiscences), in Marathi, appeared in 1949. He came out of his retirement to inaugurate the Hindu Mahasabha session of December 1949 at Calcutta. Thousands of his followers cheered him. He was again arrested in April 1950 at the time of Nehru-Liaqat Ali Agreement. The final part of his autobiography was published in 1965.

He died on 27 February 1966, leaving behind a son, Vishwas and a daughter, Prabha.

Savarkar, besides writing on political topics, was a creative writer of some merit. His poems *Kamla* and *Saptarshi,* which he composed in Andaman Cellular jail, show his literary excellence. While at Ratnagiri he wrote two novels, *Kala Pani* and *Mopla Rebellion* and three dramas *Sanyasta Khadge, Usshap* and *Uttarkria,* all in Marathi. He also started a movement for Bhasha Shuddhi and improvement in Devanagari script. As a writer, he was asked to preside over the Marathi Literary Conference in 1938 at Poona. His last work, *Shatruchya Shibarat* (In the Enemy Camp), describes his experiences in England. His complete works in Marathi were published by Maharashtra Hindu Sabha in eight volumes, as *Samagra Savarkar.*

Honours came haltingly, grudgingly. A postal stamp was issued in memory of Savarkar during his centenary celebrations in 1983 by the

Government of India. A portrait of his was unveiled in the Indian Parliament House in March 2003 which invited some amount of criticism. A commemorative plaque hangs at the entrance of the India House, London. It reads 'Vinayak Damodar Savarkar, 1883-1966, Indian patriot and philosopher lived here'. In England, during the centenary celebrations function in the House of Commons Annexe, ninety-eight year old Labour M.P. Fenner Brockway revealed that: "All charges levelled against Savarkar by British Empire were completely baseless and fraudulent". And he added that "to have a patriot like Savarkar was a matter of great pride for any country".

## References

1. Majumdar, R.C. *History of the Freedom Movement in India*, Calcutta, Firma KLM, 1988, p.401.
2. Pradhan, G.P. *India's Freedom Struggle; An Epic of Sacrifice and Suffering*. Bombay, Popular Prakashan, 1990, p.49.
3. Agarwala, B.R. *Trials of Independence*, New Delhi. NBT 1991, p.86.
4. *Collected Works of Mahatma Gandhi* Vol. 20, pp.104-5.
5. Godse, Nathuram. *May it Please Your Honour*, New Delhi, Surya Bharati Prakashan, 1993, p.46.

# Keshab Chandra Sen

## (1838-1889)

Keshab Chandra Sen was the last of the trinity of the leaders of Brahmo Samaj after Rammohun Roy (1774-1933) and Debendranath Tagore (1817-1905). Throughout his adult life he worked as a social and religious reformer and toiled for spreading education among the masses, especially women. He was tall, handsome and had a magnetic personality. He was probably the most widely known man of his time in India, though his last days, like Bipin Chandra Pal and Surendranath Banerjee, were not happy ones.

Keshab Chandra Sen was born in Calcutta on 19 November 1838, in a family of kinsmen of Sena Rajas. His was a well-to-do family. His father, Peary Mohan, was dewan of the mint. He died when Keshab was only ten years old. Thus, his mother, Sarada Devi, moulded Keshab's character more than his father could. He passed his entrance examination from Hindu School, Calcutta, in 1953 and graduated from Hindu College in 1856. The same year, he was married to Jaganmohini Devi. He was not a good student and did not study further but had developed a taste for reading books by western as well as Indian authors. He worked in Bengal Bank for two years from 1859-61. After reading a tract on Brahmonism by Rajaram Bose he was attracted towards this theistic church and joined it in 1857, and devoted the rest of his life for the propagation of Brahmonism. After the death of Rammohun Roy in 1833,

Brahmo Samaj had become almost defunct but was revived by Debendranath Tagore in 1852 as Adi Brahmo Samaj. When Keshab Chandra joined the Brahmo Samaj, Debendranath was its head. The latter was impressed by the intellect and devotion of Keshab Chandra and appointed him as *acharya* or minister of the Samaj in 1862. The following year the title of 'Brahmananda' was conferred on him. As a Brahmo minister (clergyman) he visited Bombay and Madras, and lectured on Brahmonism. He was enthusiastically received wherever he went. He was gradually turning towards more radical views which were not acceptable to Debendranath. Keshab's advocacy for intercaste marriages, widow remarriage, abolition of caste distinctions including the wearing of sacred thread, and opposition to child marriage became the matter of dispute, and the two parted company.

Keshab Chandra established a separate Samaj in 1865, calling it 'Brahmo Samaj of India', which was formally inaugurated in a new building in 1869. Under the auspices of the newly founded Samaj, Keshab Chandra once again toured various parts of the country speaking to interested audiences. He was a powerful speaker and used his oratory skills to great effect. During his lecture tours he covered most of India and established branches of his version of the Samaj at various places including Punjab, N.W. Provinces (present Uttar Pradesh), Madras and Bombay. Due to his untiring efforts, his theistic church became an all-India organization and he became a national leader. When Swami Dayanand, the founder of Arya Samaj, visited Calcutta in 1872, he met Keshab Chandra and sought his advice on several organizational matters which proved to be a turning point in the life of Dayanand and that of the Arya Samaj.

Keshab Chandra's Brahmo Samaj was broad-based as it included social reform as an important element of its work, besides preaching religious reform like anti-idolatory. Among the items of social reform which he undertook almost single-handedly were inter-caste marriage, abolition of caste restrictions including untouchability, abolition of child marriage, and making people aware of the evils of drinking. Keshab Chandra visited the viceroy, Lord Lawrence, at Simla and developed a lasting friendship with him. He induced the viceroy to introduce a bill for legalizing Brahmo marriages (which were performed without complicated Hindu rituals). Consequently, the Brahmo Marriage Act was passed in 1872. Using the provisions of this Act, Keshab Chandra was able to perform nineteen Brahmo marriages, eight of them being inter-caste.

Keshab deliberately eschewed politics and he and his followers "openly proclaimed loyalty to the British Government as an article of faith". This no doubt endeared him to the British government and Keshab was lionized both in India and England. His lectures in the Town Hall, Calcutta, were attended by high British officials and businessmen. However, he did not hesitate to put before the British government problems faced by the people of this country especially during his stay in England.

In 1870, Keshab Chandra went to England and was enthusiastically received by the people there, especially by the Unitarians as they had done four decades earlier for Rammohun Roy when he visited that country. Keshab Chandra was in England for six months. He visited several towns in England and Scotland. He was introduced to Prime Minister Gladstone, Dean Stanley, John Stuart Mill and was received by Queen Victoria in a private audience. For fifteen days he stayed with Max Muller in Oxford. Max Muller writes: "When Keshab Chandra was staying with me at Oxford, I had a good opportunity of watching him. I always found him perfectly tranquil, even most in earnest, and all his opinions were clear and settled. He never claimed any merit for the sacrifices he had made, he rather smiled at what was past, and seldom complained of his opponents".[1]

One of his most famous speeches which he made in England was 'England's Duty to India', delivered on 24 May 1870 at the Metropolitan Tabernicle in which the ex-viceroy, Sir John Lawrence, presided. In spite of his admiration for the British rule, he was bold enough to point out the lacunae in their administration and how they could set them right.

Like Rammohun Roy earlier, Keshab Chandra came in contact with Christian missionaries early in life. While Rammohun was successful in standing up against their onslaught on Hindu religion, Keshab Chandra seemed to have succumbed to it. Among all the Brahmo leaders, Keshab Chandra came nearest to accepting Christian doctrines and theology. He delivered several lectures on Christ and Christianity, the most famous being *'Jesus Christ, Europe and Asia'*, which he delivered in 1866. But it would be wrong to say that he had been formally converted to Christianity and baptized.

His tragic downfall started when he married off his minor daughter, aged thirteen, in 1873 to the maharaja of Cooch Behar who was also a minor, violating all the tenets of the Brahmo Samaj. The marriage was performed according to traditional Hindu rites and not according to the Brahmo code. Keshab Chandra tried to justify his act by saying that he had done it according to 'Adesa' (Divine Command) but his followers were not convinced and a large number of them deserted him and formed a new body called 'Sadharan Brahmo Samaj'. It proclaimed as its objective, 'the realization of the grand ideal of Rammohun Roy, from which the Brahmo Samaj had greatly departed'. Sadharan Brahmo Samaj thus moved nearer to the original Brahmo Samaj of its founder Rammohun Roy. The repeated schisms in the Brahmo Samaj and its various incarnations did not leave a permanent impact on Indian society, not even in Bengal, where it is all but a forgotten body now.

Keshab Chandra had lectured more than he had written. Many of his lectures were published as tracts by the Brahmo Tract Society, Calcutta, a dozen of them in 1860 alone. Some of them are: *True Faith; New Samhita; Yoga–Objective and Subjective; The New Dispensation; Religion of Harmony*, all in English. The Bengali ones are: *Sangat; Brahmo Gitapanishad; Jivanveda; Meghotsab* and *Sadhu Samagam*. It may be added that unlike Rammohn who knew several languages, Keshab knew only Bengali and English.

Though Keshab Chandra did not write much, he compensated it by starting at least a dozen journals and newspapers. The first one was *Indian Mirror*, started as an English fortnightly in 1861 and converted into a daily in 1871, having perhaps the longest life among all his journalistic ventures. Others followed quickly: *Dharamatatta*, a monthly religious journal in 1864; *Bamabodhini Patrika* (1864); *Sulav Samachar* (1870); *Dharma Sadhan* (1872); *Sunday Mirror* (1873); *Balakhandu*, an illustrated children fortnightly in easy Bengali (1878); *Paricharika* (1880) and *New Dispensation* in 1881. Obviously Keshab was biting off more than he could chew. None of them, except perhaps *Indian Mirror* and *Sulav Samachar*, lasted for any length of time.

From 1881 he preached the 'New Dispensation' and moved away from Brahmo Samaj. Theism was replaced by mystical doctrines, claiming special divine inspiration for himself. Apparently he had lost his moorings. During the last two years of his life he suffered from nervous depression.[2] According to Max Muller, "the declining years of his life were years of intense suffering and full of many disappointments". He died on 8 January 1884, at the young age of forty-five. However, in spite of his early death and an unexpected tragic last years, he had achieved much for the nation and for the society. People still remembered him when he died. On Keshab's death, Henry Cotton, a high British official, remarked, "The death of Keshab Sen in January, 1884 was one of the earliest occasions for the manifestation of a truly national sentiment in the country. Men and women from all parts of India, irrespective of caste and creed, united with one voice in the expression of sorrow at his loss and pride in him as a member of one common nation".

# References

1. Max Muller, Friedvich. *Indian Friends*, First pub. OUP, 1899, Indian Reprint, New Delhi, Amrit Book Co. 1982, p.88.
2. Buckland, C.E. *Dictionary of Indian Biography*, London, 1910, Indian Reprint New Delhi, Cosmo, 1999.

# Lal Bahadur Shastri

## (1904-1966)

The diminutive Lal Bahadur, with an unimpressive personality and self-effacing and gentle personality, is remembered for his toughness and tenacity as the second prime minister of India during the 1965 war with Pakistan.

Lal Bahadur was born on 2 October 1904 at Mughalsarai, near Varanasi. His father, Sharda Prasad Srivastava, was a school teacher who later became a clerk in the Revenue Office at Allahabad. It was a lower middle-class family. Lal Bahadur was the youngest of the three children of his parents, the other two were girls. His father died when Lal Bahadur was only a year and-a-half. His mother moved to her parent's house in Mirzapur where Lal Bahadur lived till his tenth year.

After finishing his primary education in Mirzapur, he came to Varanasi for further studies and joined the Harish Chandra Vidyalaya. Here he became a favourite student of his teacher, Nishkameshwar Prasad Misra, who played an important role in moulding the character of his young pupil. When the Congress led by Gandhi started the Non-Cooperation movement in 1920 and asked students to forego studies, Lal Bahadur left the school. But when the movement was suspended in 1922, Lal Bahadur joined Kashi Vidyapith, a nationalist institution founded in 1921 in Varanasi. Here, Lal Bahadur saw stalwarts like Bhagwan Das, J.B. Kriplani, Sampurnanand, Acharya Narendra Dev, who were teachers in this infant institution. From there, Lal Bahadur graduated in 1925, getting the degree 'Shastri', thus acquiring the suffix Shastri with his name. As the Shastri degree was not recognised by the government, it was not easy for Lal Bahadur to find a job. He enrolled himself as a life member of Servants of the People Society founded by Lajpat Rai earlier. The main function of the society was to train nationalist missionaries whose duty was to work for educational and social upliftment of the people. Shastri was assigned to work for the upliftment of Harijans at Muzzaffarabad and Meerut. He worked there for two years. In 1928, Lal Bahadur was married to Lalitadevi, whose parents also lived in Mirzapur.

After the death of Lajpat Rai in 1928, Purushottam Das Tandon became the president of the Servants of People Society. Tandon became Lal Bahadur's first political guru and asked him to move to Allahabad. On the advice of Tandon, Shastri joined the Congress. His journey towards a political career had begun. At Allahabad, he came in close contact with Jawaharlal Nehru which propelled his political career with the passage of time. He was elected as secretary, and later president, of the Allahabad District Congress Committee. He moved one step higher by becoming general secretary of the U.P. Provincial Congress Committee (1935-1937). In 1937, Shastri was returned to the U.P. Legislative Assembly, and came in contact with Govind Ballabh Pant who became the first chief minister of Uttar Pradesh under the 1935 Act. Pant was to be a great influence on Shastri, next only to Nehru. Shastri became the secretary of the U.P. Parliamentary Board. When Gandhi started the individual Satyagraha in 1940, Shastri was selected as a satyagrahi by Gandhi and was imprisoned. Shastri went to jail thrice and spent nine years in various jails. In the 1946 elections, the Congress had won majority in several states including Uttar Pradesh. Pandit Pant had again become the chief minister of U.P. Pant had liked Shastri's unassuming and un-controversial nature, unlike most of the political workers in the Congress. Besides, he was very hard-working, sincere and honest. Pant asked Shastri to move to Lucknow in 1946 and made him his parliamentary secretary. In 1947, when India had become independent, a greater responsibility had fallen on the Congress ministries and Pant was looking for efficient and honest persons who would deliver the goods. Shastri was an obvious choice. He was made the police and transport minister in Pant's cabinet.

In 1951, Shastri moved to the national scene at the behest of Prime Minister Jawaharlal Nehru, who made him general secretary of the Congress party. Shastri shifted to Delhi. During the first general elections of 1952, Shastri worked hard as general secretary. The Congress won majority in the states and in the Parliament. Shastri was inducted by Nehru in his cabinet as minister of Railways and Transport, the portfolio which he held till 1956, when he resigned, taking moral responsibility for the train accident near Ariyalur in the south in which 144 persons were killed, setting an embarassing precedent for the future railway ministers. Even after almost five decades, whenever there is a railway accident the opposition vociferously begin to urge the railway minister to resign reminding him of the precedent set by Shastri in 1956. So far no railway minister has resigned though there have been hundreds of railway accidents since 1956 in which thousands of passengers have lost their lives. That speaks highly of the man that Shastri was. In the 1957 elections, Shastri was returned to the Parliament from the Allahabad constituency and Nehru inducted him again in his cabinet. He held various portfolios successively as minister of Transport and Communications, Commerce and Industry and became the Home minister in 1961. Once again Shastri resigned, this time under the Kamraj Plan in 1963. But Nehru called him back. Soonafter, Nehru suffered a massive heart attack at the Bhubaneshwar Congress session and could never fully recover from it. He wanted someone to share his burden and appointed Shastri as minister without portfolio. That Nehru selected Shastri for this important post from among the stalwarts of Congress party, showed the immense faith Nehru had developed in the modest, self-effacing but hard-working Shastri.

Nehru died on 27 May 1964. Who would succeed Nehru? The nation was perplexed. Even before Nehru's death, books and articles had been written hazarding guess about Nehru's successor. But by appointing Shastri as a minister without portflio, Nehru had given a glimpse of what was in his mind. Just a day before his death, he had asked Shastri to be prepared to attend the Commonwealth Conference scheduled to be held in June. The election of the successor of Nehru was surprisingly quite smooth. The Congress president, Kamaraj, played a crucial role in Shastri's election as leader of the Congress Parliamentary Party. Shastri inherited many problems, the major ones being food shortage and menacing postures of Pakistan and China. He gave the slogan '*Jai Jawan, Jai Kissan*' (Hail the Soldier; Hail the Farmer) to meet the challenge on both the fronts. To meet the food shortage, he imported foodgrains from wherever he could and took steps to increase the domestic production. That was the beginning of 'Green Revolution' which made India self-sufficient in food grains in due course.

Soon after Shastri's taking charge as the prime minister, Pakistan got onto the offensive. Pakistan was being ruled by General Ayub Khan at that time. They started with a probing attack in the Rann of Kutch in April, 1965 as the boundary between the two countries was not clearly marked there. The Indian side suffered as they were not prepared for such an eventuality. Emboldened by this, the Pakistan army crossed the international border in Chhamb area of Kashmir in September, 1965. This time India did not take it lying down. Shastri went on air to address the nation. "We are at war," he declared, "but the war will not be fought on Indian soil," Shastri assured the nation. The country stood up and cheered their leader. Shastri gave full freedom to the armed forced to retaliate as they thought fit. The Indian army crossed the international border in Panjab and within days had reached the outskirts of Lahore and Sialkot. Pakistan air force was badly mauled. Their armoured units suffered heavy losses in the tank warfare near Ferozpur. The war lasted for twenty-two days. The matter went to the United Nations. A resolution moved by both U.S.A. and Soviet Union demanded cease fire, which came into effect soonafter. The Soviet premier, Alexei Kosygin, offered his good offices to settle the dispute.

Shastri and Ayub Khan were invited to Tashkent, capital of Uzbekistan. After lot of deliberations and discussions, in which Kosygin played the mediator, an agreement was signed on 10 January 1966 between Shastri and Ayub Khan. According to the agreement, which has come to be known as Tashkent Agreement, the armed forces of the two countries were to go back to the position they held before the hostilities broke out. The two countries also had to restore diplomatic relations. India had to surrender about 2000 sq. kms. of Pakistan's territory which their forces had conquered after a great sacrifice. Immediately after signing the agreement, Shastri, it seems, realized that he had committed a mistake by giving back territory which had been acquired at the cost of many lives by the armed forces. Within hours, he had a massive heart attack and died on the morning of 11 Janauary 1966 at Tashkent. His body was brought to Delhi and was cremated on the banks of the Yamuna river, at a spot which is now called Vijay Ghat.

Shastri signed the Tashkent Agreement with considerable misgivings. He knew that when he went back home he would have to face an angry Parliament and a resentful nation. This overpowering thought may have been bothering him. But the nation has forgiven him. He is remembered today for his slogan *Jai Jawan Jai Kissan;* for taking moral responsibility for a train accident when he was the railway minister. He is remembered for the way he conducted the Indo-Pak 1965 war. And he is remembered as an honest and sincere man. "No one in such high office ever displayed such modesty and humility. It was not something put on like a garb for public display. It was something innate to the man. He fully realised that he was stepping into the shoes of a great man and that he had neither the qualities not the upbringing which would make it possible for him to play the same distinguished role that Nehru had done. But Shastri's distinction lay in the clear realization of this fact, and in his acting in a manner well suited to the limitations of his character and personality".[1] But surprisingly he overcame these limitations during the 1965 war. Those who used to jest about his unimpressive personality and his humble ways, suddenly realized that there was greatness in the man, and while the war lasted, he became immensely popular — almost an idol of the people. And in many ways he still is.

# References

1.  Chagla, M.C. *Roses in December; An Autobiography,* Bombay, Bharatiya Vidya Bhawan, 1973, p.445.

# Swami Shraddhanand

## (1856-1926)

Swami Shraddhanand was born at Talwandi, District Jalandhar in Punjab, as Munshi Ram. His father, Nanak Chand, was a small-time businessman. But soon he closed his business and entered the police service as inspector (1957) and was posted in the North-Western Province (present Uttar Pradesh), when Munshi Ram was a year old. Munshi Ram had three brothers and two sisters. Due to his father's frequent transfers, Munshi Ram's education was often interrupted and the boy had to change many schools in different cities. However, he did pass the matriculation examination in 1877, at the age of twenty-one. The same year he was married to Shiv Devi, daughter of Salig Ram, a prosperous landlord of Jalandhar city.

For higher studies, Munshi Ram was sent to Banaras and joined Queen's College, one of the oldest colleges in Uttar Pradesh. But due to his indulgences he did not keep good health and his father called him back to Bareilly after a year, where he was posted at that time. In 1882, Munshi Ram joined the University Law College at Lahore and passed the law examination in due course. But the year 1882 proved to be a turning point in his life when he heard Swami Dayanand speaking on the nature of God and about the Vedas during his visit to Bareilly. He contacted the swami later and decided to follow his precepts. When Munshi Ram returned to Lahore, he formally joined the Arya Samaj, which had been inaugurated by the swami a few years earlier. He read *Satyarth Prakash*, written by Swami Dayanand, and met several leading Arya Samajists at Lahore and elsewhere.

By then, Munshi Ram was a qualified lawyer and he started a legal practice at Jalandhar in 1885. Soon, he became a successful lawyer. At the same time he was an active member of the Arya Samaj and due to his organizational ability and eloquence he was emerging as a leading Arya Samajist of Punjab, and became the president of the Representative Assembly (Arya Pratinidhi Sabha) of Punjab in 1889. Along with the removal of untouchability, child marriage, caste system and spreading the message of the Vedas, the Arya Samaj movement was concerned with the education of boys and girls to make them better 'Aryas'. With this in view, Shraddhanand, in collaboration with his brother-in-law Lala Devraj, founded a girls college at Jalandhar in 1886 and named it Kanya Maha Vidyalaya. It was a residential school for girls where they were brought up 'in an intensively Hindu or Aryan atmosphere'. The school was raised to the level of a college in due course of time and attracted students not only from various parts of India but also from some foreign countries where Hindus were in a sizeable number Today it is a leading post-graduate college for girls in Punjab.

A split occurred in the Arya Samaj on the issue of the type of education which the Arya Samaj educational institutions should render. One wing supported the Dayanand Anglo-Vedic (D.A.V.) institutions, which offered courses in Western sciences, philosophy, English literature etc. with some courses covering Hindi and Sanskrit literatures. The other section was all for the ancient type of institutions called gurukuls with emphasis on ancient Hindu culture through the medium of Hindi and Sanskrit. Munshi Ram emerged as the leader of the gurukul wing. To propagate his views, he started a weekly newspaper, the *Satya Dharam Pracharak*, from Jalandhar, with himself as editor. The foundation of the Gurukul became the mission of his life and he started collecting the required funds for the purpose. By 1902, he was able to collect thirty-two thousand rupees, which included his own contribution, and founded the Gurukul at Hardwar. He abandoned his legal practice at Jalandhar and moved to Hardwar to look after the working of the gurukul. The medium of instruction at the gurukul was Hindi and Sanskrit with emphasis on Sanskrit classics including scientific works. The boys were to observe *brahmcharya* (celibacy) during their gurukul days and live a simple and religious life. It was difficult to find students for the education given in the gurukul because it was not job-oriented. Among the four students in the first batch, two were Munshi Ram's own sons. The gurukul did succeed and gradually the number of students increased. It became a trendsetter for other gurukuls to come up in various places in north India. The gurukul education also inculcated a nationalist feeling among the students and pride in the ancient culture of India. When Gandhi started a satyagraha in South Africa, the inmates of the gurukul collected a modest amount and the money was sent by Munshi Ram to Gandhi in South Africa, earning Gandhi's gratitude and friendship. The success of the gurukul could be gauged from the fact that when Gandhi returned to India from South Africa in 1915, along with about a hundred 'Phoenix boys', they had to be accommodated in the gurukul for several weeks. Gandhi also stayed there for sometime and discussed various matters with Munshi Ram. In fact, C.F. Andrews had written to Gandhi while he was still in South Africa that he should meet three great men of India on his return to India — Rabindranath Tagore, Sushil Kumar Rudra (the Christian principal of St. Stephen's College, Delhi) and Swami Shraddhanand. Gandhi was impressed by the working of the gurukul and years later, he wrote in *Young India:* "Whenever I see a Punjabi youth capable of reading and writing Devanagari, I immediately conclude that he must have had his training in one of the Gurukuls. They have done more than any other institution in these parts to revivify Sanskrit learning and Aryan culture.' Munshi Ram had built this institution almost single-handedly and served as its Governor-Director. The Gurukul has a beautiful campus on the bank of the Ganges and in the initial stages it resembled the ashrams of the ancient *rishis*. Today, however, it is a 'deemed university' like any other university in India, perhaps with more emphasis on Sanskrit learning as compared to others. Munshi Ram remained the guiding spirit of the gurukul till 1917. When he turned sixty, he decided to enter the last stage of the life of a Hindu — sanyas ashram. He became a *sanyasi* and changed his name to Shraddhanand, the name by which he became famous. He now moved to Delhi where his son Indra Vidyavachaspati lived and was a journalist in the Hindi paper *Arjun*.

At Delhi, he started organizing social work under the aegis of the Arya Samaj. He organized famine relief work in Garhwal in 1918 and the other places. Wherever there was a calamity there was Shraddhanand with a small band of his Arya followers. The year 1919 turned out to be the most memorable in the life of Shraddhanand. Rowlatt Acts which empowered the Government to arrest and imprison Indians without trial and inflict on them most humiliating punishments and much more, was passed on 21 March 1919 in spite of opposition of Indian members in the Imperial Legislative Council. Gandhi exhorted all Indians to observe 30 March as a protest day (actually he had fixed the day as April 6 but because of some misunderstanding, people in Delhi observed it on 30 March). There was demonstration in Chandni Chowk, a busy market place in Delhi. In panic, the police opened fire on demonstrators, killing ten persons, both Hindus and Muslims. Many more were injured. From the crowd, Shraddhanand emerged in saffron robes and a staff in hand, and faced the gurkha soldiers who were ready to continue firing. '*Main tun ko ched dun ga*' (I will pierce you with bullet) said a gurkha. Shraddhanand bared his chest and shouted '*Goli chalao*' (fire at me). Better sense prevailed and the gurkhas withdrew. The procession was then allowed to proceed. Muslims, who were also demonstrating against the treatment meted out to the Khalifa of Turkey by the British, were so moved by this act of bravery on the part of Shraddhanand that they lifted him on their shoulders and took him to the nearby Jama Masjid where Shraddhanand delivered a soul stirring speech. Then happened the Jallianwala Bagh tragedy on 13 April 1919, followed by other atrocities on the innocent people of Punjab, including the crawling order. Gandhi's indifference to the plight the people of Punjab, mostly Hindus and Sikhs, shocked Shraddhanand and on 30 May 1919 he withdrew from the satyagraha movement started by Gandhi. In *Young India* (11.6.1919) Gandhi wrote: "By my complete silence over the Punjab disturbances I have allowed myself to be misunderstood by many friends and, as is now well known, I have been desired of the cooperation, though never the friendship, of so respected and renowned a leader and coworker as Sanyasi Swami Shri

Shraddhanandji". The swami did not sit idle and straight went away to Punjab and visited several places in the province including Amritsar, Lahore Gujranwala, where ghastly massacres had occurred. He tried to trace out the families whose male members were killed in Jallianwala Bagh and other places and tried to give them solace and monetary help after collecting funds for the purpose. Madan Mohan Malaviya joined Shraddhanand in this humanitarian venture. Shraddhanand persuaded the Congress party to hold its annual session of 1919 December in Amritsar, hoping that the Congress would wake up to the immensity of the Punjab tragedy. He acted as chairman of the Reception Committee and in a memorable speech he told the gathering what had happened in Punjab.

After that, Shraddhanand concentrated on the social work launched by the Arya Samaj, like educating people about the curse of untouchability and caste system. He started taking part in the *Shuddhi* (purifying) movement; bringing back those Muslims to the fold of Hinduism who had been forcibly converted to Islam. In the first half of 1923 more than eighteen thousand Malkana Rajputs, Gujjars and Bania converts were brought back to the Hindu fold. Under the *Sanghatan* movement, great efforts were made to elevate the depressed classes and 'untouchables'. This antagonised the Muslim community who believed that conversion was only their exclusive right. On this issue, fresh differences cropped up between him and Gandhi when the latter criticized the *Shuddhi* movement and also Swami Dayanand and *Satyarth Prakash* written by Dayanand. Early in 1926, Shraddhanand started a paper, *Liberator*, with the purpose of propagating against untouchability and the treatment suffered by the depressed classes. Thus, the last years of Shraddhanand's life were spent for the cause of the upliftment of the depressed classes, reconversion of the former Hindus to Hindusism and bringing Hindus of various views together. By such activities he had earned the ire of the Muslim fanatics. On 23 December 1926 a Muslim came to the residence of Shraddhanand, who was ill and was lying down. He sent Shraddhanand's servant to fetch a glass of water and shot Shraddhanand twice on the chest. Shraddhanand died in the spot. The nation was stunned. The assassin, Abdul Rashid, was caught, tried in a court and was sentenced to be hanged. The Muslim press and leaders came forward in his defence. On the eve of the implementation of the capital punishment to the murderer, Muslim crowds collected at the Delhi jail and the following morning thousands joined the funeral procession. En route, many processionists went out of control and started attacking the Hindus.

During the Gauhati session of the Congress (26 December) a resolution was passed which was drafted by Gandhi. Gandhi asked Mohammad Ali to move the resolution, who refused. Gandhi then himself moved the resolution: "This Congress expresses its horror and indignation at the cowardly and treacherous murder of Swami Shraddhanand and places on record its sense of the irreparable loss the nation has sustained by the tragic death of a brave and noble patriot who dedicated his life and his great gifts to the service of his country and of his faith and espoused with fearless devotion the cause of the lowly, the fallen and the weak". It was followed by a speech by Gandhi who called the murderer Abdul Rashid his brother. "I do not even regard him as guilty of Swami's murder. Guilty indeed, are all those who excited feelings of hatred against one another".

However, Jawaharlal Nehru wrote in a different vein in his *Autobiography*: "The end of the year 1926 was darkened by great tragedy, which sent a shrill of horror all over India. Always I have admired sheer physical courage, the courage to face physical suffering in a good cause, even unto death. Most of us I suppose, admire it. Swami Shraddhanand had an amazing amount of that fearlessness. His tall and stately figure, wrapped in a sanyasin's robe, perfectly erect in spite of advanced years, eyes flashing, sometimes a shadow of irritation or anger at the weakness of others passing over his face — how I remember that vivid picture, and how often it has come back to me".[1]

# References

1. Nehru, Jawaharlal. *An Autobiography*, New Delhi, Jawaharlal Nehru Memorial Fund, 1980, p.160. (First published, London, Bodley Head, 1936).

# Bhagat Singh

## (1907-1931)

Bhagat Singh was born in 1907 (exact date not known) at Banga, a village in Lyalpur district (now in Pakistan) in a Sikh family. He was the second of five children of his parents, Kishan Singh and Vidya Vati. He had three brothers and a sister. The family was quite well-off as peasant proprietors. They had nationalistic inclinations and also took part in reform movements led by Arya Samaj and the Singh Sabha. The most famous member of the family was, of course, Ajit Singh, uncle of Bhagat Singh, who was deported to Mandalay for six months along with Lala Lajpat Rai in 1907 for leading an agitation against the Colonisation Bill. Bhagat Singh was very attached to his uncle and was obviously inspired by his self-sacrifices as a nationalist. Ajit Singh had left India and spent many years working for India in self-exile while in foreign lands.

After completing his primary education in a village school Bhagat Singh joined the D.A.V. High School at Lahore. After passing the matriculation examination, he joined D.A.V. College. There he was influenced greatly by his history teacher, Bhai Parmanand (who was later sentenced to life imprisonment in the 1915 Lahore conspiracy case and was sent to Andaman where he spent six years). From his early days Bhagat Singh had qualities of leadership and founded the College Student Union, and served as its president. He also joined the Indian National Congress while still a student but left it finding it 'supine and ineffective'. When Lajpat Rai founded the

National College in 1921, Bhagat enrolled in it leaving D.A.V. College and graduated from it in 1923.

Bhagat Singh had developed an interest in reading. He read widely, especially literature about socialism, Marxism and revolutionary movements while studying in college. At a young age he decided to devote his life for the country's cause through revolutionary activities.

In 1924, the family of Bhagat Singh, specially his grandmother, started pressing him for marriage. As he did not want to be saddled with family life which would hamper his activities as a revolutionary, he left home and reached Kanpur, armed with a letter of introduction from one of his teachers for the Congress leader Ganesh Shankar Vidyarthi. Bhagat Singh stayed in Kanpur for five months, working for the Hindi paper *Pratap* edited by Vidyarthi. In spite of being president of the U.P. Congress, Vidyarthi had a soft corner for the revolutionaries and his office served as a meeting-point for them. There Bhagat Singh met revolutionaries like Batukeshwar Dutt, Chandershekhar Azad and others. He also wrote articles and pamphlets under the name, Balwant. The stay at Kanpur served as an apprenticeship in journalism for him and for writing revolutionary literature. Early in 1925 Bhagat Singh returned to Lahore after being assured that his family would not force him to marry.

While still a student of the National College he had joined the Hindustan Socialist Republican Association (1923) and was soon elected as its general secretary. After his return from Kanpur, he founded the Nav Jawan Bharat Sabha in 1925 in Lahore to inculcate a spirit of revolution in the youth. He came in touch with several revolutionaries in Lahore like Sukhdev, Yashpal, Bhagwati Charan besides those he had met at Kanpur. On the Dussehra day of 1926 a bomb exploded in Lahore. Bhagat Singh was arrested and prosecuted but was released in the absence of valid proof. By 1928 the Hindustan Socialist Republic Association (HSRA) had created a network of branches throughout north India.

Lajpat Rai, as leader of the Nationalist Party in the Central Legislative Council, moved a resolution on 16 February 1928 to boycott the Simon Commission which was carried by sixty-eight to sixty-two votes. To live upto his conviction, he led a demonstration in Lahore when the Commission members arrived there on 30 October 1928. Lajpat Rai was assaulted by the police and a British officer hit him on the chest. Lajpat Rai died on 17 November presumably of injuries. This shocked the nation and the members of the HSRA decided to take revenge, and kill Scott, deputy superintendent of police who they thought had hit Lajpat Rai. Bhagat Singh with his two associates, Rajguru and Azad, reached Scott's office on 17 December 1928. Mistaking Saunders, assistant superintendent of police, for Scott, Raj Guru fired a shot followed by four shots from close quarter by Bhagat Singh. Saunders died on the spot. All three escaped. Bhagat Singh reached Calcutta incognito.

This was followed by two bombs thrown in the Legislative Assembly Hall in Delhi by Bhagat Singh and B.K. Dutt on 8 April 1929. The bombs did not kill any one but a few persons were slightly injured. Bhagat Singh and Dutt did not run away but offered themselves for arrest. They had also thrown a red pamphlet earlier from the gallery and shouted revolutionary slogans like '*Inquilab Zindabad*' and '*Long Live Revolution*'. Both of them were arrested and put in solitary confinement in Delhi jail. They were committed to the sessions in the first week of June. Bhagat Singh made an historic statement in the court drafted by himself which 'forms a glorious chapter in the history of the revolutionary movement'. An excerpt from it reads: "The bomb was necessary to awaken England from her dreams. Our sole purpose was to make the deaf hear and give the timely warning. We have only marked the end of an era of utopian non-violence of whose futility the rising generation has been convinced beyond the shadow of doubt".

Jawaharlal Nehru was so moved by the statement made by Bhagat Singh that he published it in the *Congress Bulletin*. The sttlement of Bhagat Singh and Dutt did not have any effect on the judge and he sentenced the two of them to transportation for life. An appeal in the high court was rejected.

While they were undergoing sentence, the Lahore Conspiracy Case (murder of Saunders) was also opened. There were large scale arrests before that and almost all the revolutionaries were arrested. Some of them became approvers and the role of Bhagat Singh was disclosed. Thus Bhagat Singh was charged with murder and brought to Lahore jail from Delhi. While in prison, Bhagat Singh and his colleagues started a hunger strike on 15 June 1929. They were demanding better facilities as political prisoners. The hunger strike went on for several weeks. The prolonged fast created great commotion among the public and huge demonstrations were held all over India. Jawaharlal Nehru met the prisoners in jail on 9 August 1929. In a speech at Lahore he said, "The hunger-strikers in Lahore jail are undergoing this magnificent suffering, suffering which it is in the power of few men to endure, not for themselves but for all political prisoners. The sacrifice of these young men has roused us to a new consciousness of political life and once more made all of us yearn for liberty of the country. What a contrast this is, compared with the unfortunate wrangles among Congressmen and the fighting for securing positions in the Congress and the reception committee. I am ashamed to hear of these internecine differences among the Congressmen."[1]

Gandhi in a letter dated 1 July 1929 reprimanded Nehru for publishing the statement of Bhagat Singh which he thought was written by his counsel, and for eulogising Bhagat Singh and his colleagues for undergoing fast.[2] Nehru in his reply on 13 July 1929 informed Gandhi: "I am sorry you disapproved of my giving Bhagat Singh and Dutt's statement in the *Congress Bulletin*. I found that there was very general appreciation of it among Congress circles, I decided to give extracts. It was difficult however to pick and choose and gradually most of it went in. You are mistaken in thinking that the statement was the work of their counsel. My information is that counsel had nothing or practically nothing to do with it".[3]

As Bhagat Singh and his comrades were charged with murder and were not cooperating with the Court and were shouting revolutionary slogans in the Court, a Special Tribunal was appointed to prosecute them. The trial thus became a farce. Bhagat Singh, Sukhdev and Rajguru were sentenced to death. The rest of them were sentenced to transportation for life. A petition was filed in the Privy Council by prominent public men which was rejected. On 14 February 1931, Pandit Madan Mohan Malaviya submitted an appeal to the viceroy seeking his prerogative of mercy in commuting the death sentence to transportation for life on grounds of humanity. The Viceroy was not moved.[4]

The three, Bhagat Singh, Rajguru and Sukhdev, were hanged in the Lahore jail on 23 March 1931, at 7 p.m. Their bodies were secretly taken out and cremated on the bank of Sutlej river the same night.

The nation was stunned. There were huge demonstrations throughout the country. There was a general feeling that Gandhi did not do enough to use his influence with the Viceroy, to save the lives of Bhagat Singh and his two comrades. Some believed that he did his best, but the facts do not support their contention. Gandhi, during his meeting with Viceroy Lord Irwin on 18 February 1931, raised the question of the death sentence of Bhagat Singh and his two comrades, as an afterthought but according to Irwin, Gandhi did not plead for commutation, only for postponement. On 23 March 1931, the day fixed for the hanging, Gandhi wrote to the viceroy in the morning in Delhi (the hanging had to take place in Lahore). It is not certain at what time the viceroy received Gandhi's letter. In the letter Gandhi wrote: "Though you were frank enough to tell me that there was little hope of your commuting the sentence of death on Bhagat Singh and two others, you said you would consider my submission on Saturday ... Popular opinion rightly or wrongly demands commutation. When there is no principle at stake it is often a duty to respect it". The strangest part of the tragic episode is that the same evening (on 23 March 1931) Gandhi issued a statement: "Bhagat Singh and his companions have been executed (they were executed at 7 p.m. in Lahore jail) and have become martyrs. Their death seems to have been a personal loss to many. I join in the tributes paid to the memory of these young men. And yet I must warn the youth of the country against following their example".[5]

Gandhi left for Karachi on 26 March to attend the Congress session there. He was warned about the anger of youth against him for not saving Bhagat Singh, Sukhdev and Rajguru. He alighted at Malir, a wayside station fifteen miles from Karachi, for fear of the angry demonstration. The demonstrators had reached Malir station also and received Gandhi with black flags and shouts of 'Gandhi murdabad' and 'Gandhi go back'.

Gandhi drafted a resolution to be passed in the Congress session. He asked Nehru to move the resolution, who refused, but later agreed due to his regard for Gandhi. The significant part of the resolution reads: "The Congress while dissociating itself from and disapproving of political violence in any shape or form, places on record its admiration of the bravery and sacrifice of the late Sardar Bhagat Singh and his comrades Syts. Sukhdev and Rajguru, and mourns with the bereaved families the loss of these lives".[6] While moving the resolution, Nehru said, "Why is everyone thinking of Bhagat Singh today? Even children in villages know about him. Many before him have made sacrifices and many more are still doing so. But why is the name of Bhagat Singh on every tongue? There must be some reason for this. He was a clean fighter who faced his enemy in the open field. He was a young boy full of burning zeal for the country. He was like a spark which became a flame in a short time and spread from one end of the country to the other, dispelling the prevailing darkness everywhere".[7]

The author of the official history of the Congress, an ardent Gandhian, wrote: "At the time of the Karachi Congress in 1931, it was doubtful whether Gandhi or Bhagat Singh occupied the chief attention of India". As late as 30 July 1931 Gandhi wrote: "The Bhagat Singh worship has done and is doing incalculable harm to the country".

Notwithstanding Gandhi's disapproval, Bhagat Singh has become a legend and will continue to be praised by generations to come.

## References

1. *The Tribune* August 11, 1929.
2. *Collected Works of Mahatma Gandhi* Vol. 41, pp.152-53.
3. Nehru, Jawaharlal. *Selected Works of Jawaharlal Nehru*, First Series, Vol. 4, p.157.
4. Agarwala, B.R. *Trials of Independence*, New Delhi, National Book Trust, 1991, p.136.
5. *Collected Works of Mahatma Gandhi*, Vol. 45, p.335.
6. Ibid, p.363.
7. Nehru, op. cit., pp.505-06.

# Bhagat Puran Singh

## (1904-1992)

Puran Singh was an embodiment of unselfishness and service. Khushwant Singh called him Mother Teresa with a beard.

Puran Singh was born in a Hindu family in Rajewal village near Ludhiana, Punjab, in 1904. His father Shibu Mall named his son Ramji Das. While still a child, Ramji helped his mother in bathing the idols of the local Shiva temple. He grew up under the influence of his mother who encouraged him to hear *kirtans* (devotional songs) in a *gurdwara* (Sikh temple) also. His visits to the *gurdwara* became more frequent and he sensed a certain degree of warmth which he found lacking in a temple. He learnt more about Sikh gurus and their sacrifices and preachings. What impressed him most was the humility and *sewa* (service) to society which the *gurus* preached.

Ramji was put in the village school but he was not interested in attending classes and had gone only half-way to primary level when his formal education ended. When the family moved to Lahore, gurdwara Dera Sahib became his second home and he started doing *sewa* (service) in the gurdwara as a *sevadar* (volunteer). Still in his teens, he was converted to Sikhism and his uncut hair and gradually growing beard became the external symbols of his adopted religion. His name was changed to Puran. His urge to know more about Sikhism led him to libraries, the most important being Dayal Singh Library managed by the Brahmo Samaj. He read widely and did not confine his study to the tenets of Sikhism. Soon he became a well informed man. What a school and classroom could not give him, the library did, proving the dictum that real education is self education. Besides reading about the lives of Sikh gurus he read about history, population explosion, family planning, environment, pollution, social welfare and myriad other subjects.

An unexpected incident changed his life. Impressed by his selfless service, Puran Singh was entrusted with the responsibility of bringing up a three-year-old crippled child abandoned by his parents outside Gurdwara Dera Sahib at Lahore. This was in 1924 when Puran Singh himself was hardly twenty. The child was named Piara Singh, and had suffered paralysis of the arms and legs. He also suffered from speech deficiency. It became Puran Singh's mission to look after this unfortunate child. This was the beginning of a lifelong mission to serve and save thousands of India's physically challenged people. He had no money and often had to carry the crippled child on his back from place to place. He was subjected to public ridicule but he persisted, ignoring the mockery and banter of society. Puran Singh found time to roam about the roads and lanes of Lahore picking up nails, horseshoes, spikes, bricks and pebbles so that people did not get hurt. For more than two decades Puran Singh thus roamed the streets of Lahore, often carrying Piara Singh on his back.

Then came the partition of the country (1947). More than half of Lahore was burnt down. Thousands of Hindus and Sikhs were killed or converted and the lucky ones were driven out. Puran Singh crossed over to India, with Piara Singh on his back. He came to Amritsar and found refuge in the Khalsa College refugee camp where thousands of unfortunate refugees from (what was now Pakistan) were huddled like sheep. Puran Singh saw misery writ large on their faces. There were old people who had no one to look after them; there were women who could not bear the shock and humiliation and had gone insane. There were sick and infirm people for whom nobody seemed to care. Puran Singh decided to do something for those unfortunate individuals in an organized way. His sincerity of purpose attracted people's attention. Soon a group of service minded youth joined him. Puran Singh and his devoted small team of workers then took under their wing more physically challenged and the mentally ill. That was the beginning of the institution called 'Pingalwara' (literally home for the cripples). It was formally inaugurated in 1948. To finance his venture Puran Singh put hundreds of small black wooden boxes at strategic places like bus-stands, road crossings, gurdwaras, railway stations bearing crude messages in Hindi, Gurumukhi, Urdu and English reminding people about their duty to their fellow beings who were invalid and needed help. When he ran out of money, Puran Singh would sit outside the Golden Temple (Harmandar Sahib) begging people to donate money for the noble cause. Within seven years Pingalwara moved to its own building on the G.T. Road, Amritsar. Pingalwara is non-sectarian. 'People are my God', Puran Singh used to say. The number of inmates in Pingalwara grew. Those who were without resources, without anyone to look after them, those who were the discards of the society were all welcome in the Pingalwara — the insane, the paralytic, the seriously injured and infected, the invalid, aged and deaf-and-dumb — all found an abode in Pingalwara. They were fed and looked after by *sewadars* (volunteers) who got meagre salary. Puran Singh saw to it that no helpless patient would die on the roadside unattended and uncared for. Thus Pingalwara also served as a sort of boarding house for patients who were being treated in hospitals and private nursing homes, who could not afford to stay in hospitals and nursing homes.

Puran Singh had a much wider vision than caring for the crippled. To spread his message, which covered many areas like conservation, environment, pollution, family planning, dowry, drug menace, Hindu-Sikh unity, care of animals etc., he had established a printing press within the precincts of the Pingalwara. Here he got printed pamphlets, booklets, posters and placards on recycled paper for distribution for a farthing among general public. A tall, sturdy man with a flowing snow-white beard and clad in loose white khadi shirt and wearing an untidy huge saffron turban, he would sit cross-legged distributing such useful literature on topics dear to his heart. Their contents would shock you, educate you and 'seek the milk of kindness out of you'. His writings are the result of deep study. He used to subscribe to two dozen regional, national and international dailies and magazines and scanned all of them. "What obsesses us most — the daily obscenities of politicians and editorial homilies of journalists — did not occupy his attention, but he read avidly the news which concerned the people, the society at large and the values that ought to govern us. Through wide reading he had developed a scientific and rational thinking yet so deeply rooted in the soil of our glorious history, culture and religion. As he talks one could see the zeal of a child eager to learn. He is gentle, soft and sublimely uncritical of anything around him. To him all of God's creations are sacred, be they animal, vegetable or mineral or whatever".[1] Today, besides Amritsar, Pingalwara functions at five other places, Jalandhar, Pandori, Goindwal Sahib, Palsora and Sangrur, all in Panjab. There are over five hundred inmates in these Pingalwaras where they are looked after by 250 *sewadars*. Food, beddings, clothes and even medicines are provided gratis. Early in life, Puran Singh had taken the vow of celibacy so that he could devote his life for the welfare of the people.

Bhagat Puran Singh had become a legend in his lifetime. Nobody in living memory has done so much for the poor and the crippled in the Punjab. Hundreds of unbearable lives were made worth living by him. Puran Singh became a metaphor of help and self-sacrifice in a world full of misery. His main source of money was the common man. He worked single-handedly braving all odds. He did not perform miracles to earn a sainthood. The only miracle he performed was the Pingalwara which has transfigured and immortalized him. His was a life of compassion, service and humility.

Few honours were bestowed on him. In 1980, the Government of India awarded him the Padam Shri (which he surrendered after Operation Blue Star in 1984), Punjab government awarded him the Lok Kala Academy Award. He was nominated for the Nobel Peace Prize in 1991, but did not get it. He died in Chandigarh in 1992 at the age of eighty-eight. In 1986, Bhagat Puran Singh in his will had made Dr. Bibi Inderjit Kaur (his adopted daughter) the life-president of the Pingalwara Society. Though a practicing doctor, she has been devoting much of her time for the management and expansion of the Pingalwaras.

## References

1.   Narayanan, V.N. *Humility is My Mace. The Tribune*, 30 March 1991.

# Ranjit Singh

## (1780-1839)

Ranjit Singh was born on 13 November 1780 in Gujranwala (now in Pakistan). His father, Maha Singh, was the leader of the Sukerchakia misle (an Arabic word meaning equal or alike). Not much is known about Ranjit's childhood accept that he had no interest in reading or writing and spent his childhood riding, hunting and other such wild games. Early in childhood, he had an attack of small-pox which affected one of his eyes and left deep scars on his face. He was short and slight of built but he compensated these shortcomings with his daring, innate shrewdness and ample commonsense. In addition to listening to the recitation of Sikh scriptures (Granth Sahib), he was influenced by the preachings of Brahmins whom he continued to respect throughout his life, giving them generous offerings and gifts. Due to their influence, he had banned beef eating and *azans* (calling Muslims from the minarets of mosques) as was done by the Mughal emperor, Akbar, earlier. Indeed, in many ways, he lived like an orthodox Hindu, often going to Hardwar for a holy dip in the Ganges and celebrating all the Hindu festivals like Holi, Diwali and Basant with enthusiasm and devotion.

At the early age of ten he accompanied his father on a campaign. During the skirmish his father fell ill, leaving his forces under the charge of the young lad. Ranjit led his army bravely and the enemy was routed. His father died soon after leaving Ranjit to head the Sukerchakia misle, convinced of the qualities which his young son possessed. Ranjit had no interest in administering the estate and continued spending time in hunting, shooting and riding. To check his wayward ways, he was married at the age of fifteen to Mehtab Kaur of the Kanhaya misle. The marriage was not a happy one and in 1798, he married again, this time to Raj Kaur of Nakhais misle. The matrimonial alliances between two powerful misles added to his strength and at the age of seventeen, he began to dream of greater deeds.

In 1776, came his chance to prove himself when the Afghan ruler, Shah Zaman, grandson of Ahmed Shah Abdali, invaded Punjab. Instead of yielding and running away to the hills as was often done during earlier invasions, Ranjit Singh collected the Sikh forces and led them to victory against the Afghans. With this victory Ranjit Singh's reputation rose from that of an obscure Sikh chieftain to leader of the Sikhs. The following year, Zaman Shah again invaded Lahore and Sikhs under Ranjit Singh's command repulsed his attack and drove him back to Kabul once again.

When Ranjit Singh had taken over the Sikh leadership, he had found them divided into twelve misles of varying strength, always quarrelling and devoting themselves to intrigues and worse. "Ranjit Singh laboured; with more or less of intelligent design, to give unity and coherence to diverse atoms and scattered elements; to remould the increasing Sikh nation into a well-ordered state or commonwealth as Gobind had developed a sect into a people".[1] In 1799, at the age of eighteen, he captured Lahore, the largest and oldest city of Punjab. He made Lahore his capital and ruled from there for the next forty years. The following year, Ranjit was proclaimed a Maharaja by the highly respected Sahib Singh Bedi, a descendent of Guru Nanak. He, however, remained unaffected by this. New coins were struck but they did not have his effigy or his name but that of Guru Nanak and he named his government as Nanak Shahi. Even the government seal did not bear his name; it bore only the words Sarkar Khalsaji; his court was called Darbar Khalsaji.[2]

He was shrewd enough to learn that to channelize the energies of the warlike Sikhs, he must regularly engage them in war in remote corners. In 1802, Ranjit Singh took over Amritsar, the holy city of the Sikhs from the Bhangi misle. The same year he annexed Jhang, defeating

Ahmad Khan Sial. From then on he started reorganizing his army on European lines as he was convinced that the victories of the British army over superior arms and numbers of Indians was due to their training and discipline. He divided his army into separate units of cavalry, infantry and artillery and supervised their training himself. He realized early that it would be dangerous to antagonize the British whose disciplined army was superior to what the Indians had. To ensure their friendship and non-interference, he sacrificed a few states east of Sutlej, called Malwa or cis-Sutlej states, which had come under his suzerainty. He signed a treaty of friendship with the British in 1809 at Amritsar, demarcating spheres of influence of each; the East India Company were to confine their activities east and Ranjit Singh to the West of the Sutlej river. Consequently, cis-Sutlej states came under the protection of East India Company. The treaty was adhered to as long as Ranjit Singh lived. This treaty gave him a free hand to expand his empire to the West, but shattered his dream of a united Punjab. In 1818, he captured Multan and extended his territory right up to the Sindh desert. The following year his generals took over Kashmir from the Afghans, and Peshawar in North-West Frontier in 1823. Though it was occupied by the Wahabis around 1828, they were defeated and Peshawar was finally annexed in 1830 with his forces reaching the gates of Afghanistan. In 1835, Amir Dost Mohammad of Afghanistan attacked Peshawar. The Sikh army led by general Hari Singh Nalwa defeated him and chased the Afghans upto the streets of Jamrud and Nalwa's name became a terror for the Afghans for decades to come. However, Nalwa was fatally wounded in the battle.

In 1822, two French soldiers came to Ranjit to enlist in his army and train it on European lines. They were Francois Allard and Bapiste Ventura, who claimed to have fought for Napoleon Bonaparte in the French army. After some hesitation, Ranjit employed the two on a generous salary. Allard was to train the cavalry and Ventura, the artillery. In 1827, two other Europeans joined Ranjit's army and held important positions: Henri Court, a Frenchman and Avitabile, an Italian. Gradually, the number of Europeans serving in Ranjit's army rose to fifty. "Ranjit Singh looked upon his European officers as highly paid drill sergeants. Most of his conquests had been made before 1822 by men like Mokham Chand, Hari

Singh Nalwa and Misr Diwan Chand. Even after 1822 the real commanders of the Durbar army were Punjabi officers of the Maharaja's sons".[3] Thus it is not true, as many historians claim, that the superiority of Ranjit Singh's army was due to these European officers. "In truth the Sikh owes his excellences as a soldier to his own hardihood of character, to that spirit of adaptation which distinguishes every new people, and to that feeling of a common interest and destiny implanted in him by his great teachers".[4]

In 1831, Ranjit Singh met Governor General Lord William Bentinck at Rupar on the banks of Sutlej. The meeting lasted for a week and negotiations with the agents continued for several more months. On 26 December 1832, a commercial treaty was signed between the East India Company and the Lahore Durbar. It was agreed that Ranjit Singh was not to annex Sindh 'renouncing his ambition to extend his empire to the sea'. He also agreed to give navigational rights to the Company in the rivers in his empire. But he was free to extend his empire towards the north. His general, Zorawar Singh, a Dogra, crossed the almost impassable mountain ranges of Kashmir in 1936 and annexed Ladakh without much fighting.

There was an interesting interlude about the diamond Koh-i-Noor (mountain of light) perhaps the most brilliant diamond in the world. The diamond was taken by Nadir Shah from the Mughals in 1739 along with the famous peacock throne. It passed on to Ahmad Shah Abdali after the assassination of Nadir Shah in 1747. Abdali's grandson, Shah Shuja, who had acquired the diamond, came to Lahore to seek sanctuary. Ranjit Singh got the diamond from him as compensation for providing sanctuary. It was in the Lahore Durbar when Sikhs were defeated in the Second Sikh War in 1849 by the British. Punjab was annexed by Dalhousie and the Koh-i-Noor passed on to the British. In a letter to John Hobhouse, Chairman, East India Company, Dalhousie wrote after annexing Punjab: "You at least will find no fault with my having regarded the Koh-i-Noor as a thing by itself; and with my having caused the Maharaja of Lahore in token of submission, to surrender it to the Queen of England. The Koh-i-Noor has become in the lapse of ages a sort of historical Emblem of Conquest in India. It has now found its proper place".[5] Even today it is the principal jewel in the crown of the British Queen. In spite of repeated requests by the Indians, the British government refuses to part with it. While on his deathbed in June 1839 Ranjit Singh desired that Koh-i-Noor be presented to the temple of Jagannath at Puri but his courtiers dissuaded him from doing so saying that it was too precious a thing to be given to an unguarded temple. Had the courtiers obeyed the Maharaja, the diamond may still be in the possession of the Indians.

Ranjit Singh built an empire conquering those areas in the western part of India which none of the earlier kings could do, and had become the most powerful Indian ruler of his time. He was the first Indian in a thousand years to stem the tides of invasions from western passes. His conquests, however, have overshadowed his other qualities as a ruler. He never coerced his subjects with heavy taxes. "He took from the land as much as it could readily yield, and he took from merchants as much as they could profitably give". His rule was founded on the feelings of the people but it must be admitted that the central theme of his rule was war and annexations. "The whole wealth and energies of the people were devoted to war, and to the preparation of military means and equipment. It suited the mass of the Sikh population, and they were pleased that city after city admitted the supremacy of the Khalsa and enabled them to enrich their families".[6] He was, however, always generous to his friends and forgiving to his foes. Though most of his generals were Sikhs and Hindus, he had employed many Muslims in his army, especially the gunners. He is rightly called a secular ruler.

He impressed many Europeans who came in close contact with him. In the words of Alexander Burnes, an agent of the East India Company, who had visited Ranjit Singh at Lahore and was his guest for a month in 1832:

'I never quitted the presence of a native of Asia with such impressions as I left this man; without education, and without a guide, he conducts all the affairs of his kingdom with surpassing energy and vigour, and yet he wields his power with a consideration unprecedented in an Eastern prince'.[7]

Lt. Col. James Skinner, who was with Governor-General William Bentinck at Rupar, wrote after the meeting which had included the inspection of troops on both sides; (1600 Sikh cavalry and a sizable company's horse artillery):

'In every way Ranjit proved himself to be a far superior soldier to any other native. He seemed as if gifted with the intelligence of an English Field Marshal and in fact be moved about as if he was himself in command of the troops'.[8]

The picture of Ranjit Singh without its warts will be incomplete. He was fond of wine and women. He was also taking opium in large quantities, which affected his health over the years. As was customary with the rulers of the time, he had well large harem besides his forty-six-odd official wives. It is alleged by some historians that he poisoned his mother while still a teenager due to her infidelities. However, there is no valid proof of this allegation.

Ranjit Singh suffered a fatal stroke, though he had survived two earlier ones, and died on 27 June 1839. Millions of Punjabis wept on that day. His last rites were performed according to Hindu tradition. While a thousand miles to the east Ram Mohan Roy had succeeded in getting the custom of sati declared illegal and punishable as a crime by the Governor General Lord William Bentinck in 1829, it was not applicable to the Lahore Durbar. Four 'ranis' (queens) and seven slave girls underwent the ritual of sati and were burnt on the pyre of the Maharaja. That was an ignoble end of a noble maharaja. Ashes of all twelve were collected and immersed in the holy Ganga at Hardwar, the sacred place for the Hindus.

Ranjit Singh left for his successors fifty thousand disciplined soldiers, fifty thousand well-armed militia and more than three hundred pieces of cannon. But after Ranjit's death, Sikh chiefs lapsed into jealousy, intrigues and murder. It required a genius to build an empire and lesser men to wreck it.

# References

1. Cunningham, J.D. *History of the Sikhs*. 1849, Indian reprint, Delhi, Low Price Publications, 1990, p.120.
2. Singh, Khushwant. *Ranjit Singh, Maharaja of the Punjab*. London, George Allen & Unwin, 1962. (Indian reprint 1973), p.47.
3. Ibid, p.141.
4. Cunningham, J.D. op. cit., p.153.
5. Hasrat, Bikram Jit. *The Punjab Papers*, Hoshiarpur, V.V. Research Institute, 1970, p.229.
6. Cunningham, op. cit., p.152.
7. Burnes, Alexander. *Travels into Bokhara*, 3 Vols, London, John Murray, 1834, Vol. 2, p.28.
8. Skinner, Lt. Col. James. *Military Memoirs*, 2 Vols, London, 1851.

# Dwarkanath Tagore

## (1794-1845)

Dwarkanath belonged to one of the most illustrious families of Bengal. He was the father of Maharishi Debendranath and grandfather of Rabindranath Tagore.

Dwarkanath was born in 1794 in Calcutta. His parents were Ram Mani and Meneka. As his mother died soon after his birth, he was brought up by his uncle Ramlochan, a rich zamindar and his wife Alaka, who legally adopted Dwarkanath, thus becoming his foster parents. He started his studies under a private tutor and at the age of ten joined the Sherbourne's school in Calcutta, where he studied for six years. He learnt Persian, the court language of the time. He soon realized that under the East India Company rule one had to know the English language. So he brushed up on his English under Rev. William Adams and some other Britishers who were friends of his father. He rounded it off by studying law. Dwarkanath thus equipped himself for a life working in cooperation with the East India Company and its European officials.

Ramlochan, his foster father, died in 1807, bequeathing all his property, including some houses in Calcutta and a large estate in Nadia and Pabna districts to Dwarkanath. However, this financial security did not dampen his aspirations to achieving something great on his own. Even his marriage at the age of seventeen (1811) did not detract him from the aim which he had envisioned. On coming of age, Dwarkanath started managing his estates independently. He also trained himself in the rudiments of land tenure and revenue systems and educated himself on British law and court practices under the supervision of Robert Fergusson, a leading barrister of the time.

Dwarkanath began his career as an entrepreneur, in buying and selling land (in the process extending his estate) and lending money to low-paid employees of the East India Company. In partnership with a leading European firm, Mackintosh & Co., he engaged in export and import. Through export of silk and indigo he made good profit. Further, he started earning thousands of rupees per month by way of fees and charges in lieu of legal advice which he rendered to rich zamindars and landlords and also by drafting legal petitions in Persian and English for them. His knowledge of legal procedures and his all round ability came to the notice of the East India Company and they appointed him as a *sarishtedar* to the collector and salt-agent of 24 Parganas and later in 1829 as dewan to the Board of Customs, Salt and Opium. He resigned in 1834 to concentrate on his industrial, commercial and financial ventures.

His experience in Mackintosh & Co. taught him that no progress could be made by his countrymen unless they took to business and industry and learnt to depend less and less on agriculture. Commerce and industry became his passion. He had the ability, and had the means to give concrete shape to his vision. He helped in the establishment of the Union Bank, a joint-stock venture to mop-up money and offering it for commercial and industrial use. In 1834, he opened a business firm Carr, Tagore & Co. with European friends as partners. Sometime earlier, another Indian gentleman, a Parsi settled at Calcutta, Rustomjee Cowasjee (1792-1852), had started a joint-stock company Rustomjee, Turner & Co. which may have inspired Dwarkanath to start a similar company. His firm prospered under efficient administration and earned huge profit. It had branches all over the country. Thus encouraged, Dwarkanath launched a number of industries and commercial ventures. He started a sugar factory at Ramnagar, and a silk factory at Kumarkhali. Then came the Bengal Coal Company which started the extraction of coal at Raniganj, the first venture of its kind in India. Using steam power, he introduced river navigation with the help of tugs and founded the Steam Tug

Association in 1837. He also set up a dock at Kidderpore for the repair of ships. He thus became a pioneer in some new types of industrial and commercial undertakings. For decades afterwards, Indian leaders went on preaching swadeshi; Dwarkanath put it into practice and proved that Indians could compete with the West. He was a dreamer and pathmaker. He was a true *karmayogi*.

Dwarkanath put some of his money to social work and nation building and the rest for living lavishly and in style. First the social reforms. Dwarkanath stood by Rammohun Roy in his crusade for social and religious reforms and considered him his 'guru'. He jointed Ram Mohun's 'Atmiya Sabha' and helped him and his friend William Adams to form the Unitary Mission of Calcutta by his donation. He also helped Ram Mohun's Brahmo Samaj (1828) and continued to support it with monetary help even after Ram Mohun left for England in 1831. He had also cooperated with Ram Mohun in getting the Act passed against sati in 1829. Like other leaders of the time, he encouraged the spread of English education and worked, along with David Hare, Ram Mohun and others, in the founding of the Hindu College in 1817, and was an active member of its managing committee. He was also one of the founders of the Gaudiya Samaj (1823) to promote Bengali language and culture. Dwarkanath gave tremendous impetus to the study of western system of medical science and paid for the expenses of two students to study medicine in England. He persuaded the government to establish a medical college in Calcutta. In 1835, along with other distinguished Indians and Europeans, he raised subscription for establishing the Fever Hospital. Dwarkanath helped in founding of the Calcutta Public Library through money and books and was its first proprietor. The library was later converted into India's National Library which at present is situated in the former governor general's residence, with several additions. A memorial in the form of his marble bust greets the visitors at the entrance of the Library. In 1835, Dwarkanath was made a Justice of Peace. In April 1838, he established the Landholder's Society for the preservation of landholders' rights and ventilation of their grievances. Out of it grew the British Indian Association, the precursor of the Indian National Congress.

As if these achievements were not enough, he contributed in the field of journalism also. Dwarkanath helped Rammohun Roy to launch *Sambad Kaumudi* (1821), a Bengali weekly and continued to support it even after Ram Mohun's death. He had substantial proprietorial rights in three papers, *Bangadoot* (Bengali), *Bengal Herald* (English) and *Bengal Harkara*, which was one of the leading journals of Calcutta in those days. He took active part, along with Rammohun Roy and others, against the Adam's Press Laws of 1923. He spent thousands of rupees to get the 'Black Act' repealed. Eventually, the Adams Press regulations were amended in 1835 to the jubilation of Indians and Europeans who fought for the freedom of the press.

His lavish style of living was reflected in the grand parties which he hosted in his Belgachia Villa in Calcutta, which were attended by the elite of Calcutta, both Indian and European, including, at times, Lord Auckland, the governor general and his sister Emily. He was one of the most popular figures in Calcutta society and was famous for his generosity and philanthropy. He maintained his lavish lifestyle on his two visits to England and Europe, staying in expensive hotels. In England, he was honoured by Queen Victoria who invited him to a dinner. The English aristocracy vied with each other to get introduced to him. In Paris also, he was well received. He developed intimate friendship with the famous Indologist Max Muller. Max Muller's observations about Dwarkanath are interesting and revealing and justify a rather longish quotation:

"Indians do not travel so freely fifty years ago as they do now. The crossing of the black water and all its consequences had not lost its terrors. When, therefore, in the year 1844, a real Hindu made his appearance in Paris, his visit created a great sensation, and filled me with a strong desire to make his acquaintance. He was a handsome man, and, as he took the best suite of apartments in one of the best hotels in Paris, he naturally roused considerable curiosity —— Dwarkanath Tagore was not a Sanskrit scholar but he was not unacquainted with Sanskrit literature. He was not an antiquarian, nor a student of his own religion or of the language of his own sacred books. —— My Indian friend Dwarkanath Tagore, though not learned, was very intelligent, and a man of the world. He rather looked down on the Brahmans and when I asked him whether he would have to perform penance, or *Prayaskitta* after his return to India, he laughed and said, 'No. I am all this time feeding a large number of Brahmans at home, and that is quite penance enough'. But if he took a low view of his Brahmans, he did not show much more respect for what he called black-coated English Brahmans. Much as he admired everything English, he had a mischievous delight in finding out the weak points of English society, and particularly of the English clergy".

Max Muller continues: "Dwarkanath Tagore lived in a truly magnificent Oriental style while at Paris. The King, Lois Philippe, received him, nay, he honoured him, by his presence and that of his Court at a grand evening party. The room was hung with Indian shawls, then the height of ambition of every French lady. And what was their delight when the Indian Prince placed a shawl on the shoulders of each lady as she left the room".[1]

While in England he fulfilled a sacred duty towards his 'guru' Rammohun Roy by getting his remains transferred to the beautiful cemetry of Arno's Vale near Bristol and got a memorial built there in the shape of a Hindu temple, which stands there even today along with an inscription. Little did he know that he too would soon die in a foreign land. He died in Surrey on first August 1846. He was only fifty-one years old.

# References

1. Max Muller, Friedrich. *Indian Friends*, First published Oxford as *My Indian Friends*. (Reprint, New Delhi, Amrit Book Co. 1982), pp.4-12.

# General Zorawar Singh

## (1784-1841)

Zorawar Singh was one of the greatest military generals India has produced. If Ladakh, the most spacious district of India, is today a part of India it is due to the daring and gallantry of one man, Zorawar Singh.

The early life of those who become famous in later life is usually shrouded in obscurity. Such is the case with Zorawar Singh. Very little is known about his birth and early life. The information which has been gathered about him is from descendants of his elder brother, Sardar Singh. He did not leave any male heir. He did not write about himself as he was almost an illiterate.

Zorawar Singh was born in September 1784 at Bilaspur, now in Himachal Pradesh. His father's name is believed to be Thakur Harji Singh, belonging to a family of Kahluria Rajputs. Zorawar had two brothers, elder, Sardar Singh and younger, Daler Singh. As a boy, he was mischievous and troublesome. He was fond of horse riding and swordmanship. When he was still a teenager, he killed a cousin over some property dispute. After that he ran away from home and reached Hardwar, the sacred city of the Hindus. There he met Rana Jaswant Singh, a *jagirdar* of Galihan, near Jammu. Rana brought Zorawar to his estate and engaged him in his service. While serving there, Zorawar Singh got trained in the use of weapons and perfect in horsemanship. But after a few years he left the service of the Rana and joined that of Raja Gulab Singh, who was emerging as a favourite satrap of Maharaja Ranjit Singh. That was in 1815. Soon his personal valour, keen intelligence and integrity made him a favourite of the new master. He was put incharge of the Riasi fort. Zorawar Singh got a chance to show his valour there when the fort was attacked by the forces of Mian Dewan Singh, another contender for the possession of the Riasi estate. The fort was besieged by superior force but, though hard-pressed, Zorawar held out with great courage and fortitude till relief came from Jammu. Riasi was saved to the delight of Gulab Singh, and the career of Zorawar as a brave and resourceful soldier received a big boost, and earned him quick promotions.

Soon after he showed another aspect of his character; an efficient and ingenious organiser. Zorawar Singh made a careful study of Gulab Singh's Commissariat and found its management wasteful. He put up a scheme for better utilization of supplies to the troops. When implemented, it resulted in considerable saving. Gulab Singh was so impressed by Zorawar that he appointed him inspector of Commissariat supplies in all the forts north of Jammu under Dogra control. By 1823, he was appointed governor of Kishtwar and Kussal and after sometime he was given the title wazir i.e. general.[1] Gulab Singh had already been recognized as Raja of Jammu by Maharaja Ranjit Singh with full powers to levy taxes and employ forces for the conquest of independent smaller states around. Most of these powers and authority were transferred to Zorawar Singh, his Wazir, by Raja Gulab Singh, who had by now full faith in him. Zorawar Singh lived upto the expectations of Gulab Singh and even surpassed what his master had expected. The following ten years Zorawar Singh, an organizing genius that he was, devoted in consolidating the territories which now belonged to Gulab Singh. He revised the tax structure which increased the revenue yield considerably. He renovated the Kishtwar fort to make it a formidable base of his troops for his exploits in the north. He used the high mountains around Kishtwar for imparting physical training to his sturdy Dogra soldiers. With the increase in state revenue, he was able to increase the strength of his forces and equip them properly. The fertile valley of Maru Wardwant provided the much needed provisions for his army which were stocked in the Fort. Thus Kishtwar served as a very useful base of operations for the conquest of Ladakh, Baltistan and

Western Tibet.[2] Zorawar was now ready to extend the boundaries to the Jammu state.

Ladakh at that time was ruled by an indolent and easygoing prince, Tse-pal Namgyal, who cared little for the administrative affairs and even less for the welfare of his subjects. There were also dissensions going on between two petty rulers. Zorawar Singh wanted to take advantage of the disturbed state of affairs in Ladakh and demanded the restoration of an estate supposedly held by a Kishtwar chief in former times. During the summer when the passes were open and the weather was congenial for Dogra soldiers, Zorawar advanced at the head of four to five thousand Dogra army in 1834 and entered the Purig province of Ladakh, now part of Kargil Tehsil. The Ladakhis were completely taken by surprise because they could never imagine that the Dogra army could cross over a 14,000 feet high pass. They could thus offer little resistance initially. But soon a hastily collected force of about five thousand men faced the Dogra army and tried to stem their advance at Sankho. However, they were defeated as the Dogras had better arms and were superior in war-tactics and discipline as they had participated in many battles earlier. The victorious Dogra army occupied Kartse, capital of Purig province, and marched down the Suru river in the lower Ladakh. They inflicted another defeat on the Ladakhis at Paskkym and their leader was killed. From Paskkym, the Dogras marched to Shergol and thence to Mulbeh. There they met an envoy of the Ladakhi king with a letter from King Tse-Pal praying for peace. Zorawar assured the king of safe conduct if the latter accepted to pay Gulab Singh an annual tribute. Under the peace settlement, the kingdom was restored to Tse-Pal but he now became a vassal of Raja Gulab Singh and through him of Maharaja Ranjit Singh. The Ladakhi king, in addition to paying a yearly tribute of Rs. 20,000, was also asked to pay Rs. 50,000 as war indemnity. By then the Dogras had penetrated up to Leh and the peace terms were settled there. This, however, was not to be the end of confrontation. The Dogras had hardly returned to Kishtwar when news came of an insurrection in Ladakh. Zorawar, therefore with characteristic energy and celerity again marched to Leh in November 1935 and subdued the rebels, collecting further war indemnity. To strengthen the Dogra position in Leh, Zorawar Singh got built a strong fort there. There were two more insurrections which Zorawar Singh had to subdue, the last one being in May 1939. Finally, the Ladakhi resistence was broken and they became peaceful subjects of the Dogra rule which lasted upto 1947, when it became part of India as a district of Jammu and Kashmir state.

Ladakh now became a convenient base for invading Baltistan and Western Tibet. To keep the Ladakhis away from further mischief, Zorawar decided to utilize them for the conquest of Baltistan on the western side of Ladakh. The people of Baltistan were Mohammedans of Shia faith. When compared to the peace loving Ladakhis, they were warlike and aggressive. Baltistan contains enormous mountain chains, most of which are eighteen thousand to twenty thousand feet high. Thus, the conquest of Baltistan was not an easy task but the indomitable General Zorawar Singh made the conquest of this region feasible. Zorawar's advance was perfectly timed and an excuse for intervention was already there. Relations between its ruler, Ahmed Shah and his eldest son, Mohammad Shah, were far from cordial as Ahmed Shah had declared not the eldest son but another son as his heir. This had offended Mohammad Shah who sought the help of Dogra ruler, and Zorawar Singh found a valid reason for invading Baltistan. As in Ladakh so in Baltistan there was no standing army. Except for the cruel weather, which was the greatest enemy of the Dogras, the hurriedly formed Balti force was no match for the disciplined and better armed Dogra army. After undergoing some harrowing experiences, the Dogra army was able to subdue Baltistan including the district of Shardu. Before returning, Zorawar installed Mohammad Shah as the ruler of Baltistan but left a Dogra garrison in the fort to assert Dogra authority. This was in 1840.

In early 1841, he planned to invade Western Tibet and raised a force of about six thousand, comprising mostly Ladakhis and Baltis. He sent an ultimatum to the Tibetan governor at Gortok to submit on the ground that his province, Rudok, had once been a dependency of Ladakh. The latter tried to put him off by sending him presents but that did not mollify the Dogra general, who advanced upto the Indus and overran the territory as far as the holy Mount Kailas and Lake Mansarowar, meeting little opposition on the way. While Zorawar camped at Tirathpuri, his trusted

Colonel Basti Ram was sent to Taklakot, near the Nepal border. The small Tibetan force at Taklakot was subdued and the conquest of Western Tibet was complete. Zorawar and other high Dogra dignitaries proceeded to take a holy bath in Lake Mansarowar and made offerings at the Kailas temple.

In the meanwhile, news reached Lhasa about the Dogra conquest of Western Tibet. An army of about ten thousand soldiers, having a strong unit of artillery, was sent. Zorawar apparently did not expect any confrontation with the Tibetan army during the winter. But the Tibetan army knowing the topography and accustomed to the snowy landscape, managed to reach the Western part of Tibet. Zorawar Singh realised the gravity of the situation. He was surrounded in the depth of winter by an army three times the strength of his own. He could not expect any help from Leh as all the passages were blocked by snow. Zorawar broke up his camp at Tirathpuri and advanced towards Taklakot with the intention of effecting a junction with Colonel Basti Ram. But he could not reach Taklakot as all the by-paths had been blocked by the Tibetans. His own army was suffering due to frostbite and was being incapacitated due to extreme cold. The wazir, a man of indomitable courage as he was, fell upon the enemy. The first action was fought on 10 December, 1841 and fighting continued for three days. On the fateful day of 12 December, Zorawar personally led his troops in a final assault. He fought like a lion and might have defeated the army, but a bullet hit him on the shoulder. He fell down from his horse and before he could rise to his feet the Tibetans had closed in upon him. A Tibetan soldier impaled a spear through his chest. The brave general fell in the battlefield, sword in hand. Zorawar had lost his last battle not so much to the Tibetans as to the rigours of the Tibetan winter at a height of over fifteen thousand feet above sea level. Even the enemy pays respect to the brave. The Tibetans built a *smadhi* (memorial) called '*Singhba ka Chorten*' outside the small village Toye, near Taklakot, where Zorawar was killed. The monument is merely a pyramid of small stones collated together in multiple layers without the use of cement or clay, with the top layer whitewashed. The monument is maintained by the local villagers. The Hindu pilgrims who go annually to pay homage to Mount Kailas and to have a dip in the sacred

Mansarovar, have started visiting '*Singhba ka Chorten*' to enliven the memory of the brave general whose contribution to history was to bring Ladakh within the political domain of India.[3]

The Tibetans, encouraged by their victory over Zorawar's forces, tried to take over Ladakh in 1842 but were repulsed by the Dogras trained by Zorawar Singh who were entrenched in the forts built by the great general. The Tibetans went back and agreed to a peace treaty which was signed by the Tibetans with the Dogra chiefs by which Ladakh became permanently a part of India.

Zorawar Singh had no son to perpetuate his line. He married thrice. His first wife died early. Then he married two sisters, Asha Devi and Lajwanti. Asha Devi accompanied her husband on his Tibetan expedition and had performed pilgrimage to Mount Kailas and Mansarovar lake in the company of her husband. Before the final battle, Zorawar had sent Asha Devi back to Leh. When she heard the news of her husband's death, she performed sati. Several legends have sprung up about the great general and his wives in the Ladakh and Jammu region.[4]

The brave Zorawar has not found his rightful place in Indian history. However, K.M. Panikkar pays tribute to him in the following words: "Besides being an intrepid commander, as the Ladakh and Baltistan campaigns had shown him to be, he was also gifted with considerable political ability. His settlement of the newly conquered provinces bears witness to this. To have marched an army, not once or twice but six times, over the snow-clad ranges of Ladakh and Baltistan, 15,000 feet above sea-level, is a wonderful achievement. To have conquered that country after successive campaigns and reduce it to a peaceful province is an exploit for which there is no parallel in Indian history. His greatness will shine through the pages of Indian history as that of a great noble warrior".[5]

# References

1.  Smyth, G.C. *A History of Reigning Family of Lahore*, Calcutta, 1847, p.199.
2.  Datta, C.L. *General Zorawar Singh*, New Delhi, Deep & Deep, 1984, pp.20-21.
3.  Punj, Balbir K. *Unsung Hero. The Pioneer*, 15 October 2003.

4. Charak, Sukhdev Singh. *General Zorawar Singh*, New Delhi, Publications Division, 1983, p.126.
5. Panikkar, K.M. *Founding of Kashmir State*, London, 1953, p.82.

# Rabindranath Tagore

## (1861-1941)

"Tagore family has played a leading part in various reform movements in Bengal during the nineteenth century. There were men of spiritual stature in it and fine writers and artists, but Rabindranath towered among them all, and indeed all over India his position gradually became one of unchallenged supremacy".[1] So wrote Jawaharlal Nehru in *Discovery of India*. This talented family lived in a sprawling house called Jorasanko House in north Calcutta, where Rabindranath or Rabi was born on 6 May 1861, the fourteenth child of his parents, Debendranath Tagore and Sarada Devi. In this big house a joint family of scores of people lived while exploring their talents in writing, music, drama and philosophy. It was impossible for Rabi not to absorb the atmosphere of the place. The family was rich and owned huge estates in east Bengal (now Bangladesh).

Rabindranath hated going to school. Thus, his formal education was only basic. For brief periods he studied in Oriental Seminary, Bengal Academy and later St. Xavier's High School. Tutors were arranged for him to study at home but he hated the tutors as much as he hated schools. However, he learnt fast with his own efforts imbibing the intellectual atmosphere of his house. Early in life he started writing poetry in Bengali. He was composing verses on a slate, 'happy in the thought that errors could be wiped away'. Soon he was writing songs full of tenderness of his country, about the people who inhabited it and about the bounties of nature. About this early urge to write poetry Tagore later said, "In early dawn of mind's first urge of expansion, I instinctively chose my own true path which, I believe, was to give rhythmic expression of life on a colourful background of imagination". The songs continued to pour spontaneously out of his unusually fertile mind in scores, in hundreds. He began to compose music for his songs, resulting in the now famous Rabindra Sangeet. Along with poetry, he started writing short stories, plays, novels and essays on various topics as he grew up.

At the age of seventeen, his elder brother Satyendranath (the first Indian I.C.S.) took him to England, where Rabindranath studied English literature at the University College, London for more than a year. On his return, his family wanted him to go to England again to get a degree in law but he foiled their attempt and spent the next three years in the house of his brother who was a judge at Ahmedabad. Rabindranath experienced the maturity of his poetic vision which he immortalized in a poem '*The Awakening of the Waterfall*'.

In late 1883, Rabindranath was married to Mrinalini Devi who was barely eleven years old, who bore him five children; three daughters and two sons. Of them, only the eldest son, Rathindranath (born 1888) and the youngest daughter, Mira (born 1893) survived him. All the others died young.

His early writings were published in the family magazines *Bharati* and a little later in *Balak*, of which he was editor for sometime. In 1890, Rabindranath visited England for three months in the company of his brother. On his return, he was entrusted with the management of the family estate in Rajshahi with its headquarters at Shilaidah (now in Bangladesh) where he spent a very fruitful decade and was able to develop many of his ideas about education and rural development. Here he came in close contact with nature and the rustic rural folk. He came to believe that many of the ills of society were so because of faulty education or no education. He also realized the need for rural upliftment; the two areas on which he spent his time and energy in later life, besides writing and travelling. During this period, he wrote a number of stories including the famous *Post Master*.

In 1891, he started his own magazine *Sadhana*, a monthly, which survived till 1895. In it were published some of his best writings like *Sonar*

*Tari* and *Panchbhuter Diary*. Tagore moved to Santiniketan near Bolpur in 1901 where his father had founded an *ashram* earlier (1863) and started a school there with five students including his son. Here Rabindranath tried to put into practice his ideas about educating the youth in free atmosphere. The school steadily grew into an institution of repute.

The four years, 1902-1905, brought a series of tragedies for him. His wife died in 1902; his second daughter, Renuka, in 1903 and his father, Debendranath, in 1905. Tagore bore these tragedies stoically and concentrated on the development of his educational experiment in Santiniketan. Then came the partition of Bengal in 1905 which stirred up the people of Bengal, resulting in a powerful movement against the British rule. Tagore's emotional attachment to Bengal came to the fore. Abandoning his tranquil life at Santiniketan he came to Calcutta and took active part in the movement, preaching *swadeshi*, composing stirring nationalistic songs, writing incisive essays, addressing meetings and even leading protest demonstrations. But when the movement took a violent turn he retired to the tranquility of Santiniketan. This he did throughout his life: 'short spells of whirlpool of activity and then retreating to the solitude of Santiniketan'. He loved solitude but could not endure it for any length of time, and was drawn back into intense public activity.

Back in Santiniketan Tagore entered upon another creative period. His novel *Gora,* one of his most popular ones, appeared in a serialized version in the monthly *Prabasi*, Bengali literary magazine, edited by Ramananda Chatterjee, in 1907. In 1908, came out a collected edition of his prose writings. The period 1908-11 saw the appearance of his plays the *Autumn Festival* (1908), *Atonement* (1909), *Raja* (1910) and *Post Office* (1911) besides *Jivansmriti* (1911) the English version of which was published as *My Reminiscences* a little later. The same year (1911), Tagore wrote the song '*Jana, Gana, Mana*' on the anniversary of the Brahmo Samaj of which he was a secretary for many years, which is now the national anthem of India. His most famous book *Gitanjali* in Bengali was also published in 1911. Tagore himself rendered it into English, the manuscript of which he took to England in May 1912. When some songs of it were read out in the London literary circles headed by the Irish poet W.B. Yeats, it created a mild sensation. The English version of *Gitanjali* was published the same year in a limited edition by India Society and soon after by Macmillan, the publishing house which went on to publish almost all of Tagore's English works. From London, Tagore left for a lecture tour of the United States where his son Rathindranath was studying agriculture at the University of Illinois. Tagore lectured at several universities but the series of lectures at the Harvard University engaged him for a longer period. The lectures were later published as *Sadhana* in book form.

After this tour, Tagore came back to Santiniketan when he received the news that he had been awarded the Nobel Prize for Literature for 1913. A train load of people from Calcutta reached Santiniketan to felicitate him. These included even reviewers who had so far seen only his faults and professors who had used his poems as examples of bad Bengali. Tagore refused to meet them saying that it required a foreign prize for them to know his worth. The worst came from the notorious and unscrupulous London *Times* correspondent Valentine Chirol who while addressing a Muslim gathering in Calcutta told the audience that *Gitanjali* was actually written by W.B. Yeats, the famous Irish poet, who later wrote a moving introduction to *Gitanjali*. *Gitanjali* contains over one hundred short poems, collectively called 'song offerings'. "There are many virtues in these poems — an intense and yet sober patriotism; a femininely subtle understanding of love and woman, nature and man; a passionate penetration into the insight of India's philosophers; and a Tennysonian delicacy of sentiment and phrase; a Shelley who refused to die young or to grow old. If there is any fault in them it is that they are too consistently beautiful, too monotonously idealistic and tender".[2]

Tagore suddenly found himself on a world stage. Overnight he became famous. His first reaction to the fame thrust on him was 'I would never again have any peace'. So it was. He began to be honoured by universities, parliaments, presidents and kings and literary societies the world over. He was conferred a knighthood in 1915, which he renounced in 1919 through a personal letter written by him in his own hand to Viceroy Lord Chelmsford on 30 May 1919 after the Jallianwala Bagh massacre by the British troops at Amritsar, in Punjab.

He was fifty-two when he received the Nobel Prize. His creative period of writing almost came to an end. The remaining years of his life were devoted to building up his school at Santiniketan which was transformed to a university, Visva Bharati, the foundation stone of which was laid in 1918. It soon earned name and fame, attracting students and teachers from different parts of India and some foreign countries. Here Tagore experimented with his theories of education. In the convocation address at the Banaras Hindu University in 1935, he spelled out his ideas on education as being followed in Visva Bharati: "Education came by living part of nature, from cosmic environment. To him the true ideal of education was infinite peace, infinite wellbeing, the infinite one". He did try to bring education near nature by holding classes in the open, amidst flowering trees, chirping of birds and by celebrating each change of season with music, dance and drama. Tagore gave a new orientation to Indian education and tried to stem the tide unleashed by Macaulay almost a century ago.

Tagore toured several countries, some more than once, with dual purposes: 1) to spread the message of universal love for mankind and building a bridge between East and West, and 2) to raise funds for Visva Bharati, which was not getting any government aid. After his first tour of America in 1912, he again went on a tour during 1916-17 to Japan and America. The theme of his lectures was 'nationalism' which was later published in book form with the same title in 1917. In 1921, Rabindranath tried to give concrete shape to his ideas of village reconstruction by converting the Surul Kuthi (which he had purchased earlier) into the Institute of Rural Reconstruction. But his first love remained Visva Bharati, for the development of which he devoted the rest of his life. He used to say that his educational projects at Bolpur was his 'chief and most enduring poem'.

The following two decades, Tagore spent touring different parts of India and several countries of the world: in 1922 Ceylon and south India; in 1923 Western India; in 1924 China, Japan and Argentina (where he met Victoria O' Campo, the leading poetess of Argentina in Buenos Aires and stayed in her country house for two months and had a harmless romantic interlude); in 1925-26 Europe and Egypt; in 1927 Southeast Asia; in 1928 Pondicherry and Ceylon; in 1929 Canada and America. The year 1930 proved more rewarding when he visited several countries of Europe and America once again. In May 1930, he delivered Hibbert Lectures at Oxford which were later published in book form as *The Religion of Man*. During this tour, Rabindranath had taken with him a number of his paintings. He had an urge to paint at the age of sixty-eight. Tagore called his paintings 'Versification in lines.' Although many of his paintings and drawings "had the air of having been done on the spur of the moment, were lacking in technical discipline, and in some instances were as primitive in medium as they were in concept and execution, some critics found in them a dramatic and haunting quality".[3] When these paintings were exhibited in art galleries of London, Paris, Berlin, Moscow, Copenhagen, New York and Boston they created a sensation in art circles. Some of these paintings were bought by art lovers.

In December 1931, Rabindranath's seventieth birthday was celebrated in Calcutta where glowing tributes were paid to him by Indian and foreign admirers which were collected in a volume titled *Golden Book of Tagore* edited by Ramananda Chatterjee, his old friend and editor of *Modern Review*.

Tagore first met Gandhi in 1915 when Gandhi came back to India from South Africa, and stayed at Santiniketan for about a month. Though there was hardly anything common between the two they continued to be friendly and respectful to each other though there were unpleasant skirmishes between the two from time to time. The first one came when Gandhi started the Non-Cooperation movement in 1920. Tagore was in America at the time. From there he wrote to Charles Andrews in Santiniketan: "What irony of fate is that I should be preaching 'Cooperation of Cultures' between East and West on this side of the sea just at the moment when the doctrine of non-cooperation is preached on the other side". He ridiculed Gandhi for 'going back to crude spinning wheel in the age of modern machines'. Tagore was opposed to burning of foreign clothes and the boycott of schools and colleges as preached by Gandhi.

In 1933, Tagore belatedly learnt that Bengal had been treated unjustly in the Poona Pact. He sent a cable to Sir S.N. Sircar who was in London to get the Pact modified and even held a press conference on 24 July 1933 in Calcutta pointing out that no 'responsible representative of Bengal' was present during the negotiations and that 'justice has certainly been sacrificed in the case of Bengal in the Poona Pact'. Tagore wrote to Gandhi about his feelings on 8 August 1933 but Gandhi was adamant and was not moved by Tagore's plea. When Gandhi attributed the earthquake in Bihar in 1934 as the 'divine chastisement' for the sin of untouchability, Tagore expressed his 'painful surprise' that Gandhi could hold such unscientific view of things. Obviously the two great men had different intellectual levels of thinking and the love-hate relationship lasted throughout their lives.

In 1937, Gandhi in a letter to Tagore termed the latter's fund raising lecture tours as 'begging expeditions'. Tagore was hurt. He wrote to Gandhi on 26 February 1937: "I must refuse to accept the term 'begging expedition' as an accurate or worthy expression coming from your pen". He explained that, "If I have to receive contribution in the shape of admission fees from the audience, I claim it as very much less than what is due to me in return for the rare benefit conferred upon them".[4]

Tagore often used to say that he was not a politician but whenever he felt that injustice was being done he did not hesitate to express his opinion. In 1939, when Gandhi manipulated the Congress Working Committee to oust Subhas Chandra Bose as president of the Congress, Tagore was aggrieved. He sent a telegram to Subhas encouraging and consoling him: "The dignity and forbearance which you have shown in the midst of a most aggravating situation has won my admiration and confidence in your leadership. The same perfect decorum has still to be maintained by Bengal for the sake of her own self-respect and thereby to turn your apparent defeat into a permanent victory".[5] Did Tagore want Subhas to lead the nation at that stage? It becomes somewhat clear then during the foundation stone laying ceremony for the proposed Mahajati Sadan in August 1933. Tagore blessed Subhas, "I feel that you have come with an errand to usher a new light of hope in our motherland —— My days have come to an end. I may not join him in the fight that is to come (prophetic words these) I can only bless him and take my leave".[6]

But in spite of so many idiosyncrasies and quirks which Tagore found in Gandhi and frankly pointed these out to him from time to time, both loved and respected each other. Gandhi and Kasturba's last visit to Santiniketan was in March 1940. In a brief welcome speech Tagore said, "I hope we shall be able to keep close to a reticent expression of love and reverence in welcoming you into our ashram and never allow it to overflow into any extravagant display of phrases —— Let us make our meeting today a simple meeting of hearts".[7]

On 14 April 1941 on his eightieth birthday address, Tagore gave his last message to the world in which he reiterated his faith in man for fostering peace and unity. He passed away on 7 August 1941 in the same Jorasanko House where he was born. His death was mourned by people all over the world.

Tagore was undoubtedly one of the greatest intellect this country has produced. He was a poet, writer, actor, composer, painter, educationist and India's 'conscious keeper'. He has left a phenomenal literary output which is not easy to count: fifty dramas, a hundred books of verse containing three thousand poems, about forty works of fiction, innumerable songs, about fifteen books of literary, political and religious essays and scores of other books. Add to these his hundreds of paintings, sketches and doodlings, a hobby which he acquired late in life.

In spite of Tagore's occasional foray into politics, he was essentially an apolitical man, founder of the anti-politics movement. And in spite of his internationalism, he was, at heart, a nationalist. When in millions of places today *Jana, Gana, Mana* is sung the voice of Tagore is heard. Decades back he had written in his book of poems, *Gardener:*

None lives for ever, brother, and Nothing lasts for long. Keep that in mind and rejoice.

## References

1. Nehru, Jawaharlal. *Discovery of India*, OUP, 1946, p.340.
2. Durant, Will. *Our Oriental Heritage*, New York, Simon and Schuster, 1954, p.620.
3. Deed, Joseph Lister. *Tagore and America*, New Delhi, U.S. Information Service, 1961, p.29.
4. Bhattacharya, S.ed., *The Mahatma and the Poet*, New Delhi, National Book Trust, 1997, p.166.
5. Bose, A.N. *My Uncle Netaji*, Bombay, Bhartiya Vidya Bhavan, 1989, p.179.
6. Ibid, p.184.
7. Bhattacharya, S.ed, op. cit. p.208.

# Purushottam Das Tandon

## (1882-1961)

Purushottam Das Tandon was born at Allahabad (U.P.) on 1 August 1882 in a middle-class family. His father, Salig Ram Tandon, was an accountant in government service. His mother, Saranpiari, was not much educated and was a traditional God-fearing Hindu lady. Purushottam started his education in a *madarasa* (Muslim school) near his home and learnt Urdu and Persian there. But soonafter he joined the City Anglo-vernacular school from where he passed his eighth class in first division in 1895. He then joined Government School and passed the matriculation examination in 1897, again in first division. He graduated from Muir Central College in 1904. Subsequently, he got a degree in law in 1906 and also passed his M.A. history.

While still a student, he was married to Chandramukhi Devi in 1897, immediately after passing his matriculation. Early marriages of boys and girls were customary during those days. His happy married life did not interfere with his education or his political and social activities. He started his legal career in 1906 and joined the Allahabad High Court Bar in 1908, as a junior of Sir Tej Bahadur Sapru. He had become a successful lawyer but on the advice of Madan Mohan Malaviya, he joined Nabha state in Punjab as law minister. He resigned after three years to devote himself to political and social activities, the important part of which was the propagation and development of Hindi. In fact, he had taken active part to get the status of one of the court languages for Hindi in U.P. The agitation had started in 1901 and the government agreed to accept applications in Hindi in Devnagari script in 1905. Propagation of Hindi became his life's mission for which he devoted a major part of his time and energy. Besides Madan Mohan Malaviya, he had great respect and admiration for Lala Lajpat Rai who persuaded him to accept an executive position in the Punjab National Bank at Lahore. He worked there from 1923 to 1929, after which he became an active member of the Congress party.

He had joined the Indian National Congress in 1899 when he was still a student. Due to his active participation in nationalistic activities, he was expelled from the Muir College for one year when he was an undergraduate student. He was an active member of the Seva Dal formed by Madan Mohan Malaviya to undertake social work during epidemics and religious gatherings at the Sangam. In 1906, he represented Allahabad at the All-India Congress Committee (AICC). In 1918, he organized the Allahabad District Peasants Committee for improving the economic condition of the farmers. In 1919, he was elected as chairman of the Allahabad Municipal Board where he did some valuable work providing essential services, like drinking water, for the common man. He displeased the white residents of the Cantonment area by compelling them to pay water-tax like other residents, which they were not paying earlier. He took part in the Non-Cooperation movement started by Gandhi. He was arrested in 1921 and was imprisoned for eighteen months. He was emerging as an important leader of the Congress party not only in Allahabad but in Uttar Pradesh. He was elected president of the Gorakhpur District Congress Committee in 1923 and the same year he presided over the Provincial Congress Committee. In 1930, the Allahabad District Peasant Committee became very active and started a no-tax campaign on the lines of the Bardoli satyagraha led by Sardar Patel in 1928. About this campaign Nehru writes: "I also functioned as a member of the Allahabad District Committee. This Committee under the leadership of its president Purushottam Das Tandon played an important part in the development of the agrarian situation. In 1930, it had given the lead in starting the no-tax campaign in the province".[1] From 1932 onwards, Tandon was arrested several times for organizing peasant agitations through the Kisan Sabha. In 1937-38 he was elected speaker of the U.P. Legislative Assembly, a job which he did with great distinction.

Purushottam Das Tandon is remembered most as a lover and propagator of Hindi. This was the greatest mission of his life and he devoted almost all his life for the success of his mission. In May 1910, writers and lovers of Hindi assembled in Banaras (Varanasi) as a result of which the Nagri Pracharni Sabha came into being. Its aim was to conduct research and the publication of seminal works in Hindi. For the propagation of Hindi, an auxillary body, Hindi Sahitya Sammelan, was also formed with Madan Mohan Malaviya as president and Purushottam Das Tandon as secretary. After a year, the office of the Sammelan was shifted to Allahabad, and Tandon started to develop this institution with a missionary zeal. During its fourth annual session at Bhagalpur, (Bihar) it was decided to conduct examinations and award degrees. For this, several branches of the Sammelan were opened in different places. For over twenty-five years, Gandhi was closely associated with the working of the Hindi Sahitya Sammelan. He presided over the 1918 session of the Sammelan at Indore. With the efforts of Purushottam Das Tandon a building was constructed for the Sammelan to house its office, library and museum. While performing the opening ceremony of the library and museum on 5 April 1936, Gandhi appealed for donations and was pained that the "response had to be so small in a matter which concern what India had declared was its national language".[2] Upto this time Gandhi was very much involved in the propagation of Hindi. But soon after Gandhi changed his views and started supporting Hindustani (Hindi plus Urdu) to be written both in Devnagari and Persian scripts. To propagate this spurious language the Hindustani Prachar Sabha was formed with the blessings of Gandhi as a rival to the Hindi Sahitya Sammelan. But Hindustani, as a written language, could never become popular in a country where illiteracy (people not knowing even one script) was as high as seventy percent. To expect them to learn two scripts was rather contrary to reason. When the question of national language came up in the Constituent Assembly in September 1949, Hindustani was also suggested as the national language. It was the greatest day for Purushottam Das

Tandon when Hindi in Devnagari script was declared as the *rashtra bhasha* (national language). His single-minded devotion and love for Hindi bore fruit.

During the 1937 elections to the provincial assemblies Tandon was elected unopposed from the Allahabad constituency. The Congress won and formed a ministry with Govind Ballabh Pant as chief minister. Purushottam Das Tandon was elected speaker of the Assembly. With the start of the war (1939), the Congress ministries resigned in October 1939. Gandhi started the individual satyagraha. Many leaders were arrested including Vinoba Bhave, Jawaharlal Nehru. Tandon was also arrested in 1940 and was sentenced for one year and was kept in Fatehgarh jail. In August 1942, started the Quit India movement. Most of the Congress leaders were arrested. Tandon was also arrested on 9 August and was sent to Naini Jail. This was his seventh imprisonment. Tandon had his first heart attack in 1939 and he did not recover fully when he was imprisoned. When his health deteriorated further, he was released in 1944 on health grounds.

The year 1947 brought the freedom of the country as well as the catastrophe of partition. The Muslim League had started 'Direct Action', resulting in communal riots in many parts of the country starting with Calcutta and Noakhali in Bengal. Hindus, wedded to the concept of non-violence, bore the brunt. Only in Bihar they retaliated. In the Interim Government (1946-47) the Muslim League cabinet ministers saw to it that it did not function. The Congress leaders, including Gandhi, were now in favour of accepting the 3 June 1947 proposal of the British government which promised freedom along with partition of the country. The All-India Congress Committee met on 14-15 June 1947 to discuss the 3 June proposal as approved by the Working Committee. Among the opponents, the most impressive and impassioned speech was made by Purushottam Das Tandon. He said, "Acceptance of the resolution will be an abject surrender to the British and the Muslim League. The Working Committee has failed you, but you have the strength of millions behind you and you must reject the resolution. The decision of the Working Committee was an admission of weakness and the result of a sense of despair. The Partition will not benefit either community — the Hindus in Pakistan and the Muslims in India would both live in fear".[4] However, the majority of members were for accepting the Partition Plan, and it came into force on 15 August 1947.

Purushottam Das Tandon was very distressed by the communal riots between Hindus and Muslims which had started in the early twenties and the frequency and intensity of which went on increasing. For Tandon, it was very painful that in spite of being in majority in many states, Hindus were at the receiving end most of the time. He advised Hindus to take up the sword to defend themselves which angered Gandhi. In the prayer meeting on 16 June 1947, Gandhi broached this topic, and criticized Tandon for going against preaching of non-violence, which had become the creed of the Congress. However, Purushottam Das could not accept the philosophy of Gandhi that getting killed without raising an arm was the highest form of bravery — non-violence of the brave.[5] The schism between Tandon and Gandhi widened. A similar skirmish occurred between Gandhi and K.M. Munshi in 1941 when after the Bombay riots Munshi advised Hindus to join *akharas* (gyms) to defend themselves. It so angered Gandhi that he advised Munshi to leave the Congress, which he did.

In 1946, Tandon was elected member of the Constituent Assembly where he was active in getting Hindi recognized as the national language. In free India, Nehru became the prime minister but the Congress party was controlled by Sardar Patel. The result was that many decisions which the Congress Party took were not to Nehru's liking. In spite of Nehru's opposition, Rajendra Prasad was elected as the first president of India in 1950. The same year Purushottam Das Tandon was elected president of the Congress party in spite of Nehru's opposition. Nehru's choice was J.B. Kriplani. Nehru expressed his anger by writing a letter to Purushottam Das Tandon on 8 August 1950. Nehru wrote: "You have become to large numbers of people in India some kind of a symbol of this communal and revivalist outlook". Nehru was not always in touch with the party feeling, but that did not prevent him from putting out his own view as that of 'large number'. There is no doubt that Purushottam Das Tandon commanded a large following, and had the support of majority of the members. As Tandon was supported by Sardar Patel, his election also affected the relations between Nehru and Patel also. Nehru did not forgive Patel for lending support to Tandon and the last two months of Sardar's life were spent in an uncomfortable position of receiving pin-pricks from him whenever he could get an opportunity of giving them".[6] Nehru refused to join the Working Committee while Tandon was president of the Congress and threatened to resign as prime minister. Being a true gentleman Tandon resigned as Congress president in 1951 and Nehru himself took over from him. This was the most agonising and humiliating experience in Tandon's life. Besides his active participation in the Hindi Sahitya Sammelan and the Congress party, Tandon was actively involved in the functioning of the Servants of People's Society founded by Lajpat Rai and was elected president of the Society after Lajpat Rai's death in 1928.

Tandon was elected member of the Lok Sabha in 1952 and of Rajya Sabha in 1956. But in 1956 due to his indifferent health he could hardly attend any meeting of the Rajya Sabha and almost retired from public life. Tandon did not write much but was a successful journalist. He edited the influential Hindi paper, *Abhyudaya* for many years. On 3 October 1960, in a public ceremony at Allahabad, *Tandon Abhinandon Granth* was presented to him by Rajendra Prasad, president of India. The following year, in 1961, the Bharat Ratna was conferred on him. He died on 1 July 1961.

Tandon was a man of integrity and principles. He and his family suffered long spells of privation and suffering which they bore stoically. He refused to accept monetary help from Seth Jamnalal Bajaj and Shiv Prasad Gupta of Banaras and preferred to live in poverty. In his personal life he was austere, almost ascetic, and did not wear Western clothes even when he was general manager of the Punjab National Bank at Lahore, the fashion capital of India at the time. For these qualities he was endeared by the people who started calling him 'Rajashri'. He can be regarded 'as the lineal successor of Madan Mohan Malaviya and Lajpat Rai, who influenced him most in his life.

## References

1. Nehru, Jawaharlal *An Autobiography*, New Delhi, Jawaharlal Nehru Memorial Fund, 1936, p.208.
2. *Collected Works of Mahatma Gandhi*, Vol. 62, p.314.
3. Ibid, Vol. 88, p.162.
4. Majumdar, R.C. *Struggle for Freedom*, Bombay, Bharatiya Vidya Bhavan, 2nd ed. 1988, p.780, (Vol. 11 of *The History and Culture of the Indian People*).
5. *Collected Worked of Mahatma Gandhi*, Vol. 88, pp.162-63.
6. Shankar, V. Ed. *Select Correspondence of Sardar Patel*, 1945-50, Vol. 2, Ahmedabad, Navajivan, 1977, pp.392-93.

# Jamsetji Nusserwanji Tata

## (1839-1904)

The small Parsi community in India has produced political leaders, freedom fighters, scientists, educationists, philanthropists, musicians, artists, cine and stage artists, high-ranking defence personnel and jurists. Jamsetji Nusserwanji Tata added one more dimension by creating an industrial empire which helped India towards economic independence.

Jamsetji Tata was born at Navsari, Gujarat on 3 March 1839. His father, Nusserwanji Tata, a businessman had an export-import trade with China. During his early years in Navsari, Jamsetji did not receive any formal education. However, at the age of thirteen, he was taken to Bombay by his father to acquire an English education. He joined Elphinstone College in 1852. As he showed exceptional promise he was awarded a free studentship by his college. There he underwent a liberal education and developed a passion for reading, which remained with him all his life. While still in college, Jamsetji was married to a Parsi girl Heerabai, five years his junior. They had two sons, Dorab born in 1859 and Ratan in 1871. In 1858, Jamsetji obtained his degree and left the college. That was the end of his formal education. After leaving college Jamsetji joined a solicitor's office but left after a few months to look after his father's business in China. A new branch of the firm was opened in Hong Kong under the name Jamsetji and Ardeshir. A branch was also opened at Shanghai. Always keen to observe and learn, Jamsetji studied the potential of the eastern market while in China. Early in 1864 he left for England to represent the firm of Nusserwanji and Kalyandas, which was dealing in Indian cotton. However, the cotton prices came down crashing after the end of the Civil War in America and the firm suffered heavy losses. While in England, Jamsetji visited Lancashire frequently to study the working of the cotton textile industry. Back in India, he, along with his father, worked hard for three years to put their firm on a sound footing once again. When a 'derelict and bankrupt oil mill' was put up for sale at Chinchpokly, Jamsetji, in collaboration with a few friends, purchased the mill and renamed it Alexander Mill. It was converted into a cotton mill after the installation of new machinery. After making it a profitable venture, the mill was sold off after two years. As the mill was under the sole charge of Jamsetji, quite a tidy sum came to his share as profit.

In 1873, Jamsetji decided to revisit England and once again studied the working of the Lancashire textile industry more intimately. He saw how the Indian cotton was being transformed into cloth, which was then exported to India. Why not manufacture cloth in India itself, using Indian cotton and save transport cost both ways? Armed with this resolve, he returned to India in 1874. While managing the Alexander Mill he had gained some experience of the cotton industry at home. He now wanted to invest in cotton industry in a big way. After studying the suitability of a cotton growing district for his new venture he selected Nagpur which had a proximity to Warora Coal mines. The mill became functional in January 1877 and was named Empress Mills. Jamsetji was continuously in touch with the new developments in cotton-textile machinery and was quick to buy the latest machinery to compete with the imported cloth from England. Huge profits started coming in. One secret of his success was the care and consideration with which he treated his labour force, providing them facilities which were unknown in other mills and industries. With money flowing in, Jamshetji started investing in real estate, not only in Bombay but also at other places like Ootacamund, Bangalore and also at his native place, Navsari. He got a magnificent house built for the family at the Esplanade in Bombay where the extended family of uncles, aunts, sisters, nephews and nieces lived happily for decades. He also had an extensive collection of books. Jamsetji's father Nusserwanji died in 1886 and all his property passed into the hands of Jamsetji.

Jamsetji was always thinking of new projects though the Empress Mills had made him rich and famous. So far Indian mills, including his own, were producing coarse cloth and coarse yarn and all the finer cloth was being imported from England. Jamsetji now planned to start a mill which could produce fine cloth to compete with Lancashire mills. He was confident that people would buy *swadeshi* cloth in preference to the imported one as the *swadeshi* concept was gaining ground in India at the time. The result was the founding of the Swadeshi Mills Company, Limited. The company acquired Dharamsi Mills at Kurla in 1886, which was running at a loss; reorganized the whole set-up, replaced the old machinery with the newly imported one and made it a profit making concern after naming it Swadeshi Mills. The newly floated company, Tata and Sons, became the agents of the mill. Later another cotton mill, Advance Mills, at Ahmedabad, was added. After reorganization and modernization it started making a profit adding to the wealth of the Tatas and the prestige of the country.

In 1890, Jamsetji decided, with usual foresight, to invest in property on a large scale. Buying one piece of land after another, he became one of the leading landowners in Bombay. But he did not use his landed property for profit-making. He strove tirelessly for the development of Bombay, the city which he loved. Many impressive buildings in the city owe their existence to his munificence including the Parsi Gymkhana. He also built homes for middle-class Parsi families and established many educational institutions in Bombay and Navsari. He also felt the need for a modern hotel in Bombay. After great planning he built the Taj Hotel opposite the Gateway of India in Bombay. Its interiors were done up with what was best available in Europe. Many renowned persons have stayed in this hotel and it has found a place in many novels and other works written during the Raj.

Jamsetji was always thinking and planning new ventures. One such was the development of sericulture in Mysore which he had thought of after his visit to Japan and France. He was a compulsive traveller and visited Europe, England and America several times. He would not miss an industrial exhibition whether it was in Paris, London or Chicago to see and learn about new techniques and machinery. In 1893, while Vivekananda was telling the world about Hindu religion and philosophy in the Parliament of Religions, Jamsetji was busy in inspecting new machines and techniques at the Chicago Exhibition.

Jamsetji was a nationalist to the core though he never used a political platform. However, he was an active member of the Bombay Presidency Association through which the Indian National Congress was working in Bombay Presidency. He created an endowment to help the bright students to get into I.C.S. in greater number so that the administration of the country could be controlled by Indians gradually. In those days the Indian Civil Service examination was held only in London and many deserving students could not afford the passage to Britain to appear in the examination. Through the endowment, financial assistance was given to young aspirants who wanted to appear in the I.C.S. examination. His biographer, Harris, writes that twenty percent of the Indian members of the I.C.S. had been Tata scholars at one time.

He had planned and worked for three of his dream projects whose completion he did not live to see: a hydro-electric scheme near Bombay; a scientific research institute and an iron and steel manufacturing plant. He visited the United States in 1902 to work out the details of these projects after studying them in detail. He visited several cities and was received with respect and admiration wherever he went. The press eulogized him. *The Washington Post* described him, not inaccurately, as 'merchant prince', manufacturer and importer, and likewise 'philanthropist, scholar and philosopher.' Other papers wrote about him with 'strange blend of fact and fiction'.[1] He visited Pittsburg, the foremost centre of iron and steel production. He visited Niagara Falls with his hydro-electric scheme in mind. He met and discussed with leading industrialists of America like George Westington and Julian Kennedy. On the recommendation of Kennedy, he hired C.P. Perin as consulting engineer for his proposed iron and steel works. His meeting with Perin was full of drama and show. Perin later wrote about this meeting: "I was poring over some accounts in the office when the door opened and a man in strange garb entered. He walked in, leaned over my desk and looked at me for fully a minute in silence. Finally, he said in deep voice, 'Are you Charles Page Perin?' I said, 'Yes'. He stared at me again silently for a long time. Then slowly he said, 'I believe I have found the man I have been looking for. I want you to come to India with me to find suitable iron ore and cooking coal and the necessary fluxes. I want you to take charge as my consulting engineer. Mr. Kennedy will build the steel plant wherever you advice and I will foot the bill'".[2]

It took quite sometime to complete the preliminaries; to choose the site, to import the machinery and to build the iron and steel mill. The site chosen after a series of investigations was Sakchi in Bihar where the present day Jamshedpur stands. It was only in 1911 that iron began to flow from the blast furnaces of the Tata Iron and Steel Company. The dreamer had died seven years earlier.

On his way back to India, he visited England and met Lord George Hamilton, secretary of state for India, in connection with his proposed Research Institute. Nothing concrete came out of the meeting. It took time for this dream of his to materialize. Lord Minto, the viceroy, approved the constitution of the Institute of Science at Bangalore in 1909. It started functioning in 1911 and became a leading scientific research institute in the country. It is also called the Tata Institute. Scientists like C.V. Raman and Bhabha have taught and worked in the institute.

Jamsetji also left the details of the scheme for hydro-electric power generation at Lonavala near Bombay. It took much longer for the scheme to materialize because the involvement of the government was required. But he had shown that hydro-electric generation was feasible to meet the power requirements of the country. The number of hydro-electric generation plants built later on bear the testimony of his foresight.

For quite some time Jamsetji was not keeping well. He was an incorrigible gourmand though a teetotaller. As time passed, his condition worsened. He developed shortness of breath and a sick heart, which worked under increasing strain. On 19 May 1904, he died at Bad Nauheim in Germany. His body was brought to England and the last rites were performed according to Zoroashtrian customs.

At Jamshedpur (named after him) stands an imposing statue of Jamsetji Tata. At the foot of the statue are the words, 'If you seek a monument, look around'.

## References

1. Saklatvala, B.S. and K. Khosla. *Jamsetji Tata*, New Delhi, Publications Division, 1970, pp.116-17.
2. Ibid, p.118.

# Mother Teresa

## (1910-1997)

Mother Teresa is the most famous and at the same time most controversial Catholic nun of the twentieth century.

Agnes Gonxha Bojaxhiu (her real name) was born on 27 August 1910 in Skopje or Skoplje, a city in S.E. Yugoslavia, (which was part of the Turkish Empire at the time) to an Albanian mother and father, Nikola, of unknown background, giving rise to a debate which Agnesa, even as Mother Teresa, never bothered to resolve in her lifetime. 'Both her parents were born in Skopje' was all that Pina Markovska, a relative of Agnes, would say about the ongoing dispute over whether she was a Macedonian or Albanian. But to the millions of her admirers it matters little as to which nationality she belonged to. Actually, Macedonia and neighbouring Albania did not even exist when Agnes was born. However, at present, Skopje is the capital of Macedonia. She had an elder brother and a sister whom she was attached to in childhood, besides her mother.

When Agnes was seven years old (1917), her father Nikola died, leaving the family in dire financial straits. Agnes was looked after by the parish of the Sacred Heart, (a denomination of the Catholic Church). She was so influenced by the religious atmosphere of the Parish that at an early age of twelve she decided that she wanted to be a nun. At the age of fourteen, she heard about the Irish Order of the Sisters of Loreto. She went to Ireland in 1928 to join the Institute of the Blessed Virgin

Mary but soon after decided to come to India to join the Sisters of Loreto. What inspired her to come to India is not recorded but she must have learnt that the Sisters of Loreto were working in India. She reached India on 6 January 1929. She was eighteen at the time, a short (four feet ten inches tall) frail little girl. After her arrival she was sent to Darjeeling to teach in the Loreto Convent. Before coming to India she had learnt English; and had acquired a smattering of Bengali. She started with teaching history and geography to junior students. On 24 May 1931, she took her vows as a nun and changed her name to Teresa, borrowing the name from a French nun, Therese Martin. To avoid confusion, she changed the spelling to its Spanish version 'Teresa'.

From Darjeeling, Teresa was sent to Loreto School for girls (Entally) in Calcutta, again as a history and geography teacher. From there she was sent to teach at St. Mary's at Calcutta and in due course she became the headmistress of the school. She worked in this school for sixteen years. During these years she learnt to speak, read and write Bengali. From her room's window at St. Mary's School she could see the vast expanse of the slum of Moti Jheel area where thousands of Calcutta's poor lived without proper sanitation and medical facilities. She was troubled to see these unfortunate members of humanity. Later on, during a train ride from Darjeeling to Calcutta, where she had gone on an annual retreat, "she went through a spiritual discernment, which made her realize that her calling was to serve the poorest of the poor".[1] On 16 August 1946, Teresa left for Patna to get training as a nurse under Mother Denger, the medical nun who had started the Order to heal the sick. There Teresa decided that she would launch her own Order which would be called Missionary Sisters of Charity. An 'Order' in Christian parlance is a body or society of persons living by common consent under the same religious, moral and social regulation. A person joining the religious Order is 'ordained'. She discarded her black and white attire of a Christian nun and started wearing a white sari with blue border, head covered with a tiny white cap and on her left shoulder dangled a small black crucifix. Every Sister of Charity now wears this dress and can be identified by this simple yet unique attire.

On her return to Calcutta, she started her mission of mercy in the Moti Jheel area. Sister Teresa was soon to become a mother to the masses.

She started with opening in a small house, the first 'Nirmal Hriday' (a home of the kind heart.) This was the home for the dying who had nobody to look after them. In 1952, the home was shifted to Kalighat. Mother Teresa started collecting funds for creating new modes of service to the poor and the downtrodden. Soon after a shed was started in Dhaba where children suffering from were housed and looked after. It was followed by homes for lepers in Balgachia and Titagarh, all located in Calcutta and its suburbs. A Mobile Leprosy Clinic was also started to help those afflicted with leprosy in far flung areas in Howrah, Tilijala and other areas. It must be remembered that leprosy has been a special concern for Christian missionaries who are inspired from Jesus Christ himself who cured lepers with his 'miraculous powers'.

In 1955, Mother Teresa opened 'Shishu Bhavan', a home for orphans and abandoned children. The older children were sent to one of the schools run by the Missionaries of Charity and the younger ones were kept in the 'Shishu Bhavan'. The children were given food and clothes. Many of them were given to foreign couples for adoption. In 1963, she founded the Missionary Brothers of Charity to help the Sisters of Charity in their work. She was media friendly and encouraged correspondents and journalists to visit her. She could expand her charitable work with amazing speed and in many countries. Her diminutive figure and her wrinkled face became one of the most familiar faces of the twentieth century. The *Time* magazine in August 1983 carried a profile of Mother Teresa and also some statistics: 2000 Sisters and 400 Brothers working in 257 bases in at least 152 countries; 70 Homes looking after 4000 children and arranging at least a 1000 adoptions every year; 154 slum schools feeding 50,000 children; 81 Homes caring for 13,000 dying destitutes. It is claimed that these statistics are now drastically outdated, and that there are at least 4000 Sisters working in some 561 missions spread out in 180 countries of the world.

In the 1970s, Mother Teresa added AIDS patients to her mission of charity and care. In 1986, she opened the 'City of Peace' in Washington, D.C. to look after and help AIDS patients. In fact she opened several centres in the so-called developed countries in Europe and North America besides those in countries in Asia, Africa and Latin America. When a correspondent asked her 'why are you opening centres in developed countries where there is hardly any poverty.'? 'Poverty of spirit', she replied.

Mother Teresa had become an Indian citizen way back in 1950 and started calling herself an Indian. The government, in turn, showered privileges and honours on her. She was issued a 'red passport' which is reserved for diplomats. On receiving it she said, "It is a gift from the Government of India. They have been very helpful." Honours came in quick succession: Padmashree (1962); Pope John XXIII Peace Prize (January 1971); John F. Kennedy International Award, (September 1971); Jawaharlal Nehru Award for International Understanding (1972); Templeton Prize for Progress in Religion (1973); Nobel Peace Prize (1979); Bharat Ratna (1980); Order of Merit, from Queen Elizabeth (1983); Gold Medal of the Soviet Peace Committee (1987); U.S. Congressional Gold Medal (June, 1997).

Individuals, the corporate sector and even the governments have been her generous donors. Tatas, Lever Brothers, Jet Airways are some from the Indian corporate sector who have donated hundreds of thousands of rupees to Mother Teresa and her Missionaries of Charity to 'spiritualize' their billions. A network spread out in most of the countries of the world providing housing, clothing, food and medical care to thousands of needy and destitutes required money and Mother Teresa got what her mission required without asking.

However, it was not praise and glorification all the time. She had to face many critics. Many have expressed reservations about the proselytising work her organization has allegedly carried out in the name of altruism. Shankracharya of Puri, Nischalanand Saraswati, in a scathing attack on Mother Teresa said that: "She is engaged in conversion in the name of *manav seva* (service to mankind.)"[2] In reply to this accusation she did not deny it but said, "Not even God almighty can convert unless that person *wants* it." She has also candidly confessed, "My life is devoted to Christ. It is for him that I breathe and see. I can't bear the pain when people call me a social worker. Had I been a social worker, I would have left it long ago."[3] She is also accused of giving unclaimed children to only Catholic couples for adoption.

Many Bengalis have lamented the negative image of Kolkata, and by extension, the country which the association with the Catholic nun made inevitable. It has been said that her extraordinary fame itself worked India's 'packaging' as a site of aesthetic devastation: disease, poverty, want and sloth. The contribution of Kolkata towards Indian renaissance, towards Indian art, literature, music and freedom movement stands unrivalled. To depict this city as a vast gutter and consequently getting the appellation 'Saint of the Gutters' is nothing but defaming a great city. Her opposition to contraception and abortion invited ridicule. The most devastating and detailed criticism of Mother Teresa came from the writer Christopher Hitchens. He questioned her sources and use of funds, "her deeply orthodox views on a range of issues and the 'imperialistic' underpinnings of her evangelising mission. Apart from decrying her role as conscience-salver of the world's rich, he has sought to 'expose' what he thinks is the cultural myth-making that has gone into the nun's apotheosis as messiah of the downtrodden". Similar charges have been documented in celluloid in the film titled *Hell's Angel* which was telecast by BBC in November 1994.

Mother Teresa's beatification on 19 October 2003 led to another controversy. For beatification it has to be proved that he or she was capable of performing 'miracles'. In this case a tribal girl named Monika Besra was 'cured' of a cancerous growth in her stomach by putting a 'miraculous medal' bearing the image of Mother Teresa, to her stomach. The incident occurred on 5 September 1998 according to the spokesperson of the Missionaries of Charity. Overnight, Monika became famous. And rich. She was flown to the Vatican as a proof of the 'miracle' during the beatification ceremony which was attended by 2,50,000 people. Monika converted to Christianity after the 'miracle'. Another 'miracle' and Mother Teresa will be declared a saint. Prabir Ghose, founder of Science and Rational Society of India suggested to the Missionaries of Charity: "Why don't you close your *Nirmal Hridayas* and all other homes providing medical facilities to the sick and the destitute and open a huge medal manufacturing factory instead." He calls the 'miracle' of Monika Besra as 'one of the world's biggest lies of the modern times, unflinchingly believed and broadcast by a profit-hunting media'.[5] Incidentally, beatification in the Catholic religion (which means blessing of the soul of the deceased by the Pope) is not as rare as is made out to be. She will be number 1319 in the row of those beatified earlier. Article 51A(h) of the Indian Constitution assigns Indian citizens a fundamental duty to develop the scientific temper, humanism and the spirit of inquiry and reform. However, it is difficult to fight with faith and superstition especially in a country where a large section of the population is extremely poor, illiterate and superstitious. Laws don't change blind faith. Only reason can.

In spite of all the criticism and antagonism, Mother's halo has remained intact. A diminutive figure became one of the most famous personalities of our age. When she died on 13 September 1997, at the age of eighty-seven at Calcutta, she was accorded a state funeral. "Princes, Presidents, Prime Ministers, Ambassadors, celebrities, special representatives of heads of States and three queens attended the funeral. India was represented by her Prime Minister I.K. Gujaral accompanied by his wife".

## References

1. Singh, Amitabh. *Famous Missionaries in India*, Delhi, Indian Society for Promoting Christian Knowledge, 1997, pp.39-40.
2. *Daily Telegraph*, 21 October, 1995.
3. Joseph, Babu, Ed. *Tracing the Footsteps of Mother Teresa: New Delhi*, Dept. of Public Relations, Catholic Bishops Conferences of India (CBCI), 2003, p.99.
4. *The Indian Express* (Daily), 22/3/2001.
5. *The Pioneer* (Daily) 2 November 2003.

# Bal Gangadhar Tilak

## (1856-1920)

Bal Gangadhar Tilak was born on 23 July 1856 at Ratnagiri in Maharastra in a Chitpawan Brahmin family, the caste made famous by the Peshwas. His father, Gangadhar Shastri, was a school teacher who rose to become assistant deputy inspector of schools at Poona. As the only son, Tilak inherited all his father's property after his father's death in 1872 and thanks to this legacy, was liberated from pecuniary anxiety during most of his life. His mother had died earlier and he was an orphan at the age of sixteen.

Tilak was educated at the Deccan College, Poona, getting his B.A. degree in 1876 with a first class with mathematics and Sanskrit as subjects and passed B.L in 1879. He chose teaching as his career in preference to legal practice. Tilak, along with Chiplonkar, Agarkar and Namjoshi, started the New English School in 1880 with nineteen students, believing that the right education was the sure panacea for the country's ills. Within a year the school enrolment multiplied tenfold. The young teachers soon ventured into journalism and started two newspapers in January 1881, the English language weekly *Mahratta*, which was initially edited by Tilak and a Marathi weekly, *Kesari*, edited by Agarkar (1856-1895). Within a year, the fame of both the editors spread throughout Maharastra lending them a sort of heroic trait. A lawsuit filed by the Dewan of Kolhapur for defamation sent the two editors to four months in prison in July 1882 making them martyrs in the eyes of many and thus adding to their popularity.

Encouraged by the success of the New English School, Tilak and other founders of the school decided to establish the Deccan Education Society in 1884. The aim of the society was to open a chain of schools and colleges on the lines of Christian missionaries. The most famous of the institutions started by the society was Fergusson College, named after the governor of Bombay, Sir James Fergusson, who personally laid the foundation of the college on 5 March 1885 in Poona. The college has flourished and continues to be one of the leading colleges in the country. Tilak did not favour educating girls and opposed the opening of a girl's school in Poona in 1884 as he believed that 'a woman's role was to look after the house'. Tilak started teaching mathematics in Fergusson College. But soon Tilak resigned from the Deccan Education Society as well as the college due to differences with other members, especially Gokhale and Agarkar who were liberal in their thinking. After severing relations with the society, Tilak acquired the sole proprietorship of the two papers, *Mahratta* and *Kesari* and used the paper for spreading his message on various political, economic and social issues. He gained immense popularity among the masses while earning the antagonism of the government. In October 1887, Agarkar resigned as editor of *Kesari* due to differences with Tilak on political and social issues like child marriage and age of consent and joined the reformer group led by Ranade and Gokhale. Henceforth, Tilak took editorial charge of the *Kesari* also thus facing many tribulations as a result and at the same time earning fame and gratitude of the masses. In 1889, Tilak joined the Congress but found that its working was confined to a small section of the English educated elitists who lacked nationalistic spirit. "Very early in public career Tilak discovered the need for bringing a spiritual element to the politics of the country by infusing into them (sic) a religious fervour".[1] He also found that the Congress leaders were ignorant of the true source of popular inspiration. With that purpose in mind, Tilak started celebrating the Ganpati festival annually from September 1893. Soon this festival became the best attended festival of western India lasting for a week; industrial and agricultural labour taking part in it in large number with enthusiasm. This gave Tilak a mass following which none of the Congress leaders could boast of. Today this festival is celebrated throughout the country. Encouraged by the success of the Ganpati festival, Tilak and his supporters sponsored another festival, the Shivaji festival. "The integral political and religious motivation of this festival was made explicit since its inception. Its inauguration in 1896 marked the maturing and increased self-confidence of Tilak's new party. The two festivals imparted to Hinduism a congregational character which helped to unite the masses under religious-political banner".[2]

Tilak's orthodoxy came to the fore when the Age of Consent bill was moved in the Assembly by Sir Andrew Scoble. The bill proposed to raise the age for consummation of marriage from ten to twelve years for girls. Tilak vehemently opposed the Bill in an editorial in *Kesari*. He wrote that if the Bill was passed 'it will damage our traditions and shastras'. By propagating such orthodox views he crossed swords with reformers like Ranade, Gokhale, Telang and the famous Sanskrit scholar R.G. Bhandarkar. Politically, also these reformers differed from Tilak. While they believed in political reforms through constitutional means, Tilak believed in militant agitation. The reformers were controlling the Poona Sarvajanik Sabha through which they were propagating their views. But in 1895, Tilak and his group seized control of the sabha by outvoting the reformers. Tilak thus got control of a popular organization in addition to his two papers *Kesari* and *Mahratta*. The ousted reformers led by Ranade, Gokhale and their liberal allies then founded another sabha called the Deccan Sabha.

Tilak's next target was the National Social Conference started by Ranade in 1887 to rid the Hindu society of social evils. Its annual sessions were held along with the Congress sessions in the same venue. At the time of 1895 Congress session in Poona, Tilak opposed the holding of the Social Conference in the Congress pandal in the capacity of a secretary. "The majority of the people of Poona", he asserted, "and I might say of the Deccan generally, are not in favour of the social reform." He believed that social reform would distract the people from political aim — freedom of the country. The opposition of Tilak and his men to the Social Conference compelled the reformers to erect a separate pandal on the grounds of Fergusson College. The schism between the two factions, started in 1893, kept on widening and erupted dangerously during the

Surat Congress in 1907. The Congress all this time continued to be controlled by the 'Moderates' led by Pherozshah Mehta and Gokhale.

Plague, the Black Death, arrived in western India in 1896 and continued its toll for over a year, affecting the business interests of the Empire. Governor Sandhurst of Bombay appointed Walter Charles Rand, 'the strong man', to control the epidemic in Poona. Rand acted as a dictator without any concern for the inconvenience and agony of the inhabitants. Tilak wrote against the tyrannical methods adopted by Rand in *Kesari*. As luck would have it, Rand was murdered in June 1897 by Damodar Chapekar. Though there was no evidence of Tilak's hand in the murder, he was charged with seditious writings in *Kesari* and was sentenced to eighteen months of rigorous imprisonment. After eight months in jail, Tilak had lost twenty-five pounds and decided to appeal for clemency. He was released after one year in September 1898. After his release, he gained fame as a martyr.

The partition of Bengal in 1905 by Curzon put new life into the agitational approach for the salvation of the country. In the 1906 session of the Congress in Calcutta, Tilak, along with Lajpat Rai, Bipin Chandra Pal and others succeeded in getting a resolution passed to implement a four-fold programme of *swaraj, swadeshi*, boycott and national education. However, during the Surat session of 1907, the resolution was not taken up for confirmation by the 'moderates' led by Pherozshah Mehta, Gokhale and others who controlled the Congress. Tilak tried to get the resolution taken up and went up the rostrum to move an amendment. All hell broke loose. Chairs and shoes were hurled at the rivals. The result was that Tilak and his followers were expelled from the Congress which proved to be a turning point in his life.

On 29 April 1908, a bomb was thrown by Khudi Ram Bose aimed at the carriage of District Judge Kingsford at Muzaffarpur. But it killed two English ladies who happened to be in the carriage. Tilak wrote an article '*The Country's Misfortune*' in *Kesari* of 12 May 1908, in which he dealt with the Muzaffarpur incident describing it as the 'result of exasperation of the people who were subjected to repression by the ruling power.' Soon, Tilak was arrested in Bombay on charge of sedition. He was tried by the jury and was sentenced to six years imprisonment. He was shipped to Mandalay jail in Burma where he languished. The news of Tilak's conviction spread throughout the city. The labour class who had been participating enthusiastically in Ganpati and Shivaji festivals and were his devoted followers struck work in scores of mills. The cloth, grain, freight and stock markets were closed down. This was the first mass political strike in recent Indian history and 'a dramatic demonstration of Tilak's influence on the masses'. While he was in jail, his name was on the lips of every Maratha in the Deccan and his portrait was hung in countless houses like a deity.

Tilak returned from Mandalay jail in June 1914 after serving a full term of his imprisonment. "If in 1898 he had returned from prison a martyred hero, with his restoration to India in June 1914, he appeared to his followers as little less than the reincarnation of a deity". After a brief rest, he again plunged into active politics. He started a new movement under the banner of the Home Rule League in April, 1916. Annie Besant also started a Home Rule league later in the same year. The two leagues did not merge but worked in cooperation with each other, demarcating the territory of their work; Tilak confining his activities to the Deccan and northwest while Besant operating in the rest of India. Tilak took a whirlwind tour of the territory making the slogan 'Freedom is my birthright and I must have it' popular throughout the country.

In 1916, another sedition case was filed against Tilak for delivering speeches during his tour to explain the meaning of Home Rule. M.A. Jinnah defended him as his counsel. The case was ultimately withdrawn by the Bombay high court. Thus Jinnah earned the gratitude of Tilak which he encashed during the 1916 Congress session. The Lucknow session of the Congress in December 1916 proved to be a turning point in the history of the country as the notorious Lucknow Pact between Congress and the Muslim League was signed during the joint session. The Pact bestowed on the Muslims a separate electorate (only Muslims electing Muslim legislators for the assemblies) and weightage in councils and other bodies, 'thus converting an insignificant minority, into effective minority in the Muslim minority provinces'. There was a strong reaction to these clauses from a section of the Congress leaders. Strangely, Tilak, a person who was the father of militant Hindu nationalism, defended the

Pact and silenced its critics. Tilak said, "It has been said gentlemen by some that we Hindus have yielded too much to our Mohemmedan brethren. I am sure I represent the sense of the community all over India when I say that we would not care if the rights of self-government were granted to the Mohemmedan community only —— Then the fight will be between them and other sections of the community and not as at present a triangular fight".[3] C.S. Ranga Iyer, who was in close touch with Tilak during the time, later observed that Tilak would not listen to any argument against the pact. The pact was drafted by Jinnah who was masquerading as a nationalist at the time. A political blunder of high magnitude was thus committed by Tilak. The British parliament recognized the Lucknow Pact as the only agreement between Hindus and Muslims and put their seal on the sinister provisions of the pact in the Acts of 1919 and 1935. Once the basis of the division of the electorates was accepted, the recognition of the division of the country was inevitable.[4]

Before the Lucknow session, the Congress united once again. The 'moderate' leaders like Gokhale and Pherozeshah Mehta were dead by that time. Tilak and his followers were now controlling the destiny of the Congress. However, Tilak was more interested in propagating the message of Home Rule League for which he had toured the country. Now he wanted to explain it to the British people. He also wanted to file a libel case against a British author and journalist, Valentine Chirol, who in his book *Indian Unrest* had blamed Tilak for subversive activities. Tilak sailed for London late in September 1918 accompanied by Namjoshi, legal adviser Karandikar and Vasukaka Joshi. Tilak used his stay for meeting influential people who were considerate to Indian aspirations, especially those in the Labour Party. But the libel case dragged on and ultimately Tilak lost the case and had to pay a heavy fee to British solicitors and counsel. In addition, he had to pay the costs of Chirol's defence. Tilak was now financially ruined for the first time in his life and had to pawn every thing to raise money. He was stranded abroad, draining the reservoir of his remaining energy in a hostile environment. "Gray robed with gray shadows of death already upon him, to me Tilak in London is a tragic memory", wrote Sarojini Naidu who was in London at the time. Tilak stayed in London for thirteen months and returned to India in December, 1919 a dejected man. He was to live only seven more months.

Immediately after returning from England, Tilak attended the Amritsar session of the Congress (December 1919). There he came to know about the Reforms Act of 1919 which gave a little more share of administration of the country to the Indians. Tilak immediately wired the government declaring his 'responsive cooperation' during the implementation of the Act. He seemed to have veered towards the policies advocated by the 'moderates' all these years. He did not live long to implement this policy. Soon, Gandhi emerged as the leader of the Congress and started the Non-Cooperation movement on 1 August 1920. The same day Tilak died of high fever caused by malaria and later pneumonia. He was cremated in Bombay's Back Bay cremation ground. Gandhi, Lajpat Rai, Kitchlu, Shaukat Ali, N.C. Kelkar were among a crowd of leaders who walked as part of the two-mile-long procession as pallbearers.

Tilak was short, dark, stout and remarkably physically fit. He used to shave his head except for the long tuft. He had a thick bushy moustache, 'which stood out in his portraits'. His short stature was not the only similarity with Napoleon Bonaparte. Like Napoleon, he was a man determined to lead. His remarkable fortitude and courage would have singled him out as a mover of the masses in any country. He was, as Gokhale said of him, "the kind of man who in the days before British rule, would have carved out an Indian kingdom for himself".

Tilak has left three important books for the generations to come. The first one was *Orion: Researches into the Antiquity of the Vedas* published in 1893. In it Tilak used astronomical data recorded in the *Rig Veda* to establish its antiquity which he pushed back to 8000 BC. The book received praise from Max Muller and others and established Tilak as a serious Sanskrit scholar. His second book was *Arctic Home in the Vedas; A New Key to the Interpretation of Many Vedic Texts and Legends*. In this book Tilak used geology instead of astronomy to prove the Polar attributes of the Vedic deities. The book was completed in 1901 but was published in 1903. Tilak's most ambitious and important book remains *Gita Rahasya* (secret meaning of the *Gita*), which he wrote during prison life in Mandalay. Through the book, Tilak tried to teach the doctrine of *karma yoga,* the religion of action. It is still considered as one of the best commentaries of the *Gita*. Though the book was completed in 1910 it was published in 1915 in Poona. While the first two books were written in English, *Gita Rahasya* was in Marathi, and has been translated into English and many Indian languages.

Tilak had forestalled Gandhi in all the movements which Gandhi launched — no-rent campaign, boycott of government service, *swadeshi*, national education etc. In 1921, someone sent an anonymous letter to Gandhi praising him for toeing Tilak's line in fighting for India's freedom and at the same time called him an imposter for claiming that he was a disciple of Gokhale, which provoked Gandhi to write a reply in his paper *Young India*. In his reply Gandhi praised Tilak saying that: "Of all the men of modern times, he captivated most the imagination of his people. He breathed into us the spirit of swaraj. And in all humility, I claim to deliver his message to the country as truly as the best of his disciples. But I am conscious that my method is not Mr. Tilak's method".[5] Be as it may, with the death of Tilak passed away an era in Indian history. It was the turn of his disciple Gandhi to take over.

# References

1. Tahmankar, D.V. *Lokmanya Tilak*, London, John Murray, 1956, p.315.
2. Wolpert, Stanley A. *Tilak and Gokhale*. Oxford India Paperback. 1989, p.80.
3. Indian Annual Register, 1920.
4. Nagarkar, V.V. *Genesis of Pakistan*, Allied, 1975, p.106.
5. *Young India*, 13 July 1921, and *Collected Works of Mahatma Gandhi*, Vol. 20, p.369.

# Tatya Tope

## (1814-1859)

Tatya Tope is a forgotten hero of the 1857 uprising. He had an extraordinary skill as a military strategist and was an expert in guerilla warfare without having any formal training. Along with Rani Lakshmibai of Jhansi, he fought the British forces in central India with extraordinary perseverance and resolve, harassing the much superior forces of the British for almost a year. Sir Hugh Rose, the British commander, said about him: "Of all the rebel chiefs Tatya Tope possessed the greatest enterprise as regards initiative and the most enduring resolution of character. His talent for organisation was remarkable".[1]

Not much is known about the early life of Tatya Tope. His real name was Ramchandra Pandurang, son of Pandurang Rao and Rukma Bai. His family belonged to the Nasik district in Maharashtra. In the statement made by him during his court-martial in 1859 he stated that he was forty-five years old; his year of birth may, therefore, be assumed to be as 1814. His father was among the retainers of Peshwa Baji Rao II who had settled at Bithur, near Kanpur. Tatya Tope grew up in the Peshwa's palace in the company of Peshwa's adopted sons, Nana Saheb and Bala Saheb. Later Manu, who later became famous as Lakshmibai of Jhansi, joined them as their playmate. It seems Tatya knew Hindi, Gujarati, besides his mother-tongue Marathi. While still a teenager, he learnt riding, shooting and other martial arts. It seems 'he had inherited the natural instincts of his race for guerilla tactics'. John Lang (1817-1864), a British barrister and fiction writer, who was also employed by Rani Lakshmibai as her counsel, had met Tatya Tope at Bithur before the uprising and described him thus: "He was a man of about the middle height — say five feet eight — rather slightly made, but very erect. He was far from good-looking. The forehead was low, the nose rather broad at the nostrils, and his teeth irregular and discoloured. His eyes were expressive and full of cunning, like those of most Asiatics; but he did not strike me as a man of eminent ability".[2]

Tatya was and was bound to Nana Sahib by ties of loyalty and gratitude. Tatya Tope came into limelight only after his master Nana Sahib's defeat and flight from Kanpur on 17 July 1857. Now the real authority and initiative had passed into the hands of Tatya Tope, 'his able and devoted lieutenant'. Tatya gathered a force of four thousand men at Bithur itself and marched to Kanpur. But he was defeated by General Havelock on 16 August 1857. Tatya then proceeded to Gwalior and won over the sepoys of the Gwalior contingent and with this increased strength, he seized Kalpi. Henceforth, Tatya took orders from Rao Sahib, nephew of Nana Saheb. Rao asked Tatya to seize Kanpur. Leaving a small detachment for defence at Kalpi. Tatya advanced to Kanpur which was being defended by General Windham with the help of a small force, as major part of the British forces were engaged in Lucknow and Awadh. After an initial setback at Pandu river, Tatya managed to attack Kanpur the following day (27 November) and after a fierce fight lasting two days he overwhelmed the British forces and the whole city of Kanpur; all the baggage and store fell into his hands. This was his greatest victory but it proved to be short-lived. On hearing the capture of Kanpur by rebel troops under Tatya Tope, Sir Colin Campbell, British commander-in-chief, who had gone to Lucknow with his strong contingent to relieve the city rushed back towards Kanpur and defeated Tatya Tope's forces. That was the last battle fought for Kanpur. Tatya fell back on Kalpi extracting cleverly almost all his forces. Henceforth his activities were confined to the region further.[3] The defeat at Kanpur had not dispirited Tatya Tope and he soon appeared in Char-Khari, the capital of a small Bundela state of the same name, whose Raja was a friend of the British. There he received a message from Rani Lakshmibai for help as her fort was under siege by the British forces. On 31 March 1858, Tatya marched to Jhansi leading a force of twenty thousand men. Before his men could salvage the Jhansi fort, Tatya was defeated after a hard-fought battle outside Jhansi itself. He fell back on Kalpi where Lakshmibai and Rao Saheb joined him. But on 23 May, the rebels were compelled to evacuate Kalpi, after a series of hard-fought actions. Their last stronghold was thus lost. From there, Tatya stealthily went to Gwalior and was successful in engineering a revolt of the forces there who joined the rebel forces when they approached Gwalior. Gwalior fell without a shot. But the victory was shortlived. Soon the British commander, Hugh Rose's army marched to Gwalior. Rani Lakshmibai fell while fighting and the rebel forces dispersed. Tatya Tope escaped to Central India and from then on he changed his fighting strategy and engaged the British forces in guerilla tactics, resorting to attacking enemy bases and destroying their line of communication, while keeping his troops intact 'by carrying out rearguard action to cover the retreat of his troops'. Pursued by his enemies, Tatya Tope escaped his capture for almost a year and moved from Central India to Rajasthan, back and forth. He fought his last battle at Sikar in Rajasthan in January 1859.

At last, worn out with fatigue and thoroughly disheartened, he crossed the Chambal and hid himself in the jungles near Seronge which belonged to Man Singh, a feudatory of Sindhia. Being deprived of his estate by the latter, Man Singh had rebelled, but was defeated by a British detachment. He was wandering in the forest when he chanced upon Tatya, and the two became very friendly. As soon as the British commander learnt of this, he won over Man Singh by holding out the hope of restoring his wealth and position. Man Singh not only surrendered, but led a few sepoys of the British detachment to Tatya Tope's hiding place. The sepoys, guided by Man Singh, found Tatya asleep, seized him and carried him to the British camp at Sipri. The only arms that Tatya had with him were a sword and a 'kukri'. He was court-martialled on 15 April 1859 on the "charge of having been in rebellion and having waged war against the British Government between January 1857 and December 1858 especially at Jhansi and Gwalior". The result was a foregone conclusion. "He was found guilty of the heinous offence charged, and accordance with the law, he was sentenced to death". He was hanged three days later on 18 December in the presence of a large crowd.

The capture of Tatya Tope and his execution was the last important act by the British in the suppression of the revolt in Central India. The wonderful guerilla warfare which Tatya had carried on for almost a year against a powerful enemy elicited admiration even from his enemies and "may be looked upon as a fitting end to a struggle which was hopeless almost from the very beginning". His death certainly brought an end to the uprising of 1857-58 but the revolt which was the first great challenge to the British rule in India, shook the British Empire. The memory of 1857-58 sustained the later freedom movements, infused courage into the hearts of freedom fighters who were prepared to lay down their lives for the emancipation of the country, following the example of Rani Lakshmibai and Tatya Tope. The inspiration which the revolt inculcated in the hearts of later revolutionaries did more damage to the cause of the British rule in India than the revolt itself.

Apart from its impact on the Indian mind the revolt had a permanent after-effect on the British mind also: they could never trust the Indians in their army. From the very beginning of their rule the British were ruling the country with the help of the Indian soldiers. "Though the British could not do without the native portion of their Indian army, and despite its gallant performance in two world wars, never again would they wholly trust it". The raising of Indian National Army by Subhas Chandra Bose in 1943 consisting mainly of the Indian prisoners-of-war in Malaya and Singapore and the revolt of the British Indian Navy and Air Force in 1946 confirmed their suspicion. "There is no doubt that the fear of another, and greater Mutiny had its effect upon the negotiations that ended with India's independence in 1947".[4] It took almost a century for the sacrifices of the like of Tatya Tope and Lakshmibai to bear fruit.

## References

1.   Letter of Hugh Rose to Richard Meade, 14 January 1860, Quoted by Rajni Kant Gupta in his *Military Traits of Tatya Tope*, New Delhi, S. Chand, 1987, p.155.

2. Lang, John. *Wanderings in India and Other Sketches of Life in Hindoostan*, London, 1859, Quoted by S.N. Sen in *Eighteen Fifty-Seven*. New Delhi, Publications Division, 1957, p.231.
3. Majumdar, R.C. *History of the Freedom Movement in India*, Vol. 1, Calcutta, Firma KLM, 1988, pp.180-81.
4. Edwardes, Michael. *Battles of the Indian Mutiny*, London, B.T. Batsford, 1963, p.202.

# Uday Shankar

## (1900-1977)

Uday Shankar was born in 1900 at Udaipur (Rajasthan). His father Shyama Shankar Chowdhary, a barrister, was educational adviser to the Maharaja of Jhalawar, a petty state in Rajasthan. Later he became the private secretary of the Maharaja and also minister of Education. The family originally came from Bengal but had settled in northern India. They had a house in Banaras and Uday's maternal grandfather was a big landlord settled at Ghazipur, a town near Banaras. Uday spent several years of his childhood in these two places. It was a talented family. Shyama Shankar, in addition to being an educationist, was a multifaceted personality who spent several years in London trying his luck as a stage artist and composer. He had married a British lady and settled there, resigning from the Jhalawar state job. Uday was the eldest of the four brothers. Among the three of his brothers, the youngest Ravi Shankar is a sitarist of international repute. The others were Rajendra and Devandra.

Uday had no interest in studies. He would play truant and would avoid going to school. He would watch Matadin, an amateur folk dancer for hours, sometime till late in the night. Matadin was a cobbler and a landless labourer in his grandfather's zamindari in Ghazipur. Uday was fascinated by the movements of Matadin's hands and feet and facial expressions. At Jhalawar, the court dancer Kuki Bai, was another dancer who inspired the dancer in Uday. As he had no sister, Uday's mother would often dress little Uday as a girl and he would try to imitate sometime Matadin and at other times Kuki Bai.

Being an educationist, Uday's father soon understood that his son had no interest in studies and it would be futile to inflict formal education on the child. As Uday had shown interest in drawing and painting at an early age his father took him to England and got him admitted to the Royal College of Arts, London. His teacher, Sir William Rothenstein, trained him in painting and plastic arts and impressed upon Uday not to ape the Western painters, but to seek his style in the rich Indian cultural heritage. This applied to other arts also, he was told; a lesson which Uday never forgot. Uday graduated, with honours, from the Royal College of Arts in 1923. During that period, he often danced at private gatherings. The dance form was his very own and not conforming to any rigid classical mould. At twenty-three, Uday Shankar was a very handsome man with finely chiselled features, large expressive eyes and beautiful hands. Even his unrehearsed movements, imparted an elegance and easy grace which earned the admiration of the people. As luck would have it, the great Russian-born ballerina, Anna Pavlova (1885-1931), saw him dancing and was charmed by his movements. She was considered as the greatest ballerina of her time and was famous throughout the Western world. Some of her ballets like *Giselle* and *The Dying Swan* have seldom been excelled. She wanted to add a few ballets with Indian theme in her repertoire. She offered Uday Shankar the lead role in the ballet *Radha-Krishna*, and *Hindu Marriage*. Uday Shankar thought it was a chance of a lifetime and joined her troupe. Pavlova as Radha and Uday as Krishna presented a scene of unrivalled grandeur and something of a novelty on the Western stage. After adequate rehearsal, Pavlova took Uday as a member of her troupe, for a coast to coast tour of America. This was in 1923. The first performance of *Radha-Krishna* was held at the Manhattan Opera House, New York. Though the media concentrated their eulogies on Pavlova and her famous ballet *The Dying Swan*, the *Radha-Krishna* ballet did not go unnoticed. So also Uday as Krishna. Some critics called him the 'Indian dancing wizard'. Being in Pavlova's troupe was a great honour for any dancer but Uday felt that he was in a way tied to her apron strings and that his own personality and genius were being thwarted.

On his return from America, he left Pavlova's troupe and decided to make it on his own. During his short stint in her troupe he had learnt a few things which were very helpful in his future career as a dancer. He learnt discipline, team work, punctuality, stage craft and above all, showmanship.

Taking advantage of his association with Pavlova, he started giving solo performances. The dance compositions were based on Indian mythology. Some unknown stage artists joined him and he started performing amateur stage shows. From London, he moved to Paris where he was more successful. He also performed at Berlin, Vienna, Budapest, Geneva. His solo item, Nataraja, was appreciated the most. In Paris, he met Alice Boner, a Swiss lady, who was a lover of Indian art and culture and had settled in Banaras. She told Uday that he should know more about India and its varied art forms before he started his professional dance career for which he had unlimited talent which she could discern. The two came back to India. That was in 1929. Alice travelled with Uday from village to village, from one corner of the country to the other: Malabar, Manipur, Orissa, Lucknow, Panjab, collecting a variety of musical instruments used in folk dances. They also studied the costumes of folk dancers. They travelled for several months, on this 'educative' tour, Alice Boner bearing all the expenses. The following year, with her help, Uday assembled a company of Indian dancers and musicians and took them to Europe. It was an immediate success and his future was now assured. He took his troupe to several countries in Europe and America and was applauded everywhere.

This success brought several aspiring artists who wanted to join his troupe, the most important of them being Simone or Simkia and Shirali, both young French girls. Then there was Amala Nandi, who met Uday Shankar in Paris where she was with her father on a visit. She joined Uday's troupe and was a female partner in many of his ballets. Ultimately both of them fell in love and married after several years, in 1942.

Uday Shankar had by then a team of hundred and fifty artists, dancers, musicians and other sundry craftsmen. No Indian dancer had earlier assembled around him such an impressive team of artists and workers. He now started composing ballets for which he earned unmatched fame and applause. Some of his unforgettable ballets were: *Shiva Tandav, Shiva*

*Parvati Nritya Dwanda; Rhythm of Life; Eternal Melody; Labour and Machinery; Great Renunciation, Lord Buddha* and *Pramila and Arjuna*. Every ballet was a chapter in the life of the artist in Uday. He had also created some solo items like *Kartikeya* (son of Shiva) and *Indra*, but his genius was more discernible in the ballets than in solo items. He had studied the basics of various Indian dance forms like Kathakali, Manipuri, Odissi, and Kathak and blended them into his own creations thus creating a new dance form. The costume and make-up Uday adopted in his stage performances were entirely in the clsssical tradition.

His creations were like lyrical poems on the stage. In his movements and expressions were depicted different moods, in his gestures and postures were a strange freedom and grace, and in his smile was hidden the mysteries of the Orient. He had brought a revolution on the Indian stage through his intrinsic talent and well-thought out showmanship. The stage craft, the lighting, the orchestra were all on a lavish scale. After seeing his stage show an American art critic once wrote: "Perhaps the showmanhisp on which we in America pride ourselves is more universal than we think. At any rate Shankar had it". Surprisingly, Uday was the product of no school. His art was strictly his own and was not bound by the tedious rules of the classical form. That is why there was a freshness in his art.

He took his troupe around the world — Europe, America and East Asia. Even after several shows, the enthusiasm of the viewers never waned. In San Francisco, there was a seating capacity for four thousand and five hundred in the hall where he performed. Not one seat was available, with thousands waiting outside. Seeing the rush, tickets continued to be sold. Five hundred art lovers were made to stand in the passage. That space was soon filled. A few hundred were allowed to sit in the orchestra pit. Still a large number were standing outside and could not be accommodated. When Amala told Uday, after the performance, about the rush at the theatre, Uday modestly said, "I think I am deceiving them. I should give them more."[1] This enthusiasm was witnessed in city after city, in country after country. The media joined in to eulogize the Indian dancer of ethereal beauty. In New York, S. Hurok, art critic of *New York Herald Tribune*, came to Uday's hotel and presented an album with the inscription 'Uday Shankar's Indra Dance'. On each page was a painting that depicted Uday's movements — lotuses, chakras, bows and arrows, his facial expressions and a series of *alpana* designs. Such was the impact of his dances on the Western viewers.

India also started appreciating and admiring this new form of dance that was steeped in Indian culture but not following the essential grammar of Indian classical dances. After his long absence from India, Uday performed in Calcutta's First Empire Theatre. Rabindranath Tagore occupied a middle seat in the first row. When Uday finished his dance and was bowing to the crowd who were cheering him, the great poet gave him a standing ovation. Uday jumped from the stage and bowed and touched Tagore's feet. From Santiniketan the poet wrote to Uday Shankar: "Uday Shankar! You have made the art of dancing your life's companion. Through it you have won the laurels of the West. Now you are back home after a long absence. Your Motherland has kept ready for you her love and blessings, and the poet of Bengal offers them on her behalf".[2] In 1953, during Buddha Jayanti, Uday performed at the National Stadium, New Delhi. The ballets were *'Buddha's Shadow Play'* and the *'Great Renunciation'*. Among the audience were Jawaharlal Nehru, the Chinese Prime Minister Chou En Lai and the Dalai Lama. The stadium was full. After the performance Nehru and Chou En Lai rushed to the stage to congratulate Uday and the Chinese prime minister greeted him with a wreath on behalf of the people of China.

Earlier he had an urge to establish a cultural center for the propagation of Indian arts. When some people learnt about Uday's plans they came forward to help him; above all, the Leonard Elmhirst family of Dartington Hall, England. They gave a large donation for setting up an Indian Culture Centre. The surprised Uday Shankar was told by Mrs. Dorothy Elmhirst that it was nothing in comparison to what Indian art had given them. The Centre was opened at Almora, Kumaon Hills, in mid-1930s. Uday had big plans for the Centre. He collected under one roof great artists from various parts of India to train the aspiring artists: Guru Shankaran Namboodri of Travancore, Ustad Allauddin Khan of Maihar, Guru Kandappa Pillai of Madras and the wizard of Manipur dance, Guru Amobi Singh, from Imphal. They joined as the teaching staff. Students came from far and near, some of them very talented. Several of the students got married and left. Two sisters, Zohra and Uzra, were among the talented ones. Zohra even toured East Asia, playing the role of Radha with Uday as Krishna. But on her return she married one of her classmates, Sehgal, and left. Later, she became famous as a stage artist and actress Zohra Sehgal. Simkie, the French girl whom Uday had trained for the roles of Parvati and Radha and had toured Europe with the troupe, married one Prabhat Ganguli and left. So also many others. The lavish set-up and expensive paraphernalia added to the financial problems. One day the Centre caught fire and that was the end of Uday's dream. However, while he was at the height of his career and money was flowing in, he had built a palatial building at 14, Boag Road, Madras, had a limousine, and a of servants etc. He lived a fabulous life, though it lasted only for a few years.

He married Amala in 1942. For several years they travelled together, Amala performing the female roles. Along with Uday, she had also earned fame as an artist of exquisite beauty and grace. They had two children, son Anand Shankar and daughter Mamta. Ananda earned fame as a music composer, blending Western and Indian music, conducting his own orchestra. Mamta became an actress. Gradually Amala took over the management of the troupe. She loved Bengal and the couple moved to Calcutta. The house at Madras was sold out. The cosmopolitan nature of the troupe changed as Amala was now recruiting only Bengali girls and boys. Age was catching up with Uday. The agility of his younger days had gone. Uday became a heavy drinker, and spent some unhappy years in Calcutta. He and Amala separated and Uday started living alone. He was shattered. He died on 26 September 1977 at Calcutta. Before his death, the Government of India conferred the Padma Vibhushan on him.

# References

1.  Banerji, P. *Uday Shankar and His Art*. Delhi, B.R. Publishing, 1982, p.46.
2.  Ibid, pp.61-62.

# Raja Ravi Varma

## (1848-1906)

No other Indian artist blazed as many trails as did Raja Ravi Varma. He was the first Indian artist to master perspective, the first to use human models to depict gods and goddesses of the Hindu pantheon. He was the first Indian artist to study and learn from the European artists and then use oil as a medium unlike other Indian artists who were using temperas. He was the only artist who tried to bring his art to the homes of the rich and the poor alike. He was the first artist whose works were exhibited in galleries of Europe and America, though he never ventured beyond Indian shores. To this day his works are in great demand in India as well as in London and Paris.

Ravi Varma was born on 29 April 1848 in Kilimanoor Palace, his mother's home, which is about forty kilometers from Thiruvananthapuram. His father was Sreekantan Bhattathiripad and mother was Princess Uma Amba Bai. The family was related to the Travancore royal family and had easy access to the durbar.

Ravi Varma did not have any formal education but his parents taught him Sanskrit and his mother introduced him to the rich mythological lore of India. She also taught him some classical music. Ravi started learning the rudiments of art at the age of six from his uncle Raja Varma who was an artist of some repute. He also studied the working of the court artists of Travancore among whom was a European, Theodore

Jenson. All this helped Ravi Varma's artistic talents to blossom and by the time he was fourteen he was able to secure the patronage of the Maharaja of Travancore. The Maharaja was an ardent lover of art and could see the making of a great artist in the young lad. On the suggestion of the Maharaja, Ravi moved to Thiruvananthapuram from Kilimanoor. The Maharaja set up a studio for the young artist and managed to get European art books for him. "Western painting fascinated Ravi Varma. He instinctively sympathized with its vigorous realism, so different from the stylized, contemporary Indian tradition. He also preferred oil paints, then new in India, to tempera, the traditional Indian medium".[1] Ravi had to teach himself the technique of oil painting as no artist around was using oil as a medium. He started mixing oils perfectly by trial and error. He was doing portraits to begin with and showed remarkable ability to depict a variety of skin tones and fabrics, the variety which abounds in India. His portraits not only revealed the likeness of the subject but also the character. With diligence and an innate talent his proficiency improved; so also his fame. He was introduced to distinguished visitors to the court and he got invitations from many Indian princes to do their portraits: Mysore, Baroda, Gwalior, Bhavnagar, Udaipur. In 1888, he was commissioned by the Majaraja of Baroda to do fourteen paintings which fetched Ravi Rs. 50,000, a fabulous amount at that time.

One of the paintings which outshone his other paintings was of Shakuntala writing a love-letter to King Dushyanta. It won the Madras Governor's Gold Medal and was purchased by the then governor, the Duke of Buckingham. Sir William Jones, the famous Orientalist used this painting titled 'Shakuntala Patra Lekhan' as a frontpiece of his translation of Kalidasa's *Shakuntala*. Ravi Varma's paintings started leaving the shores of India, making him famous in distant lands. Not only the Indian rulers but also British dignitaries commissioned him for doing their portraits. The Duke of Buckingham asked him to paint a life-size portrait of him and was very much impressed by the quality of his work. Another governor, Sir Arthur Havelock, governor of Madras (1895-1900) commissioned Ravi Varma to paint his portrait from a photograph which he did, earning high praise from his distinguished subject.

A hardworking and a meticulous artist, he studied his subjects carefully and did not confine his activities to Travancore. He travelled widely in India and even learnt several regional languages to interact freely with the people. While he painted Nair people, especially their women in the beginning, he was equally fascinated by the women of Maharashtra and their style of wearing the sari. It is claimed that he made the sari popular even in Kerala where it was not part of a woman's attire. However, Ravi Varma is best known for his paintings of Hindu gods and goddesses as well as scenes from Sanskrit epics like *Ramayana* and *Mahabharata*. This came naturally to Ravi Varma as he was a highly religious man. His paintings of deities like Krishna, Saraswati, Lakshmi look sublime though in human form. "So popular were these paintings that, ever since, Hindus have visualized their gods very much the way Ravi Varma depicted them". He was so touched by the response of the common people to his paintings that he wanted the reprints of his paintings to be available at a reasonable price to them. For that purpose he set up a colour press in Bombay with the name Ravi Varma Press and opened a picture depot at Lonavala, where the press was shifted later. The prints became very popular and were displayed in innumerable houses and shops. Even today the imitations of his paintings are selling throughout the country. After initial success the press ran into difficulties and in 1901 he had to sell the press. He lost a tidy sum in this venture but he never regretted the loss as through the reproductions 'his genius came to be more widely known and appreciated'.

In 1873, at the International Art Exhibition, Vienna, Ravi Varma's painting of a Nair lady won a gold medal and a diploma. Again in 1893, in Chicago, at the International Art Exhibition, he sent ten of his paintings. They secured the first prize, two gold medals and two diplomas and brought him international fame.[2] The Maharaja of Travancore bestowed on him the Vira Sringhala (Bangle of Valour), the highest decoration of the state, the first time a painter had been so honoured. In 1904, Edward VII of England awarded him the Kaiser-i-Hind Gold medal.

Ravi Varma died in 1906 at the age of fifty-seven. In 1866, he had been married to Poorooruttathi Nal, a princess of Mavelikara Palace. They had five children. One of his sons, Rama Varma also became a noted painter and in 1915 he set up the Ravi Varma Institute of Fine Arts at Mavelika.

Ravi Varma had been criticized by art critics as a "mere illustrator, and an unimaginative copier of the European tradition". However his popularity during the last hundred years has never waned. In 1992, a special exhibition of Ravi Varma's paintings was held at the National Gallery of Modern Art, New Delhi. During a recent auction of Indian paintings in London, Ravi Varma's paintings fetched the highest price, several times more than those of M.F. Husain.

# References

1.  Sivanand, Mohan. *Ravi Varma; Prince Among Painters*. Reader's Digest, December 1992, p.141.
2.  Sankara Menon, T.C. *Raja Ravi Varma in Dictionary of National Biography* ed. by S.P. Sen. Calcutta, Institute of Historical Studies, Vol. 3, 1974.

# Shyamji Krishna Varma

## (1857-1930)

Shyamji Krishna Varma was one of those freedom fighters who spent a major part of their lives in self-exile fighting for the freedom of the country from foreign shores. Besides, he was a reputed Sanskrit scholar and a social reformer.

Shyamji Krishna Varma was born on 4 October 1857 at Mandavi, a small town in the former state of Kutch, in a Bhansali family. His parents, father Krishna Varma (whose name was added to his son's as is customary in Gujarat) and mother, Ramadevi, belonged to a lower-middle class family. His father, soon after Shyamji's birth, moved to Bombay to better his lot and that of the family and started a small business, leaving his family in Mandavi. Shyamji started his education in a local primary school. He proved to be a precocious child and stood out among the children. For further education he was put in a school at Bhuj, then the capital of the Kutch state. Tragedy struck the family when his mother, Ramadevi, died in 1867 and the responsibility of bringing up the child fell on his mother's parents. Later, he was taken to Bombay by a friend of the family and was admitted to Wilson High School. In addition to reading for his matriculation examination, he was advised to join a Sanskrit pathshala (school), where he learnt Sanskrit under a learned *shastri* and soon became proficient in the language. He won the Seth Gokuldas Kahandas scholarship by standing first in Sanskrit, enabling him to join

Elphinstone High School, a better school, where the boys of the Bombay elite studied. He topped in the high school examination also. In the school he befriended one Ramdas, son of Seth Chhabildas Lalubhai, a rich merchnt of Bombay. Impressed by the character and qualities of the young Shyamji, the Seth married his daughter Bhanumati to him. That was in 1875, when Shyamji was eighteen and Bhanumati fourteen. They led a happy married life for fifty-five years, Bhanumati standing alongside her husband through good times and bad. However, the couple died childless.

The same year Swami Dayanand founded the first Arya Samaj in Bombay at the invitation of some social reformers and enlightened citizens of Bombay. The swami preached against idolatory, child marriage, mistreatment of widows and other evils prevailing in the Hindu society. Shyamji attended several lectures of the swami who spoke in Sanskrit and was very much impressed by Dayanand's personality and his sermons. Shyamji decided to carry on propaganda on behalf of the Arya Samaj and became quite close to the swami, regularly corresponding with him and discussing various matters. He went on a propaganda tour in 1877 in western and northern India. He delivered lectures in Sanskrit at Nasik, Poona, Ahmedabad, Bahruch, Vadodra, and in 1878 at Bhuj, Mandavi and Lahore. He impressed everyone with his knowledge of Sanskrit and the *shastras*.

In 1878, Sir Monier-Williams, professor of Sanskrit at the Oxford University, visited India. On hearing Shyamji's Sanskrit scholarship he met him and suggested that Shyamji should study at Oxford. After initial reluctance, Swami Dayanand gave his blessings and Shyamji sailed for England in April 1879. He was admitted to the Balliol College, Oxford and shortly after, also to the Inner Temple for studies in Law. Shyamji was awarded the B.A. degree in 1883 at Oxford and was called to the Bar in London in 1884. While still a student at Oxford, he represented India at the Conference of Orientalists in Berlin. He also helped Monier-Williams to establish the Indian Institute at Oxford 'as a centre of Indian learning and interests' in 1883. Later, Monier-Williams wrote about Shyamji's stay at Oxford: "Without giving up one iota of his Sanskrit learning, he has opened his mind freely to the reception of all the higher forms of European culture. Assuredly no English or European teacher could possibly be his equal in expounding the grammars of Indian languages according to the principles of native grammarians. He is the first Indian Sanskrit scholar who has ever visited England and achieved so great a success. During his residence at Oxford, Pandit Shyamji acted as my assistant in Sanskrit and last year the Master and Fellow of the College appointed him to the office of Lecturer in Sanskrit, Marathi and Gujarati".[1] Shyamji returned to India in January 1885.

Like his mentor Swami Dayanand, Shyamji surmised that the part of India which was ruled by Indian princes was free India and that it would be easier to start the freedom movement and social reform in Indian states. In fact, Dayanand spent the last decade of his life trying to spread his gospel in Rajasthan — Masuda, Udaipur, Jodhpur — and had met with partial success. On his return to India, Shyamji served in Indian states — Ratlam, Udaipur and Junagadh — as diwan (minister). Intermittently he did legal practice first at Bombay and then at Ajmer, but his heart was not in the legal profession. One advantage of working in the Indian states was that he could save quite a large amount of money as the princes paid him generously. It is also believed that Shyamji had invested wisely in shares and had earned rich dividends. He was a rich man now but a disillusioned one. He had realized that even in the princely states the real power was vested in the British Resident in each state. He decided to return to England after spending twelve fruitless years of his life in the country. During his earlier stay in England he had found that Indians enjoyed more freedom in England than in their own country. He wanted to make use of that freedom for India's freedom. He left for England in 1897.

While at Oxford, he came across Herbert Spencer's *First Principles*. Besides, he had studied Spencer, who was considered as the greatest British philosopher of the nineteenth century, in depth. He was influenced most by his *Principles of Sociology* in which he had propagated the gospel of rationalism and had denounced oppression of every kind. He had opined that war was merely wholesale cannibalism and that imperialism could be sustained only through war, through that cannibalism. He developed close links with the 'radical rationalists' in London, and joined the agitation against the banning of Havelock Ellis' book *Psychology of Sex* (1897) on the charges of obscenity. He also supported the cause of Boers in the Boer War in South Africa (1899-1902). He contributed liberally to such causes. In 1903, Herbert Spencer, his idol, died. Shyamji attended his funeral and after the orations Shyamji stood up and announced a donation of one thousand pounds to Oxford for establishing a chair in memory of Herbert Spencer. The proposal was accepted.

In 1904, Shyamji announced his scheme of fellowships of Rs. 2000 each for enabling Indian students to pursue their studies in England or other foreign countries. The only condition was that on completion they shall not serve the British government in any capacity after their return to India. Moral condemnation of the British rule and non-cooperation was implicit in the condition. The scheme was heralded by many nationalists including Tilak. Many aspiring students availed of this bounty, the more prominent being V.D. Savarkar, Senapati Bapat, and Madhavrao Jadhav; B.C. Pal accepted a lectureship under the scheme.

The year 1905 was the most momentous in the life of Shyamji in England. In January 1905, he started publication of the *Indian Sociologist* — 'an organ of freedom and political, social and religious reform'. It declared as its motto, 'Resistance to aggression is not simply justifiable but imperative', obviously borrowed from Spencer. The prodigy in Sanskrit proved also to be a gifted journalist in the English language. Soon the *Indian Sociologist* took the pride of place in expressing the Indian point of view and proved to be a rallying point for freedom fighters in self-exile. Gandhi took note of it and wrote: "It (*The Indian Sociologist*) is edited by Pandit Shyamji Krishnavarma, M.A. (Oxon), sometime lecturer at Oxford, and is published in London. It is a journal fearlessly edited, and the editor is imbued with the teachings of the late Herbert Spencer. The journal is evidently intended to model Indian opinion in accordance with Spencer's teachings. The Pandit is an Indian scholar of distinction, and has a fair amount of capital at his command".[2]

Shyamji's following increased with the publication of the *Indian Sociologist*. The need for an association to coordinate the efforts of individuals was felt. Thus was born on 18 February, 1905 the 'Indian Home Rule Society' modelled on the Irish Home Rule League. The main object of the society was to secure Home Rule for India. The society was to carry on propaganda towards that end and to educate people about the advantages of freedom. Shyamji was appointed president and J.C. Mukherjee as secretary. The society made good progress and within a year the number of active members crossed the hundred mark. In 1916, both Tilak and Annie Besant also launched two Home Rule Leagues independently. But these had no connection with the Home Rule Society established by Shyamji and his friends.

On 1 July 1905, Shyamji bought a house at Highgate, Hampstead, London in the center of the city. He named it 'India House' where Indian students studying in London or passing through the city, could stay by paying nominal charges for board and lodging. It had twenty-five rooms and a conference hall, library and reading room. During the opening ceremony many prominent Indians including Dadabhai Naoroji, Lala Lajpat Rai, Madam Cama, along with some British liberals were present. In a speech Hyndman (Social Democratic Federation) said, "The institution of 'India House' means a great step in the direction of Indian growth and Indian emancipation and some of those who are here this afternoon may witness the first fruit of its triumphant success". The India House became a safe abode for revolutionaries like Savarkar, Madan Lal Dhingra and others. For other Indians it was a meeting place where they could hold cultural functions and celebrate religious festivals.

In October 1906, Gandhi came to London as part of a delegation from South Africa. He met Shyamji and had several meetings with him discussing Indian problems. 'Our conversation went on till one in the morning', Gandhi wrote later. Gandhi found his discussions with Shyamji so engaging that he even cancelled his other engagements. Gandhi was specially fascinated by an article in the October issue of the *Indian Sociologist* by Shyamji in which he had argued that the Indian government could be brought to a standstill by peaceful passive resistance movement by the Indian people to win freedom as there were no Britishers serving as policemen, postmen, clerks, drivers etc. in the country. The British were ruling India with the cooperation of Indians. If the Indians 'non-cooperate' on a massive scale the British will be left with no option but to quit India. It is not very unlikely that Gandhi got the idea of the non-cooperation movement (which he started in 1920) from these discussions with Shyamji.

The Indian Sociologist wrote extensively on the developments in Indian politics denouncing the 'moderates' like Gokhale and Dadabhai Naoroji and supporting the 'extremist' wing in the Congress led by Tilak. His attack on the governmnet as well as 'Anglo-Indians' like Hume, who had been controlling the Congress, was being increasingly severe. He was now advocating armed struggle for freeing the country from foreign rule. By then, India House had become notorious as a center of seditious activities. In 1907, a question was raised in the House of Commons enquiring whether the government proposed to take any action against Shyamji Krishna Varma. Though no action was taken, Shyamji thought it prudent to leave England and settle in Paris. Revolutionaries like Savarkar, Madam Cama, Dhingra and others continued to plan revolutionary activities from the India House; Savarkar had emerged as the leader of the group.

In July 1909, Madan Lal Dhingra, an engineering student in London, shot dead Curzon Wyllie, political ADC of secretary of state for India. He was sentenced to death and faced the gallows on 17 August 1909. The revolutionaries were expecting support from Shyamji in the columns of the *Indian Sociologist*. On the other hand, Shyamji condemned Dhingra's act unequivocally saying that he believed that "political assassinations, though quite justified in India, were worthy of utmost condemnation when perpetrated in England or any other country". He repeatedly declared that he had no hand in the assassination of Wyllie. Actually the British secret police was after Shyamji, the founder of India House and were seeking his extradition from France. Revolutionaries started feeling that Shyamji was a coward and to save his skin he had become a turncoat. He was accused as a renegade. Though he tried to make up by declaring that he was granting four scholarships in the name of Madan Lal Dhingra, the damage was done. He could never earn the same respect which was bestowed on him by the revolutionaries before 1909. By that time Madam Cama and Sardar Singh Rana had also moved to Paris as the heat was also on them in London. They started a 'truly revolutionary paper', *Bande Matram* in September 1909. Hardyal was made its editor. A similar paper

*Talwar* was started by Virendra Nath Chattopadhyay, brother of Sarojini Naidu, from Berlin. *The Indian Sociologist* was eclipsed and with it Shyamji. Till then the *Indian Sociologist* was being printed in London. But as the two printers, both White, were imprisoned on charges of sedition, Shyamji got its printing done in Paris itself. With the arrest and deportation of V.D. Savarkar in 1910, the revolutionary activities in London came to an end; Paris and Berlin became their new abode.Shyamji sold his property in London, never to return to that country or to India again. He was then fifty-three and the best and most glorious period of his life was behind him. He was still a wealthy man and had the company of his talented and dependable companion in his wife Bhanumati.

In 1914, started the European War and Britain and France joined hands to face the Germans. France was no longer a safe haven for the revolutionaries. Shyamji shifted to Geneva, Switzerland, which was a neutral country. He had given a pledge to the Swiss government of political inaction while in that country. As a result, the publication of the *Indian Sociologist* was suspended during the War. Incidentally, Madam Cama did not leave Paris and was sentenced to three years imprisonment by the French government. The War ended with the victory of Britain and France and the Indian revolutionaries lost their support not only in France but also in Germany. Shyamji decided to stay on in Geneva.

He kept in close touch with the movements in India and continued his programme of offering lectureships and scholarships to Indian students to study in foreign lands. On the death of Tilak in 1920, he donated ten thousand rupees for the purpose. He had resumed publication of the *Indian Sociologist* but the fire had gone from it. The September 1922 issue of the journal was to be the last issue in which Shyamji announced his retirement from active politics — whatever had remained of it. After the cessation of the *Indian Sociologist*, Shyamji's activity was confined to casual correspondence and still more casual meetings with Indian and foreign friends while living in Geneva.

Nehru, (who had gone to Europe in 1926-27 for the treatment of his wife Kamala who was suffering from tuberculosis) met Shyamji and his wife in their flat in Geneva and found the couple in a pathetic condition. Nehru later wrote something which deserves being quoted in full: "Shyamji Krishnavarma was living with his ailing wife high up on the top floor of a house in Geneva. The aged couple lived by themselves with no whole-time servants, and their rooms were musty and suffocating, and everything had a thick layer of dust. Shyamji had plenty of money, but he did not believe in spending it. He was suspicious of all comers, presuming them, until the contrary was proved, to be either British agents or after his money. His pockets bulged with ancient copies of his old paper, the *Indian Sociologist*, and he would pull them out and point with some excitement to some article he had written a dozen years previously. His talk was of the old days, of India House at Hampstead, of the various persons that the British Government had sent to spy on him, and how he had spotted them and outwitted them. The walls of his rooms were covered with shelves full of old books, dust-laden and neglected, looking down sorrowfully on the intruder. Over the whole place there hung an atmosphere of decay; life seemed to be an unwelcome stranger there, and, as one walked through the dark and silent corridors, one almost expected to come across, round the corner, the shadow of death. With relief one came out of that flat and breathed the air outside".[3]

One could not live in that gloomy atmosphere for long. Shyamji died on 31 March 1930. Shiv Prasad Gupta, editor of Hindi daily *Aaj*, Varanasi was the last Indian to see him. Bhanumati, now had a problem at her hand: what to do with all the money they had and the books they had collected. She donated ten thousand Swiss francs to the Geneva University, and an equal amount to a hospital in Geneva. The books were presented to Institute de Civilisation Indiennens, Sorbonne University. Finally, she made a trust for awarding scholarships to deserving Indian students for pursuing higher studies in the University of Sorbonne for which she left nearly two million French francs. After getting rid of her money, she died in peace at Geneva on 22 August 1933. The couple had been cremated in a cemetery near Geneva. There the remains of the forgotten couple lay. Suddenly in 2003 the nation remembered them and the Gujarat government brought their remains to India and a suitable memorial is planned for Shyamji Krishna Varma, the forgotten hero of the freedom movement.

# References

1. Varma, Ganesh Lal. *Shyamji Krishna Varma; The Unknown Patriot.* New Delhi, Publications Division. 1993, p.11.
2. *Collected Works of Mahatma Gandhi.* Vol. 4 (in *Indian Opinion* 3 June, 1905) p.458.
3. Nehru, Jawaharlal. *An Autobiography*, OUP, 1936, pp.148-49.

# Iswar Chandra Vidyasagar

## (1820-1891)

Iswar Chandra was born in a poor Brahmin family on 26 September 1820 in the village of Birsingha in Midnapur district of West Bengal. His parents, Thakurdas Bandhopadhyaya and Bhagwati Devi, lived in a thatched hut in extreme poverty. In spite of that, Thakurdas wanted his son to become a learned pandit. After finishing his initial study at a village pathshala, Thakurdas took Iswar Chandra to Calcutta where he underwent a year's schooling in a local pathshala and the next year (1829) he was admitted to the Sanskrit College where Iswar Chandra completed his studies by 1841 with brilliant results, winning prizes and scholarships, "sweeping in his stride the highest honours in every class examination". The title 'Vidyasagar' was used for the first time in the certificate awarded to him by the Law Committee, in May, 1839, on his passing the *Smriti* (Law) examination.

After completing his studies, Vidyasagar joined government service and started his career as head pandit in Fort William College, Calcutta in 1841. In 1846, he was appointed assistant secretary, Sanskrit College, but he resigned that post in 1849 over some differences with the secretary of the College and returned to Fort William College as head writer and treasurer. In December 1850, however, he was back in the Sanskrit College as professor of Sanskrit literature and on 22 January 1851, he rose to be the first principal of the college. As principal, he started rationalization and reorganization of the courses which included teaching of English as a compulsory subject. He was invested with "full discretion to remodel, reform and simplify Sanskrit education for the benefit of countrymen". In 1855, he was appointed special inspector of schools for Hoogly, Burdwan, Midnapur and Nadia in addition to his duties as principal of the Sanskrit College. As special inspector, he was instrumental in the establishment of twenty model schools and thirty-five girls schools in these districts starting from 1855, and a normal school on the premises of the Sanskrit College to train up teachers for these schools. In his own village, Birsingha, he opened two schools, one for boys and another for girls and bore all the expenses himself.

Vidyasagar was active in the cause of female education as already stated. An important female institution was founded by Sir Drinkwatar Bethune, president of the Education Committee in May 1849, called the Calcutta Female School (later named as Bethune Female School). Vidyasagar fully collaborated with Bethune from the beginning. On the death of Bethune, Vidyasagar took over as honorary secretary. The school developed into a Women's College, the first girl's college in Calcutta.

When the University of Calcutta was established in 1857. Vidyasagar was one of the six Indian members of the Senate. As Senate member, he was a tireless guide for the affairs of the University particularly those involving the curriculum and examinations. In other important matters of the university also he always expressed his views forcefully. He opposed a resolution to exclude Sanskrit from university courses as well as the move to abolish the Sanskrit College. He was successful in saving both Sanskrit and the Sanskrit College, as his opinion carried weight with the government. He was connected with a number of educational bodies even after his resignation from the government service and continued to be an unofficial adviser of the government, being consulted by successive lieutenant governors.

Considered as one of the best educational administrators, Vidyasagar was called upon to take up the management of the Metropolitan Institution and was made its secretary in 1861. The institution was founded in 1859 by private individuals as the Calcutta Training School, later changed to Hindu Metropolitan Institution in 1864 (now named Vidyasagar College). Vidyasagar worked hard for the institution; brought about reforms in the school, and supervised its teaching. He personally contributed towards the cost of the new building which was completed in 1886.

Education was not the only field in which Vidyasagar contributed effectively spending huge amounts of money from his own resources. In fact, he is remembered most as a reformer. "A still loftier endeavour occupied Vidyasagar when he proclaimed in 1855 that the perpetual widowhood of Hindu women was not sanctioned by the sastras, and that the marriage of Hindu widows was permitted. He quoted a couplet from *Prasar Samhita* which vindicated the remarriage of the Hindu widows".[1] He wrote two articles on the subject published in *Tattbodhini Patrika* in 1855. The articles were then issued later in a pamphlet form which raised a storm of protest by the orthodox Hindus, similar to what Rammohun Roy had to face three decades earlier on the issue of sati. In October 1855, a second tract was brought out by him in reply to the protests of his opponents. After the publication of Vidyasagar's pamphlets many others opposing his views were brought out from various associations of orthodox pandits like Dharam Sabha and Jessore Hindu Dharma Rakshini Sabha. Undaunted, Vidyasagar proceeded ahead with his campaign.

Consolidating the earlier two tracts in Bengali, he published one *Marriage of Hindu Widows* in English and gave a copy of it to the British India Association with a request to forward it to the government with their recommendation. Vidyasagar was close to many higher government officials who had been his sympathizers and supporters in his reform activities. On their advice, he submitted a petition to the government on 4 October 1855 for enactment of a legislation in favour of widow re-marriage. He got support from some influential circles of Maharashtra and south India but had to face another round of stiff opposition in Bengal. About one hundred pamphlets, for and against, were addressed to an agitated public, out of which only ten percent were in support. Several petitions were also submitted with thousands of signatures against Vidyasagar's move. But in spite of such overwhelming opposition Vidyasagar's stand was vindicated when the Legislative Council passed an act on 26 July 1856, (Act XV of 1856) which made the remarriage of Hindu widows valid. This was the happiest day in his life and an important milestone in the history of social reform in India.

With the Act passed, Vidyasagar now devoted himself in arranging widow marriages. The first such marriage was solemnized under police protection on 7 December 1856, that of Sris Chandra Vidyaratna, professor of Literature at the Sanskrit College, who married a widow Kalimati Devi. Vidyasagar bore all the expenses of the clothes and ornaments. To set an example, his only son Narayan Chandra was married to a child widow in 1870. He made no bones about his happiness at this great event. He wrote to a friend: "The most honest act of my life has been to fight for the promotion of widow remarriage in society and there cannot be any other unimpeachably conscientious act on my part than seeing through Narayan Chandra's marriage to a widow".[2] Several of such marriages were solemnized during his lifetime and each one cost him a substantial amount of money which ultimately pushed him into debt but he lived long enough to clear it. However, the taboo against marrying widows did not disappear. The Act of 1829 against sati was more successful for obvious reasons. While the Act of 1856 about widow remarriage was a 'permissive act' recognizing as legal both the remarriage of a widow and her issues by such marriage, the anti-Sati Act was a 'punitive act,' those violating it were liable to be punished. Thus the widow remarriage Act did not have much effect on society. However, to mitigate the suffering of widows who could not remarry, Vidyasagar founded the Hindu Family Annuity Fund in 1872 to ensure security for a widow.

Bengal had the largest number of widows in the country. The main reason for this proliferation of widows was a peculiar social custom of Kulinism — polygamy among the Hindus particularly among the Kulin Brahmins. Sometimes they used to have scores or even hundreds of wives. The death of the husband resulted in as many widows. To cut this source of widowhood, Vidyasagar started a crusade against polygamy among the Hindus. In December 1855, he organized a deputation for banning polygamy and a mass petition with twenty-five thousand signatures was addressed to the governor-general to that effect. A bill, which was promised by the government, had to be shelved because of the Sepoy uprising of 1857 which led to a policy shift. The campaign was revived by Vidyasagar in 1866 when once again several petitions with thousands of signatures were submitted. Taking a lesson from the uprising, the government was in no hurry to tamper with the social customs of the Hindus and used dilatory tactics to mark time by appointing a committee to look into the matter. The relentless Vidyasagar issued a tract on polygamy in 1871 and a second one in 1872, both in Bengali and later combining these two in the English version with the title *Whether Polygamy was Consonant with Hindu Shastra*. The movement failed ultimately, but not without awakening his countrymen to the curse of polygamy. The custom died down with the passage of time mainly due to economic reasons and urbanization, bringing down the number of widows in the process. Another reformer of his time, Swami Dayanand, also fought for widow remarriage and was more successful. His success was confined to Punjab and western Uttar Pradesh partly because the problem of widowhood was not so acute in that area as compared to Bengal. Also the Brahmin orthodoxy was not as powerful in that area.

As a social reformer, Vidyasagar chose his methods with restraint. Unlike the 'Young Bengal' (Derozians) or to some extent unlike Brahmos of Bengal, Vidyasagar was no rebel but a sincere and courageous reformer. He was unwilling to be alienated from the mainstream of Hindu society. At the same time he would not yield to any pressure or antagonism once he was convinced about the righteousness of the cause he was upholding. In fact he would go to any extent to achieve what he thought was morally right and spent money liberally and in the process was financially ruined. But he had no regrets for that.

Vidyasagar's contribution to journalism was quite limited, though not altogether negligible. His articles were published in *Sarbashubhankar Patrika*; he was on the Paper Committee (the Editorial Committee) of the *Tattwabodhini Patrika* and was directly associated with the *Somprakash*, a distinguished Bengali journal of the time. A greater responsibility also fell on him when it fell on bad days.

In spite of Vidyasagar's plea for learning English, he had an innate love for his mother-tongue, Bengali. Though he wrote mainly textbooks, he gave the Bengali language a fluent and elegant style. The style was a marked improvement over the earlier pompous and turgid style of the likes of Rammohun Roy. He made the Bengali prose simple and elastic, discarding the heavy weight of Sanskrit words. He was the first writer to use proper punctuation in the Bengali language. The more important of his works in Bengali are: *Belal Panchavimasi* (1847), *Banglar Itihas* (1848); *Jivan Charit* (biographies of western scientists); *Bodhodaya* (1851); *Sakuntala* (1854); *Chitravali* (1856); *Kathamala* (1860); *Sitar Vanvas*; *Akhyan Manjari* (in two parts, 1863-68); *Bhranti-Vilas* (1869). Sanskrit textbooks are: *Upakramanika* (1851); *Rijupatha*, (3 parts, 1851-53) *Vyakarana Kaumudi* (4 parts, 1853-55).

Dressed in a typical middle class attire, dhuti, chaddar and Taltola slippers, Vidyasagar walked the streets of Calcutta as a colossus and was loved, admired and hated at the same time. He became a legend in his own time. He had almost an obsession for charity and philanthropy and spent a major part of his earnings for others — for the cause of women's upliftment, for schools and hospitals, for famine relief in Midnapore, for epidemic relief in Burdwan, for the support of orphans and their education etc.

He died of high fever in Calcutta on 29 July 1891. He will always stand out prominently in the galaxy of great men of this country.

## References

1. Mitra, Subal Chandra. *Iswar Chandra Vidyasagar; A Story of His Life and Work*. 1902. Reprint. New Delhi, Ashish, 1975. p.262.
2. Sinha, Nirmal ed. *Freedom Movement in Bengal*, 1818-1904. Calcutta, Academic Publishers. 1991. p.196.

# M. Visvesvaraya

## (1861-1962)

Visvesvaraya was one of the greatest civil engineers this country has produced, leaving scores of living monuments perpetuating his memory; the dancing fountains of the Vrindaban Gardens, near Mysore, is only one of them. Visvesvaraya was also a great administrator and an educationist who tried to change the face of India through economic and intellectual regeneration. Though he did not indulge in politics during his remarkably long life, he was an ardent nationalist.

Mokshagundam Visvesvaraya (M.V. to his friends and admirers) was born on 15 September 1861 at Muddenahalli, a village near Nandi Hills in Mysore state. He belonged to an orthodox middle class Brahmin family. His father, Srinivas Sastri, was a practicing Ayurveda doctor and also a Sanskrit scholar. M.V. received his middle and high school education in the nearby town of Chickballapur. For higher education he joined the Central College, Bangalore, from where he passed his B.A. examination, with distinction, in 1880. He won a scholarship which enabled him to join College of Science at Poona for his engineering degree, which he got in 1883. He started his career as an assistant engineer in the Bombay Public Works Department. His first posting was at Nasik in 1884, but he was assigned duties in different places in the Bombay Presidency. He designed water supply scheme of Dhulia in Sind (which was part of the Bombay Presidency at that time) where he completed the special work of water supply and drainage (1894-95). He solved the problem of drinking water of Surat city by digging wells in the Tapati river bed. During this period one important piece of engineering which he devised was a system of automatic gates to raise the storage level of Lake Fife at Khadakvasla. He writes in his *Memoirs of My Working Life*: "The reservoir overflowed every year up to a height of six to eight feet above the crest of the surplus weir. A system of automatic gates was designed by me to raise the storage water level of the lake permanently by about 8 feet above the original surplus weir. This increased the storage in the reservoir by about 25 per cent without raising the dam". He took out a patent for these automatic gates which are now used the world over but he refused to accept any royalty on it.

In 1901, as sanitary engineer of the Poona Municipality, M.V. prepared a project for a modern type of sewerage system for the first time for Poona. In 1904, he was promoted to the post of sanitary engineer for the Bombay Presidency and in that capacity he made improvements in the water supply system of Karachi and Ahmedabad. When a senior engineer was required to advise for the improvement of water and drainage system of Aden (a British Protectorate), Visvesvaraya was deputed and he submitted a detailed report, which was later implemented. He also prepared water supply schemes for Kolhapur, Belgaum, Dharwar and Bijapur. Hard work matched with innovative skill, brought him accelerated promotions and soon his rank was next only to the chief engineer. As the post of the chief engineer was reserved for the Britishers his chances were almost nil. Therefore, he decided to resign from the government service in 1908 after twenty-four years of service. He was honoured with the title, Kaiser-e-Hind, by the government. His more momentous achievements had yet to come.

Immediately after his retirement from government service he was requested by the Nizam of Hyderabad to advise and assist in the reconstruction of Hyderabad city which was earlier devastated by floods of the Musi river. After careful study he submitted a plan in October 1909 to save the city from such unusual floods in the future. Thereafter started the most productive period of his career when in November 1909 he joined as chief engineer of the Mysore state at the personal request of the Maharaja. This job was much after his own heart, because the Maharaja gave him the freedom to work as he liked. He set to ameliorate the overall condition of the people through education, including technical education, and establishing a network of industries. As chief engineer, he prepared schemes for water supply, road communication and irrigation. M.V. also tried to involve more and more people, especially the intellectuals, in the regeneration of Mysore state. At his instance the Mysore Economic Conference, consisting of officials and knowledgeable non-officials, was formed to discuss the problems faced by the people of the state and to suggest solutions. But his greatest achievement was the building of the Krishnaraja Sagara Reservoir, which was made possible by building a 124 feet high dam across the Cauvery river. This extensive multipurpose project stores 48,000 million cubic feet of water for the purpose of irrigating thousands of acres of land. The Krishnaraja Sagar Dam was the largest reservoir built in India till then. It also provides an even flow of water to the Hydro-Electric Power Station at Sivasamudram, which supplied power to the Kolar Gold Mines, which were functioning at that time. The project was completed in 1915 according to schedule. The famous Vrindaban Gardens form a beautiful adjunct to the Reservoir. Gandhi visited the Dam in July, 1927 and wrote: "I saw the Krishnarajasagara Dam today and was delighted to see the wonderful engineering feat of Sir M. Visvesvaraya, the second I am told, of its kind in the world".

In November 1912, the Maharaja appointed him as the dewan (chief minister) of Mysore state and at once the sphere of his activities widened — education, industry, commerce and public works. His first preference was education, especially technical education. He got opened an Agricultural School in 1913, a Mechanical Engineering School the following year as well as several industrial schools. An Engineering College was established at Bangalore (1916) and the Mysore University was founded in 1916 which gave a fillip to the spread of education in the state. The number of schools increased from 4500 to 10,500 and the student enrollment from 1,40,000 to 3,66,000. He also offered scholarships to meritorious students, enabling them to study abroad. For girls, the Maharani's College in Mysore was founded along with a hostel.

Turning to industry, he took action for the development of sericulture, thus making Mysore silk famous throughout the country. He had a sandalwood oil manufacturing unit set up that was used for making soap thus starting a small scale industry of soap manufacture, which is continuing to this day. The construction of the Mysore Iron and Wood Distillation Works was started in 1918. He also put up plans for Bhadravath Iron Works (1918) and for harnessing hydroelectric power at Jog (1918). He took keen interest, along with Walchand, for starting the Hindustan Aircraft Factory at Bangalore. He canvassed for the Vishakhapatnam Shipyard and offered useful suggestions at the construction stage. He did not succeed in establishing an automobile industry in Mysore, but was able to help in the establishment of the Premier Automobile Company near Bombay. To provide easy finance for the growing industries in Mysore he founded the Bank of Mysore (1913).

Gradually, caste politics engulfed south India and Mysore was no exception. The Maharaja supported the move of reservations in appointments for depressed classes and backward communities. M.V. opposed the Maharaja's move on the grounds of efficiency and quality of service. When the Maharaja ignored his appeal, he resigned from the post of Dewan in February, 1918. He later took the charge of Mysore Iron and Steel Works from 1923 to 1929 on the personal request of the Maharaja, and turned it into a profitable venture for the first time. He also worked as chairman of the Committee of the Cauvery Canal System and the New Bangalore Water Supply Scheme. By that time he had earned a name as an able administrator. He advised the Bombay City Corporation (1924-25) and the Karachi Municipal Corporation (1924) about their finances and administration. Many of the cities in Western India, which have modern water supply schemes or drainage systems, owe it to Visvesvaraya. In 1937, the Orissa government requisitioned his services to suggest ways and means to solve the flood problem.

M.V. served as chairman of several committees constituted by the government: Bombay Technical and Industrial Education Committee (1921-22); Indian Economic Enquiry Committee (1925); Bangalore Political Disturbances Enquiry Committee (1929) and Irrigation Enquiry Committee, Bombay (1938). Even at age of ninety-two, Jawaharlal Nehru requested

M.V. to suggest two sites for bridges over the Ganga river from among several which the state governments of U.P., Bihar and West Bengal were canvassing for. Nehru observed that, "He is an engineer of integrity, character and broad national outlook who could take an unbiased view, resist local pressures and whose views would be respected and accepted by all".[1] Visvesvaraya visited all the proposed sites and weighed the merits and demerits of each and recommended Mokamah in Bihar and Farakha in West Bengal as the most suitable sites for the bridges in 1953. Nobody complained.

He retained his quest for knowledge and learning throughout his life. He visited foreign countries to study their advanced technologies, six times in 1898, 1908, 1919, 1926, 1935 and 1946 — the last one when he was eighty-six.

Visvesvaraya, though an engineer, wrote on economic matters extensively and was an advocate of planned economy. He elucidated his views in his two books *Reconstructing India* (1920) and *Planned Economy for India* (1934). He also wrote several tracts on village industries, rural industrialization and the automobile industry. His autobiography, *Memoirs of My Working Life* (1951), is very revealing. Honorary degrees were conferred on him by several universities. He was made a C.I.E. in 1911 and a K.C.I.E. in 1915. The Government of India conferred the Bharat Ratna on him in 1955.

M.V. had become a legend in his lifetime. People wondered how he could enjoy such good health and retain zest for life even in advanced age. Gandhi, a health faddist himself, was intrigued by Visvesvaraya's secret of good health. Gandhi wrote to him in 1944: "You have enriched the life of the country by your unrivalled engineering skill. I have also been following too your writings on planned economy. Besides your contribution as a great engineer, what has captivated me is the art you have cultivated of keeping up in old age robust physical and mental energy. I have not forgotten the way in which you used to climb up the Nandi Hill without any effort. I would like you to give the young men and women of the country the secret, as you have known it, of feeling young and vigorous even in old age. It is a rare gift in our country".[2]

M.V. died on 14 April 1962, at the age of hundred and one, mourned by millions and envied by many others.

## References

1. Murthi, R.K. *Visvesvaraya*, in *Our Leaders* Vol. 2, New Delhi, CBT, 1989. p.61.
2. *Collected Works of Mahatma Gandhi*, Vol. 78, pp.13-14.

# Swami Vivekananda

## (1863-1902)

Narendra Nath Dutta better known as Vivekananda, was born on 12 January 1863, in a well-to-do family in Calcutta. His father, Biswanath Dutta, was an attorney at the Calcutta high court, earning quite a handsome amount. His mother, Bhubaneswari Devi, was a moderately educated lady.

Narendra was educated at the Metropolitan Institution founded by Ishwar Chandra Vidyasagar (now named Vidyasagar College) from where he passed his matriculation in 1879. Later, he studied at the General Assembly Institution (now Scottish Church College), graduating from the Calcutta University in 1884. During his student days, apart from his brilliance in studies, he was very fond of physical exercise and sports. He had a beautiful voice and took lessons in music and used to sing devotional songs in his melodious voice which enthralled listeners. Narendra also studied widely both Indian and Western philosophy and literature and gradually acquired a deep knowledge of both which he used to great effect in his lectures and writings later in life. Narendra Dutta grew up to be a handsome man, with a personality that attracted attention, standing at five feet eight and half inches.

Naren's father died in 1884. Though his father used to earn a considerable amount, he was a spendthrift and had lived beyond his means. After his death, his family was in dire straits. Narendra being the eldest son, had to been the responsibility of meeting the needs of the family. During this period of turmoil, Narendra had tasted poverty and misery which made him identify himself with the miserables and the downtrodden throughout his life. He tried to find a suitable job but did not succeed. However, he took an apprenticeship in an attorney's firm and also joined a law course which he soon gave up. In 1885, he also served as a teacher in Metropolitan Institution for a brief period.

In spite of his robust physique and love for sports and physical exercise, Narendra Nath was a contemplative type. The study of Western philosophy and literature had instilled in him a profoundly questioning attitude towards God and to the nature of this world. He had joined Sadharan Brahmo Samaj where he met eminent personalities like Debendranath Tagore, Keshab Chandra Sen, Sivnath Sastri and other leading lights of Calcutta but even they could not satisfy his inquisitive mind. His search for an enlightened guru ended when he met Ramakrishna Paramhansa at the Kali temple of Dakshineswar late in 1881. After initial skepticism, Narendra gradually surrendered to the master and sought his guidance. Ramakrishna had already attracted around him a band of young men who were ready to do his bidding for any cause as ordained by the great master. Unfortunately, Ramakrishna died of cancer in 1886. By that time, Narendra Nath had become his favourite disciple in whom the guru saw tremendous potential to execute the plans which he had in mind. Before his death, Ramakrishna transferred his mantle to Narendra Nath, which did not come as a surprise to any one. All the young disciples then formed themselves into a team under the leadership of Narendra Nath to launch what is popularly known as the Ramakrishna Order. They set up a *math* (monastery) in 1887 in a rented garden-house at Baranagore, a few mile from Calcutta, to carry on their spiritual *sadhana* (quest). But their mission had to be more than just meditation. It was to spread the message of Ramakrishna to the wider public but the details were not clear to Naren or to his colleagues. To know the people whom the disciples of Ramakrishna had to serve, Narendranath set out on a wandering mission, incognito, in 1888. The mission took him to various parts of the country from the southern tip to the Himalayas. He conferred with holy men, visited sacred shrines, studied Sanskrit and the scriptures at some places, practiced incredible austerities and underwent the severest possible ordeals. Between 1888 and the early months of 1893, Naren traversed the country thrice and came in contact with all sorts of men, rajas and maharajas, the householders and the pariahs (untouchables). Reaching Kanyakumari, the southernmost tip of the mainland, he swam to a rock at some distance from the mainland and meditated there, looking up to the country remembering her past glory and present degradation. While contemplating on this rock he got the enlightenment that gave him the vision about his future mission in life. This rock is now known as the Vivekananda Rock on which a beautiful memorial has been built. The mission was now clear to him. He remembered the words of Ramakrishna, 'Religion is not for empty bellies'. The first duty of religion is to care for the poor, the hungry and raise them from their misery.

During his travels he had met maharajas of Khetri and Alwar (both in Rajasthan) and of Mysore and Ramnad in the south, who became Naren's followers. At the end of October 1892, he had made up his mind to go to the West. He learnt that a Parliament of Religions was to be held during the following year in Chicago. He thought that it would be a great opportunity to give the message of Vedanta to the august gathering and seek help 'to ameliorate the material condition of India'. When he told about it to the Maharajas of Mysore, Ramnad and later to the Raja of Khetri, they enthusiastically helped him and arranged for his passage to America. The Raja of Khetri, Ajit Singh, suggested the name Vivekananda which 'he was about to impose upon the world'. At Khetri, Naren, now Vivekananda, changed his dress to a robe of red silk and an ochre turban. Vivekananda sailed from Bombay on 31 May 1893 via Southeast Asia reaching Chicago in July. But he carried no official credentials without which he would not to be permitted into the Parliament of Religions. But with the help of Professor J.H. Wright of Harvard University and some kindly Americans who saw in Vivekananda qualities of a genius, Vivekananda succeeded in participating in the Parliament of Religions, the delegates of which represented all the religions of the world, from East and West.

The first session started on 11 September. Vivekananda spoke almost at the end. But his brief speech was 'like a tongue of fire'. "Among the grey wastes of cold dissertation it fired the souls of the listeing throngs. Hardly had he pronounced the very simple opening words 'Sisters and brothers of America' that hundreds arose in their seats and applauded".[1] He greeted the youngest of the nations in the name of the most ancient monastic order in the world — the Vedic order of Sanyasins. Vivekananda became the most sought after speaker at the Parliament of Religions. During the following few days he spoke at least ten times including at the closing session on 27 September. He was lauded by the American press. *The New York Herald* reported: "He is undoubtedly the greatest figure in the Parliament of Religions. After hearing him we feel how foolish it is to send missionaries to this learned nation".[2]

However, it was not friendly exchange of views all the time. A point was reached when sharp acerbate developed. The thin veil of courtesy was maintained, but behind it was ill feeling, especially among Christian missionaries. Rev. Joseph Cook criticized the Hindus sharply. He said that to speak of a universe that was not created is almost unpardonable nonsense and received the retort that a universe which had a beginning is a self-evident absurdity. But notwithstanding such skirmishes with Christian missionaries, Vivekananda was elated by the response which he received in America and decided to stay on, spreading the message of Vedanta and at the same time collecting money for his future plans. He stayed on for more than three years in America, lecturing and discoursing at various places from the east coast to the west coast. At New York, Vivekananda founded the Vedanta Society in 1894 (which is still functioning) and published his first philosophical treatise, *Raja Yoga*, in 1896. (Three other treatises: *Karma Yoga*, *Jnana Yoga* and *Bhakti Yoga* were published later; all were based on his lectures). From America, Vivekananda visited England, twice, in 1895 and again in 1896, where he met great Orientalists including Max Muller and Paul Deussen. He felt the seriousness of his English hearers in contrast to the 'superficial infatuation' of the American public. And it was England which gave Vivekanand some devoted disciples: Mr. and Mrs. Sevier (who built the Advaita Ashram in Mayavati, near Almora); a young man J.J. Goodwin who was a journalist and knew short-hand and noted down every word uttered by the Swami from January, 1896 to June, 1898 when he (Goodwin) died in Ottacamund,

Henrieta Mulelr (who bought a plot of land with her money for the Belur Math in 1898). There were others like Margaret Noble (Sister Nivedita) who took 'diksha' (initiation) from the swami and devoted her life for the welfare of Indian women; Ole Bull, and Josephine Macleod, who remained friends and helpers of the swami but were not initiated like Margaret Noble.

Though Vivekananda could not find disciples like Seviers, Margaret Noble and Goodwin in America, he was very impressed by the people and their way of life. He admired their economic policy, industrial organization, public instruction, their museums and art galleries, the progress in science, hygienic institutions and social welfare work. Above all, he was fascinated by the American women. In a letter to a 'brother disciple' Ramakrishnananda, Vivekananda wrote from America: "Nowhere in the world are women like those in this country. How pure, independent, self-relying and kind-hearted! It is the women who are the life and soul of this country. All learning and culture are centred in them". Then he laments that in our own country we call women 'despicable worms' and 'gateways to hell'. We are horrible sinners and our degradation is due to the way we treat our women and the poor and downtrodden who now form a majority. We have debased our sublimating religion by converting it into shameful and worthless rituals.[3]

Vivekananda voyaged back to India via Europe accompanied by the Seviers and Goodwin, reaching Colombo on 15 January 1897 and proceeding through Rameswar, Ramnad and Madras to reach Calcutta on 20 February 1897. He was accorded a rousing reception wherever he went. On 1 May 1897 he founded Ramakrishna Mission and the *math* at Belur, a few miles from Calcutta, with the objective of preaching the teachings of the Master (Ramakrishna) and to start work for the material and spiritual welfare of the people. This is by far the most enduring legacy left by Vivekananda for mankind and according to Christopher Isherwood 'the most significant religious movement of our times'. The movement has a dual character — contemplative *math* and the *mission* for social work. The latter undertakes medical service, educational work and relief work during natural disasters. It has over 120 branches spread over eighteen countries besides India. Hundreds of 'monks in orange robes devote their lives for the good of the poor and needy. Initially the funds came from voluntary charities but now the mission accepts.

Vivekananda left India for the second time on 20 June 1899 and reached New York via London to consolidate his work done earlier. Apart from giving lectures and discourses, he set up Vedanta centers at San Franciso and sowed the seeds of more centers in the West Coast. From the West Coast, Vivekananda reached New York and from there sailed for Europe on 26 July 1900. He had been invited to attend the Congress of the History of Religions to be held at Paris. There the swami spoke about the distortion of Indian history. What he said in Paris in 1900 is still relevant today because the controversy about the origin of Aryans in this country goes on unabated. Vivekananda said, "What your European pundits say about the Aryans swooping down from some foreign land, snatching away the lands of the aborigines and settling in India by exterminating them, is all pure nonsense, foolish talk. Strange that our Indian scholars too say them amen; and all those monstrous lies are being taught to our boys. In what Veda, in what Sukta do you find that the Aryans came into India from a foreign country? Where you get the idea that they slaughtered the wild aborigines?" He continued, "Wherever the Europeans find an opportunity, they exterminate the aborigines and settle down in ease and comfort on their lands; and therefore they think the Aryans must have done the same".[4]

Vivekananda returned to India via Cairo reaching Belur *Math* on 9 December 1900. He paid a hurried visit to Mayavati, the ashram founded by the Seviers near Almora. Back at the Belur *Math*, the swami was busy organizing the work of the mission and the *math* trying to put the two institutions on a sound footing. But his health was causing anxiety and he had the premonition that his end was near. In spite of his athletic physique, Vivekananda suffered from several diseases. From his early days he had diabetes and later in life he suffered from acute asthma. He also had several bouts of malaria which had weakened him. Add to these were the deprivations he inflicted on himself during the years he travelled in India. Overwork also affected his health. He died on 4 July 1902 at Belur *Math*. He was only thirty-nine when he died.

Vivekananda started or helped to start a few journals: *Brahmavadin* (1895), English monthly (now titled *Vedanta Kesari*) from Madras; *Prabuddha*

*Bharata*, English monthly started initially from Madras but later shifted to Mayavati (Almóra) and *Udbodhan* (1899), Bengali monthly from Calcutta. Some of the writings of Vivekananda in Bengali were first published in *Udbodhan*.

Vivekananda has left a legacy which is still alive. What he thought and preached is still relevant today. He believed that the misery of Indian people is because they have debased their own soul-inspiring religion, Vedanta, and have opted for meaningless and dehumanizing rituals. "He made a trumpet call to all Indians to shed fear of all kinds and stand forth as men by imbibing *shakti* (strength), reminding them that they were the particles of the Divine according to the eternal truth preached by the Vedanta". Vivekananda believed that non-violence was the cult of the weak and the impotent. He quotes the scriptures, "Thou are the house-holder, if any one smites thy cheek, and thou does not return him, and eye for an eye, a tooth for a tooth, thou wilt verily be a sinner. Heroes only enjoy the world". He often quoted the *Gita*, 'Our Lord in the *Gita* is saying. 'Always work with great enthusiasm, destroy your enemies and enjoy the world'". Of Christians he said, "The Europeans never took the words of Jesus Christ seriously. Always of active habits, being possessed of a tremendous *Rajasika* nature, they are gathering with great enterprise and youthful ardour the comforts and luxuries of different countries of the world and enjoying them to their heart's content. And we are sitting in a corner, with our bag and baggage pondering on death day and night."

We find that he did not preach religion in the conventional sense. He believed that what people in India need is not religion but service to their fellow beings. The true service of God was therefore the service of the people. This aspect of his preaching is being put into practice by the Ramakrishna Mission. However, again and again he exhorted the people to be strong and shed cowardice. "The older I grow", he said, "the more everything seems to me to lie in manliness; this is my new gospel. The vilest of crimes is not to act."

Vivekananda never participated in political movements but his preachings infused new hopes and inspiration to the masses. Thus he 'gave a spiritual basis to Indian nationalism'. As his biographer, the French savant Romain Rolland, puts it: "The master's rough scourge made her

(India) turn for the first time in her sleep, and for the first time the heroic trumpet sounded in the midst of her dream the Forward March of India, conscious of her God. She never forgot it. From that day the awakening of the torpid colossus began".[5]

# References

1. Rolland, Romain. *The Life of Vivekananda and the Universal Gospel*. Calcutta, Advaita Ashrama, 1931 p.37.
2. Quoted in *Chicago Address: Swami Vivekanand*. Calcutta, Advaita Ashrama, 1993, p.62.
3. Vivekananda. *Complete Works*. Calcutta, Advaita Ashram, 1989 (subsidized ed.) Vol. 6, pp.250-52.
4. Vivekananda. *The East and the West*. Calcutta, Advaita Ashrama, 1971, pp.104-5. (It is a translation of an article written by the Swami published serially in *Udbodhan*, the Bengali monthly (1899-1901).
5. Rolland, Romain op. cit. p.113.

# Horace Hayman Wilson

## (1786-1860)

Horace was born on 26 September 1786, in a poor family in London. After completing his primary education in a Soho Square school, London, he joined St. Thomas Hospital as an apprentice in 1804. After four years, he graduated as a qualified medical practitioner. During his early years, he often visited the Royal Mint in the company of a relative who was working there, which provided him a fair knowledge of the working of the mint. This knowledge gained in his early youth stood him in good stead in his later years.

In 1808, Wilson was appointed a military surgeon in the Indian army by the East India Company. He arrived in India in 1809, but instead of joining as a medical surgeon in the army, he was inducted as assistant assay-master in the Calcutta mint by virtue of his knowledge about the working of the London mint. At the Calcutta mint, John Leydon was the assay-master under whom Wilson had to work. Leydon was interested in Asiatic languages and literature and was also an Indologist of some repute. Leydon introduced Wilson to the famous Indologist Henry Thomas Colebrooke (1765-1837). Colebrooke encouraged and helped Wilson to learn Sanskrit and study its literature. His progress was amazing and in 1813 Wilson published an edition of Kalidasa's *Meghaduta* with Sanskrit text and English translation in verse, with explanatory notes. Wilson's edition of *Meghaduta* was the first to have been translated in a European language. It was well-received in the Western world and a reprint was published in London in 1814.

Colebrooke also inducted Wilson in the Asiatic Society of Calcutta as secretary of which he (Colebrooke) was president. Wilson worked as secretary of the Asiatic Society for twenty-one years till 1832. During his stewardship of the society, it earned considerable reputation as a learned Oriental body. For the first time, Wilson inducted a few Indian members in the society which all those years was the prerogative of only the Europeans.

In 1816, Wilson became the assay-master of the Calcutta mint and held this appointment until he left India in 1832. It is surprising how he could devote so much time and energy in furthering his Sanskrit study and research while he was serving a responsible position in the mint. He regularly contributed articles in the *Asiatic Researches*. In addition, he also conducted his own *Quarterly Oriental Journal* from 1821 to 1827.

In 1819, Wilson was sent to Banaras for organizing the Sanskrit College, where he sharpened his knowledge of Sanskrit with the help of Kashi pundits. The same year (1819), he published the first edition of his *Sanskrit-English Dictionary*. It was at the time the only dictionary for Europeans to learn Sanskrit until the publication of *Sanskrit Worterbuch* (German-Sanskrit Dictionary) in seven volumes by Rudolf von Roth and Otto von Bohtlingk (1852-75). Wilson's dictionary became so popular that it ran into three editions. In 1825, Wilson wrote the *History of Kashmir* based on Kalhan's *Rajtrangini*, which was later also translated into French.

Wilson joined hands with David Hare (1775-1842) to promote the establishment of the Hindu College (1817) and later became one of its visitors and finally its secretary. The college played a significant role in ushering in the Bengal renaissance movement. In 1823, Wilson was made secretary of the General Committee for Public Instruction with J.H. Harrington as its president. This committee was responsible for laying down the educational policy to be followed by the government, recommending the introduction of European science and English literature in the curriculum. In 1824, Wilson founded the Sanskrit College, Calcutta, which became the premier institution of Sanskrit learning in Bengal.

In spite of his official preoccupations, Wilson continued his literary pursuits. In 1827, he published *Select Specimens of the Theatre of the Hindus*, which contains English rendering of substantial portions of the famous Sanskrit dramas e.g. *Mrichakattika* of Sudraka, *Vikramorvasi* of Kalidasa, *Malti Madhava* of Bhavabhuti. Besides these three, twenty-three other plays are dealt with briefly. Thus, Wilson's work brought the Sanskrit drama to the notice of the Western scholars. It was later translated into German and French and was well-received by European readers.

After living in India for twenty-three years, Wilson left for England in 1832 to become the first Boden professor of Sanskrit at Oxford University in 1833. From 1836, he also served as the librarian of the India Office Library, London, after the death of Charles Wilkins, who was the first Britisher to acquire a thorough knowledge of Sanskrit. Wilson was associated with the activities of the Royal Asiatic Society of Great Britain and Ireland ever since he returned from India and later became its president and thereafter its Director till his death.

Wilson continued his Sanskrit studies while in England and published several important works during this period. In 1837, he published *Sankhya-Karika* with Sanskrit text and English translation; translation of *Vishnu Purana* (London, 1840). His lectures as Boden Professor were collected and published under the title *Lectures on the Religious and Philosophical Systems of the Hindus* (Oxford, 1840). He was interested in numismatics also and published a book on the ancient coins of Gandhara under the title *Asiana Antiqua; Antiquities of the Coins of Afghanistan* (London, 1841). His *Sketches of the Religious Sects of the Hindus* (Calcutta, 1846) was earlier published in part in the *Asiatic Researches* (Vols. 15-16). It dealt with many obscure religious customs of the Hindus. In 1846, he edited Dandin's *Dasakumara Charitam* with an English translation, part of which was earlier published in the *Quarterly Oriental Journal* (Calcutta). Wilson's other works include, *Grammar of the Sanskrit Language* (Oxford, 1847). Another important work is the translation of the *Rig Veda* with Sayan's commentary. Volumes one to four were published during 1850-57 while volumes five and six were published soon after his death in 1860. It is a monumental work in verse form and brought out the text of *Rig Veda* before the European scholars for the first time.[1] *Glossary of Indian Revenue, Judicial and other Useful Terms* in different Indian languages was published in 1855.

Wilson was a good singer and actor and a patron of the famous Chowringhee Theatre in Calcutta which was later purchased by Dwarkanath Tagore. He was one of the early promoters of the Bengali stage. He could speak Bengali fluently and had a working knowledge of Hindi and Tamil.

Wilson died in London on 8 May 1860. He was the greatest Sanskrit scholar of his time combining a variety of attainments as general linguist, historian, chemist, accountant, numismatist, actor and musician. His entire works, both books and articles, were collected in his Works: H.H. Wilson in twelve volumes which were edited by R. Rost (London, 1862-71).

# References

1. Sengupta, G.G. *Indology and its Eminent Western Savants*. Calcutta, Punthi Pustak, 1996, pp.51-60.

# Bibliography

Agarwal, B.R. *Trials of Independence*, New Delhi, National Book Trust 1991.

Ahluwalia, M.M. *Freedom Struggle in India*, 1858-1909. Delhi, Ranjit Printers & Publishers. 1965.

Allana, G. *Eminent Muslim Freedom Fighters*. Delhi, Low Price Publications (Reprint) 1993.

Ambedkar, B.R. *Ranade, Gandhi and Jinnah*. Bombay, Dr. Babasaheb Ambedkar Writings & Speeches, Vol.1. 1943.

_____ *Pakistan or Partition of India*, Bombay, Thackers. 1946. Reprint, Education Dept., Govt of Maharashtra, (Vol. 8 of *Writings & Speeches*).

Anderson, W.K. and Shridhar D. Damla. *The Brotherhood of Saffron*. New Delhi, Vistaar (Sage) 1987.

Atmaprana, P. *The Story of Sister Nivedita*, Calcutta, Ramakrishan Sarda Mission, 1997.

Aurobindo Ghosh *see* Sri Aurobindo.

Ayer, S.A. *Story of the INA*. New Delhi, National Book Trust, 1997.

Aziz, K.K. *Rahmat Ali; A Biography*. Lahore, Vanguard Books. 1987.

Baig, Tara Ali. *Sarojini Naidu*. New Delhi, Publications Division. 1974.

Bandopadhya, Manohar. *Prem Chand; His Life and Work*. New Delhi, Publications Division. 1981.

Banerjee, A.C. *Two Nations: The Philosophy of Muslim Nationalism*. New Delhi, Concept. 1981.

Banerji, P. *Uday Shankar and His Art*. New Delhi, B.R. Publications. 1982.

Basham, A.L. *The Wonder that was India*. New Delhi, Rupa Paperback, 1981. (Earlier pub. Grove Press, New York, 1954).

Besant, Annie. *Future of Indian Politics*. Madras, Theosophical Publishing House, 1922.

Bhattacharya, S. Ed. *Mahatma and the Poet*. New Delhi, National Book Trust. 1997.

Bose, A.N. *My Uncle Netaji*. Bombay, Bharatiya Vidya Bhavan. 1989.

Bose, Subhas Chandra. *The Indian Struggle*, 1920-1942. OUP. 1997.

_____ *An Indian Pilgrim; An Unfinished Autobiography*. OUP 1997.

Brown, Emily C. *Hardayal; Hindu Revolutionary and Rationalist*. Univ. of Arizona Press, 1975. (Indian print, Manohar, New Delhi).

Brown, Judith. *Gandhi Prisoner of Hope*. OUP. 1989.

Chagla, M.C. *Roses in December; An Autobiography*. Bombay, Bharatiya Vidya Bhavan. 1973.

Charak, Sukhdev Singh. *General Zoravar Singh*. New Delhi, Publications Division. 1983.

Chowdhuri, Satyabrata Rai. *Leftist Movements in India, 1917-47*. Calcutta, Minerva, 1977.

Collet, Sophia. *The Life and Letters of Rammohan Roy*, Calcutta, Sadharan Brahmo Samaj. 1962 (Reprint)

Collins, Larry and Dominique Lapierre. *Mountbatten and the Partition of India*. New Delhi, Vikas. 1983.

Copley, Antony. *C. Rajagopalachari; Gandhi's Southern Commander*. Madras, Indo-British Historical Society, 1986.

Crawford, S. Cromwell. *Ram Mohan Roy; His Era and Ethics*. New Delhi, Arnold Heinemann, 1984.

Crocker, Walter. *Nehru; A Contemporary Estimate*. New York, OUP. 1966.

Cunningham, J.D. *History of the Sikhs*. Delhi, Low Price Publications, 1990. (First pub. London 1849).

Dalal, Bhagubhai Chandulal. *Harilal Gandhi*. Varanasi, Sarva Seva Sangh. 1980. (Hindi)

Dar, S.L. and S. Somaskandan. *History of the Banaras Hindu University* Varanasi, B.H.U. Press. 1966.

Datta, C.L. *General Zorawar Singh*. New Delhi, Deep & Deep. 1984.

Deed, Joseph Lister. *Tagore and America*, New Delhi, U.S. Information Service. 1961.

Deogirikar, T.R. *Gopal Krishna Gokhale*. New Delhi, Publications Division. 1964.

Desai, Morarji. *The Story of My Life*. Macmillan. 2 vols.

Deshpande, G.P. ed. *Selected Writings of Jotirao Phule*. Delhi, Left Word. 2002.

Dharamvira. *I Threw the Bomb; The Revolutionary Life of Rash Behari Bose*. New Delhi, Orient Paperbacks. 1979.

Dharamvira. *Lala Har Dayal and Revolutionary Movements of His Time*. Delhi, Indian Book Co. 1970.

Dombo, Morris. *Introduction in Political Profile of Sir Sayyid Ahmad Khan* ed. By Hafeez Malik. Delhi, Adam Publishers. 1993.

Durant, Will. *Our Oriental Heritage*. New York, Simon & Schuster. 1954.

Dutt, R.C. *Romesh Chunder Dutt*. New Delhi, Publications Division. 1981.

Edwardes, Michael. *Battles of the Indian Mutiny*. London, B.T. Batsford, 1963.

Edwardes, Michael. *Nehru; A Political Biography*. London, Allan Lane. 1971. (reprint, Vikas, New Delhi)

Elst, Koenrad. *Gandhi and Godse*. New Delhi, Voice of India. 2001.

Elst, Koenrad. *Dr. Ambedkar: A True Aryan*. New Delhi. Voice of India. 1993.

Firth, C.B. *An Introduction to Indian Church Hitory*. Serampur, Senate of the Serampur College. Rev. ed. 1976.

Frank, Katherine. *Indira: The Real Life of Indira Nehru Gandhi*. London, HarperCollins. 2001.

Gandhi, M.K. *An Autobiography*. Ahmedabad, Navajivan, 1927.

_____ *Collected Works of Mahatma Gandhi*. New Delhi, Publications Division. 100 vols. 1958-1994.

Gandhi, Rajmohan. *The Rajaji Story*. Madras, Baratam Publications. 2. vol. 1978.

_____ *Eight Lives*. New Delhi. Roli. 1986.

Godse, Nathuram. *May it Please your Honour*. New Delhi, Surya Bharati Prakashan. 1993.

Gundevia, Y.D. *Outside the Archives*. Pune, Sangam Books, 1984.

Gupta, Rajni Kant. *Military Trials of Tatya Tope*. New Delhi, S. Chand. 1987.

Harvani, Ansar. *Gandhi to Gandhi: Private Faces of Public Figures*. New Delhi, Gyan. 1996.

Hatch, Alden. *The Mountbattens*. London, W.H. Allen. 1966.

Hodson. H.V. *The Great Divide*. OUP. 1985. (First pub. 1969 Hutchison, London)

Hough, Richard. *Edwina; Countess Mountbatten of Burma*. London, Weidenfeld & Nicolson. 1983.

*Indian Annual Register*, 1920-1947.

Iqbal, Mohammad. *Bange Dara* (Collection of His Poetry) Lahore, Sheikh Mubarak 1924. (Urdu).

Jaggi, O.P. *Friends of India: Biographical Profiles*. New Delhi, Munshiram. 1973.

Jayakar, M.R. *Story of My Life*. 2 vols. Bombay. 1959.

Jinarajadas, C. ed. *H.P.B. (Blavatsky) Speaks*. Madras, Theosophical Publishing House. 1951.

Jordens, J.T.F. *Dayanand Saraswati: His Life and Ideas*. OUP. 1997.

Joseph, Babu, ed. *Tracing the Footsteps of Mother Teresa*. New Delhi, Catholic Bishops Conference of India. 2003.

Joshi, V.V. *Rammohan Roy and the Process of Modernization*. New Delhi, Vikas. 1975.

Judd, Denis. *Jawaharlal Nehru*. Univ. of Wales Press. 1993.

Keer, Dhananjaya. *Dr. Ambedkar: Life and Mission*. Bombay, Popular Prakashan. 1962.

_____ *Mahatma Jotirao Phooley: Father of Our Social Revolution*. Bombay, Popular Prakashan. 1960.

Kesavan, B.S. *History of Printing and Publishing in India*. New Delhi, National Book Trust. 1985.

Khairi, Saad R. *Jinnah Reinterpreted*. Karachi, OUP. 1966.

Khaliqualzaman, C. *Pathway to Pakistan*. Lahore, 1961.

Khurshid, K.H. *Memories of Jinnah*, ed. by Khalid Hasan. Karachi, OUP. 1990.

Kondanda Rao, V. *Right Honorable V.S. Srinivasa Sastri: A Political Biography*. Bombay, Asia. 1963.

Kulkarni, Sumitra Gandhi. *Mahatma Gandhi Mere Pitamah*. New Delhi, Diamond Pocket Books. 1997. (Hindi)

Lane-Poole, Stanley. *Aurangzeb and the Decay of the Mughal Empire*. Delhi, Low Price Publications. 1990. (First Pub. 1889, London)

Lebra-Chapman, Joyce. *Rani of Jhansi*. Bombay, Jaico.

Llewellyn, Alexander. *The Siege of Delhi*. London, Macdonald & Janis. 1977.

Lohia, Rammanohar. *Guilty Men of India's Partition*. Hyderabad, Rammanohar Lohia Samata Vidyalaya Nyas. 1970.

Madhavan Kutty, V.K., *V.K. Krishna Menon*. New Delhi, Publications Division. 1988.

Majumdar, B.B. *History of Political Thought from Raja Rammohan Roy to Dayanand*. Calcutta. 1964.

Majumdar, R.C. ed. *Struggle for Freedom*. Bombay, Bhartiya Vidya Bhavan. 2nd ed. 1988.

Majumdar, R.C. *History of the Freedom Movement in India*. 3 vols. Calcutta, Firma KLM. 2nd. Ed. 1988.

_____ *On Rammohan Roy*. Calcutta. 1972.

Malik, Hafeez, ed. *Political Profile of Sir Syed Ahmed Khan: A Documentary Record*. Delhi, Adams. 1993.

Mathai, M.O. *Days With Nehru*, New Delhi. Vikas. 1979.

Max Muller, F. *Indian Friends*. OUP 1899. (Indian reprint: New Delhi, Amrit Book Co. 1982).

_____ *Ramakrishna; His Life and Sayings*. Calcutta, Advaita Ashram. 1898. (Reprint 1998)

Mehta, Ved. *A Family Affair: India Under Three Prime Ministers*. Madras, Sangam Books. 1982.

Mitra, Subal Chandra. *Iswar Chandra Vidyasagar*. New Delhi, Ashish. 1975. (First pub. 1902).

Mookerjee, Girija K. *Subhas Chandra Bose*. New Delhi, Publications Division. 1975.

Mookerjee, Syama Prasad. *Leaves from a Diary*. OUP. 1993.

Morgan, Janet. Edwina Mountbatten. *A Life of Her Own*. Macmillan. 1991.

Mukherjee, Haridas and Uma. *Bipin Chandra Pal*. Calcutta, Firma K.L. Mukhopadhya. 1958.

Mukherji, Visvapriya. *Jagdis Chandra Bose*. New Delhi, Publications Division. 1994.

Nagarkar, V.V. *Genesis of Pakistan*. Allied. 1975.

Nair, Thankappan. *James Prinsep: His Life and Work*. Calcutta, Firma K.L.M. 1999.

Nanda, B.R. *Gokhale and the Indian Moderates and the British Raj*. OUP. 1979.

_____ Witness to Partition; A Memoir. New Delhi, Rupa.

Narasimhan, V.K. *Kamaraj: A Study*. Bombay, Manaktalas. 1967.

_____ *Kasturi Ranga Iyengar*. New Delhi, Publications Division 1963,

Narayan, Shriman. *Vinoba; His Life and Work*. Bombay, Popular Prakashan. 1970.

Nehru, Jawaharlal. *An Autobiography*. OUP. 1980. (First pub. Bodley Head, London, 1936)

_____ ed. A Bunch of Old Letters. OUP. 1958.

_____ *Discovery of India*. New Delhi, Jawaharlal Nehru Memorial Fund. 1946.

_____ *Selected Works*. 1st and 2nd Series.

Netaji Research Bureau, Calcutta. *Netaji and India's Freedom; Proceedings of the International Netaji Seminar* 1973, ed. by Sisir K. Bose. Calcutta. 1975.

Nikhillananda, Swami. *Ramakrishna: A Biography*. Madras, Sri Ramakrishna Math. 1953.

Nivedita, Sister. *Complete Works*. Calcutta, Sister Nivedita Girl's School. 1967.

Pande, B.N. *Indira Gandhi*. New Delhi. Publications Division. 1989.

Pandey, B.N. ed. *The Indian National Movement, 1885-1947; Select Documents*. London, Macmillan. 1979.

Pandya, Jayant. *Gandhiji and his Disciples*. New Delhi, National Book Trust. 1994.

Pannikar, K.M. *Founding of Kashmir State*. London. 1953.

Pareekh, R.S. *Contribution of Arya Samaj in the Making of Modern India*. Delhi. 1973.

Parmanand, Bhai. *The Story of My Life*. New Delhi, Ocean Books, 2002 (First pub. Lahore, 1935)

Parvate, T.V. *Portraits of Greatness*. New Delhi, Sterlings. 1964.

Patel, Vallabhbhai. *For a United India, Speeches, 1947-50*. New Delhi, Publications Division. 1967.

_____ *Sardar's Letters: Mostly Unknown*. Ahmedabad, Sardar Vallabhbhai Samarak Bhavan. 1983.

Payne, Robert. *The Life and Death of Mahatma Gandhi*. New Delhi, Rupa. 1997. (First pub. 1969 by Dutton, New York)

Philips, C.H. and Wainwright, Mary D. eds. *Partition of India; Policies and Perspectives, 1935-47*. London, Allen & Unwon. 1970.

Pradhan, G.P. *India's Freedom Struggle: An Epic of Sacrifice and Suffering*. Bombay, Popular Prakashan. 1990.

Pradhan, R.G. *India's Struggle for Swaraj*. New Delhi, Low Price Publications, Reprint (First pub. 1930).

Prem Lata. *Swami Dayananda Saraswati*. New Delhi, Sumit. 1990.

*Radhakrishnan Reader*. Bombay, Bharatiya Vidya Bhavan. 1969.

Rolland, Romain. *Life of Ramakrishna*. Calcutta, Advaita Ashram. 1931.

Ramgopal. *Indian Freedom: Rhetorics & Realities*. Ghaziabad, Vimal Prakashan. 2nd ed. 1987.

Ranchan, Som P. *Jawaharlal Nehru: Puer Aetenus*. New Delhi, Konark. 1991.

Ravindra Kumar, ed. *Selected Documents of Lala Lajpat Rai*. New Delhi Anmol. 1992.

Rau, M. Chlapathi. *Govind Ballabh Pant: His Life and Times.* Allied, 1981.

Roy Caudhury, P.C. *Gandhi and His Contemporaries.* New Delhi, Sterling. 1972.

Roy, S. *Selected Works of M.N. Roy.* 2nd. ed. OUP. 1987.

Russell, Ralph and Khurshidul Islam. *Ghalib, 1797-1869: Life and Letters.* London, Allen & Unwin. 1969. (UNESCO Collection of Representative Works, Indian Series)

Saiyid, M.H. *Sound of Fury: A Political Study of Mohammad Ali Jinnah.* New Delhi, Akbar Publishing House. N.D.

Saklatvala, B.S. and K. Khosla. *Jamsetji Tata.* New Delhi, Publications Division. 1970.

Salvi, Dilip M. *Scientists of India.* New Delhi, CBT. 1995.

Sarda, Har Bilas. *Life of Dayananda Saraswati; World Teacher.* Ajmer, Vedic Yantralaya. 1945.

Scarfe, Allen and Wendy. *J.P.: His Biography.* Hyderabad, Orient Longman. 1998.

Schlesinger, Arthur M. *A Thousand Days: John F. Kennedy in the White House.* New York, Houghton Mifflin. 1965.

Sen, S.N. *Eighteen Fifty Seven.* New Delhi, Publications Division. 1957.

Sen, S.P. ed. *Dictionary of National Biography.* Calcutta, Institute of Historical Studies. 1972-

Sengupta, G.G. *Indology and its Eminent Savants: Collection of Biographies of Western Indologists.* Calcutta, Punthi. 1996.

Seton, Marie. *Panditji; A Portrait of Jawaharlal Nehru.* London, 1967.

Shah, A.B. ed. *Jawaharlal Nehru: A Critical Tribute.* Bombay, Manaktalas. 1965.

Shakir, Moin. *Khilafat to Partition.* New Delhi, Kalamkar Publications. 1970.

Shan Muhammad. *Sir Syed Ahmed Khan: A Political Biography.* Meerut, Meenakshi. 1969.

Shankar, V. ed. *Sardar Patel: Select Correspondence, 1945-50.* 2 vol. Ahmedabad, Navajivan. 1976.

Sharma, H.D. *100 Best Pre-Independence Speeches.* New Delhi, HarperCollins, 1998.

_____ *100 Best Letters, 1847-1947.* New Delhi, HarperCollins. 2000.

Sheth, Jayana. *Munshi: Self Sculptor.* Bombay, Bharatiya Vidya Bhavan. 1979.

Sherring, M.A. *Benares: The Sacred City of the Hindus.* Delhi, Low Price Publications. 1990 (First pub. London, 1868)

Shinde, J.R. *Dynamics of Cultural Revolution: 19th Century Maharashtra*. Delhi, Ajanta. 1985.

Singh, Jagjit. *Some Eminent Indian Scientists*. New Delhi, Publications Division. 4th ed. 1991.

Singh, Khushwant. *Ranjit Singh: Maharaja of the Punjab*. Bombay, 1973. (First pub. London, Allen & Unwin 1962)

Sinha, Nirmal. *Freedom Movement in Bengal, 1818-1914: Who's Who*. Calcutta, Acandemic Publishers. 1991.

Sinha, R.P.N. *Birth and Development of Indo-English Verse*. New Delhi, Dev Publishing House. 1971.

Smyth, G.C. *History of Reigning Family of Lahore*. Calcutta. 1847.

Spear, Percival. *History of Delhi Under Later Mughals*. Delhi, Low Price Publications. 1990.

Sri Aurobindo. *Collected Works*. Pondicherry, Sri Aurobindo Ashram Trust.

Sri Prakash. *Bharat Ratna Dr. Bhagwan Das*. Meerut, Meenakshi. 1970.

Subramanian, M.K. *Periyar E.V. Ramaswamy: His Life and Mission*. Chennai, Periyar E.V. Ramaswamy Nagammai Education and Research Trust. 2004.

Sud, K.N. *Eternal Flame: Aspects of Ghalib's Life and Works*. New Delhi, Sterling. 1969.

Syed, Anwar Hussain. *Pakistan; Islam, Politics and National Solidarity*. New York, Praeger. 1982.

Tahmankar, D.V. *Lokmanya Tilak*. London, John Murrary. 1956.

_____ *Sardar Patel*. London, George Allen & Unwin. 1970.

Tandon, V. *Acharya Vinoba Bhave*. New Delhi, Publications Division. 1992.

Tandulkar, D.G. *Mahatma*. New Delhi, Publications Division. 8 vols. 1960.

Thomas, Mark. *Gandhi and his Ashrams*. Bombay, Popular Prakashan. 1993.

Toy, Hugh. *Subhas Chandra Bose: The Springing Tiger*. Bombay, Jaico Reprint. 2001. (First pub. London, Cassel, 1957)

Uttar Pradesh Publication Bureau. *Freedom Struggle in Uttar Pradesh*: Source Material. Lucknow. 1957.

Varma, Ganesh Lal. *Shyamji Krishna Varma: The Unknown Patriot.*.New Delhi, Publications Division. 1993.

Veer, Ram Avtar. *Torch Bearer of Indian Music: Maharshi Vishnu Digambar Paluskar*. New Delhi, Pankaj Publications. 1978.

Venkataraman, G. *Raman and his Effect*. Hyderabad, Universities Press. 1995.

_____ *Bhabha and his Magnificent Obsession*. Hyderabad, Universities Press. 1994.

Wavell, Archibald. *The Viceroy's Journal*. Ed. by Penderel Moon. OUP. 1974.

Wedderburn, William. *Allen Octavian Hume: Father of the Indian National Congress*. New Delhi, Pegasus, 1951. (First pub. London 1913).

Wolpert, Stanley. *Jinnah of Pakistan*. OUP. 1984.

_____ *Tilak and Gokhale*. OUP. 1961.

Yadav, K.C. *Autobiography of Dayanand Saraswati*. New Delhi, Manohar. 3rd ed. 1987.

Zaidi, A.M. ed. *Evolution of Muslim Political Thought in India*. New Delhi, S. Chand. 1978.

Zakaria, Rafiq, ed. *A Study of Nehru*. New Delhi, Rupa. 1989.

Ziegler, Philip. *Mountbatten, the Official Biography*. London, Collins. 1985.

# Index